HANDBOOK OF PERCEPTION

Volume V

Seeing

ADVISORY EDITORIAL BOARD

This is Volume V of

HANDBOOK OF PERCEPTION

EDITORS: *Edward C. Carterette and Morton P. Friedman*

A complete list of the books in this series appears at the end of this volume.

HANDBOOK
OF PERCEPTION

VOLUME V

Seeing

EDITED BY

Edward C. Carterette and Morton P. Friedman

Department of Psychology
University of California
Los Angeles, California

ACADEMIC PRESS   New York   San Francisco   London   1975
A Subsidiary of Harcourt Brace Jovanovich, Publishers

ACADEMIC PRESS, INC.
111 Fifth Avenue, New York, New York 10003

United Kingdom Edition published by
ACADEMIC PRESS, INC. (LONDON) LTD.
24/28 Oval Road, London NW1

Library of Congress Cataloging in Publication Data

Carterette, Edward C
    Seeing.

    (Their Handbook of perception; v. 5)
    Includes bibliographies and index.
    1.   Visual perception.   I.   Friedman, Morton P.,
joint author.   II.   Title.
BF241.C35   152.1′4   74-9323
ISBN 0–12–161905–2 (v. 5)

PRINTED IN THE UNITED STATES OF AMERICA

CONTENTS

Chapter 3.   Contemporary Theoretical Problems in Seeing

P. C. Dodwell

PART II.   THE NEURAL BASES OF SEEING

Chapter 4.   Receptive Fields: Neural Representation of
The Spatial and Intensive Attributes of
The Visual Image

J. G. Robson

Chapter 5.   Neural Coding of Color

Russell L. De Valois and Karen K. De Valois

PART III.   TEMPORAL AND SPATIAL RESOLUTION

Chapter 6.   Temporal Factors in Visual Perception

Leo Ganz

Chapter 7.   Spatial Resolution and Spatial Interaction

James P. Thomas

PART IV.   PATTERN, OBJECT, AND COLOR

Chapter 8.   Pattern and Object Perception

P. C. Dodwell

Chapter 9.   Color, Hue, and Wavelength

Robert M. Boynton

PART V.   SPACE AND MOTION PERCEPTION

Chapter 10.   Visual Space Perception

Whitman Richards

Chapter 11.   Visual Motion Perception

Robert Sekuler

PART VI.   PAINTING AND PHOTOGRAPHY

Chapter 12.   Vision and Art

M. H. Pirenne

LIST OF CONTRIBUTORS

Numbers in parentheses indicate the pages on which the authors' contributions begin.

ROBERT M. BOYNTON (301), Department of Psychology, University of California, San Diego, La Jolla, California

KAREN K. DE VALOIS (117), Department of Psychology, University of California, Berkeley, California

RUSSELL L. DE VALOIS (117), Department of Psychology, University of California, Berkeley, California

P. C. DODWELL (57, 267), Department of Psychology, Queen's University, Kingston, Ontario, Canada

LEO GANZ (169), Department of Psychology, Stanford University, Stanford, California

YVES LE GRAND (3, 26), French National Museum of Natural History, Paris, France

M. H. PIRENNE (433), University Laboratory of Physiology, Oxford, England

WHITMAN RICHARDS (351), Department of Psychology, Massachusetts Institute of Technology, Cambridge, Massachusetts

J. G. ROBSON (81), Physiological Laboratory, Cambridge, England

ROBERT SEKULER (388), Cresap Neuroscience Laboratory, Department of Psychology, Northwestern University, Evanston, Illinois

JAMES P. THOMAS (233), Department of Psychology, University of California, Los Angeles, California

FOREWORD

The problem of perception is one of understanding the way in which the organism transforms, organizes, and structures information arising from the world in sense data or memory. With this definition of perception in mind, the aims of this treatise are to bring together essential aspects of the very large, diverse, and widely scattered literature on human perception and to give a précis of the state of knowledge in every area of perception. It is aimed at the psychologist in particular and at the natural scientist in general. A given topic is covered in a comprehensive survey in which fundamental facts and concepts are presented and important leads to journals and monographs of the specialized literature are provided. Perception is considered in its broadest sense. Therefore, the work will treat a wide range of experimental and theoretical work.

This ten-volume treatise is divided into two sections. Section One deals with the fundamentals of perceptual systems. It is comprised of six volumes covering (1) historical and philosophical roots of perception, (2) psychophysical judgment and measurement, (3) the biology of perceptual systems, (4) hearing, (5) seeing, and (6) feeling, tasting, smelling, and hurting.

Section Two, comprising four volumes, will cover the perceiving organism, which takes up the wider view and generally ignores specialty boundaries. The major areas will include speech and language, perception of space and objects, perception of form and pattern, cognitive performance, information processing, perceptual memory, perceptual aspects of thinking and problem solving, esthetics, and the ecology of the perceiver. Coverage will be given to theoretical issues and models of perceptual processes and also to central topics in perceptual judgment and decision.

The "Handbook of Perception" should serve as a basic source and reference work for all in the arts or sciences, indeed for all who are interested in human perception.

EDWARD C. CARTERETTE
MORTON P. FRIEDMAN

PREFACE

It has been said that three of the classical domains of physics—light, heat, and sound—were fixed by perception. E. G. Boring in his *History of Sensation and Perception in Experimental Psychology* (1942) stated:

> Thus *light* is a concept invented to explain vision, since it was perception that set the first problems for physics . . . it was only much later that imperceptibles like electricity, magnetism, invisible light, radiant and wavemotion became equally important. For this reason, then, the first important knowledge of color and its stimulus was contributed by Newton, of visual space perception by Kepler, of the tonal stimulus by Galileo.

Indeed, as Le Grand points out in the very first chapter, "until the beginning of the nineteenth century, optics and vision were intimately mixed, and light was considered only as the substrate of visual perception. . . ."

Vision may not be as primordial a sense as touch in the evolution of sensory systems (see Kruger & Stein in Volume III, this work) but in the evolution of perception and epistemology vision has held the oldest and chief role. Part I begins in a natural way with Le Grand's concise, informative history of research on seeing. Le Grand's authoritative Chapter 2 on the measurement of the visual stimulus is remarkably clear in view of the necessary, complex details. In the final chapter of Part I (Chapter 3), Dodwell maintains that the contemporary theoretical problems of seeing are just the traditional problems—the measurement of sensation, the physiological bases of perception, the role of experience in perception, and the nature of explanations of perception. We may agree that perhaps the questions have not changed, but the answers are different. Dodwell would say that our contemporary attempts at answers are better because they have become less metaphysical and less ideological, although theoretical differences exist, of course.

Part II deals with the neural foundations of vision. Robson (Chapter 4) lays out what is known about the receptive fields of the retinal ganglion cells and cortical neurons. He assesses the ability of various classes of receptive fields to represent the spatial and intensive properties of the visual image. In Chapter 5, R. and K. De Valois elucidate the neural coding of color based on evidence drawn largely from physiological studies on monkeys. They are confident in applying findings on monkey vision to human vision because the visual systems of men and monkeys are anatomically and behaviorally very similar. The Young–Helmholtz (1801, 1863) color theory which requires a limited number of receptors of different spectral sensitivity is shown to be compatible with the Hering (1872) theory of spectrally opponent interactions. The paradox is resolved by "ample direct physiological evidence to indicate that both three separate receptor types and spectrally opponent interactions are present, but at different neural levels."

Robson (Chapter 4) concludes that if the visual cortex is a spatial frequency analyzer it is "an analyzer of very modest capabilities." In Chapter 6, Ganz reviews the evidence for the relatively poor temporal resolution of the visual system and the implications for visual perception.

The resolution of spatial patterns and the phenomena of spatial interaction are separated in Thomas's Chapter 7 only because the research has been separated historically. Thomas delineates the extent of their common experimental and theoretical ground. He succinctly characterizes theories based on neural images with decision rules and those based on detectors (receptive fields). Although they lead to different interpretations of the psychophysical data, Thomas suggests that the two views are not mutually exclusive but represent neural processing at different levels of the nervous system.

Pattern, Object, and Color is the topic of Part IV. It will be seen that the central questions about patterns and objects (Dodwell, Chapter 8) are much the same as they have always been: How are perceptions organized? How do they develop? How are they learned? And how are illusions and constancies to be explained? In our attempts to confirm old answers and obtain new ones we have developed new instruments and methods, and the digital computer is at the heart of many of them. The cognitive, information-processing approach has revitalized perceptual research and encouraged the building and testing of models.

Boynton's Chapter 9 on color, hue, and wavelength is both refreshing and ambitious. He lays out the basic concepts of color and compares the subjective and physical bases of the description and ordering of colors. In assessing the psychological ordering of spectral colors, that is, the relation of perceived color to the wavelength of light, Boynton compares the three methods, color naming, hue cancellation, and multidimensional scaling of perceived color differences. Among other topics, he briefly discusses the physiological basis for the appearance of color, and color metrics.

The best way to see how an observer handles spatial information is to choose the most informative egocentric coordinate system, which Richards (Chapter 10) takes to be a spherical system centered on the observer with the forward direction the direction of the primary axis and gravity the secondary axis. Richards discusses models for the stability of the world when one moves himself actively, and for stereopsis. He points out that little is known of disparity detecting mechanisms in dynamic stereopsis nor of how this process and the dynamic cue of motion parallax are related.

In writing on visual motion perception Sekuler (Chapter 11) has chosen to break away from the classical work on motion and its attendant categories. It is necessary to go beyond the physical stimulus, "We must consider the contribution of our sensory apparatus." Accordingly, Sekuler emphasizes anomalies of motion perception, for they force us to attend to the properties of the analyzing mechanisms. His discussion is based on psychophysical findings strongly conditioned by inferences from neurophysiology. In other words, mechanisms are inferred from various classes of cells which respond selectively to movement, or velocity, or orientation, and are strongly conditioned by spatial frequency.

Pirenne in the final Part VI, consisting of but one chapter (Chapter 12), has abstracted and amplified for us the main thesis of his book *Optics, Painting and Photography*.* His purpose is to show "the significance of linear perspective in painting, and thus to demonstrate the fundamental importance of the pattern on the picture surface in our everyday perception of ordinary paintings and photographs." The notion of surface pattern is used again in the last section, on irradiation, in which Pirenne links the techniques of the pointillist painters to those of earlier mosaicists and illuminators of manuscripts.

* Pirenne, M. H. *Optics, painting, and photography*. London and New York: Cambridge Univ. Press, 1970.

CONTENTS OF OTHER VOLUMES

Volume II: Psychophysical Judgment and Measurement

I. Introduction and Overview

II. Perceptual Choice and Judgment

Part I

History, Measurement, and Contemporary Problems

Chapter 1

HISTORY OF RESEARCH ON SEEING

YVES LE GRAND

I. LIGHT AND VISION

"The nature of sight and the structure of the organ of vision rank among the foremost subjects with which the minds of thinking men have been preoccupied since the dawn of recorded history." Our best introduction is this quotation from Polyak (1941) in his outstanding history of our knowledge of the human retina.

Actually, until the beginning of the nineteenth century, optics and vision were intimately mixed, and light was considered only as the substrate of visual perception, a point thoroughly developed by Ronchi (1966). The concept of "invisible light" was meaningless until, in 1800, Herschel found that a part of the Sun's spectrum extends beyond the visible red. This invisible infrared was discovered through the heating of a thermometer. The following year Ritter established that the photochemical action of blue and violet light on silver chloride is continued in the invisible ultraviolet. The electromagnetic theory of Maxwell in 1865, its experimental confirmation by Hertz in 1887, the discovery of X rays by Röntgen in 1895, proved that light is only a very small part in the enormous range of electromagnetic radiations: It is those wavelengths to which the human eye is sensitive.

Optics is now a vast chapter of pure and applied physics. Some 20 years ago it might perhaps have seemed old fashioned. Now laser and holographic techniques have brought an extraordinary revival in optical studies. In comparison physiological optics may appear as somewhat out of date. But this is not true, and when turning over the pages of the *Journal of the Optical Society of America,* for example, the reader finds that one of every three or four papers is devoted to vision. Our modern world is predominantly visual, and research in physiological and psychological optics still must go a long way before we understand how man achieves this apparently so simple task: to see.

II. DIOPTRICS OF THE EYE

A. Classical Antiquity

Greek naturalists and physicians of the early period of classical antiquity had studied the eye, like the remainder of the body, but with little success, at least if we refer to the works that have come down to us. It is only from the writings of Rufos and Galen, in the second century A.D., that we learn of man's acquisition of important knowledge about the anatomy of the eye through dissection of animals.

For example, Galen (see Daremberg, 1854) gives a precise description of the parts of the eye we call now conjunctiva, cornea, iris, aqueous humor, crystalline lens, vitreous, retina, choroïd, and sclera. The retina was, in Galen's opinion, an expansion of the optic nerve, which itself was thought to be a protrusion of the brain, its function being to nourish the vitreous and through it the lens, which does not possess blood vessels. These descriptions anticipate modern ideas, but Galen viewed the crystalline lens as the main organ of vision (the photoreceptor in modern language), and this error would persist for many centuries. Another of Galen's views, considered by Polyak as a "fatal mistake," was his description of vision, inspired by Plato. A visual spirit ("pneuma") was supposed to originate from the brain, travel along the hollow optic nerve, and fill the crystalline lens where it met the rays of light coming from the external objects. The pneuma was thought to return to the brain, bringing with it the visual message.

It seems to me that, if retina is read instead of lens, this description anticipates modern views about the centrifugal fibers of the optic nerve and the role played by a central control of adaptation and other visual phenomena. Even the "emanation" by the eye of rays which were supposed by Galen to touch external objects, may be interpreted in modern terminology as the efferent projection, which allows a perceptive reconstruction of the world.

As to the physical nature of the rays of light emitted by the objects, Greek philosophers had anticipated both the Newtonian corpuscular theory (Pythagoras) and Huyghens's undulations (Aristotle).

B. Arab Ophthalmology

After the fall of the Byzantine Empire, the Greek knowledge was saved and developed by from the eighth through the thirteenth centuries Mohammedan ophthalmologists in Mesopotamia, Syria, Iran, Egypt, Morocco, and finally, in the Iberian peninsula. The earliest text is the *Book of the Ten Treatises on the Eye,* ascribed to Hunain Ibn Ishaq, who lived in the ninth century. [It has been edited and translated into English by Meyerhof (1928).] It contains the oldest detailed diagram of the eye (Fig. 1). The major mistakes are inherited from the Greek view of the eye's anatomy. The first one is the channeling in the axis of the optic nerve. Another one is the location of a spherical lens in the center of the eyeball. As a consequence, the anterior chamber is too spacious and the vitreal cavity too small. The cornea is correctly shown with a smaller radius of curvature than the sclera. The pupillary opening is enclosed in a curious crescent-shaped iris.

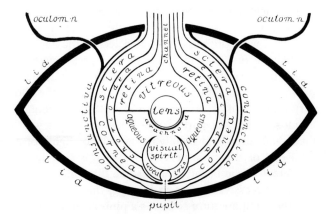

FIG. 1. Drawing of the first known diagram of the eye. [From Polyak (1957), with permission of the University of Chicago Press.]

An important treatise on physiological optics was written at the beginning of the tenth century by Ibn Al Haitham, whose name became Alhazen in the latin translation published by Vitello (1572). The lens is correctly described as flattened and with different radii of curvature for the anterior and the posterior surfaces. At first reading it may seem that Alhazen still thinks of the crystalline lens as the "chief organ of vision," but he is opposed to any emanation going out the eye, and he says that the "apex of the visual pyramid" coincides with the posterior surface of the "glacial sphere." This sentence is generally interpreted as placing the formation of the image upon the posterior surface of the crystalline lens, but Polyak points out that in Alhazen's text the "glacial sphere" sometimes includes both the lens and the vitreous. In this case the visual image should be located at the posterior surface of the vitreous, that is, on the retina, in accordance with modern concepts. In support of this viewpoint, Polyak cites the opinion of Averroës, a prominent Arab scholar of the twelfth century, who also seemed to favor retinal photoreception. In Alhazen's book there is also a precise description of the dark chamber (*camera obscura*). Alhazen does not claim to have discovered the *camera obscura,* and perhaps he found it in a now lost Greek manuscript. So without any knowledge of refraction, with only the use of the old principle of rectilinear propagation of light and the idea of the pinhole camera through the pupil aperture, Alhazen gives a presentation of the formation of the visual image which is some respects appears almost modern.

C. The Renaissance

Until the end of the fifteenth century, Western Europe remained dependent upon the ancient Greek knowledge transmitted through the Arabs. With the revival of arts and sciences in Italy, this situation began to change and historical errors were progressively corrected on the basis of dissection and new experiments. For example, in Vesalius's great anatomical treatise published in the middle of the sixteenth century, the hole in the optic nerve, which had previously been common, was not shown, and the photoreceptor role of the crystalline lens is presented as doubtful, the retina being suggested as the most important part of the eye (see O'Malley, 1965). Leonardo da Vinci had already postulated that rays of light form an image on the "frontal end of the optic nerve," but he was troubled by the false necessity of an erect image in the eye. In some diagrams of his notebooks, he conceives two successive images in the eye, the first one inverted, obtained through the pupil aperture acting as a pinhole in the *camera obscura,* the second one erected by refraction through the crystalline lens.

Progress toward the correct solution was made by Maurolycus in the mid sixteenth century. He hypothesized that rays of light from an external

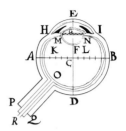

Fig. 2. Section of the human eye, after Scheiner (1619). This drawing is quite correct, except that the iris is not tangent to the crystalline lens MN.

point enter the eye and are collected on one point on the retina by refraction through the crystalline lens. It was thus necessary to postulate the photoreceptive function of the retina. This was clearly enunciated by Platter (1583), whose diagrams show a great improvement: The crystalline lens was displaced from the center of the eyeball into its anterior portion. A still better diagram is given (Fig. 2) by Scheiner (1619), with a corneal radius of curvature smaller than for the sclera, and a position of the optic nerve outside the optical axis, in the nasal direction.

D. Modern Dioptrics

One of the great achievements of Johannes Kepler (1571–1630) is his discovery of the basic facts of refraction of light and explanation of the formation of the retinal image. Another of his great achievements is the laws of planetary motion (see Frisch, 1858). Kepler's law of refraction— that there is a constant ratio between angles of incidence and refraction—is valid only for small angles; for large ones we must use the sines instead of angles (Snellius–Descartes law). But for the three main refracting surfaces in the eye, that is air–cornea, aqueous humor–crystalline lens, lens–vitreous, Kepler's law is sufficient because the geometrical form of these surfaces is not spherical and varies from one subject to another: In modern terminology, it means that spherical aberration is of no general use in the eye. Kepler was aware of the fact that the main refraction of light in the eye occurs on the first surface (air–cornea), and that the crystalline lens adds only about half of the refractive corneal power. But this supplement is essential, because it varies with the state of accommodation, that is, with the form of the lens under the influence of the ciliary muscle, which allows for sharp images on the retina at various distances. Kepler thought that this accommodation was achieved by a translation of the lens (as in a photographic camera; such a mechanism works effectively in fishes). However, in man, the main effect is due to a change in curvature of the anterior surface of the crystalline lens. The proof was given by Helmholtz (1856) by use of the so-called Purkinje images (1819) by reflection on the lens surfaces. It is interesting to note that this loss in emphasis of the crystalline lens, which is neither the photosensitive organ nor the major refracting one, might have been settled long ago from the observation of aphakic subjects, whose crystalline lens has been put out of action by cataract surgery. Cataract surgery was performed by Egyptian ophthalmologists as early as before the Christian era. Aphakics can see, but their retinal image is blurred (except in case of strong myopia) and their accommodation is totally lost.

As for the false difficulty of the inverted retinal image, Kepler gave the right answer in the early seventeenth century. Uprighting of the inverted image is due to "activity of Soul," which means that is a psychological problem and not a physical one.

Theoretical conclusions which Kepler drew from mathematical computations needed experimental verification. The test was made a few years later by Scheiner (1619). He opened a window in the back part of an animal eye, by removing a fragment of sclera and choroïd, and demonstrated the reality of an inverted image projected on the transparent retina. He constructed a model of the eye, wth cornea, lens, and retina made of glass, and the interior filled with water. He demonstrated beautifully that accommodation proceeds from a physical change inside the eye by his famous experiment of seeing a needle through three pinholes in a card put before the cornea: If these holes are all within an area the diameter of which is less than that of the pupil, there will be three images of the needle; if the eye is accommodated for a point nearer (or farther) than the needle, the knobs appear in the same relative position as the holes (or form an inverted pattern of the holes); only one image is seen if the eye is accommodated on the needle itself.

Roughly speaking, with Kepler and Scheiner, the optical story of vision is closed. Evidently, practical progress continued, and still does. For example, astigmatism, due to lack of symmetry of curvature in the cornea, and its correction by aspherical lenses, have been extensively studied since the nineteenth century. But for the study of perception, the Keplerian model of the eye is sufficient.

III. THE RETINA

A. Anatomy

Here again, as in Section II, we are most indebted to Polyak's (1941) work. A more detailed discussion of what is to follow may be found in Le Grand (1968) from which the following historical retrospect has been derived. References cited in this section can also be found in this latter book.

The name of the retina comes from classical antiquity and means a fisherman's net, because when the eye is carelessly cut and opened, the retina incloses the vitreous and lens like the catch of a fishing net. Although the retina is referred to in the oldest descriptions, its rich supply of blood vessels suggested that it had only a nutritive role, and we have seen that it was necessary to wait until the beginning of the seventeenth century for the photoreceptive function of retina to be settled definitively.

Leeuwenhoek was the first to examine a retina under the microscope in 1674 and to describe "globules" in it. In 1782 Buzzi discovered the *macula lutea,* or yellow spot, at the posterior pole of the retina. Three years later, Sömmering described a depression at the center of the macula, the *fovea centralis,* but he thought that it was Mariotte's blind spot (entry of the optic nerve); the correct explanation awaited Michaelis in 1838. The founder of the retinal histology, Treviranus, discovered in 1835 cylindrical "papillae" (our visual cells), closely packed together. He correctly attributed the role of photoreceptive ends of the optic nerve fibers to these "papillae," but thought by mistake that they were on the vitreal face of the retina. Four years later, Bidder showed that the extremities of these cells touch the choroïd, but this inverted position with respect to the propagation of light seemed to him paradoxical for receptor organs, and he assumed that they acted as reflectors to reinforce the photoreceptive response (a similar interpretation is now applied to the *tapetum* found in the choroïd of many vertebrates).

In 1850, H. Müller definitively proved the photosensitive function of the receptor cells by means of his celebrated experiment on the entoptic shadows of the blood vessels in the retina. Later, Boll gave a more direct demonstration by a modern version of Scheiner's experiment: The visual cells and the retinal image can be seen together in a microscope through a window cut in the sclera and the choroïd. In 1866 Schultze described two forms of receptor cells, the *cones* and the *rods*. Fifteen years later, this anatomical duality was taken by Parinaud and Von Kries as a basis for the functional *duplicity* of the retina: There exists a *photopic* cone retina, used at high levels of daylight and giving color sensations, and a *scotopic* rod retina, absent in the fovea, and still sensitive at low levels of light, but giving achromatic sensations.

As Kepler is the father of modern dioptrics, so Ramón y Cajal (1852–1934) is the founder of modern retinal histology. In place of the continuity of the fibers of the optic nerve and the receptor cells, previously assumed, he described a succession of separate nervous cells, the *neurons,* the impulse passing from one to the other in a definite direction through contacts called *synapses*. Each neuron possesses a fiber called the *axon,* the length of which may vary from a fraction of a millimeter to several centimeters and which transmits the message to another neuron through a synapse. There are three successive neurons in the retina. The first is the receptor cell (cone or rod), and the second is the *bipolar* cell, several cones and rods being generally connected by synapses to a single bipolar. The third neuron in the chain is the *ganglion* cell, which is connected by synapses to one or more bipolars. The axons of the ganglion cells form the fibers of the optic nerve. In the human retina there are about 7 million cones and 120 million rods, and only 800,000 fibers in the optic nerve. In the fovea, each cone is connected separately by way of one bipolar to one ganglion cell, and this enables it to send individual messages to the brain: It is the anatomical basis for *visual acuity,* as postulated by Kölliker as early as 1954. All these views of Cajal dominate current ideas concerning the retina (see Thorpe & Glickstein, 1972), although further discoveries concerning the "controller" cells of the retina (horizontal, amacrine, perhaps centrifugal and glial) have complicated Cajal's scheme with interaction, inhibition, and feedback mechanisms.

B. Photochemistry

The functional concept of the retina was, before the nineteenth century, based on an analogy with the ear: Rays of light were thought to cause, by direct stimulation, a vibratory motion in the optic nerve fibers. In modern times, such mechanical theories have occasionally been postulated again (based on radiation pressure), in parallel with numerous other hypotheses all deriving from physical phenomena (heating, piezoelectricity, photoelectricity, etc.). But the only theory of vision that is supported by experiments is the photochemical one, now universally accepted.

Photochemistry began with Scheele's studies, in 1780, on the blackening of silver salts in the violet end of the spectrum. In 1785, Berthollet observed the effect of sunlight on an aqueous solution of chlorine. (For a concise history of photochemistry, see Le Grand, 1970.) In 1818, Grotthus stated the first photochemical law: Only the radiation absorbed by a substance produces a photochemical effect. This law was confirmed by experiments made by Draper in 1839 and often carries the names of both workers. When the quantum theory was introduced at the beginning of the twentieth century, Stark and Einstein gave a precise basis to the Grotthus–Draper law in 1908: In the spectral domain where light reacts on a given molecule, the absorption of one photon (quantum of light) induces the same photochemical effect no matter what the wavelength of the light, but the probability of absorption of the photon is a function of wavelength.

The second law of photochemistry was enunciated in the middle of the nineteenth century by Bunsen and Roscoe, in relation to their study of the combination of chlorine with hydrogen under the action of light. This law of *reciprocity* states that the photochemical action depends only on the product of light intensity and the duration of exposure, or, to speak in modern language, on the number of photons absorbed. This law is valid for the primary action of light, that is to say, for exposures so short that secondary dark reactions do not have enough time to come into play.

The first visual photopigment was discovered by Boll in 1876: He detached a frog's retina from the choroïd and, observing light through it, found that the initially pink coloration rapidly became yellow. Boll called this pigment *visual purple;* it is now more commonly known as *rhodopsin.* The presence of visual purple in the human retina was proved by dissecting the eye of a criminal executed in the dark in 1877. Kühne showed in 1878 that a solution of biliary salts would liberate the purple from a retina macerated in the solution, so that it became possible to study it *in vitro.* He also discovered, in a fish, a second visual pigment, porphyropsin. Presently, a hundred visual pigments are known.

Rhodopsin is the pigment of rods. The first proof was given by König in 1894: The spectral absorption curve of rhodopsin in solution agrees fairly well with the scotopic luminous efficiency function, as measured on man by psychophysical experiments. The fit becomes better if the absorption curve is based on the number of photons absorbed and not on their energy, in agreement with Stark and Einstein's law, and also if absorption by the crystalline lens and the macula is taken into account. Instead of using extracted rhodopsin in solution, a more direct method is the study of the spectral absorption of the retina *in situ,* in the living eye, by an ophthalmoscopic principle suggested by Abelsdorff in 1897 and extensively used in modern times (see Weale, 1965). Another argument was given by Sugita in 1926: The ingestion of sodium cholate produces a temporary night blindness in rats by dissolving the rhodopsin in their ròds. We note a remarkable consequence of the quantal nature of absorption in rhodopsin: The visual threshold must bear a natural limit due to this discrete mechanism, a minimal value of two photons absorbed having been advocated as early as 1921 by Zwaaedemaker (Bouman & Koenderink, 1972).

Chemical structure of rhodopsin and of other visual pigments will be discussed by Robson, in Chapter 4 of this volume. As for cone pigments, our knowledge is very scanty, and we are not even certain that the few reported cases are really cone pigments, much less that their structure is analogous to that of rhodopsin (Le Grand, 1972). Nevertheless there is little doubt that cone vision also works through photochemistry.

C. Electrophysiology

Electrical phenomena connected with vision attracted attention long ago, and have led to extensive research. In 1755 Le Ray described the electric phosphene produced by the discharge of a Leyden jar between the head and the legs of a young man, who was blind due to a bilateral cataract, and who thereupon perceived a blaze of light. This electrical excitation of the retina is of little importance in vision, its only physiological implication being the explanation of the "blue arcs" described by Purkinje (1825) when viewing monocularly a small weak light (preferably red) in the dark, at 1° or 2° on the nasal side of the fixation point. Then one observes two blue–violet bands arching out from above and below the light, and converging toward the blind spot. These arcs follow the course of the nerve fibers in the retina running from the image of the source toward the papilla. Their explanation (Gertz, 1905) is based upon an electric phosphene induced in visual cells by action currents in the retinal fibers (see Moreland, 1969).

The complementary phenomenon of electric phosphene, that is, the electrical response of the retina, has, on the contrary, a great physiological importance (for its history, see Granit, 1947). In 1849, du Bois-Reymond discovered in vertebrates the existence of a *resting potential* between the cornea and the back of the eye, of a few millivolts. In 1865 Holmgren discovered that, superposed on this resting potential, there was a sudden *action potential* at the onset of illumination. In absence of suitable techniques, the study of these rapid and small (less than 1 mV) potentials remained difficult, and it was not until 1903 that Gotch, using a capillary electrometer, was able to record as a function of time the first *electroretinogram* (ERG). Twenty years later, valve amplification made this study quite easy. The ERG is a mass response of the whole retina and thus is more useful in clinical research than for our knowledge of vision. A better analysis is obtained with microelectrodes, which record potentials inside the retinal neurons. This work was initiated by Tomita in 1950 and is extremely helpful for retinal studies, the main difficulty being to know what retinal cell is in contact with the tip of the microelectrode at any given time. The reader will find in Chapters 5 and 7 of the present volume the main results obtained by this technique for the neural coding of perception.

IV. THE VISUAL PATHWAY

A. Historical Retrospect

Our major source of information on this aspect of vision is again Polyak (1957). The father of scientific medicine, Hippocrates (460–377 B.C.), had already acquired a vast knowledge of the anatomy and physiology of the brain, considered as the substratum of nervous action and intelligence. But half a century later, Aristotle's description of the connections of the eyes with the brain is very short, although the optic chiasma is clearly indicated. For Aristotle, the brain was only an accessory of the heart which he considered to be the seat of the soul. In Galen's medical writings, on the contrary, all sensations arrive at the brain, which is seen as the seat of imagination, comprehension, and memory, these faculties being located, respectively, in three cerebral cavities, frontal, central, and posterior. The optic nerves were described as hollow tubes originating from the lateral ventricules, in the anterior portion of the brain, which he called *thalami*. In the chiasma, their channels come together for various purposes, in particular to avoid diplopia: It is the first explanation of single vision through both eyes. This merging of the optic nerves was the prevalent idea until modern times, although there were opponents, such as Avicenna, for whom the nerves crossed completely in the chiasma, or Vesalius, who was in favor of the opposite thesis, that is, each nerve remaining on its own side.

Anatomical progress about the visual pathway was slow until the sixteenth century. Eustacchio put correctly the origin of the optic nerves in the posterior part of the thalamus. An important step is due to Descartes (1596–1650): The "animal spirits" go along thin tubes in the optic nerves from a given point in the retina to the corresponding point in the topographical representation of the retina in the brain (Fig. 3). Hence a merging of the two single monocular images is done in the pineal gland, the "seat of the soul." A hypothetical crossing of brain nerves gives a unique upright cerebral copy of the observed object. The animal spirits continue their course and the images transmitted by them are finally stored in the brain as a substratum of memory. Descartes' ideas are the forerunners of our current ideas on cerebral localizations.

B. Modern Views

With the eighteenth century the progress became more rapid. Vieussens conceived of the optic nerves as made up of bundles of fibers which continue as far as the cerebral cortex. The partial decussation of these fibers in the chiasma was first assumed by Newton in 1704 as an explanation of simple binocular vision, and experimentally demonstrated in 1755 by Zinn, who was able to follow the position of fiber bundles all along the optic nerves, which added evidence to the projection of the retina upon the brain.

Although Haller (1708–1777), founder of modern physiology, had violently struggled against functional localizations in the brain, these ideas were gaining some favor, especially through the efforts of Gall (1758–1828) on "cerebral organology." With the progress in the development of microscopes at the beginning of the nineteenth century, numerous

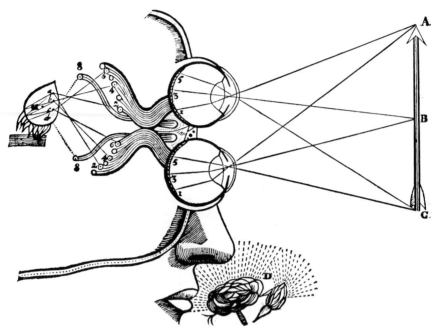

FIG. 3. Visual pathway in man, as imagined by Descartes (*Tractatus de Homine,* Amsterdam, 1686). The point B of the object projects an image at 3 on the retinas, and the "animal spirits" carry it to 4 along the optic nerves, which are represented as remaining each on its own side, as Vesalius thought. The two ventricular points 4 are then transmitting the spirits to the pineal gland H, at point *b.* The scent of the rose D is also acting on the pineal gland through the olfactory nerves 8.

discoveries about the visual pathway were made. Descriptions were given of the pulvinar of the thalamus; of the lateral geniculate nucleus (in our terms, the site of the third synapse of the visual pathway); of the separation above the chiasma of the cerebral portion of the optic nerve (optic tract) from the peripheral optic nerve; and other such. Flourens' experiments on the brain of the pigeon and chicken proved the dependence of vision on the cerebral cortex. Unilateral destruction of the cortex in the occipital region abolishes vision in the contralateral eye (in birds the optic nerves are almost completely decussated). In 1840 Baillarger demonstrated the structural variation of different parts of the cortex. In 1854 Gratiolet was able, for the first time, to follow the nervous fibers carrying the visual message. He found that the majority of the fibers, after leaving the geniculate nucleus, constitute the visual radiation which spreads like a fan until they end in the occipital lobes of the cortex. The modern scheme of the visual pathway was then obtained (Fig. 4).

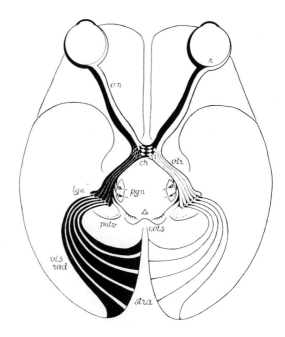

FIG. 4. Human visual pathway, after Polyak (1957). *r*, retinas; *on*, optic nerves; *ch*, chiasma; *otr*, optic tracts; *lgn*, lateral geniculate nucleus; *vis rad*, visual radiations; *stra*, striate area. [With permission of the University of Chicago Press.]

Modern studies of the optic pathway were done mainly by pathological work on scotoma and cortical blindness, with the aid of the ophthalmoscope, invented in 1851 by Helmholtz, one of the giants of physiological optics. This study began with Graefe in the middle of the nineteenth century and, after countless efforts, which the reader may find detailed in Polyak (1957), culminated with Henschen's definitive proof in 1897 of the localization of the visual center in the striate area which lies symetrically about the calcarine fissure, with Lenz's correct location in 1909 of the macular region at the posterior pole of the occipital cortex, and with Holmes's studies of the effects on vision of cranial injuries that he observed during World War I (1914–1918).

V. VISUAL FUNCTIONS

A. Form Vision

It is impossible to deal here with the history of research on all visual phenomena, so we shall limit ourselves to the most important ideas.

The ability to see small details is measured by various tasks, the oldest one being Daza de Valdes's method (1623): counting grains of mustard on a paper. This visual acuity is founded on three bases: the quality of the retinal image, the anatomy of the retina and of the visual pathway, and their physiology. As regards the quality of the retinal image, various dioptrical defects of the eye have been known for a long time, and their correction by spectacles began in the fourteenth century (Von Rohr, 1921). Contact lenses were foreseen by Herschel as early as 1827, but their first practical realization is due to Fick in 1888. A clear distinction between presbyopia, ametropia, and astigmatism was achieved by Donders in 1864. As for the aberrations of the eye, the only one to bear some practical importance is chromatic aberration, caused by variation with wavelength of the refraction index of ocular media. It was discovered and correctly explained by Newton (1704) from the colored fringes which appear at the edge of a white paper on a black ground, when one covers half of the pupil of the eye. For young subjects with good eyes, diffraction of light is, for pupil diameters less than 4 mm, the only factor which limits visual acuity in central vision, because of the heavy packing of thin foveal cones which maintain their individual pathways into the cortex. Protection against stray light which might blur the image, is obtained by a directional sensitivity of the cones, known as the Stiles–Crawford effect (1933). This phenomenon, which is rightly considered as the only new visual effect discovered since Helmholtz, is now interpreted by a dielectric waveguide theory.

In scotopic vision, acuity becomes poor because the photoreceptors are no longer independent, due to the convergence of many rods on one ganglion cell. An additional reason is the *night myopia,* mentioned by Lord Rayleigh in 1883. This difference of refraction between photopic and scotopic vision is partly explained by the chromatic aberration of the eye and the spectral shift named in honor of Purkinje (1819), one of the greatest physiologists in vision: The spectral maximum sensitivity is about 500 nm for human rods and 560 nm for cones. But the main effect is due to a position of rest of the crystalline lens in the dark, which differs from that in the day by more than 1 diopter for young subjects (Otero, 1949).

In form vision, the story of *irradiation* is interesting. The fact that a bright surface appears larger than a dark one of the same size has been known since antiquity. Galileo observed that a planet seen in his telescope seems smaller in front of the sun than on the black sky background, and Kepler explained this effect by the optical enlarging of the retinal image due to defects of the eye. In addition to this physical interpretation, Plateau (1838), following Descartes, considered a possible interaction between retinal receptors, the first time this assumption was made. Helmholtz (1856), who hated Plateau, rashly attacked this physiological interpretation which, due to Helmholtz's immense fame, was abandoned until recently. Actually both effects seem to come into play, and even cortical interaction processes have been held as operating in irradiation.

B. Space Vision

In space vision, one of the most important problems is related to depth perception obtained by binocular vision. That there must be a difference between the images of an object as seen by both eyes was already explained by Euclid, circa 300 b.c. In 1728, Robert Smith clearly described the main facts of fusion and diplopia in relation with distance. Wheatstone's invention of the stereoscope in 1833 demonstrated how much the difference between retinal images contributes to the sense of depth.

About the precision of this stereoscopic acuity, it has been believed for a long time, on the basis of rough observations and under the influence of the monocular limit of separation, that the threshold was near 1 minute of arc. Lower values were given by Stratton in 1898 and the result gradually improved, with actual limits lower than 5 seconds of arc. Stereoscopic acuity is not to be compared with monocular acuity, but with "vernier" acuity, that is the possibility of alignment of two lines. How such an extraordinary precision is compatible with the retinal mosaic of cones has been studied very often since Hering (1868), but does not seem to be satisfactorily settled.

Another possible basis of depth localization is given by the convergence angle between the two lines of sight. This idea of Descartes (Fig. 5) was supported in 1841 by Brücke and others since them. It seems (Le Grand, 1932) that, for small values of the visual angle between the two points, the depth of which is compared, retinal disparity explains stereoscopic acuity, whereas for larger values of this angle, it is the degree of convergence.

An old question is whether the relationship between corresponding points is innate, as Hering (1879) held it to be, or acquired, as conceived by Wundt in 1898 (see Le Grand, 1967). Experiments on the stability of retinal correspondence performed by Ogle (1950) in his study of artificial aniseikonia suggest that both views are true: There exists an anatomical correspondence, but with a margin of physiological adjustment that is probably achieved in the cortex by experience.

C. Color Vision

1. BEFORE YOUNG

The mystery of color has always attracted human thought. What was known in classical antiquity may be read in Seneca, who wrote in the first

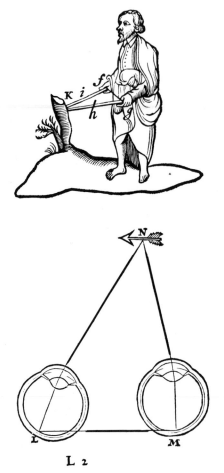

FIG. 5. Binocular depth perception, after Descartes (*Tractatus de Homine,* Amsterdam, 1686). The upper drawing represents a blind man who is measuring the position of a tree K by triangulation with two rods *h* and *i*. The lower drawing explains the depth localization of an object N through the images L and M on corresponding points of the retinas and the evaluation of the convergence angle between the lines of sight.

century A.D. He speaks about prismatic colors, which he compares to the rainbow and calls them "false colors" because, as with the dove's neck, they vary with the conditions of observation, whereas "true" colors of the objects proceed from a mixture of light and darkness "at the limit of the body." In modern terminology, colors of the first kind result from dispersion or interference of light, and those of the second kind from a selective absorption of light in a given range of wavelength. For example, an object is red not because diffusion of achromatic light by its surface adds anything to the incident light, but because it retains a larger fraction of energy in the short wavelength part of the visible spectrum than in the long wavelength region. The object is dark in violet, blue, and green lights, and this mixture of darkness with the lightness in yellow, orange, and red lights is perceived as color. On the other hand, painting and dyeing industries had found from very old experience that there are "simple colors" (red, yellow, and blue) that, by mixture, can reproduce almost any hue (visual trichromatism). The reader may find in MacAdam (1970) a collection of historical texts on color.

The famous experiment by Newton in 1666 about prismatic decomposition of the achromatic light of the sun, proved that "Light is not homogenous but consists of different kinds of rays, some of which are more refrangible than others." Colors are "original and inherent" properties of light, which in different rays are different and cannot be changed by any physical process. Mixtures of different kinds of rays give heterogenous colors.

> "The original or primary colors are red, yellow, green, blue and a violet-purple, together with orange, indigo and an indefinite variety of intermediate gradations. . . . There is no kind of rays that alone can exhibit white. White is always a mixture and to its composition are requisite all of the aforesaid primary colors, mixed in due proportions. . . . Colors of all natural bodies have no other origin than this, that they are variously constituted so as to reflect one kind of light in greater plenty than another.

Three centuries later, these lines from Newton are still true, the only exception being that a mixture of two "original" colors may sometimes give white when properly chosen (complementary) and in proper proportion. It is customary to say that Newton had divided the spectrum into seven colors, by analogy with the muscial scale, but it is evident from the preceding citation that he was conscious of the continuity of spectral hues in an "indefinite variety" and of the conventional character of any division by names.

The subjective character of color was also perfectly understood by Newton: "The rays, to speak properly, are not colored. In them there is nothing else than a certain power and disposition to stir up a sensation of this or that color." Newton remains vague about the nature of this "power," but by comparison with sound he suggests that it is through "this or that motion" of the light on retina that the "sensorium" feels a color sensation.

The main difficulty in Newton's synthesis was its disparity with the old visual trichromatism, which was, at the time, thought to be based on an unknown property of light. For instance, in 1757 Lomonosow postulated, in the framework of the particle theory of light, three kinds of "ether particles," the large ones being seen as red, the medium-sized ones as yellow, and the small as blue (see Weale, 1957). In 1777 Palmer writes, in the framework of the wave theory of light, "Each ray of light is compounded of three other rays only: one of these rays is analogous to the yellow, one to the red and the other to the blue. . . . The surface of retina is compounded of fibers of three kinds and each of these is moved by its own way by one of the three rays of light . . . . I venture to affirm that we never saw the primary colors in an absolute degree of purity," which is true. "Any deficiency of sensibility of these three classes of fibers as well as an excessive sensibility of any class constitute false vision," or color anomaly, in modern language. "Of these persons was the poet Colardeau," a French writer who died in 1776, 30 years before the famous self-analysis of Dalton. In opposition to these pioneer concepts, Palmer repudiated the explanation of white light given by Newton, for poor reasons that anticipate those that were to be advanced by Goethe (1810).

2. YOUNG AND HERING

Thomas Young (1773–1829) was one of the greatest men of genius. He was a doctor, wrote a thesis on audition, and his experiments on interference had convinced him of the wave nature of light. Light waves, like sound waves, form a continuous spectrum. "As it is almost impossible to conceive each sensitive point of the retina to contain an infinite number of particles, each capable of vibrating in perfect unison with every possible undulation, it becomes necessary to suppose the number limited for instance to the three principal colors, red, yellow and blue." We must note here that the fact considered by Young as "almost impossible" is actually realized in the ear, but this organ does not localize the sources in space, or does so only in a rudimentary way, by the time difference between the sounds arriving at the two ears. Conversely, the ear is capable of delicate spectral analysis: A musician can recognize the component notes in a chord. The eye cannot perform such a spectral analysis. The image must be spatially analyzed, but it is impossible for the eye also to transmit a message for each frequency of light. The information-transmission capacity of either acoustic or optic nerves is inadequate for carrying a message with both temporal and spatial spectra so large. Nature must choose: The ear is an excellent temporal analyzer of frequencies and a bad spatial one, the eye performs the opposite job.

In the 1801 citation of Young's theory, the "principal" colors were, as seen above, red, yellow, and blue, which are good primaries for subtractive mixtures, such as those done by an artist with oil pigments: He obtains green by mixing blue and yellow. But for additive mixtures obtained through the retinal mosaic of three types of cones (or the juxtaposition of three kinds of fluorescent dots on the TV screen), better primaries are red, green, and blue. Superposition of green and red lights gives yellow. Later on, Young said, in effect, that the "three simple sensations" are red, green, and violet (see MacAdam, 1970).

Young's idea, that trichromatism is physiological and not physical, was very slow to gain favor until Helmholtz in 1852, after some reluctance, gave to Young's theory the weight of his personal authority. The basic laws of colorimetry, founded on the trivariance of color vision, were established by Grassmann in 1853, and between 1852 and 1857 Maxwell performed the measurements of the solar spectrum with his "color box" which gave a firm foundation to trivariance (see Le Grand, 1968). A few years later, Maxwell realized the first trichromatic synthesis by superposition on a screen of the images from three photographic slides, projected through suitable filters. Curiously enough, the photographic emulsion used by Maxwell was not sensitive to red light, but happily the dyes used both in the Scotch ribbon photographed and in the liquid filter of the red primary, had also a transparency band in ultraviolet. Strictly speaking, Maxwell's experiment was more suitable for bees than for men, because bees possess a trichromatic vision, one primary of which is in the ultraviolet!

The existence in the human retina of three types of cones sensitive, respectively, to the long, the medium, and the short wavelengths of the visible spectrum, was the simplest way to give a biological basis to Young's theory. But anatomically all cones seem to be identical, except for a gradual change in form from the fovea to the peripheral retina. To overcome this difficulty, it was sometimes postulated that every cone was impregnated with a mixture of the three photopigments. Their decomposition products after light absorption would have a selective action on three types of bipolars. Recent progress in microspectrophotometry (see Chapter 6 in this volume) has settled the question: There are really three kinds of cones, each one with a different photopigment. So Young's theory works at the retinal level.

But two difficulties remain. First, yellow does not appear subjectively as a greenish red, it seems as "simple" as the primaries. And second, it is difficult to understand how the responses of the three kinds of cones can add their luminosities and yet on the contrary cancel their color attributes when simultaneously excited. In white light there is even a total loss of color. To deal with these difficulties, Hering assumed in 1872 (see Hering, 1905) six distinct sensations arranged in three opponent pairs, white–black, yellow–blue, red–green. For Hering, these pairs were due to two opposing actions of light on three substances in the retina, which is an error. But microelectrode recordings in the retina and all along the visual pathway, particularly in the lateral geniculate nucleus and in the visual cortex, have proved the reality of a color coding at these levels, which is of Hering's type (see Chapter 6 in this volume). It is a confirmation of the compromise, historically known as *zone theory* and developed by Donders in 1881. Young's theory is valid for the photoreceptors in the retina and Hering's scheme applies at some later stage in the visual transmission. Much work is still to be done before a thorough explanation of color vision is obtained. Nevertheless data collected during the last 10 years begin to reveal the mystery of this old and fascinating problem.

References

Bouman, M. A., & Koenderink, J. J. Psychophysical basis of coincidence mechanisms in the human visual system. *Ergebnisse der Physiologie,* 1972, **65**, 126–172.

Daremberg, C., *Oeuvres anatomiques, physiologiques et médicales de Galien,* 2 vols. Paris: Baillière, 1854.

Frisch, C., *Joannis Kepleri astronomi Opera omnia,* 8 vols. Frankfort: Heyder & Zimmer, 1858–1871.

Goethe, J. W. von, *Zur Farbenlehre.* Weimar: 1810. [Translated and published under the title *Theory of color.* London: Murray, 1840. Reprinted with an introduction by D. W. Judd, Cambridge, Massachusetts: M.I.T. Press, 1970.]

Granit, K., *Sensory mechanisms of the retina.* London: Oxford Univ. Press, 1947.

Helmholtz, H. von, *Handbuch der Physiologischen Optik.* Hamburg: Voss, 1856–1866. [A translation by Southall from the 3rd German edition appeared in 1924, and has been re-edited, New York: Dover, 1962. 2 vols.]

Hering, E., *Die Lehre vom binocularen Sehen.* Leipzig: Engelmann, 1868.

Hering, E., Der Raumsinn und die Bewegungen des Auges. In L. Hermann (Ed.), *Handbuch der Physiologie,* Vol. 3. Leipzig: Vogel, 1879.

Hering, E. Grundzüge der Lehre vom Lichtsinn. In A. Graefe & E. T. Saemich (Eds.), *Handbuch der ges. Augenh.,* Vol. 3, Ch. 13. Leipzig: Engelmann, 1905. [Translation by L. M. Hurvich & D. Jameson. *Outlines of a theory of the light sense.* Cambridge, Massachusetts: Harvard Univ. Press, 1964.]

Le Grand, Y. Convergence et sens du relief. *Rev. d'Optique* 1932, **11**, 313–323.

Le Grand, Y. *Form and space vision.* Bloomington: Indiana Univ. Press, 1967.

Le Grand, Y. *Light, colour and vision* (2nd ed.). London: Chapman & Hall, 1968.

Le Grand, Y. *An introduction to photobiology.* London: Faber & Faber, 1970.

Le Grand, Y. About the photopigments of colour vision. *Modern Problems in Ophthalmology* 1972, **11**, 186–192.

MacAdam, D. L. *Sources of color science.* Cambridge, Massachusetts: M.I.T. Press, 1970.

Meyerhof, M. *The book of the ten treatises on the eye, ascribed to Hunain Ibn Ishaq.* Cairo: Government Press, 1928.

Moreland, J. D. Retinal topography and the blue arcs phenomenon. *Vision Research,* 1969, **9**, 965–976.

Newton, I. *Opticks.* London: Smith & Walford, 1704. [Reprint, New York: Dover, 1952.]

Ogle, K. N. *Researches in binocular vision.* Philadelphia: Saunders, 1950.

O'Malley, C. D. *Andreas Vesalius of Brussels.* Berkeley: Univ. of California Press, 1965.

Otero, J. M. *Sobre las causas de las ametropias naturales de la Vision nocturna.* Madrid: Instituto de Optica, 1949.

Plateau, J. A. F. Mémoire sur l'irradiation. *Nouveaux Mémoires de l'Académie de Bruxelles,* 1838, **11.**

Platter, F. *De corporis humani structura et usu libri tres.* Basel: König, 1583.

Polyak, S. L. *The retina.* Chicago: Univ. of Chicago Press, 1941.

Polyak, S. L. *The Vertebrate visual system,* H. Klüver (Ed.). Chicago: Univ. of Chicago Press, 1957.

Purkinje, J. *Beobachtungen und Versuche sur Physiologie des Sinne.* Praha: Reiner, 1819–1825.

Rohr, M. von, *Die Brille als optisches Instrument* (3rd ed.). Berlin: Springer, 1921.

Ronchi, V. *L'optique, science de la vision*. Paris: Masson, 1966.

Scheiner, C. *Oculus hoc est: Fundamentum Opticum*. Innsbrück: Agricola, 1619.

Stiles, W. S. & Crawford, B. H. The directional sensitivity of the Retina. *Proceedings of the Royal Society, Series B,* 1933, **112,** 428–468.

Thorpe, S., & Glickstein, M. *"The Structure of the retina" by Santiago Ramón y Cajal, compiled and transplated in English*. Springfield, Illinois: Thomas, 1972.

Vitello, *Opticae thesaurus Alhazeni arabis libri septem*. Basel: Risnero, 1572.

Weale, R. A. Trichromatic ideas in the seventeenth and eighteenth centuries. *Nature,* 1957, **179,** 648–651.

Weale, R. A., Vision and Fundus Reflectometry. *Documenta Ophthalmologica,* 1965, **19,** 252–286.

Chapter 2

MEASUREMENT OF THE VISUAL STIMULUS

YVES LE GRAND

I. LIGHT AND RADIATION

Visual sensations are induced by the excitation of neurons at any point of the so-called visual pathway, from the retina to the occipital cortex in the brain. For instance a blow on the eye results in a *phosphene*. This "seeing stars" arises from the mechanical pressure on the retina; the blow, of course, does not produce any luminous radiation. Electrical excitation of the visual cortex also produces hallucinatory phosphenes. But these phenomena are mere curiosities, and the appropriate stimulus for vision is, evidently, the absorption by retinal photoreceptors of *light*, that is, a narrow band in the enormous range of electromagnetic radiations. All these radiations have the same speed in vacuum, the best value of which (Blaney *et al.* 1974) is

$$c = 2.9979246 \times 10^8 \text{ m sec}^{-1}.$$

This universal constant is independent of the kind of radiation, its intensity, and of any movement of the source or the observer.

Electromagnetic radiations may be considered as an assembly of *monochromatic components,* each of them being periodic with respect to both time and space. At any fixed point, a given component may be thought of as having the same value a large number of times per second; the maximum of this number is called the *frequency, ν,* the unit of frequency being reciprocal seconds (sec^{-1}) or hertz (Hz). Similarly, at any given time the same given component has the same value at a number of points which are distant from one another by an integral number of a length, the minimal value of which is the *wavelength, λ,* its unit being the meter (m). Frequency and wavelength are bound in a vacuum by the relation

$$\lambda = c\nu^{-1}. \tag{1}$$

For convenience, wavelengths are generally expressed by smaller units, such as the micron (μm) or 10^{-6} m, and the nanometer (nm) or 10^{-9} m.

When electromagnetic radiation travels through a medium other than a vacuum, the velocity is reduced and becomes c/n, where n is the *refractive index* of the material for the monochromatic component; this index is defined as the ratio of the sines of the angles of incidence and refraction when radiation enters in the medium from a vacuum. Frequency remains constant and wavelength is divided by n. Visible light comprises radiation of wavelengths from about .4 to .7 μm. In visual studies wavelengths are well enough defined by three significant figures, so the most convenient unit is the nanometer. There is no need, at this precision, to specify whether the wavelength is measured in vacuum or in air, because the refractive index of air is about 1.0003 for visible light. Frequencies of visible light range approximately from 4×10^{14} to 7×10^{14} Hz, which is very difficult to imagine, whereas the order of magnitude of wavelengths may be reached by electron microscopic techniques, so that it is more easily conceivable.

Wavelengths just shorter than .4 μm are known as ultraviolet, those just longer than .7 μm as infrared, and both are emitted by most sources of visible light, such as the sun and incandescent lamps. By means of oscillating electrical circuits, radiation with frequencies ranging from several thousand to several thousand million hertz can be produced, these are used in radio transmission, television, and radar. The corresponding wavelengths are spread out between kilometers and a few centimeters. It has been possible to generate radiation with wavelengths of less than a millimeter, which are also emitted as extreme infrared by hot bodies. At the other end of the scale, by shooting high-speed electrons at metal targets in a vacuum, radiation is emitted from about 10 nm (soft X-rays) to .01 nm (hard X-rays). Radiation of shorter wavelength (gamma rays) is emitted in nuclear processes, with wavelength sometimes less than 10^{-7} nm.

This continuous range of wavelengths covers, in musical terminology, no less than 70 octaves; that is, the range of frequencies is 2^{70}, but visible light occupies slightly less than one octave. However it is sometimes possible to "see" radiations outside the visual range of .4–.7 μm. By carefully eliminating stray light, Helmholtz (1855) was able to see up to 810 nm and this limit has been extended beyond 1 μm. It is also possible to see in the ultraviolet as far as 300 nm, especially by young subjects whose crystalline lenses are less yellow than those of adults. X rays, too, can affect the retina, probably through light emitted by fluorescence inside the eye, as is also the case for ultraviolet. It is perhaps through a Cherenkov light flash generated by cosmic radiation within the eye that astronauts perceive these high-energy particles (Fazio, Jelley, & Charman, 1970). However, visual research is generally limited to visible light and we shall deal only with such radiation in the present chapter.

II. SOURCES OF RADIANT ENERGY

A. Radiometric Concepts

1. RADIANT FLUX

For a precise definition of a visual stimulus, it is necessary to deal with quantities based upon the energy of radiation, that is, *radiometric* quantities, which do not involve the special properties of the visual receptor, as do *photometric* quantities, which will be considered later on. The definitions adopted here are those of the Vocabulary of the International Commission on Illumination (CIE), 2nd ed. (1971). The reader may also consult Le Grand (1968), which I follow very closely.

Consider a real or imaginary surface on which an area A is bounded by a closed curve. The radiation which passes through this surface in a given sense carries a certain amount of energy per unit time, which is called the *radiant flux* through A and is represented by the symbol P, because it is of the same nature as a mechanical power; hence the unit is the watt (W). The word *flux* suggests a fluid moving through A, and it is more than an image: Modern physics considers that the energy carried by any electromagnetic component of the radiation is concentrated in discrete particles, the quanta of light or *photons*. The elementary energy of one photon is equal to $h\nu$, where h is the Planck's constant the value of which is

$$h = 6.62517 \times 10^{-34} \text{ W sec}^2.$$

Thus in a radiant flux P of a monochromatic component λ, with the use of Eq. (1) we may write for the flux N of photons per unit time

$$N = P\lambda/hc. \tag{2}$$

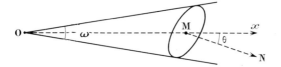

FIG. 1. The definition of radiant intensity. [From Le Grand, 1972a.]

If around a given point on the surface we consider an elementary area dA and if dP is the elementary radiant flux through dA, *irradiance* at this point is defined by the quotient

$$E_e = \frac{dP}{dA}. \tag{3}$$

The unit of irradiance is the watt per square meter.

2. POINT SOURCES

Any surface or volume that emits radiant energy is a source. Every source has finite size, but when size is small compared with the distance of the observer the source is called a *point source;* the matter is a question of ratio of the size of the source to its distance from the observer, that is of the angle subtended by the major dimension of the source from the point of view. An incandescent lamp seen at a few meters cannot be regarded as a point source whereas a star is a typical point source despite its enormous size. A planet viewed with the naked eye is a point source because the apparent angle is less than 1 minute of arc (40″ for Jupiter), but when viewed with a telescope it is no longer a point source.

Consider a spherical surface S having a point source O at its center. If the irradiance E_e is the same all over S, the source is said to be *uniform,* but if it is not the same, we must define the emissive properties of the source in various directions, which gives rise to the concept of *radiant intensity.* Consider a direction Ox (Fig. 1) and a cone of solid angle ω having Ox as axis. Since the radiation travels in straight lines, the radiant flux P traversing any cross section of the cone is constant, if the medium of propagation does not absorb the radiation. The ratio P/ω is therefore independent of the position of the cross section and, if ω is small in relation to the nonuniformity of the source, P/ω is also independent of the value of ω. This ratio is, therefore, a measure of the energy emission of the point source in the direction Ox. Thus the radiant intensity I_e of the source in the direction being considered, is defined by the limit of this ratio when ω tends to zero

$$I_e = \frac{dP}{d\omega}. \tag{4}$$

As the unit of solid angle is the *steradian* (solid angle subtended at the center of a sphere of 1 m radius by an area of 1 m² of the sphere surface), the unit of radiant intensity is the watt per steradian ($W\ sr^{-1}$).

If M is the point at which Ox meets the cross section and $OM = r$, if dA is the area of the elementary cross section and θ the angle between Ox and the normal MN, then

$$d\omega = dA \cos \theta r^{-2}, \tag{5}$$

and using Eqs. (3)–(4) the irradiance is given by

$$E_e = I_e \cos \theta r^{-2}. \tag{6}$$

It is the classical law of the inverse proportionality to the square of the distance.

3. EXTENDED SOURCES

As radiant intensity is not applicable to extended sources, we shall use two different quantities, depending on whether the radiation considered is that emitted in all directions, or only that close to one particular direction.

In the first case, if from an elementary area dA around a point M on the emitting surface, the total radiant flux emitted in all directions (that is within the solid angle of 2π bounded by the plane tangential to the surface at M) is dP, then the *radiant emittance,* or better *radiant exitance, M_e* of the source at M is defined by the ratio

$$M_e = \frac{dP}{dA}. \tag{7}$$

Radiant exitance, like irradiance, is radiant flux per unit area, but the former refers to the radiant energy emitted and the latter to the energy received. The units are the same, watts per square meter.

In the second case, if we consider a given direction Mx and if θ is the angle between Mx and the normal MN, we may consider that at a sufficient distance the elementary area dA behaves as a point source of radiant intensity dI_e in the direction Mx; then *radiance* in this direction is defined as

$$L_e = \frac{dI_e}{dA \cos \theta}. \tag{8}$$

The unit of radiance is the watt per steradian per square meter ($W\ sr^{-1}\ m^{-2}$).

The reader may wonder about the presence of $\cos \theta$ in this definition. Actually Eq. (8) means that L_e is the quotient of the intensity divided by the orthogonal projection of the elementary area on a plant perpendicular to the direction of observation. There are two reasons for such a definition. The first is that, in many real cases, L_e is nearly constant no matter what the direction Mx: Such a source is said to obey *Lambert's law*. The second is that if at a point O at the distance OM $= r$ (Fig. 1) we consider a plane perpendicular to OM, the irradiance in O on this plane is, after Eq. (6)

$$dE_e = dI_e r^{-2}$$

and since the elementary solid angle $d\omega$ subtended by dA at O is given by Eq. (5), Eq. (8) becomes

$$L_e = \frac{dE_e}{d\omega}. \tag{9}$$

This new definition has the advantage that it is applicable to a luminous volume without any boundary surface. A third reason will be given later on.

When a source obeys Lambert's law, there exists a very simple relation between radiant exitance and radiance, that is

$$M_e = \pi L_e. \tag{10}$$

4. SPECTRAL QUANTITIES

The radiometric concepts discussed so far have concerned integral radiation, that is, the total radiant energy of all monochromatic components of the radiation. By means of a dispersing apparatus, such as a prism or a grating, it is possible to split up the radiation into a *spectrum* where the monochromatic components are separated. There are two different types of spectra.

a. LINE SPECTRA. The spectrum appears as a finite number of *lines,* which are, in fact, images of the entrance slit of the dispersing apparatus, each line corresponding to a monochromatic component, and separated by regions in which there is no radiation. Such a source (gas made luminous by an electric discharge, for example) may be thought as a number of superimposed sources each emitting a monochromatic radiation; each of these fictitious sources can be measured in terms of the appropriate radiometric quantity, radiant intensity or radiant exitance.

b. CONTINUOUS SPECTRA. Here, every wavelength is present, at least over certain spectral domains (incandescent solids, for example). It is no longer possible to consider fictitious sources emitting monochromatic radiation, because the number of these sources should be infinite and, therefore, the energy of each nil. Actually, we isolate in the radiant exitance M_e, that is, the total radiant flux emitted per unit area of the source, an elementary

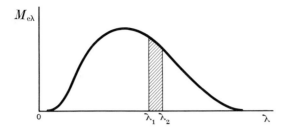

FIG. 2. A spectral energy distribution curve. [From Le Grand, 1972a.]

flux dM_e representing the energy of radiations with wavelengths within the range λ to $\lambda + d\lambda$. The *spectric exitance* is then defined as

$$M_{e\lambda} = \frac{dM_e}{d\lambda}.$$

It is important to note that spectric exitance is very different from the total radiant exitance, for the unit is not watts per square meter, as for this last quantity, but watts per cubic meter. It is the reason for this new term being recommended by the CIE, "spectric" meaning a derivative with regard to wavelength (it is frequently more convenient to measure wavelengths not in meters, but in microns or nanometers: the unit would then be, respectively, watts per square meter per micron or watts per square meter per nanometer). If we plot $M_{e\lambda}$ against λ, M_e is equal to the area between this *spectral energy distribution curve* (Fig. 2) and the λ-axis. The area shaded in the figure represents the radiant flux emitted by unit area in the form of radiation having wavelengths between λ_1 and λ_2, and if $\lambda_2 - \lambda_1$ is equal to the unit of wavelength employed, then the partial radiant exitance for this wavelength interval is numerically equal to the spectric exitance at a point near the middle of the interval; hence spectric exitance is sometimes called *radiant exitance per unit wavelength*. We must note that the choice of the variable λ is arbitrary, and if frequency had been used instead, the result would have been *radiant exitance per unit frequency* M_{ev}, related to $M_{e\lambda}$ by the relation

$$M_{ev} \, d\nu = -M_{e\lambda} \, d\lambda$$

the minus sign indicating that frequency decreases as wavelength increases. Using Eq. (1), it follows that

$$M_{ev} = c^{-1}\lambda^2 M_{e\lambda}. \tag{11}$$

If a spectral energy distribution curve is plotted as M_{ev} against ν the shape of the curve differs from the preceding one, and the monochromatic component corresponding to the maximum of the curve is different. Hence the position of "maximum spectric exitance" in a continuous spectrum has no signification, as it depends on an arbitrary choice in the method of plotting. Furthermore, if, following Eq. (2), the flux of photons was used instead of the radiant flux, two new spectric exitances might be defined, and again with different spectral energy distribution curves.

Instead of radiant exitance, one can consider radiance, or for a point source radiant intensity, and in a similar way define *spectric radiance* or *spectric intensity,* and in each case at least four different curves of spectral energy distribution are possible, depending upon the method of plotting.

B. Main Sources

1. DAYLIGHT

The sun is the most important natural source of radiation, but its spectral energy distribution is continually changing because atmospheric absorption and diffusion depend on many factors (latitude, season, hour, meteorological conditions, etc.). For biological reasons, it would certainly be useful to study vision under daylight conditions, but the lack of precision in definition and reproduction of natural daylight is a major difficulty which has not been completely solved. A first step has been the standardization by the CIE of spectral energy distributions for various types of daylight (Henderson, 1970; Wyszecki & Stiles, 1967). The next step will be to find a practical means for the artificial reproduction of these standard illuminants, so that they may be used in laboratory work, and progress is being made in this direction.

2. THERMAL RADIATORS

Heated solids emit radiation in a continuous spectrum. At room temperatures, this radiation is in the infrared region, but at high temperatures visible radiation is also emitted. The spectral energy distribution depends on the nature of the hot body, but there exists a very important theoretical body for which radiation depends only on temperature, such a body is called a *full radiator* or *black body*. This curious name denotes a hollow cavity, completely closed except for a small opening through which the radiation is emitted. At low temperatures the opening looks black because the light which enters the cavity can only be returned through it after a large number of successive reflections and diffusions, and these effectively absorb all the radiation. The smaller the opening compared with the size of the cavity, the better will be the approximation of a true full radiator.

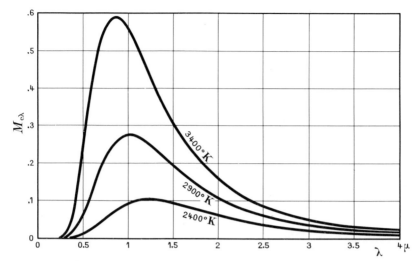

FIG. 3. Spectric exitance of the full radiator (in watts per square centimeter per nanometer). [From Le Grand, 1972a.]

In 1900, Planck showed that the spectric exitance of a full radiator should obey the law

$$M_{e\lambda} = c_1\lambda^{-5}[\exp(c_2/\lambda T) - 1]^{-1}, \tag{12}$$

where T is the *absolute temperature* (degrees Celsius $+ 273.15$), c_1 and c_2 are two constants which it is usual to evaluate with microns as units of wavelength and watts per square centimeter as unit of the radiant exitance:

$$c_1 = 3.7413 \times 10^4; \qquad c_2 = 1.43878 \times 10^4.$$

The full radiator obeys Lambert's law at every wavelength, so, from Eq. (10), the spectric radiance is given by

$$L_{e\lambda} = \pi^{-1}M_{e\lambda}. \tag{13}$$

In Fig. 3 spectral energy distribution curves are shown for full radiators at absolute temperatures in the range used in incandescent lamps (the letter K, after Lord Kelvin, is used for absolute temperatures). Each curve exhibits a maximum at a wavelength λ_m given by Wien's law,

$$\lambda_m T = 2898, \tag{14}$$

and shows a sharper fall on the short wavelength side of λ_m than on the long one. The value of M_e falls to one hundredth of its maximum at .33 λ_m

and $6.5\lambda_m$, whatever the temperature. The areas under the curve on either side of λ_m are almost exactly in a ratio of 3, so that only a quarter of the total energy radiated by a full radiator is of wavelength shorter than λ_m.

As explained before, energy distribution curves like those of Fig. 3 are mere conventions. For example at 5200°K, which is roughly similar to the solar radiation filtered by the atmosphere, Eq. (14) gives for the maximum λ_m the value 557 nm; we shall see later on that the maximum photopic spectral sensitivity of the human retina is very near to this value, and accordingly, one might conclude to a biological precise adaptation of photopic vision on the solar light. But it is possible to use frequency instead of wavelength through Eq. (11) and the maximum falls then at 981 nm, in the infrared. Moreover, as vision is a quantal process, the most rational choice should be to use the number of photons in ordinates and frequency in abscissas, which puts the maximum at 1737 nm! Teleological arguments are thus very dangerous.

For nonfull radiators, the spectric radiance $L'_{e\lambda}$ is always lower than the value of Eq. (13), at the same temperature, and thus

$$L'_{e\lambda} = \alpha(\lambda)L_{e\lambda}, \tag{15}$$

where $\alpha(\lambda)$ is a function of wavelength and temperature, always less than unity, and which may also depend on the direction of observation if the body does not obey Lambert's law. According to the law demonstrated by Kirchhoff in 1859, $\alpha(\lambda)$ is the *spectral absorption factor,* that is, the proportion of energy received by the body (for wavelength, temperature, and direction considered) which is retained and transformed into heat in its interior. It is to be noted that $\alpha(\lambda)$ is a function of λ, and not a derivative with respect to λ, so we use the word "spectral," and put λ in brackets, instead of writing it in subscript as in a spectric quantity. For a spectral quantity, the curve has an absolute signification, and the maximum is always obtained for the same monochromatic component, independently of any choice either for ordinates or for abscissas.

If $\alpha(\lambda)$ is independent of λ, the source is a *gray body* and its radiative properties are the same as for a black body $[\alpha(\lambda) = 1]$, except that all energies are reduced by the factor $\alpha(\lambda)$.

3. INCANDESCENT LAMPS

The filaments of these lamps are made of tungsten, because this metal has a high melting point, near 3700°K. To reduce evaporation the bulb is filled with an inert gas, such as argon or krypton. Sometimes a small quantity of iodine is added to the gas in the bulb, it is gaseous at the temperature of the filament, but it combines with the tungsten deposited inside the bulb at the relatively low temperature of the glass to form gaseous WI_2, which itself is decomposed on the filament to which tungsten returns. An ordinary 60 W lamp having a life of 1000 hours, generally works at about 2800°K, an iodine lamp may work at 3200°K, and "photoflood" lamps used in photography work near 3400°K but last only a few hours.

The spectral absorption factor of tungsten increases when λ decreases: At 2800°K, for example, $\alpha(\lambda) = .25$ for $\lambda = 2$ μm and .45 for .45 μm, which is an advantage because the proportion of visible light increases. As $\alpha(\lambda)$ varies slowly with wavelength throughout the visible spectrum, by multiplying by a constant factor the ordinates of the spectral energy curve it is possible to make it very similar to that of a full radiator having the temperature T_c which is called the *color temperature* of the source. Except for a gray body, T_c is not equal to the real temperature of the source, and for incandescent lamps, it is some 50 higher than the actual temperature.

For laboratory purposes, the CIE has defined a *standard illuminant* A which is an incandescent lamp operating at a color temperature of 2848°K if the c_2 constant in Eq. (12) has the value 1.435×10^4. With the now recommended value (1.438×10^4) we obtain $T_c = 2854$°K. With the interposition of liquid filters, other standard illuminants B and C had been defined, but their use is now almost abandoned (see Le Grand, 1968).

As stimuli for visual research, incandescent lamps are by far the most useful sources. In precision work, it is necessary to stabilize carefully the electrical power source, because the percentage change of spectric quantities of the lamp in the visible range is about 3.6 times that of the voltage and 6 to 7 times that of the current, so that voltage control is the more sensitive. In some experiments it may be also necessary to eliminate the fluctuating component (at 120 Hz for a 60-Hz current) by use of a direct current source.

4. DISCHARGE LAMPS

For special purposes it is often useful to employ the electric discharge in gases as source of radiation. Sodium vapor emits principally a doublet composed of two monochromatic components (589.0 and 589.6 nm). Xenon emits a large number of wavelengths throughout the visible spectrum, so that the xenon arc is a powerful source of white light. Mercury emits some 20 wavelengths ranging from the ultraviolet to the infrared. By coating the inside of the glass tube with a fluorescent layer, the absorption of the intense 253.7-nm ultraviolet radiation of mercury gives a continuous spectrum of longer wavelengths. The spectric exitance of this fluorescent light, with wavelength as variable, is a maximum at about 440 nm for a coating of calcium tunstate, 480 nm for magnesium tungstate, 540

nm for zinc silicate, 615 nm for cadmium borate, and 665 nm for magnesium germanate. It is thus possible to produce a great variety of stimuli
with different spectral energy curves.

Emission of radiation by the *laser* effect is possible with a large variety
of solids, semiconductors, and gases. In physical optics, such sources are
important because of the coherence of light emitted. In visual research,
it is because they offer the possibility of brief and intense flashes of monochromatic radiation that they may be of interest.

C. Receptors of Radiation

1. NEUTRAL RECEPTORS

Neutral receptors give the same response for equal radiant flux P, no matter what the spectral composition of the flux. They are based on the rise
of temperature of a black surface which completely absorbs P, when a
state of equilibrium is reached, i.e., when the heat given by the surface
to its surroundings, per unit time, is equal to the flux P absorbed. Such
receptors are somewhat delicate, because it is necessary to protect them
from all extraneous fluctuations of temperature, and they are never perfectly neutral except within certain wavelength limits. *Thermocouples* make
use of the property that junctions between different metals produce electro-
motive forces when they are at different temperatures; one series of junctions if blackened and receives the radiation, whereas the other is carefully
screened, the entire device being enclosed in an evacuated glass envelope.
Bolometers consist of two identical thin strips of platinum, each blackened
on one side. One strip is screened; the other receives the radiation and
rises in temperature, and, hence, in electrical resistance. Resistances of the
strips are compared on a Wheatstone bridge. *Golay cells* are pneumatic
receptors where temperature variations are recorded through differences
in pressure. For further discussion of all detectors mentioned in this section, the reader may consult Kingslake (1965, Vol. II).

Thermal receptors are the only ones that operate in infrared, but in the
visible range their use is limited to absolute measurements. Otherwise it
is preferable to use *selective* receptors, which are more convenient and
sensitive, but in which equal amounts of flux give different responses according to the wavelength. For the comparison of radiant fluxes of different
spectral composition, it is therefore necessary to know the *spectral radiant
sensitivity* of the receptor, that is, for a constant radiant flux, the response
for each wavelength; this sensitivity may be given in milliamperes per watt
($mA\ W^{-1}$). As for all spectral quantities, the choice of frequency or wavelength does not change the monochromatic radiation that elicits the maxi-

mal response, but here, the use of the flux photons N instead of the flux of energy P according to Eq. (2) would change the result.

2. PHOTOELECTRIC RECEPTORS

In these devices, the absorption of photons results in an electric current.

a. PHOTOTUBES. In photoelectric cells, the radiation falls on a *photocathode,* which emits electrons. The cathode is either a metal electrode coated with a suitable photoemissive material or a layer of such material inside an evacuated glass envelope. Electrons emitted are collected by an anode in the envelope, a potential difference of the order of 100 V being maintained between the cathode and the anode. Typical curves of various coatings are given in Fig. 4 for radiant spectral sensitivity versus wavelength. In gas tubes, there is an inert gas, usually argon, at low pressure; this gives an amplification factor of about 10.

b. PHOTOMULTIPLIERS. A secondary emission from the primary photoelectrons falling on *dynodes* coated with magnesium oxide, beryllium oxide, or tricesium antimonide, gives a large amplification of the current emitted from the photocathode. As it is necessary to accelerate the secondary electrons emitted by each dynode, it must have a higher voltage than the preceding one. Sometimes multiplier phototubes are operated at low temperature in liquid air to reduce noise due to the thermionic emission.

c. PHOTOCONDUCTIVE CELLS. These are made with a semiconductor, the electrical conductivity of which increases on exposure to radiation. Pure crystals (CdS and CdSe) exhibit a sharp maximum in spectral radiant sensitivity, but cells made of particles show a broader spectral response and

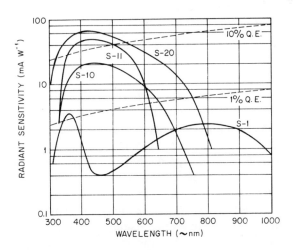

FIG. 4. Spectral responses of photoemission devices. [From Kingslake (1965).]

a higher sensitivity, which depends on small concentration of impurities. However, they have a relatively long response time, of more than .1 sec. The photoresponse is proportional to the radiant flux received.

d. PHOTOVOLTAIC CELLS. These are rectifying junctions (metal–semiconductor) which transform a fraction of the flux into electric power, in close proportionality. The highest efficiency is achieved with Si single crystals, but cells made with this material are small and expensive. More frequently, photovoltaic cells are composed of an iron substrate coated with a polycrystalline layer of selenium in its gray hexagonal form, coated in turn with a thin layer of noble metal (*Barrier layer cells, solar cells*). Such a device is robust, convenient, and needs no external power supply; the current is measurable directly with a portable microammeter.

3. PHOTOGRAPHIC EMULSION

This extremely useful receptor is affected cumulatively, although the reciprocity law is not strictly valid. The emulsion acts as an amplifier: The absorbed photons only trigger a reaction, the energy of which is supplied by the developer. Radiant spectral sensitivity of nonsensitized emulsions extends from about 360 to 510 nm, with a maximum near 450 nm. In orthochromatic emulsions, sensitivity is extended to 580 nm and in panchromatic to 650 nm. Emulsions sensible to infrared possess, in addition to the nonsensitized domain, a second range between 680 and 880 nm. Sensitivity may even be extended to more than 1200 nm, but blackening appears due to heat.

III. THE VISUAL RECEPTOR

A. The Retina as a Receptor of Radiation

1. RETINAL HETEROGENEITY

It is difficult to obtain a receiver whose sensitive surface possesses the same properties all over. In the case of the retina there is extreme heterogeneity. Vision has maximum acuity when the image falls on the *fovea,* a region of the retina which has its center coincident with the image of the point of *fixation,* i.e., the point that the subject looks at fixedly (in daylight conditions). To project a circular source on the fovea only, its apparent diameter u must be about $1°$ and its center must coincide with the fixation point. When the image on the retina covers only the fovea, vision is said to be *central*. In *lateral* vision, the position of the test object is given by its *eccentricity* η, that is, the angle between the point of fixation and the center of the test object. Vision is said to be *parafoveal* when

η is less than 4–5°, *perifoveal* until 9–10°, and then *peripheral*. At a first approximation retinal properties depend only on η, whatever may be the position of the test in the visual field. But closer examination shows this not to be so. If the words temporal, nasal, above, and below refer to the field as seen by the observer (due to image inversion, regions of the field are reversed on the retina), the limits of the monocular visual field are about 60° for the nasal side, 70° above, 80° below, and more than 100° on the temporal side. In each eye, there exists a *blind spot* (scotoma), corresponding to the entry of the optic nerve; its center is at $\eta = 15°$ on the temporal side and 2–3° below the horizontal meridian, and its dimensions are 7–8° vertically and 5–6° horizontally.

2. DURATION OF THE STIMULUS

Consider a certain monochromatic radiation of which a radiant flux P falls on a receptor. Let us suppose that this flux is zero until zero time, assumes the constant value P immediately afterward, and returns to zero at time t. For a photoelectric cell with no lag, the electric current is a function of P and not of t. Naturally, if t is small, this current must be measured by an instrument without inertia (as by a cathode ray oscillograph). For a photographic emulsion, the blackening is, on the contrary, a function of the product Pt only: If P is small, this can be made up by prolonging the exposure correspondingly. The case of thermometric receptors is more complicated: Each has a characteristic time t_0 for equilibrium. If the time t during which the flux acts is small compared with t_0, the response is a function of Pt only, whereas if t is large compared with t_0 it is a function of P only. Between these two conditions there is an intermediate zone in which the response is a function of both P and t but not of their product.

The visual receptor behaves like thermometric receivers, with a characteristic time t_0 of some hundredths of a second. For flashes shorter than this, only the product Pt is significant (Bloch's law), whereas if t exceeds several seconds, P is the only variable, because a state of equilibrium is attained, which involves a concentration of photoproducts in the retinal receptors and other nervous phenomena.

3. ADAPTATION

Like all living organs, the eye is affected by its past history. Upon entering a dark room from bright sunlight, at first, nothing at all can be seen; gradually, the eye becomes accustomed to the new conditions and after a few minutes objects in dim light can be seen. Such phenomena of *temporal adaptation,* partly photochemical and partly nervous, are of utmost importance in visual work. But there exists also a *simultaneous adaptation* due to interaction between different parts of the retina. In some cases it facilitates the visual response. Neighboring elements of the retina help each other, which can appear as a *summation* effect: total, when the flux distributed over all the elements is integrated whatever the distribution, partial in other cases. In some circumstances the interaction is an *inhibition,* the excitation of one area of the retina counteracting that of others.

4. ACTION OF LIGHT ON THE RETINA

It is universally agreed that vision is mediated through absorption of photons in photopigments located in the *rods* and *cones* of the retina. If N is the flux of photons of wavelength λ falling on the cross section of one of the photoreceptors, and $\alpha(\lambda)$ is the spectral absorption factor inside the photoreceptor, the effective number of photons (per unit time) which may act on the rod or cone is $N\alpha(\lambda)$. But if a photon must be absorbed in the photoreceptor in order to induce a visual process, this necessary condition is not sufficient. For example, in rhodopsin, which is the photopigment of rods, there is a strong absorption band at 278 nm, but it has no role in vision, because it belongs to the protein and not to the chromophore (retinal). Accordingly, we must introduce the quantum efficiency Q, a number always less than unity and which may be a function of wavelength, so that the number of photons which actually play a role in vision is $NQ\alpha(\lambda)$. On the other hand, if the observer is looking with central vision at a steady monochromatic source, the radiance of which is L_e, in the direction of the eye, it is easy to show (see, for example, Le Grand, 1968, Chap. 5) that the irradiance on the retina is

$$E_e = L_e f^{-2} S \tau(\lambda), \tag{16}$$

where f is the focal length of the eye, S the surface of the entrance pupil, and $\tau(\lambda)$ the *spectral transmission factor* for the media of the eye, that is, the ratio of any monochromatic energy that reaches the retina to that which entered the eye. This result is a new argument in favor of the definition of L_e by Eq. (8). It is also important to note that the distance between the object and the eye does not appear, obviously this can be so only if atmospheric absorption is taken as negligible. When this distance increases, the dimension of the retinal image of the object decreases but in this image, E_e remains constant so long as the source is seen as extended.

The radiant flux P that enters a cone or rod is equal to the product of E_e by the cross section area of the photoreceptor. Using also Eq. (2), we may write for the number N_a of photons actually active for vision and relative to one photoreceptor and unit time

$$N_a = kL_e QS\lambda\alpha(\lambda)\tau(\lambda), \tag{17}$$

where k is a constant factor.

B. Spectral Sensitivity of the Eye

1. NATURE OF THE PROBLEM

It is evident that radiometric quantities, such as radiant flux or radiance characterize the radiation of a source independently of any receptor, but give no idea of the effect on the eye. It is therefore necessary to introduce *photometric quantities* especially for visual problems, and first, as the eye is an extremely selective apparatus, to study the efficiency of various different wavelengths radiation in producing vision. This is referred to as *luminous efficiency* of monochromatic radiations.

In given conditions of temporal and spatial adaptation, it seems natural to admit that the visual effect of a monochromatic radiation is only a function of the number N_a of active photons given by Eq. (17). It follows that radiance L_e is the fundamental quantity for vision. This conclusion is experimentally verified: If two sources of uniform radiance are placed so that they appear in juxtaposition, the observer sees them as two identical patches if λ and L_e are the same, even though the distances may differ for both sources. In particular if the apparent contours of the sources overlap, the two patches merge into one and the line of separation disappears. If on the other hand the sources have unequal radiances L_{e1} and L_{e2}, but always the same λ, the source with greater L_e will appear brighter and the other darker; whatever the apparent diameters of the sources provided they are seen as extended.

If we now have sources that emit monochromatic radiations of wavelengths λ_1 and λ_2, the problem becomes more complicated. We must use a device with a control knob which allows a change of L_{e2} while L_{e1} remains constant, and adopt an *equivalence criterion* to define the equality of visual effects between the sources that are compared. This choice is more or less arbitrary. When equivalence is reached, there is no reason for L_{e1} and L_{e2} to be equal if $\lambda_1 \neq \lambda_2$, and actually this happens only by chance. But it is always possible to write

$$V_1 L_{e1} = V_2 L_{e2}, \tag{18}$$

V_1 and V_2 being positive weighting factors. The choice of symbol V is historical: These quantities were called "visibility factors" by Nutting in 1908, and although the terminology is obsolete, the symbol remains.

If the argument is continued in the same way to compare λ_2 and λ_3, it is possible to assign to each wavelength a factor $V(\lambda)$. As these factors have so far been defined only by their ratios, it is possible to fix $V(\lambda_m)$ as unity for its maximal value, which yields values less than unity for all other wavelengths, and thus to define *relative luminous efficiency* as a function of λ. The plot of the relative luminous efficiency curve is usually done with $V(\lambda)$ in ordinates and λ in abscissae. As it is a spectral quantity, the choice of frequency instead of wavelength does not change λ_m, but if radiances were expressed in photons instead of energies, a new λ_m value would result, as for all spectral radiant sensitivities.

It is interesting to note that the equality $V_2 L_{e2} = V_3 L_{e3}$ combined with Eq. (18) does not necessarily mean that $V_1 L_{e1} = V_3 L_{e3}$ unless the mathematical condition of *transitivity* is obeyed. Experience shows that it is true to a reasonable approximation, so that we may speak of a single-valued function $V(\lambda)$ without giving the sequence $\lambda_1 \lambda_2 \ldots \lambda_n$ used in the actual measurements. On the contrary, it is essential to specify conditions of adaptation. With high light levels, in central vision, cones predominate and vision is said to be *photopic*. On the other hand, with a dark-adapted retina, low light levels, and a large peripheral test area, vision is mediated by rods and conditions are said to be *scotopic*.

2. PHOTOPIC VISION

The first equivalence criterion to be used for a statistical determination of the photopic efficiency was the *flicker* method: A circular field is uniformly and successively filled with constant white light and monochromatic light λ of radiance L_e. The rate of alternation, without dark interruption, was 10–20 Hz; L_e was adjusted until flicker was at a minimum.

A second equivalence criterion was that of *direct comparison:* A bipartite photometric field (for example a 2° circular test area divided by a vertical diameter) is uniformly filled with light λ_1 on one side and λ_2 on the other; if these wavelengths are well apart in the spectrum, the equivalence criterion is highly subjective, due to difference in color. To overcome this difficulty the *step-by-step* method compares wavelengths differing only between 2 and 5 nm so that difference in hue remains slight. This comparison is made for about 20 points in the visible spectrum.

There is a systematic deviation between results of these methods, but much smaller than the spread between different subjects using the same method, so a mean curve based on about 200 observers was adopted in 1924 by the International Commission on Illumination and is universally used under the name of *CIE Photopic Standard Observer*. Corresponding $V(\lambda)$ values may be found in Table I. The maximum is at $\lambda_m = 555$ nm. The curve (Fig. 5) is bell-shaped, and if we fix arbitrarily the limits of the visible spectrum at $V(\lambda) = .001$ we obtain 410 and 720 nm: this convention is the origin of the round values .4 and .7 μm given usually.

For practical purposes the choice of a 2° field is rather small, and the light level was not very high. Measurements done with a 10° field and

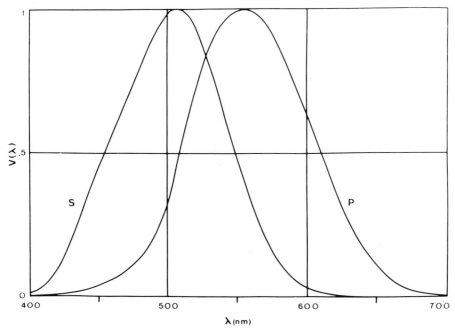

FIG. 5. Relative luminous efficiency curves: p, CIE standard photopic observer; s, CIE standard scotopic observer.

a much higher level by a rather indirect colorimetric method (see Le Grand, 1972b) were used to define in 1964 a *CIE Supplementary Standard Observer* (see Table I), which differs from the 1924 standard mainly in the short wavelengths; CIE experts think that both observers may be used in photopic conditions, depending on the field dimensions.

Many other criteria have been proposed for the present problem, but the only one which gives results in agreement with the flicker, step-by-step, and colorimetric methods is based on electrophysiology (see Chapter 5 in this volume). We shall not deal with the complicated problem of spectral sensitivity in peripheral vision (Le Grand, 1972b).

3. PHOTOMETRIC QUANTITIES

Standard observers having been defined, it is possible to link up photometry with radiometric quantities. When the observer looks centrally at a source emitting monochromatic radiation, Eq. (18) implies that the luminous appearance depends on the product $V(\lambda)L_e$. Therefore, *luminance* is defined by the relation

$$L = K_m V(\lambda) L_e, \tag{19}$$

TABLE I

C.I.E. STANDARD OBSERVERS: a, PHOTOPIC; b, SUPPLEMENTARY; c, SCOTOPIC

λ(nm)	a	b	c
380	0.00004	0.00002	0.0006
390	0.00012	0.00025	0.0022
400	0.0004	0.0020	0.0093
410	0.0012	0.0088	0.0348
420	0.0040	0.0214	0.0966
430	0.0116	0.0387	0.1998
440	0.023	0.0621	0.3281
450	0.038	0.0895	0.455
460	0.060	0.1282	0.567
470	0.091	0.1852	0.676
480	0.139	0.2536	0.793
490	0.208	0.3391	0.904
500	0.323	0.4608	0.982
510	0.503	0.6067	0.997
520	0.710	0.7618	0.935
530	0.862	0.8752	0.811
540	0.954	0.9620	0.650
550	0.995	0.9918	0.481
560	0.995	0.9973	0.3288
570	0.952	0.9556	0.2076
580	0.870	0.8689	0.1212
590	0.757	0.7774	0.0655
600	0.631	0.6583	0.0332
610	0.503	0.5280	0.0159
620	0.381	0.3981	0.0074
630	0.265	0.2835	0.0033
640	0.175	0.1798	0.0015
650	0.107	0.1076	0.00068
660	0.061	0.0603	0.00031
670	0.032	0.0318	0.00015
680	0.017	0.0159	0.000072
690	0.0082	0.0077	0.000035
700	0.0041	0.0037	0.000018
710	0.0021	0.0018	0.000009
720	0.00105	0.00085	0.000005
730	0.00052	0.00041	0.000003
740	0.00025	0.00020	0.000001
750	0.00012	0.00010	0.000001
760	0.00006	0.00005	
770	0.00003	0.00003	
780	0.000015	0.000013	

where K_m is a constant factor depending of the choice of the units for L and L_e, since $V(\lambda)$ is a dimensionless number. The CIE recommends using the same symbols for photometric and radiometric quantities, but to add, respectively, the subscripts "v" (visual) or "e" (energetic). Then the first member of Eq. (19) is L_v. But it is possible to drop the subscript "v" when no confusion is possible, and we shall use this simplification.

For a group of monochromatic radiations or for a continuous spectrum, luminance is defined by assuming the additivity law and writing

$$L = K_m \int V(\lambda)L_{e\lambda} \, d\lambda; \qquad (20)$$

limits of the integral are 380 and 780 nm since $V(\lambda)$ is nil outside. Experiment shows that the additivity law is verified (*Abney's law*), at least with a sufficient approximation for practical purposes.

Once luminance has been connected with radiance, other photometric quantities can be derived from luminance by the same relations that apply to corresponding radiometric concepts. Thus the *luminous intensity I* is such that the intensity dI of an element of projected area dA (on a plane perpendicular to the direction of observation) is given by a formula similar to Eq. (8)

$$dI = L \, dA. \qquad (21)$$

The *luminous flux F* is related to a solid angle by a formula analogous to Eq. (4)

$$dF = I \, d\omega. \qquad (22)$$

The *illumination E* is the surface density of flux received (this becomes the *luminous exitance M* in the case of emitted flux) and, similarly to Eqs. (3)–(7),

$$E \text{ or } M = dF/dA. \qquad (23)$$

The story of photometric units is curious. In early years, the starting point was a unit of luminous intensity called the "international candle," represented by electric lamps kept in test laboratories. In 1939 the CIE defined a new unit, the *candela* (cd), such that a full radiator at the temperature of solidification of platinum had a luminance of exactly 6×10^5 cd m^{-2}, this value being chosen because this round number is near the experimental value of luminance when measured in international candles per square meter. Then other photometric units derive from Eqs. (22) and (23): The unit of luminous flux is the *lumen*, lm (candela $\times$ steradian), and the unit of illumination the *lux*, lx (lumen per square meter). Sometimes illumination is measured in lumen per square foot, or foot-

candle, which is equal to 10.764 lx. The unit of luminance is expressed
as candelas per square meter, sometimes called *nit,* and also in candelas
per square foot (10.764 nit). But other units, which depend not on intensity, but on luminous exitance, are still used: The *lambert* is the luminance
of a surface which obeys Lambert's law and of which M is equal to one
lumen per square centimeter. From Eq. (13), 1 lambert = 3183 nit. Another unit is used in Germany, the *apostilb* = 1 lm m^{-2}. = .3183 nit. In
lighting practice, we find also the *foot-lambert* = 1 lm ft^{-2}. = 3.426 nit.
We hope that all these units will soon be obsolete.

The value of K_m in Eq. (20) may be calculated by putting $L = 6 \times 10^5$
and taking for $V(\lambda)$ the values for the photopic standard observer, and
for $L_{e\lambda}$ the spectric radiance of the full radiator at the temperature T of
solidification of platinum. In fact T is measured by optical pyrometry, so
that the only constants in Eq. (12) are c_1 and c_2/T. I made the calculation with $c_1 = 3.7413 \times 10^4$ and $c_2/T = 7.04212$, and using for $V(\lambda)$
tables at every nanometer given by Wyszecki and Stiles (1969). The
result is $K_m = 680.23$ lm W^{-1} for the CIE photopic standard observer
and 654.45 for the supplementary one. In the first case, this means that
to a radiant flux of 1 watt there corresponds 680 lm for 555 nm, and less
in all other cases. For the full radiator, the maximal luminous flux F
emitted per watt is obtained at about $T = 6500°$K (90 lm W^{-1}), iodine
incandescent lamps may give 24 lm W^{-1}, fluorescent tubes attain 70 and
sodium discharge lamps more than 100.

4. SCOTOPIC VISION

The problem here is much easier to solve than it was with photopic
vision. The retina is now fully dark adapted by at least 20 min of darkness,
luminous levels are kept low, test fields are large to favor the cooperative
properties of rods, and they are presented peripherally at about 10° eccentricity, where the rod population is most dense. As for the equivalence
criterion, flicker is inaccurate because fusion is reached quickly in peripheral vision. Direct comparison is possible because color differences disappear in scotoptic vision. A threshold method is also usable, because there
is only one kind of rod for man, and, therefore, no difficulties arise from
a multiplicity of responses, as would be the case for the three kinds of
cones.

The *CIE scotopic standard observer* is based on Crawford's measurements by direct comparison and Wald's threshold results (see Le Grand,
1968), on subjects under 30 years of age. Values are found in Table I,
and λ_m occurs at 507 nm instead of the 555 nm found for the photopic
observer (Fig. 5). This displacement is the well-known Purkinje shift.

As will be shown in Chapter 4 of this volume, scotopic luminous efficiency $V'(\lambda)$ is closely related to the absorption curve of rhodopsin, the photopigment of rods. There is a good fit between $V'(\lambda)$ and the product $\lambda\alpha(\lambda)\tau(\lambda)$ in Eq. (17), which shows that Q is a constant in the visible range. But as $\tau(\lambda)$ is smaller in short wavelengths when the crystalline lens becomes more yellow with age, scotopic observers change from year to year more than the photopic observers.

Photometry in scotopic vision proceeds along the same lines as photopic photometry. Equation (20) becomes

$$L' = K_m' \int V'(\lambda)L_{e\lambda}\, d\lambda. \tag{24}$$

If we put $L' = 6 \times 10^5$ for the full radiator at the solidification point of platinum (about $T = 2042°K$), we find $K_m' = 1746.70$, which is 2.6 times the K_m value. Photometric quantities and units have the same name in scotopic vision, with the addition of the adjective "scotopic" and a prime on the symbol. It may seem quite simple, but it is the origin of many difficulties. Let us suppose, for example, a source of luminance L, this value being expressed in photopic vision. We insert between this source and the observer a neutral filter whose transmission factor $\tau(\lambda)$ is constant throughout the visible spectrum and very small, so that the observer must now, in order to see the source, be dark adapted and use scotopic vision. The relation

$$L' = L\tau(\lambda) \tag{25}$$

in valid only if the color temperature of the source is near $2042°K$. For most sources used in visual work, color temperature is higher than this value and the scotopic luminance will be greater than the L' value of Eq. (25), by a factor of about 1.4 for the standard illuminant A and about 2.3 for a color temperature of $6500°K$ which may be taken for daylight.

It is generally agreed that vision is scotopic between the absolute threshold (about 10^{-6} cd m^{-2}) of scotopic luminance and 10^{-3} cd m^{-2}. It is photopic above 10 cd m^{-2}. Between these limits, vision is said to be *mesopic* and no precise photometry is possible. So it is extremely important in visual research to give, if possible, radiometric absolute quantities in addition to photopic or (and) scotopic ones, depending on the level of light used in the experiences. Otherwise results may be meaningless.

5. PUPIL OF THE EYE

If we refer to Eq. (17), which expresses the number of active photons in vision, the spectral transmission factor of the eye $\tau(\lambda)$ may vary from one observer to the other and explain deviations between a given subject and the standard observer. In addition, the gradual yellowing of the crystal-

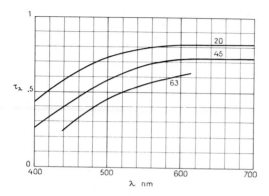

Fig. 6. Spectral transmission factor of the human lens at various ages, after Said and Weale (1959). [From Le Grand, 1972a.]

line lens with age alters $V(\lambda)$ in a way that may be predicted from Fig. 6. Another important factor is the surface S of the entrance pupil of the eye: It is not a small factor, as the diameter d of the pupil may vary between 2 and about 10 mm, which corresponds to a ratio of 25 for areas. It is, therefore, very important in visual research to specify values of d, which may be measured with *pupillometers*. A large number of devices have been used for this purpose, the best ones using infrared photography in order to avoid the effect of light on the pupil. In a first and very crude approximation, it is possible to calculate the diameter d when the subject is adapted to a level of luminance L; that is, when his visual field has this mean value to which he is accustomed for a sufficient time, and if glare is avoided. The following empirical formula has at least the advantage of simplicity,

$$d = 5 - 3 \tanh(.4 \log L), \qquad (26)$$

where d is expressed in millimeters, L is candelas per square meter, and the log being the common one.

From Eq. (17) and the definition of luminance in Eq. (19), it may be concluded that illumination of the retina (which is the true physical stimulus for an extended source) is proportional to LS. Thus, this product may be used to express the *luminous level* in a given experiment. The unit for this level is the *troland* (td) if L is given in candelas per square meter and S in square millimeters. It may be noted that a troland, which corresponds to a luminance of 1 cd m^{-2} seen through a pupil of 1 mm^2, corresponds also to a luminance of 1 apostilb or .1 millilambert seen through a pupil of 1 mm radius.

In visual research, it is very frequent to use an artificial pupil, the observer looking through a slit or a hole put a short distance before his cornea, and in such a case, S is the area of this artificial pupil. It may also happen that, although there is no physical aperture immediately in

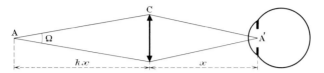

FIG. 7. Diagram of the Maxwellian view. [From Le Grand, 1972a.]

front of the eye, light nevertheless enters the eye through only a small part of the pupil. This is known as the *Maxwellian view,* after James Clerk Maxwell who used this method in his color box. The principle is shown in Fig. 7. A lens C forms an image A' of a point source A in the plane of the observer's pupil; the observer focuses on the lens C, the entire surface of which he sees uniformly illuminated, provided that the luminous intensity I of the source is constant throughout the solid angle Ω. It is easy to show (see Le Grand, 1968) that the retinal illumination, instead of being proportional to LS, is now proportional to Ik^{-2}, where k is the ratio of the distances from the lens to the source and the eye, so that the level in trolands is given by $10^6\ Ik^{-2}$, the numerical factor coming from the unit used for S (square millimeters instead of square meters) in the definition of the troland.

In 1933, Stiles and Crawford discovered that two point sources of equal luminous intensity, imaged on different points of the pupil in Maxwellian view, appeared of unequal luminous values. For example, if one image was in the center of the pupil and the other at the edge, with a pupil diameter of 8 mm, it was necessary to increase the intensity of the second source by a factor of about five to make it appear equal to the first. The *relative directional efficiency* ψ of two points of entry of light in the pupil is measured by the ratio of the corresponding luminous intensities for apparent luminous equality. The point of maximum efficiency ($\psi = 1$) is not necessarily the center of the pupil, but it is generally near it. At a distance r from this point, the efficiency may be represented by

$$\log \psi = -ar^2, \qquad (27)$$

the log being of base 10 and r expressed in millimeters, a is then of the order of .05. The Stiles–Crawford effect is not caused by absorption in the ocular media, but arises from a property of the retina itself, which is more sensitive to rays which strike it normally than to those which are slightly oblique (whence the name "directional" efficiency), probably by a waveguide effect in the cones (in rods, the effect is small or absent).

As a consequence of this phenomenon, the pupil behaves as though its area

$$S = \pi d^2 / 4$$

were replaced by a *reduced area* S_r. If the point of maximum efficiency is assumed to be at the center of the pupil, this area is given by

$$S_r = 2\pi \int_0^{d/2} \psi r \, dr. \tag{28}$$

In Table II, mean values of pupil diameter d are given in function of luminance L, using Eq.(26), and also values of the true area S of the pupil and of its reduced area S_r calculated by Eqs. (27) and (28). In scotopic vision where no Stiles–Crawford effect exists, the level is expressed in trolands LS, but in photopic vision we must use *reduced trolands* LS_r. If in addition we remember that in the first case we deal actually with "scotopic trolands" $L'S$ where luminance is expressed through the retinal sensitivity of the scotopic standard observer, we realize all the complexity of visual specifications.

a. *Photometry and Physical Receptors.* The same difficulties that we met when trying to compare the responses of the two biological receptors mixed in the retina (cones and rods) arise when we try to use physical receptors to measure photometric quantities. Results have no significance, except in rare cases where the radiant spectral sensitivity of the receptor has been corrected with a filter so that the resultant curve approximates (more or less) the CIE standard luminous efficiency. Sometimes with the apparatus curves are given that allow for a correction factor when color temperature of the source is known. But most frequencly, one reads illumination in lux of foot-candles directly, without considering any correction! The same remarks apply to definition of sensitivities of the receptors. For example, vacuum diode phototubes, whose spectral properties are plotted on Fig. 4, when exposed to tungsten light at a color temperature of $2870°K$, have, respectively, the following responses: 25 μA lm^{-1} for S_1, 40 for S_{10}, 60 for S_{11} and 150 for S_{20}; but at a lower color temperature, S_1 may be more sensitive than the others, owing to its response in infrared.

For photographic emulsions, blackening is measured by the *optical density* D which is the common logarithm of $\tau(\lambda)^{-1}$. Since silver grains in gelatine constitue a neutral filter, this spectral transmission factor is practically constant in the visible range. For a transmission of .1 we have, thus, $D = 1$, for .01 $D = 2$, etc. The optical density D is plotted again the common logarithm of the exposure $E \times t$ (in lx sec) and the lowest end of the toe of this curve is the *fog* density D_f. The speed of the emulsion is defined by the ASA (American Standards Association) as .8 divided by the exposure for which density is equal to $.1 + D_f$, for a specified method of development. ASA speeds of about 100 are common, and values higher than 1000 are obtainable; but it is evident that the spectral energy distribu-

TABLE II[a]

L (cd m^{-2})	d (mm)	S (mm^2)	S_r (mm^2)	$L \cdot S$ (td)	$L \cdot S_r$ (reduced td)
1×10^{-6}	7.95	49.5	24.5	5.0×10^{-5}	
2×10^{-6}	7.94	49.4	24.5	9.9×10^{-5}	
5×10^{-6}	7.91	49.2	24.5	2.5×10^{-4}	
1×10^{-5}	7.89	48.9	24.4	4.9×10^{-4}	
2×10^{-5}	7.86	48.5	24.4	9.7×10^{-4}	
5×10^{-5}	7.81	47.9	24.3	2.4×10^{-3}	
1×10^{-4}	7.77	47.4	24.2	4.7×10^{-3}	
2×10^{-4}	7.70	46.6	24.1	9.3×10^{-3}	
5×10^{-4}	7.60	45.4	23.8	2.3×10^{-2}	
1×10^{-3}	7.50	44.2	23.6	4.4×10^{-2}	
2×10^{-3}	7.38	42.8	23.3	8.6×10^{-2}	
5×10^{-3}	7.18	40.5	22.8	0.20	
1×10^{-2}	6.99	38.4	22.3	0.38	
2×10^{-2}	6.77	36.0	21.6	0.72	
5×10^{-2}	6.43	32.4	20.5	1.6	
0.1	6.14	29.6	19.5	3.0	1.95
0.2	5.82	26.6	18.3	5.3	3.7
0.5	5.36	22.5	16.4	11.3	8.2
1	5.00	19.7	15.0	19.7	15
2	4.64	16.9	13.4	34	27
5	4.18	13.7	11.3	69	57
10	3.86	11.7	9.96	117	100
20	3.57	10.0	8.72		174
50	3.23	8.17	7.30		365
1×10^2	3.01	7.12	6.46		646
2×10^2	2.82	6.24	5.73		1.15×10^3
5×10^2	2.62	5.39	5.01		2.5×10^3
1×10^3	2.50	4.91	4.59		4.6×10^3
2×10^3	2.40	4.52	4.25		8.5×10^3
5×10^3	2.30	4.15	3.92		1.96×10^4
1×10^4	2.23	3.90	3.70		3.7×10^4
2×10^4	2.19	3.77	3.58		7.2×10^4
5×10^4	2.14	3.60	3.43		1.72×10^5
1×10^5	2.11	3.50	3.34		3.3×10^5
2×10^5	2.09	3.43	3.27		6.5×10^5
5×10^5	2.06	3.33	3.18		1.59×10^6

[a] From Le Grand, 1972a.

tion of the source that produces the exposure must be carefully defined, otherwise speed is meaningless.

C. Color Vision

1. SPECIFICATION OF COLOR

The use of color stimuli is routine in visual research. Monochromatic stimuli are, theoretically, the most simple. They are produced by discharge lamps—sodium, for example. Sometimes, as in the case of mercury, there are a small number visible of spectral lines (405, 436, 546, and 578 nm) which are easy to isolate with colored filters that absorb all these rays except one.

Another method for creating monochromatic stimuli is to use dispersion by a prism or grating in order to split the continuous radiation of incandescent tungsten into a spectrum in which any monochromatic component may be isolated by a slit in a screen. An apparatus that does this is called a *monochromator* (see Fig. 8). The image of the filament of an incandescent lamp L is thrown onto the entrance slit F_1 by a condenser C; the emergent light is dispersed by a prism functioning in parallel light between two objectives; in the plane where the spectrum is formed, there is a second slit F_2, which selects a small group of radiations centered about a wavelength λ, and the displacement of F_2 controls the monochromatic light utilized. But stray light is also present, due to diffusion and reflection in the prism and objectives, which mars the purity of the monochromatic radiation. This stray light is especially troublesome when λ is at the ends of the visible spectrum, but can be eliminated by a double monochromator. The exit slit F_2 of the first monochromator is also the entrance slit of a second monochromator, exactly symmetrical with the first with respect to the plane of F_2. Under these conditions, only light of the desired wavelength λ

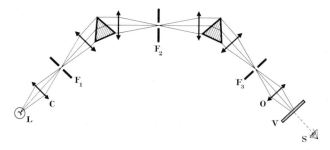

FIG. 8. Double monochromator (schematic). [From Le Grand, 1972a.]

will emerge from the slit F_3; stray light will form a spectrum in the plane of F_3 and will be stopped.

With such an apparatus it is possible to study statistically the limits of the main colors in the spectrum. An objective, O, forms an image of the lens following the second prism on a ground-glass, V, so that a bright circular spot of monochromatic light is formed on V and seen by the subject. The rounded mean of the limits of spectral colors in nanometers are the following (Le Grand, 1968): violet–blue, 450; blue–green, 500; green–yellow, 570; yellow–orange, 590; orange-red, 610. Naturally this division of the spectrum in six bands is arbitrary and reflects habits of speech rather than reality. In fact the change of color is continuous, and under good conditions, about 250 hues can be distinguished in the spectrum.

The most convenient way of obtaining nearly monochromatic light is to use optical filters. These are made of glass or gelatin in which coloring agents are dissolved, and their spectral transmission factor, or spectral transmittance $\tau(\lambda)$, may be chosen among very numerous possibilities commercially available. For narrow passbands, necessary for near monochromatism, *interference filters* are more suitable, and in the form of multiple all-dielectric layers they may have high peak transmittances (of the order of 80% for a half-width less than 10 nm); but they are expensive, and their properties depend strongly on the angle of incidence of light on the filter.

The physical specification of any light source is given by its spectral energy distribution curve, and the resulting color may be calculated by colorimetry (see, for example, Wyszecki & Stiles, 1967, or Le Grand, 1968). As a consequence of the trivariant nature of color vision (existence in the retina of three kinds of cones of different spectral sensitivities), three numbers are necessary and sufficient for this specification. Examples are the so-called *tristimulus values* X Y Z in the CIE colorimetric system, or the tristimulus value Y and two *chromaticity coordinates* x and y (ratios of tristimulus values to their sum), or a photometric quantity (such as L) and two colorimetric quantities (*dominant wavelength* and *purity*).

The specification of the color of an object is given by its spectral reflectance curve, that is, the energy distribution of the light diffused by its surface when it receives the light of a theoretical source whose spectric properties (as a function of λ) are constant in the visible spectrum. In addition, it is necessary to know the energy distribution of the real source that illuminates the object. Specification is the same as for sources, except for the photometric quantity (Y), which is now the *luminance factor:* That is, Y is the ratio of the luminance of the object to the luminance of a *perfect diffuser* (which reflects all the light received and obeys Lambert's law) assuming the same illuminant and the same conditions of view.

2. PSYCHOLOGICAL CONCEPTS

Once again, it is useful to stress the importance of physical specifications in visual stimuli. For example, in color, the basic apparatus is the spectro-photometer and not visual colorimeters, because there are large variations even between "normal" subjects and also because the proportion of anomalies in color vision is high (about 8% of male subjects). But, naturally, in a handbook of perception, it is also necessary to introduce psychological concepts, but with great care so as not to confuse them with the quantities used until this juncture.

About this difficult point the best I can do is to quote the CIE Vocabulary:

> *Hue* is the attribute of a color perception denoted by blue, green, yellow, red, purple, and so on. An *achromatic* color perception is defined as one not possessing a hue. *Saturation* is the attribute of a color perception determining the degree of its difference from the achromatic color perception most resembling it. *Brightness* (of an area perceived as self-luminous) is the attribute of a color perception permitting it to be classed as equivalent to some member of the series of achromatic color perceptions ranging from very dim to very bright or dazzling. *Lightness* (of an object perceived as nonself-luminous) is the atttribute of a color perception permitting it to be classed as equivalent to some member of the series of achromatic object–color perceptions ranging from black to white.

It is clear that hue is mainly related to the physical quantity dominant wavelength, saturation to purity, brightness to luminance, and lightness to luminance factor, but actually it is more complicated. Hue varies also with purity (the Aubert effect) and with luminance (the Bezold–Brücke effect), saturation with hue (at unit purity, that is, for spectral colors, yellow is less saturated than red, and red less than violet) and luminance (Purdy), and brightness varies with dominant wavelength and purity (the Helm-holtz–Kohlrausch effect).In addition, temporal and spatial adaptations also have enormous effects upon the color appearance, and, on the other hand, psychological "constancy" phenomena maintain a constant appearance in various conditions.

References

Blaney, T. G. *et al.,* Measurement of the speed of light. *Nature,* 1974, **251,** 46.
Fazio, G. G., Jelley, J. V., & Charman, W. N. Generation of Cherenkov light flashes by cosmic radiation within the eyes of the Apollo astronauts. *Nature,* 1970, **228,** 260–261.

Helmholtz, H. von, *Handbuch des Physiologischen Optik.* Hamburg: Voss, 1856–1866. [A translation by Southall from the 3rd German edition appeared in 1924 and has been reedited, New York: Dover, 1962, 2 vols.]

Henderson, J. T., *Daylight and its spectrum.* London: Hilger, 1970.

Kingslake, R. (Ed.) *Applied optics and optical engineering.* New-York: Academic Press, 1965, 5 vols.

Le Grand, Y. *Light, colour, and Vision* (2nd ed.). London: Chapman & Hall, 1968.

Le Grand, Y., *Optique physiologique,* Vol. 2, 2nd ed., Paris: Masson, 1972. (a)

Le Grand, Y. Spectral luminosity. In *Handbook of sensory physiology,* Vol. VII/4. Berlin: Springer, 1972. Pp. 413–433. (b)

Said, S., & Weale, R. A. The variation with age of the spectral transmissivity of the living human crystalline lens. *Gerontologia,* 1959, **3,** 213–231.

Wyszecki, G., & Stiles, W. S. *Color science,* New York: Wiley, 1967.

Chapter 3

CONTEMPORARY THEORETICAL PROBLEMS IN SEEING

P. C. DODWELL

I. INTRODUCTION

The contemporary theoretical problems about seeing—about visual perception—are the traditional problems. Such an apparently paradoxical statement is best justified by asking the question: What theoretical problems exercised visual scientists a century ago, in the very early years of the experimental psychology of perception? They were problems concerning the role of experience in perception, the measurement of sensation, the physiological bases of perception, and the nature of explanations of perception. One can view all of these as parts of a single question: What is the correct theoretical framework within which to gain an understanding of the nature of perception? Although the central issues have not changed, there is an important shift of emphasis in the way these matters are approached today, compared with 100, or even 20, years ago. It is probably correct to say that explanatory attempts tend now to be far less metaphysical, less ideological, than in the past; there are no longer the schools of psychology which were so prominent some decades ago (Woodworth, 1948), and where such schools flourish, their impact on the psychology of perception seems to be relatively slight. This may be contrasted with the situation in the much newer field of psycholinguistics, where there have recently been deep theoretical differences, and where sharp partisan exchanges between adherents of different ideologies are not unknown (Mac-Corquodale, 1970). There are, of course, theoretical differences and discussions within the field of perception, but it can be taken as evidence of the maturity of the field that these are now less abstract, more devoted to specific issues, than before. I shall argue, however, that despite their lack of prominence in contemporary theorizing and research, the larger issues are by no means all dead or settled, and it would be a mistake to dismiss them completely as being irrelevant to the scientific enterprise of understanding visual perception. Moreover, they influence the ways in which the more specific theoretical and practical questions are approached, even though the influence is not always explicit, as I shall try to show.

What have been the main areas of theoretical interest and progress in recent years? The record is, of course, contained in the different chapters of this volume. At the risk of appearing partisan I shall not attempt to review every such area, but rather will select a few that appear to me to have most furthered theoretical understanding of the processes of seeing. Detailed presentations of the technical aspects of the research to be discussed can be found in appropriate places in this volume; the reader will find here more an overview of some of the major campaigns, than a discussion of the tactics and minutiae of individual battles.

Concerted attempts have been made to understand the visual system as:

(i) the *detector* of signals in a normally "noisy" ambient stimulus environment,
(ii) the *organizer* of information contained in optical arrays,
(iii) the *processor* or *user* of information gleaned from the visual world.

These three correspond approximately to the traditional labels of psychophysics and sensation, pattern recognition, and object and event perception.

Theoretical advances in these fields can be distinguished from the practical and technical innovations which have made them possible. As in most fields of psychology, the technical developments that have furthered our progress have usually occurred outside psychology; to a very great extent we have been borrowers of others' tools and discoveries. This is nowhere so true as in the electrophysiological recording of events in the visual nervous system and its bearing on the understanding of visual perception.

II. PHYSIOLOGICAL BASES OF SEEING

A major question for psychologists and physiologists has been that of sensory quality. How many different qualities can be distinguished, how may they be described, how are they detected, and what is the physiological mechanism of their encoding? There can be little doubt that most of the important advances in answering questions about visual coding in the past 20 years or so have occurred because of advances in optics and electronics which made possible the detailed study of the action of single cells. In certain cases, it has been possible to reach definitive solutions to questions about sensory coding. Thus the whole basis for understanding color vision and color theory was given a new status by discoveries about the visual pigments of retinal cones (Marks, Dobell, & MacNichol, 1964; Wald, 1964). Technically formidable, although conceptually straightforward, these experiments demonstrated that individual cones of the primate retina contain one of three different photopigments, selectively absorbing light energy with maxima at about 445, 535, and 570 nm. These correspond to blue, green, and orange–red regions of the visible spectrum and apparently confirm the theory, first put forward by Thomas Young in 1802 and subsequently elaborated on by Helmholtz, that color vision is mediated by three types of receptors, or channels, with maximum sensitivities (accoring to Helmholtz) for spectrally pure blue, green, and red lights.

As is well known, the *opponent process* theory of color vision first elaborated by Hering, and more recently placed on a solid quantitative basis by Hurvich and Jameson (1955), was posed as a major competitor to the trichromatic theory of Young and Helmholtz. Remarkably enough, electrophysiological evidence has been found in the visual nervous system which evidently supports this theory: Opponent-type color-coding has been recorded in individual neurons of the lateral geniculate bodies and visual cortices of certain mammals, including primates. These cells respond with an increased rate of firing (excitation) when light of one wavelength strikes the retina and with a reduced rate (inhibition) to a different wavelength (Tomita, 1963; de Valois & Jacobs, 1968). The data give general support to the notion of green–red and blue–yellow opponent processes, as the theory specifies.

It seems that the two sorts of evidence support different and conflicting theories. However, as Hurvich and others have emphasized, the opponent-process theory is compatible with—indeed, in his formulation, requires—the concept of three differentially sensitive photopigments. Thus the physiological discoveries support nicely a theory which was based initially on psychophysical data. The state of the art of theorizing about color coding is now sophisticated and precise; for details the reader is referred to Chapter 5 of this volume. Here I shall pursue the broader question of whether the physiological discoveries contribute to solving theoretical problems of color *perception,* as opposed to color coding.

One might characterize the foregoing description by saying that, once the requisite recording techniques had been developed, physical and electrophysiological facts could displace psychological theory. In one sense this is obviously true, and yet in terms of the tripartite division suggested in the Introduction to this chapter, it is clear that these advances have been mainly in the first area characterized: studying the visual system as *detector* of signals with specifiable qualities. The detailed physiological responses of single units to color tell us almost nothing in themselves about the organization of color information or its uses. Here is a fascinating and fundamental fact about seeing: Studying processes at one level of the system, which are certainly necessary prerequisites for the occurrence of other ("higher") processes, does not automatically lead to understanding of the latter. On the other hand, visual scientists, like others, wield Occam's razor, and will explain as much of a given phenomenon at as low a level as possible, provided the explanation is adequate. In the present case one must ask: How much of color perception is adequately explained by the findings on photopigments and electrophysiological opponent processes?

It has been argued, for instance by Land (1959), that the generally accepted theories of color coding are adequate only so long as one considers homogeneous patches of colored surfaces, or lights viewed under specialized and highly artificial conditions. Perception of real objects in a visually rich environment is a far different matter. However Land's ideas may shock the orthodox (e.g., Walls, 1960), it is evident that a comprehensive account of the perception of color must encompass a variety of spatial and temporal interaction effects which range well beyond the question of coding of the simple sensory quality: color. For example, simultaneous and successive contrast are well-known and much-investigated phenomena of color vision, and the enhancement of brightness contrast found in the familiar Mach band demonstrations is another. Brightness and color constancy are commonly observed facts about the visual world and they too seem to require more complex explanations than a physiologically based model of color coding can provide.

It is instructive to consider the wide range of explanations that have been offered, from Helmholtz's notion of "unconscious inference," an explanatory device based on the conviction that perception is a cognitive activity and is so to be understood, to the opposite view that all such phenomena can be comprehended in terms of the immediate processing capacities of the visual system and hence will—ultimately—have a physiological explanation. Each different sort of explanation has its own appeal, and yet no one of them seems both tight enough and comprehensive enough to be fully satisfactory.

Nearly 100 years ago Ernst Mach proposed a mechanism of reciprocal inhibition to account for border enhancement effects, and the discovery of physiological mechanisms subserving this function gave a powerful boost to explanations of spatial and temporal interactions based on the principle (Ratliff, 1965).* Investigation of the contrast modulation transfer function of the (human) visual system in terms of its Fourier components (Cornsweet, 1970) has yielded plausible explanations of a great many of the known contrast phenomena and perhaps can be extended to account for some aspects of constancy. Similarly, attempts to explain constancy in terms of invariants in the stimulus array such as luminance ratios have met with some success (Wallach, 1948). These explanations are instances of our second level: attempts to understand the *organization* of information in optical arrays. Visual scientists are happy to accept the more "basic" explanation for a fact of color vision in terms of coding or neural organization, so long as it is adequate, rather than appeal to "higher order" factors. Yet it is undeniably true that cognitive influences such as knowledge of the stimulus object, set, or value *can* influence what is seen: A gray patch seen against a red background appears green, and this is a straightforward demonstration of the perceptual phenomenon of simultaneous color contrast. The fact that the patch appears greener if it is in the shape of a leaf rather than when it resembles a donkey is just as valid a perceptual phenomenon, and it is difficult to see how anything but a cognitive explanation can account for it. This is a basic and crude demonstration, and, of course, much more elaborate examples could be cited. What is important is the realization that different *sorts* of perceptual process are involved, even in so simple a case as this. Physiological processes must underlie the phenomenon as necessary conditions for simultaneous contrast to occur; they are not, however, sufficient to explain exhaustively everything about the phenomenon. It is important to know what the physiological basis may be, but this is not equivalent to saying that the phenomenon can be understood wholly in terms of those processes. Thus explanations at the third proposed level—attempts to understand the *uses* of visual information—go beyond explanations at the earlier levels, but do not in any sense *displace* them.

A second place where physiological discoveries made during the last decade have had a profound influence in the theorizing of psychologists is in the field of contour coding and pattern recognition. (See, for example, Dodwell, 1970, for an introduction to this area.) The basic finding on contour vision in the mammalian visual system is that single cells in the visual cortex have well-circumscribed retinal receptive fields, and are tuned to

---

* At the same time it should be pointed out that most of the detailed information on physiological inhibitory mechanisms of the type required to explain border contrast enhancement and similar effects comes from the study of invertebrate visual systems which in many respects are quite differently organized from vertebrate and particularly mammalian systems.

respond to contours or edges in particular orientations (so-called simple receptive field units) but in some cases with position on the retina not highly specified (complex units); other cells (hypercomplex) respond to more restricted pattern elements, such as a contour of a specified length, or moving in a particular way (Hubel & Wiesel, 1962, 1968). This sort of information has been seized on avidly by psychologists, who have not been slow to seek out, and find, psychophysical parallels to many of the electrophysiological results. Perhaps the most celebrated of these is the McCollough effect, in which adaptation to a square wave grating in one orientation and color is produced simultaneously with adaptation to a second grating at 90° to the first and in a different color; when an achromatic grating is then viewed, orientation-specific colored aftereffects are observed (McCollough, 1965). The effect has been explained in terms of the selective adaptation of units in the visual cortex specifically tuned to contours of a given orientation and color. (See Chapters 4 and 7 for a review of these findings.) Adaptation effects of a more complicated kind have been observed, such as color-contingent motion aftereffects, and even three-way contingencies. The tendency has been to identify the effect with selective adaptation of neurons that are specifically tuned to identify the complex of features for which the contingent effect occurs, and so long as a type of cell so tuned has been detected independently by other means this strategy seems reasonable. But things get out of hand if *any* type of selective effect is immediately identified with adaptation of the unit that detects the particular conglomerate of features in question: The yellow VW detector is now an old joke. What about simple curvature adaptation, for example? This can be even more readily obtained than the McCollough effect—yet curvature detectors have not been identified by physiological methods. If we postulate curvature detectors to explain a contingent adaptive effect, as Riggs (1973) has done, we are coming close to MacDougall's problem with instincts: For each possible motive, posit an instinct; for each possible visual adaptation, posit a neural detector. The proof of existence of these detectors rapidly degenerates into circularity and is of no real significance for the development of perceptual theory. At best the experimental demonstration of a particular type of selective adaptation might suggest what to look for with an exploratory electrode; the trouble is that the visual system has an enormous range of adaptive capacity (Helson, 1964). It will adapt to just about anything: Therefore, anything visible must have a neural correlate that is subject to adaptation—hardly a powerful or novel theoretical discovery! There are other problems: The time-course of the psychophysically demonstrated contingent adaptations may be of the order of hours, or even days which are not even remotely like the normally observed time courses for neural (single unit) adaptations. This difficulty remains to be resolved, and theorizing such as that of Mayhew and Anstis (1972), has moved toward the position that the contingent aftereffects have more in common with a process of perceptual learning or conditioning than with simple neural adaptations.

These arguments are made not to belittle the importance of neurophysiological discoveries in furthering understanding of vision. Rather, their point is to caution against overenthusiastic invocation of hypothetical physiological processes to explain psychophysical phenomena. A great many facts about visual perception are compatible with the neurophysiological findings, but the instances where an interpretation of the former in terms of the latter is forced on us by the tightness of the relationship are quite rare, and, for the most part, are at the first level of visual *detection*. The phenomena of scotopic and photopic vision and their relationship to rod and cone function are the outstanding example of such a tight association (see, e.g., Cornsweet, 1970). In particular, the physiological findings on contour coding should be viewed with caution, so far as pattern and object recognition are concerned. They tell a great deal about the probable mechanism of pattern element detection, but almost nothing about pattern organization, or synthesis [Level (*ii*)] or object recognition [Level (*iii*)]. Attempts have been made to integrate the neurophysiological findings into models for visual pattern recognition following the Hebbian notion of associative neural networks (e.g., Dodwell, 1970) but these efforts are, at present, somewhat speculative, and the same can be said of the Artificial Intelligence approach to pattern recognition (e.g., Barlow, Narasimhan, & Rosenfeld, 1972). The important point to realize is that the neurophysiological findings can supplement, but do not displace, theoretical attempts to understand pattern and object recognition.

At present, the firmly established facts about cortical cell response to visual stimulation are confined mainly to responses to simple elements such as lines oriented in a particular direction and moving in a specified way. The fact that virtually all cortical cells have a "preferred" orientation is agreeably in harmony with the very extensive psychophysical demonstrations of orientationally tuned visual channels (e.g., Blakemore & Campbell, 1969, Campbell & Kulikowski, 1966). This, together with the fact that such channels tend to be frequency-specific (Sachs, Nachmias, & Robson, 1971), has added impetus to the search for an understanding of visual processing in terms of Fourier analysis (Campbell & Robson, 1968; Glezer, Ivanoff, & Tscherbach, 1973). This view is not without difficulties of its own (Nachmias, Sansbury, Vassilev, & Weber, 1973) but is appealing because it suggests a powerful way to bridge the gap between pattern element or contour detection on the one hand and the synthesis (organization) of patterns on the other (Glezer *et al.,* 1973; Rosenfeld, 1969). Even so, one is still dealing with processes at Levels (i) and (ii), and by methods that are not obviously amenable to rendering an account of pattern recognition in its more cognitive aspects. As in the case of color perception, one would like to account for as much as possible in terms of "basic" processes for which a physiological explanation seems possible in principle, yet pattern perception serves cognitive ends, which, even in principle, are not fully explainable in these terms. This is a theme to which I shall return in detail later.

There is a creative antithesis between physicalist or reductionist theorizers on the one hand, and those with a leaning toward cognitive explanations on the other. To the extent that enormous advances in understanding visual physiology have occurred in recent years, one might argue that the formers' star is in the ascendant. Yet detailed knowledge of visual physiology is only one step in the understanding of seeing. As understanding of the coding of visual sensory qualities progresses, the need to integrate them into coherent models of visual processing becomes pressing, and this is, in my view, one of the major contemporary issues.

III. THE NATURE–NURTURE CONTROVERSIES

Perhaps the single most pervasive theoretical argument in perception has been about the role experience plays, particularly in perceptual development. The philosophical controversy has existed since Plato's time, at least, and was a major area of dispute between Rationalist and Empiricist philosophers of the seventeenth and eighteenth centuries. The interested reader can find an excellent historical résumé in a paper by Hochberg (1962), who also traces its development as a scientific issue in the opposing viewpoints of Helmholtz and Hering in the nineteenth century, and indeed into some more recent developments of the first half of the twentieth. A detailed account of the philosophical antecedents of modern perceptual theory is given by Hamlyn (1961); Armstrong (1964) is another useful sourcebook in this area. Nature versus nurture is still a lively point at issue in the biological sciences generally; see Lehrman (1970).

Posed as the general question: "Does experience affect perception?" the answer seems obvious. If you drive a car, you do not observe the same things on the road as someone who has never used mechanical transport; if your livelihood depends on using a microscope, you will see things with it that the layman does not. These are not the points at issue, of course. What one really wants to ask is whether particular sorts of experience are necessary conditions for achieving a stable, three-dimensional perceptual world, a frame of reference evidently common to all normally reared human beings. Beyond this, one may inquire into the detailed similarities and differences in the perceptual capacities of individuals brought up in environments whose optical ecologies are quite diverse (see the review in Section V of Chapter 8), but empirical investigations of this sort have not led to striking advances in our understanding of perception. Of much more immediate impact on the status of the nature–nurture question have been two other lines of research. The first of these is the study of pattern and object recognition in human infants, and the second is the study of the electrophysiology of single cells in the visual system. These topics are reviewed elsewhere in this volume (Chapter 4; Chapter 8, Section V); the discussion here will concentrate on their relevance to the development of an adequate theoretical treatment of nature and nurture.

The study of infants and certain aspects of electrophysiology are so relevant to nature–nurture problems because they address questions about the initial conditions from which normal adult perceptual abilities develop. Thus when it was discovered that young kittens without visual exposure have essentially the same elementary physiological contour coding system as adult cats (Hubel & Wiesel, 1963) this was a strong blow for nativism. Despite a large amount of research showing that deprivation and selective exposure can bias the system in important ways (e.g., Pettigrew, Olson, & Barlow, 1973), it still remains true to say that visual scientists are now convinced that a great deal more of the mammalian visual system's information processing capacity is built in, or prewired, than was thought possible before the advent of the single cell studies of cortical function. Similarly, discovery that young human infants display pattern preferences (Fantz, 1961) led to a line of inquiry that established discriminative capacities hitherto unsuspected and tending to support a nativistic position. The early work in infant perception was much influenced by the ethological findings on key stimuli in an organism's environment which trigger specific forms of behavior (the so-called innate releasing mechanisms; Eibl-Eibesfeldt, 1969; Tinbergen, 1951). Again, there has been much controversy about the validity and interpretation of ethological discoveries, and attempts to find correlates of the trigger stimuli in human infants' vision have not been too successful, yet the effects on theoretical discussions of perception have been considerable, tending to increase the force of nativistic arguments.

Certainly no psychologist today would espouse a simple nativistic or empiricist theory of perception: Perhaps the last major attempts of this sort were made by the *Gestalt* psychologists on the one hand, and J. G. Taylor on the other (Taylor, 1962), but one can recognize strong leanings toward one side or the other in contemporary writers. A novel approach to the issue, and one with genuine theoretical impact, was generated some time ago by the Gibsons (Gibson & Gibson, 1955). It was that most of the controversies over nativism versus empiricism, both philosophical and psychological, are misguided because of a deep misunderstanding of the nature of perception. They argued that the "contructivism" typical of empiricists is forced on them because of a belief in sensory "atoms," the simple elements from which complex perceptions must be formed. Denial of the importance of experience is forced on the nativist if he accepts the empiricist's account of what perceptual organization is all about (construction of a perceptual world from simple sensory elements) and this he is likely to do because he shares the same misconception about the nature of perception. For the nativist however, the atoms include the perceptual features the empiricist thinks must be learned. In the Gibsons' view there are no sensory atoms, and no need, therefore, for associations, interpretations, or constructions; this does not deny the fact of perceptual learning, or its importance. Instead it entails a redefinition of what perceptual learning is.

J. J. Gibson's contribution in this area has actually been twofold. First, he has argued strongly for a broadening of the concept of visual stimulation. By pointing to the enormous richness of information inherent in a natural visual environment and stressing the importance of such hitherto neglected static and dynamic variables as gradients of texture, movement parallax, binocular disparity and so on, he has successfully convinced most perceptual theorists that the broadening was necessary (Gibson, 1950, 1966). Second, he has argued that the broader concept is sufficient (together with his notion of information pickup) to explain the veridical perception of the visual world. In this he has been less successful, and has been branded an obstinate nativist, despite his own claims to the contrary (Taylor, 1962). Three observations are in order here: First, Gibson's conception of the global nature of sensory stimulation is quite out of tune with the atomistic findings of sensory neurophysiology. It seems that the visual system does, in fact, operate in the first instance as the detector of small elements of pattern information; although it is possible that some sort of automatic synthesis (of Fourier components, for example) occurs, physiological evidence of the more elaborate processing that would be required in Gibson's system is so far lacking. Second, experimental evidence reported by Ericksson (1970) shows fairly conclusively that perceptual judgments based on texture, perspective, and movement gradients are not as uniform as Gibson's theory predicted, nor even always in the expected direction. In other words, perceptual judgments are not as stimulus bound as the theory requires them to be. Third, insofar as perceptual learning, in the Gibsonian view, consists of perception coming into ever-greater correspondence with stimulation, or the detection of ever finer and more sophisticated aspects of the presented stimulation, it attempts to limit perceptual activity to Levels (i) and (ii) of the scheme suggested earlier. There are strong grounds for thinking that this limitation cannot be sustained (see the following section). Nevertheless, Gibson's theoretical innovations have had the great merit of forcing psychologists to think afresh about the nature–nurture issue, and have certainly led to some interesting new types of experiments (see, for instance, E. J. Gibson, 1969). Gibson's claim to cut across the traditional issues is in part correct, and, to this extent, the experimental work stemming from his ideas sidesteps those issues. On the other hand, his insistence on the "completeness" of information available in the optical array gives his theorizing a strongly nativistic flavor, which probably has had some influence on the general move toward that position in recent years. Be that as it may, by far the most important point to make about the nature–nurture controversy at present is that no one regards any particular question as paramount, and no one attempts to perform the crucial experiment that will settle the issue definitively one way or the other. Rather, a great many experiments, particularly on infant visual capacities and on visual physiology, are seen as bearing on the matter and, usually by small increments in knowledge, tend to elucidate the nature of the interaction of hereditary and environmental factors. Theoretical alignment with a position such as Gibson's or Piaget's (1969) certainly influences the sorts of experiment which will be done, and how they are interpreted. But experimental evidence in itself will not resolve, or bury, the nature–nurture controversy. It is certainly a contemporary issue, but psychologists in vision research tend to be less dogmatic about it than in the past.

IV. LEVELS OF FUNCTIONING

Having surveyed some of the areas where basic and continuing theoretical discussion are prevalent, the reader may feel a certain sense of dissatisfaction with the state of our science. Increasing knowledge about sensory coding at the physiological level improves our understanding of such processes, but in itself promises no major theoretical breakthrough in understanding perception. The same is true of the solution of nature–nurture questions. One might think that this lack of resolution of the large traditional issues is a sign of weakness, or lack of progress. The point I want to make is quite to the contrary: What looks like a stalemate from one viewpoint can be seen as the essence of psychological science from another. In particular, the nature of visual perception is such as to preclude the sorts of major development in theory which characterize other branches of science, unless it be considered a breakthrough to recognize this very fact. I shall now attempt to clarify that notion.

Let us consider for a moment what might be thought to constitute a theoretical advance in understanding vision. Three prime candidates would be the discovery of some new principle of physiological coding in the visual nervous system, the observation of a radical change in perceptual capability as a result of some particular intervention or experience, or the finding that some strategy of perceptual information pickup was uniformly employed, but had hitherto gone undetected. Exciting in themselves, such discoveries would not alter in any profound way our understanding of the *nature* of perception. They imply no revolutionary insights of the sort that have transformed physics and biology in this century. Advances of the type described have certainly occurred since the study of perception became a scientific, experimental enterprise, and have led to new understanding; not, however, to fundamental theoretical breakthroughs. Is it failure in our own imaginations that leads to the conclusion that no profoundly new insights will revolutionize our understanding of perception? I think not, because perception is a multilevel phenomenon, and its attainment depends on many different kinds of process. Theoretical and practical discoveries occur within the different levels. This may change our understanding of what happens at a particular level, may revolutionize our knowledge of the process, but this is not the same as a radical change in understanding the nature of perception per se.

Further discussion of the three examples just given will make this point clear. First of all, consider the example of a new physiological discovery in sensory coding. As we have already noted, discoveries of this sort have been made frequently in recent years, and have vastly changed our knowledge of sensory coding. Although such results are quoted with almost monotonous regularity in relation to perceptual phenomena studied by psychologists, their theoretical impact is usually quite moderate at best, and can at worst be rather misleading. It has been understood for a very long time that visual perception depends on transduction of physical energy, electromagnetic radiation of certain frequencies, into physiological activity within the nervous system, and that this transduction involves particular types of coding. How we perceive things must depend, at least in the first instance, on what the coding process is. Knowledge of sensory coding grows, and with it our understanding of the constraints it places on perception; but this does not cause a fundamental shift in our view of how the two are related, nor should it. There is a misleading tendency evident in some quarters to *equate* knowledge of electrophysiological coding with theoretical understanding of perception. My point is that the understanding of electrophysiological coding occurs at one level, or one stage, of processing; it contributes to understanding perception, but is not itself the whole story. The discoveries of recent years have vastly improved our knowledge of that coding, but the theoretical issues were understood, and had been debated for many years before the electrophysiological break-throughs were made. Progress in understanding the necessity for a concept of coding for shape, for instance, can be traced from work of the nineteenth century and from *Gestalt* psychology, but substantial new progress was made by Lashley (1942) with his notion of reduplicated interference pat-terns, by Pitts and McCulloch (1947) with their computing networks, and by Deutsch (1955), who first produced a testable model for shape coding. Emphasis since that time has shifted in two directions, one toward the factual, atheoretical, questions of how visual coding occurs physiologically, the other toward finding more adequate models, for example, ones that do not involve circular definition of the pattern recognition operation (Dodwell, 1970). These developments do not entail radical changes in our understanding of the nature of perception, but do lead to sharper defi-nition and knowledge of certain underlying perceptual processes, at Levels (*i*) and (*ii*), according to the scheme proposed earlier.

Our second example of a theoretically important discovery is the finding of some new effect of perceptual experience, or lack of it, such as visual deprivation or exposure to distorted visual environments. The now classical work of Held and Hein (1963) on the breaking of the visuomotor feedback loop and its effect on visual guidance, and that of Walk and Gibson (1961) on the "visual cliff" serve as fine examples. How much change is wrought by such studies on our understanding of perception as a whole? In fact, not very much. They may nudge us toward some more centralist or periph-eralist point of view, just as some electrophysiological discoveries have done, but in neither case is there a profound change in our conception of what perception is all about. There are pendulum swings from side to side in response to some new discovery or particularly persuasive writer; but the oscillations tend now to be well damped, and to expect a definitive "solution" in favor of nature or nurture would be absurd. It is their detailed interaction that is of contemporary interest, not the question of dominance by one over the other.

Our third example is the discovery of a new strategy of information pickup: Suppose it were found that learning to read involves some hitherto quite unsuspected process of extracting meaning from symbols, and that exploitation of that process resulted in greatly improved methods of teach-ing reading and similar skills. Exciting as this would be, it would not qualify as a discovery that alters our grasp of the nature of reading; after all, read-ing is a human invention, and in its conventional aspects is well understood. When we study reading we are really studying some of the psychological processes that allow us to *use* the conventions of the written and spoken word. Those processes are but part of the activities of reading, writing, and speaking, and will not, in themselves, lead to radical alterations of our understanding of those activities.

The three illustrations exemplify my point that different processes, at different levels of abstractness, are involved in typical perceptual activity; theoretical advances occur in understanding the processes, not perception as such. Certainly, discoveries about these processes can have a profound influence on the direction which experimental investigation takes. Good examples of this are the rediscovery of short-term visual storage by Sperling (1960) which led to the development of the concept of iconic memory, and the recent burgeoning interest in imaginal operations, which followed the discovery that they can be studied objectively (e.g., Pylyshyn, 1973; Shepard & Metzler, 1971).

Reading, writing, and speaking are human inventions, but this fact does not guarantee that we understand them intuitively and perfectly, or do not need to study them. Great strides have been made in understanding language during the past two decades, particularly in its developmental aspects. Yet the *purpose* of language is not affected by such new discoveries, only the processes that allow the purpose to be fulfilled. That seems obvious. What is not so obvious is that the same logic applies to many other cognitive functions, including perception. It is not so obvious there because perception is not so clearly an invention of mankind.

The way we perceive, and in particular the way we see, is constrained by the physiological apparatus of the visual system; it is shaped in some degree by experience, but also is a major factor in the genesis of human communication. The ability to classify, to name, to describe and refer, rest on the discrimination of common perceptual features of the environment in the first instance. This point was driven home to me some years ago by watching a linguist, a specialist in nonliterate languages, establish communication with the speaker of a completely unknown language, in that language, in the space of an hour or so. Not only this, but the major structure of the language was also laid bare. All this was done, basically, by appealing to common perceived attributes of the environment, familiar objects, events and actions. The modern linguistic tradition makes much of the universality of certain features of language, thereby claiming that the competence for language inheres in the human species. No less a case can be made for the similar *shaping* of languages by a common physical environment. Perception shapes language, our major tool of communication, but the achievement of language in turn widens the scope of perception (Urmson, 1956). To this extent, perception also is a human artifact. Without language, there would be no perception as we understand it: perception of objects, people, social situations, etc. Our perception of the world requires, then, at least the tools of language to be available for its expression. In this sense, it is a distinctively human achievement. To call it a human invention is to invoke too deliberate a process of rational search; nevertheless one cannot fully comprehend perception without realizing the human purposes it serves.

To point to discriminative behavior in animals or young children which is similar to that of the normal adult, as the *Gestalt* psychologists and others have done, is to show that the discriminative powers are similar, or that the same organization of cues is utilized; it surely does not prove identity of perception. Similarly, teaching a chimpanzee to "read" strings of symbols identifies a process similar to human reading; it throws no light on the activity of reading, only on the abilities of chimps. To understand reading requires a *conceptual analysis* of what is involved before any empirical investigation is worthwhile. This appears to be an overstatement, but only because we take so much for granted; we have an implicit understanding of reading and what it involves. This does not alter the fact that conceptual clarity about the nature of reading is prerequisite to studying it in other ways, and this prerequisite is in the province of epistemological, or philosophical, analysis. Another way of saying this is to say that no amount of empirical study of people reading will improve our understanding of the *purpose* of reading. The same is true of perception. Thus, to the antitheses described earlier we can add a third: the antithesis between perception as biological activity, and as cognitive, intellectual achievement.

Comparison with the psychologist's study of chess—another highly cognitive, purposive human activity—can be illuminating here. A recent major effort to understand the psychological processes underlying ability at chess has met with considerable success (Simon & Chase, 1973). The actual behavior of chess players is analyzed in detail, and hypotheses about certain activities, particularly those of a visual-perceptual nature, investigated. This leads to some insight into the *how* of chess mastery, but advances our understanding of *why* chess is engaged in as a challenging intellectual activity not at all. The investigation does not help in the understanding of chess as a game: It helps in understanding how chess as a game is mastered. That is, it helps in understanding the processes that underlie ability at chess. It would be absurd to inquire into the evolution or biological utility of chess, its origins are not those of perception. Yet, comparison between the study of chess and of perception can tell us something about the sorts of explanatory schemata it is fruitful for the psychologist to propose for the latter. Psychologists study and try to explain *process,* not *purpose;* yet should not lose sight of the fact that purpose is of the essence of the activities they seek to understand.

V. LEVELS OF EXPLANATION

What have the arguments proposed in the previous section to do with the practical activities of visual scientists? In one sense, very little; the modern theoretical emphasis is on explaining the role particular factors—physiological, experiential, or cognitive—play in perception. These do not aim at a grand new design, but rather at filling in a picture whose main structure is already known. The emphases shift and analogies alter, usually in accordance with the latest technology, but these cause relatively minor changes in our understanding of perception. However, in another sense, it is important to acknowledge the limits within which theoretical advances in perception can occur; it is important because it leads to the realization that those limits are conceptual and depend on our implicit understanding of the role perception plays in human life. No amount of empirical investigation or theoretical speculation will alter that role. In this sense, no breakthroughs are possible.

Philosophers concerned with explanations in psychology frequently make the point that psychologists' models and theories bear little relation to the ordinary uses of "psychological" words, and hence are mistaken in their attempts at explanation of activities such as seeing and remembering (e.g., Malcolm, 1971). My arguments of the previous section are addressed to the same problem, but approach it in a manner more sympathetic to the activities of scientific psychology. The typical psychological model, couched in physiological, engineering or information-theoretical terms, is not sufficient to *entail* statements about perception or memory as commonly understood (Dodwell, 1960, 1970, 1971) because process and purpose have different explanatory roles in normal linguistic usage. This again is another way of emphasizing the difference between scientific and everyday discourse about psychological activities. Philosophers have argued that, because of this hiatus, psychologists misjudge what it is that needs explanation in psychology. I would argue, on the contrary, that philosophers have missed the point of what psychologists are attempting to achieve with their explanations; admittedly psychologists themselves have not shown convincingly what role their explanations should play, particularly in understanding cognitive behavior. To be explicit, it can be said that psychologists investigate and theorize about certain conditions that are *empirically necessary* if perception (for instance) is to occur. That is, they argue about and investigate processes that are parts of, or stages in, the activity of perception; they certainly affect perception in definite ways, and that is why their models are testable, scientific. But those process models can be distinguished sharply from general theories of the *nature* of perception. The latter may be epistemological, metaphysical, existential; they have little empirical content, and hence small interest for the scientist.

Thus there are different levels of explanation for perceptual processes, different sorts of processes that can be investigated, and no one of them is exhaustive in accounting for perceptual phenomena. Elsewhere I have used an analogy with music to give the matter sharper emphasis (Dodwell, 1971b), and it might be valuable to reiterate the arguments here.

Consider the nature of a sophisticated audience's enjoyment of a classical work, say a Beethoven symphony: The appreciation of the music will vary in depth and variety even within such a group. Some will simply enjoy the fine melodies, others will recognize and appreciate the tonality typical of this composer's middle period, yet others will pay attention particularly to the richness and variety of thematic and contrapuntal skill displayed, and so on. The extent to which the music is a vehicle of communication for different people will depend on their previous training, experience, and involvement with music. They may be said to be necessary conditions of their appreciation of classical music, but certainly not sufficient in themselves to explain that appreciation. At an entirely different level, one may note that the production of music depends on the acceptance and use of a large measure of technical symbolism, conventions having to do with musical notation, conducting technique and similar matters. At yet another level, it is dependent on the skills of the musicians, both manual and artistic. These, too, are necessary conditions for the production and appreciation of music. The acoustic properties of musical instruments and the physics of sound constitute a further level of facts and phenomena that underlie the production of music. The list could be extended in various ways, but the point should now be obvious: To understand music and music appreciation must necessarily involve understanding and explanation at several different levels. Processes at one level, acoustics, for instance, can be studied and understood in their own right, and as necessary conditions for the production of musical sounds, without being sufficient as explanations of music. No one would think to understand a composition in any real sense by pure acoustical analysis. Music is a *multilevel* phenomenon; the underlying processes are of different sorts and to be understood according to different conventions and models of the world. To think that a single, exhaustive, monolithic "explanation" of music—or theory of music—is possible is to mistake entirely the nature of what it is that we seek to understand.

This same argument holds with perception, and specifically with seeing. In many respects, the differences of level are obvious enough, as in the physics of light, physiological energy transduction, the biological utility of seeing, and the cognitive ends which perception serves; earlier I made the distinction between detection [Level (*i*)], organization [Level (*ii*)], and use [Level (*iii*)] of visual signals, which complements this classification. The relationships between the levels have been ill-defined, and, in particular, the role that explanation at different levels should play in understanding perception as a whole has scarcely been analyzed explicitly. I do not propose to make such an analysis here, only to point out that it is a matter worthy of thought, and should constitute a major theoretical goal for the psychology of perception. My contention is that this is, or should be, the avenue to explore in attempting to answer the general question raised at the beginning of this chapter: What is the correct theoretical framework within which to gain an understanding of perception? If we accept this, it is at once clear why the antitheses described earlier arise. It is because different levels within the system are selected as the sites of processes held to underlie particular phenomena. In the case of nature–nurture the choice (or pseudochoice) is between innately determined mechanisms on the one hand and environmentally shaped processes on the other. Once it is recognized that the levels of discourse for these two sorts of process are different, and, in fact, the former must contain some empirically necessary conditions for the development of the latter, it becomes easier to accept the coexistence of different explanatory schemes or models that are related in important ways, but not completely reducible to a single common level. Similarly with the other two antitheses, between the physiological–cognitive and biological–rational aspects of perception; an appreciation of the different types of discourse appropriate to the different levels of the antitheses eases our problems. One can say that such antitheses have only appeared to create philosophical and scientific problems for the psychology of perception because we had mistakenly thought them to involve antagonistic rather than complementary schemes of explanation. This is where the analogy with the understanding of music should be most useful.

An implicit acceptance of the multistage nature of perception has developed in recent years; certainly attempts at theorizing have become less metaphysical, more technical, more specialized and, of course, more testable by experiment. Systematists have made useful contributions, but the need for all-embracing theories in visual perception is now probably over. The change of emphasis in our attempts to understand perception has thus been a change toward stressing the need to understand particular underlying processes. If it has led to a certain fragmentation of attempts at explanation, the present analysis of the situation should make clear why this is almost inevitable.

The traditional theoretical problems of perception, as I said at the beginning of the chapter, are still the problems and questions that exercise us today. The reason for this should now be clear. What have been taken to be the major questions have often been posed as if they were amenable to definitive empirical solution, and this is particularly true for questions to do with nature and nurture, and the physiological bases of perception. I have tried to show why, in many cases, definitive solutions are not merely unlikely, but actually not possible, hence why the problems are still with us, and how theoretical questions should be rephrased to take account of the many different sorts of process and activity that underlie—that are empirically necessary conditions of—perception. Increased understanding comes· about through increased understanding of the component processes. Understanding of perception per se is not a matter for empirical investigation so much as for conceptual analysis, whose tradition, so far as perception is concerned, goes back over 2000 years. There have been philosophers who maintain that, because of the primacy of conceptual analysis, experimentally based investigations necessarily fail to achieve any adequate grasp of the explanatory tools required to understand perception. It would, of course, be absurd to belittle the scientific advances that have been made in understanding visual perception, but the analysis given here should help to make clear which sorts of questions about perception can reasonably be tackled scientifically and experimentally, and which cannot. Let us give the philosopher his due, but not at the expense of derogation of the visual scientists' achievements.

References

Armstrong, D. M. *Perception and the physical world.* New York: Humanities Press, 1964.

Barlow, H. B., Narasimhan, R., & Rosenfeld, A. Visual pattern analysis in machines and animals. *Science,* 1972, **177,** 567–575.

Blakemore, C., & Campbell, F. W. On the existence of neurons in the human visual system selectively sensitive to the orientation and size of retinal images. *Journal of Physiology,* 1969, **203,** 237–260.

Campbell, F. W., & Kulikowski, J. J. Orientational selectivity of the human visual system. *Journal of Physiology,* 1966, **187,** 437–445.

Campbell, F. W., & Robson, J. G. Application of Fourier analysis to the visibility of gratings. *Journal of Physiology,* 1968, **197,** 557–566.

Cornsweet, T. N. *Visual perception,* New York: Academic Press, 1970.

Deutsch, J. A. A theory of shape recognition. *British Journal of Psychology,* 1955, **46,** 30–37.

De Valois, R. L., & Jacobs, G. H. Primate color vision. *Science,* 1968, **162,** 533–540.

Dodwell, P. C. Causes, and explanation in psychology. *Mind,* 1960, **69,** N.S., 1–13.

Dodwell, P. C. *Visual pattern recognition.* New York: Holt, 1970.

Dodwell, P. C. Is a theory of conceptual development necessary? In T. Mischel (Ed.), *Cognitive development and epistemology.* New York: Academic Press, 1971.

Eibl-Eibesfeldt, I. *Grundriss der Vergleichen den Verhaltensforschung.* 2nd ed. Munich: R. Piper & Co Verlag, 1969. [Translated as: *Ethology: The biology of behavior.* New York: Holt, 1970.]

Ericksson, E. S. A cognitive theory of three-dimensional motion perception. *Report No. 75. Department of Psychology, University of Uppsala, Sweden, 1970.*

Fantz, R. L. The origin of form perception. *Scientific American,* 1961, **204**, (No. 5), 66–72.

Gibson, E. J. *Principles of perceptual learning and development.* New York: Appleton, 1969.

Gibson, J. J. *The perception of the visual world.* Boston: Houghton-Mifflin, 1950.

Gibson, J. J. *The senses considered as perceptual systems.* Boston: Houghton-Mifflin, 1966.

Gibson, J. J., & Gibson, E. J. Perceptual learning: Differentiation or enrichment? *Psychological Review,* 1955, **62**, 1–32.

Glezer, V. D., Ivanoff, V. A., & Tscherbach, T. A. Investigation of complex and hypercomplex receptive fields of visual cortex of the cat as spatial frequency filters. *Vision Research,* 1973, **13**, 1875–1904.

Hamlyn, D. *Sensation and perception: A history of the philosophy of perception.* New York : Humanities Press, 1961.

Held, R., & Hein, A. Movement-produced stimulation in the development of visually guided behavior. *Journal of Comparative & Physiological Psychology,* 1963, **56**, 872–876.

Helson, H. *Adaptation level theory.* New York: Harper and Row, 1964.

Hochberg, J. Nativism and empiricism in perception. In L. Postman (Ed.), *Psychology in the making.* New York: Knopf, 1962.

Hubel D. H., & Wiesel, T. N. Receptive fields, binocular interaction and functional architecture in the cat's visual cortex. *Journal of Physiology,* 1962, **160**, 106–154.

Hubel, D. H., & Wiesel, T. N. Receptive fields of cells in striate cortex of very young visually inexperienced kittens. *Journal of Neurophysiology,* 1963, **26**, 994–1002.

Hubel, D. H., & Wiesel, T. N. Receptive fields and functional architecture of monkey striate cortex. *Journal of Physiology,* 1968, **195**, 215–243.

Hurvich, L. M., & Jameson, D. Some quantitative aspects of an opponent-colors theory. II. Brightness, saturation, and hue in normal and dichromatic vision. *Journal of the Optical Society of America,* 1955, **45**, 602–616.

Land, E. H. Color vision and the natural image. *Proceedings of the National Academy of Science,* 1959, **45**, pt. I, 115–126; pt. II, 636–644.

Lashley, K. S. The problem of cerebral organization in vision. *Biological Symposia,* 1942, **7**, 301–322.

Lehrman, D. S. Semantic and conceptual issues in the nature–nurture problem. In L. Aronson (Ed.), *Development and evolution of behavior: Essays in memory of T. C. Schneirla.* San Francisco: Freeman, 1970.

MacCorquodale, K. On Chomsky's review of Skinner's Verbal Behavior. *Journal of Experimental Analysis of Behavior,* 1970, **13**, 83–99.

Malcolm, N. The myth of cognitive processes and structures. In T. Mischel (Ed.), *Cognitive development and epistemology.* New York: Academic Press, 1971.

Marks, W. B., Dobell, W. H., & MacNichol, J. R. The visual pigments of single primate cones, *Science,* 1964, **143**, 1181–1183.

Mayhew, J. T., & Anstis, S. M. Movement after-effects contingent on color, intensity and pattern. *Perception & Psychophysics,* 1972, **12**, 77–85.

McCollough, C. Color adaptation of edge-detectors in the human visual system. *Science,* 1965, **149,** 3688.

Nachmias, J., Sansbury, R., Vassilev, A., & Weber, A. Adaptation to square-wave gratings; in search of the elusive third harmonic. *Vision Research,* 1973, **13,** 1335–1341.

Pettigrew, W. J., Olson, C., & Barlow, H. B. Kitten visual cortex: Short-term stimulus-induced changes in connectivity. *Science,* 1973, **180,** 1202–1203.

Piaget, J. *The mechanisms of perception* G. Seagrim (trans.). London: Routledge & Kegan Paul, 1969. (Original French version, 1961.)

Pitts, W. H., & McCulloch, W. S. How we know universals: The perception of auditory and visual forms. *Bulletin of Mathematical Biophysics,* 1947, **9,** 127–147.

Pylyshyn, Z. W. What the mind's eye tells the mind's brain: A critique of mental imagery. *Psychological Review,* 1973, **80,** 1–24.

Ratliff, F. *Mach bands: Quantitative studies on neural networks in the retina.* San Francisco: Holden-Day, 1965.

Riggs, L. A. Curvature as a feature of pattern vision. *Science,* 1973, **181,** 1070–1072.

Rosenfeld, A. *Picture processing by computer.* New York: Academic Press, 1969.

Sachs, M. B., Nachmias, J., & Robson, J. G. Spatial-frequency channels in human vision. *Journal of the Optical Society of America,* 1971, **61,** 1176–1186.

Shepard, R., & Metzler, J. Mental rotation of three-dimensional objects. *Science,* 1971, **171,** 701–703.

Simon, A. H., & Chase, W. G. Skill at chess. *American Scientist,* 1973, **61,** 394–403.

Sperling, G. The information available in brief visual presentations. *Psychological Monographs: General and Applied,* 1960, **74,** 1–29.

Taylor, J. G. *The behavioral basis of perception.* New Haven: Yale Univ. Press, 1962.

Tinbergen, N. *The study of instinct.* Oxford: Clarendon Press, 1951.

Tomita, T. Electrical activity in the vertebrate retina. *Journal of the Optical Society of America,* 1963, **53,** 968–974.

Urmson, J. O. Recognition. *Proceedings of the Aristotelian Society,* 1955–1956, N.S. **56,** 259–280.

Wald, G. The receptors for human color vision. *Science,* 1964, **145,** 1007–1017.

Walk, R. D., & Gibson, J. J. A comparative and analytical study of visual depth perception. *Psychological Monographs,* 1961, 75, No. 15 (Whole No. 519).

Wallach, H. Brightness constancy and the nature of achromatic colors. *Journal of Experimental Psychology,* 1948, **38,** 310–324.

Walls, G. Land! Land! *Psychological Bulletin,* 1960, **57,** 29–48.

Woodworth, R. S. *Contemporary schools of psychology.* Rev. ed. New York: Ronald Press, 1948.

Part II

The Neural Bases of Seeing

Chapter 4

RECEPTIVE FIELDS: NEURAL REPRESENTATION OF THE SPATIAL AND INTENSIVE ATTRIBUTES OF THE VISUAL IMAGE

J. G. ROBSON

I. INTRODUCTION

It must be admitted that we still have no real understanding of how visual perception may be related to the activity of nerve cells in the visual system. Indeed we cannot even be really certain that visual perception is solely related, as is often assumed, to the activity of cells in the retinogeniculostriate pathway. However, since geniculostriate lesions cause more or less complete blindness in man (see Brindley, 1970), there can be little doubt that the integrity of this pathway is a necessary prerequisite for anything other than the most rudimentary visual sense. Although claims continue to be made that residual visual performance following destruction of the striate cortex in man may not be as minimal as commonly supposed (e.g., Sanders, Warrington, Marshall, & Weiskrantz, 1974) it is not clear that subjects with complete destruction of the striate cortex can be unequivocally demonstrated to retain any visual ability other than to distinguish sudden light from sudden darkness.

The other main visual projection, from the retina to the tectal region of the midbrain (superior colliculus), will not be discussed in detail for, although it may seem unlikely that the activity of this system has no role in visual perception, it is still far from clear what that role might be. Recent neurophysiological studies (e.g., Schiller & Stryker, 1972; Wurtz & Goldberg, 1972) have all tended to support the idea that the colliculus may be involved in the visually guided control (and possibly interpretation of the effects) of eye movements. In this context, it is interesting to find that the cat's superior colliculus appears to be the central destination for signals from those retinal ganglion cells which respond specifically to moving retinal images (Cleland & Levick, 1974b), whereas those retinal ganglion cells which send information about fine spatial detail in the image (X-cells, Enroth-Cugell & Robson, 1966) project mainly in the retinogeniculate pathway (Cleland & Levick, 1974a).

The great increase in knowledge of the neurophysiology of the retinostriate system which has occurred in the past two decades has resulted mainly from the use of extracellular microelectrodes to monitor the activity and responses to visual stimulation of individual neurons at different levels in the pathway. Although this technique has been extensively employed in many different species, the information available from its direct application in man is still very slight (Marg, 1973). We must therefore rely heavily on results obtained from other animals with all the attendant questions regarding their reliability as a guide to what happens in man. In order to minimize this problem, we shall restrict our attention so far as possible to results obtained from primate species but, since the amount of work done on monkeys is still relatively small, we shall have to consider information obtained from studies on other species, principally the cat, as well. Except where it is stated otherwise, it can be assumed that the findings discussed in this chapter relate to the monkey visual system.

II. RETINAL IMAGE AND ITS ANALYSIS

Although the function of the visual system is to provide information about the three-dimensional world around us, the visual signal available to the nervous system is simply a two-dimensional pattern of light on the retina (or rather two slightly different patterns on the two retinas). The spatial arrangement of the elements of the retinal image pattern is directly determined by the shape and orientation of the objects in the external world and their geometric relation with the eye, but the illuminance and wavelength distribution of the light falling on the retina depend not only upon the surface characteristics of the diffusely illuminated objects around us but also upon the relative position, intensity, and spectral characteristics of the source of light.

The retinal image is discretely sampled by a densely packed mosaic of photoreceptors to give the signal array which the nervous system must subsequently process to provide an inferential reconstruction of the outside world (or some equivalent result). Even allowing for the availability of two slightly disparate retinal images this is a formidable task, which we certainly do not fully understand and cannot simulate. However, we can reasonably expect that the signal processing will occur in several successive stages, the first retinal stages probably being mainly involved with transforming a luminance-related signal to one related more nearly to the variation in surface reflectivities of the external objects and less dependent upon the intensity and other characteristics of the light source. Such a transformation would have the further desirable effect of greatly reducing the dynamic range of the signals required, since the possible variation in the luminance of an object's surface is many orders of magnitude greater than the possible variation in reflectivity.

Before considering how the output of the retina is, in fact, related to external visual stimulation it is worth noting that the relation must partly depend upon the characteristics of the optical image-forming process as well as on the nervous mechanism of the retina itself. The actual retinal image is inevitably a degraded version of the ideal image which would be formed by a perfect optical system, and it has been suggested (see Ratliff, 1965) that it is one of the functions of the retinal mechanism to correct for this degradation. However, the magnitude of the blurring (loss of fine detail in the image) and its importance have probably been exaggerated. Measurements of the optical quality of the retinal image which do not suffer from certain methodological difficulties have shown that in man (Campbell & Green, 1965) and in the cat (Enroth-Cugell & Robson, 1974) the degradation of the image may be little greater than that inevitably resulting from diffraction at the pupil. Although the fine details of an external visual stimulus may be rather well reproduced on the retina the amount of stray light in the eye is quite substantial and is probably important in determining the maximum ratio of retinal illuminances that can be achieved.

III. RETINAL GANGLION CELLS—RECEPTIVE FIELDS

The first study of the spatial extent of the retinal area which could be stimulated to produce a response in a mammalian ganglion cell was made by Kuffler (1953) who used an intraocular microelectrode to record the action potentials of the cell bodies in the cat's retina. Using a small spot of light which could be projected onto different parts of the retina, Kuffler was able to show that each ganglion cell was most sensitive to stimulation at a point close to the cell body. However, the response of a cell to stimulation at this point might be either one of two kinds. Some cells responded more or less transiently by increasing their discharge frequency when the small spot of light was turned on (giving "on" responses), whereas others were activated when the spot of light, after being on for some time, was turned off (giving "off" responses). Nothing Kuffler could do changed this characteristic of a cell's behavior and he therefore concluded that there were two distinct kinds of ganglion cells: on-center and off-center cells.

Although each ganglion cell was most readily stimulated when the spot of light was projected onto the retina close to it, it could also be influenced by a spot of light falling anywhere within a roughly circular region around the optimum position. This region is the "receptive field" of the cell. Kuffler found also that the response of each ganglion cell to stimulation in the peripheral (surround) part of its receptive field was the opposite to that caused by stimulation in the receptive field center. Thus an off-center cell would give on-responses to stimulation of its receptive field surround and an on-center cell would give off-responses. Moreover, it was apparent from experiments involving simultaneous stimulation of both center and surround regions of the receptive field that the stimulation of each region reduced the response to stimulation of the other. This antagonism is best seen in cells which maintain a high frequency of discharge even when their receptive field is uniformly illuminated, a common feature of the behavior of a majority of retinal ganglion cells but not of those illustrated in Kuffler's papers.

Figure 1b shows how little affected the discharge frequency of a retinal ganglion cell may be if the illumination of its receptive field surround is changed in the same way as the illumination of the center even though differentially changing the illumination of these two regions may produce a large and well sustained response (Figs. 1a and 1c). The figure also shows very clearly how increasing the illumination of that region of a receptive field giving off-responses can inhibit the maintained discharge. Because of the slow time scale of the records shown in Fig. 1 the very brief transient

FIG. 1. Discharge of an off-center ganglion cell in the cat retina with different
static patterns of light and dark in the
receptive field. (a) Successive 5-min intervals alternating black and white annuli
in the receptive field surround. (b) Alternating large black and white disks each
covering the whole receptive field. (c)
Alternating small black and white disks
each confined to the receptive field center.
All stimuli were presented against a gray
background. [From P. O. Bishop and
R. W. Rodieck. In P. W. Nye (Ed.),
*Symposium on information processing
in sight sensory systems,* California Institute of Technology, 1965.]

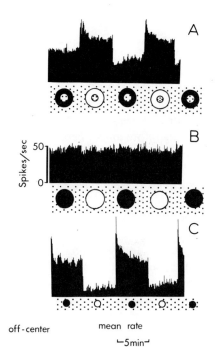

off-center   mean rate

⊢5min⊣

disturbance of the discharge which follows any sudden change in illumination is not visible.

The receptive fields of ganglion cells in the monkey retina (e.g., Gouras,
1968, 1969; Hubel & Wiesel, 1960) appear to be organized rather similarly
to those in the cat retina. However, the receptive fields of monkey ganglion
cells are often much smaller than those of the cat, and the cells may also
show wavelength specific effects suggesting that they receive signals from
more than one type of cone receptor. In some cells the wavelength specificities of center and surround regions of the receptive field are different,
whereas in other cells, they are the same (Gouras, 1968).

A. Varieties of Retinal Ganglion Cells

Since Kuffler (1953) classified the retinal ganglion cells of the cat into
on- and off-center types, it has become clear that there are other important
differences shown by the cells with concentrically organized receptive fields,
as well as other kinds of cells altogether. It was shown by Enroth-Cugell
and Robson (1966) that the cells with concentrically organized receptive
fields could be divided into two groups on the basis of the extent to which

they displayed apparently linear spatial summation over their receptive fields. Subsequently, it was shown (Cleland, Dubin, & Levick, 1971) that the X-cells, which had the more linear behavior, differed from the more nonlinear Y-cells by giving more "sustained" and less "transient" responses to step changes in the luminance of a spot stimulus in the center of their receptive field. By this latter criterion the retinal ganglion cell whose behavior is shown in Fig. 1 would be classified as a "sustained" (and presumably therefore an X) cell.

X-cells are the predominant type in the central retina (Cleland & Levick, 1974a; Stone, 1973); their axons appear to project mainly to the lateral geniculate nucleus (Hoffman, 1973), although a few may also terminate in the midbrain (Fukuda & Stone, 1974). Y-cells, on the other hand, have axons which bifurcate to send branches to both lateral geniculate nucleus and superior colliculus (Fukuda & Stone, 1974). The receptive fields of Y-cells are rather larger than those of X-cells and their cell bodies and axons are also probably of greater diameter. Since the axons of Y-cells are larger than those of X-cells their activity is more easily recorded with microelectrodes, and, thus, studies in which recordings have been made from fibers in the optic nerve or tract have undoubtedly tended to reveal the behavior of Y-cells. Intraocular recordings made directly from the cell bodies of ganglion cells in the central retina do not show such a marked bias in favor of Y-cells, and, thus, studies in which this recording technique has been employed can reasonably be assumed to reveal the behavior of X-cells, even when no direct classification has been made. It is interesting to note that, although Y-cells have the faster conducting axons, the latency of Y-cell responses is so much longer (Ikeda & Wright, 1972b) that signals from X-cells almost certainly reach the cortex first.

Direct recordings from the retina, particularly recordings made with very fine microelectrodes, have revealed the existence of ganglion cells with still more slowly conducting axons and presumably smaller cell bodies as well (Stone, 1973). These cells (grouped together as W-cells by Stone) have been described as showing several different kinds of behavior (Cleland & Levick, 1974a,b). They include cells that respond specifically to moving targets and show directional specificity similar to that shown by cells first studied in the rabbit's retina (Barlow, Hill, & Levick, 1964). The retinal ganglion cells with slowly conducting axons all appear to project directly to the superior colliculus and not to the lateral geniculate nucleus (Fukuda & Stone, 1974; Hoffman, 1973). Although the identification is still only based upon circumstantial evidence, it seems likely that the principal retinal ganglion cell types that can be differentiated on the basis of their physiological behavior correspond to morphologically distinguishable groups of cells (Boycott & Wässle, 1974).

The ganglion cells of the monkey retina have been found by Gouras (1968, 1969) to be divisible into two classes, "tonic" and "phasic," on the basis of their response to a prolonged stimulus. Although Gouras was principally interested in the difference between these cells in terms of the different cone mechanisms which were involved in determining their behavior, he showed (Gouras, 1969) that the tonic cells had smaller axons than the phasic cells and that they were more concentrated in the foveal region of the retina. It seems probable that the resemblance of these classes of retinal ganglion cells in the monkey to the X- and Y-cells of the cat may extend also to the greater ability of the tonic and X-cells to summate linearly over their receptive fields (De Monasterio, Gouras, & Tolhurst, pers. comm.).

IV. MAINTAINED ACTIVITY OF CELLS AND THE SIGNALING OF ILLUMINATION

Although retinal ganglion cells are relatively insensitive to changes in the light falling uniformly on their receptive field, their maintained discharge frequency can be made to change if the illumination is varied over a sufficiently wide range. This effect has been examined in both cats (e.g., Barlow & Levick, 1969b) and monkeys (Marrocco, 1972) with rather similar results (Fig. 2). On-center cells, which discharge spontaneously at a

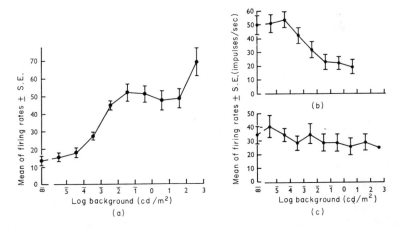

FIG. 2. The relation between mean frequency of the maintained discharge and luminance of adapting field in cat retinal ganglion cells. (a) Average of 14 on-center cells. (b) Average of six off-center cells whose discharge frequency showed a marked decline with luminance. (c) Average of six off-center cells showing little change with luminance. [From Barlow & Levick (1969b).]

low frequency even in the dark, increase their discharge frequency as the retinal illumination is raised toward photopic levels; but in cats, at least, the frequency may then remain roughly constant over several decades of luminance at mesopic and low photopic levels. Conversely, off-center cells are most active in the dark and their maintained discharge frequency declines progressively as the uniform illumination of their receptive field is increased. All these changes are, however, relatively insignificant when compared with the changes that can be readily evoked by patterned stimuli of modest contrast.

The maintained discharge of retinal ganglion cells is not fully characterized by its mean frequency, since the discharge is not regular. Moreover, measurements of the statistical distribution of intervals between successive nerve action potentials (Barlow & Levick, 1969b) have shown that the form of the distribution may change with the mean level of illumination, the discharge of on-center cells usually becoming more regular at higher light levels.

Although it might have been supposed that the frequency of the maintained discharge of ganglion cells would convey information about the general level of retinal illumination, it will be clear from the preceding description of the way in which the frequency depends on light level that neither the on-center nor the off-center cells could provide any good indication of this level. In fact, it is not really clear to what extent information about mean retinal illumination is transmitted along the cat's retinogeniculostriate pathway at all. However, the existence in the unanesthetized monkey striate cortex of cells whose maintained discharge frequencies are regular functions of the intensity of diffuse light has been reported (Bartlett & Doty, 1974).

Barlow and Levick (1969b) and Cleland and Levick (1974a) have described a rarely encountered type of retinal ganglion cell in the cat. Its maintained discharge frequency varies much more regularly with illumination; but it is not unlikely that these cells have extrageniculate projections and are involved in controlling the diameter of the pupil rather than contributing to brightness perception.

A. Significance of the Maintained Discharge in Neural Signaling

Although the frequency of the maintained discharge of retinal ganglion cells may not be important in signaling the general level of retinal illumination, the existence of an ongoing discharge is of undoubted significance in the signaling of small differences between center and surround illumination of the receptive field. Since the discharge of every neuron is always somewhat irregular, it must be assumed that there is inevitably a significant level of intrinsic noise associated with the transmission of nervous signals.

This makes it impossible for nerve cells to be completely inactive in the absence of an appropriate stimulus without sacrificing their ability to transmit information about weak stimuli, that is without displaying a threshold type of nonlinearity. However, a large majority of retinal ganglion cells and, indeed, most of the nerve cells in the lower levels of the visual pathway appear to exhibit maintained discharges and, therefore, do not necessarily show threshold behavior.

Since the center of a ganglion cell's receptive field can be either more or less strongly illuminated than its surround, it may well be desirable for the cell to be able to signal both positive and negative contrast. This it can do because the frequency of its discharge can be either increased or decreased with respect to the level maintained in the absence of specific stimulation; clearly no decrease in frequency would be possible if there were initially no discharge. In fact, it is not certain that a decrease in frequency is ever a physiologically significant signal in the visual system, because, for every cell whose frequency of discharge is decreased by a stimulus, there is probably another cell whose activity is increased. Although a good case could be made for the desirability of information being conveyed in the nervous system by the difference in activity of oppositely responding cells, there seems to be little evidence to suggest that the nervous system makes direct use of such differential signaling.

Although the existence of a maintained discharge may permit the transmission of information about low contrast stimuli, the irregularity of the discharge must inevitably limit the rate at which information can be transmitted. Moreover, since the maximum time over which the signals in the visual system can be effectively integrated is, by all accounts, rather limited, the irregularity of the maintained discharge is likely to be an important factor in setting a lower limit to the magnitude of even a long-duration stimulus that can be reliably detected. Barlow and Levick (1969a,c) and Barlow, Levick, and Yoon (1971) have studied in some detail how the detection threshold for a brief stimulus is determined in the situation in which the only information available is contained in the discharge of a single cat ganglion cell. These studies not only make clear just how important the irregularity of the maintained discharge is in determining threshold, but they also show how exquisitely sensitive the retina can be in the dark-adapted state (the absorption of even a single photon is sufficient to result in the generation of several extra nerve impulses). However, although the irregularity of the maintained discharge must remain a limiting factor at all levels of light adaptation, it is apparent from Barlow and Levick's work that the increase in threshold for incremental stimuli brought about by increasing the luminance of a continuous background field comes mainly from a reduction in responsiveness rather than from changes in the noisiness of the maintained discharge.

V. QUANTITATIVE ASPECTS OF RETINAL GANGLION CELL BEHAVIOR

Although there have been a number of investigations of the stimulus–response relation of cat retinal ganglion cells* using as a stimulus a spot or disk of light located in the receptive field center (e.g., Creutzfeldt, Sakmann, Scheich, & Korn, 1970; Stone & Fabian, 1968), most have concentrated on the approximately logarithmic relation between response magnitude and stimulus luminance that obtains when the response is large. But if the stimulus is weak enough for the response (a rise in the frequency of the cell's discharge) not to exceed about one quarter of the maximum possible (i.e., not greater than about 80 impulses per second), the response is found to be proportional to the stimulus luminance (e.g., Barlow & Levick, 1969a). Moreover, if the stimulus polarity is reversed so that it results in a fall in firing frequency the stimulus–response relationship remains unchanged.

Investigations of the summation of stimuli falling within a receptive field center have shown that, at "threshold" (Cleland & Enroth-Cugell, 1968) and within the linear range of response magnitudes (Creutzfeldt et al., 1970), linear spatial summation occurs. However, when the stimuli are strong enough to give responses in the quasi-logarithmic range, linear spatial summation of responses no longer obtains (Creutzfeldt et al., 1970; Stone & Fabian, 1968). Spatial summation of stimuli confined to the receptive field surround does not appear to have been studied, although the interaction between center and surround stimulation has been. Enroth-Cugell and Pinto (1972) found that responses evoked by combined stimulation of center and surround were the (algebraic) sum of the responses evoked by stimulation of the two regions separately, but they only seem to have tested this with stimuli that were sufficiently weak not to cause nonlinear operation.

Although linear summation of responses only seems to occur when the stimuli are weak enough for the cell to be operating altogether linearly for incremental stimuli, it has been suggested (Enroth-Cugell & Robson, 1966) that the (weighted) illuminance distribution over a ganglion cell's receptive field is initially integrated linearly, even if the cell's response is then nonlinearly related to this integral. But this formulation is clearly incomplete, since it does not take into account the well-known phenomenon of light adaptation. Studies of the responses of retinal ganglion cells to

---

* Few investigators have reported whether the retinal ganglion cells that they have studied have been X- or Y-cells, but it is likely that most studies (particularly those in which intraocular microelectrodes have been used to record directly from cells in, or close to, the area centralis) have, in fact, been carried out on X-cells.

incremental stimuli confined to the receptive field center (e.g., Barlow & Levick, 1969a; Enroth-Cugell & Shapley, 1973a) clearly show that the magnitude of the response is reduced when the steady background illumination is increased above some minimum level. Incremental responsiveness (measured with stimuli giving small responses) has usually been found to be inversely related to some power of the background luminance, the exponent commonly lying between .7 and 1. Although the factors involved in determining the exact value of the exponent have not been fully elucidated, they probably include both temporal and spatial parameters of the stimulus as well as the particular response measure that is employed. Certainly the measurement of a ganglion cell's sensitivity at different levels of light adaptation is complicated by the change in the temporal characteristics of the response to a stimulus of standard form (Enroth-Cugell & Shapley, 1973b). Insofar as the responsiveness of a ganglion cell to incremental stimuli is inversely related to the first power of the background luminance, it is appropriate to think of the cell as responding to the *contrast* of the stimulus pattern rather than to the mean difference in illumination of center and surround regions of its receptive field.

When measured with a small spot of light presented in different positions the sensitivity (or responsiveness) is not constant across the center region of a ganglion cell's receptive field, but falls off radially from a maximum at the very center of the field (Cleland & Enroth-Cugell, 1968, Creutzfeldt *et al.,* 1970). The measured sensitivity profile and, at least within the linear range of incremental operation, the response profile can be used to predict the behavior of a ganglion cell when it is stimulated with a disk of light.

Response profiles showing the surround as well as the center response component have been measured using annular stimuli (Hammond, 1973), whereas sensitivity profiles (spatial weighting functions), derived from measurements of contrast sensitivity using sinusoidal grating stimuli (Enroth-Cugell and Robson, 1966 and see Section XI), have been used to predict the responses to "edge" stimuli (Fig. 4) and also to simple two-dimensional patterns (Kaji, Yamane, Yoshimura, & Sugie, 1974). The magnitude of a cell's response is, of course, a function of the position of the stimulus pattern relative to the cell's receptive field. This function can be thought of not only as describing the behavior of a single cell, but also as an estimate of how the responses of an array of similar cells are distributed over space or, in other words, as a representation of the "neural image" existing in the cellular array. As would be expected, the spatial differentiating effect of the antagonistic center-surround organization of ganglion cell receptive fields causes the neural image transmitted along the retinostriate pathway to show marked enhancement of luminance contours in the stimulus pattern.

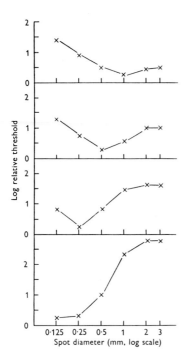

FIG. 3. Changes in threshold of center responses with area of illumination measured on four different retinal ganglion cells in the cat, all on-center units. Abscissa: diameter of spot on the retina. Ordinate: threshold, relative logarithmic scale; 0 corresponds to a stimulus 2 log units lower in luminance than the background on which it was superimposed. [From Wiesel (1960).]

A. Sizes of Receptive Fields of Ganglion Cells

The sizes of ganglion cell receptive fields have been measured in a number of studies, and several different methods were employed. The simplest method is to "map" the receptive field with a small spot of light projected onto a screen set at a suitable distance from the eye (Hubel & Wiesel, 1960). The experimenter listens to the discharge of the cell relayed over a loudspeaker as the light spot is flashed on and off in different positions on the screen. While the spot is within the cell's receptive field the experimenter hears a change in the discharge frequency as the light goes on and off. He can locate the middle of the receptive field as the point at which the response is greatest (or can be elicited with the dimmest test spot) and the central area of the receptive field as the region over which similar, though perhaps weaker, responses can be obtained. Responses characteristic of the surround (opposite to those of the center) may be heard if the test spot is within an appropriate range of distances from the middle of the receptive field.

An alternative approach to determining the size of a receptive field is to measure the sensitivity of the cell to an illuminated disk as a function

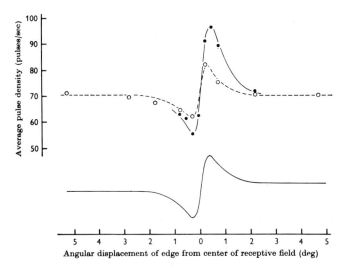

FIG. 4. Static response of an on-center X-cell to an edge. The edge was presented is different positions with respect to the center of the ganglion cell's receptive field and the average discharge frequency measured over the period 10–20 sec after turning on the contrast of the pattern without changing the mean luminance. Two contrast levels were used: filled circles, .4; open circles, .2. Shown below is the edge sensitivity calculated from values of the cell's contrast sensitivity function measured using sinusoidal gratings. [From Enroth-Cugell & Robson (1966).]

of the diameter of the disk (Wiesel, 1960). As the disk is increased in size to fill the receptive field center more completely, the sensitivity of the cell increases and a just detectable response is evoked by stimuli of lower luminance (Fig. 3). However, when the diameter of the disk is enlarged sufficiently for it to invade the antagonistic surround region of the receptive field, the cell's sensitivity starts to fall. Eventually, when the stimulus is large enough to cover the whole receptive field, the cell may be almost completely unresponsive when the luminance of the stimulus is changed. The diameter of the disk giving the greatest sensitivity can be taken as a measure of the diameter of the receptive field center, although it should be noted that the underlying neural mechanism responsible for the center-type response of the ganglion cell probably responds to some extent to stimuli falling outside this area. Equally, stimuli that are confined to the center region of a ganglion cell's receptive field probably stimulate the surround mechanism to some extent. The diameters of receptive field centers have been estimated by other methods as well (e.g., Cleland & Enroth-Cugell, 1968; Enroth-Cugell & Robson, 1966; Fischer, 1973). In view of the number of different methods used and because of their different implicit definitions of what constitutes the receptive field center, it is not surprising that there has been considerable diversity in the reported values of receptive field diameters.

It became apparent as soon as the first extensive measurements of the sizes of receptive field centers were made that, both in the cat (Wiesel, 1960) and monkey retina (Hubel & Wiesel, 1960), there is a wide range of center diameters. The existence of a range of diameters is partly explained by the receptive fields in the peripheral retina being larger than those in the area centralis or foveal region. But it is also clear that in any one retinal region there are ganglion cells with different size receptive fields. The interpretation of this finding is complicated by the inhomogeneity of the ganglion cell population, different ganglion cell types (see Section III,A) coexisting in all regions of the retina. The receptive fields of the various cell types differ not only in their size but also in the way in which the size varies with the retinal eccentricity (e.g., Cleland & Levick, 1974a,b; Stone & Fukuda, 1974).

In the cat, the receptive fields of both X- and Y-cells are smallest in the area centralis and progressively increase in size toward the periphery of the retina. However, whereas in the area centralis, the X-cell receptive fields are considerably smaller than those of Y-cells, the difference is less marked in the peripheral retina (Cleland & Levick, 1974b; Stone & Fukuda, 1974). Boycott and Wässle (1974) have shown histologically two morphologically distinguishable groups of ganglion cells in the cat's retina, the dendritic field diameters of which are related in the same kind of way with retinal eccentricity. On this and other grounds they have suggested that these (beta and alpha) morphological types can be identified with X- and Y-cells.

Much less is known about the sizes of receptive fields of ganglion cells in the monkey retina, although the general picture (De Monasterio & Gouras, 1975; Hubel & Wiesel, 1960) seems to be rather similar, apart from the much smaller actual diameters of the monkey fields. Histological studies of ganglion cells close to the fovea in the monkey retina (Boycott & Dowling, 1969) have revealed three groups of cells with very different dendritic spreads. The relationship between these groups and functional classes is unknown.

B. The Retinal Ganglion Cell Array

Since ganglion cells respond poorly to stimuli that are either much smaller or much larger than the diameter of their receptive field center, an array of cells all having the same size receptive fields would be unable to transmit information about either very fine or very coarse detail in the retinal image. Thus, it is clearly necessary for the retinal image to be sampled by arrays of cells of different sizes if as much information as possible is to be made available to the higher levels of the visual system.

But the ability of a homogeneous array of ganglion cells to transmit information about the fine detail in the retinal image is not only limited by the size of the cells' receptive fields; it is also limited by the spacing between the cells in the array. Thus we might expect to find that the spacing between the cells forming an array would be related to the diameter of their receptive field centers. Without making a large number of doubtful assumptions it is impossible to be precise about the optimum relation between receptive field size and spacing. However, it would be surprising if the receptive field centers were less in diameter than the distance between them, as this would result in an unnecessary loss of sensitivity as well as introduce problems of spurious resolution. On the other hand, it would be surprising if the cells were much more closely spaced than the radius of their receptive field center since the transmission of fine detail in the image and freedom from spurious resolution would not be significantly improved by closer spacing, despite the increased number of cells involved.

Fischer (1973) has pointed out that the overall density of ganglion cells in each region of the cat's retina (Stone, 1965) is inversely related to the average area of the receptive field centers in that region. This, of course, implies that the relation between receptive field size and spacing is constant, even though there is a wide variation in the actual sizes of receptive fields in different parts of the retina. Unfortunately, Fischer did not take into account the existence of different ganglion cell types with different receptive field sizes and his calculations cannot therefore give an accurate picture of any of the coexisting arrays of cells. However, we can quite easily use the available information to get an estimate of the separation between ganglion cells of one type.

Let us consider, for example, the X-cells of the area centralis in the cat retina. These cells account for about two thirds of all ganglion cells in the middle of the area centralis (Cleland & Levick, 1974a) and thus, since the density of all cells in this region is about 6000 mm^{-2} (Stone, 1965), we can estimate the density of the X-cells at about 4000 mm^{-2}. Assuming that it is appropriate to consider on-center and off-center cells separately and that they are equal in numbers, we get a figure of 2000 mm^{-2} as the cell density. If the cells are arranged in a hexagonal lattice then we can easily calculate that they will lie about 24 μm apart, equivalent to about .11° visual angle. The receptive field centers of the X-cells in the middle of the area centralis are probably not much more than .3° in diameter so that the field centers of these cells appear to be about three times larger in diameter than the distance between adjacent cells. Similar calculations suggest that separation between X- and Y-cells bears much the same relation to their receptive field center diameter all over the retina. Thus it seems that the retinal image is sufficiently frequently sampled by the arrays of ganglion cells for all the information available to individual cells to be transmitted to higher levels. The spatial sampling density does not, however, seem to be much greater than is minimally required to achieve this.

VI. LATERAL GENICULATE NUCLEUS

It has been shown that each cell of the cat's lateral geniculate nucleus (LGN) receives its main excitatory input from only one, or at most a small number, of similar retinal ganglion cells whose receptive fields are located close together (Cleland, Dubin, & Levick, 1971). Thus, it is not surprising that LGN cells behave rather similarly to retinal ganglion cells and, though their responses are all rather more transient, can be classified into the same X and Y (sustained and transient) types. In the monkey, also, the cells of the LGN respond to visual stimuli in much the same way as retinal ganglion cells (Wiesel & Hubel, 1966) and it is still not clear which, if any, of the relatively subtle differences in behavior which have been described are of functional significance.

Like retinal ganglion cells, the cells of the LGN show a maintained discharge in the absence of specific visual stimulation, although their discharge is generally more irregular and of rather lower frequency than that of retinal cells, the frequency being even less dependent upon the mean level of illumination (Marrocco, 1972). It has been suggested that these differences could result from the convergence on LGN cells of inhibitory influences from a ring of retinal ganglion cells surrounding the central excitatory group, in other words, from a further stage of center–surround processing. A similar explanation has been offered for the finding that in the cat LGN there is functional surround antagonism at light levels lower than those at which retinal surround antagonism becomes ineffective (Maffei & Fiorentini, 1972). Hammond (1973) has offered the same explanation also for his observation of an "outer" surround synergistic with the receptive field center of cat LGN cells. It is not clear, however, that stray light scattered within the eye may not have been responsible for this finding as well as a similar one reported for retinal Y-cells (Ikeda & Wright, 1972a). Further support for the possibility of an antagonistic center–surround organization of the connections between optic tract fibers and LGN cells is provided by the demonstration of double-opponent-color cells in the LGN of the ground squirrel (Michael, 1973). In these cells antagonism between long- and short-wavelength stimuli is found in both center and surround regions and must depend upon separate inputs from different color-opponent retinal ganglion cells.

Since the behavior of LGN cells in experimental animals is so frequently found to be similar to that of retinal ganglion cells, it has often been suggested that the function of the LGN may be less to transform routinely the visual signals being relayed to the cortex than to permit them to be modified by nonvisual influences. However, little good experimental evidence has emerged to support any substantial physiological effect of this kind. In particular, suggestions that transmission through the LGN may be gated by oculomotor signals (to permit visual signals generated by retinal image motion resulting from eye movements to be differentiated from signals resulting from actual object movement) do not seem to be consistent with the observation that only a very few neurons in the monkey LGN are influenced at all by saccadic eye movements (Büttner & Fuchs, 1973).

The cells in the LGN are arranged in layers supplied by fibers from each eye alternately so that there is little possibility of direct binocular interaction, and the cells were thought for a long time to be affected by stimuli in only one eye. However, it has been found that, in the cat (see Sanderson, Bishop, & Darian-Smith, 1971), stimulation of the other eye can partially suppress the activity of many LGN cells, although a few may be excited instead. In either case, the receptive field in the nondominant eye corresponds rather well in retinal position with the excitatory field in the dominant eye. It is not known whether this binocular arrangement obtains in primates, nor what its functional significance may be.

VII. VISUAL CORTEX

The principal destination of the efferent fibers from the LGN in the monkey is the striate cortex (Wilson & Cragg, 1967; Garey & Powell, 1971); the output from the striate cortex, apart from interhemispheric connections, is widely distributed to prestriate regions (Cragg, 1969; Zeki, 1969). In the cat, the fibers from the LGN project not only to the striate cortex, but also to the prestriate regions (see Stone & Dreher, 1973).

At all cortical levels the activity of individual neurons remains correlated with the visual pattern falling on a restricted region of the retina, though the receptive fields of cortical neurons, especially those in the more remote prestriate areas, may be much larger and less easily delineated experimentally than those of the retina and LGN. At the higher levels, too, the point-by-point topographical organization seems to become less rigid than at lower levels and the clustering of cells with characteristics other than position in the visual field in common is frequently noted (e.g., Zeki, 1974).

All the cells in the striate and prestriate cortex can probably be stimulated visually when an appropriate stimulus pattern has been found. However, it has been reported that many of the cells in the cat striate cortex may also respond to auditory stimulation (Fishman & Michael, 1973), the most effective sound being one located in the same direction from the animal as the visual receptive field of the cortical cell (Morrell, 1972).

The neurons of the striate cortex of paralyzed anesthetized monkeys have been found to respond to patterned visual stimuli in much the same way as the neurons of the more extensively studied cortex of cats similarly anesthetized and paralyzed (Hubel & Wiesel, 1968). Moreover, the technically more difficult studies of visual cortical neurons in awake unrestrained cats (Hubel, 1959) and monkeys (Wurtz, 1969) suggest that anesthesia has no specific effect on their characteristic behavior, although it may reduce the frequency of the discharge maintained in the absence of specific stimulation as well as the responsiveness to appropriate stimulation. As might be expected, the striate cortex of the monkey differs from that of the cat in having a substantial proportion of color-sensitive cells often responding poorly or not at all to white and black patterns (Hubel & Wiesel, 1968; Dow & Gouras, 1973).

Within the striate cortex of the monkey, only a fairly small proportion of the neurons from which microelectrode recordings have been made have the circularly organized receptive fields characteristic of the LGN and retina. These units, unlike all others in the striate cortex, respond equally well to line or bar patterns of any orientation when they are moved across the receptive field. Moreover, unlike the majority of cortical cells, these circular units only respond to stimuli presented to one of the two eyes (Hubel & Wiesel, 1968; Dow & Gouras, 1973; Gouras, 1974) and it may still be questioned whether many of these responses have not in fact been recorded from terminals of fibers from the LGN (but see Poggio, 1972).

In contrast, the majority of neurons in the visual cortex show distinctive behavior characterized by the way in which their response to a line, bar, or edge stimulus is critically dependent upon its orientation. Hubel and Wiesel (1968) have described these cells in the monkey cortex as clearly falling into the same three classes—simple, complex, and hypercomplex—as those of the cat cortex (Hubel & Wiesel, 1962). Since this classification has become so firmly established, we shall discuss the three types separately. However, it is worth bearing in mind that characteristics of cortical neurons other than those emphasized by Hubel and Wiesel in making this classification may be of greater functional significance. Work on the striate cortex of unanesthetized monkeys (Bartlett & Doty, 1974; Poggio, 1972) has indicated that the application of Hubel and Wiesel's classification scheme may result in very nearly all the cells from which recordings can be made being lumped together as complex cells.

A. Simple Cells

Of the different types of orientation-specific cortical neurons, the so-called "simple cells" (Hubel & Wiesel, 1959, 1962, 1968) appear most like the cells of the LGN in that they have receptive fields with directly demonstrable excitatory and inhibitory regions. However, instead of being arranged concentrically, these antagonistic regions form parallel strips that may be several times as long as they are wide. The receptive fields of simple cells have one or more excitatory regions flanked by inhibitory areas, although the existence and extent of the inhibitory areas cannot always be determined simply by examining the responses to isolated stimuli. This is both because off-responses may be weak or even absent and because the low frequency and irregularity of the maintained discharge can make it difficult to appreciate the direct effect of inhibitory stimulation in reducing it. In such cases, the inhibitory regions can be identified by observing the effect of stimulating them on the simultaneously induced response to an excitatory stimulus, a method extensively employed by Bishop and his colleagues (see Bishop, Coombs, & Henry, 1973). Even when distinct inhibitory regions cannot easily be mapped, the presence of strong inhibitory influences can usually be inferred from the weakness of the response to changes in the illumination of the whole receptive field.

In their earliest investigations Hubel and Wiesel found that moving bars and edges were very convenient stimuli for studying the behavior of cortical cells, such stimuli being most effective when they were orientated parallel to the long axis of the receptive field. In general terms, it seemed to be possible to correlate the response of a simple cell to a moving stimulus with the layout of its receptive field as determined with stationary flashing stimuli (Hubel & Wiesel, 1962). Indeed it seemed that it would be possible to predict in detail how a cell would respond to a moving stimulus by taking into account the time course of the responses to stimuli presented in different positions within the receptive field as well as variations in sensitivity. However, attempts to obtain sufficiently detailed information about cortical cell behavior to make quantitative predictions possible (e.g., Bishop, Coombs, & Henry, 1973) have emphasized not only the difficulties of obtaining sufficient data about a single cell but also the complexity of the underlying processes which have to be taken into account.

B. Complex Cells

The majority of cells in the monkey striate cortex (Hubel & Wiesel, 1968) either do not respond at all strongly to stationary stimuli even if they are flashed on and off, or they give both on- and off-responses to such stimuli wherever they are presented in the receptive field. These cells do, however, respond well to moving bars or edges if they are correctly oriented, although, in cats, at least, they usually require a faster moving stimulus than simple cells to give the best response (Pettigrew, Nikara, & Bishop, 1968a). Many of these cells are direction-specific, that is, their response to a correctly oriented bar or edge moving in one direction may be very much greater than the response to the same stimulus moving in the opposite direction; indeed, movement opposite to the preferred direction may produce no response at all or even inhibit the maintained discharge (which tends to be higher in frequency in these than in simple cells). The direction-specificity usually persists unchanged if the contrast of the stimulus is reversed and may also be evident in cells which respond well to spots of light.

C. Hypercomplex Cells

For most cortical cells, the magnitude of the response evoked by a moving bar or edge increases as the length of the stimulus is increased up to some limiting value. If the length is increased still further then the response of cells classified by Hubel and Wiesel as simple or complex shows no further change. However there are some cells whose response is clearly reduced or even suppressed when the stimulus becomes too long. In Hubel and Wiesel's studies cells showing this behavior otherwise behaved most like complex cells and were therefore called "hypercomplex." However, it seems that in the cat (Dreher, 1972) the defining behavior of hypercomplex cells can be associated with characteristics that would otherwise result in the cells being classified as simple.

D. Hierarchical Organization

It has commonly been supposed (e.g., Hubel & Wiesel, 1965) that the different cell types, even within a single division of the cortex, represent successive hierarchical stages in the processing of visual signals. However, there is very little direct evidence for this interpretation and it seems equally likely that the different kinds of cells lie in separate, though possibly associated, parallel signal paths. Stone (1972) has emphasized the need to take into account the parallel organization of the cortical input, particularly with respect to the X- and Y-types of ganglion cells, which probably project more or less independently via the LGN to the simple and complex cells of the striate cortex in the cat (Cleland, Dubin, & Levick, 1971; Stone & Dreher, 1973). In the monkey, the color- and space-opponent systems may also remain relatively separate in their retinocortical course, although this is less certainly established (Dow & Gouras, 1973).

VIII. ORIENTATION SPECIFICITY IN THE VISUAL CORTEX

Except for those units with circularly symmetric receptive fields, which resemble the cells of the LGN, the cells of the striate cortex characteristically respond maximally to line or edge stimuli having some particular orientation. Although cells with all possible optimum orientations can be found in the cortex, they do not seem to be haphazardly arranged. Rather it appears that the cells are organized into columns or sheets which extend through the thickness of the cortex perpendicular to the surface. The cells in each column or sheet have the same optimum orientation, and this optimum orientation changes progressively in small but fairly regular steps from column to column (Hubel & Wiesel, 1968). The orientation-related columnar organization appears to be superimposed on a rather coarser local grouping of cells, according to which of the two eyes primarily provides their excitation. It has also been suggested that cortical cells may show some segregation on the basis of their responsiveness, or lack of it, to movement in both directions as well as their relative responsiveness to different stimulus patterns (bars or edges) and their color specificity (Hubel & Wiesel, 1968).

Although the orientation specificity of primate cortical cells has not been studied quantitatively, some idea of their degree of selectivity can be gained from Fig. 5. It has been reported that in cats, the orientation specificity of simple cells is somewhat greater than that of complex cells (Watkins & Berkeley, 1974), although the same observation does not seem to have been made with regard to cells in the monkey cortex.

Several claims have been made that the optimum orientation of cortical cells is not fixed (with respect to the retina) but can change either spontaneously or in a compensatory manner in response to rotation of the animal about its visual axis. It has also been suggested that the degree of orientation specificity can change spontaneously during the course of an experiment. The most comprehensive report of such effects (Horn, Stechler, & Hill, 1972) can perhaps best be interpreted as indicating that the behavior of at least an overwhelming majority of cortical cells in the cat is remarkably stable. It is, of course, widely accepted that the general responsiveness of cortical cells can vary with changes in the level of anesthesia or arousal and it is, therefore, unfortunate that quantitative investigations of cortical cell characteristics have rarely employed methods of measurement that would minimize the confusing effects of such nonspecific changes in sensitivity. The better designed an experiment is to counteract these changes the more stable the measured characteristics seem to be (see Henry, Bishop, Tupper, & Dreher, 1973).

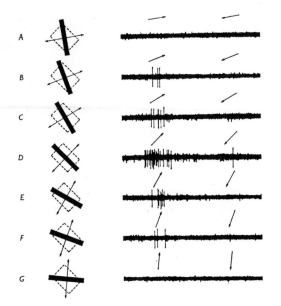

FIG. 5. Responses of a complex cell in monkey striate cortex to various orientations of a black bar. The receptive field is indicated by the interrupted rectangles. The arrows above the action potential records on the right indicate the direction the bar was moving in during the period in which it was crossing the receptive field. The duration of each record is 2 sec. [From Hubel & Wiesel (1968).]

Those cat cortical cells which respond to stimuli moving in one direction only thereby resemble the direction-specific ganglion cells of the retina that probably project to the superior colliculus (Cleland & Levick, 1974b). However, it is worth remarking that the orientation selectivity of the cortical cells is substantially better than that of any retinal cells so far reported (see Grüsser & Grüsser-Cornehls, 1973).

IX. BINOCULAR INTERACTIONS AND STEREOPSIS

Many of the cortical neurons that show orientation specificity have connections to both eyes, although in the monkey striate cortex, there is a marked tendency for one eye to be very dominant, particularly in the case of simple cells (Hubel & Wiesel, 1968; Poggio, 1972). It has been shown in the cat that if a cortical cell can be stimulated through each eye alone, then the characteristics of the cell's receptive field nearly always appear to be very similar whichever eye is used; the retinal position of the receptive field is also always very nearly the same in both eyes (Hubel & Wiesel, 1962; Nikara, Bishop, & Pettigrew, 1968). When both eyes are stimulated together, it is often possible to obtain a greater response than with either eye alone, though this may require the stimuli to be rather precisely located within the receptive fields. On the other hand, if one of the stimuli is displaced from its optimum position the response to binocular stimulation can become less than the response to monocular stimulation (Barlow, Blakemore, & Pettigrew, 1967; Pettigrew, Nikara, & Bishop, 1968b). Hubel and Wiesel (1971) have reported that this kind of behavior is particularly marked in certain of the cells in the peristriate cortex of the monkey. Some of these peristriate cells (which may hardly respond at all to monocular stimulation) respond strongly when exactly corresponding areas of the two retinas are stimulated together, whereas others require the stimuli in the two eyes to be slightly disparate. In fact, it is rather difficult to give any precise meaning to the idea of exact retinal correspondence, but what is important is that different cells respond maximally to stimulus pairs with different degrees of binocular disparity.

A spread in the optimal stimulus disparities for cat cortical cells has also been reported (Barlow, Blakemore, & Pettigrew, 1967; Pettigrew, Nikara, & Bishop, 1968), although Hubel and Wiesel (1973) have found that only a very small proportion of the cells in the cat striate cortex are preferentially stimulated by binocularly presented patterns with a significant disparity.

The existence of cells with different optimal binocular stimulus disparities provides a possible neurophysiological basis for stereoscopic vision, since objects at different distances from the eyes will give rise to pairs of retinal images with different disparities and will therefore preferentially stimulate different subsets of cortical cells.

Although most binocularly activated cells in the cortex have the same stimulus specificities in both eyes, a few direction-specific cells in prestriate cortex of cat (Pettigrew, 1973) and monkey (Zeki, 1974) have been found to respond to opposite directions of movement in the two eyes. If such cells show the appropriate binocular interactions, they could be expected to respond preferentially to objects more or less directly approaching, or receding from, the head.

A phenomenon well-known from subjective experience is binocular rivalry, the alternating perception of dissimilar images presented to the two eyes; but no instabilities in the interactions of binocularly presented stimuli have been reported in neurophysiological studies.

X. SPATIAL FREQUENCY ANALYSIS OF THE VISUAL SYSTEM

Many single-unit studies of the visual system have been based on the idea that the activity of a neuron signals the presence of a particular simple geometric feature in the visual image. These studies have concentrated on

identifying the optimum stimulus or "trigger" feature for each neuron (see
Barlow, 1972) rather than on quantifying their responses to a wide range
of possible visual inputs. But it may well be doubted whether the spots,
blobs, bars, or edges commonly used as stimuli are likely to be the elementary features which the nervous system is wired up to detect. Moreover,
little attention has been paid in such studies either to the relationship between the magnitude of the response and the strength (contrast) of the
stimulus or to the interactions between multiple simple stimuli in different
parts of a receptive field. Thus we often have little idea of how visual cells
can be expected to respond to natural stimuli of reasonable complexity.

An alternative approach to describing the operation of the visual system
is to view the activity of the arrays of nerve cells at each level in the visual
pathway simply as a generalized transform of the visual input. The task
of the investigator is then to identify the transformation and, ideally, to
describe it in such a way as to make it possible to predict the activity
in each array that would be produced by any arbitrary input pattern. One
way to attempt this involves considering the visual input to be made up
of a large number of elementary spots of light of different intensities. This
suggests characterizing a neuron's behavior by its response to a single small
spot as a function of the spot's intensity and position, a method already
discussed.

But there are many other ways to analyze a visual stimulus pattern be-
sides using a point-by-point measure of intensity. One other particularly
simple way (because the components are again orthogonal) is spatial frequency analysis, the pattern being considered as the sum of a number of
spatial frequency (Fourier) components. Each of the components is a sinusoidal grating of particular spatial frequency, phase (lateral displacement),
orientation, and contrast, and the behavior of a neuron may then be characterized by its response to a simple grating as a function of these variables.

Spatial frequency methods have already been extensively employed in
describing the optical performance of the eye as well as in psychophysical
studies of human vision (see review of Campbell, 1974), whereas behavioral studies of vision in both monkey (DeValois, Morgan, & Snodderly,
1974) and cat (Bisti & Maffei, 1974; Blake, Cool, & Crawford, 1974)
using the same methods have demonstrated the similarities in visual performance of these different animals.

The existence, and unified nature, of this optical and behavioral information itself provides a good reason for using spatial frequency methods to
study single neurons. However, there are other more direct reasons for
choosing this approach. Neurons at all levels in the retinocortical pathway
respond well to grating patterns drifting across their receptive field (Maffei
& Fiorentini, 1973), whereas they certainly do not all respond well to spots

of light. Moreover, the continuous nature of the grating stimulation can greatly increase the rate at which information about the magnitude of a cell's response can be acquired—an important practical advantage. Also, since visual neurons often have receptive fields with large areas of low sensitivity which still, because of their large extent, contribute importantly to the response to extended patterns, it is basically more appropriate to use an extended test stimulus to analyze the behavior of such cells. Again, the use of a drifting sinusoidal grating has the advantage not only that the temporal change in luminance at each point in the receptive field is the same (sinusoidal), but also that this waveform is an appropriate one for investigating temporal aspects of the cell's behavior.

Although frequency-response methods are particularly simple to apply if the system being studied behaves linearly (e.g., the optics of the eye), it should be emphasized that the adoption of these methods in studying the visual nervous system no more implies that the nervous system is believed to operate linearly than does the use of the point-by-point approach. In either case, the linearity of operation must be explicitly investigated and appropriate methods devised for dealing with any nonlinearities that are uncovered. In fact, nonlinear operation can be very easily recognized if frequency response analysis is used, since it results in the appearance at the output of frequencies not present in the input of the system. If the input is sinusoidal the resulting harmonic distortion in the output may be readily detected.

A. Responses of Neurons to Drifting Gratings

The effect of stimulating a visual neuron with a drifting grating pattern is twofold. First, the frequency of the neuron's ongoing discharge may be modulated in synchrony with the passage of the bars of the grating across the receptive field. Second, the mean frequency of the discharge may be raised by the stimulation. X-cells of the cat retina (Enroth-Cugell & Robson, 1966) and LGN (Maffei & Fiorentini, 1973) show only the first of these effects. Y-cells, on the other hand, show both effects, unless the spatial frequency is greater than the optimum, in which case, only the second effect (an unmodulated increase in the discharge frequency) is produced.

Maffei and Fiorentini (1973) have described simple cells of the cat striate cortex as responding to drifting gratings with a modulated discharge; complex cells respond only with an overall increase in activity unrelated to the position of the pattern, unless the period of the pattern is greater than the whole width of the receptive field. Simple and complex cells thus appear to behave rather as might be expected if they were driven by X-

and Y-cells, respectively. Although it has not been established that X- and Y-cells of the LGN do in fact project exclusively to simple and complex cells in the cortex, there may be a substantial segregation of this kind (Stone & Dreher, 1973). In conflict with this simple correlation, Ikeda and Wright (1974) have claimed that both simple and complex cells can show either sustained or transient responses which might be presumed to reflect X- and Y-cells inputs, respectively.

The use of moving gratings (as opposed to stationary patterns turned on and off) has the advantage that the pattern is automatically used in every possible position successively. But it might be argued that moving patterns are not directly comparable with stationary ones. In fact, a stationary pattern whose contrast is modulated sinuosoidally in time is the superposition of two uniform gratings drifting with constant velocity in opposite directions, the position of the stationary pattern being determined by the phase difference between the two moving ones. Thus an exact comparison of the responses of neurons to moving and stationary patterns can easily be made and any difference can readily be interpreted in terms of specific responsiveness to *moving* stimuli. X-cells in the retina (Enroth-Cugell & Robson, 1966) and some cortical (probably simple) cells (Cooper & Robson, 1968) respond to appropriately positioned time-modulated gratings just as well as they do to the equivalent moving patterns. However, Cooper and Robson found that other cortical cells respond much more vigorously to moving gratings than to any equivalent stationary ones.

The orientation-specificity of cat cortical cells measured using drifting grating patterns as stimuli (Campbell, Cleland, Cooper, & Enroth-Cugell, 1968) appears very much the same as when other stimulus patterns are used. Comparison of measurements of orientation-specificity using moving and stationary patterns shows that movement per se has little effect on the degree of specificity, even if it causes the response to be greatly enhanced (Cooper & Robson, 1968).

B. Signaling of Contrast

The magnitude of the response of visual neurons to a grating pattern is a function of the contrast of the stimulus. In the case of retinal X-cells and X-cells in the LGN, the response is directly proportional to the contrast at low-contrast levels, but becomes more nearly proportional to the logarithm of the contrast at higher levels (Fig. 6). These cells with a spontaneous maintained discharge give no sign of any threshold-type of nonlinear behavior, the exponent of the relation between stimulus and response never being greater than unity. However, this may not apply in the case of the simple cells of the cat cortex (Maffei & Fiorentini, 1973), though

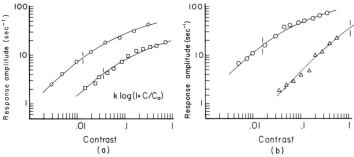

Fig. 6. The magnitude of the responses of (a) retinal ganglion cells and (b) cells in the LGN to grating patterns of optimum spatial frequency drifting across their receptive fields at approximately optimal velocity. The response is measured as the amplitude of the variation in the cell's discharge frequency synchronized with the passage of the bars of the grating across the receptive field. All curves are of the form: response amplitude = $k \log(1 + C/C_0)$, where k and C_0 are constants and C is the contrast of the grating stimulus. C_0, which can be considered to be the limit of approximately linear operation, is indicated by the vertical lines. [Right-hand curves redrawn from Maffei & Fiorentini (1973); left-hand curve from Enroth-Cugell & Robson, unpublished results.]

even here the appearance of a threshold contrast below which no response is evoked may only be related to the absence of a spontaneous discharge in the particular experimental situation.

Since the response of visual neurons is not simply proportional to stimulus contrast at all levels, it is to be expected that the way in which their response varies with any other stimulus variable, e.g., spatial frequency or orientation, will depend upon the contrast level at which the measurements are made. A similar difficulty is involved in measuring the frequency selectivity of auditory neurons (see Evans, 1974). To the extent that visual neurons behave as though they were linear spatial filters followed by a space-independent nonlinearity (Enroth-Cugell & Robson, 1966), the effect of the nonlinearity can be nullified by measuring the way in which stimulus contrast has to be adjusted to maintain a constant response as the other variable of interest is changed. Measurements made in this way provide information about the initial filtering process alone; they are frequently referred to as "sensitivity" rather than "response" measures. Although no systematic study of the relation between sensitivity and response measures has been reported, it can be expected that response measures will underestimate (with respect to sensitivity measures) the degree of orientation and spatial frequency selectivity of visual neurons because the nonlinearity normally observed is a compressive one, the response increasing less rapidly with contrast at high than at low levels. It is more appropri-

ate to compare psychophysical results based on threshold measures with
neurophysiological results based on sensitivity measures.

C. Spatial Frequency Selectivity of Visual Neurons

The magnitude of the response of a visual neuron to a drifting grating
is a function of the spatial frequency of the pattern (Fig. 7). At all levels
in the retinocortical pathway individual neurons respond best at some intermediate spatial frequency, the response falling off at frequencies both above
and below the optimum.

At the retinal level the fall-off in response at low spatial frequencies
is always fairly slow, but in the cortex the low-frequency attenuation may

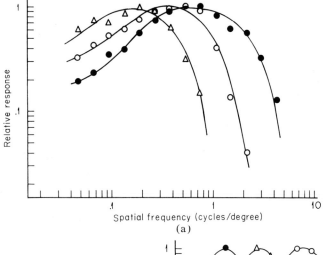

(a)

FIG. 7. Responses of cat (a) retinal
ganglion cells and (b) striate cortical
cells to drifting grating patterns of
different spatial frequencies. The gratings had a contrast of .5 and drifted
across the receptive field at about the
optimum velocity. In the case of the
cortical cells, the orientation of the
grating was also optimal. The response measured was the amplitude
of the fluctuation in discharge frequency synchronized with the passage
of the bars of the grating across the
receptive field. [From Cooper & Robson (1968).]

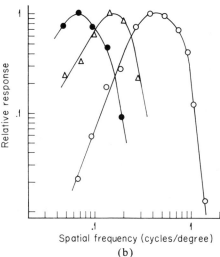

(b)

be much more rapid and profound, so making the cells more selectively responsive to just a small range of spatial frequencies (Cooper & Robson, 1968; Maffei & Fiorentini, 1973). Maffei and Fiorentini (1973) have reported that the spatial frequency selectivity of simple cells in the cat striate cortex is often greater than that of complex cells, though Ikeda and Wright (1974) believe that the cells showing the greater spatial frequency selectivity are those which can be classified as "sustained" rather than "transient" cells. In any case, it should be emphasized that not all cortical cells have the same degree of spatial frequency selectivity. Some cells in the monkey striate cortex have also been found to be rather selectively tuned with respect to spatial frequency (DeValois, personal communication), and it may even be supposed that the cell in the monkey inferotemporal cortex, which Gross, Rocha-Miranda, and Bender (1972) found to respond best to the silhouette of an appropriately oriented hand (with more or less equally spaced digits), was also simply rather precisely tuned to a particular spatial frequency.

The spatial frequency selectivity of retinal X-cells has been shown to be directly explicable in terms of receptive fields with center–surround antagonism (Enrogh-Cugell & Robson, 1966), but the greater spatial frequency selectivity of some cortical cells has yet to be related in any exact way to receptive field organization. However, it seems very probable that the several parallel excitatory and inhibitory strips of simple cell receptive fields can at once account for the observed orientation and spatial frequency selectivity.

D. The Visual Cortex as a Spatial Frequency Analyzer

It has been suggested (e.g., see Pollen & Taylor, 1974; Glezer, Ivanoff, & Tscherbach, 1973) that the visual cortex may operate as a spatial frequency analyzer, an as yet rather ill-defined notion, which has, however, gained wide circulation. The most extreme interpretation of this idea is that the visual image is subject, in its entirety, to some form of discrete two-dimensional Fourier transformation, the value of each of the required spectral coefficients being represented by the activity of a neuron or group of neurons. This interpretation neither seems inherently plausible nor does it gain any support from neurophysiological results. However, it may not be too fanciful to suggest that the visual system does perform some rudimentary piecewise (patch by patch) spatial frequency analysis of the visual image and that the activity levels of at least some of the neurons in the visual cortex can usefully be thought of as local spectral coefficients (Glezer, Ivanoff, & Tscherbach, 1973). Although we do not have sufficiently detailed information about the characteristics of cortical cells to evaluate this suggestion very critically, it is perhaps worth considering how what we do know of cortical cells fits in with the idea of the cortex as a spatial frequency analyzer. Contrary to the point of view adopted by Pollen and Taylor (1974) and Glezer *et al.* (1973) we shall assume that it is the simple cells rather than the complex cells that primarily carry information about the magnitudes of the spatial frequency components of the visual image.

It seems clear that any given patch of the visual image will be conjugate with the receptive fields of a considerable number of neurons in the visual cortex. It is this set of neurons, all having receptive fields of the same size in the same location, whose activities might constitute a representation of the spatial frequency spectrum of the patch of image corresponding to the receptive field. In the simplest case the activity of each individual cell in this set would represent the magnitude of one of the coefficients of the two-dimensional spatial frequency spectrum of the image patch. Each cell would therefore need to show both orientation and spatial frequency selectivity, characteristics which all cortical cells do, in fact, demonstrate. What is not clear is whether the degrees of both orientation and spatial frequency selectivity, which the cells would have to have for it to be reasonable to think of them as signaling the values of spectral coefficients, are, in fact, characteristic of real cortical cells. The problem comes about because the required degree of selectivity depends upon the number of spectral components it is supposed are isolated. It is therefore important to make some estimate of this number. But at the moment we really do not have enough information about the orientation and spatial frequency selectivity of cortical neurons (or the relation between them) to make it very useful to discuss this problem as directly as we could wish possible. Rather, it may be more helpful to consider the question in terms of the receptive field organization of simple cortical cells.

The receptive fields of simple cells can have different numbers of excitatory and inhibitory regions side-by-side, and we can probably reasonably assume that sets of neurons with the same receptive field size but different numbers of excitatory subdivisions can exist. A member of such a set having a receptive field with m excitatory regions flanked by inhibitory regions can be expected to respond optimally to a grating (of the appropriate orientation) having a spatial frequency such that m periods of the grating span the receptive field. That is, the cell can be expected to respond best at the frequency of the mth harmonic component of an image patch corresponding in size to its receptive field. If the excitatory and inhibitory regions are all about equally sensitive then the cell will respond rather selectively to the mth harmonic component, and its activity can be considered to represent the amplitude of this component. In fact, the amplitude of the component can only be completely represented by the activity of two cells, not one. This is because the phase of the component is essentially arbitrary with respect to the boundaries of the image patch. However, the representation of the complex amplitude of each frequency component will come about quite naturally if, for each frequency, there are two cells having the same number of excitatory regions but differing from each other in having these regions arranged with either odd or even symmetry with respect to the receptive field. We may recall that Hubel and Wiesel (1962) described some simple cell receptive fields as having a single excitatory region flanked by a single inhibitory one, whereas others had an excitatory region sandwiched between two inhibitory ones. In the present context the activities of a pair of such cells (having odd and even symmetry) can be thought of as together representing the complex amplitude of that first harmonic component having the orientation appropriate to the cells. Other cell pairs would be needed to represent the first-order harmonics at other orientations (minimally four pairs of cells are needed altogether for this order), whereas a minimal number of $4m$ pairs of cells would be required to represent the amplitudes of the differently oriented mth harmonic components. But not only would more cells be needed to represent the amplitudes of a set of higher-order components, the orientation selectivity of these cells would have to be sufficiently good to isolate the individual components. If the receptive fields of such cells had excitatory and inhibitory regions of equal width and uniform sensitivity over their whole area then the required selectivity would be achieved; however, it should be noted that the orientational separation of adjacent mth-order harmonic components will only be about $45/m°$ and that cells capable of responding to only one of these components must display this degree of orientation selectivity.

We now have several ways in which we can hope to get some idea of the maximum value that m might really have, that is, the number of spectral frequency components into which a patch of the visual image might be analyzed by the cortex. First, and we must allow that descriptions of simple cell receptive fields do not really suggest that they are often divided into excitatory and inhibitory regions of equal width, there does not seem to be much evidence that receptive fields ever have more than three excitatory regions. Second, the orientation selectivity of cortical neurons never seems to exceed a value (negligible response at angles greater than about 15° from the optimum) appropriate to the isolation of third-order harmonic components. Third, we may note that the optimum orientations of cortical neurons have been reported (Hubel & Wiesel, 1968) to jump from one value to another, a range of 180° being covered in 10–15 jumps. This is consistent with analysis of the image into its first three harmonic components, though it should be noted that the observations primarily relate to complex and not simple cells. Fourth, what little information we have about the frequency selectivity of cortical neurons (e.g., Maffei & Fiorentini, 1973) makes it difficult to suppose that any higher-order harmonic components than the third can be usefully isolated from any patch of the visual image.

Despite the rather insubstantial nature of the neurophysiological evidence which can be brought to bear on the problem, we can probably safely conclude that, if the visual cortex is a spatial frequency analyzer, it is certainly an analyzer of very modest capabilities, able to do no more than analyze patches of the visual image into their first three harmonic components. It may be that even such a simple analysis could be an important step in the visual process, especially if the analysis is carried out simultaneously on a large number of image patches in different locations and of different sizes. However, it seems premature to speculate about the functional significance of what is still only a rather free interpretation of some aspects of known cortical neurophysiology. At this stage we should probably be satisfied with any suggested functional description which can suggest lines of attack on the many complex problems of visual perception which still await any kind of neurophysiological interpretation.

References

Barlow, H. B. Trigger features, adaptation and economy of impulses. In K. N. Leibovic (Ed.), *Information processing in the nervous system*. New York: Springer-Verlag, 1969. Pp. 209–226.

Barlow, H. B. Single units and sensation: A neuron doctrine for perceptual psychology. *Perception*, 1972, **1**, 371–394.

Barlow, H. B., Blakemore, C. B., & Pettigrew, J. D. The neural mechanism of binocular depth discrimination. *Journal of Physiology*, 1967, **193**, 327–342.

Barlow, H. B., Hill, R. M., & Levick, W. R. Retinal ganglion cells responding selectively to direction and speed of image motion in the rabbit. *Journal of Physiology*, 1964, **173**, 377–407.

Barlow, H. B., & Levick, W. R. Three factors limiting the reliable detection of light by retinal ganglion cells of the cat. *Journal of Physiology*, 1969, **200**, 1–24. (a)

Barlow, H. B., & Levick, W. R. Changes in the maintained discharge with adaptation level in the cat retina. *Journal of Physiology*, 1969, **202**, 699–718. (b)

Barlow, H. B., & Levick, W. R. Coding of light intensity by the cat retina. In W. Reichardt (Ed.), *Processing of optical data by organisms and machines*. New York: Academic Press, 1969. (c)

Bartlett, N. R., & Doty, R. W. Response of units in striate cortex of squirrel monkeys to visual and electrical stimuli. *Journal of Neurophysiology*, 1974, **37**, 621–641.

Bishop, P. O., Coombs, J. S., & Henry, G. H. Receptive fields of simple cells in the cat's striate cortex. *Journal of Physiology*, 1973, **231**, 31–60.

Bisti, S. & Maffei, L. Behavioral contrast sensitivity of the cat in various visual meridians. *Journal of Physiology*, 1974, **241**, 201–210.

Blake, R., Cool, S. J., & Crawford, M. L. J. Visual resolution in the cat. *Vision Research*, 1974, **14**, 1211–1217.

Boycott, B. B., & Dowling, J. E. Organization of the primate retina: Light microscopy. *Philosophical Transactions of the Royal Society, Series B,* 1969, **225,** 109–176.

Boycott, B. B., & Wässle, H. The morphological types of ganglion cells of the domestic cat's retina. *Journal of Physiology,* 1974, **240,** 397–419.

Brindley, G. S. *Physiology of the retina and visual pathway.* London: Edward Arnold, 1970.

Büttner, U., & Fuchs, A. F. Influence of saccadic eye movements on unit activity in Simian lateral geniculate and pregeniculate nuclei. *Journal of Neurophysiology,* 1973, **36,** 127–141.

Campbell, F. W. The transmission of spatial information through the visual system. *The neurosciences, Third study program.* Cambridge, Massachusetts: M.I.T. Press 1974. Pp. 95–103.

Campbell, F. W., Cleland, B. G., Cooper, G. F., & Enroth-Cugell, C. The angular selectivity of visual cortical cells to moving gratings. *Journal of Physiology,* 1968, **198,** 237–250.

Campbell, F. W. and Green, D. G. Optical and retinal factors affecting visual resolution. *Journal of Physiology,* 1965, **181,** 576–593.

Cleland, B. G., Dubin, M. W., & Levick, W. R. Sustained and transient neurones in the cat's retina and lateral geniculate nucleus. *Journal of Physiology,* 1971, **217,** 473–496.

Cleland, B. G., & Enroth-Cugell, C. Quantitative aspects of sensitivity and summation in the cat retina. *Journal of Physiology,* 1968. **198,** 17–38.

Cleland, B. G., & Enroth-Cugell, C. Quantitative aspects of gain and latency in the cat retina. *Journal of Physiology,* 1970, **206,** 73–91.

Cleland, B. G. & Levick, W. R. Brisk and sluggish concentrically organized ganglion cells of the cat's retina. *Journal of Physiology,* 1974, **240,** 421–456.

Cleland, B. G., & Levick, W. R. Properties of rarely encountered types of ganglion cells in the cat's retina and an overall classification. *Journal of Physiology,* 1974, **240,** 457–492.

Cleland, B. G., Levick, W. R., & Sanderson, K. J. Properties of sustained and transient ganglion cells in the cat retina. *Journal of Physiology,* 1973, **228,** 649–680.

Cooper, G. F., & Robson, J. G. Successive transformations of spatial information in the visual system. *I.E.E./N.P.L. Conference on Pattern Recognition,* 1968, I.E.E. Conference publication **47,** 134–143.

Cragg, B. G. The topography of the afferent projections in the circumstriate visual cortex (c.v.c.) of the monkey studied by the Nauta method. *Vision Research,* 1969, **9,** 733–747.

Creutzfeldt, O. D., Sakmann, B., Scheich, H., & Korn, A. Sensitivity distribution and spatial summation within receptive field center of retinal on-center ganglion cells and transfer function of the retina. *Journal of Neurophysiology,* 1970, **33,** 654–671.

De Monasterio, F. M., & Gouras, P. Functional properties of ganglion cells of the Rhesus monkey retina. *Journal of Physiology,* 1975.

De Valois, R. L., Morgan, H., & Snodderly, D. M. Psychophysical studies of monkey vision—III Spatial luminance contrast sensitivity tests of macaque and human observers. *Vision Research,* 1974, **14,** 75–81.

Dow, B. M., & Gouras, P. Color and spatial specificity of single units in Rhesus monkey foveal striate cortex. *Journal of Neurophysiology,* 1973, **36,** 79–100.

Dreher, B. Hypercomplex cells in the cat's striate cortex. *Investigative Ophthalmology,* 1972, **11,** 355–356.

Enroth-Cugell, C. & Pinto, L. H. Properties of the surround response mechanism of cat retinal ganglion cells and centre-surround interaction. *Journal of Physiology,* 1972, **220,** 403–439.

Enroth-Cugell, C., & Robson, J. G. The contrast sensitivity of retinal ganglion cells of the cat. *Journal of Physiology,* 1966, **187,** 517–552.

Enroth-Cugell, C., & Robson, J. G. Direct measurement of image quality in the cat eye. *Journal of Physiology,* 1974, **239,** 30-31P.

Enroth-Cugell, C., & Shapley, R. M. Adaptation and dynamics of cat retinal ganglion cells. *Journal of Physiology,* 1973, **233,** 271–309.

Evans, E. F. Physiological studies of the cochlear nerve and cochlear nucleus. In W. D. Keidel & W. D. Neff (Eds.), *Handbook of sensory physiology,* Vol. V/1. New York: Springer-Verlag, 1974.

Fischer, B. Overlap of receptive field centres and representation of the visual field in the cat's optic tract. *Vision Research,* 1973, **13,** 2113–2120.

Fishman, M. C. & Michael, C. R. Integration of auditory information in the cat's visual cortex. *Vision Research,* 1973, **13,** 1415–1419.

Fukuda, Y., & Stone, J. Retinal distribution and central projections of X-, Y-, and W-cells of the cat's retina. *Journal of Neurophysiology,* 1974, **37,** 749–772.

Garey, L. J., & Powell, T. P. S. An experimental study of the termination of the lateral geniculo-cortical pathway in the cat and monkey. *Proceedings of the Royal Society (London) Series B.,* 1971, **179,** 41–63.

Glezer, V. D., Ivanoff, V. A., & Tscherbach, T. A. Investigation of complex and hypercomplex receptive fields of visual cortex of the cat as spatial frequency filters. *Vision Research,* 1973, **13,** 1875–1904.

Gouras, P. The effects of light-adaptation on rod and cone receptive field organization of monkey ganglion cells. *Journal of Physiology,* 1967, **192,** 747–760.

Gouras, P. Identification of cone mechanisms in monkey ganglion cells. *Journal of Physiology,* 1968, **199,** 533–547.

Gouras, P. Antidromic responses of orthodromically identified ganglion cells in monkey retina. *Journal of Physiology,* 1969, **204,** 407–419.

Gouras, P. Opponent-colour cells in different layers of foveal striate cortex. *Journal of Physiology,* 1974, **238,** 589–602,

Gross, C. G., Rocha-Miranda, C. E., & Bender, D. B. Visual properties of neurons in inferotemporal cortex of the macaque. *Journal of Neurophysiology,* 1972, **35,** 96–111.

Grüsser, O. J. & Grüsser-Cornehls, U. Neuronal mechanisms of visual movement perception and some psychophysical and behavioral correlates. *Handbook of sensory physiology,* Vol. VII/3A New York: Springer-Verlag, 1973. pp. 333–429.

Hammond, P. Contrasts in spatial organization of receptive fields at geniculate and retinal levels. *Journal of Physiology,* 1973, **228,** 115–137.

Henry, G. H., Bishop, P. O., Tupper, R. M., & Dreher, B. Orientation specificity and response variability of cells in the striate cortex. *Vision Research,* 1973, **13,** 1771–1779.

Hoffman, K.-P. Conduction velocity in pathways from retina to superior colliculus in the cat: A correlation with receptive-field properties. *Journal of Neurophysiology,* 1973, **36,** 409–424.

Hoffman, K.-P., Stone, J., & Sherman, S. M. Relay of receptive field properties in dorsal lateral geniculate nucleus of the cat. *Journal of Neurophysiology,* 1972, **35,** 518–531.

Horn, G., Stechler, G., & Hill, R. M. Receptive fields of units in the visual cortex of the cat in the presence and absence of bodily tilt. *Experimental Brain Research,* 1972, **15,** 113–132.

Hubel, D. H. Single unit activity in striate cortex of unrestrained cats. *Journal of Physiology,* 1959, **147,** 226–238.

Hubel, D. H., & Wiesel, T. N. Receptive fields of single neurones in the cat's striate cortex. *Journal of Physiology,* 1959, **148,** 754–591.

Hubel, D. H., & Wiesel, T. N. Receptive fields of optic nerve fibres in the spider monkey. *Journal of Physiology,* 1960, **154,** 572–580.

Hubel, D. H., & Wiesel, T. N. Receptive fields, binocular interaction and functional architecture in the cat's visual cortex. *Journal of Physiology,* 1962, **160,** 106–154.

Hubel, D. H., & Wiesel, T. N. Receptive fields and functional architecture in two non striate visual areas (18 and 19) of the cat. *Journal of Neurophysiology,* 165, **28,** 229–289.

Hubel, D. H., & Wiesel, T. N. Receptive fields and functional architecture of monkey striate cortex. *Journal of Physiology,* 1968, **195,** 215–243.

Hubel, D. H., & Wiesel, T. N. Stereoscopic vision in macaque monkey. *Nature,* 1970, **225,** 41–42.

Hubel, D. H., & Wiesel, T. N. A re-examination of stereoscopic mechanisms in area 17 of the cat. *Journal of Physiology,* 1973, **232,** 29–30P.

Ikeda, H., & Wright, M. J. The outer disinhibitory surround of the retinal ganglion cell receptive field. *Journal of Physiology,* 1972, **226,** 511–544. (a)

Ikeda, H., & Wright, M. J. Receptive field organisation of sustained and transient retinal ganglion cells which subserve different functional roles. *Journal of Physiology,* 1972, **227,** 769–800. (b)

Ikeda, H., & Wright, M. J. Evidence for "sustained" and "transient" neurones in the cat's visual cortex. *Vision Research,* 1974, **14,** 133–136.

Kaji, S., Yamane, S., Yoshimura, M., & Sugie, N. Contour enhancement of two-dimensional figures observed in the lateral geniculate cells of cats. *Vision Research,* 1974, **14,** 113–117.

Kuffler, S. W. Discharge patterns and functional organization of mammalian retina. *Journal of Neurophysiology,* 1953, **16,** 37–68.

Maffei, L., & Fiorentini, A. Retinogeniculate convergence and analysis of contrast. *Journal of Neurophysiology,* 1972, **35,** 65–72.

Maffei, L., & Fiorentini, Adriana. The visual cortex as a spatial frequency analyser. *Vision Research,* 1973, **13,** 1255–1267.

Marg, E. Recording from single cells in the human visual cortex. *Handbook of sensory physiology;* Vol. VII/3B. New York: Springer-Verlag, 1973. Pp. 441–450.

Marrocco, R. T. Maintained activity of monkey optic tract fibres and lateral geniculate nucleus cells. *Vision Research,* 1972, **12,** 1175–1181.

Michael, C. R. Opponent-color and opponent-contrast cells in lateral geniculate nucleus of the ground squirrel. *Journal of Neurophysiology,* 1973, **36,** 536–550. (a)

Morrell, F. Visual system's view of acoustic space. *Nature,* 1972, **238,** 44–46.

Nikara, T., Bishop, P. O., & Pettigrew, J. D. Analysis of retinal correspondence by studying receptive fields of binocular single units in cat striate cortex. *Experimental Brain Research,* 1968, **6,** 353–372.

Pettigrew, J. D. Binocular neurones which signal change of disparity in area 18 of cat visual cortex. *Nature, New Biology,* 1973, **241,** 123–124.

Pettigrew, J. D., Nikara, T., & Bishop, P. O. Responses to moving slits by single units in cat striate cortex. *Experimental Brain Research,* 1968, **6,** 373–390. (a)

Pettigrew, J. D., Nikara, T., & Bishop, P. O. Binocular interaction on single units in cat striate cortex: Simultaneous stimulation by single moving slit with receptive fields in correspondence. *Experimental Brain Research,* 1968, **6,** 391–410. (b)

Poggio, G. F. Spatial properties of neurons in striate cortex of unanesthetized macaque monkey. *Investigative Ophthalmology,* 1972, **11,** 368–376.

Pollen, D. A. & Taylor, J. H. The striate cortex and the spatial analysis of visual space. *The neurosciences, Third study Program.* Cambridge, Massachusetts. M.I.T. Press, 1974. Pp. 239–247.

Ratliff, F. *Mach bands: Quantitative studies on neural networks in the retina.* San Francisco: Holden-Day, 1965.

Sanders, M. D., Warrington, E. K., Marshall, J., & Wieskrantz, L. "Blindsight": vision in a field defect. *Lancet,* 1974, **i,** 707–708.

Sanderson, K. J., Bishop, P. O., & Darian-Smith. The properties of binocular receptive fields of lateral geniculate neurones. *Experimental Brain Research,* 1971, **13,** 178–207.

Schiller, P. H., & Stryker, M. Single-unit recording and stimulation in superior colliculus of the alert rhesus monkey. *Journal of Neurophysiology,* 1972, **35,** 915–924.

Stone, J. Morphology and physiology of the geniculo-cortical synapse in the cat: The question of parallel input to the striate cortex. *Investigative Ophthalmology,* 1972, **11,** 338–346.

Stone, J., & Dreher, B. Projection of x- and y-cells of the cat's lateral geniculate nucleus to areas 17 and 18 of visual cortex. *Journal of Neurophysiology,* 1973, **36,** 551–567.

Stone, J., & Fabian, M. Summing properties of the cat's retinal ganglion cells. *Vision Research,* 1968, **8,** 1023–1040.

Stone, J., & Fukuda, Y. Properties of cat retinal ganglion cells: A comparison of W-cells with X- and Y-cells. *Journal of Neurophysiology,* 1974, **37,** 722–748.

Stone, J., & Hoffmann, K.-P. Very slow-conducting ganglion cells in the cat's retina. *Brain Research,* 1972, **43,** 610–616.

Wässle, H., & Creutzfeldt, O. D. Spatial resolution in the visual system: A theoretical and experimental study on single units in the cat's lateral geniculate nucleus. *Journal of Neurophysiology,* 1973, **36,** 13–27.

Watkins, D. W., & Berkley, M. A. The orientation selectivity of single neurones in cat striate cortex. *Experimental Brain Research,* 1974, **19,** 433–446.

Wiesel, T. N. Receptive fields of ganglion cells in the cat's retina. *Journal of Physiology,* 1960, **153,** 583–594.

Wiesel, T. N., & Hubel, D. H. Spatial and chromatic interactions in the lateral geniculate body of the rhesus monkey. *Journal of Neurophysiology,* 1966, **29,** 981–1166.

Wilson, M. D., & Cragg, B. G. Projections from the lateral geniculate nucleus in the cat and monkey. *Journal of Anatomy,* 1967, **101,** 677–692.

Wurtz, R. H. Visual receptive fields of striate cortex neurons in awake monkeys. *Journal of Neurophysiology,* 1969, **32,** 727–742.

Wurtz, R. H., & Goldberg, M. E. The role of the superior colliculus in visually evoked eye movement. In J. Dichgans & E. Bizzi (Eds.), *Cerebral control of eye movement and motion perception.* Basel: Karger, 1972.

Zeki, S. M. Representation of central visual fields in prestriate cortex of monkey. *Brain Research,* 1969, **14,** 271–291.

Zeki, S. M. Functional organization of a visual area in the posterior bank of the superior temporal sulcus of the rhesus monkey. *Journal of Physiology,* 1974, **236,** 549–573.

Chapter 5

NEURAL CODING OF COLOR

RUSSELL L. De VALOIS AND
KAREN K. De VALOIS

I. INTRODUCTION

Whenever one attempts to understand some aspect of human function by studying other animals, as is so often done in physiological psychology, the problems of interspecies comparisons become of prime importance. It is probably no more extreme a problem in the case of color vision than elsewhere, but is immediately obvious because of the wide recognition of the fact that animals differ greatly in their color vision. Although it now appears unlikely that as many domestic animals are completely color blind as was once thought, there are nonetheless enormous quantitative and qualitative variations in color vision among species, and indeed within man. Thus, whereas the cat, for instance, has some ability to discriminate colors (Mello & Peterson, 1964; Sechzer & Brown, 1964), it has great difficulty in distinguishing even the 150-nm wavelength difference between green and red and can do so only under optimal conditions. Such a miniscule sensory capability can play little if any role in the cat's ordinary behavior. A macaque monkey or normal human, on the other hand, can, with ease, discriminate, say, a 5-nm wavelength difference between 590 and 595 nm, and color differences are so dominant in our vision (and that of macaques) that it is notoriously difficult for us to make brightness judgments between objects of different colors. It is thus unlikely that the physiology of such common laboratory species as cats, rats, or dogs will tell us much about the neural basis for color vision.

There are numerous animals with excellent color vision, especially among the birds and fish. Most of these species differ so greatly from man, however, that interspecies comparisons become quite difficult. Birds, for example, have oil droplets on their retinas which act as filters and significantly affect the transmission of colored light. And fish, whereas they show some neural mechanisms that are very similar to ours, have retinas that differ greatly in structure from those of man. In order to try to infer the nature of the human visual system, it would obviously be of great advantage to study an animal with which we could make direct anatomical, physiological, and behavioral comparisons. The more similar to man a given species is, the more accurate our inferences are likely to be. In addition to the obvious fact of the closeness of macaque monkeys to man on the phylogenetic scale, there is the advantage of the knowledge we possess about their visual abilities. A series of behavioral tests has been made (De Valois, Morgan, Polson, Mead, & Hull, 1974; De Valois & Morgan, 1974) of macaque monkeys and human observers on many classical visual psychophysical tasks, using the same apparatus and procedures for the two species. On each task (spectral sensitivity, wavelength discrimination, purity discrimination, anomaloscope tests, spatial frequency discrimination) the performance of the macaques was very similar, if not identical, to that of the humans. Thus, in view of the anatomical and behavioral similarities of their respective visual systems, we can with confidence extrapolate to the human visual system from physiological studies on macaque monkeys. For this reason, we have chosen to restrict our discussion here largely to the results of physiological studies conducted on monkeys. A thorough review of color processing in other animals can be found in Daw (1973).

An initial requirement for color vision is the presence of at least two different receptor types containing pigments of different spectral sensitivity. When a photopigment molecule absorbs a photon of light, it is isomerized and starts the chemical events that lead eventually to neural activity. But this isomerization is quite independent of the energy level (or wavelength) of the photon captured. The spectral sensitivity of a pigment is an expression of the probability that photons of different wavelengths will be captured by the pigment, but any photon absorbed has exactly the same effect on the photopigment. Thus, wavelength information (independent of intensity) is lost to a receptor with the initial visual response, the photopigments being capable of signaling only how many photons they have captured.

How then can the wavelength of a light be identified? Clearly, it can only be on the basis of a comparison of the outputs of two or more receptors of different spectral sensitivity. If one absorbs long-wavelength photons more readily, and the other absorbs short-wavelengths photons better, then a long-wavelength light, regardless of intensity, will activate the first receptor type more than the second, and a short-wavelength light more the second than the first. The critical information for specifying the wavelength, clearly, is not the extent to which the receptors are activated, but the *relative* activation of the two receptor types. On the other hand, the intensity of the light is obviously related to the total receptor output. As we shall see, it is just these two types of information that are extracted in retinal interactions, in parallel neural systems.

Color vision requires, then, a limited number of receptors of different spectral sensitivity, plus a neural system that compares the output of different receptor types. Each of these essential basic components was postulated over a century ago, by Helmholtz (1863) and Hering (1872), respectively. But they and their numerous followers, even to the present, saw their respective theoretical contributions as being mutually exclusive (a position aided by the fact that Hering postulated that the opponent process occurred at the receptor level). There is now ample direct physiological evidence to indicate that both three separate receptor types and spectrally opponent interactions are present, but at different neural levels. It would seem that a reluctance to let a good argument die plus an apparent need for mystery in color vision mechanisms act to keep this old pseudoissue alive. Certain terminologies that have tenaciously maintained their hold have also helped to generate some mystification in what would otherwise be a straightforward problem.

In his book on audition, Helmholtz (1863) postulated that the analysis of complex tones into their sine wave components was accomplished by independent resonators in the cochlea, each of which could be set into vibration only by a particular sound frequency. The sound frequency would be recognized, then, on the basis of which resonator was activated. (We now know, above all from the work of Békésy, that this is not the case; rather each section of basilar membrane vibrates to a broad frequency range.) Helmholtz's model of how color vision takes place had much the same characteristics as his tonal theory; he postulated three types of color receptors—red, green, and blue—with independent paths to the brain. The color of an object would be recognized, then, on the basis of which color receptor was activated. He postulated three receptor types from considerations of the trichromacy of normal human color matches. The actual receptor curves he postulated have considerable overlap in their spectral sensitivity (thus raising questions about his giving them color names), but in general peak at distinctly different spectral regions. Actual cone pigments in man (and monkey) we now know, are quite different.

As a heuristic exercise, we might extend such a Helmholtzian receptor-specific color vision system to its logical limit (which he did not do) and postulate a set of color receptors, each sensitive to a different discrete spectral band. Such receptors we could truly term "red receptors," "yellow receptors," "green receptors," etc., since they would only respond to wavelengths that we see as those particular colors. Such a system would have the virtue of requiring no neural processing. Which receptor was activated by a light would immediately signal the wavelength. But such a system would have major disadvantages, such crippling ones that no known animal has ever evolved such a system. First, color vision itself would be very poor. One spectral range could readily be discriminated from another, but within the range covered by one receptor type there would be no color discrimination at all: As already discussed, a single receptor responds identically to any photon it captures. So with three color receptors, we could only discriminate three colors from each other (instead of the hundreds we in fact can); there would be no discrimination among the various reds or between them and oranges or yellows. One could, in principle, compensate for this by having many color receptors, but that would magnify the second problem, which is that visual acuity and form vision would seriously suffer in colored light. If long wavelengths were only absorbed by "red receptors" among three or more color receptor types, then the retinal mosaic would be very coarse in long-wavelength light, since only a scattered receptor here and there would respond. The same would obviously be true in any other monochromatic light. Since white light, on the other hand, would activate all receptors, one would predict from such a formulation that visual acuity with white light would be far better than with monochromatic. In fact, the reverse is the case (as one would predict from purely optical considerations: The image of a white object is necessarily a little more blurred than a monochromatic one because the human cornea and lens cannot simultaneously bring all the wavelengths in white light to a focus at the same plane). Having more than three color receptors would of course make acuity in monochromatic light even worse.

In fact, the human visual system does not have color receptors, each sensitive to a selective spectral range. Rather, each receptor type responds to lights of almost any wavelength (the short-wavelength cones are something of an exception to this, as to most other general statements about color vision, but they seem to be quite rare in the retina). Under ordinary conditions, then, all receptor types are stimulated by light from any visual object whether white or monochromatic, thus providing for high visual acuity and form perception. The spectral sensitivities of the various receptor types are slightly different from each other, however, and the later neural processing detects and magnifies this difference to extract the color information. Later neural elements, then, are color-specific, but receptors are not.

This mode of operation, with broadly tuned receptors feeding into neural circuits that compare and contrast the outputs of different receptors to extract specific information, seems to be general to all sensory systems. The auditory receptors respond to a wide range of frequencies, but later neural interactions produce a great narrowing of tuning curves so that many cells higher in the pathway respond only to narrow frequency bands. In the gustatory and olfactory systems, higher centers have not been extensively investigated, but the receptors certainly show very broad tuning to tastes and smells, not the specificity one would expect from nineteenth century notions of sensory physiology. And, of course, within vision such an organization characterizes not just color vision: We do not have form-specific receptors responding only to lines of particular orientation. Rather, the receptors fire to any shape of object and the shape is detected later in the neural pathway by comparing the output of different receptors. Quite the same holds for color vision, although this fact is hidden by tenacious old theories and the continued use of color names for receptor types.

II. NEUROPHYSIOLOGY OF COLOR SYSTEMS

A. Receptors

1. PHOTOPIGMENTS

Four critical questions, from the point of view of color vision, about the visual photopigments are (a) the number of photopigments involved, (b) their spectral sensitivities, (c) their photosensitivity and prevalence in the retina, and (d) whether they are segregated into separate receptor types or sometimes combined in one. No single experimental procedure has provided definitive answers to any of these questions, but a variety of quite different approaches, each with its own limitations, have converged on the same answers to these questions. Such agreement reached among psychophysical, physiological, and optical approaches is perhaps even more convincing than apparently definitive answers from just one procedure.

The trichromacy of vision has been adequately established in extensive psychophysical studies over the last century. It was first clearly realized by Young (1807) that this requirement for three and only three physical variables to match all colors could be explained by the presence of just three receptor types each containing a different photopigment. Such an explanation is hardly without other plausible alternatives, however. There could be more than three photopigments but combined into only three different receptor types; or there could be more than three photopigments and receptor types, but only three different pathways to the brain, etc. But Young's explanation is the simplest and, without much doubt, the correct one since other lines of evidence lead to the same conclusion.

A very direct spectrophotometric approach to answering this question for the primate was taken by Marks, Dobelle, and MacNichol (1964), following a successful application of those procedures to goldfish receptors (Marks, 1963). A tiny spot of monochromatic light was focused on the receptor outer segment in a fragmented mixture of retinal components on a microscope slide. The spectral absorption of the receptor was directly measured by measuring with a photocell the amount of light that passed through the outer segment while sweeping across the spectrum with the monochromator. This was done for each of a sample of receptors from macaque monkey and human eyes. Although the procedure is straightforward in concept, it has its difficulties in practice, among them that the spectral light used to measure the spectral sensitivity of the receptor bleaches it at the same time, and the amounts of light involved were so extremely small as to be at the limits of measurement. The net result of these limitations was that one could not be absolutely certain about either the shape of the absorption curve or the point in the spectrum at which it peaked.

Despite these limitations, however, several interesting findings did emerge. They found evidence for three (and only three) separate pigments with peak absorptions in the region of 445, 535, and 570 nm, and with broad spectral sensitivity. These results from the macaque monkey and the human eyes were virtually identical. Furthermore, their results suggest that only one pigment is found in any given cone, although Wald and Brown (1965), on the basis of similar experiments, suggest that some cones may possibly contain two long-wavelength pigments. Both of these studies found many more cones containing the medium- and long-wavelength absorbing pigments than the short-wavelength pigment. Marks, Dobelle, and MacNichol, for example, found only two cones with the short-wavelength pigment in a sample of 56 receptors. (We may term the three receptors contaning pigments with long-, middle-, and short-wavelength maxima, the L, M, and S cones, respectively.)

Further support for these findings comes from physiological studies of the responses of single cells at the LGN or ganglion cell level after chromatic adaptation. For various reasons that will be discussed later, it seems probable that spectrally opponent cells in the LGN receive their inputs from two cone types. If this is so, and if each cone type contains only one photopigment, then one should be able to reveal the shape of the absorption curve of one pigment input by selectively chromatically adapting the other input to a given cell. When this is done, three separate spectral sensitivity functions are revealed, corresponding to photopigments with absorption peaks at approximately 445, 540, and 570 nm, respectively (Abramov, 1968; De Valois, 1965).

Still other evidence for the existence and better evidence for the shape of the two long-wavelength pigments comes from Rushton's (1963, 1965) studies on the human eye using reflection densitometry. This technique involves shining lights of various wavelengths into the eye, then measuring the light which is reflected back out. By taking the difference between the light which was shone in and that which is reflected out and then correcting for various interfering factors (absorption by nonphotopigments, light scatter, etc.), one can obtain an estimate of the amount of light at each wavelength that was absorbed by the photopigments. Rushton utilized the fact that no rods and few S cones are present in the fovea and that the S cones do not absorb at longer wavelengths, so the normal fovea contains just two pigments sensitive at long wavelengths. Furthermore, color-blind protanopes and deuteranopes, according to the most prevalent theory of color blindness, which his data strongly support, are missing one or the other of the two longer wavelength pigments. Therefore, foveal reflection densitometry on protanopes and deuteranopes should (and did) reveal just a single pigment absorption, that of the M and the L cones, respectively. His results show that these pigments have peak absorptions at about 540 and 570 nm, respectively, and that they have broad spectral sensitivity functions.

Cone pigment curves have also been determined from psychophysical measurements of protanopes and deuteranopes (Pitt, 1944) and, indirectly, from other types of psychophysical experiments. The vast majority of studies agree rather well with those reported here. Thus there are, apparently, three cone pigments, and their peak absorptions are approximately 440–450, 530–540, and 560–570 nm, respectively. Figure 1 gives the best estimate of the absorption curves of the three human (and macaque) cone types based on the consideration of many of these factors (Vos & Walraven, 1971).

2. RECEPTOR RESPONSE

Receptors differ from most later neurons in the visual system in that they do not show all-or-none spikes but rather graded depolarization or hyperpolarization responses. In an elegant recording from single receptors

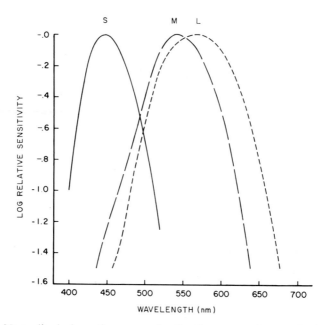

FIG. 1. Normalized absorption curves for the three cone pigments in the macaque monkey (and human) eye. Based on spectrophotometric, physiological, and psychophysical evidence.

in *Necturus* and *Gekko,* Toyoda, Nosaki, and Tomita (1969) demonstrated that they respond with graded hyperpolarization to light. In consideration of the surprise often expressed at the fact that vertebrate photoreceptors show a hyperpolarizing response to light (that is, to light increments), we should note that the visual world as often consists of objects darker than the mean luminance level as of objects lighter than the mean light level. And the one type of stimulus is as important for the organism to detect and characterize as the other. In response to decrements in light the photoreceptors show depolarization (and secretion of synaptic chemicals). Under normal circumstances, the light falling on any given receptor is constantly fluctuating up and down as our eyes scan a scene. The receptor responds with a fluctuating polarization of the receptor membrane (depolarizing to decrements and hyperpolarizing to increments in light), which results in a fluctuating amount of synaptic chemical being released to activate the bipolar and horizontal cells with which the receptor synapses.

Although the direction of the receptor response is determined by whether the stimulus is incremental or decremental, its magnitude depends on both the intensity of the stimulus and the adaptation state of the receptor. For very small changes in intensity, the graded receptor response is approximately linear. But when the intensity change is of greater magnitude, the receptor output becomes roughly proportional to the log of the intensity. Boynton and Whitten (1970) argue that the intensity–response function of receptors can be best fitted by a power function.

In our later description of spectrally opponent cells, we will discuss the fact that these cells seem to difference the outputs of two cone types. Since, as we have just noted, the receptor intensity–response function is quasi-logarithmic, the opponent cells are, thus, approximately responding to the ratio of the absorbances.

B. Ganglion and Lateral Geniculate Cells

The single most important—if by now commonplace—finding of twentieth-century sensory physiology is that every neuron in the sensory pathways has a combination of excitatory and inhibitory influences playing on it. Before evidence from single neurons was available, many theorists postulated "private" lines from receptors to the brain, that is, noninteracting pathways. Thus, for instance, Polyak (1957) postulated a private path from each foveal cone in primates to the brain by way of midget bipolars and ganglion cells, one cone to one bipolar to one ganglion cell, to account for our high visual acuity. And Helmholtz (1866) postulated separate noninteracting paths for each cone type to the brain. Neither of these nor other similar notions has any basis in fact. We can now see, on the contrary, that it is the comparison of the excitatory and inhibitory inputs at each synaptic level which forms the very basis of the information processing that takes place in sensory systems.

The most important interaction involved in analyzing wavelength information is the comparison of the outputs of different cone types seen in the responses of spectrally opponent cells. These were first seen in the primate visual system in recordings from single cells in the lateral geniculate nucleus (LGN) (De Valois, Smith, Karoly, & Kitai, 1958). But the principal interactions clearly do not take place there, but earlier, since ganglion cells show very similar behavior (Gouras, 1968; Marrocco, 1972). Spectrally opponent ganglion cells are also found in goldfish (MacNichol & Svaetichin, 1958); similar interactions (involving depolarization and hyperpolarization) are seen even earlier in this animal, at the level of horizontal and bipolar cells (Svaetichin & MacNichol, 1958). Thus it is entirely possible—in fact likely—that the spectrally opponent interactions in primates also take place before the ganglion cell level in the retina, but there is a paucity of direct evidence from primates. Since evidence is lacking about earlier interactions, and since ganglion and LGN cells are highly similar in respect to color processing, only the evidence from these latter two levels will be considered, and they will be treated as one.

Two principal interactions take place before the cortex in the primate visual system: (*a*) a comparison by later neurons of the receptor activity in different spatial locations, to form a spatially opponent organization, and (*b*) a comparison of the receptor activity among different cone type to form a spectrally opponent organization. Some cells show just one and others just the other, but most show both types of interactions.

1. Spatially Opponent Organization

The spatially opponent organization of visual neurons was first seen by Kuffler (1953) and Barlow (1953) in the responses of single ganglion cells of cat and rabbit, respectively. The vast majority of cells in these animals (and of others with little or no color vision) consist of one or the other of two types. Both cell types show either excitation (an increase in firing from the maintained discharge rate seen in the absence of stimulation) or inhibition (a decrease in firing), depending on the location of a tiny stimulus within their receptive field (RF: that limited portion of the environment about which the cell is signaling or equivalently, those particular receptors from which the cell is receiving its input).

One of these cell types, commonly but misguidedly called on-center cells, responds to a tiny light spot (a tiny incremental stimulus) with excitation, or on-responses, when the spot is in the center of the RF, and inhibition (with off-responses at the termination of stimulation) when the spot is anywhere within an annular surround. The responses to a tiny dark spot would be just the reverse, that is, off responses in the RF center and on responses in the surround. It is only if one ignores decremental stimuli (which, fortunately, the visual system does not do) that one could call such cells on-center cells. One might better think of the conventional RF map in Fig. 2 as indicating whether an increment ($+$) or a decrement ($-$) produces firing in that portion of the RF. It can be seen that the optimal stimulus for firing such a cell would be an incremental spot on a decremental background or, in other words, a white spot on a black background. The reverse stimulus, a black spot on white background, would produce the maximum inhibition. We (De Valois, 1972) have thus termed such cells $+$Wh $-$Bl cells, since they fire to white and inhibit to black spots.

Found equally frequently are mirror image cells, see Fig. 2, which show inhibition in the RF center and excitation in the surround to incremental stimuli, and hence were called by Kuffler (1953) off-center cells. They might better be termed $+$Bl $-$Wh cells, since they fire to black spots on a white background, and inhibit to white spots.

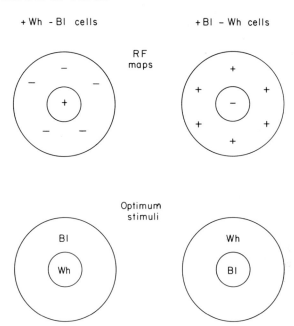

FIG. 2. Receptive field maps for spectrally nonopponent cells, and optimal stimuli to fire the cells. The + and − signs conventionally refer to on or off responses, respectively, to (incremental) stimuli. They might better be thought of as areas in which incremental (+) or decremental (−) stimuli fire the cell. The size of RFs vary enormously; the area represented in the RF map might encompass anything from a dozen to tens of thousands of receptors.

The centers of the RFs are dominant over the surrounds, if both are stimulated, in the case of ganglion cells and of most LGN cells (Jacobs & Yolton, 1968), so a +Wh −Bl cell will fire to an increment of light covering the whole RF (but much less so than to a discrete white spot) and a +Bl −Wh cell will also fire to a uniform decrement. These two cell types, which constitute virtually the whole population of cat ganglion or LGN cells, are also found in the macaque (and presumably human) visual system (De Valois, 1960), but make up less than 30% of the total (De Valois, Abramov, & Jacobs, 1966; Wiesel & Hubel, 1966).

All of the preceding discussion is with respect to responses to increments and decrements in the intensity of light, and it is clear that the visual system is roughly symmetrically organized into cells responding to increments and to decrements (De Valois, Jacobs, & Jones, 1962; Jacobs, 1965; Jung, 1961). After examining the spectral responses of such cells, we have termed them together *spectrally nonopponent cells,* since such a cell gives the same type of response to monochromatic lights of any wavelength. The

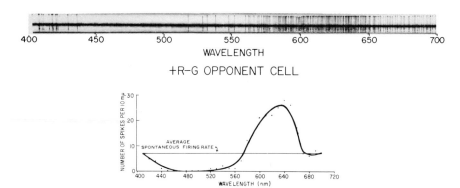

FIG. 3. Example of responses to different spectral lights of an opponent cell. On the top line are the spikes evoked in a $+R$ $-G$ cell by sweeping across the spectrum with a monochromator. Below is a graph of the record at top, in which is plotted the number of spikes fired to each 10-nm section of the spectrum. It can be seen that this cell fires to long wavelengths (red) and is inhibited by shorter wavelengths (green).

$+Wh$ $-Bl$ cells fire to any incremental monochromatic light; the $+Bl$ $-Wh$ cells inhibit to any incremental monochromatic light (and fire to any decremental lights), see Fig. 4. The basis for this is that the same cone types feed into both the center and surround of such cells (De Valois, 1969) and the center and surround thus have the same spectral sensitivity (Wiesel & Hubel, 1966).

2. SPECTRALLY OPPONENT ORGANIZATION

Far more commonly found in the macaque visual system than the cells just discussed are those we have termed *spectrally opponent cells:* those that fire to some wavelengths and inhibit to others (De Valois *et al.,* 1958; De Valois, 1965; Gouras, 1968; Wiesel & Hubel, 1966). See Fig. 3 for an example of the responses of one such cell to lights of various wavelengths. Since opponent cells show different responses to various spectral regions, they would appear to be carrying color information.

As one samples the responses of a large number of ganglion or LGN cells, one encounters a wide variety of different opponent cells, with considerable variation in the wavelengths that produce peak excitation and inhibition. Whether there is truly a huge number of different cell types, or a much more limited number, with some random variation in their interconnections, is a difficult question to answer definitively. We have presented evidence from the distributions of peak response and of crosspoints from excitation to inhibition which suggests the presence of just four spectrally opponent cell types (De Valois, Abramov, & Jacobs, 1966; Abramov,

1968). One of these cell types, an example being the cell in Fig. 3, we have termed *red-excitatory, green-inhibitory* (+R —G) cells, so named because the spectral region to which the cell fires maximally is that which appears red to us, and it inhibits to those wavelengths we see as green. Found equally frequently are cells which are mirror images of these, in terms of the spectral regions to which they fire or inhibit: +G —R cells. Together we can class these as the RG system. There are other cells that show maximum excitation to somewhat shorter wavelengths than the +R —G cells, to that region we see as yellow; and their maximum inhibition is also to wavelengths we see as blue rather than green. These cells we have termed +Y —B cells; together with their mirror-image cells +B —Y, they constitute what we may call the BY system. In Fig. 4 are the average firing rates of a sizable sample of each of these six opponent and nonopponent cell types in response to flashes of monochromatic light of different wavelengths. (It should be noted that in every case their response to a *decrement* would be opposite.)

The receptive fields of these various cell types found in a given location in the LGN overlap, and it is highly probable that each small section of the central retina projects up to cells of each of these varieties. Furthermore, both opponent and nonopponent cells of a particular type vary considerably in RF size, some +R —G cells having tiny receptive fields, others somewhat larger, still others quite large, etc. So it is likely that some dozens of LGN cells receive inputs from each small central region, reporting on the color and size of objects in that portion of the environment.

3. RECEPTOR INPUTS TO LGN CELLS

It is clear that the spectrally opponent cells must be receiving inputs from at least two different receptor types, containing photopigments of different spectral sensitivity. Thus the +G —R cells have a short-wavelength excitatory and a long-wavelength inhibitory input. But since the spectral sensitivities of the cones probably overlap to a great extent, it is by no means obvious which particular cone types feed into these cells, or what their spectral sensitivities are. There have been several attempts (De Valois, 1965; Wiesel & Hubel, 1966; Abramov, 1968; Gouras, 1968) to determine this, with somewhat conflicting results.

Chromatic adaptation can be used to isolate the individual cone inputs to an LGN cell, in much the same fashion as it was used psychophysically by Stiles (1949). A long-wavelength light, in the case of the +R —G cell in Fig. 3, would be mainly absorbed by the longer wavelength pigment feeding into it and should thus desensitize the long-wavelength excitatory input to the +R —G cell, revealing the short-wavelength inhibitory input more or less in isolation. When this is done, it is found that the cell now

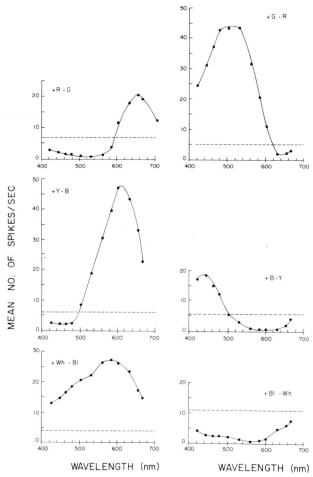

Fig. 4. Plots of the average firing rates of a large sample of cells of each of the six LGN cell types in response to flashes of monochromatic light. The top four are spectrally-opponent cells which fire to some wavelengths and inhibit to others. The bottom two are spectrally nonopponent cells (it should be noted that these are responses to increments; the +Bl −Wh cells fire to decrements).

inhibits to wavelengths across virtually the whole spectrum and gives its maximum inhibition not to 500 nm, as before adaptation, but to about 530–540 nm. The spectral sensitivity of the cell now corresponds very closely to a 535-nm cone pigment, that is, to the sensitivity of the M cone. When the converse experiment is done, using a short-wavelength adaptation, one sees excitation all across the spectrum, with the point of maximum excitation shifted from about 640 nm to approximately 570 nm, or the point of maximum absorption of the L cone. Thus, in a +R —G cell, the M pigment is presumably feeding in an inhibitory manner, and the L pigment gives an excitatory input. In +G —R cells the same two pigments are implicated, but the M cones now give an excitatory input, while the L cones feed in an inhibitory manner.

The same conclusion, namely that the RG cells are differencing the M and the L cones, is supported by two other approaches. Wiesel and Hubel (1966) measured the spectral sensitivity of LGN cells using discrete stimuli in either the center or surround of the RF to attempt to isolate the separate cone inputs, which are nonuniformly distributed spatially. They found that the L and M cones fed into these cells. Abramov (1968) tested the responses of units of mixtures of two wavelengths equated for absorption by these two putative cone inputs and found equal responses, thus confirming the same conclusion.

Although there is general agreement concerning the cone inputs to cells in the red–green opponent system, the cone inputs to blue–yellow cells are in dispute. When the chromatic adaptation procedure just discussed was used with a sizable sample of BY cells, it revealed isolated opponent inputs with peak absorptions at 445 and 570 nm, or the S and L cone types (De Valois, 1965). Wiesel and Hubel (1966), however, again measuring sensitivity to spots in discrete areas in the center or surround of the cells' RFs, concluded for the two by cells they studied that the cone inputs were from the S and M cones. Gouras (1968) has presented evidence from ganglion cell recordings of macaque that also suggest that it is the S and M cone types that are involved. Abramov (1968), on the other hand, has argued on both theoretical and experimental grounds that the S and L cone types provide the inputs to these BY cells. So although most of the data suggest that the BY cells are differencing the outputs of the S and the L cones, this can not be considered a firm conclusion. It is conceivable, of course, that both the S–L and the S–M types of connections exist.

From this evidence, it should be clear that the pathway from receptors to brain has nowhere the outputs of single cone types. All LGN cells have inputs from at least two cone types: the nonopponent cells summing the outputs of L and M cones (and rods and, perhaps, S cones); the opponent cells differencing the outputs of the different cone types in pairs, see Fig. 5.

The spectral sensitivities of the L and the M cones are very nearly the same, peaking as they do at about 530–540 and 560–570 nm (both in the part of the spectrum we see as greenish yellow, compounding the absurdity of calling them "green" and "red" receptors as too many people do). But the +R —G and +G —R cells, by differencing the outputs of these cone types, have maximum activity rates at about 500 and 640 nm (which *are*

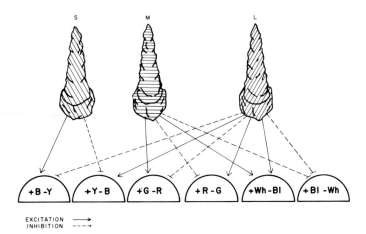

EXCITATION ⟶
INHIBITION ----┤

FIG. 5. A model of how the three cone types interact to form the six LGN cell types. Note that the L cones feed into all pathways.

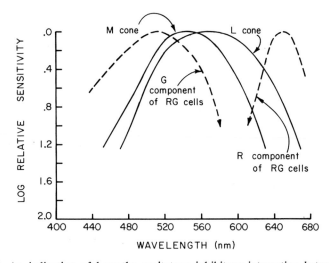

FIG. 6. An indication of how the excitatory–inhibitory interaction between L and M cones in the RG opponent cells leads to a narrowing of the spectral response curves and a shift toward the spectral extremes. The cones absorb all across the spectrum and both peak at middle wavelengths (greenish-yellow); the RG cells by differencing their outputs respond to only narrow spectral regions, peaking at 500 nm (green) and 640 nm (red).

the regions we see as green and red, respectively); see Fig. 6. That is, although the L cone is maximally sensitive to 565 nm, the *difference* between the sensitivities of the L and M cones, which is what fires the $+R$ $—G$ cells, is greatest at around 640 nm.

4. COMBINED SPATIALLY AND SPECTRALLY OPPONENT ORGANIZATIONS

As was already stated, the two main types of neural interactions seen in the precortical visual system are a spatial-opponent organization and a spectral-opponent organization. We have seen how the one is characteristic of spectrally nonopponent cells, and the other of spectrally opponent cells. But almost all spectrally opponent cells also have spatial opponency in the organization of their RFs. This was first shown by Wagner, Mac-Nichol, and Wolbarsht (1960) for goldfish ganglion cells, and by Wiesel and Hubel (1966) for the primate retina. If one measures the spectral sensitivity of a +G −R cell, for instance, with a spot covering the center of the RF one may find that the cell fires to increments across virtually the whole spectrum, and shows maximum sensitivity at about 530 nm. On the other hand, an annular stimulus of almost any wavelength covering all but the RF center would evoke inhibition from the cell and the maximum sensitivity might now be to, say, 590 nm. This is what one might expect if this +G −R cell had an excitatory input from M cones in the RF center and an inhibitory input from L cones in the RF surround, see Fig. 7.

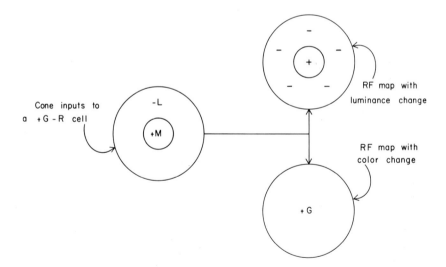

FIG. 7. Receptive field map for a spectrally opponent cell that also shows spatial opponency. Such a cell responds to both luminance changes and color changes, but with entirely different receptive field maps for the two types of stimuli. When mapped with a luminance change, the cell shows a spatial antagonism and a RF like a +Wh −Bl cell; when mapped with a color change the RF is uniform in sign, the cell firing to a shift toward green (and inhibiting to red) anywhere in the field.

Since the cone pigments—particularly the L and M cones—respond to wavelengths across virtually the whole spectrum, a +G —R cell with an RF like that depicted in Fig. 7 would be expected to respond to a black–white figure virtually the same as would a nonopponent +Wh —Bl cell. And so it does (De Valois & Pease, 1971; De Valois, 1972), firing to a small white spot on a black background. It would respond thus, of course, not just to black–white patterns, but to almost any stimulus based on luminance (as opposed to color) differences. The maximum inhibition, with such luminance-difference patterns, would be to a black spot on a white background.

If one now examined the RF organization of this same cell with patterns containing not luminance differences, but only color differences, one would obtain quite a different RF organization and size. The optimum *color* stimulus would not be a small spot, but a large field and the direction of the response would be the same throughout the field, i.e., there would be no center–surround organization. It can be seen, Fig. 7, that a green light would also produce minimum inhibition from the RF surround. So the optimal color stimulus would be green on green, that is, a uniform green stimulus across the whole RF (such as that used in the experiments of De Valois *et al.,* 1958; De Valois, 1965, etc.). Of course, the maximum inhibition from a pure color stimulus would correspondingly be a uniform red field.

A spectrally opponent cell can thus be thought of as having two quite different RF organizations depending on the nature of the stimulus: an antagonistic center–surround RF from luminance-based stimuli, and a uniform RF for pure-color stimuli. As a result, it responds both to luminance changes and to color changes, but with quite different spatial tuning in the two cases, see Fig. 7. To a luminance change, the cell responds optimally to small bars, the response falling almost to zero for large bars, but for a color change the optimum stimulus is large.

Other spectrally opponent cells have inhibitory centers and excitatory surrounds to luminance stimuli; that is, they act like +Bl —Wh cells to those stimuli. A few—Wiesel and Hubel's (1966) Type II cells—have no center–surround organization even to luminance figures. It is not clear whether such cells are in fact a discrete class or extreme examples of overlapping receptive field inputs. Most of the evidence from studies of goldfish ganglion cells (Wagner, MacNichol, & Wolbarsht, 1963) and macaque LGN cells (Mead, 1967) indicates that even in the case of cells like that just discussed and depicted in Fig. 7 (and the nonopponent cells discussed earlier), the excitatory and inhibitory inputs overlap spatially. That is, a +Wh —Bl cell (or the +G —R cell, which responds like that to luminance figures) would have both excitation and inhibition in the RF center and surround, but the excitation would dominate in the center and the inhibition in the surround. Since the cells vary considerably in the spatial distribution of excitatory and inhibitory inputs, a Wiesel and Hubel Type II cell might be just an extreme example in which the distribution of the two inputs was virtually the same.

C. Cortex

The visual cortex at least equals in complexity of organization the whole earlier retinal and thalamic centers, yet has been investigated far less, particularly with respect to color. It is not surprising, then, that we have only the most rudimentary idea of what happens to color information when it reaches this level. Any statements made in this discussion should be viewed even more skeptically than those in earlier sections.

There have been fewer than a dozen studies of the color responses of cortical cells in monkeys (Andersen, Buchmann, & Lennox-Buchthal, 1962; Hubel & Wiesel, 1968; Gouras, 1968; Boles, 1971; Poggio, Mansfield, & Sillito, 1971; Zeki, 1973; Dow & Gouras, 1973; Michael, 1973; Hepler, Yund, & De Valois, in preparation). In many of these, the color investigations were incidental to studies of other aspects of visual processing. As a result, nothing approaching a complete account of cortical color processing can be given. But the evidence suggests to us the following picture: LGN color information may go into two directions in the cortex: (a) into color-specific channels that separate color and luminance information, and (b) into multiple-color channels that generalize across many color inputs while extracting form information.

1. COLOR-SPECIFIC STRIATE CELLS

As we have already pointed out, one of the problems in understanding the physiological basis for color vision from the LGN results is that the spectrally opponent cells are carrying not only color but luminance information, and $+G$ $-R$ cell, for instance, responding in the same way to a white spot on black as to an extended green surface. Since we can obviously distinguish between these stimuli, one would expect that at some cortical level cells should be found that respond to color changes but not to luminance changes. Unfortunately, most investigators have only tested cells with flashes of colored light, which consist of both color and luminance changes. With such a technique one cannot tell which aspect of the stimulus is driving the cell. (It is as if one were to test a person's color vision by asking him whether he can see various flashes of colored light projected in turn on a screen. Even a totally color-blind individual could of course do so, detecting the flashes on the basis of the brightness change. To detect presence or absence of color vision, one must eliminate luminance differences and test detection of pure color figures, as in the Ishihara or HRR color-blindness plates.) Nonetheless, reports of cells in striate cortex (area 17), which respond to monochromatic lights but not to white light (Hubel & Wiesel, 1968; Boles, 1971; Dow & Gouras, 1973) indicate an increase in color specificity from the LGN. As will be discussed, this is particularly true for a poststriate region of cortex (termed V4), in which Zeki (1973) reports finding all of the cells to be color-specific.

Hubel and Wiesel (1962), in their pioneering studies of cat cortex cells, found that virtually all striate cortex cells were responsive to lines of some orientation, rather than having radially symmetrical RFs like ganglion and LGN cells. They classified these orientation-specific cells as simple, complex or hypercomplex according to their apparent position in a hierarchical order of processing. Nonoriented cells, however, have been reported in cat (Baumgartner, Brown, & Schulz, 1965), and such cells are clearly very prevalent in monkey cortex forming perhaps 40% of cells related to the fovea (Poggio, 1972). Although such cells superficially resemble LGN cells, it should not be assumed that they are the earliest cells in the cortical chain. In many respects, such cells are quite unlike LGN cells or other cortical cells; they may in fact constitute several levels of a side-chain in the cortical information processing scheme.

In addition to cortical cells that appear similar to LGN cells in their color responses, two types of color-specific cells have been reported in monkey striate cortex. One variety consists of nonoriented cells, which both respond to narrower spectral bands than do LGN cells, and are less responsive to achromatic patterns (Boles, 1971; Poggio et al., 1971; Dow & Gouras, 1973). There may well be many such cells within the sample of units in mangabey cortex studied with diffuse light flashes by Anderson et al. (1962). Unfortunately, little is known of how such cells are related to LGN opponent cells, or of how they respond to pure color figures.

A second variety of color-specific cell that has been reported in the monkey striate cortex are termed double-opponent cells (Hubel & Wiesel, 1968; Michael, 1973). Cells of these characteristics were first found by Daw (1968) in the goldfish retina, where they apparently constitute the majority of the ganglion-cell populations. Such cells in goldfish have a concentric center–surround organization like the monkey LGN cells already described, but, in addition, a large far surround of the opposite spectral response characteristic to the near center–surround. Thus, a $+R$ $-G$ cell would have a $+G$ $-R$ far surround. It is clear that such a cell would not respond to a uniform red surface but would to a red on a green background.

The monkey cortical double-opponent cells appear mainly to be "simple" cells, with line-orientation specificity and discrete RFs. The central region responds like a LGN opponent cell and the flanks like opponent cells of the mirror-image type. Such a cell will clearly not respond to a large colored surface, as LGN cells optimally do, for such a surface would produce antagonistic responses from the center area and the flanks.

2. MULTIPLE-COLOR STRIATE CELLS

The color-specific cells found in monkey striate cortex form only a small proportion of striate cells—far fewer than the 70–80% of LGN cells that are carrying color information. This poses the question of what happens to all the color information that reaches the cortex. One answer (Hepler, Yund, & De Valois, in preparation) seems to be the presence of many cortical cells which are receiving a color input, but in such a manner that they have doubtless been misclassified previously.

To understand the nature of these cells, we must make a few observations about geniculate cells. They are all, in the broadest sense, opponent cells: The spectrally opponent cells fire to one spectral range and inhibit to another; the spectrally nonopponent cells fire to white (luminance increment) and inhibit to black, or vice versa. If one flashes lights of different wavelengths on a screen (as Hubel and Wiesel did in their experiments), the spectrally nonopponent cells will respond to them, but in the same way to lights from each spectral region—+Wh —Bl cells, for example, will fire to them all. Such a stimulus differs from the background both in color and in luminance. Since the nonopponent cells fire to all the different colors, one may presume that it is the luminance increment accompanying each to which they are responsive. We have shown that this is indeed the case, since if one matches the different wavelengths for luminance the nonopponent cells cannot detect a change in wavelength (De Valois, 1971).

In their recordings from striate cells, Hubel and Wiesel again examined the responses to colored flashes of light. Finding that almost all cortical cells responded to flashes of any wavelength, they concluded that they were all nonopponent cells with no color input. A far better way to establish that, however, would be to equate various wavelengths for luminance, and then see whether the cells can detect a pure color change (a sort of Ishihara color blindness test). We have done that with a considerable population of cells in monkey striate cortex and find that, quite contrary to first impressions and to Hubel and Wiesel's (1968) conclusions, many of these cells clearly can discriminate wavelength differences. However, they seem quite indifferent to the particular colors involved. That is, a cell will fire to a red line on an equal-luminance green background (to which a nonopponent cell would be quite blind), but will also fire to a green line on a red background. It appears to us that such cells must be receiving excitatory inputs from multiple geniculate cell types, opponent and nonopponent, and thus can discriminate color differences quite indifferently to the particular colors involved.

The presence—and great prevalence—of such multiple-color cells leads us to the view that the form or shape discriminating systems in the cortex must operate on visual stimuli in large part quite independent of color or contrast. One can suggest that such multiple-color cells are responding to a particular form—a line of a particular orientation and width or spatial frequency—regardless of whether the line differs from its background in color or in brightness, and regardless of the particular color differences involved or whether the lines are white or black. That is, it is abstracting out "form" information and generalizing across color.

3. Color-Specific V4 Area Cells

The visual path from the striate cortex is very complex, with multiple pathways to other cortical areas in the occipital and temporal lobes as well as to subcortical regions such as the superior colliculus and pulvinar. Of particular importance for color processing is an area, termed V4, anterior to the classically described visual areas 17, 18 and 19 (V1, 2 and 3). In the first recordings from single cells in this area, Zeki (1973) found all the cells to be color specific. Not only, like geniculate cells, do they fire only to light from a particular spectral region, but they also are reported not to respond to white light, thus showing greater color specificity than LGN cells. The color responses have not analyzed in detail to see whether the range of wavelengths to which they respond is narrower or different from that of LGN cells. Nor have they been tested with pure color versus luminance stimuli, but the fact that those cells which respond to limited spectral regions do not respond to white suggests that luminance and color information have been separated by this stage. (It should be noted that Zeki also finds cells in this area which respond just to white light but not to any narrow spectral band, so the color specificity apparently extends to the white–black domain.)

This visual area V4 appears to be organized into color columns. Zeki (1973) finds that the cells in a given column will all respond to the same color, e.g., red, but have different demands as to the shape of the red object. For some cells, any red light in the appropriate visual location suffices; others require a red object of a particular shape, or a red border of a particular orientation before they will fire. The cells in a neighboring column might be similarly diverse in their shape requirements but all demand that the objects be blue.

Our conclusion, then, is that color information in the cortex must go two ways: into color-specific paths, which maintain and even increase the color specificity seen at the LGN, and into multiple-color cells, which use color (and luminance) information to detect form but do not care what colors are involved.

D. Summary of Physiology of Color Vision

There is now very convincing evidence from many types of experiments indicating the presence in trichromatic man and monkey of rods plus three types of cones, containing photopigments peaking at about 505 nm for rods, and about 445, 535, and 565 nm for the S, M, and L cones, respectively. These cone pigments have a very broad spectral sensitivity, the M and the L cones, at least, being stimulated by lights of virtually all wavelengths. It is very misleading to consider the cones as color receptors or give them color names, both because of their lack of anything approaching the color selectivity associated with color names, and because they are involved in signaling many other things—black and white, movement, etc.—as well as color. Rather, the cones should be thought of as light receptors, responding to increments and decrements in light regardless of color, or form, whether the light is moving or stationary, etc. The specific information about color, brightness, form, movement, etc., comes from later neural interactions which in every case involve a comparison of activity in different receptors.

There appear to be six principal types of cells between the retina and cortex: four types of opponent cells and two types of nonopponent cells. Color information is extracted from the cones by spectrally opponent cells, which subtract the (log) output of one cone type from that of another. The responses of these cells, then, do not correspond to the responses of any cone type, but rather to the extent that one cone type absorbs more light than another. The $+R$ $-G$ cells, for instance, difference the L and M cones; although each of these cone types fires across the whole spectrum, the $+R$ $-G$ cells fire only to very long wavelengths (those we see as red), since it is only at these wavelengths that the L cones absorb more than the M cones. The four opponent cell types ($+R$ $-G$, $+G$ $-R$, $+B$ $-Y$, $+Y$ $-B$) appear to difference the L and M and the L and S cones.

Black–white information is extracted by a spatially opponent organization in the spectrally nonopponent cells. These cells receive the same type of input from all cone types (and from rods) but have an antagonism between the center and surround of their RFs. They fire, then, not to the extent to which the receptors are activated, but to the extent to which the receptors in the centers of their RF are activated more than those in the surround ($+$Wh $-$Bl), or vice versa ($+$Bl $-$Wh). Most of the spectrally opponent cells have a similar center–surround RF and thus can be thought of as multiplexing color and luminance–contrast information.

In the cortex, it appears that color information goes in two directions: into color-specific cells, which extract specific color information, and into multiple-color cells, which appear to combine the outputs of various LGN cell types to extract form information from either color or luminance differences, but generalize across colors.

III. RELATION TO COLOR VISION

In order to claim that the physiological organization just described actually underlies our color vision, one must be able to show a relationship between the physiology and the characteristics of color vision that have been derived psychophysically. In the following subsections, we examine these relationships between physiology and psychophysics. We will also see to what extent we can explain various aspects of color vision, to try to give a comprehensive picture of where we stand at present in being able to understand the physiological underpinnings of color vision. We are clearly far from being able to explain all the intricacies and the second and third-order effects that have been found in a century's study of color vision in man. But our current understanding of the primate visual system is sufficient to account for many of the primary, first-order aspects of our color vision.

A. Color Discrimination

1. Cells Responsible for Color Vision

The term *color vision* implies the ability to discriminate among lights of different wavelengths regardless of whether or not they differ in intensity. If color vision is present, then one should be able to discriminate between lights of, say 640 and 520 nm even if they were perfectly matched in luminance, or if they were mismatched in either direction.

Since photopigments obey the law of invariance—they give the same type and size of response to any captured photons, regardless of their wavelength—then single receptors obviously cannot be responsible for color vision. In order to obtain the same response from a receptor to lights of 520 and 640 nm, their relative intensities would only have to be adjusted so that the probability of capturing a given number of photons would be the same in each case.

Correspondingly, the nonopponent cells found in the LGN also are not responsible for color vision. They respond in the same manner (either excitation or inhibition, depending on the particular cell) to light from any part of the visible spectrum. In order to evoke the same response from lights of, say, 520 and 640 nm, all one must do is equate those lights in luminance. When they are luminance-equated so that the shift from one to the other is thus a pure color change, the nonopponent cells are unable to discriminate between them, giving no response to the shift between two lights of different colors or between white and a monochromatic light (De Valois, 1971).

The opponent cells in the LGN, on the contrary, can discriminate between lights from different spectral regions whatever their respective luminances. A $+R -G$ cell, for example, will show excitation to a 640-nm light and inhibition to a 520-nm light, regardless of whether they are matched in luminance or whether they are mismatched in either direction. Thus, these and the other three types of spectrally opponent cells all meet the requirements for carrying color vision information and provide, therefore, the precortical basis for our color vision.

The spectrally opponent cells, however, can only discriminate between wavelengths in the case of fairly large stimuli or, more accurately, for low spatial frequency stimuli. With high spatial frequency stimuli (in which stimulus changes would occur *within* the extent of the RF of a single opponent cell) the spectrally opponent and nonopponent cells become alike in their responses: The opponent cells lose their ability to discriminate colors and instead become responsive to luminance differences. The loss of color discrimination on the part of the opponent cells does not cause an embarrassment for our argument that they are responsible for our color vision because under these circumstances we behaviorally lose our color vision (van der Horst & Bouman, 1969). Roughly speaking, we cannot see nearly as fine detail in a scene possessing only color differences as we can in one with luminance differences, and a fine color grid becomes uniform in color.

What does pose a problem is the fact that an opponent cell will respond identically to, say, a tiny white spot as to a large green surface, as seen in Fig. 8. Since the opponent cells give every evidence of true color discrimination with extensive figures, we can best think of them as carrying both color and luminance information, but multiplexed in such a way that it can be separated at later levels. This is perhaps what happens in the organization involving color-specific cells in the cortex.

The multiple-color cells present an interesting problem for classification. Many can clearly discriminate pure color changes, but respond similarly to changes in different spectral directions, e.g., responding the same to a

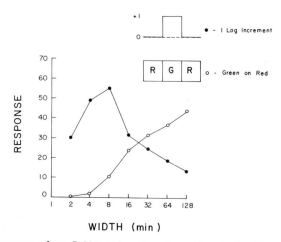

Fig. 8. Responses of an LGN +G −R cell to stimuli of different widths, each centered on the RF. This experiment was carried out with two types of stimuli: a 1-log-unit increment in white light (solid dots); and a shift from a red field to a green line on a red field, the red and green being equated for luminance to produce a pure color change (open dots). Spatial tuning is seen for the luminance but not the color stimulus.

shift from red to green as to a shift from green to red. They can thus discriminate colors yet cannot tell which color is which.

One could predict that a brain lesion which destroyed the color-specific cells of V4 but spared the multiple-color cells of the striate cortex would leave a patient with a color agnosia. He should have an unimpaired ability to discriminate color differences (i.e., to point out, in an Ishihara chart, the numbers which can only be seen on the basis of color differences) but would be unable to name colors. In fact, patients with such a color agnosia have often been reported (e.g., Kinsbourne & Warrington, 1964). Such patients have perfectly normal color vision as shown by the Ishihara or HRR tests, for instance, but when asked to name the colors of objects do so at random. They are as likely to call a red shirt green or blue as they are to call it red. It has been argued that patients with such brain lesions may not have a true color agnosia (loss of the percept or recognition of color but merely a language problem, an inability to associate color names with the various color percepts. But the physiological evidence for two separate cortical regions concerned with color, one containing color-specific and the other mainly multiple-color cells, makes it entirely conceivable that true color agnosias might in fact occur, since a loss of the color-specific region would leave a patient with cells which can use color differences to detect form but which do not carry information about the particular colors involved.

2. WAVELENGTH DISCRIMINATION

The classical technique for measuring wavelength discrimination is to present a subject with a bipartite field, the two halves of which are matched in luminance and variable in wavelength. The subject's task is to adjust the wavelength of the test field until hue is just discriminable from that of the standard field. The difference between the wavelength of the two fields $(\lambda_a - \lambda_b)$ defines the wavelength discrimination threshold $(\Delta\lambda)$ at that point in the spectrum. When $\Delta\lambda$ is obtained for many wavelengths across the entire visible spectrum, the result is the standard wavelength discrimination function. This function (Judd, 1932, for example) which we have replicated (De Valois et al., 1974) with both human observers and macaque monkeys in a four-alternative forced choice procedure, shows two minima (i.e., regions of best discrimination) at approximately 490 and 590 nm. It rises to essentially infinity at both extremes and shows a secondary maximum around 540 nm.

It is interesting to note that the two minima in the wavelength discrimination function occur in the same spectral regions as the crosspoints of the two pairs of spectrally opponent cell types in the LGN, the $+R -G$ and the $+G -R$ cells having their crosspoint at approximately 590 nm, and the $+B -Y$ and $+Y -B$ at approximately 500 nm. If, as one might reasonably expect, fine discriminations are based on the activity of the cell type which is most sensitive, then one would predict just such a double minimum in the wavelength discrimination funtion. Since the RG cells have their crosspoints around 590 nm, they should be extremely sensitive to small changes in wavelength in that region. A wavelength shift of, say, 5 nm might be sufficient to shift a $+R -G$ cell from inhibition to excitation if it occurred near the crosspoint, where the cell is most sensitive. A shift of 5 nm in a spectral region where the cell is *not* particularly sensitive, however, might have little or no effect.

De Valois, Abramov, and Mead (1967) examined the wavelength-discrimination ability of spectrally opponent and nonopponent cells. The nonopponent cells were found to be quite unable to discriminate (by a change in firing rate) among different wavelengths. The opponent cells, on the other hand, were extremely sensitive to wavelength changes in certain spectral ranges, see Fig. 9. As can be seen (middle line of the top trio, Fig. 9), this $+G -R$ cell shows a large firing change to a shift between 560 and 593 nm, firing to the 560 and inhibiting to the 593 (in fact, it showed in other tests a considerable response to even a 5-nm wavelength change). It also responds to the 27-nm wavelength difference between 593 and 620 nm with a large change in firing (middle line of bottom trio, Fig. 9). As can be seen in the top and bottom lines in each group, the discrimination

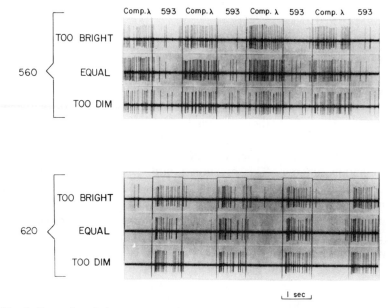

FIG. 9. Examples of the responses of a $+G\ -R$ cell to shifts in wavelength around 593 nm. The middle line in each shows the wavelength discrimination is in the same direction even if the intensity is varied up or down a half-log-unit.

between these wavelengths occurs even in the presence of large intensity differences, the direction of the firing change being determined by the wavelength not the intensity relations.

From data, like the sample shown in Fig. 9, obtained for different size wavelength shifts around each of several spectral points for each of a large number of opponent cells of various types one can determine, for each spectral point, the minimum wavelength difference necessary to produce a criterion change in firing rate in whatever cell type was most sensitive at that spectral point. The function they found fit quite well the classical wavelength-discrimination function described by Judd (1932), with the shapes of the two functions being quite similar and their maxima and minima occurring at the same spectral loci. In general, the RG cells account for our wavelength discrimination at long wavelengths and the BY cells for it at short wavelengths. This relationship is reinforced by a comparison of macaque and squirrel monkeys (De Valois & Jacobs, 1968). Squirrel monkeys have color vision similar to that of severely protanomalous human color defectives (Jacobs, 1963). Their wavelength-discrimination function shows the short but not the long wavelength minimum; their color discrimination is extremely poor at long wavelengths (De Valois & Morgan,

1974). A sampling of a large population of LGN cells in this species shows that most of the (limited number of) opponent cells are of the BY cell types (+Y —B and +B —Y). The presence of these BY cells accounts for the squirrel monkey's good wavelength discrimination at short wavelengths, and the absence of many RG cells accounts for their poor discrimination among long-wavelength lights.

3. SATURATION

Saturation is a psychophysical quality of light that might be described as the degree to which a color appears to be free of whiteness or blackness, or the extent to which it is colored as opposed to achromatic. Although many variables can affect saturation (for example, intensity, retinal locus of stimulation, stimulus size, temporal factors), the two most important determinants are colorimetric purity and wavelength. The colorimetric purity of a white–monchromatic light mixture is specified by the proportion of colored light, with a pure monochromatic light have a purity of 1. For a given white–monochromatic mixture, saturation varies with purity, generally increasing as a power function (Onley, Klingberg, Dainoff, & Rollman, 1963).

The second important variable affecting saturation is wavelength. The plethora of studies investigating this relationship (Jones & Lowry, 1926; Purdy, 1931; Martin, Warburton, & Morgan, 1933; Wright & Pitt, 1937; Priest & Brickwedde, 1938) have agreed that saturation is greatest at the spectral extremes and decreases to a minimum in the region of 570 nm. Thus, no yellow light will appear as saturated as a red or blue light of the same purity and luminance.

Appropriate behavioral tests have shown that macaque monkeys have a purity discrimination ability that is essentially identical to that of normal human observers (De Valois & Jacobs, 1968; De Valois, Morgan, & Snodderly, 1974), and physiological studies of the responses of single cells in the LGN of macaques have demonstrated a mechanism which could account for the classical purity discrimination function (De Valois, Abramov, & Jacobs, 1966; De Valois & Marrocco, 1973). Consider first the spectrally nonopponent cells in the LGN. A +Wh —Bl or +Bl —Wh cell will give the same response to any light, regardless of its spectral composition, if its luminance is matched for that of the light to which it is being compared. If, say, a mixture of white and any monochromatic light is systematically varied in purity from 0 (pure white) to 1 (pure monochromatic), while its total luminance is kept constant, the response of a nonopponent cell will not change (De Valois & Marrocco, 1973). Since these cells cannot discriminate even the grossest changes in purity, they cannot be responsible for our perception of saturation differences among lights.

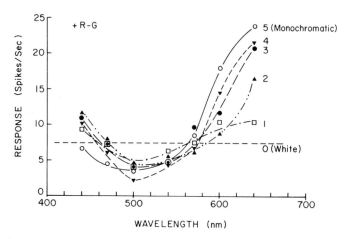

F𝘪ɢ. 10. Saturation discrimination data from a sample of +R —G cells. Shifts were made from white light to various white–monochromatic mixtures, all equated for luminance. This was done at each of several spectral points. It can be seen especially clearly in the responses to 640 nm that the greater the purity (i.e., the more monochromatic light in the white–monochromatic mixture) of the red light the more the +R —G cells fire.

The responses of the spectrally opponent cells, on the other hand, change quite systematically with both purity and wavelength. For any shift from, say, a white light to a white–monochromatic mixture equated for luminance, the direction in which a given opponent cell responds (i.e., excitation or inhibition) will be determined by the wavelength of the monochromatic component, and the magnitude of its response will be determined by its purity (De Valois & Marrocco, 1973). See Fig. 10 for an example. The response rate of these +R —G cells to the various 640-nm–white mixtures, for instance, is monotonically related to the purity of the mixture.

De Valois and Marrocco (1973) also examined the sensitivity of the various cell types to changes in purity at different points across the spectrum. Since the +R —G cells and the +G —R cells show virtually identical curves, they were combined into one RG system for purposes of this study. The same was true of the +B —Y and +Y —B cells. When one compares their sensitivities to purity changes at various spectral loci, and then assumes that the most sensitive cell type is responsible for threshold discrimination at any given point, the classical purity discrimination function can be replicated by plotting for each point the discrimination ability of the cell types most sensitive at that point. By adopting different criteria for detection of a change in a cell's response rate the curve can be pushed up or down, but its shape remains the same. One can argue, therefore, that our ability to discriminate purity differences among equally bright lights (and thus, probably, our perception of saturation) is dependent on the activity rate of the spectrally opponent cells seen in the LGN.

Another approach to the problem is to consider, for any given wavelength, what proportion of total activity occurs in the nonopponent versus the opponent cells. For a given luminance level and purity, the proportion of total response produced by the nonopponent cells is least at the spectral extremes and greatest around 570 nm, the least saturated portion of the spectrum. The opponent cells, on the other hand, give large responses to light from either spectral extreme, more so than to the middle of the spectrum. If one plots the log ratio of the opponent and nonopponent spectral sensitivities as a function of wavelength, the resulting curve closely resembles the purity discrimination function (De Valois, Abramov, & Jacobs, 1966). Thus, saturation is greatest in spectral regions to which the spectrally opponent cells are most sensitive, and the saturation of lights corresponds to the relative activity rate of these two groups of cells.

One can argue strongly to this same point from comparative studies. In macaque monkeys, spectrally nonopponent cells make up less than 30% of the LGN cell population (the remainder being, of course, opponent cells). In squirrel monkeys (De Valois & Jacobs, 1968) nonopponent cells make up some 80% of the LGN cells; in cats nonopponent cells make up perhaps 99% of the population. If the saturation of lights depends on the proportion of the total activity produced by opponent versus nonopponent cells, one would expect that the spectrum must be much more saturated overall for macaque monkeys (and man) than for squirrel monkeys, and far, far more saturated for macaques than for cats. Direct behavioral comparisons have been carried out on macaques and squirrel monkeys (De Valois & Morgan, 1974) confirming this prediction: Over most of the spectrum macaques can discriminate a considerably smaller admixture of monochromatic light with white from a pure white than can squirrel monkeys. Such direct comparisons have not been made with cats, but the great difficulty cats have in discriminating even a pure monochromatic light from white indicates that the whole spectrum must be of a vanishingly small saturation to them.

B. Color Appearance

1. COLOR SPACE

We can think of perceptual color space as being a three-dimensional solid, and, in fact, it was often represented as such in early phenomenological accounts of vision. Imagine three axes, each at right angles to the others, see Fig. 11a, in which one axis consists of the white–black lightness

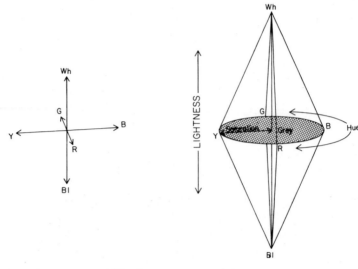

Axes formed by activity of LGN cells types   Color space

Fig. 11. A suggestion of how the location of a stimulus in color space (right) might be determined by the relative activity rates of each of the six LGN cell types (left). The hue would be determined by the activity rates among the four opponent cell types, i.e., which were most active; the lightness by the two activity rates of the two nonopponent cells; and the saturation by the relative activity rates of the opponent and nonopponent cells.

dimension, another the red–green dimension, and the third the yellow–blue dimension. Since intermediate points can occur between these axes, what one obtains is a three-dimensional solid something like a double cone. The axis from tip to tip would be the white–gray–black dimension; distance from this axis to the outside would correspond to the saturation; and location around the circle in any cut at right angles to the black-white axis would give the hue, see Fig. 11b.

We can postulate that the relative activity rate to a stimulus of the LGN cell types already discussed (Wh–Bl, RG, and BY cell pairs) give the location of the stimulus in this perceptual color space. Thus, if a stimulus activated the $+R$ $-G$ cells but none of the other cell types to any great extent we would see it as red; if the $+R$ $-G$ and $+Y$ $-B$ cells were equally activated, we would see it as orange, etc. If some light of 500 nm were added to the 640-nm red light, this would have the effect of decreasing the activity of the $+R$ $-G$ cells (and decreasing the inhibition of the $+G$ $-R$ cells). Such a stimulus would be perceived as a desaturated red, or pink. If white were added to the red (e.g., by means of adding a dark surround) it would also lighten and desaturate the red because now the

+Wh —Bl cells would be highly active as well as the +R —G cells. The red appearance of the 640-nm light could also be desaturated by the addition of black (e.g., by adding a light surround) to produce a brown appearance. In terms of the cell activity we can see that both +R —G and +Bl —Wh cells would now be active.

The validity of such postulated relationships between the color appearances of objects and which cell types are active in the visual pathway could be semiquantitatively tested a number of ways. One such test that has been examined is the color naming of spectral lights.

2. COLOR NAMING

If the spectrally opponent cells in the primate LGN do indeed constitute the physiological system at that level which underlies our color vision, then it should be possible to correlate the outputs of these cells when stimulated with various monochromatic lights with the color names which are given to those same stimuli.

Boynton and Gordon (1965) studied color naming by presenting subjects with various monochromatic lights and then recording the color names given to them. Subjects were allowed to specify the color as red, yellow, green or blue, using the color names either singly or in combinations of two. The results were combined across subjects to look at the proportion of times a given color name was used to describe a flash of light of a specified wavelength.

De Valois, Abramov, and Jacobs (1966) looked at the relative contributions of each of the four spectrally opponent cell types by summing all of the spikes given to a flash of light of a particular wavelength by a large sample of LGN cells, and then calculating the proportion of the total spike discharge which had been contributed by each of the cell types. If one compares these psychophysical and physiological data, a very good correspondence is seen between the incidence of the color name "red' given by subjects to different wavelengths and the proportion of the LGN activity to different wavelengths contributed by the +R —G cells, see Fig. 12a,b. The occurrence of the color name "yellow" corresponded with the contribution to the total spikes of the +Y —B cells, etc. The correlation is quite high for stimuli of 500 nm or higher wavelength; below 500 nm there are some disparities: Although the color name "green" is essentially never used for very short wavelengths, the RG cells continue to contribute a large proportion to the total spike discharge. The later cortical processing (which we have indicated must take place to separate color and luminance information) must also introduce some modifications in the responses to short wavelengths. But at long wavelengths, at least, the schema given here for color space seems to be supported.

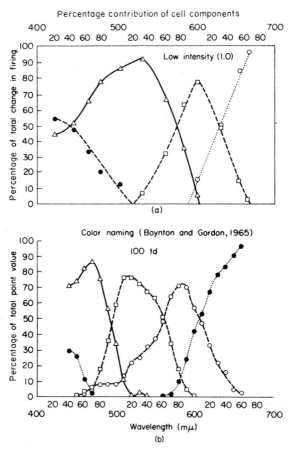

FIG. 12. Comparison of the color names given spectral lights by human observers (bottom) with percentage of the total opponent cell firing-rate contributed by each of the four opponent cell types. At long wavelengths the agreement is good, knowing that the +R −G cells fired far more to a stimulus than any other cell type, one could predict that a human observer would see it as red, etc.

A further test can be made of this schema in the modifications introduced by chromatic adaptation. Jacobs and Gaylord (1967) systematically examined the shift in color produced by chromatic adaptation, using the Boynton and Gordon color-naming technique. Dramatic changes in color appearance take place with chromatic adaptation. For instance, adaptation to a green light of 500 nm produces a shift of longer wavelengths toward red so that a 500-nm light that was previously called greenish–yellow would now be seen as a yellowish red. The changes that are produced in the relative firing rates of various LGN opponent cell types with chromatic adaptation are in excellent qualitative agreement with the perceptual changes (De Valois, 1973). Thus, for instance, in the example just discussed, a 500-nm adaptation light produces changes in the firing of RG cells such that a 500-nm light, which previously inhibited a +R —G cell, will now fire it; and the +G —R cell, which previously fired to this light, is now inhibited by it.

C. Contrast and Similitude

1. SUCCESSIVE COLOR INTERACTIONS

a. DESCRIPTION OF PHENOMENA. As is well known, the brightness and color of a surface are determined not only by the present stimulation but by the aftereffects of previous stimulation. These aftereffects are also sometimes termed *successive induction* or *successive contrast effects*. An excellent summary discussion of the phenomena and of the variables involved can be found in Brown (1965).

If one looks at a uniform gray surface after inspecting a red square for a period of time, one sees a rapidly fading image of a blue–green square. This is termed a *negative afterimage,* since it is of approximately the complementary hue to the original inducing image. Correspondingly, a blue–green square would induce a red afterimage; a yellow square a blue afterimage, etc. The same is true for black and white; the afterimage of a black square is white, and vice versa. All such aftereffects are termed *negative aftereffects;* since the effects result from successive stimulation and produce changes in a direction opposite in color to the original stimulus they are also termed *successive color contrast.*

Afterimages can also be of the same color as the original stimulus. These positive afterimages might also be termed *successive color assimilation* or *similitude.* The conditions that promote positive versus negative afterimages are complex, and often both positive and negative afterimages appear, in alternation. Short intense flashes produce predominantly positive afterimages; following longer-duration stimuli, one is more likely to see negative afterimages. An easy way to see a positive afterimage is to look at a light bulb briefly, then turn off the light.

The afterimage and color of the subsequently presented surface combine in determining the color seen, so if, in the example above, one projected the afterimage of a red square not on a gray surface but on a yellow one, the color of the afterimage would be yellowish–green rather than blue–green. Or if the inspection surface were blue–green the result would be a more saturated blue–green (one can thereby get supersaturated colors: more colored than monochromatic light).

b. PHYSIOLOGICAL BASIS. There are at least three physiological processes that are likely involved in producing the various types of afterimages: (a) photopigment bleaching and receptor adaptation; (b) neural rebound combined with an opponent-color organization; and (c) receptor afterdischarge. The first two of these would lead to negative afterimages; the last to positive afterimages. There is independent evidence from various types of experiments for the existence of each of these processes; how they combine together to produce various types of afterimages has not been thoroughly investigated.

Helmholtz (1866) offered a physiological explanation for successive color contrast or negative afterimages in terms of photopigment depletion. His explanation, for instance, of the example of looking at a gray surface after prolonged inspection of a red square, would be that the inspection of the red square would lead to bleaching of the photopigments in the long wavelength receptors. Subsequent stimulation with the gray surface would therefore set off all but these receptors, and one would therefore see this area as being blue–green (since the adapted retinal area and that in the surround would be responding differently, simultaneous contrast effects would also enter into the picture).

There is ample evidence from psychophysical, physiological, and spectrophotometric studies of retinal function to support the existence of such photochemical bleaching and resulting retinal adaptation (or desensitization). Such a process, then, doubtless forms one basis for negative afterimages. But, as pointed out long ago by Hering (1872) and amply supported since, such a process cannot be the whole story. One sees powerful negative afterimages and successive contrast effects at light levels at which little receptor bleaching could have occurred; high intensity levels, which produce much bleaching, are, in general, more likely to lead to positive rather than negative aftereffects. But most tellingly, one does not need subsequent retinal stimulation to see negative afterimages. Turning off all stimuli after an exposure to a red surface can lead to the appearance in the dark of the negative afterimage. Since there is here no stimulation in the dark to set off all but the long-wavelength receptors, that can hardly account for the percept.

It can now be seen that a second, quite different physiological process is also involved in producing successive color contrast or negative aftereffects: the spectrally opponent neural organization of visual cells combined with neural rebound. A fairly ubiquitous property of neurons anywhere in the brain is that at the termination of prolonged stimulation their firing rate rebounds into the opposite state. Thus, if a stimulus which excited the cell is turned off, one sees a rebound into inhibition; termination of an inhibitory stimulus evokes rebound excitation. Since cells in the visual

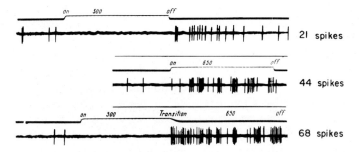

FIG. 13. Example of neural rebound in a +R —G opponent cell. Such a rebound must contribute to successive color contrast. Top record: Response to a 500-nm (green) light. Note the inhibition during the light and rebound firing at the termination of the light. Middle record: response to a 650-nm (red) light, which fires the cell. Bottom record: green light followed by red. Note the larger response than to the red light alone.

path to the brain are organized in terms of either spectral or black–white opponency, such rebound produces firing changes which should lead to negative afterimages quite in the absence of any further receptor stimulation. Thus, a +R —G cell fires to a red light and inhibits to a green. At the termination of prolonged stimulation with a red light (even at quite low, nonbleaching intensities) the cell rebounds into inhibition, giving the same response that it would to a green light. At the same time, a +G —R cell would be rebounding from inhibition to excitation. The effect of these firing changes at the termination of the red stimulus must be indistinguishable to higher centers from those produced by the onset of a green stimulus. We have shown that such neural changes corresponding to successive contrast do occur at the level of the LGN (De Valois & Jones, 1961) and that the off-responses to the termination of one color add together with the on-responses to the initiation of the complementary color to produce more firing than the on-response alone, see Fig. 13. This would be comparable to a greenish surface appearing to be a more saturated green after a red surface had been viewed for a time.

Neural rebound, or off-responses, in opponent-color systems should produce very powerful, but quite brief, negative afterimages, which are not dependent on subsequent stimulation. Receptor adaptation or bleaching, on the other hand, would provide a long-duration process that would also tend to produce negative afterimages, but ones dependent on subsequent retinal stimulation to "reveal" the desensitized receptors. Under ordinary conditions, with fairly brief exposures to the light from low-intensity colored objects, neural rebound in the opponent cells is doubtless the dominant process; with exposures to intense lights, such as looking at a light bulb, or with very long fixation of brightly lit colored objects, receptor adaptation is dominant.

As is the case with simultaneous induction of colors, the fact that there is not only successive color contrast but also sometimes changes in the anticontrast (or what we have termed *similitude*) direction is often forgotten. But such positive aftereffects—or an alternation of positive and negative aftereffects—often occur.

The effects of light on the receptor outer segments (Falk & Fatt, 1972) is probably to open holes in the receptor disk membranes as the isomerized photopigment molecules break away. This in turn leads to Ca^{++} ion flow which diffuses to the receptor outer membrane and there acts to decrease the Na^+ permeability of the membrane (which eventually leads to decreased synaptic chemical release at the receptor–horizontal-cell–bipolar-cell synapse). Since it takes a considerable time (a half life of about 4 min in cones and 8 min in rods) for the photopigment molecule to be regenerated, one would expect continued receptor output after the termination of a stimulus. Such continued receptor activity has indeed been recorded (Brown, Watanabe, & Murikami, 1965), and should lead to positive aftereffects. In response to a brief intense flash of light, the late receptor potential (LRP) shows an extended hyperpolarizing response, with duration far longer than the stimulus. When a long-duration flash is used, the LRP response falls abruptly at stimulus offset, but not completely back to the resting membrane potential (Brown *et al.,* 1965). Rather, there is an after-hyperpolarization (larger with rod than with cone stimulation) which takes some seconds at least to die away.

These three processes are ordinarily involved to some extent at the termination of any stimulation. Whether one sees positive, or negative, or an alternation between positive and negative afterimages depends on the extent to which the conditions of the initial and the subsequent stimulation promotes one or another of the underlying processes. Some of the complexities of the interactions, as well as a partial dissection of the separate processes can be seen in the situation studied by De Valois and Walraven (1967). They inspected an intense spot of red light with the right eye, then measured the color of monochromatic lights seen subsequently with that and with the other eye. When test stimuli are presented to the adapted (right) eye, all three of the processes we have been discussing are involved, with receptor adaptation being dominant due to the prolonged stimulation. One therefore sees large negative afterimages or successive contrast effects: Monochromatic lights from anywhere in the middle of the spectrum (ordinarily seen as green or yellow) appear a spectacularly supersaturated emerald green. The nonadapted (left) eye has, of course, no receptor adaptation; only rebound and receptor afterdischarge from the other eye, mixing at cortical levels, can influence the color seen upon subsequent stimulation of that eye. When neural rebound has died away, a few seconds after stimulus offset, one sees large positive aftereffects and successive color similitude: Lights that would ordinarily appear yellow now look orange when viewed with that eye. And the region of the spectrum complementary to the (red) adaptation light appear quite colorless when viewed with the nonadapted eye. That this is due to continued afterdischarge from the adapted eye mixing with the stimulus light can be seen by the fact that temporarily blinding the adapted eye by pressing on it abolishes the color shift seen with the unadapted eye (Gestrin & Teller, 1969).

Most of us devote only limited portions of our day to looking at burning light bulbs or staring fixedly for minutes at colored papers under a spot light, so these powerful successive color changes play a small role in our perceptual life. But extrapolations from experimental studies show that even the fleeting glances we give to naturally lit objects should produce much larger effects than they apparently do in everyday life. One should expect that our percepts of the world would be an indecipherable melange of color and forms from present and past stimuli. That this does not occur reflects the presence of inhibitory interactions between different forms or contours. Daw (1962), examining this specific question, noted that the colored afterimages of a scene to which one adapts for a few seconds can be readily seen, as in the usual demonstration, when one subsequently views a uniform surface. If, however, one subsequently views a black–white scene in which the contours do not coincide with those of the adaptation stimulus, the colored afterimages are not seen at all. On the other hand, if the contours in the second stimulus coincide with those in the first (as when one adapts to a colored photograph and then views a black and white reproduction of the same photograph maintaining the same fixation point throughout) the negative color afterimages are the strongest of all. All this would follow if there were inhibitory interactions (presumably at cortical levels) between cells signaling the presence of different forms in the same location. When the adaptation and the present stimuli are identical in form, there is no inhibition and the full-blown afterimages are seen; when the present stimulus is an uncontoured surface that afterimages are only slightly weakened, but when the contours of the present stimuli are different from those of the adaptation stimuli, the (weaker) afterimage is inhibited to oblivion. (Of course, one could doubtless arrange a situation in which the afterimage was more powerful than a blurred scene seen subsequently; one would then expect the afterimage to obliterate the percept of the subsequent stimulus.) Since under normal conditions we are constantly looking from one scene to a different one, such a process would have the adaptive value of having the information from each new percept cancel the after-effect from the previous one.

2. SIMULTANEOUS COLOR INTERACTIONS

a. PERCEPTUAL PHENOMENA. The color seen in a region of space is determined not only by the characteristics of the stimuli in that region, but also by those simultaneously present in surrounding regions. These lateral interactions can affect both the color and the brightness (or better, the whiteness–blackness or lightness) of a region. And the direction of the effects can be such as to change the region in a direction opposite to the surround (color and lightness contrast), or in a direction toward that of the surround (color and lightness assimilation).

Contrast effects are widely known and extensively investigated. In a popular textbook demonstration of color contrast, one can see that a gray square on a red background looks slightly greenish, whereas on a green background it appears reddish. And, in demonstrations of lightness contrast a gray square on a white background appears blackish and on a black background appears whitish.

These textbook demonstrations suffice to give one the flavor of contrast effects but do not adequately demonstrate their enormous influence (particularly that of lightness contrast) in ordinary vision. Most people, when asked what characterizes a black object, would say an absence of light, but this is totally false. As the Gestalt psychologists emphasized, what appears as white or black is almost completely independent of the amount of light it reflects to the eye, but rather is determined by the amount it reflects relative to its surround. Thus, a piece of coal in bright sunlight may reflect thousands of times the amount of light (per unit area) to the eye as does a white piece of paper in an adjacent shadow. But the coal is seen as black and the paper as white. Whether we see an object as white, gray, or black, then, is almost totally determined by the relative amounts of light it and its surround reflect; it is almost totally a function of the contrast rather than of the intensity of the light. This is less true for color contrast, although the demonstrations of Land (1959a,b) show the power of color contrast, too.

Although, under most visual conditions, simultaneous color and lightness induction is in the contrast direction, there are circumstances in which the lateral interactions produce perceptual changes in quite the opposite direction. These anticontrast changes have been called variously the *spreading effect of von Bezold* and *assimilation*. Although they probably do not need a third name, we (De Valois, 1973) have referred to them as *similitude effects* to emphasize that the lateral interactions operate to make objects more similar to their backgrounds in color and/or lightness, as opposed to contrast interactions, which operate to make them more dissimilar.

There have been relatively few studies of the factors determining whether the lateral interactions operate in the contrast or similitude direction. A major factor is the size of the inducing surround: When it is large, contrast induction is seen; when it is small, the tendency is toward similitude (Helson & Rohles, 1959). Blurring of the visual image, as, for instance, would happen along certain planes with astigmatism, also tends to produce similitude effects (Wright, 1969).

Both similitude and contrast interactions are primarily determined by the immediately adjacent surround of an object. That is, the color and lightness of an object are determined by the wavelength and intensity of light coming from that object in relation to that of the background on which it lies. The characteristics of more distant objects also play a role, but it is a secondary one, involving as it does not only direct interactions between the object and the far surround but also the influence of the far surround on the immediately adjacent surround of the object. Many classical studies of contrast effects (Leibowitz, Mote, & Thurlow, 1953; Fry & Alpern, 1953) have only concerned themselves with such second-order interactions.

An important characteristic of contrast effects—and one which presents an intriguing puzzle to understand physiologically—is that objects of virtually any size have their lightness and color determined by their relation to the surround. Thus, when we look at a nearby white wall, it may subtend 20° or more visual angle. Yet our percept of it as being white (rather than gray or even black) depends completely on the amount of light from it with respect to other surrounding objects, that is, on the contrast relationships. Furthermore, our immediate percept of the wall is of its being uniformly white. This may seem like a nonproblem until we consider, as we discuss further later, that all the likely retinal processes for explaining contrast effects only operate over much smaller distances—a degree or less of visual angle. So the white appearance of the center of the wall is determined by the contrast situation 10° or more in the periphery, whereas neurons signaling information about the center of the visual field are quite uninfluenced by stimuli even 1° away.

b. PHYSIOLOGICAL BASIS. The first point to be made about the physiological basis for simultaneous lateral interactions is that the retinal image is such as to produce similitude rather than contrast effects. The retinal image is blurred, due to the limitations of the optics of the cornea and lens even in the best of eyes. There is also some light scatter in the course of passage through the eye. Both of these effects are greatly enhanced by such com-

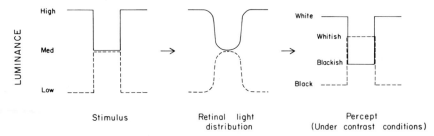

FIG. 14. Diagram of a classical lightness contrast situation: a gray disk on a white (solid line) versus on a black (dotted line) background. The optics of the eye produce some light scatter so the gray on white is lighter, in the image at the receptors, than the gray on black. Under similitude conditions it is so seen. More frequently, however, contrast operates and the percept on the right is seen, with the gray on white looking blacker than the gray on black.

mon optical effects as myopia or presbyopia, or by astigmatism and by diseases, such as cataracts or intraretinal hemorrhages. As a result, the image of a gray square on a white surround, see Fig. 14, will actually be lighter than that same square on a black surround. So also, a gray square on a red background actually has some long-wavelength ("red") light scattered onto it, whereas on a green background it would be slightly greenish. There are some circumstances, as we have mentioned (and termed similitude), when we actually see a gray square on a white background as lighter than when it is on a black background; or when we see a gray on a red background as redder than the same gray on a green background. Under these similitude conditions, then, our percept corresponds to the actual retinal stimulation.

That we do not always see similitude effects—in fact, seldom do—implicates the existence of very powerful neural interactions operating in the contrast direction. Such interactions indeed take place (as far as the achromatic lightness–darkness processing is concerned) at the first retinal synapse. The first evidence for such a process was found by Kuffler (1953), in ganglion cell recordings in the cat. He found evidence for two different types of neurons in the cat (these correspond to the two types of spectrally nonopponent cells in the primate visual system). As already discussed, one variety fires to a light increment in the center of its receptive field and is inhibited by a light increment in the surround; a light decrement in the center of the RF, on the other hand, inhibits such a cell, whereas a light decrement in the surround fires it. Thus, the optimal stimulus for firing the cell is an increment in the RF center combined with a decrement in the surround. The total amount of light is almost irrelevant; it is the difference between the amount of light in center and surround (i.e., the contrast) that is critical. We have termed such cells $+$Wh $-$Bl for the good reason that they fire to those objects we see as white, i.e., more light in the center than in the surround, and inhibit to black.

Such cells would completely counter the blur-induced similitude effects. Consider the response of a $+$Wh $-$Bl cell to the light distributions in Fig. 14. The gray on a white background would provide an excitatory stimulus, but the high-intensity background, falling on the inhibitory surround would more than counteract this excitation and the net effect would be inhibition, signaling black. But consider now the gray on the black background. The gray would produce less excitation than the gray on white, but the black background would produce no inhibition, so the net effect would then be excitation, signaling white. This is, of course, how we would see the two grays under most conditions.

The surround of RFs of cells are far more extensive than the centers and are relatively less sensitive per unit area than the centers. Even in the case of stimuli with extensive surrounds, the center tends to dominate the surround, but if the surround is made very small the center would be totally dominant. In the example of the gray on white and black backgrounds, the gray area, stimulating the RF center of our hypothetical cell, would produce responses in the similitude direction; it is only the counteracting influence of the background on the RF surround that produces the contrast-like response. If the effect of the surround would be lessened, as with narrow borders around an area, one might very well expect the responses of retinal neurons to shift in the similitude direction.

Found equally frequently in cat (and primates) are mirror-image cells, which also respond to contrast rather than to the amount of light, but these cells fire to a decrement in the RF center and are inhibited by an increment. Again, the RF surround is opposite. Such cells we have termed $+$Bl $-$Wh because they fire optimally to black objects, i.e., ones which reflect less light than their surrounds.

Among each of these classes of nonopponent cells there is a wide variation in receptive field size (Wiesel, 1960). (This presumably acts as the first step in an analysis of the size or spatial frequency characteristics of objects.) But even the largest receptive fields found in the central part of the primate visual system are scarcely larger than a degree, and most are far smaller, averaging around 8′ of arc (De Valois & Pease, 1971). So, although such cells show strong lightness contrast effects, it is only for very small stimuli or at the borders of large stimuli; the 20° white wall discussed earlier would cover uniformly the RFs of all central neurons, presenting them with no contrast stimulus. The retinal center–surround organization is just a partial step toward explaining perceptual lightness contrast.

As we have discussed, a center–surround organization is also seen in the case of most spectrally opponent cells. The difference here is that the opposing center and surround inputs are from different cone types. For instance, the $+G -R$ cell diagrammed in Fig. 7 has M cones feeding into the RF center in an excitatory way, and L cones feeding into the surround in an inhibitory fashion (in response to increments in light). Since the spectral sensitivity of L and M cones are not very different and each is responsive to light from virtually all spectral regions, such a cell will respond to luminance changes in a way very similar to $+Wh -Bl$ cells (De Valois, 1972), showing strong contrast effects. That is, the optimal achromatic excitatory stimulus will be a light object on a dark surround.

Such a center–surround organization of spectrally opponent cell RFs does *not* produce color contrast, however. Quite the contrary: it acts in the anticontrast or similitude direction, as far as color differences are concerned. The $+G -R$ cell fires optimally to a green object on a green surround, i.e., with no contrast. A maximum color contrast stimulus of green on red would be a quite ineffective stimulus, the green producing excitation from the RF center, but the red evoking inhibition from the surround. Or, consider the classical example of gray on green versus gray on red (the latter appearing greener by contrast). The gray center would produce some excitation in each case, but the red background would produce more inhibition from the RF surround than would the green. Therefore this $+G -R$ cell would fire more to the gray on a green background than to the gray on red, i.e., in the similitude direction.

The center–surround antagonism of spectrally opponent cells thus gives them the property of responding to lightness contrast but not to color contrast. We are therefore left with two puzzles with respect to simultaneous lateral inductions: the absence of a process (before the cortex) for producing color contrast; and the fact that the precortical processes producing lightness contrast operate only over very limited distances, only for small stimuli. For neither of these are there, as yet, certain physiological solutions.

What we are led to in considering the physiological basis of contrast is a two-stage model: a very powerful lightness contrast process, in the center–surround organization of retinal cells, operating over short distance; and a weaker but long-distance cortical process operating for both lightness and color contrast. Such a proposal would be in accord with the fact that color contrast effects are far weaker than lightness contrast effects. Békésy (1968) proposed something similar from phenomenological and psychophysical considerations: a strong, narrow, "Mach" lateral inhibition and a weak, diffuse, "Hering" lateral inhibition, as he termed them. At stimulus discontinuities one sees lightness (and saturation) differences—Mach bands—but not hue shifts. So the "Mach"-type inhibition operates in the achromatic but not the chromatic domain. But the weaker "Hering" inhibition he believed operated for both lightness and color.

A double-opponent organization, such as found in fish retina (Daw, 1968), has been put forth as a possible basis for color contrast. But such double-opponent cells as have been found in monkey cortex (Hubel & Wiesel, 1968; Michael, 1973) have far too small fields to account for long-distance color interactions. A model based on colored-edge detectors, such as that proposed by Yund (1970), would seem more plausible, but the physiological evidence for such is weak as yet.

c. CONTRAST AND CONSTANCY. One might finally consider the functional significance of lightness contrast mechanisms for the organism, what makes it of such importance that it constitutes the very first step of retinal processing. The answer would appear to be to maintain object constancy. There are two types of visual objects: those that are self-luminous and those that merely reflect some part of whatever light strikes them. With the exception of such things as the sun and fireflies, most self-luminous objects are recent human inventions, and even now the vast majority of visual objects we encounter are just reflective.

A self-luminous object puts out a constant amount of light and can therefore be characterized by its absolute intensity. If we lived in a world filled with self-luminous objects, we might well have developed a visual system that gave absolute intensity information. But reflective objects, which is what we are mainly concerned with detecting and identifying, send wildly varying amounts of light to the eye, depending on the illumination conditions. A black piece of paper may reflect 8% of what light falls on it; if 100 photons per unit area are shined on it, it will reflect 8; if 1,000,000, it will reflect 80,000. A white piece of paper may reflect 80% of the light and in the same two situations send 80 and 800,000 photons per unit area to the eye. It is clear that what would allow us to identify and characterize these two papers is not the absolute amount of light from either, but the relative amounts or the contrast: The white always reflects 10 times the amount as the black. To maintain object constancy in a self-luminous visual world, then, one would want a visual system that signals absolute intensity, but in our actual reflective visual world what is required is relative intensities or contrast. And that is what is, in fact, signaled to the brain by both nonopponent and opponent cells.

The same argument can be made for color contrast, but with a different conclusion. If our world were lit by monochromators which were constantly fluctuating in wavelength (instead of by sunlight which fluctuates massively in intensity with time of day and cloud cover but not much in spectral characteristics), it would be advantageous for us to develop a completely relative-wavelength encoding system. But color variations are relatively small, and objects can be well characterized by their absolute-wavelength characteristics. Therefore, a largely absolute color signaling system preserves object constancy in the color domain.

References

Abramov, I. Further analysis of the responses of LGN cells. *Journal of the Optical Society of America,* 1968, **58**, 574–579.

Anderson, V. O., Buchmann, B., & Lennox-Buchthal, M. A. Single cortical units with narrow spectral sensitivity in monkey (*Cercocebus torquates atys*). *Vision Research,* 1962, **2**, 295–307.

Barlow, H. B. Summation and Inhibition in the frog's retina. *Journal of Physiology (London),* 1953, **119**, 69–88.

Baumgartner, G., Brown, J. L., & Schulz, A. Responses of single units of the cat visual system to rectangular stimulus patterns. *Journal of Neurophysiology,* 1965, **28**, 1–18.

Békésy, G. v. Mach- and Hering-type lateral inhibition in vision. *Vision Research,* 1968, **8**, 1483–1499.

Boles, J. Colour and contour detection by cells representing the fovea in monkey striate cortex. Paper presented at Society for Neuroscience First Annual Meeting, Washington, D.C., October, 1971.

Boynton, R. M., & Gordon, J. Bezold–Brücke hue shift measured by colornaming technique. *Journal of the Optical Society of America,* 1965, **55**, 78–86.

Boynton, R. M., & Whitten, D. N. Visual adaptation in monkey cones: Recordings of late receptor potentials. *Science,* 1970, **170**, 1423–1426.

Brown, J. L. Afterimages. In C. H. Graham (Ed.), *Vision and visual perception.* New York: Wiley, 1965.

Brown, K. T., Watanabe, K., & Murikami, M. The early and late receptor potentials of monkey cones and rods. *Cold Spring Harbor Symposium on Quantitative Biology,* 1965, **30**, 457–482.

Daw, N. W. Why after-images are not seen in normal circumstances. *Nature,* 1962, **196**, 1143–1145.

Daw, N. W. Goldfish retina: Organization for simultaneous color contrast. *Science,* 1968, **158**, 942–944.

Daw, N. W. Neurophysiology of color vision. *Physiological Review,* 1973, **53**, 571–611.

De Valois, R. L. Color vision mechanisms in the monkey. *Journal of General Physiology,* 1960, **43**, 115–128.

De Valois, R. L. Analysis and coding of color vision in the primate visual system. *Cold Spring Harbor Symposium on Quantitative Biology,* 1965, **30**, 567–579.

De Valois, R. L. Physiology of color vision. In *Tagungsbericht Internationale Farbtagung COLOR 69,* Stockholm, 1969, Pp. 29–47.

De Valois, R. L. Contributions of different lateral geniculate cell types to visual behavior. *Vision Research,* 1971, **11**, 383–396.

De Valois, R. L. Processing intensity and wavelength information. *Investigative Ophthalmology,* 1972, **11**, 417–427.

De Valois, R. L. Central mechanisms of color vision. R. Jung (Ed.), In *Handbook of sensory physiology,* Vol. VII/3A. New York: Springer-Verlag, 1973. Pp. 209–253.

De Valois, R. L., Abramov, I., & Jacobs, G. H. Analysis of response patterns of LGN cells. *Journal of the Optical Society of America,* 1966, **56,** 966–977.

De Valois, R. L., Abramov, I., & Mead, W. R. Single cell analysis of wavelength discrimination at the lateral geniculate nucleus in the macaque. *Journal of Neurophysiology,* 1967, **30,** 415–433.

De Valois, R. L., & Jacobs, G. H. Primate color vision. *Science,* 1968, **162,** 533–540.

De Valois, R. L., Jacobs, G. H., & Jones, A. E. Effects of increments and decrements of light on neural discharge rate. *Science,* 1962, **136,** 986–988.

De Valois, R. L., & Jones, A. E. Single-cell analysis of the organization of the primate color-vision system. In R. Jung & H. Kornhuber (Eds.), *The visual system.* Berlin: Springer, 1961.

De Valois, R. L., & Marrocco, R. T. Single-cell analysis of saturation discrimination in the macaque. *Vision Research,* 1973, **13,** 701–711.

De Valois, R. L., Morgan, H. C., Polson, M. C., Mead, W. R., & Hull, E. M. Psychophysical studies of monkey vision: I. Macaque color vision and luminosity tests. *Vision Research,* 1974, **14,** 53–67.

De Valois, R. L., & Morgan, H. C. Psychophysical studies of monkey vision: II. Squirell monkey wavelength and saturation discrimination. *Vision Research,* 1974, **14,** 69–73.

De Valois, R. L., Morgan, H. C., & Snodderly, D. M. Psychophysical studies of monkey vision: III. Spatial luminance contrast sensitivity tests of macaque and human observers. *Vision Research,* 1974, **14,** 75–81.

De Valois, R. L., & Pease, P. L. Contours and contrast: Responses of monkey lateral geniculate nucleus cells to luminance and color figures. *Science,* 1971, **171,** 694–696.

De Valois, R. L., Smith, C. J., Karoly, A. J., & Kitai, S. T. Electrical responses of primate visual system. I. Different layers of macaque lateral geniculate nucleus. *Journal of Comparative & Physiological Psychology,* 1958, **51,** 662–668.

De Valois, R. L., & Walraven, J. Monocular and binocular aftereffects of chromatic adaptation. *Science,* 1967, **155,** 463–465.

Dow, B. M., & Gouras, P. Color and spatial specificity of single units in the rhesus monkey foveal striate cortex. *Journal of Neurophysiology,* 1973, **36,** 79–100.

Falk, G., & Fatt, P. Physical changes induced by light in the rod outer segment of vertebrates. In H. J. A. Dartnall (Ed.), *Handbook of sensory physiology,* Vol. VII/1. New York: Springer-Verlag, 1972. Pp. 200–244.

Fry, G. A., & Alpern, M. The effect of a peripheral glare source upon the apparent brightness of an object. *Journal of the Optical Society of America,* 1953, **43,** 189–195.

Gestrin, P. J., & Teller, D. Y. Interocular hue shifts and pressure blindness. *Vision Research,* 1969, **9,** 1267–1272.

Gouras, P. Identification of cone mechanisms in monkey ganglion cells. *Journal of Physiology (London),* 1968, **199,** 533–547.

Helmholtz, H. L. F. von. *Die Lehre von den Tonempfindungen als physiologische Grundlage für die Theorie der Musik.* Brunswick: Viewig, 1863.

Helmholtz, H. L. F. von *Handbuch der Physiologischen Optik.* Hamburg-Leipzig: Voss, 1866.

Helson, H., and Rohles, F. H., Jr. A quantitative study of reversal of classical lightness contrast. *Amer. J. Psychol.,* 1959, **72,** 530–538.

Hepler, N., Yund, E. W., and De Valois, R. L. In preparation.

Hering, E. *Zur Lehre vom Lichtsinn. Ueber successive Lichtinduction.* Sitzungber. Akad, Wissensch., Wien, math. nat. Kl., 1872.

Hubel, D. H., & Wiesel, T. N. Receptive fields, binocular interaction and functional architecture in the cat's visual cortex. *Journal of Physiology (London)*, 1962, **160**, 106–154.

Hubel, D. H., & Wiesel, T. N. Receptive fields and functional architecture of monkey striate cortex. *Journal of Physiology (London)*, 1968, **195**, 215–243.

Jacobs, G. H. Spectral sensitivity and color vision of the squirrel monkey. *Journal Comparative & Physiological Psychology*, 1963, **56**, 616–621.

Jacobs, G. H. Effects of adaptation on the lateral geniculate response to light increment and decrement. *Journal of the Optical Society of America*, 1965, **55**, 1535–1540.

Jacobs, G. H., & Gaylord, H. Effects of chromatic adaptation on color naming. *Vision Research*, 1967, **7**, 645–653.

Jacobs, G. H., & Yolton, R. L. Distribution of excitation and inhibition in receptive fields of lateral geniculate neurons. *Nature (London)*, 1968, **217**, 187–188.

Jones, L. A., & Lowry, E. M. Retinal sensibility to saturation differences. *Journal of the Optical Society of America*, 1926, **13**, 25–37.

Judd, D. B. Chromaticity sensibility to stimulus differences. *Journal of the Optical Society America*, 1932, **22**, 72–108.

Jung, R. Korrelation von Neuronentätigkeit und Sehen. In: R. Jung and H. H. Kornhuber (Eds.), *Neurophysiologie und Psychophysik des visuellen Systems*, New York: Springer, 1961. Pp. 410–435.

Kinsbourne, M., & Warrington, E. K. Observations on colour agnosia. *Journal of Neurology Neurosurgery & Psychiatry*, 1964, **27**, 296–299.

Kuffler, S. W. Discharge patterns and functional organization of mammalian retina. *Journal of Neurophysiology*, 1953, **16**, 37–68.

Land, E. H. Color vision and the natural image, Part I. *Proceedings of the National Academy of Science, U.S.*, 1959, **45**, 115–129. (a)

Land, E. H. Color vision and the natural image, Part II. *Proceedings of the National Academy of Science, U.S.*, 1959, **45**, 636–644. (b)

Leibowitz, H., Mote, F. A., & Thurlow, W. R. Simultaneous contrast as a function of separation between test- and inducing-field. *Journal of Experimental Psychology*, 1953, **46**, 453–456.

MacNichol, E. F., Jr., & Svaetichin, G. Electric responses from the isolated retinas of fishes. *American Journal of Ophthalmology*, 1958, **46**, 26–39.

Marks, W. B. Difference spectra of the visual pigments in single goldfish cones. Unpublished doctoral dissertation. Baltimore: Johns Hopkins University, 1963.

Marks, W. B., Dobell, W. H., & MacNichol, E. F, Jr. Visual pigments of single primate cones. *Science*, 1964, **143**, 1181–1182.

Marrocco, R. T. Responses of monkey optic tract fibers to monochromatic lights. *Vision Research*, 1972, **12**, 1167–1174.

Martin, L. C., Warburton, F. L., & Morgan, W. J. The determination of the sensitiveness of the eye to differences in saturation of colors. Great Britain Research Council Special Report Series, 1–42, 1933.

Mead, W. R. Analysis of the receptive field organization of macaque lateral geniculate nucleus cells. Unpublished doctoral dissertation. Bloomington, Indiana: Indiana University, 1967.

Mello, N. K., & Peterson, N. J. Behavioral evidence for color discrimination in cat. *Journal of Neurophysiology*, 1964, **27**, 323–333.

Michael, C. R. Double opponent-color cells in the primate striate cortex. Paper presented at the Association for Research in Vision and Ophthalmology Spring Meeting, Sarasota, Florida, May, 1973.

Onley, J. W., Klingberg, C. L., Dainoff, M. J., & Rollman, G. B. Quantitative estimates of saturation. *Journal of the Optical Society of America,* 1963, **53,** 487–493.

Pitt, F. H. G. The nature of normal trichromatic and dichromatic vision. *Proceedings of the Royal Society (London), Series B,* 1944, **132,** 101–117.

Poggio, G. F. Spatial properties of neurons in striate cortex of unanesthetized macaque monkey. *Investigative Ophthalmology,* 1972, **11,** 368–376.

Poggio, G. F., Mansfield, R. J. W., & Sillito, A. M. Functional properties of neurons in the striate cortex of the macaque monkey subserving the foveal region of the retina. Paper presented at Society for Neuroscience First Annual Meeting, Washington, D.C., October, 1971.

Polyak, S. L. *The vertebrate visual system.* Chicago: University of Chicago Press, 1957.

Priest, I. G., & Brickwedde, F. G. The minimum perceptible colormetric purity as a function of dominant wavelength. *Journal of the Optical Society of America,* 1938, **28,** 133–139.

Purdy, D. M. On the saturation and chromatic thresholds of the spectral colours. *British Journal of Psychology,* 1931, **21,** 283–313.

Rushton, W. A. H. A cone pigment in the protanope. *Journal of Physiology (London),* 1963, **168,** 345–359.

Rushton, W. A. H. A foveal pigment in the deuteranope. *Journal of Physiology (London),* 1965, **176,** 24–37.

Sechzer, J. A., & Brown, J. L. Color discrimination in the cat. *Science,* 1964, **144,** 427–428.

Stiles, W. S. Increment thresholds and the mechanisms of color vision. *Documenta Ophthalmologica den Haag),* 1949, **3,** 138–165.

Svaetichin, G., & MacNichol, E, F., Jr. Retinal mechanisms for chromatic and achromatic vision. *Annals of the New York Academy of Science,* 1958, **74,** 385–404.

Toyoda, J., Nosaki, H., & Tomita, T. Light induced resistance changes in single receptors of *Necturus* and *Gekko. Vision Research,* 1969, **9,** 453–463.

van der Horst, G. J. C., & Bouman, M. A. Spatiotemporal chromaticity discrimination. *Journal of the Optical Society of America,* 1969, **59,** 1482–1488.

Vos, J. J., & Walraven, P. L. On the derivation of the foveal receptor primaries. *Vision Research,* 1971, **11,** 799–818.

Wagner, H. G., MacNichol, E. F., Jr., and Wolbarsht, M. L. The response properties of single ganglion cells in the goldfish retina. *Journal of General Physiology,* 1960, **43,** Suppl. 6, part 2, 45–62.

Wagner, H. G., MacNichol, E. F., Jr., & Wolbarsht, M. L. Functional basis for "on"-center and "off"-center receptive fields in the retina. *Journal of the Optical Society of America,* 1963, **53,** 66–70.

Wald, G., and Brown, P. K. Human color vision and color blindness. *Cold Spring Harbor Symposium on Quantitative Biology,* 1965, **30,** 345–359.

Wiesel, T. N. Receptive fields of ganglion cells in the cat's retina. *Journal of Physiology,* 1960, **153,** 583–594.

Wiesel, T. N., & Hubel, D. H. Spatial and chromatic interactions in the lateral geniculate body of the rhesus monkey. *Journal of Neurophysiology,* 1966, **29,** 1115–1156.

Wright, W. D. *The measurement of colour,* 4th ed. London: Hilger, 1969.

Wright, W. D., & Pitt, F. H. G. The saturation discrimination of two trichromats. *Proceedings of the Physical Society, London,* 1937, **49,** 329–331.

Young, T. On the theory of light and colours. In *Lectures in natural philosophy,* Vol. 2. London: Printed for Joseph Johnson, St. Paul's Church Yard, by William Savage, 1807.

Yund, E. W. A physiological model for color and brightness contrast effects. Unpublished doctoral dissertation. Boston: Northeastern University, 1970.

Zeki, S. M. Colour coding in rhesus monkey prestriate cortex. *Brain Research,* 1973, **53,** 422–427.

Part III
Temporal and Spatial Resolution

Chapter 6

TEMPORAL FACTORS IN VISUAL PERCEPTION

LEO GANZ

I. INTRODUCTION

Time, as a parameter of examination in research on visual perception, is so universal that it cannot really be contained satisfactorily within the confines of a single handbook chapter. In order to bring the subject down to a manageable chunk, we have addressed ourselves really to only one issue: the relatively poor temporal resolution of the visual system. Consider the "picture" generated by a television screen. A single beam creates a small spot which moves across the entire screen in approximately 1/60 sec. The fact that we do indeed see a picture rather than a single spot suggests immediately that the visual system integrates over time periods of the order of 17 msec or longer. Or consider reading. Our eyes execute saccades which take an insignificant amount of time, interspersed by 200 msec or so of fixation. If we attempted to increase our reading rate by shortening the fixation time to 100 msec or less, we would soon find interference effects of one fixation on another both backward and forward in time. In other words, the visual system can be considered time-integrative: It is so constructed that light quanta are integrated in time bins of 17–100 msec, or longer.

This chapter will concern itself with this time bin property and its implications for visual perception.

II. BLOCH'S LAW OF TEMPORAL SUMMATION

The basic law underlying a wide variety of temporal perceptual phenomena is Bloch's law (1885):

$$I \cdot t = k, \qquad t < \tau. \tag{1}$$

where I is the threshold intensity, t is the duration of the test, and k is a constant. It states simply that, for threshold phenomena, the same visual effect will be obtained if the product of intensity and duration is maintained constant, so long as the duration time is less than the *critical duration* τ. Phrased differently, the law states that below the critical duration, the magnitude of a visual effect near threshold is constant when the total number of quanta absorbed from light pulse(s) is constant; this constancy is not affected by the wave shape of the light pulse(s). An example of the operation of Bloch's law is shown in Fig. 1, taken from an experiment by Baumgardt and Hillmann (1961). The task involved the threshold detection of a fairly large disk (48.6 square degrees of visual angle). When the logarithm of the threshold intensity is plotted against the logarithm of the light-pulse duration, as is done in Fig. 1, Bloch's law predicts a negative linear slope of 1.0. We see in the figure that this is indeed true for both observers up to a duration of 100 msec. The function assumes a shallower slope with flashes of longer duration, indicating less than perfect temporal integration above 100 msec. The estimate of τ, the critical duration, is therefore 100 msec.

Estimates of the critical duration of about 100 msec have been obtained in a wide variety of experimental determinations. In foveal vision, Herrick (1956) found $\tau = 99$ msec; Barlow (1958) reports perfect temporal summation for pulse durations up to 100 msec. Blackwell (1963) reports ex-

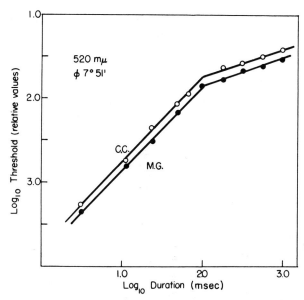

FIG. 1. An illustration of Bloch's law. The logarithm of the intensity of a flash threshold (units are arbitrary) plotted against the logarithm of its duration. For durations under 100 msec the slope $= -1$. This slope indicates $I \times t = k$ at threshold. Data for two observers. Flash wavelength $= 520$ nm. Target size $= 7°51'$. [From Baumgardt & Hillmann (1961).]

periments suggesting $\tau = 87$ msec at threshold. Johnson and Bartlett (1956) used the b-wave of the human electroretinogram, measuring flash intensity needed to obtain a standard-sized b-wave, and varying pulse duration as an experimental parameter. They found Bloch's law held up to the critical duration of 100 msec.

Although earlier studies suggested that the critical duration becomes very small when large targets are used (Graham & Margaria, 1935), more recent investigations such as Baumgardt and Hillmann's (1961), illustrated here in Fig. 1, show, in fact, that critical duration remains constant— about 100 msec—for fairly sizable targets. One variable that does affect the critical duration is the luminance of the background. As shown in Fig. 2, light pulses presented against bright backgrounds yield shorter critical durations than against dark backgrounds (Graham & Kemp, 1938; Barlow, 1958; Sperling & Jollife, 1965; Roufs, 1972a). More specifically, it has been shown that the inverse of the critical duration, τ^{-1}, varies logarithmically with adaptation level (Matin, 1968). This is of theoretical interest because, as we shall see in Section IV, the impulse response of the visual system also becomes more rapid at high background luminances.

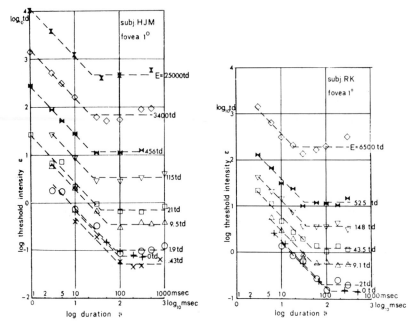

FIG. 2. Threshold intensity as a function of duration. The intensity of the background against which the flashes are presented is the parameter of the experiment. The break in each curve marks the critical duration τ. Note that τ increases when background luminance diminishes. Data from two observers are shown. [From Roufs (1972a).]

Another variable that has been found to affect the critical duration is the nature of the visual task. Apparently, integration time has been found to increase markedly, to values as high as 400 msec during movement of the test target (van den Brink, 1957) and for shape-recognition tasks such as judgments involving Landolt-C acuity test targets (Kahneman & Norman, 1964). Obviously more data is needed on this issue, but the pattern of results suggests that perceptual tasks involving higher stages of the perceptual system yield larger critical durations.

There is a resemblance between Bloch's law and the Bunsen–Roscoe law of photochemistry ($I \times t = k$), but as Boynton (1972) has pointed out, the resemblance does not imply that the basis of the critical duration's magnitude is photochemical. The photochemical events within the photopigments, namely isomerization by light, are extremely rapid events relative to the critical duration. Yet the temporal property of the visual system, a critical duration in the range of 100 msec, does suggest that at relatively peripheral portions of the visual system a very brief pulse of light elicits

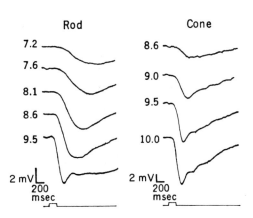

FIG. 3. Intracellular recording from within individual rods and cones of the mudpuppy. A comparison of the receptor potentials of rods and cones to pulses of light, 180 msec in duration. The numbers to the left of each record is the log intensity of the flash. Note the slow decay of the responses; the records on the right are plotted on a slower time scale to illustrate this. Rods are slower both in onset and decay than cones. [From Fain & Dowling (1973).]

a comparatively long response. For example, Fig. 3 shows a *receptor* potential recorded from within a single cone or single rod receptor of the mudpuppy retina, and obtained with brief flashes (Fain & Dowling, 1973). The voltage envelope rises and decays much more slowly than the stimulus pulse. In fact, as we might expect from Bloch's law, when the stimuli are much briefer than the critical duration, the rise and decay function is independent of the duration or wave shape of the light pulse. Thus, in large measure, the temporal properties that comprise Bloch's law are determined within the visual receptors themselves, presumably at a stage in the chain of events after the isomerization itself. The relative slowness of the critical duration suggests a mechanism such as the diffusion of ions within the outer segments of the rods and cones. Note in Fig. 3 that the temporal parameters of rods are considerably slower than cones.

The change in time constant with background luminance can also be attributed to receptor mechanisms, or receptor interactions. In Fig. 4 we see the receptor potential of cones recorded extracellularly from the monkey eye (Whitten & Brown, 1973). In the dark-adapted state (record 0) the cone shows a very slow decay of its receptor potential. As background intensity increases (records 10, 20, . . . etc.), the decay becomes more rapid. It should also be noted that the decay is exponential in shape, which may explain some characteristics of metacontrast and masking. This is discussed in Sections IX and X.

III. TEMPORAL SUMMATION WITH DOUBLE PULSES

If instead of presenting a subject with a single light pulse of variable duration, we substitute a double pulse varying in stimulus onset-to-onset

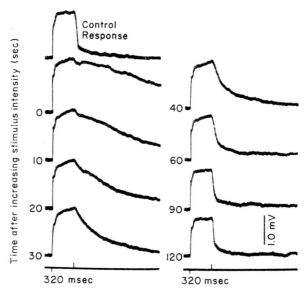

FIG. 4. Cone receptor potentials from monkey retina. A 320-msec flash is presented every 10 sec. Record 0 is obtained under dark adaptation. Records 10, 20, 30, . . . etc. are obtained with successively brighter backgrounds. Note that the decay becomes more rapid as background level increases. [From Whitten & Brown (1973).]

asynchrony (SOA), the results obtained are no longer as simple. The main complication appears to be that, in response to a very brief light pulse, the visual system goes through a bivalent sequence of excitation followed by inhibition which, if the interval is appropriate (40–70 msec) will attenuate the impact of the second pulse. For example, Baumgardt and Segal (1946), working at suprathreshold levels presented pairs of equiluminous 10-msec light pulses in the shape of two concentric squares of unequal size to the same retinal region. They obtained temporal summation only if they kept SOA very short, below 40 msec. If the asynchrony was within the range 50–80 msec, then the inner square was dimmed relative to its appearance when presented alone. At an asynchrony above 100 msec, the inhibitory interaction diminished progressively. Using a detection threshold measure, Ikeda (1965) reported similar results (see also Rashbass, 1970). Two pulses of 12.5-msec duration were presented against a brighter or a dimmer background. Both positive (lighter than the background) and negative pulses (darker than the background) were used. Results are shown in Fig. 5, expressed as a summation index that equals 1 when temporal integration is complete and .10 when the pulses are exerting independent effects. The figure shows that temporal integration is complete when

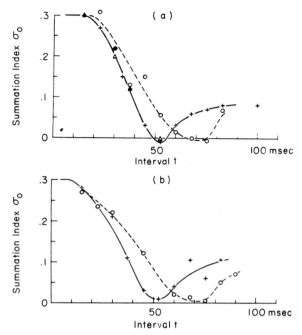

FIG. 5. Summation obtained at threshold between two pulses of light as a function of their temporal separation. Results for one subject are shown. Crosses represent a 328-td adapting level and open circles a 61.2-td adapting level. Part (a) is for positive pulses and (b) for negative pulses. [From Ikeda (1965).]

SOA is below 20 msec. When SOA = 50–70 msec, the index is below .10, indicating inhibition between the two. When SOA is increased still further, the two pulses become increasingly independent. It was also shown that when background luminance was diminished, this sequence of excitation–inhibition–independence unfolded more slowly. With regard to inhibition, Ikeda showed that when pulses of unequal intensity are used, the stronger completely inhibits the weaker, with little inhibition in the opposite direction.

One of the fascinating aspects of the Ikeda study was his demonstration that if a pair of pulses are presented with SOA = 50–70 msec, with one of the pair positive and the other negative, then summation rather than inhibition occurs. Therefore, a brief pulse of light initiates a bivalent response in the visual system with a periodicity of about 50–70 msec. One obtains inhibition in this SOA range if both pulses are positive or if both are negative, because the second pulse finds the visual system out-of-phase. Rashbass (1970) has reported the same phase periodicity, with a similar experiment.

IV. LINEAR SYSTEMS ANALYSIS OF THE RESPONSE TO TEMPORAL TRANSIENTS

A. Fourier Analysis

The concept of Fourier analysis states simply that a periodic phenomenon of any wave shape whatsoever can be analyzed into a series of sinusoids made up of the fundamental frequency and of integer multiples thereof, of that frequency (i.e., harmonics), each harmonic having a particular amplitude and phase.

Inversely, the concept of Fourier synthesis states that by combining a fundamental frequency with a series of harmonics with designated amplitude and phase for each, one can reconstruct any designated periodic wave shape. Linear systems analysis begins with the assumption that the visual system is linear. Specifically, it is assumed that the principle of linear superposition holds in the visual system:

$$F(a + b) = F(a) + F(b), \tag{2}$$

namely that the output resulting from two inputs combined equals the sum of the outputs to the separate components. The response of the visual system is certainly nonlinear. Nevertheless, over small dynamic ranges, the superposition assumption proves to be a workable and convenient approximation.

B. The Sensitivity of the Visual System to Sinusoidally Modulated Light

One can predict the response of a linear system to any temporal transient if one knows the system's response to the sine wave components into which the transient can be decomposed by Fourier analysis. The visual system is viewed as a filter network that can transfer sinusoidal inputs of varying frequencies with differing efficiencies. This transfer characteristic is called the *temporal modulation transfer function* (TMTF). It is determined by presenting observers with sinusoidally flickering light and measuring, for each frequency of flicker, what amplitude is needed to obtain a standard amplitude response. A visual stimulus that is flickering sinusoidally has a luminance function,

$$f(t) = L(1 + m \sin \omega t), \tag{3}$$

where t is time, L is the average luminance, ω is the flicker frequency in radians, and m is the amplitude of modulation. Thus, m represents the height of the peak above the mean luminance level. The terms are depicted in Fig. 6. Ives (1922a,b) performed some of the earliest experiments using

FIG. 6. An illustration of the terms used to describe a stimulus varying in time sinusoidally. The light has a constant component L and a sinusoidal component mL, where L is the background luminance or adaptation level, m is the modulation, and $2\pi/\omega$ is the period. [From Kelly (1972b).]

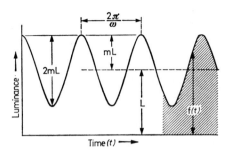

sinusoidally flickering stimuli. He showed that it was indeed possible to predict the response to different waveforms of flicker, once the response to sinusoids had been measured. DeLange (1958) performed similar measurements using different average luminance levels and different wave shapes of flickering stimulation. The results are shown in Fig. 7. Examining first the 4.3 td average luminance function, we note that relative log sensi-

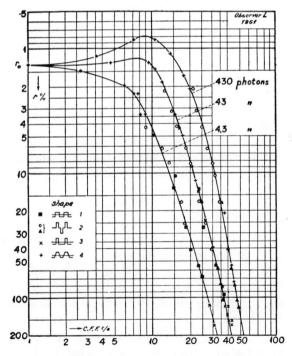

FIG. 7. Sensitivity to flickering light. Logarithm of percentage of modulation of the fundamental ($r\%$) is plotted against logarithm of flicker frequency (C.F.F., c/s), for three different adaptation levels. Although different wave shapes of flicker were used, the data points fall along the same line when plotted in terms of the sensitivity to the first Fourier component. [From DeLange (1958).]

tivity (i.e.,—log % modulation) is high at low frequencies and then drops almost linearly on this log–log plot at high frequencies, from 7 Hz upward. At an average retinal illuminance of 4.3 td, the visual system is responding as a simple low-pass filter with a corner frequency of 7 Hz. One of the interesting aspects of the DeLange results is that the data points with differing symbols all fall along the same function. As the legend indicates, they refer to flickering stimuli with different wave shapes (square wave, rectangular wave, trapezoidal wave, etc.). The fact that their threshold modulation is the same proves that above 10 Hz the threshold of a flickering target of any waveform is entirely predictable from the threshold to the fundamental frequency of the sinusoid of that waveform. The higher harmonics evidently do not affect the threshold. This great simplification confirms Ives, and lends support to the rationale for applying linear systems approaches.

Figure 7 demonstrates that with higher average luminance levels (43, then 430 td) relative sensitivity to higher frequency improves and a peak of sensitivity develops at 8–10 Hz. This means that at higher photopic adaptation levels, the visual system begins to resemble a filter with both low- and high-frequency cutoff properties. Kelly (1959) has shown that the low-frequency cutoff is very sensitive to the spatial properties of the flickering field. In Fig. 8 it can be seen that the low-frequency cutoff is more profound when a large flickering field with blurred edges is used (curve b in Fig. 8) than when a small, sharp-edged field is used (curve a in Fig. 8). In other words, we are less sensitive to slow flicker when the field is large. It is thought likely that the mechanism responsible for these spatially dependent phenomena is lateral inhibition with an appropriately slow time-constant (Levinson, 1964; Kelly, 1969).

C. Kelly's Linear Model

It is beyond the scope of this chapter to consider theories of flicker in any depth (the reader interested in becoming acquainted with more theoretical treatments should consult the following: Ives, 1922b; Matin, 1968; Levinson, 1968; Sperling & Sondhi, 1968; Kelly, 1971a,b). A few brief comments, however, may be useful. If TMTF functions of the sort shown in Fig. 5 are plotted not in relative terms, but in absolute units, one obtains functions such as those in Fig. 9 (Kelly, 1971a). Once more, the differing curves are obtained at different levels of adaptation, the lowest one depicting the highest photopic background level against which flicker is measured. Note particularly that the highest frequency portions fall very close to the $[G_1(\tau\omega)]^{-1}$ function (see Kelly, 1971a, for a derivation of this function). This high-frequency asymptote expresses, it is believed, some physical pro-

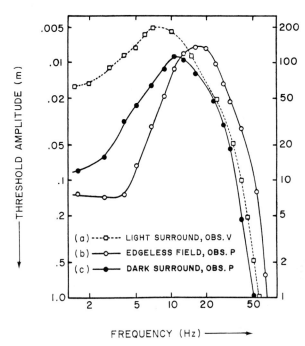

FIG. 8. The effect of target size on sensitivity to flicker. (a) 2° sharp-edged target with steady surround; (b) 65° flickering target with blurred edges; (c) 4° sharp-edged target with dark surround. [From Kelly (1959).]

cess in the visual system, which is incapable of following high oscillations, specifically a linear diffusion process (Ives, 1922b; Veringa, 1970; Kelly, 1971a). Presumably this diffusion process actually entails the transport of photoproducts and/or ionic currents initiated by the action of a light pulse, transport of these within the receptor cell and its surrounding medium. Such physical diffusion involves temporal dispersion. As a result, the visual system cannot faithfully follow higher frequencies of flicker. Such temporal dispersion probably underlies all phenomena involving temporal integration. Therefore, this one fact has a surprisingly variegated set of consequences for perception, e.g., Bloch's law, the phenomena of masking, and metacontrast.

A second aspect of flicker that Kelly (1971a) has analyzed (see also Sperling & Sondhi, 1968) is that at high photopic background luminance levels (e.g., the filled circles in Fig. 9) there is a pronounced drop in low-frequency sensitivity; by way of contrast, at low luminance levels (e.g., filled squares), low-frequency sensitivity is level from 5 Hz down. In other words, the visual system contains an inhibitory mechanism, which operates predominantly with stimuli flickering at low frequencies, and which only

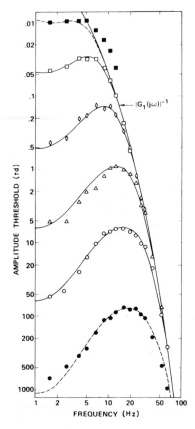

FIG. 9. Sine wave flicker thresholds plotted in terms of absolute sensitivity against flicker frequency for six different adaptation levels. [From Kelly (1971a).]

comes into operation at higher background luminance levels. We have a strong hint as to the character of this inhibitory mechanism from a fact depicted in DeLange's results shown in Fig. 5, namely that the three curves, representing different background levels, all join at low flicker-frequencies. This means *relative* thresholds are independent of background level, at those frequencies. In other words, Weber's law ($\Delta I/I = k$) operates particularly at low flicker-frequencies. In turn, Weber's law inplies that a momentary stimulus input is divided by current levels of input. In Kelly's (1971a) model of flicker this is conceptualized as a negative feedback loop (or several) that passes low frequencies and has a gain that increases with background luminance.

D. The Unit Impulse Response

Once the transfer function for sinusoidal waveforms is known, one can predict the response to any temporal pattern of visual stimulation (bearing

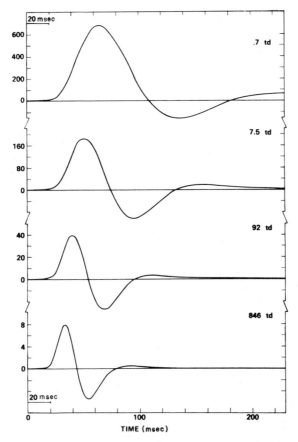

FIG. 10. Impulse response functions at four different adaptation levels, as derived from a theoretical model of sensitivity to sinusoidal flicker [From Kelly (1971a).]

in mind that the amplitude of the signal should be small enough so that considering the visual system as a linear system will remain a reasonable assumption). In particular, it is instructive to examine the predicted response of the system to a transient visual stimulus, i.e., a very brief pulse of light. This is the so-called *unit-impulse response*. It is simply the Fourier transform of the temporal modulation transfer function. One computational realization of this transform is shown in Fig. 10, taken from Kelly (1971a; see also Sperling & Sondhi, 1968). The inferred impulse response of the visual system to a brief transient pulse is shown for four levels of background luminance. For the highest background level (846 td) the visual system responds, after a latency of about 20 msec, with a positive–negative sequence, which occupies some additional 60 msec, even when the light pulse is extremely brief. Note also that the impulse response becomes considerably *slower* as background luminance diminishes. For example, at a background luminance of .7 td, the positive–negative sequence acquires a duration of some 160 msec. Comparing Figs. 5 and 10 reveals a striking convergence between flicker and two-pulse experiments.

E. The Relationship between Bloch's Law and the Temporal Modulation Transfer Function

Bloch's law can be deduced from the linear analytic system as follows: When a light pulse is shortened but kept constant in total energy, the Fourier analysis of these shortened pulses remains unchanged, except for the addition of some very high frequencies. If the duration of the original flash was quite brief relative to the total length of the unit-impulse response, then these added high frequencies will be in a range of the transfer function to which the observer is insensitive, and therefore will not contribute significantly to the detection of the flash. However, when the duration of such a constant-energy flash exceeds the critical duration τ, then low frequencies are added which are prone to inhibition by the Weber-law mechanism, thus, less than perfect summation can be expected, and Bloch's law will no longer apply.

Both psychophysical studies (Matin, 1968; Sperling & Sondhi, 1968; Kelly, 1971a,b; Roufs, 1972a,b) and physiological studies (DeVoe, 1967a,b) have had some success in predicting the visual system's response to single flashes from the TMTF extracted from sinusoidal-flicker studies.

V. VISUAL PERSISTENCE

The studies of critical duration and the unit-impulse response inferred from two-pulse interaction and sinusoidal flicker experiments leaves little doubt that a visual sensation will outlast any brief light pulse by at least 60–100 msec. In a sense, the unit-impulse response, with its minimum duration of 60–100 msec, means there is a *perceptual time quantum*. No matter how short the stimulus, perceptual experience will be no briefer than 60–100 msec. As we have already seen, the response of the peripheral generator mechanism of that perceptual experience is never briefer than the 60–100-msec unit-impulse response. In this section, we will review a number of approaches to measure the duration of perceptual experience.

Some of the earliest observations have been described elsewhere (Boynton, 1972) and will therefore not be repeated here, except to mention d'Arcy's (1773; see Boynton, 1972) experiment, in which he mounted a luminous source on a rotating wheel and noted that with a rotation time

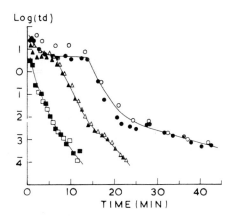

FIG. 11. The luminance of a positive afterimage (solid symbols) as a function of time elapsed since the bleaching flash. The more rightward curves represent the effects of more complete bleaches. [From Barlow & Sparrock (1964).]

of .133 sec., the subject reported essentially a complete circle. This constituted a simple but effective measurement of visual persistence. Figure 11 shows that in the dark, positive afterimages may persist for very long periods of time, waxing and waning in brilliance, but decaying exponentially over time with a rate suggesting they are part-and-parcel of the mechanism of dark adaptation (Barlow & Sparrock, 1964). Note that this last study used intense bleaching flashes. Much longer durations of visual persistence were obtained than in other studies.

Another approach to the measurement of visual persistence comes from Sperling's partial report technique (Sperling, 1960). A display such as shown in Fig. 12 is presented briefly. After a delay, this is followed by a tone instructing the subject as to which row to report on: A high tone instructs the subject to report the top row, a middle tone requires a report on the middle row, etc. The main result is that the number of available letters is *greater* than the number reported by the subject. As the subject reports the content of the icon, the icon decays. The results show that as the time interval between stimulus flash and instruction tone is increased, the subject does more poorly. The reason, presumably, is that the visual information persists, but decays. Thus, we are, in effect, mapping the decay of visual persistence (although the measurements as shown are not quite sufficient). The decay function is slower when the pre- and postadapting fields are dark. This is of theoretical interest, in view of parallel changes in the unit-impulse response with changes in adaptation level. The relationship to the impulse response suggests that visual persistence originates within the visual receptors themselves. Some recent physiological studies pinpoint the origin of the persistent icon within the outer segment of the visual receptors (Sakitt, personal communication).

In a visual persistence experiment, Haber and Standing (1969) alternated two display fields: A black outline form was shown against a white

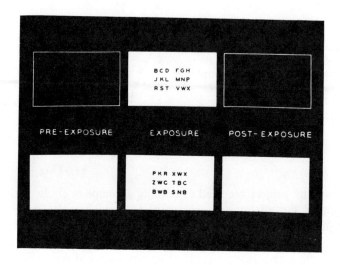

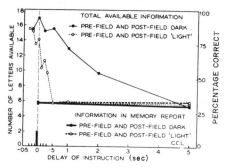

FIG. 12. Partial report technique for estimating the decay of visual (i.e., iconic) information. Three horizontal arrays of letters are presented, very briefly, followed by a tone. A high, middle, or low tone-pitch instructs the subject whether to report the top, middle, or bottom array. The proportion of letters reported correctly is plotted against the length of the delay between visual exposure and tone. The decay in recognition performance as the tone is progressively delayed presumably reflects the decay of iconic information. It might be noted that this decay is considerably slower when pre- and postexposure adaptation level is low. [From Averbach & Sperling (1960).]

background, then an intervening white background, then the form returned for 10 msec, etc., alternating in this way for 10 cycles. The duration of the intervening blackground was lengthened until the subject reported perceiving the form as having completely faded away before it reappeared (a technique similar in strategy to d'Arcy's). Complete fading required

FIG. 13. The subject adjusts a click so its onset appears to coincide with the onset of the light flash. On other trials he does the same with the offset of the flash. The interclick interval estimates directly visual persistence. As the duration of the light flash diminishes, apparent persistence also diminishes, reaching a plateau at about 400 msec in the dark-adapted state (Dark|F|Dark) and 200 msec in the light-adapted state (AF|F|AF). AF and dark refer to a light and dark background field, respectively. The field prior to the stimulus or following it could be either light or dark. Paradigm 1 to 4 represents the four permutations. [From Haber & Standing (1970).]

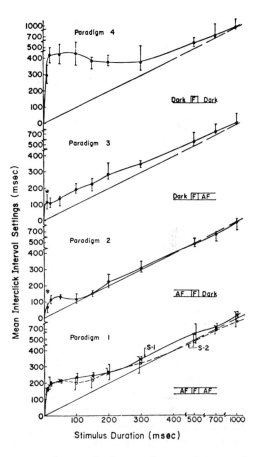

about 250 msec. When the background was dark, persistence increased to 400 msec. More recently, these same authors (Haber & Standing, 1970) used a technique first described by Sperling to measure visual persistence. A form was presented briefly. On some trials the perceiver was asked to set a tone so that the onset of the tone seemed to occur simultaneously with the onset of the figure. On other trials he was asked to set the tone so its onset synchronized with the offset of the figure. The difference between the two task-settings measures the apparent persistence of the visual form. Figure 13 shows how the duration of perceptual experience is related to the duration of the visual stimulus. As the duration of the stimulus diminishes, the phenomenological duration drops. Note, however, that apparent duration drops down to an asymptotic value of 200 msec in the light-adapted state and 400 msec in the dark adapted state, even with the briefest stimuli. (The drop in persistence at very low duration is an

Fig. 14. Split stimulus pattern used to measure visual persistence. The two upper dot patterns appear random. When superimposed, subjects can read the letters VOH. Visual persistence permits the letters to be recognized even with some asynchrony between the two presentations. [From Eriksen & Collins (1967).]

artifact, due to absence of Intensity $\times$ Time constancy.) Increased persistence under dark-adapted conditions implicates the unit-impulse response as underlying visual persistence. It should be noted, however, that their perceptual estimates of persistence are twice as long as those obtained from retinal responses to pulses.

A split stimulus presentation of letters has also been used to estimate visual persistence (Eriksen & Collins, 1967, 1968). As shown in Fig. 14 dots are placed on a background of two separate stimulus fields in such a way that when the two are optically superimposed, they form letters against a pattern of dots. According to the notion of a decaying trace, the subject should do more poorly if the two fields are separated by a time interval, since the subject must integrate the dimmed dots of the first with the fresh trace of the second field. Figure 15 (Eriksen & Collins, 1968) shows this is indeed what is found, the results indicate a trace decaying over at least 100 msec. It is also apparent, in comparing the 1967 and 1968 studies that the rate of trace decay is slower when the background is darker, results reminiscent of Sperling (1960), and anticipatory of Haber and Standing (1969). The rate changes with adaptation level provide strong evidence that retinal mechanisms, specifically *the unit impulse of the receptor generator* (see Section IV) *provides the basic pacesetter for more central mechanisms of pattern recognition.*

VI. THE PERCEPTION OF SUCCESSION

We have noted the relatively lengthy persistence of visual sensations. Such persistence must interfere with the perception of visual asynchrony. Schmidt and Kristofferson (1963) measured the threshold for visual–audi-

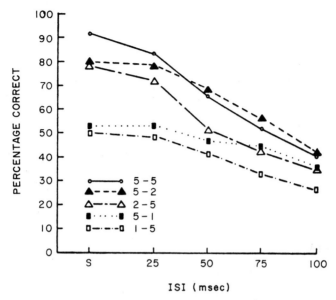

FIG. 15. Probability of correct recognition of spatally superimposed stimulus halves (see Fig. 14) as a function of their temporal asynchrony, i.e., their interstimulus interval (ISI). The different curves, e.g., 5–5, represent the intensities of the first and second halves, respectively. [From Eriksen & Collins (1968).]

tory asynchrony by presenting subjects with a click–flash pair. Subjects were at chance levels for asynchronies of 10 msec or less and were virtually perfect at asynchronies of 60 msec or more. In between, their performance was almost linearly related to asynchrony.

VII. VISUAL NUMEROSITY

One of the interesting consequences of the 60–250 msec range of visual persistence is that when trains of flashes are presented within that range, a subject will predictably underestimate the number in the train (Cheatham & White, 1952; Forsyth & Chapanis, 1958). Two or three light pulses presented at a rate of three or four per second can be counted veridically. But if the flicker rate of the train of flashes is increased, perceived numerosity approaches asymptote at six to eight per second, no matter how high the flicker rate. An asymptote of eight per second represents a perceptual grouping of events into 125 msec time bins. For example, when 14 flashes were presented at 30 flashes per second (a flash-train duration of 430 msec) subjects most frequently reported seeing four flashes, a flash being perceived approximately every 100 msec of stimulation (White, 1963).

At least two factors appear to affect numerosity judgments. The duration of perceptual integration, i.e., the complement of the asymptotic numerosity rate, is of the same order of magnitude as the duration of the unit-impulse response. Moreover, background luminance levels lower perceived numerosity (White, 1963), implicating peripheral determinants such as the unit impulse response of the rod and cone receptors. More centrally, cycles of cortical excitability have been implicated since in man the excitability cycles average 100 msec in duration (Ciganek, 1964; see also Gastaut, Roger, Corriol, & Naquet, 1951). Visual evoked potentials often show a 100-msec periodicity (Harter & White, 1967).

VIII. HOMOGENEOUS LIGHT MASKING

A. Empirical Studies

It is well known that our sensitivity to an increment of light (ΔI) is much reduced when ΔI is superimposed on a larger luminous background (I). For low background-luminances the Rose-DeVries law operates: $k = \Delta I/\sqrt{I}$ (Kelly, 1972a). At higher background luminances Weber's law operates: $k = \Delta I/I$ (Kelly, 1972a). If ΔI and I are presented as brief flashes, we can predict that their impacts on the visual system will follow a time course enduring 100 msec or longer, dictated by the unit impulse response. If the detection of light is not instantaneous, then we can expect substantial interactions between ΔI and I, even if the two are presented asynchronously. We should expect interactions so long as SOA is briefer than the unit impulse response (UIR), since when SOA < UIR there is some duration of temporal overlap between ΔI and I.

An early, and by now classical, study of masking was performed by Crawford (1947). A fairly large conditioning field was turned on for about .5 sec. A small circular test target of .01 sec duration was sometimes presented just before and sometimes just after the onset of the conditioning field. The detection threshold for the test target was measured. Results taken from one subject are shown in Fig. 16. As might have been expected, the detection threshold for the test flash was raised when the test was superimposed on the conditioning field. What was surprising, however, was the fact that even when the test preceded the mask by as much as 50–60 msec, the test was still masked. Crawford concluded that such *backward masking* could only occur if: (1) the conditioning field is more intense and therefore its conduction time is less to the brain locus where the detection judgment is made (the so-called *overtake hypothesis*), or (2) ". . . the process of perception of the test stimulus, including the receptive processes in the

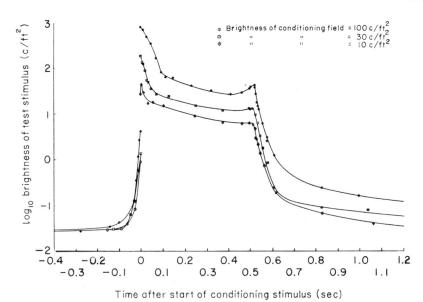

FIG. 16. Masking by homogeneous light. A small circular target is presented very briefly at some asynchrony relative to a large masking field of 500-msec duration. Log brightness of the test target at threshold is plotted against the asynchrony. Negative asynchrony represents trials where the mask preceded the test; positive asynchrony represents the reverse sequence. [From Crawford (1947).]

brain, takes an appreciable time of the order of 0.1 sec., so that the impression of a second (large) stimulus within this time interferes with perception of the first stimulus [p. 285]." Crawford also observed a similar threshold rise at the offset of the conditioning field. The decay of this threshold rise might represent the decay of the neural equivalent of the brightness of the conditioning field. He set out to measure this brightness decay, utilizing an ingenious technique. He found the brightness of steady fields needed to induce various amounts of threshold rise. The "equivalent brightness" values were then substituted into the off-decay portion of curves like Fig. 16. The results are shown in Fig. 17, giving the inferred brightness of the decaying conditioning field as a function of time; on a log–log plot the function is approximately linear. In effect, Crawford had measured the visual persistence function.

Sperling (1965) has conducted a similar experiment, except that the conditioning field (or mask) was very brief in duration. His results are shown in Fig. 18, for three intensities of masks. They show that even a virtually instantaneous mask raises the threshold for tests that precede it by 40 msec and which follow it by as much as several hundred milliseconds.

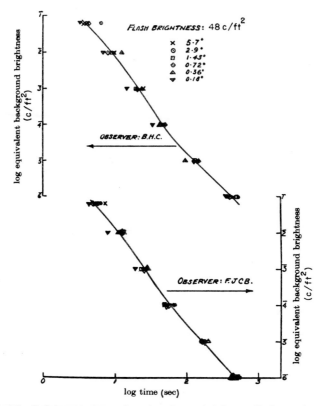

FIG. 17. The brightness decay function for a brief test flash as determined by the equivalent background brightness technique. [From Crawford (1947).]

In addition, his results followed Weber's law, since the magnitude of the threshold rise is proportional to the intensity of the mask.

Does masking by homogeneous light occur at the periphery of the visual system, at the retina, or more centrally? Addressing themselves to this question, Battersby, Oesterreich, and Sturr (1964) have isolated some of the factors that determine whether masking by light will be monocular or binocular (or dichoptic). In dichoptic masking, the test target can be masked by a conditioning field presented to the other eye; in monocular masking both are presented to the same eye. In their experiment, the detection threshold for a small disk (1°20′) was measured, presented at various asynchronies to a larger concentric masking annulus (whose outer diameter was 6°40′).The magnitude of the threshold rise measured the masking effect. The geometry of the conditioning field was varied: It could be an annulus with a large distance separating the outer circumference of the concentric test target from the inner diameter of the conditioning annulus,

FIG. 18. Masking by homogeneous light. After preadaptation a smaller masking disk and an even smaller concentric probe spot (both very brief) are presented at some SOA value. The results depict the log threshold energy for the detection of the spot as a function of SOA. Asynchrony convention as in Fig. 16. Three intensities of mask are used. Results of two subjects are shown. [From Sperling (1965).]

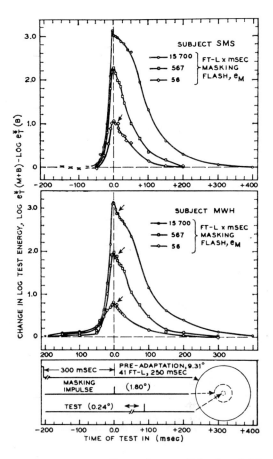

or an annulus where that distance was very small, or the conditioning field could be a solid disk on which the small test was superimposed and centered. It was found that dichoptic masking was greatest when the outer circumference of the test and inner contour of the conditioning field abutted, i.e., when intercontour separation was smallest. This latter case is essentially a metacontrast display (which is dealt with in Section IX). For monocular masking, this restriction is not necessary. Hence, masking effects involving large homogeneous conditioning fields are largely monocular phenomena, probably generated predominantly at the retina. Those masking effects which are generated more centrally involve inhibition among contour-sensitive elements of the visual system.

Masking by homogeneous light has been demonstrated within single neurons of the cat lateral geniculate nucleus (Schiller, 1968). The paradigm involves the superposition of a small test stimulus (.3 log intensity above

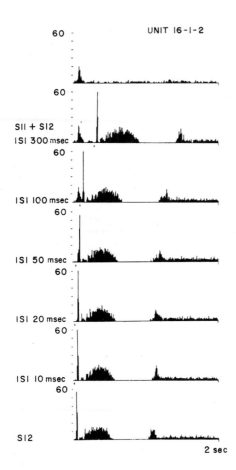

60 ·   UNIT 16-1-2

60 ·

SI1 + SI2
ISI 300 msec
60 ·

ISI 100 msec
60 ·

ISI 50 msec
60 ·

ISI 20 msec
60 ·

ISI 10 msec
60 ·

SI2

2 sec

FIG. 19. Masking by homogeneous light in single neurons of the lateral geniculate nucleus. Each record depicts a poststimulus histogram, i.e., spike frequency as a function of time following the stimulus presentation. In the top record, a weak (.3 log above threshold) 1° disk is flashed briefly in the middle of the on-center, off-surround receptive field. In the bottom record a larger and more powerful masking disk (3 logs above threshold) is flashed again centered on the receptive field. The records in between show combined presentations at interstimulus intervals of 10–300 msec. The vertical arrow shows the onset of the second stimulus. [Schiller (1968).]

threshold) presented on a large more intense background field (3.0 log intensity above threshold). The results are shown in Fig. 19. Each graph depicts a poststimulus histogram, the ordinate representing spike frequency and the abcissa 2 sec of time following the stimulus. The top record, which is labeled *St 1*, shows that the test stimulus, when presented alone, produces a small number of action potentials with a peak latency at 60 msec. The masking stimulus alone, *St 2*, gives the record at the bottom of Fig. 19: a large sharp response with a peak having a latency of about 25 msec. When *St 1* is followed by *St 2* at an interstimulus interval (ISI) of 300 msec (second record from the top), both responses to *St 1* and to *St 2* can be clearly discerned. At an ISI of 50 msec (middle record) the response to the second begins to infringe on the first. At shorter ISIs, only the second response is present—the one to the masking stimulus. These effects neatly parallel in every respect the psychophysical effects.

The experiments also provide a confirmation of Boynton's (1958, 1961) conceptualization that masking by homogeneous light is predominantly related to the massive on- and off-discharge caused by the masking stimulus.

We began this section on homogeneous light masking by attributing the effects to poor temporal resolution, or, if the reader prefers, to extensive temporal integration in the visual system. Suppose a test and mask stimulus are presented at an asynchrony such that at threshold intensity levels, the test target is more difficult to detect. If the test target is now increased in intensity to suprathreshold levels, and presented at the same asynchrony, the test stimulus is found to be brighter in the test–mask presentation than in the test-alone presentation (Donchin & Lindsley, 1965). Although the results seem paradoxical, they are not, since the effect is simply a reflection of the temporal summation of the test and mask. More specifically, it seems paradoxical that, at threshold, the test target is harder to detect, but at suprathreshold levels, it is brighter than when presented alone. However, the difference in results is inherent in the subject's task. In a detection task the observer must distinguish between background-alone trials and test-plus-background trials. Any temporal integration of the two makes their resolution more difficult for the subject. In a brightness-matching task, the subject need not resolve test from background. Any temporal integration of the two will enhance both.

IX. METACONTRAST

A. Empirical Studies

Metacontrast involves the masking of one contour by another closely adjoining it. One of the sources of fascination of this phenomenon is that when the test contour and masking contour are of approximately the same intensity, optimal masking is not obtained when the two contours are presented together, but rather when the test contour precedes the mask by some 50–100 msec (so-called Type B metacontrast, Kahneman, 1968). It is puzzling that one needs to separate two causal agents in time in order to obtain a maximum interaction between the two. The fact that the effect appears retroactive, the masking stimulus coming after the test stimulus, has also intrigued investigators.

A study by Alpern (1953) investigated many of the essential parameters underlying metacontrast. Subjects were presented a brief test object (b in Fig. 20) to the right eye, while fixating the point z. At some asynchrony relative to the test object, two abutting, contrast-inducing rectangles (or masks) were presented briefly (c and c' in Fig. 20) also to the right eye.

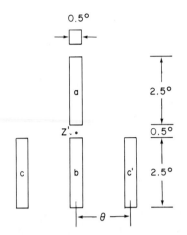

FIG. 20. Display used in a metacontrast experiment. *a* is the comparison standard seen by the left eye. *b* is the test patch seen by the right eye. *c* and *c'* are the masks also shown to the right eye. *z* is the fixation point seen binocularly. In Alpern's experiment (1953), the observers adjusted *b* until it was equally bright to *a*, for various *b–cc'* asynchronies and intercontour distances. In a dichoptic experiment, *b* would be shown to one eye and the masks *c* and *c'* to the other eye.

The subject's task was to adjust the intensity of the test object *b* until it matched the brightness of the comparison object *a* presented to the other eye. (Methodologically, it would have been preferable to keep the test object's intensity constant and to have had the subject vary the comparison object, because the test object interacts with the contrast-inducing rectangle, thus confounding independent and dependent variables.) Results are shown in Fig. 21. Positive abcissa values in Alpern's figure represent trials when the mask follows the test, i.e., backward masking; negative abcissa values signify the reverse order. The main effect is that the test object had to be greatly intensified to remain constant in perceived brightness when followed after about 100 msec by the contrast-inducing rectangles. Note especially that only relatively small effects are obtained when test and abutting masking rectangles are presented together, i.e., at a flash onset asynchrony of zero. The different curves in Fig. 21 represent different intensities of the contrast-inducing rectangles. As mask intensity increases, the metacontrast effect increases. This latter experiment is, of course, very reminiscent of simultaneous contrast in which the inhibiting force of the inducing figure is increased if its intensity is increased relative to the test figure. In fact, when Alpern presented the entire display simultaneously, he found an increase in brightness contrast as the contrast-inducing patches were increased in intensity (see also Kolers, 1962). This is shown in Fig. 22. The intensity of test object needed to keep it constant in perceived brightness increases as the intensity of the masking rectangle increases; more specifically, plotted on log–log coordinates, we have approximately linear relationship with a slope of about 1 (slightly less, actually). This in turn implies the relationship

$$k = T/I. \tag{4}$$

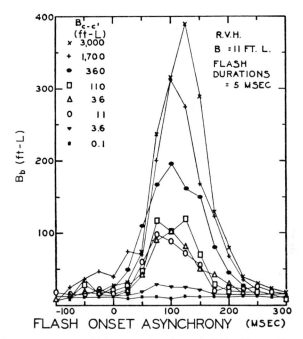

FIG. 21. Metacontrast masking as a function of SOA. The ordinate depicts the intensity of the test patch (B_b) needed to match a constant comparison standard. Therefore, high values reflect masking by the abutting masks. The different curves represent different mask intensities ($B_{c-c'}$), a parameter of the experiment. Luminance of the standard was about 11 ft-L. All flashes were 5 msec. Positive asynchrony represents a test-then-mask sequence. Data for one observer are shown. [From Alpern (1953).]

The perceived brightness of a test object (T) is constant when its *intensity ratio* to an adjoining inducing field (I) is kept constant (see also Heinemann, 1955). This recalls Weber's law ($k = \Delta I / I$), and suggests that metacontrast is a temporal manifestation of simultaneous contrast.

The metacontrast phenomenon is known to be highly sensitive to intercontour distance between test and inducing figure. For example, Werner (1935) observed that when a disk-shaped test object is followed by a half-annulus-shaped masking stimulus, only the portion of the disk near the half annulus was masked. Similarly, Alpern (1953) observed that metacontrast was markedly reduced when intercontour distances were increased beyond .75° of visual angle. And it will be recalled that Battersby et al. 1964) found that masking by light is not sensitive to intercontour distance, whereas metacontrast is. Thus, it is likely that metacontrast involves lateral inhibition particularly among contour-sensitive mechanisms.

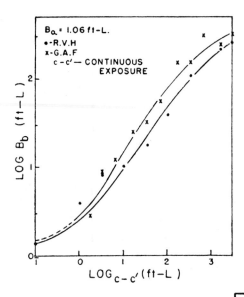

FIG. 22. Similarities between metacontrast and simultaneous contrast. Intensity of the test patch needed to match the comparison standard when the test patch is accompanied by two abutting masking patches, presented simultaneously. Strength of masking as a function of mask intensity is depicted for two observers. [From Alpern (1953).]

FIG. 23. Effect of distance between the test patch contours and mask patch contours on strength of metacontrast. Ordinate and abcissa are as in Figure 21. For clarity the curves have been displaced upward: $\theta = .5°$ shifted up 50 ft-L, $\theta = 0.75°$ up 30 ft-L, $\theta = 1.0°$ up 20 ft-L, $\theta = 1.5°$ up 10 ft-L. [From Alpern (1953).]

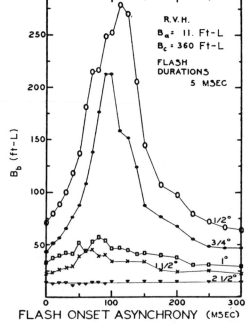

The degree of sensitivity to intercontour distance can be observed in Alpern's results in Fig. 23. The masking effect of the adjoining contrast rectangle drops markedly as their separation from the test object increases.

One aspect of the intercontour separation experiment which is of some theoretical interest is that the flash onset asynchrony (SOA) at which maximum metacontrast is obtained shifts with changes in test-mask contour separation. Figure 23 shows that at an intercontour distance of .50°, peak metacontrast occurs at SOA = 110 msec; at .75°, the peak is at SOA = 90–100 msec; and at 1.00°, the peak is at 80 msec. Thus, the flash onset asynchrony at which maximum metacontrast occurs decreases as intercontour distance increases. The results suggest that as the intercontour distance is increased, the inhibitory influence of the mask is delayed. This delay, in turn, makes it necessary to present the mask sooner, to regain an optimal effect. Since the presumed delay of the mask's inhibitory effect increases, as intercontour distance increases, it is plausible to suggest that the inhibitory process (presumably cortical) requires time to move across neural (cortical) tissue. In fact, that data permits an estimation of the velocity of .25° of visual angle (or its equivalent as projected onto neural tissue) in 10 msec. For example, assuming the effects in Alpern's experiment were primarily cortical and assuming a projection of 1° of visual angle to 6 mm of cortex, we obtain an estimated propagation velocity of .25° × (6 mm/1°)/10 msec = .15 m sec⁻¹, for the spread of the lateral inhibition. This seems slow, but not unreasonable.

Metacontrast can be generated dichoptically to the same degree as monoptically (Kolers & Rosner, 1960; Schiller & Wiener, 1963; Schiller, 1965; Battersby et al., 1964; Weisstein & Growney, 1969; Weisstein, 1971). It differs conspicuously in this regard from masking by homogeneous light (Battersby et al., 1964), reflecting, no doubt, the fact that metacontrast is a contour effect, as it is only obtained with test-mask contours abutting, and with the fact that contours are processed cortically, where binocular interactions occur.

The metacontrast paradigm can be used to measure the speed of perceptual processing. One can conceptualize form recognition as beginning with a dynamic iconic phase, in which an isomorphic representation of the stimulus is generated within the visual system. It ends with the encoding and storing of that information in a nonisomorphic representation (e.g., a verbal code), or in a structural (nontransient) iconic form. Once a form is encoded, masking can no longer operate. Hence, encoding time is the smallest test-mask asynchrony at which no metacontrast is obtained. Weisstein (1966) used the metacontrast paradigm to examine whether several letters can be encoded in the same time as a single letter. This would be the case were encoding performed in parallel. She presented subjects with a letter **O** or a letter **D** followed by a concentric masking ring. The subject's task was to recognize the letter. Figure 24 shows that an inverted U-shaped metacontrast function is generated. Moreover, the presentation of numerous forms clearly generates a broader metacontrast function than presenta-

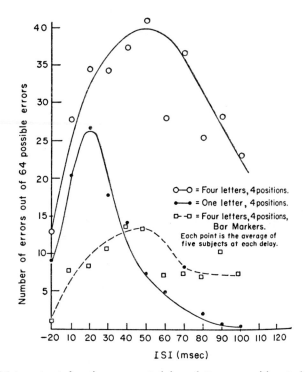

Fig. 24. Metacontrast functions generated in a letter recognition task. The filled circles represent data from an experiment in which a letter **D** or **O** was shown in one of four positions, followed by a masking ring. The unfilled circles are from an experiment in which four letters were shown, followed by a single masking ring concentric with one of the letters. The squares represent an experiment in which a bar marker was used as a masking stimulus rather than a ring. The subject's task in each case was to identify the letter within the ring or near the bar. Metacontrast is seen to extend over a longer delay between letter and mask when several letters must be processed. [From Weisstein (1966).]

tion of a single form. Hence, total encoding time is longer when numerous forms must be processed, suggesting either than the forms are encoded sequentially or by a parallel encoder with limited energy.

Typically, studies involving masking by homogeneous light generate functions where masking is most intense at SOA = 0, and greater asynchronies yield smaller masking effects, whether the test precedes or follows the mask (see Fig. 18 for an illustration of a peak SOA = 0 function). We have seen that numerous experiments with adjoining contours generate U-shaped functions with maximum masking at SOA $\simeq$ 30–100 msec. A study (Weisstein, 1971) elucidates some of the factors predisposing to one or the other. The geometry of the stimulus display partook of both masking

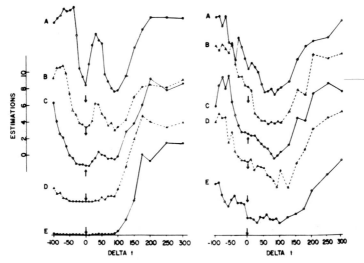

FIG. 25. An experiment containing both masking by homogeneous light and by adjoining contours. A 1° white disk is followed by a concentric 1°20′ white disk. Observers estimate the completeness of disk remaining. The geometric mean of completeness ratings is plotted against the asynchrony between test and mask. Positive asynchrony denotes a test-then-mask sequence. The functions A–E represent decreasing target energy. For clarity, each function has been offset two estimation points. Left functions: monoptic viewing. Right side: dichoptic viewing. [From Weisstein (1971).]

by homogeneous light and masking by adjoining contours. A white test disk (1°) was followed by a somewhat larger white masking disk (1°20′). Fig. 25 depicts brightness estimates as a function of onset asynchrony (called delta in the figure) between test and mask. A metacontrast effect is manifested as a *low* brightness estimate. The curves on the right represent results obtained with a dichoptic presentation. Curves from A to E describe masking functions in which the test disk is made progressively weaker. We see that the functions become broader, with more masking at SOA = 0 when the test/mask intensity ratio becomes smaller. In other words, obtaining metacontrast with a peak effect at SOA = 100 msec depends on the test and mask being of approximately equal intensities. The left-hand curves A–E represent masking functions obtained with the same test/mask energy relations, but with a monocular presentation. Note especially curve A where two troughs are obtained, one at SOA = 0 and one at SOA = 100 msec. Weisstein reasons that the SOA = 0 trough represents masking effects generated at the retina (and possibly LGN), because it is not obtained dichoptically. She also shows that the SOA = 0 trough is not obtained where the test disk fits concentrically inside the mask annulus so that test and mask share adjoining contours. The SOA = 100-msec trough is obtained under the latter conditions. In other words, the two asynchronies where masking is obtained—one at SOA = 0 and one at SOA = 100 msec—reflect different sorts of visual processing at different levels within the visual system: the first generated by homogeneous masking stimuli presumably at the retina (and possibly LGN); the second generated by contour-sensitive mechanisms within the visual cortex.

B. Neurophysiological Indices

Experimental evidence of the correlates of metacontrast masking in the human visual evoked response (Vaughan & Silverstein, 1968) has been obtained. A white disk, 1° in diameter, was briefly presented to the subject's fovea, followed by a white, concentric ring also shown very briefly. Optimal suppression occurred when ring followed disk, by 70–80 msec. Visual evoked responses were collected from an electrode near the visual cortex. When the disk was presented alone, a negative response at 100–150 msec was obtained, followed by a positive response at about 200 msec (see Fig. 26). At 50 msec SOA, subjects saw the disk as very dim, an instance of powerful metacontrast suppression. At this same 50 msec SOA, a positive component of the visual evoked potential having a latency of 200 msec (P200) is smaller. The area under the curve delineated by the dashed line correlates very closely with the brightness of the disk. The

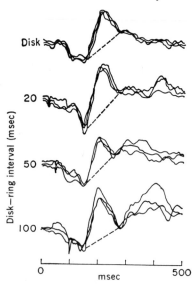

Fig. 26. Visual evoked potentials derived from a human observer; scalp electrodes near visual cortex. Test target: 1.5° disk; mask: abutting annulus. Stimulus duration: 10 msec. Each family of curves represent evoked potentials recorded for a particular disk–ring asynchrony: disk alone, ISI = 20, 50, and 100 msec. At ISI = 50 msec the suppression of the disk's brightness is maximal. The area encompassed by the evoked potential and the dashed line correlates highly with the apparent brightness of the test disk. [From Vaughan & Silverstein (1968).]

Vaughan and Silverstein experiment suggests a possible link between meta-contrast and the unit-impulse response generated at the visual cortex. If the potentials generated at the visual cortex have a basic 100-msec period-icity, (cf. Harter & White, 1967), then the disruptive effect of the annulus is related to the fact that the masking ring is presented 180° out of phase. For example, consider what occurs at ISI = 50 msec (as illustrated in Fig. 26). P200 (a positive component of 200-msec latency) generated by the disk is added to N150 (a negative component of 150-msec latency) generated by the ring. The net effect is that the potentials cancel each other to some extent. It is suggested that metacontrast is the perceptual correlate of this cancellation. A theory of metacontrast utilizing similar concepts has been formulated (Bridgeman, 1971). It fails to explain, however, why the masking ring is not itself suppressed, since its P200 also is greatly di-minished, as can be seen in Fig. 26 at the 50-msec ISI. Phrased differently, the approach fails to predict the primarily retroactive character of metacontrast.

C. Theories

1. Fast Inhibitory Component, Slow Excitatory Component

It has been difficult to explain why, under appropriate circumstances, maximum masking is obtained not at SOA = 0, where it would be ex-pected, but at SOA values as large as 80–100 msec. One recurring type of theory is exemplified by the *overtake hypothesis*, suggested by Crawford (1947) as an explanation of backward masking. It states that because latency at synaptic junctions of the CNS is inversely related to intensity, the more intense conditioning stimulus overtakes the masking stimulus in its race to the visual cortex. This makes it possible to present the mask earlier than the test stimulus and still obtain an inhibitory interaction be-tween the two. We have noted, however, that metacontrast is best obtained when test and mask are of equal intensity. Crawford's explanation is inap-plicable under those conditions.

Alpern (1953) modified Crawford's hypothesis, while retaining the same logic. Instead of assuming different transmission times, he postulated two separate processes generated by both test and mask at the retina: a fast inhibitory component (which might be photochemical) and a more delayed excitatory component (which would be neural). According to this explana-tion, metacontrast results from an interaction between the delayed excita-tory component generated by the test object and the fast inhibitory compo-nent generated by the mask. Since metacontrast effects are obtained with

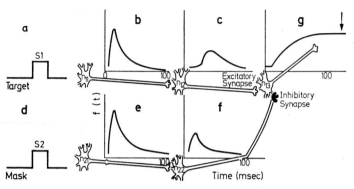

FIG. 27. A neural network with temporal properties which Weisstein has shown could account for metacontrast. The target S_1 stimulates in turn neurons n_{11}, n_{12} (which has a slow course) and then excites n_{13} (their individual time courses are shown in a, b, c, g). The mask S_2 stimulates in turn neurons n_{21}, n_{22} (n_{22} has a relatively fast time course compared to neuron n_{12}) and then inhibits neuron n_{13} (their individual time courses are shown in d, e, f, g). Neurons n_{11} and n_{21} are "peripheral" and n_{12}, n_{22}, and n_{13} are central. The excitatory contribution of n_{12} and the inhibitory contribution of n_{22} summate algebraically at the synapse with n_{13}, a decision neuron, whose cummulative frequency of firing is then translated into a response measure, e.g., percentage of detection, or magnitude estimation. [From Weisstein (1972).]

full efficacy in dichoptic presentations, the test–mask interactions must be cortical. Hence Alpern's theory of two types of retinal processes cannot explain metacontrast.

Weisstein has formulated a theoretical model retaining the notion of fast-inhibition and slow-excitation (Weisstein, 1968, 1972). The model assumes that the test and mask interact at some central locus of the visual system, with the mask exerting lateral inhibition. The key assumption is that, with equally intense stimuli, excitation and inhibition develop at different rates, the inhibitory process developing more quickly than the excitatory process. A schematic illustration of the model is shown in the five-neuron network depicted in Fig. 27. We see that the test (S_1) and mask (S_2) are presented simultaneously as a flash, activating their respective "peripheral" neurons n_{11} and n_{21}. These in turn activate n_{12} and n_{22}, which are more central. And finally, the interaction occurs at neuron n_{13}. Neuron n_{12} has an excitatory effect on n_{13} and a slow time-course; neuron n_{22} has an inhibitory effect on n_{13} and a faster time-course (50–60 msec faster than the excitatory neuron n_{12}). Hence, to obtain maximum inhibition, one presents the mask some 50–60 msec after the test. Fitting time constants to the five neurons, and simulating a metacontrast presentation,

FIG. 28. A comparison between observed monoptic metacontrast and metacontrast predicted from a neural-net (see Fig. 27). The solid connected curves are empirical metacontrast functions obtained by presenting a 16-msec, 1° disk and a 16-msec concentric, abutting annulus. The vertical lines are the output of a simulated neural network similar to Fig. 27. Vertical coordinates represent brightness of the disc and the horizontal coordinates represent disk–annulus SOA, as shown by the time calibration lines in the lower right of each frame. The numbers 1–5 represent target/mask luminance ratios of 1.0, .5, .2, .125, and .0625, respectively. Data from two subjects are shown. [From Weisstein (1972).]

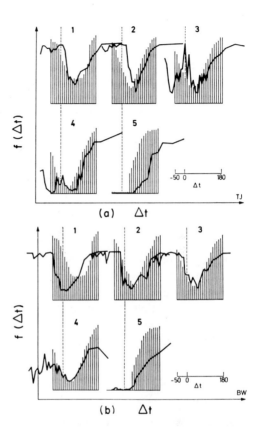

one obtains the results shown in Fig. 28, where prediction and observed metacontrast is compared for two subjects (TJ and BW). The curves numbered 1–5 represent five different ratios of test/mask intensity. The model is moderately successful.

Two serious weaknesses are apparent. The first concerns the assumption that inhibitory processes develop more quickly than excitatory, by a difference of some 50 msec or more. This would be a very striking neurophysiological phenomenon if it were true, easily measured, yet there is no neurophysiological evidence to support it, and much evidence against it. Intracellular recording in neurons of the visual cortex shows that both depolarizing (EPSP) and hyperpolarizing (IPSP) postsynaptic potentials can be elicited by electrical stimulation of the LGN (Li, Ortiz-Galvin, Chou, & Howard, 1960). The latency of IPSPs is consistently .8 msec *longer* than the initial EPSP (Watanabe, Konishi, & Creutzfeldt, 1966). This is not only much too small a difference to account for metacontrast

masking at SOA = 80–100 msec, but the difference is in the wrong direction. Furthermore, this difference in latency is true whether the locus of
stimulus is the optic chiasm, LGN or the optic radiation fibers. Hence,
the difference is not one of conduction time, but a difference between an
EPSP generated in visual cortex monosynaptically and an IPSP generated
after mediation by an internuncial neuron, and hence disynaptically. The
picture of visual cortex network connectivity that emerges is one in which
all afferent input to visual cortex from LGN is excitatory directly onto
pyramidal and stellate cells and that inhibition is then generated intrinsi-
cally within visual cortex. (An excellent discussion of these issues can be
found in Bishop, Coombs, and Henry, 1971.) These neurophysiological
observations are consistent with anatomical observations that all specific
afferent synaptic endings on both stellate and pyramidal cells are excitatory
(Colonnier & Rossignol, 1969; Jones & Powell, 1970). These facts are
simply incompatible with the postulation of an inhibitory process some
50 msec or more faster than its accompanying excitatory process.

A second weakness of Weisstein's model concerns its lack of parsimony.
Six constants are fitted to each of five neurons, making a total of 30 constants to fit a simple U-shaped function to empirical data with a resulting
fit that is far from perfect. Might not other models work as well with that
many fitted constants, or fewer?

2. NETWORKS OF MUTUAL LATERAL INHIBITION
AMONG DECAYING TRACES

It is possible to explain the fact that metacontrast is optimal at SOA
as high as 50–100 msec without recourse to inequalities in the velocity
of inhibitory and excitatory components. A different group of theories proceeds from characteristics of reciprocal lateral inhibition.

Figure 29 shows how the brightness of a disk is affected by a simultaneously presented annulus (Heinemann, 1955). Each curve represents a
particular intensity of the test disk. The abcissa represents the annulus intensity; the ordinate represents a measurement of the perceived brightness
of the disk. The functions show that there is little inhibition of the disk's
brightness until test and disk are equal in intensity. As the intensity of
the annulus surpasses that of the disk, the disk drops precipitously in perceived brightness. Metacontrast can be conceptualized as the temporal re-
creation of these relationships. When the test disk and masking annulus
are of equal intensity and presented together, they only exert moderate
inhibiting effects on each other. If the test disk is shown first, it decays
in intensity by the time the annulus is presented. The two traces then decay
together, with the annulus more intense throughout the subsequent decay,

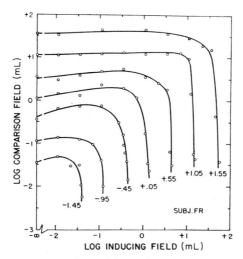

FIG. 29. Simultaneous contrast in a disk-annulus display. The stimuli are arranged as in Fig. 20. A white comparison standard is viewed by the left eye. A white test-disk is viewed by the right eye. The white mask-annulus is concentric with the test-disk with contours abutting. The subject is asked to adjust the intensity of the comparison standard until it matches the test disk in brightness. Various intensities of mask-annuli are used. In the figure, the ordinate (L_c) represents log luminance of the comparison standard when it matches the test; the abcissa (L_i) represents log luminance of the mask-annulus. The parameters on the curves are the luminances of the test fields in Log millilamberts. The results show that the brightness of the test pattern (as measured by the comparison standard) is little affected as the mask-annulus increases in brightness until test and mask are equal. Thereafter, test brightness drops precipitously with further increases in mask brightness. Results are from one observer. [From Heinemann (1955).]

and therefore exerting more suppression of the test disk. If disk and annulus are presented at a large asynchrony, then the brightness of the disk has been encoded prior to the arrival of the annulus and the two do not interact. Thus three factors need to be known to account for metacontrast: lateral inhibition between simultaneously presented test objects and masks of unequal intensity, their rate of decay, and encoding time. In a recent study, some of these factors have been examined with a disk–annulus stimulus pair (Sukale-Wolf, 1971). As to lateral inhibition, this is shown in Fig. 30 for two subjects. Subjects fixated the small cross shown in the figure and were asked to recognize a letter **D** or **O** presented for 20 msec at various intensities, sometimes surrounded by a masking annulus and sometimes not. Actually, on masking trials two annuli were used, left and right of fixation; the test letter could thus be presented either to the left or right of fixation, but this is not essential. The results show that,

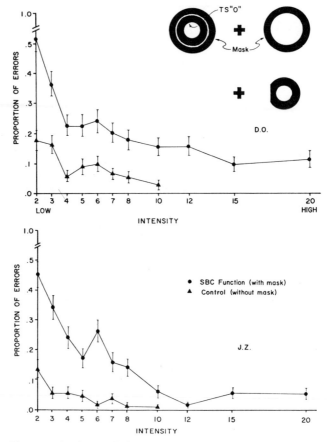

Fig. 30. First step in the prediction of metacontrast from simultaneous brightness contrast. Subjects are asked to identify a white letter **D** or **O** presented very briefly at various energy levels. The triangles represent percentage of error of recognition as a function of the energy level of the letters. The circles represent the same task, but with a white standard annulus presented simultaneously with the letter. SBC = Simultaneous Brightness Contrast. Results of two observers are shown. [From Sukale-Wolf (1971).]

as expected, recognition is poorer if the test is weaker and that the mask further diminishes performance. If we transform the recognition probabilities into Z-transforms using cumulative Gaussian distributions, and plot against log intensity, we obtain fair approximations to linear functions shown in Fig. 31. In other words, when no mask is shown we obtained

$$Z_{\overline{\mathrm{ms}}} = 1.35(\log I) + .606, \tag{5}$$

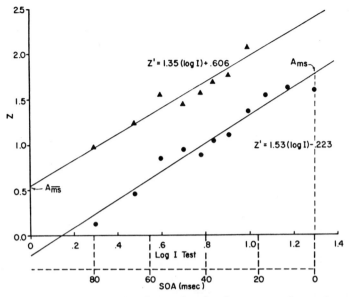

FIG. 31. The results shown in Fig 30 plotted using a z-transform of percent correct and a log intensity abscissa. The two-recognition functions (with annulus, A_{ms}, and without annulus, $A_{\overline{ms}}$,) are approximately linear and equal in slope. The main effect of the mask is to change the vertical position of the functions. The SOA abcissa is explained in the text. Results of three observers. [From Sukale-Wolf (1971).]

and when the disk was presented with a masking annulus, we obtained

$$Z_{ms} = 1.53(\log I) - .223. \qquad (6)$$

The major effect of the mask is to lower Z about .8, for all intensities of test objects.

The next step in the analysis is to measure the temporal decay of the **O** test object. This was done using Crawford's (1947) equivalent background technique. There were two steps to the decay analysis. In Step A, subjects were asked to detect a small probe spot that was superimposed spatially on the **O** (see the display in Fig. 32), but presented at various asynchronies. Figure 32 shows that detection of the probe improves as time after **O** offset increases. In Step B, the same probe spot was superimposed on the **O**, the two were presented together, but the intensity of **O** was varied. Results are shown in Figure 33. Combining Steps A and B, we can find for each SOA_i value in Step A the equivalent **O** brightness in Step B that produced the same probability of a correct probe spot detection. Figure 34 depicts the log of that equivalent brightness plotted against time, for three individual subjects. The equation $\log I = 1.3 - .01\ SOA_i(msec)$ fits the data

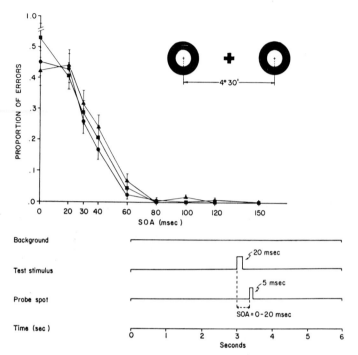

FIG. 32. The next step in the prediction of metacontrast is to measure the decay of the test letter using Crawford's (1947) equivalent brightness method. In Step A, a small white spot of 5-msec duration is superimposed spatially on test letter **O,** but presented at various asynchronies. On half the trials only the letter is shown. The subject's task is to detect the spot. The results show that detection of the spot improves as SOA increases. [From Sukale-Wolf (1971).]

of all three subjects. The semilog plot suggests the test object decays linearly as an exponential function of time. Substituting into (6), we obtain for the masking condition:

$$Z_{\mathrm{ms}} = 1.53[1.3 - .01\ \mathrm{SOA_i}] - .223 = 1.77 - .0153\ \mathrm{SOA_i}. \qquad (7)$$

Since we now know the rate of decay of the test figure, and we know the probability of recognition of a letter of a particular intensity whether inhibited by the annulus mask or not, then recognition probability under metacontrast presentation should equal

$$Z_{\mathrm{SOA_i}} = [Z_{\overline{\mathrm{ms}}} \cdot p_{\mathrm{E_{SOA_i}}}] + [Z_{\mathrm{ms}} \cdot (1 - p_{\mathrm{E_{SOA_i}}})], \qquad (8)$$

where $p_{\mathrm{E_{SOA_i}}}$ is the probability that encoding is completed at time $\mathrm{SOA_i}$. This states simply that the Z-transform of a correct recognition probability at some stimulus onset asynchrony ($\mathrm{SOA_i}$ in msec) equals the product of

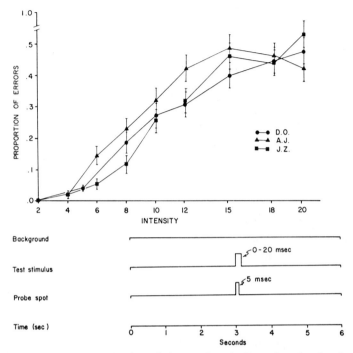

FIG. 33. Step B in the derivation of the test letter's decay function involves measuring how well the small probe spot is detected when superimposed spatially on the test letter, the two being shown simultaneously. The results show that detection of the probe spot improves as the test letter **O** is made less intense. [From Sukale-Wolf (1971).]

Z-transformed probability of recognition under no-masking conditions [$Z_{\overline{ms}}$ from Eq. (5)] times the probability that encoding is completed at time (SOA$_i$) plus the product of Z-transformed probability of recognition under masking conditions [Z_{ms} from Eq. (7)] times the probability that encoding is not completed at time (SOA$_i$).

If we assume that encoding time averages E msec, with a standard deviation σ_E, and that encoding time follows a Gaussian error function, then at any SOA$_i$, the probability that the test letter is encoded by the time the mask is presented is given by

$$p_{E_{SOA_i}} = \frac{1}{\sigma_E \sqrt{2\pi}} \int_{-\infty}^{SOA_i} \exp\left(\frac{-(E-t)^2}{2\sigma_E^2}\right) dt. \qquad (9)$$

The concept of encoding time is examined again in Section X, where its empirical determination is described.

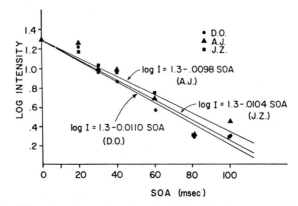

Fig. 34. To derive the decay function of the test letter, we combine the results of Figs. 32 and 33. We find, for each SOA value in Fig. 32 the equivalent letter **O** brightness in Fig. 33 that yields the same probability of a correct probe spot detection. The results shown here plot the log equivalent brightness of the test letter as a function of SOA. This derivation estimates the decay of the test letter through time. Since the logarithm of the intensity is approximately a linear function of time, we deduce that the test letter decays as approximately an exponential function of time. [From Sukale-Wolf (1971).]

The advantage of the model is that once the characteristics of lateral inhibition and temporal decay (the inverse of visual persistence) are known, two aspects on which considerable data are already available, then metacontrast can be predicted using only two constants, E and σ_E, estimated from the data. The fit of the model to a set of observations pooled from three subjects is shown in Fig. 35. Note that Eq. (8) predicts metacontrast for $0 < \text{SOA} < 60$ msec without need of even these two empirical constants.

Metacontrast is an interesting phenomenon, because, once understood, several aspects of the recognition of form become clear. As we understand it, the sequence is as follows. Suppose a test letter is followed after some asynchrony SOA_i by a mask annulus. Both initiate cortical representations that decay exponentially with time. When the moment arrives that the mask is shown, either of two possible events may have already occurred. Either the test letter has already been encoded or it has not. If it has already been encoded, then no masking can occur. If it has not, then the masking occurs between the fresh trace of the mask and the exponentially decayed trace of the test letter. If SOA is very small, then it is possible that the test will not be encoded before the mask is shown, hence the probability of mask–test interaction is high. However, because SOA is very small, the two traces will be comparable in intensity, and we know this predisposes to weak lateral inhibition of letter by mask (Heinemann, 1955), If SOA

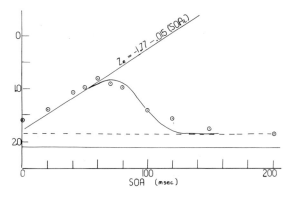

FIG. 35. A comparison between empirical results of a metacontrast experiment and prediction from a model involving lateral inhibition between two decaying traces. In the experiment (Sukale-Wolf, 1971), a test letter **D** or **O** is presented briefly, followed after some asynchrony by a concentric masking annulus. The subject fixated a cross, and the test figures were shown either right or left of fixation, followed by a pair of masking annuli. The circular symbols are obtained from pooled data ($N =$ 3; 128 observations per subject). The Z-transforms of the probability of an error in letter recognition is plotted against SOA. $Z_e = -1.77 - .015(SOA_i)$ is Eq. (7) in the text, derived from measurements of the decaying iconic representation. The continuous curve is from Eq. (8) and (9) (see text for details) with two fitted constants: Encoding time $E = 90$ msec and SD of encoding time $\sigma_E = 15$ msec.

is very large, then fresh trace of the mask interacts with a very weak trace of the test letter; however, the probability is great that the test letter is already encoded and thus the eventual interaction does not affect recognition probability. Between these two SOA values, masking is greater. Hence, it is simple to see why a curvilinear relationship of masking to SOA emerges when test and mask are equal in intensity.

The metacontrast effect suggests that the iconic representation of the test figure can be fully generated, then decay, and then be strongly inhibited by the subsequent fresh trace of the mask, before transfer to an encoded memory region occurs. This supports the concept of "erasure" (Averbach & Sperling, 1960). Metacontrast implies that it is the status of the iconic storage at the moment of encoding transfer which is critical for pattern recognition.

X. VISUAL NOISE MASKING

A. Empirical Studies

The third type of masking stimulus that has been used to analyze temporal factors in perception is the visual-noise mask, consisting of a random

Fig. 36. An illustration of the differential masking effects of superimposed regular and random patterns. [From Coltheart & Arthur (1972).]

assortment of odds-and-ends arrayed in an irregular manner. An example is shown in the lower part of Fig. 36. Note that when the word "stove" is superimposed on such a random-array, it is effectively camouflaged, i.e., masked. To study temporal factors, investigators have introduced an asynchrony between test object and visual noise. The general characteristics of visual-noise masking are that it is maximal when test and mask are synchronous, that it can be obtained when the mask precedes the test as when the mask follows the test, and that it can be readily obtained with a dichoptic presentation (Kinsbourne & Warrington, 1962a,b; Schiller, 1965; Schiller & Wiener, 1963; Smith & Schiller, 1966). However, dichoptic forward masking is reported to be fairly weak, whereas dichoptic backward masking is strong (Smith & Schiller, 1966; Greenspoon & Eriksen, 1968). The fact that visual-noise masking is obtained in a dichoptic presentation represents a distinct difference from masking by homogeneous light, which can only be obtained monocularly. Presumably, it reflects the fact that visual-noise masking involves forms interacting with each other at a cortical locus.

The results of an extensive parametric study of visual-noise masking by Kinsbourne and Warrington (1962a) are depicted in Fig. 37. Letters were presented in a tachistoscope followed after some particular asynchrony by a 'random masking pattern. Letters and masks were of equal luminance and contrast, but the duration of each was varied. Each datum in Fig. 37 shows the combination of test duration, mask duration, and SOA at which consistent perceptual recognition was just obtained. In other words, these are all isorecognition contours. The data points are medians of seven subjects. At short SOAs, the strength of the mask is approximately proportional to the strength of the test letter, as shown in Table I, taken from Fig. 37 at SOA = 10 msec. Except for the 6.4-msec test duration, the other values give approximately test duration/mask duration $\simeq \frac{1}{2}$. Thus, for very small SOA values, visual noise masking follows Weber's law. This in turn suggests that what is involved in visual noise masking is a subject's ability to discriminate those contours belonging to the test object from those belonging to the mask. The fact that this occurs under

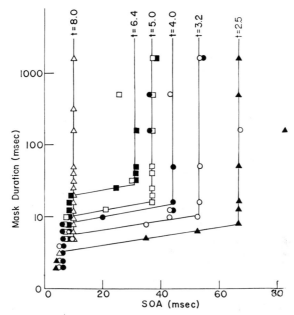

FIG. 37. Results of an experiment on visual-noise masking. Letters were presented in a tachistoscope followed after some particular asynchrony by a random masking pattern. Letters and mask were of equal luminance and contrast, but the durations of each as well as their asynchrony were varied independently. Every point in the figure represents a triplet of test duration, mask duration, and SOA where observers are just beginning to be consistently correct. Thus all points represent the same level of performance. The symbols are medians of seven subjects. Log mask duration is plotted against SOA. The different symbols represent different test-letter energy levels. [Adapted from Kinsbourne & Warrington (1962a).]

TABLE I

THE RELATIONSHIP BETWEEN TEST LETTER AND VISUAL NOISE MASK ENERGY LEVEL
FOR EQUAL PERFORMANCE LEVELS AT A SHORT SOA (10 msec)

Test duration (msec)	Mask duration (msec)
2.5	4.2
3.2	5.8
4.0	8.5
5.0	11.3
6.4	20.0

Data extrapolated from Fig. 37.

TABLE II

THE RELATIONSHIP BETWEEN THE TEST LETTER ENERGY LEVEL AND ENCODING TIME[a]

Log test letter duration (log msec)	Encoding time (msec)	Product
.398	66.5	26.5
.505	53.0	26.8
.602	44.0	26.5
.699	37.0	26.0
.806	31.5	25.4
.902	10.0	4.0

[a] Encoding time is defined by the SOA at which an arbitrarily intense mask still does not affect recognition performance. These are represented by vertical asymptotes in Figure 37, adapted from Kinsbourne and Warrington (1962a).

test mask asynchronies larger than zero is due to the visual persistence of the unit impulse response.

At larger SOA values, the curves in Fig. 37 rise linearly and then become vertical. The SOA value at which the functions become vertical Kinsbourne and Warrington call the *critical interval,* since at this SOA, a mask, however intense, will not affect recognition. It could also be termed the *encoding time,* since, once exceeded, the visual representation is evidently no longer in its dynamic visual iconic stage. The test stimulus is now encoded in some form, presumably noniconic. Table II shows that (except for the .902 log msec duration) log encoding time varies inversely with log test intensity: encoding time $\times$ log test intensity $= k$. It would appear that a process is initiated within visual cortex which must reach some threshold level before transfer from iconic to noniconic store can occur. The velocity with which that threshold is reached is proportional to the logarithm of stimulus strength.

A third aspect of Fig. 37 which deserves attention is the steady rising linear portion prior to the critical interval. The different test durations yield a family of lines of approximately equal slope. What do these linear slopes signify? As SOA increases, the mask must be made more powerful to keep performance equivalent, presumably because when SOA is large the mask has only just gotten started by the time encoding is completed. Put in other words, the linear rising function in Fig. 37 measures the temporal decay of the icon initiated by the masking stimulus. Since the function is linear on a semilogarithmic plot, it implies that some segment of the mask's unit-impulse response is an exponetial function: e^{at} or e^{-at}, with a as a rate parameter. In other words, the mask's trace decays exponentially with time.

B. Theories

1. PROCESSING INTERRUPTION

The original impetus for the use of random-patterned masks was to attempt to control the length of time during which a visual form was available to a subject in an iconic representation in order to measure encoding time. Sperling (1963, 1967; Averbach & Sperling, 1960) recognized that visual persistence was so lengthy that for brief visual displays icon–availability–duration was independent of the duration of the display. Therefore, the duration of the test stimulus gave no insight into the length of time needed for processing the iconic representation. He suggested that by presenting a visual-noise mask, one could interrupt the process of encoding the icon. Interruption theories emphasize the notion that time is needed for encoding the icon. If there is insufficient time, because a masking stimulus is presented before encoding is completed, processing will be interrupted, and the subject will be unable to identify the stimulus. Closely related is the notion that the mask *erases* the test stimulus icon, replacing the test stimulus, and thus terminating its processing and delegating it to oblivion (Averbach & Coriell, 1961). If this assumption were true, one could clock the encoding process by noting how many letters in an array could be identified for a particular test–mask SOA. For example, Sperling (1963) reported that when an array of letters was presented followed by a visual-noise mask, the subject could identify an additional letter for each additional 10 msec SOA, up to a maximum of 4.5 letters, which represents a short-term memory limitation. He interpreted these results to mean that the iconic representation is processed sequentially at the rate of 1 letter/10 msec. Although interruption theory seems appropriate in metacontrast phenomena, several weaknesses have been evident in its application to visual-noise masking. First, it cannot deal with forward masking, especially where test and mask are approximately equal in energy. During forward masking, the test would follow the mask, and thus interrupt the processing of the mask, but there would be no stimulus to interrupt the processing of the test, and thus interruption theory would not predict any forward masking effect. Yet, as we have already noted, it is readily obtained. Similarly, instances where SOA is zero or near zero cannot be handled. Is processing time really zero or near zero in these instances? Kinsbourne and Warrington's results (see Fig. 37) show that recognition probability follows Weber's law in such cases, a result more consonant with integration theory.

2. INTEGRATION THEORY

This theory assumes that the masking stimulus summates with, rather than replaces, the test stimulus, so long as the interval between the two is less than the *critical duration* (see the section on Bloch's law). For example, Kinsbourne and Warrington (1962b) maintain that when the time between onset of target and onset of masking stimulus is sufficiently brief, ". . . the two stimuli are treated as 'simultaneous' and are recorded as a composite image, without temporal differentiation. When this composite image includes a random pattern . . . it may prove too complex for retrospective analysis [p. 245]." Eriksen has presented a very closely related conceptualization of "luminance summation-contrast reduction" initially to explain masking by homogeneous light (Eriksen & Hoffman, 1963; Eriksen & Lappin, 1964; Eriksen, 1966; see also Thompson, 1966). He and his colleagues suggested that masking effects under certain experimental arrangements could be attributed to a reduced effective contrast from the stimulus figures arising from luminance summation. Eriksen (1966) formulates it this way: Suppose that a black letter on a white surround is presented for 10 msec and is followed immediately by a white masking background also for 10 msec. Because the total 20 msec is still below the *critical duration,* the eye integrates the two perfectly. The white background is 10 mL in luminance and the black letter is 1 mL, so that the contrast ratio of the letter against its background, when presented alone is 1:10. When presented with the subsequent white mask, the white areas summate to give total equivalent to a 20-mL flash, and the 1-mL black letter and 10-mL white background summate to give 11 mL in the letter area, giving a contrast ratio of 11:20. Therefore, contrast is much reduced compared to the single stimulus presentation, and hence, the level of letter recognition performance may well drop in the combined presentation. As SOA between test and mask increases (either in the forward or backward masking direction) the critical duration is approached, temporal integration becomes imperfect, and the results are now part way between what is expected for a simultaneous or near simultaneous presentation, on the one hand, and presentation of the test stimulus alone, on the other. Their studies indicate that integration theory can make a fairly accurate prediction of how much performance will decrease for masks presented at small SOA values.

Subsequently, the same approach has been used to account for the integration of two patterned stimuli presented sequentially. Integration theory predicts the visual-noise mask is effective in lowering recognition performance to the extent that the mask and test stimulus integrate temporally, so that the features of the mask become added to those of the test, which causes errors of recognition. Thus, an oblique feature from the mask random pattern becomes integrated with a letter **P** in the test pattern when SOA is not too high, and the subject reports **R**, which is scored as an error. Such an analysis yields a critical difference between interruption theory and integration theory. For interruption theory, the mask need only be sufficiently intense to interrupt ongoing processing; its pattern characteristic is not critical. For integration theory, the form characteristic is highly critical, since it must be possible to take pieces of the mask and integrate them with the test figure so as to create one of the character sets the subject is set to recognize, a letter **R**, etc. Coltheart and Arthur (1972) have tested the theory by examining the effects of masks differing in confusability. In Fig. 36 we see that a regular checkerboard pattern is a poorer simultaneous mask of the word **STOVE** than an irregular checkerboard. If masking at various asynchronies involves integration of test and mask, then the irregular pattern in Fig. 36 should be the better mask. Interruption theory would predict both regular and irregular checkerboards would be equally efficient in interrupting processing of the test (if mask follows test), and hence, no difference in masking efficiency would be expected. Coltheart and Arthur (1972) found the irregular pattern considerably more efficient as a mask, at several SOAs, thus supporting integration theory.

A similar line of reasoning concerns the strength of the test stimulus vis-à-vis the mask. According to interruption theory, test intensity should not affect the level of masking, since it is presumably because the mask ends processing that recognition fails. Integration theory predicts performance will be related to the integrated test/mask intensity ratio. Kinsbourne and Warrington's results and later studies (Spencer & Shuntich, 1970) indicate that increasing test intensity diminishes mask effectiveness. This is shown in Fig. 37 by the fact that when the test is intensified, the mask must be intensified to produce equivalent performance, thus corroborating integration theory.

Another test of the interruption–theory–integration–theory controversy in visual noise masking involves the presentation of trios of asynchronous figures, at varying SOAs (Eriksen & Eriksen, 1971). Three stimuli were presented to the same foveal region in rapid succession—a letter, a number, and an arrow at one or another orientation—and the subject was asked to identify all three. At no SOA value did performance drop to chance for the first and second stimuli, as would be expected if they were being erased by the succeeding stimuli. Rather, at small SOA values, all three stimuli appear to be present at the same time, giving the effect of a composite. It was also evident from their results that longer than 10 msec is necessary for each stimulus to be seen because even at 200-msec SOA, some mutual interference among the trio was still evident. It seems reasonable that encoding time be defined as the shortest SOA at which virtually no masking is obtained. Sperling, Budiansky, Spivak, and Johnson (1971) using multiple sequential masks, have also reported encoding times substantially above 10 msec.

The evidence reviewed indicates that many of the facts of visual noise masking cannot be parsimoniously predicted by the notion that the mask terminates the processing of the test figure. Indeed, the evidence indicates that when test and mask are presented at SOA < 50 msec, the test and mask form a composite icon which continues being decoded for 100–200 msec more, the duration being governed by visual persistence as determined by the peripheral visual system and encoding time as determined by the central visual system.

Although perceptual integration does explain many aspects of masking by random patterns, it should be recalled that masking by adjoining contours, i.e., metacontrast (see Section IX), does indeed constitute a form of erasure. Therefore, whether icon integration or icon erasure occurs depends essentially on the spatial relationships between test and mask. Erasure occurs when test and mask contours are closely adjoining, equal in intensity and SOA = 50–100 msecs. Integration occurs where SOA is between —50 and +50 msec and test and mask contours are not closely adjacent.

3. ENCODING TIME HYPOTHESIS

Integration theory, as it has been postulated is probably insufficient to account for the facts of visual-noise masking without the concept of encoding time. The vertical asymptotes in Fig. 37 indicate that the iconic representation of a test stimulus is transferred to some other memory buffer after a critical interval has elapsed—an interval inversely related to the log intensity of the test stimulus. That other buffer can be iconic or noniconic, but its information cannot be destroyed by a subsequent masking stimulus (for a similar conclusion, see also Eriksen and Collins, 1968).

We suppose that the shape of the visual-noise masking function must reflect the trailing edges of the unit impulse response (as already described). Masking functions often have an exponential trailing edge (Crawford, 1947; Sperling, 1965; Thompson, 1966), or a close approximation thereof. (A theory of metacontrast dependent on an exponential decay function has also been discussed in Section IX.) If true, we would expect visual-noise masking to show exponential properties. We assume that cortical feature encoders are sensitive to subparts of the iconic representation. These encoders accumulate energy proportionately to the momentary intensity of the icon.

We suppose further that the transfer of information to another memory buffer occurs, as in a computer operated by program interrupt, at the instigation of the peripheral device, which in our case, is the feature encoder. In other words, once some of the feature encoders have reached threshold, a transfer of information occurs between all encoders (i.e., in parallel) and their associated memory buffers.

The sequence begins with the presentation of a test object at time instant $j = 0$, which initiates an impulse response with, we assume, an exponentially decaying trailing edge. If the intensity of the test stimulus is I_t, then the rate of activation of an appropriate feature encoder at any moment j is $I_t e^{-aj}$, where a is a rate constant. Therefore, the accumulated activation by such a feature encoder at time j is

$$E_t = I_t \int_0^j e^{-aj} \, dj = \frac{-I_t}{a} [e^{-aj} - 1].$$

Let E_t^* represent threshold activation. Once this point is reached, a non-iconic buffer is transferred information by energized feature encoders. Hence, test stimulus encoding time j_t^* is given by

$$j_t^* = \frac{1}{a} \log \left(\frac{aE_t^*}{I_t} - 1 \right), \tag{10}$$

which states, in part, that encoding time is inversely related to log test intensity. This deduction is in accord with the results cited in Table II within a range of test intensity values. If the visual-noise mask is presented at $\text{SOA}_i > j_t^*$, then there is no masking, since the test icon information has already been transferred to another memory buffer before the start of the mask. This accounts for the vertical asymptotes in Figure 37. If $\text{SOA}_i < j_t^*$, then there will be a drop in recognition probability, because, at the moment of transfer, both mask-related feature encoders and test-related feature encoders will be energized to some extent. Specifically, at some moment in time, j_m^*, the mask-related feature encoders will reach transfer threshold, and will initiate a transfer to another memory buffer. At that moment, a mask-related feature encoder will be energized an amount

$$E_m^* = \frac{-I_m}{a} [\exp(-aj_m^*) - 1].$$

At this moment of data transfer, a test-object-related feature encoder will have received an energy given by

$$E_t = \left[\frac{-I_t}{a} \exp[-a(j_m^* + \text{SOA}_i)] - 1 \right].$$

We suppose, in accordance with the luminance-summation contrast-reduction hypothesis, that a masking situation resembles a Weber-ratio situation, as suggested by the results in Table I. In other words, the probability of a correct response p_c is directly related to the ratio of test-to-mask activation:

$$p_c = \frac{E_t}{E_t + E_m{}^*}$$

Simplifying, we get

$$\frac{p_c}{1 - p_c} = \frac{I_t}{I_m} \cdot \frac{\exp(-aSOA_i) - \exp(aj_m{}^*)}{1 - \exp(aj_m{}^*)},$$

which, if encoding time is not too long, gives the following approximately linear law of visual noise masking:

$$\log[p_c/(1 - p_c)] \simeq \log(I_t/I_m) + aSOA_i + k. \tag{11}$$

Equation (11) states that when performance is plotted in terms of logarithm of probability correct divided by probability incorrect, a linear function of SOA is obtained, in which the intensity of the mask or the intensity of the test does not change the slope, but only the height of the intercept with the vertical axis. Figure 38 shows the results of a masking study (Ganz & Morrison, unpublished data) plotted in terms of $\log[P_c/(1 - p_c)]$. Subjects were asked to identify a letter **G**, **C**, **P**, **R**, or **T** followed by a visual-noise mask at one of several SOA values. Results represent recognition performance for all letters combined. Two levels of intensity were used, an 8- and a 16-msec duration presentation. Note that three of four subjects show a fairly good approximation to a linear function. Moreover, the slopes are the same for the two intensity levels. The rate constant a is approximately .05.

To apply Eq. (11) to Kinsbourne and Warrington's results, we recall that they plotted combinations of test intensity, mask intensity, and SOA (see Fig. 37) with performance maintained constant. In other words, $\log[p_c/(1 - p_c)] = k'$, yielding, where SOA is less than the test object's encoding time,

$$\log I_m = \log I_t + aSOA + k'.$$

Again, we get log masking intensity a linear function of SOA, with log test intensity determining the intercept with the vertical axis. Thus, the equation predicts the linear slope sections of Fig. 37. They are, to a first approximation, of equal slope when test intensity is changed.

To reiterate, the encoding time hypothesis of visual-noise masking employs three assumptions. First, feature encoders are activated by test figures

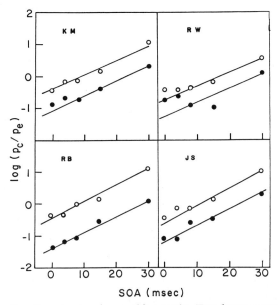

FIG. 38. Results of a visual noise masking study. Test letters were followed by a random-contoured field. Data are plotted in terms of $\log(p_e/p_c)$ against SOA; p_c is the probability of correct recognition and $p_e = 1 - p_c$. Two levels of intensity were used: 8 msec (filled circles) and 16 msec (unfilled circles). Four observers results are depicted. Three of four subjects show approximately linear functions with slopes which are highly similar from subject to subject and across intensity levels. These effects may reflect exponential decay functions of the iconic representations. [From Ganz & Morrison, unpublished results.]

along a time function dictated by the unit-impulse response. The trailing edge of that function is approximately exponential, with a rate constant a, which is independent of the test stimulus intensity. The rate constant a should increase with increased adaptation level. Second, when feature encoders reach a threshold level, this triggers a transfer of information of all active feature encoders to some other (i.e., nonerasable memory buffer. Encoding time is simply the latency with which this point is reached for some particular stimulus intensity. Where masking occurs, it is because the mask-related feature encoder reaches transfer threshold first. Third, the subject's task is to discriminate the test-related feature encoders from the others. This is done successfully to the extent that test-related feature encoder activation exceeds mask-related feature encoder activation, i.e., it follows Weber's law. The extent of activation is a function both of stimulus intensity and of activation time, as shown by Eq. (11). Thus, the model combines Integration theory's notion of luminance summation-contrast reduction with Interruption theory's emphasis on encoding time as defined by Eq. (10).

XI. SPATIO–TEMPORAL INTERACTIONS

The mechanism of motion direction perception probably involves a sequence-discriminating circuit (Barlow & Levick, 1965; Bishop *et al.*, 1971), which integrates two or more impulse responses from two different spatial locations. Therefore, a form of Bloch's law must operate for moving objects because this temporal integration operates over an amount of time comparable to the unit impulse response. The fact that integration time is fixed means that for a periodic stimulus such as a square-wave grating, there should be a relationship between spatial frequency and velocity, namely,

$$\text{spatial frequency (cycles/degree)} \times \text{velocity (degrees/sec)}$$
$$= [\text{critical duration (sec/cycle)}]^{-1}. \tag{12}$$

For example, a grating with wide bars will be visually optimal when moved quickly, since a high velocity is needed to bring a new edge to the sequence-discriminator by the time the critical duration τ has elapsed. Conversely, a grating with fine spacing must move slowly to allow an interval of time τ to elapse before the sequence-discriminator is stimulated by a new edge. In this section, we will review some of the evidence bearing on this reciprocity.

Some years ago, Crook (1937) determined the contrast threshold for the perception of direction of motion of a square wave grating. Using a range of spatial frequencies and velocities, his results suggest that the threshold is lowest when the product of grating spatial frequency and velocity is approximately constant. Van Nes, Koenderink, Nas, and Bouman (1967) also report an inverse relationship between spatial frequency and velocity. Figure 39, drawn from that study, shows that motion enhances the visibility of sinusoidal patterns. More specifically, as the figure demonstrates, the lower the spatial frequency, the higher the velocity which enhances visibility. More recently, Pantle (1970) demonstrated the inverse relationship using a selective adaptation paradigm. After subjects had been exposed to a stationary adaptation target of low spatial frequency, moving stimuli, particularly those of high velocity, were harder to see. Conversely, after adaptation to a stationary target of high frequency, moving stimuli particularly at low velocities were harder to see. Breitmeyer (1972, 1973)

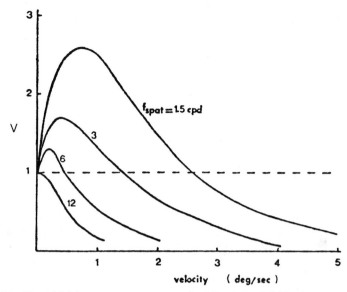

FIG. 39. Sinusoidal bar patterns are moved while their visibility is measured. The observer fixates a stationary fixation point and adjusts the modulation of the moving sinusoid until threshold is reached. We see first that for low spatial frequencies, movement enhances visibility, while for high spatial frequencies (12 cycles/degree of visual angle) movement diminishes visibility. Secondly, the velocity at which optimal visibility is obtained is higher when spatial frequency is lower. [After van Nes *et al.* (1967).]

has corroborated and extended this finding. His results are shown in Fig. 40. Subjects were exposed to a stationary square-wave for several minutes and then their threshold for the detection of a moving visual-noise texture was determined. The stationary adapting grating was either 4 cycles/degree (filled circles) or 1.5 cycles/degree (unfilled circles) in spatial frequency. The results demonstrated that with a 4-cycle/degree grating the velocity most affected (i.e., the largest threshold rise) was at 3 degrees/second. Substituting his values of spatial frequency and velocity into Eq. (12) yields a critical duration of $1/4 \times 3$ sec or 82.5 msec. Whereas, with a 1.5-cycle/degree grating, the peak threshold rise is at a velocity of 7 degrees/second, yielding a critical duration of $1/1.5 \times 7$ sec = 105 msec. Note that a reciprocal relationship exists between adapting spatial frequency and velocity of peak threshold rise. The estimated critical duration which results is clearly within the range of Bloch's law.

Breitmeyer, in the same study, also performed the inverse experiment. Subjects adapted to a visual-noise pattern moving at a particular velocity.

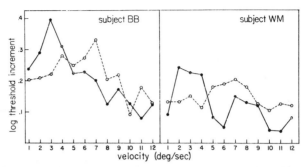

FIG. 40. Observers adapted to a stationary square wave grating of 4 cycles/degree (filled circles) or 1.5 cycles/degree (unfilled circles) in spatial frequency. Then they were required to detect a random texture pattern moving at some particular velocity. The log *increment* in threshold for detecting the moving pattern is plotted against the velocity of the pattern. Note that adapting to a lower spatial frequency diminishes sensitivity for higher velocities. [From Breitmeyer (1972).]

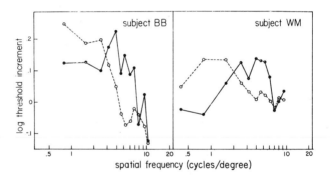

FIG. 41. The inverse experiment of that shown in Fig. 40. Observers adapt to a random texture moving at 2.5 deg/sec (filled circles) or 6.5 deg/sec (unfilled circles). After adaptation they are required to detect a stationary square wave pattern at some particular spatial frequency. The log increment in threshold for detecting the stationary grating pattern is plotted against the spatial frequency of the grating. Maximum effects are obtained when a higher velocity of adaptation is coupled with a lower spatial frequency in the test grating and lower velocity coupled with higher spatial frequency. [From Breitmeyer, 1972.]

Then, the contrast threshold needed to detect a stationary grating was measured for a range of spatial frequencies. The results are depicted in Fig. 41. Again, the inverse relationship is evident. The high-velocity adapting pattern increases the threshold, particularly for the lower spatial frequency stationary grating; the lower velocity adapting pattern increases the threshold, particularly for the higher spatial frequency stationary grating. The associated critical durations, calculated as before, are 77 and 83–100 msec, respectively.

In the initial sections of this chapter, we observed that the impulse response generated peripherally in the visual system slows down considerably under dark adaptation. Therefore, if this response sets the time window within which integration within the motion mechanism occurs, then we should expect the critical duration extracted from a selective adaptation paradigm such as used by Pantle and Breitmeyer, will yield a larger value when conducted at scotopic luminance levels. Breitmeyer (1972) performed the luminance level selective adaptation experiment in both directions. In one experiment, a stationary square wave pattern of 1.6 cycles/degree was the adapting pattern. Its effect on the detection of a texture moving at a number of different velocities was tested. Both patterns, adaptation and test, were shown at three different adaptation levels corresponding to those used by Kelly (1971a,b) see Fig. 10 (p. 181). The results are plotted in Fig. 42. As the luminance level drops, the peak threshold rise occurs at a progressively lower velocity. The product of spatial frequency and velocity yields the complement of the critical duration [see Eq. (12)], which is given in Fig. 42 by the numbers in parentheses. For subject SG the critical durations are 104, 139, and 204 msec at luminance levels of 1670, 167, and 16.7 td, respectively. As expected, the critical duration increases as the adaptation luminance diminishes. These critical

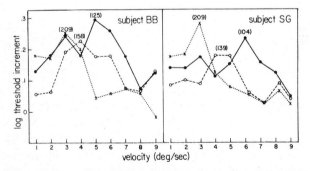

FIG. 42. The effect of varying background luminance on the spatial frequency–velocity association. *Os* adapted by viewing a stationary grating under three background luminance levels: 1670 td (filled circles), 167 td (unfilled circles), and 16.7 td (× symbols). They were then tested for the detection of a random texture pattern moving at some particular velocity. The log *increment* in threshold detection is plotted against the velocity of the random texture pattern. Numbers in parentheses above threshold peaks indicate *critical duration, d,* in msec, estimated according to the formula: Spatial Frequency × Velocity = 1/critical duration (see text for details). Note that the extracted critical duration becomes longer as background luminance diminishes. [From Breitmeyer (1972).]

durations are approximately comparable, at each adaptation level, to the duration of a single positive–negative wave of the unit-impulse response in Fig. 10 for the corresponding luminance level. These results prove that the unit-impulse response of the eye is the pacemaker for the cortical sequence-discrimination mechanism, which mediates motion perception.

Several predictions follow from the hypothesis that the unit-impulse response constitutes the pacemaker of the mechanism underlying motion perception. An object that moves too slowly, say at velocity v_1, will exceed the critical duration and therefore be suboptimal. One that moves at a velocity v_2 so as to just fill the integration time will activate the mechanism optimally. At a still higher velocity, v_3, the object will pass so quickly that less than complete integration will occur, and thus the mechanism will be less than maximally activated. When background luminance drops (see Fig. 10), the unit-impulse response becomes slower. Therefore, it is now v_1 the slower velocity that maximally activates the mechanism, with v_2 becoming suboptimal. We assume that perception is somehow related to maximally activated analytic mechanisms. It follows that under reduced background luminance, v_1 should yield the perception of velocity that v_2 does under higher background luminance. In other words, it is predicted that moving object of constant velocity should appear more rapid under diminished background luminance, which is in fact what is reported (Brown, 1931, see especially his Table II).

A prediction regarding apparent motion follows from a similar argument. At the level of the sequence-analyzing mechanism which underlies movement perception (Barlow & Levick, 1965; Bishop *et al.*, 1971) an apparent motion sequence is almost as effective as real motion. A drop in background luminance slows the unit-impulse response, which in turn increases integration time for the sequence-analyzing mechanisms. Therefore, we would expect a subject to see apparent motion for larger SOA values between the successfully presented strobed stimuli. A recent study (Ganz & Rose, unpublished results) shows this to be the case. Subjects made magnitude estimates of the perceived vividness of motion in a classical apparent movement display involving a pair of successively presented stationary light pulses. Stimulus onset asynchrony was varied over a wide range of values from zero to above 200 msec. The stimuli were presented against a background at photopic luminance level and also at scotopic luminance level but contrast was kept constant. Apparent motion was consistently seen at longer onset asynchronies under scotopic luminance conditions. The entire function of apparent motion vividness was displaced toward higher SOAs under scotopic luminance levels. This indicates that for any SOA above 40–50 msec the same vividness of motion is perceived under photopic and scotopic luminance level, if a *fixed constant* is added to the scotopic SOA. This is precisely what we should expect if the unit-impulse response paces the mechanism underlying motion perception.

References

Alpern, M. Metacontrast. *Journal of the Optical Society of America,* 1953, **43,** 648–657.

Averbach, E., & Coriell, A. S. Short-term memory in vision. *Bell System Technical Journal,* 1961, **40,** 309–328.

Averbach, E., & Sperling, G. Short-term storage of information in vision. In C. Cherry (Ed.), *Information theory.* London: Butterworth, 1960. Pp. 196–211.

Barlow, H. B. Temporal and spatial summation in human vision at different background intensities. *Journal of Physiology (London),* 1958, **141,** 337–350.

Barlow, H. B., & Levick, W. R. The mechanism of directionally selective units in rabbit's retina. *Journal of Physiology,* 1965, **178,** 477–504.

Barlow, H. B., & Sparrock, J. M. B. The role of after-images in dark adaptation. *Science,* 1964, **144,** 1309–1314.

Battersby, W. S., Oesterreich, R. E., & Sturr, J. F. Neural limitations of visual excitability. VII Non-homonymous retrochiasmal interaction. *American Journal of Physiology,* 1964, **206,** 1181–1188.

Baumgardt, E., & Hillman, B. M. Duration and size as determinants of peripheral retinal response. *Journal of the Optical Society of America,* 1961, **51,** 340–344.

Baumgardt, E., & Segal, J. La fonction inhibitrice dans le procéssus visuel. *Comptes Rendus de Séances de la Société de Biologie (Paris),* 1946, **140,** 231–233.

Bishop, P. O., Coombs, J. S., & Henry, G. H. Interaction effects of visual contours on the discharge frequency of simple striate neurones. *Journal of Physiology,* 1971, **219,** 659–687.

Blackwell, H. R. Neural theories of simple visual discriminations. *Journal of the Optical Society of America,* 1963, **53,** 129–160.

Bloch, A. M. Expérience sur la vision. *Comptes Rendus de Séances de la Société de Biologie (Paris),* 1885, **37,** 493–495.

Boynton, R. M. On-responses in the human visual system as inferred from psychophysical studies of rapid adaptation. *American Medical Association, Archives of Ophthalmology,* 1958, **60,** 800–810.

Boynton, R. M. Some temporal factors in vision. In W. A. Rosenblith (Ed.), *Sensory communication.* New York: Wiley, 1961. Pp. 739–756.

Boynton, R. M. Discrimination of homogeneous double pulses of light. In D. Jameson & L. M. Hurvich (Eds.), *Handbook of sensory physiology,* Vol. VII/4, *Visual psychophysics.* Berlin: Springer-Verlag, 1972. Pp. 202–232.

Breitmeyer, B. G. The relation between the detection of size and velocity in human vision. Unpublished doctoral dissertation, Stanford University, 1972.

Breitmeyer, B. G. A relationship between the detection of size, rate, orientation and direction in the human visual system. *Vision Research,* 1973, **13,** 41–58.

Bridgeman, B. Metacontrast and lateral inhibition. *Psychological Review,* 1971, **78,** 528–539.

Brown, J. F. The visual perception of velocity. *Psychologische Forschung,* 1931, **14,** 199–232.

Cheatham, P. G., & White, C. T. Temporal numerosity: I. Perceived number as a function of flash number and rate. *Journal of Experimental Psychology,* 1952, **44,** 447–451.

Ciganek, L. Excitability cycle of the visual cortex in man. *Annals of the New York Academy of Science,* 1964, **112,** 241–253.

Coltheart, M., & Arthur, B. Evidence for an integration theory of visual masking. *Quarterly Journal of Experimental Psychology,* 1972, **24,** 262–269.

Collonier, M., & Rossignol, S. Heterogeneity of the cerebral cortex. In H. H. Jasper, A. A. Ward, & A. Pope (Eds.), *Basic mechanisms of the epilepsies.* Boston: Little, Brown, 1969.

Crawford, B. H. Visual adaptation in relation to brief conditioning stimuli. *Proceedings of the Royal Society, London,* 1947, **134B,** 283–302.

Crook, M. N. Visual discrimination of movement. *Journal of Psychology,* 1937, **3,** 541–558.

DeLange, H. Research into the dynamic nature of the human fovea–cortex systems with intermittent and modulated light. I. Attenuation characteristics with white and colored light. *Journal of the Optical Society of America,* 1958, **48,** 777–784.

DeVoe, R. D. Non-linear transient responses from light adapted wolfspider eyes to changes in background illumination. *Journal of General Physiology,* 1967, 1961–1991. (a)

DeVoe, R. D. A non-linear model for transient responses from light adapted wolfspider eyes. *Journal of General Physiology,* 1967, **50,** 1993–2030. (b)

Donchin, E., & Lindsley, D. B. Retroactive brightness enhancement with brief paired flashes of light. *Vision Research,* 1965, **5,** 59–70.

Eriksen, C. W. Temporal luminance summation effects in backward and forward masking. *Perception & Psychophysics,* 1966, **1,** 87–92.

Eriksen, C. W., & Collins, J. F. Some temporal characteristics of visual pattern perception. *Journal of Experimental Psychology,* 1967, **74,** 476–484.

Eriksen, C. W., & Collins, J. F. Sensory traces versus the psychological moment in the temporal organization of form. *Journal of Experimental Psychology,* 1968, **77,** 376–382.

Eriksen, C. W., & Eriksen, B. A. Visual perceptual processing rates and backward and forward masking. *Journal of Experimental Psychology,* 1971, **89,** 306–313.

Eriksen, C. W., & Hoffman, M. Form recognition at brief duration as a function of adapting field and interval between stimulations. *Journal of Experimental Psychology,* 1963, **66,** 485–499.

Eriksen, C. W., & Lappin, J. S. Luminance summation-contrast reduction as a basis for certain forward and backward masking effects. *Psychonomic Science,* 1964, **1,** 313–314.

Fain, G. L., & Dowling, J. E. Intracellular recordings from single rods and cones in the mudpuppy retina. *Science,* 1973, **180,** 1178–1181.

Forsyth, D. M., & Chapanis, A. Counting repeated light flashes as a function of their number, their rate of presentation, and retinal location stimulated. *Journal of Experimental Psychology,* 1958, **56,** 385–391.

Gastaut, H., Roger, A., Corriol, J., & Naquet, R. Étude éléctrographique de cycle d'éxcitabilité corticale. *Electroencephalography & Clinical Neurophysiology,* 1951, **3,** 401–428.

Graham, C. H., & Kemp, E. H. Brightness discrimination as a function of the duration of the increment intensity. *Journal of General Physiology,* 1938, **21,** 635–650.

Graham, C. H., & Margaria, R. Area and the intensity–time relation in the peripheral retina. *American Journal of Physiology,* 1935, **113,** 299–305.

Greenspoon, T. S., & Eriksen, C. W. Interocular non-independence. *Perception and Psychophysics,* 1968, **3,** 93–96.

Haber, R. N., & Standing, L. G. Direct measures of short-term visual storage. *Quarterly Journal of Experimental Psychology,* 1969, **21,** 43–54.

Haber, R. N., & Standing, L. G. Direct estimates of apparent duration of a flash followed by visual noise. *Canadian Journal of Psychology,* 1970, **24,** 216–229.

Harter, M. R., & White, C. T. Perceived number and evoked cortical potentials. *Science,* 1967, **156,** 406–408.

Hecht, S., Schlaer, S., & Pirenne, M. H. Energy, quanta, and vision. *Journal of General Physiology,* 1942, **25,** 819–840.

Heinemann, E. G. Simultaneous brightness induction as a function of inducing and test-field luminances. *Journal of Experimental Psychology,* 1955, **50,** 89–96.

Herrick, R. M. Foveal luminance discrimination as a function of the duration of the decrement or increment in luminance. *Journal of Comparative & Physiological Psychology,* 1956, **59,** 437–443.

Ikeda, M. Temporal summation of positive and negative flashes in the visual system. *Journal of the Optical Society of America,* 1965, **55,** 1527–1534.

Ives, H. E. Critical frequency relations in scotopic vision. *Journal of the Optical Society of America,* 1922, **6,** 254–268. (a)

Ives, H. E. A theory of intermittent vision. *Journal of the Optical Society of America,* 1922, **6,** 343–361. (b)

Johnson, E. P., & Bartlett, N. R. Effect of stimulus duration on electrical responses of the human retina. *Journal of the Optical Society of America,* 1956, **46,** 167–170.

Jones, E. G., & Powell, T. P. S. An electron microscopic study of the laminar pattern and mode of termination of afferent fibre pathways in the somatic sensory cortex of the cat. *Philosophical Transactions of the Royal Society,* 1970, **B257,** 45–62.

Kahneman, D. Method, findings, and theory in studies of visual masking. *Psychological Bulletin,* 1968, **69,** 404–425.

Kahneman, D., & Norman, J. The time–intensity relation in visual perception as a function of observer's task. *Journal of Experimental Psychology,* 1964, **68,** 215–220.

Kelly, D. H. Effects of sharp edges in a flickering field. *Journal of the Optical Society of America,* 1959, **49,** 730–732.

Kelly, D. H. Flickering patterns and lateral inhibition. *Journal of the Optical Society of America,* 1969, **59,** 1361–1370.

Kelly, D. H. Theory of flicker and transient responses. I. Uniform fields. *Journal of the Optical Society of America,* 1971, **61,** 537–546. (a)

Kelly, D. H. Theory of flicker and transient responses. II. Counterphase gratings. *Journal of the Optical Society of America,* 1971, **61,** 632–640. (b)

Kelly, D. H. Adaptation effects on spatio-temporal sine-wave thresholds. *Vision Research,* 1972, **12,** 89–101. (a)

Kelly, D. H. Flicker. In D. Jameson & L. M. Hurvich (Eds.), *Handbook of sensory physiology,* Vol. VII/4, *Visual psychophysics.* Berlin: Springer-Verlag, 1972. (b)

Kinsbourne, M., & Warrington, E. K. The effect of an after-coming random pattern on the perception of brief visual stimuli. *Quarterly Journal of Experimental Psychology,* 1962, **14,** 223–234. (a)

Kinsbourne, M., & Warrington, E. K. Further studies on the masking of brief visual stimuli by a random pattern. *Quarterly Journal of Experimental Psychology,* 1962, **14,** 235–245. (b)

Kolers, P. A. Intensity and contour effects in visual masking. *Vision Research,* 1962, **2,** 277–294.

Kolers, P. A., & Rosner, B. S. On visual masking (metacontrast): Dichoptic observation. *American Journal of Psychology,* 1960, **73,** 2–21.

Levinson, J. Nonlinear and spatial effects in the perception of flicker. *Documenta Ophthalmologica,* 1964, **18,** 36–55.

Levinson, J. Flicker fusion phenomena. *Science,* 1968, **160,** 21–28.

Li, Ch.-L., Ortiz-Galvin, A., Chou, S. N., & Howard, S. Y. Cortical intracellular potentials in response to stimulation of lateral geniculate body. *Journal of Neurophysiology,* 1960, **23,** 592–601.

Matin, L. Critical duration, the differential luminance threshold, critical flicker frequency, and visual adaptation: A theoretical treatment. *Journal of the Optical Society of America,* 1968, **58,** 404–415.

Pantle, A. J. Adaptation to pattern spatial frequency effects on visual movement sensitivity in humans. *Journal of the Optical Society of America,* 1970, **60,** 1120–1124.

Rashbass, C. The visibility of transient changes of luminance. *Journal of Physiology (London),* 1970, **210,** 165–186.

Roufs, J. A. Dynamic properties of vision. I. Experimental relationships between flicker and flash thresholds. *Vision Research,* 1972, **12,** 261–278. (a)

Roufs, J. A. Dynamic properties of vision. II. Theoretical relationships between flicker and flash thresholds. *Vision Research,* 1972, **12,** 279–292. (b)

Schiller, P. H. Monoptic and dichoptic visual masking by patterns and by flashes. *Journal of Experimental Psychology,* 1965, **69,** 193–199.

Schiller, P. Single unit analysis of backward visual masking and metacontrast in the cat lateral geniculate nucleus. *Vision Research,* 1968, **8,** 855–866.

Schiller, P. H., & Wiener, M. Monoptic and dichoptic visual masking. *Journal of Experimental Psychology,* 1963, **66,** 386–393.

Schmidt, M. W., & Kristofferson, A. B. Discrimination of successiveness: A test of a model of attention. *Science,* 1963, **139,** 112–113.

Smith, M. C., & Schiller, P. H. Forward and backward masking: A comparison. *Canadian Journal of Psychology,* 1966, **20,** 191–197.

Spencer, T. J., & Shuntich, R. Evidence for an interruption theory of backward masking. *Journal of Experimental Psychology,* 1970, **85,** 198–203.

Sperling, G. The information available in brief visual presentations. *Psychological Monographs,* 1960, **74,** 1–29.

Sperling, G. A model for visual memory tasks. *Human Factors,* 1963, **5,** 19–31.

Sperling, G. Temporal and spatial visual masking: I. Masking by impulse flashes. *Journal of the Optical Society of America,* 1965, **55,** 541–559.

Sperling, G. Successive approximations to a model for short-term memory. *Acta Psychologia,* 1967, **27,** 285–292.

Sperling, G., Budiansky, J., Spivak, J. G., & Johnson, M. C. Extremely rapid visual search: The maximum rate of scanning letters for the presence of a numeral. *Science,* 1971, **174,** 307–311.

Sperling, G., & Jollife, C. L. Intensity-time relationship at threshold for spectral stimuli in human vision. *Journal of the Optical Soicety of America,* 1965, **55,** 191–199.

Sperling, G., & Sondhi, M. M. Model for visual luminance of flicker detection. *Journal of the Optical Society of America,* 1968, **58,** 1133–1145.

Sukale-Wolf, S. The prediction of the metacontrast phenomenon from simultaneous brightness contrast. Unpublished doctoral dissertation, Stanford University, 1971.

Thompson, J. H. What happens to the stimulus in backward masking? *Journal of Experimental Psychology,* 1966, **71,** 580–586.

van den Brink, G. Retinal summation and the visibility of moving objects. Thesis, Utrecht, 1957. Report WW 1957–1959, Institute for Perception RVO-TNO, Soesterberg, Netherlands.

Van Nes, F. L., Koenderink, J. J., Nas, H., & Bouman, M. A. Spatio-temporal modulation transfer in the human eye. *Journal of the Optical Society of America,* 1967, **57,** 1082–1088.

Vaughan, H. G., Jr., & Silverstein, L. Metacontrast and evoked potentials: A reappraisal. *Science,* 1968, **160,** 207–208.

Veringa, F. Diffusion model of linear flicker response. *Journal of the Optical Society of America,* 1970, **60,** 285–286.

Watanabe, S., Konishi, M., & Creutzfeldt, O. D. Post synaptic potentials in the cat's visual cortex following electrical stimulation of afferent pathways. *Experimental Brain Research,* 1966, **1,** 272–283.

Weisstein, N. Backward masking and models of perceptual processing. *Journal of Experimental Psychology,* 1966, **72,** 232–240.

Weisstein, N. A Rashevsky-Landahl neural net: Simulation of metacontrast. *Psychological Review,* 1968, **75,** 494–521.

Weisstein, N. W-shaped and U-shaped functions obtained for monoptic and dichoptic disk–disk masking. *Perception & Psychophysics,* 1971, **9,** 275–278.

Weisstein, N. Metacontrast. In D. Jameson & L. M. Hurvich (Eds.), *Handbook of sensory physiology,* Vol. VII/4, *Visual psychophysics.* Berlin: Springer-Verlag, 1972. Pp. 233–272.

Weisstein, N., & Growney, R. L. Apparent movement and metacontrast: a note on Kahneman's formulation. *Perception & Psychophysics,* 1969, **5,** 321–328.

Werner, H. Studies on contour: I. Qualitative analyses. *American Journal of Psychology,* 1935, **47,** 40–64.

White, C. T. Temporal numerosity and the psychological unit of duration. *Psychological Monographs,* 1963, Whole No. 575.

Whitten, D. N., & Brown, K. T. Slowed decay of the monkey's cone receptor potential by intense stimuli, and protection from this effect by light adaptation. *Vision Research,* 1973, **13,** 1659–1667.

Chapter 7

SPATIAL RESOLUTION AND SPATIAL INTERACTION[*]

JAMES P. THOMAS

This chapter discusses two spatial aspects of visual perception: the resolution of spatial patterns and phenomena of spatial interaction. The two topics are treated separately, just as historically they have been pursued as separate research areas. As will be seen, however, the two areas share some common ground, particularly with respect to theoretical interpretation.

I. SPATIAL RESOLUTION

The discussion of spatial resolution is in three sections. The first describes the two kinds of measures—acuity and contrast sensitivity—that are used to assess the resolving power of the visual system. The second section discusses the effects of several stimulus variables upon performance. The third section considers some theoretical questions.

A. Types of Measures

1. ACUITY

Measures of acuity test the resolving power of the visual system by determining the smallest spatial pattern or the smallest detail of a pattern that

* Preparation of this chapter was supported in part by USPHS Research Grant EY 00360 from the National Eye Institute.

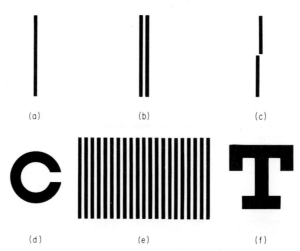

FIG. 1. Patterns used to measure acuity. (a) Minimum visible. (b) Minimum separable. (c) Vernier. (d) Landolt ring. (e) Grating. (f) Snellen letter.

can be resolved. The test pattern is usually black on a white background, as illustrated in Fig. 1. The contrast, i.e., the difference in luminance between the black and white areas, is made as great as possible. In testing acuity, the size of the test pattern is reduced until the pattern, or a critical detail, is just resolvable. This threshold size is stated in terms of the angle which it subtends at the eye of the viewer. Visual acuity, or decimal acuity, is the reciprocal of the threshold when the latter is expressed in minutes of arc. Nominally, normal acuity is 1.0: the ability to resolve a pattern whose critical dimension subtends 1 minute of arc. Higher acuities are regularly observed in the laboratory, however. In Snellen notation, acuity is expressed as the ratio of the distance, in feet, at which a detail is resolved to the distance at which the detail would subtend 1 minute of arc. Thus, 20/10 indicates that a detail that is just resolved at 20 feet would subtend 1 minute of arc if viewed from 10 feet. The equivalent decimal acuity is 2.0.

Several kinds of test patterns have been used. They are illustrated in Fig. 1 and discussed separately in what follows. Sloan (1951) gives a more extensive treatment of the different patterns, with special reference to clinical use.

a. MINIMUM VISIBLE. The target is a single dark line, usually formed by stretching a fine wire across a bright background. The width of the line is varied to establish the resolution threshold. The length is constant and usually is several degrees of arc. Under optimal conditions, threshold width is .5 sec (Hecht & Mintz, 1939). The corresponding acuity, 120, is more than an order of magnitude greater than acuities obtained with other patterns. The minimum visible task is clearly different from other types of acuity tasks.

b. MINIMUM SEPARABLE. The target consists of two points or two lines, separated by a narrow gap. The width of the gap is varied to find the separation at which the points or lines are resolved as two. Craik (1939) used dark lines on a bright background. The width of each line was so varied as to keep it equal to the width of the gap. In his best conditions, the just resolvable gap was .5 min, corresponding to an acuity of 2.0.

c. VERNIER ACUITY. The vernier pattern consists of two line segments which can be aligned on a common axis or offset by various amounts. The threshold is the minimum perceivable misalignment, and ranges down to between 1 and 2 sec (Berry, 1948).

d. LANDOLT RING. The Landolt ring is a black circle with a single break or gap. The width of the circle or ring and the breadth of the gap are each equal to one fifth the outer diameter of the ring. The entire figure is varied in size, maintaining the proportionalities, to determine the smallest gap that can be resolved. Under optimal conditions, gaps of somewhat less than .5 min can be resolved, yielding acuities around 2.5 (Shlaer, 1937; Shlaer, Smith, & Chase, 1942).

e. GRATING ACUITY. The target is a series of alternating black and white bars of equal widths. The bars are varied in width in order to determine the minimum width at which the striations are resolved. The width of a single black or white bar is taken as the threshold. Shlaer (1937) obtained thresholds near .5 min (visual acuity = 2.0). The threshold target can also be described in terms of its spatial frequency, i.e., the number of cycles or black–white pairs in each degree of width.

f. SNELLEN LETTERS. Letters of the alphabet are also used, the test being how small they can be made and still be identified. Sloan (1951) discusses different standardized forms that have been used. Threshold is based not upon overall size, but upon such critical features as stroke width, length of arms, and width of gaps between arms. Visual acuities range up to about 2.0 (Ludvigh, 1941).

2. CONTRAST SENSITIVITY

Another way to assess the resolving power of the visual system is to determine the minimum contrast needed to perceive a particular pattern (Schade, 1956). For example, consider a grating pattern. A grating of any coarseness can be made imperceptible by reducing the difference between the luminance of the light bars and the luminance of the dark bars. The difference at which the striations are just resolved is the contrast thres-

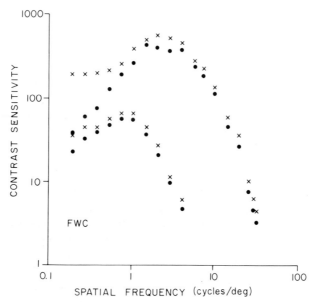

FIG. 2. Contrast sensitivity for square-wave gratings ($\times$) and sine-wave gratings ($\bullet$). The space-average luminance of the grating was 500 cd m^{-2} for the upper pair of curves and .05 cd m^{-2} for the lower pair. [Data from Campbell & Robson (1968).]

hold, and the reciprocal of the threshold is the contrast sensitivity. Campbell and Robson (1968) obtained contrast sensitivities for a variety of grating patterns. Some of their results are shown in Fig. 2. Contrast is defined as $(L_{max} - L_{min})/(L_{max} + L_{min})$, where L_{max} is the luminance of the brightest part of the grating and L_{min} is the luminance of the darkest part. The fineness of the grating is expressed in cycles (number of dark–light pairs) per degree. There are separate curves for two mean luminance levels and for two types of modulation. One type is square-wave modulation, in which luminance steps abruptly between its maximum and minimum values; the other type is sinusoidal modulation, in which luminance varies continuously between its maximum and minimum values according to a sine function of distance across the grating. Sensitivity is greatest for patterns of intermediate frequency, and decreases for patterns that are either very coarse or very fine. Less than 1% contrast is needed to resolve the most visible pattern.

The curves in Fig. 2 are called *contrast sensitivity functions*. It may be seen that grating acuity is but a single point on the contrast sensitivity function, namely, the point at which threshold contrast equals the contrast of the acuity grating (usually 1.0).

B. Variables Affecting Resolution

Performance in resolution tasks is affected by several experimental variables. The values given in the last section were for optimal conditions. This section describes the relevant variables and their effects on resolution.

1. INTENSITY OF ILLUMINATION

Acuity for minimum visible (Hecht & Mintz, 1939), minimum separable (Craik, 1939), vernier (Baker, 1949), and Landolt ring (Shlaer, 1937) targets depends upon the luminance of the background on which the dark target is superimposed. Similarly, grating acuity is dependent upon the space-average luminance of the grating target, i.e., the average of the luminances of the bright and dark bars (Shlaer, 1937). Figure 3 shows the relationships between intensity of illumination and acuity that Shlaer found for Landolt rings and gratings. Log acuity increases as a negatively accelerating function of log intensity and becomes asymptotic at high intensities. Each curve has two segments. The lower segment represents acuity mediated by rods and the upper segment represents cone vision (Shlaer, 1937; Shlaer et al., 1942). Contrast sensitivity also depends upon the intensity of illumination. As can be seen in Fig. 2, increasing the space-average luminance of the grating has two effects: There is an overall rise in contrast sensitivity, i.e., there is a decrease in the contrast needed for resolution; and the peak of the contrast sensitivity function shifts to a higher frequency. Similar effects of illumination occur in rod vision (Daitch & Green, 1969).

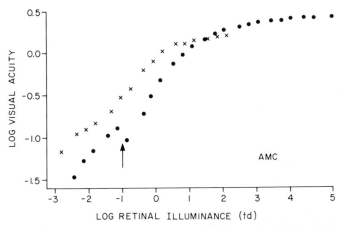

FIG. 3. Effect of intensity of illumination on acuity: ($\times$) grating target; ($\bullet$) Landolt ring target. Arrow indicates point at which subject began using central fixation when viewing Landolt ring. [Data from Shlaer (1937).]

These results were obtained in experiments in which a large part of the visual field was illuminated at an intensity level similar to that of the target area and in which the observer was adapted to the intensity of the target area. Acuity suffers when these conditions are not met, as when a small, bright area containing the target is surrounded by darkness (Lythgoe, 1932) or as when the observer is adapted to an intensity that is substantially lower or higher than that of the test area (Craik, 1939).

2. RETINAL LOCUS

At photopic levels of illumination, acuity is highest when the target is viewed with the center of the fovea and decreases rapidly as the image of the target is displaced toward the periphery (Ludvigh, 1941; Mandelbaum & Sloan, 1947; Sloan, 1968). There is a significant drop even within the fovea (Miller, 1961). Acuity and the number of cones per unit of retinal area both decrease as a function of distance from the center of the fovea; however, a precise quantitative relationship between acuity and cone density has not been satisfactorily established. The relationship between acuity and intensity of illumination varies with retinal locus: In the peripheral retina, as compared to the central retina, acuity increases more slowly as intensity increases and becomes asymptotic at lower intensities (Mandelbaum & Sloan, 1947; Sloan, 1968).

When illumination is dim and rods mediate resolution, acuity is highest for targets located about 4 deg from fixation (Mandelbaum & Sloan, 1947). Thus, there is no simple relationship between scotopic acuity and the distribution of rods, for the greatest density of the rods occurs about 20 deg from fixation.

3. PUPIL SIZE

Strictly speaking, the size of the pupil is an aspect of the subject's physiological reaction to the stimulus, rather than an experimental variable. Normally, pupil size is determined by such stimulus variables as the intensity of illumination and the distance of object viewed. In most acuity experiments, however, artificial pupils are used to provide independent control of the effective entrance aperture to the eye.

The size of the pupil affects resolution in two ways. First, as the pupil opens, more light enters the eye and the intensity of the retinal image increases. Were the intensity of the image the only factor involved, large pupils would favor acuity. However, the quality of the retinal image varies with pupil size and this relationship also affects resolution.

The quality of the retinal image is assessed in two ways. One is in terms of the point-spread function or the line-spread function of the eye, i.e., the image which is formed of a point of light or of a bright line of negligible width. The narrower and more sharply peaked this function is, the more faithfully the stimulus is reproduced in the retinal image. The second way to assess image quality is in terms of spatial frequency components. By application of Fourier techniques, the stimulus and the retinal image can each be treated as a linear combination of sinusoidal luminance patterns of various spatial frequencies, modulations, and phases. The fidelity with which each frequency component in the stimulus is reproduced in the retinal image determines the quality of the latter. One measure of quality is the modulation transfer function, which gives the ratio of the modulation in the image to the modulation in the stimulus for each frequency component. The modulation transfer function is the Fourier transform of the spread function and either one can be computed if the other is known.

The size of the pupil affects the quality of the retinal image in two opposing ways. Because of the nature of the diffraction processes by which images are formed, the size of the pupil (or entrance aperture) places an inherent limit on the quality of the image (Westheimer, 1964). Specifically, in an optical system that is limited only by diffraction, the width of the spread function is inversely proportional to the diameter of the pupil. In terms of spatial frequency, the pupil acts as a low-pass filter whose cutoff frequency (above which nothing is passed) is proportional to pupil diameter. The modulation in the image of each frequency component below the cutoff is reduced from the modulation in the stimulus by a factor related to the nearness of the frequency to the cutoff frequency. That is, even among those frequencies that are passed by the pupil, fidelity depends upon pupil size. Thus, in a diffraction limited system, image quality increases as the size of the pupil increases. The human eye is not merely diffraction limited, however. It is also subject to spherical and chromatic aberration and to errors of focus. These degrade the retinal image by amounts that increase as the size of the pupil increases. As pupil size is increased from a small diameter, such as 1 mm, the gains due to diffraction initially outweigh the losses due to aberration and focus errors, and image quality increases. At some point, however, the losses begin to outweigh the gains and further increases in pupil size degrade the image. Thus, from an optical standpoint, a pupil of intermediate diameter is optimal.

Several investigators have measured the line-spread function of the human eye by an ophthalmoscopic technique (Campbell & Gubisch, 1966; Krauskopf, 1962; Westheimer & Campbell, 1962). The procedure is difficult and there is some variation in results from study to study, particularly as methodology improves. However, there is general agreement that the best image is obtained with a pupil between 2 and 4 mm in diameter. These results are generally consistent with the results of psychophysical studies in which the intensity of retinal illumination was held constant while pupil size was varied. Both grating acuity (Cobb, 1915; Leibowitz, 1952) and contrast sensitivity (Campbell & Green, 1965) are best when pupil diameter is between 2 and 5 mm.

4. SPECTRAL COMPOSITION OF ILLUMINATION

Two questions concerning spectral composition have been examined. The first is whether acuity is better when the illumination includes only a narrow band of wavelengths than when the illumination includes wavelengths from the entire visible spectrum, i.e., white light. Narrow-band illumination reduces chromatic aberration and thus would be expected to yield higher acuities. Such improvement has been observed for minimum visible (Shlaer et al., 1942) and vernier (Baker, 1949) acuities. In the case of Landolt ring acuity, which appears to have a different dependence upon retinal image quality than either minimum visible or vernier acuity, there is no marked difference between acuities measured in narrow-band and wide-band illumination (Shlaer et al., 1942).

The second question is whether acuity depends upon wavelength when narrow-band illumination is used. At intensities high enough that acuity no longer varies with intensity, and for pupils of moderate diameter, acuity shows no marked variation with wavelength. If the pupil is small enough that diffraction becomes a limiting factor, then acuity is higher for short than for long wavelengths. If the intensity of illumination is low enough that acuity varies with intensity, then the luminous efficiency of each wavelength becomes a factor. In cone vision, wavelengths must be adjusted for photopic sensitivity, i.e., made equal in luminance, for acuity to be equal across wavelengths (Hecht, 1949). In rod vision, the adjustment is for scotopic sensitivity (Brown, Phares, & Fletcher, 1960).

For a given state of accommodation, the shorter the illuminating wavelength, the closer the image is formed to the lens of the eye. The effect is most marked for wavelengths shorter than 500 nm and it is common practice to compensate for it at these wavelengths by providing the subject with a negative correction of about 1 diopter.

5. ORIENTATION

Resolution is better for striations or lines that are oriented vertically or horizontally than for ones which are oblique. Minimum visible acuity (Ogilvie & Taylor, 1958), grating acuity (Higgins & Stultz, 1948; Shlaer, 1937) and contrast sensitivity (Campbell, Kulikowski, & Levinson, 1966; Watanabe, Mori, Nagata, & Hiwatashi, 1968) are all reduced when the test pattern is oblique. The effect is not optical in origin (Mitchell, Freeman, & Westheimer, 1967). Furthermore, although oblique gratings are less effective than vertical or horizontal ones in evoking responses recorded from scalp electrodes over the occipital region, no such difference is seen in the electroretinogram (Maffei & Campbell, 1970). Thus, the source of this phenomenon appears to be at some more central site than the retina.

6. Viewing Distance

The lens of the eye changes shape (accommodates) in order to keep a target focused on the retina as viewing distance changes. There are limits to accommodation, however. For every eye there is a critical distance, called the near point, such that objects closer than the near point cannot be properly focused on the retina. Myopic or short-sighted eyes also have a far-point: Objects farther than it cannot be properly focused. Both near and far points can be altered artificially by the use of corrective lenses. Obviously, acuity will suffer if the target is either closer than the near point or more distant than the far point. Excluding this circumstance, no clear relationship between acuity and viewing distance emerges from the evidence at hand. However, the question is complicated by the fact that errors and fluctuations in accommodation are likely to occur when the visual display has a minimum of structure, as is the case in most acuity experiments, and are also more likely to occur at short than at long viewing distances (Westheimer, 1963). Another complication is that performance varies with the overall angular size of the target, e.g., the width and height of a grating (Pokorny, 1968), and this factor is not always held constant as viewing distance is changed. These problems may account for the occasional reports that acuity is better at one viewing distance than at another.

C. Theoretical Issues

1. Effect of the Intensity of Field Illumination

Acuity and contrast sensitivity increase markedly as the intensity of illumination increases. As the light level rises, the natural pupil contracts, yielding an improved retinal image, and there is a change from rod to cone vision. Both of these factors contribute to the increased visual performance. However, substantial improvement occurs even when these two factors are eliminated. The sources of this remaining improvement have been the subject of much theoretical speculation.

Hecht (1928) introduced the notion that the functional grain of the retina changed with illumination. The numerical density of the photoreceptors places one limit upon resolution, i.e., the finer the grain of the receptor mosaic, the better the resolution. Hecht suggested that the intensity threshold varies considerably from receptor to receptor, receptors with different thresholds being randomly intermixed in each area of the retina. When the background is dim, it activates only those few receptors with the lowest thresholds. Only the active receptors can contribute to resolution, because only they can respond differentially to the background and the dark test pattern. As the luminance of the background increases, the number of active receptors and the possible resolution increase.

Pirenne (1967; Pirenne & Denton, 1952) modified the notion in two ways. First, he pointed out that the concept of varying thresholds is unnecessary. Given the low proportion of quanta actually absorbed by the receptors, not all receptors will absorb quanta until the background luminance is relatively high. Below that level, the mosaic of quantum absorptions becomes denser as luminance increases, and finer resolution becomes possible. Second, Pirenne noted that many receptors converge upon each optic nerve fiber and that the contribution of each fiber toward resolution depends upon the number of receptors or the size of the retinal region it serves. The smaller the receptive field of the fiber, the greater its contribution to resolution. The size of the receptive field varies greatly from one fiber to another and the receptive fields overlap, so that small receptive fields are contained within large fields. According to Pirenne, when field luminance is low, only large receptive fields absorb enough quanta to activate their fibers and resolution is correspondingly crude. At higher illuminations, fibers with smaller receptive fields are activated and resolution improves.

There is evidence that the organization of the receptive field itself changes with the light level to which the eye is adapted. It should be noted that the resolving power of a cell depends not only upon the size of its receptive field, but also upon how the field is divided into antagonistic parts. Barlow, Fitzhugh, and Kuffler (1957) studied the antagonism between the central and peripheral parts of the receptive fields of cat ganglion cells. They found that the antagonistic response of the surround disappeared after prolonged dark adaptation. Jacobs and Yolton (1970) studied the effect of light level on the balance between the central and peripheral parts of the receptive fields of cells in the lateral geniculate body of the squirrel monkey. They found that the balance changed with the intensity of illumination, but that the presence and direction of the effect varied from cell to cell. That is, an increase in field illumination either had no effect, increased the strength of the surround response, or decreased the strength of the surround response, depending upon the cell. It appears that changes in receptive field organization do occur, but full knowledge of the nature of the changes and how they affect visual resolution is lacking.

2. OPTICAL AND NEURAL LIMITATIONS

The interplay of optical and neural limits on resolution has been the subject of much theoretical analysis. The balance varies with the experimental conditions, of course. When an artificial pupil is used, the optical quality of the retinal image changes little with level of illumination. Thus, the decrease in visual performance at reduced illumination must represent biochemical and neural limitations. On the other hand, when illumination is high and a small artificial pupil is used (less than 1.5 mm in diameter), acuity conforms to predictions based solely on diffraction (Riggs, 1965); thus, optical limitations appear to dominate in this situation. However, most speculation has been directed toward situations in which conditions are optimized for both optical and neural mechanisms.

Hecht and Mintz (1939) estimated the distribution of light in the retinal image of a single dark test-line of threshold width (.5 sec of arc). The breadth of the retinal image of such a narrow target is fixed by the spread function of the eye and is not affected by the width of the test line. Reducing the latter merely reduces the contrast in the image. Hecht and Mintz estimated that, for a test width of .5 sec, the illumination in the darkest part of the image was about 1% less than the illumination of surrounding areas. Because this difference approximates the lowest difference thresholds for intensity discrimination, Hecht and Mintz concluded that contrast sensitivity, the ability to detect small variations in intensity, was the limiting factor in minimum visible acuity.

The situation is different for grating acuity. Shlaer (1937) calculated that the contrast in the retinal image of a just-resolvable grating was more than an order of magnitude greater than in the case of a fine line. Furthermore, he found that large variations in the contrast of the image had little affect upon acuity. He concluded, therefore, that the coarseness of the retinal mosaic, rather than contrast sensitivity, limited grating acuity. The resolution of Landolt ring targets seems to be similarly limited (Shlaer et al., 1942). At the limit of resolution, the width of a single bar of the grating or of the gap of the Landolt ring is a little less than 30 sec of arc. The similarity between this figure and the diameter of a foveal cone, about 20 sec, has often been noted.

Campbell and Green (1965) examined the roles of optical and neural factors in contrast sensitivity for grating targets. They formulated the problem as one in which optical and neural mechanisms constitute the two successive parts of a cascaded transmission system. That is, the contrast required to resolve a given pattern depends upon (a) the contrast required in the retinal image in order for the receptor–neuron system to resolve the image; and (b) the contrast required in the stimulus in order for the optics to yield a retinal image of the required contrast. The contrast sensitivity function of the entire optical–neural system is the product of the contrast sensitivity function of the neural component and the modulation transfer function of the optical component.

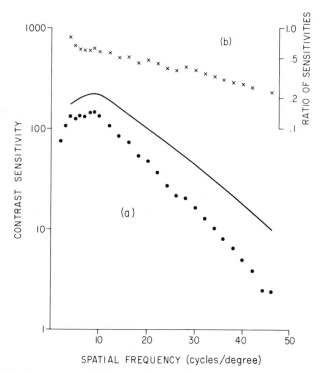

FIG. 4. (a) Contrast sensitivity of whole visual system (●), as measured with sinusoidal gratings presented on oscilloscope. Smooth curve is contrast sensitivity of receptor–neural component, as measured by interference fringes formed on retina. (b) Ratio of contrast sensitivity obtained with oscilloscope patterns to that obtained with interference fringes. [Data from Campbell & Green (1965).]

Campbell and Green used sinusoidal gratings because such patterns are only reduced in modulation, not changed in waveform, as they pass through the optics; and because such gratings can be formed directly on the retina as interference patterns that are largely independent of the optical limitations of the eye. The contrast sensitivity function for the entire visual system was obtained by presenting the sinusoidal gratings on the face of an oscilloscope. This function is shown in Fig. 4a. Then, the interference pattern was formed on the retina by imaging two coherent points of light, derived from the beam of a single laser, in the subject's pupil. Spatial frequency of the grating pattern was varied by changing the separation of the points of light and contrast was varied by superimposing a uniform wash of light. If scattering of light by the media of the eye is ignored, the contrast of the retinal image is easily calculated and the contrast sensitivity function of the isolated receptor–neuron system is obtained. This function is also shown in Fig. 4a. Figure 4b shows the ratio of the contrast sensitivity obtained with the gratings formed on the oscilloscope (entire visual system) to the sensitivity obtained with the interference fringes (neural component). Except for the fact that it does not reflect the scattering of light by the media of the eye, Fig. 4b is the modulation transfer function of the optics of the eye. It agrees well with the transfer function that Campbell and Gubisch (1966) obtained by ophthalmoscopic measures, although it indicates somewhat better optical performance, as would be expected because of the scattering factor.

Improving either the optical or neural component of the visual system by a given factor would increase overall sensitivity by the same factor. However, as Campbell and Green note, at high spatial frequencies the proportionate rate of decrease in performance is twice as great for the neural component as for the optical component. The steepness of the receptor–neuron curve at the high frequency end indicates that large changes in retinal contrast are needed in order to advance even a small way along the spatial frequency axis, which is probably why Shlaer (1937) found that changing the modulation of the retinal image had little effect upon grating acuity.

3. SPATIAL FREQUENCY TUNING

A variety of evidence indicates that the neural channels which mediate the resolution of gratings are selectively sensitive with respect to spatial frequency, different channels responding to different frequency components of the stimulus. The first evidence of separate channels was provided by Campbell and Robson (1968). They measured contrast sensitivity using complex gratings (rectangular and saw-tooth waveforms), each of which contained not only a fundamental frequency but harmonic components as well. They found that the harmonic components did not contribute as much to resolution as would be expected if the nervous system were acting as a single, broadband spatial filter. Indeed, over a wide range of frequencies resolution was determined strictly by the fundamental component. For example, in Fig. 2, the sine- and square-wave curves differ over most of the spatial frequency range by a factor which is within error of 1.273, the sensitivity ratio at which the amplitudes of the fundamental frequencies are equal. Only at very low frequencies does the factor change, indicating that the harmonic components of the square-wave are beginning to affect resolution.

Sachs, Nachmias, and Robson (1971) pursued the question using gratings composed of two superimposed spatial frequencies. They found that, for frequencies greater than about 3 cycles/degree, the two components were resolved independently, unless their frequencies differed by less than about 25%. Independence could also be demonstrated among low frequency components, provided that the difference in frequency was great enough. Graham and Nachmias (1971) found that neither the phase difference between the components nor their relative amplitudes affected the finding of independence.

A different kind of evidence for many independent neural channels, each tuned to a different narrow range of frequencies, was provided by Blakemore and Campbell (1969). The contrast threshold for a grating is raised by prior viewing of a high contrast grating of the same frequency. Blakemore and Campbell showed that the adaptation effect is highly selective with respect to frequency, the amount by which the threshold shifts decreasing as the frequencies of the test and adapting stimuli become different. No substantial effect occurs when the test and adapting frequencies differ by more than an octave.

Individual neurons that are selectively sensitive with respect to spatial frequency have been observed in the retina, lateral geniculate body, and cortex of the cat (Campbell, Cooper, & Enroth-Cugell, 1969; Enroth-Cugell & Robson, 1966; Maffei & Fiorentini, 1973). The range of frequencies to which each is sensitive varies from cell to cell in a manner which is generally consistent with the psychophysical results for human observers. The antagonism between the central and peripheral portions of the receptive field of each cell appears to generate the selectivity (Enroth-Cugell & Robson, 1966) and variation in the dimensions of the receptive fields, even within a given part of the visual field, provides the differing bands of sensitivity.

II. SPATIAL INTERACTION

The perceptual effect produced by illuminating a given spot in the visual field depends upon and varies with the stimulation delivered to neighboring regions. This dependency is called *spatial interaction* or *simultaneous contrast,* and is the subject of the second half of this chapter.

Two types of spatial interaction occur. In one, called *positive interaction,* illumination at one point reinforces or enhances the effect of stimulation at a second point. Thus, a spot of light may be seen more easily if a second, dim spot of light is exposed near it (Beitel, 1936); or a disk of light may brighten when it is surrounded by a dimmer annulus (Heinemann, 1955). In the second kind of interaction, called *negative interaction,* stimulation at one point diminishes the effect of illumination at a second point. For example, the brightness of a lighted square of fixed luminance decreases when a more intense square is exposed nearby (Leibowitz, Mote, & Thurlow, 1953). The type of spatial interaction that occurs between two points in the visual field is not fixed, but may be either positive or negative, depending upon such factors as the absolute and relative intensities of illumination at the two points and the presence of other stimuli. Both types of interactions exhibit spatial summation. That is, the change in perception of the affected stimulus may be increased by enlarging the stimulus that produces the change, or by adding new conditioning stimuli.

The dependent variable in studies of spatial interaction is some measure of the perceptual effect of illuminating a given region of the visual field. The two most common measures are visibility, as measured by the luminance increment threshold, and brightness, as measured by brightness matches between the test region and a stimulus that is not subject to varying spatial interactions. Other perceptual characteristics, such as apparent size, are less frequently used. Spatial interactions can also affect perceived hue and saturation, but such color-contrast effects are not included in this chapter.

The independent variable in studies of spatial interaction is the spatial distribution of light, either within the test stimulus itself or in one or more conditioning or inducing stimuli. For example, the visibility or brightness of the test stimulus may be studied as a function of its own area, the distribution of light within its boundaries, or the sharpness with which its edges are defined. Conditioning stimuli may take the form of a background on which the test stimulus is superimposed, a contiguous surround, or noncontiguous stimuli exposed near the test stimulus. The visibility or brightness of the test stimulus is studied as a function of the luminance and area of the conditioning stimuli and, in the case of noncontiguous stimuli, the separation of the test and conditioning stimuli. The temporal relationship between the exposures of the test stimulus and the conditioning stimuli is an important variable which is discussed in Chapter 6 of this volume.

The discussion of spatial interactions is divided into two parts. The first examines the effects of specific independent variables; the second discusses general theoretical concepts which bear upon a variety of contrast phenomena.

A. Effects of Specific Independent Variables

1. Test Stimulus Variables

a. Size of test stimulus. The luminance threshold (least flux per unit area required for detection) varies with the size of the test stimulus, being lower for large stimuli than for small ones. This dependence is known as areal summation or spatial summation. How much summation occurs depends upon the part of the retina involved, the duration of the stimulus, and the luminance of the background against which the test stimulus is exposed. There is less summation in the fovea than in the periphery (Gra-

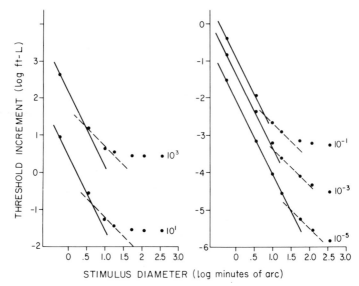

Fig. 5. Luminance threshold as a function of stimulus diameter. Background lumi-nance for each curve is indicated to right of curve in foot-lamberts. Solid lines represent Ricco's law, broken lines represent Piper's law. [Data from Blackwell (1946).]

ham, Brown, & Mote, 1939). Summation also decreases as the duration of the stimulus increases (Barlow, 1958) and as the luminance of the back-ground increases (Barlow, 1958; Blackwell, 1946). Figure 5 illustrates the variation in luminance threshold as a function of stimulus size for several background luminances. The exposure duration for these data was long (15 sec) and summation is therefore minimal. Subjects scanned the stimu-lus field, so viewing was probably parafoveal for the lowest backgrounds and foveal for the higher ones.

The suprathreshold brightness of a stimulus, in contrast to its visibility, is relatively independent of size (Diamond, 1962; Willmer, 1954). Only among stimuli less than 5 min in a diameter does brightness increase as a function of stimulus size.

Several empirical laws of areal summation have been proposed, but each holds over only a limited range of conditions. Ricco's law states that area and threshold luminance are inversely proportional, i.e., that detection is determined by the total flux presented. This relationship is represented by solid lines in Fig. 5; it holds only for small stimuli. The angular subtense of the largest stimulus for which Ricco's law holds is called the critical angle. Beyond the critical angle, threshold luminance decreases more slowly than Ricco's law requires (and total flux increases). As shown in Fig. 5, the critical angle decreases as background luminance increases. The critical angle is also smaller for long stimulus durations than for short ones (Barlow, 1958) and smaller in the fovea than in the periphery (Graham *et al.,* 1939).

Piper's law states that threshold luminance is inversely proportional to the square root of stimulus area. Piper's law is represented by the broken lines in Fig. 5. Piéron (1929) suggested a more general law: Threshold luminance is inversely proportional to the nth power of stimulus area, where $n \leq 1.0$. However, even this formulation holds over only limited ranges (Barlow, 1958; Graham *et al.,* 1939).

Theoretical discussion of areal summation has centered on two questions. The first is the role of quantal fluctuations. The number of quanta the receptors absorb from the background is inherently variable and the test stimulus, if it is to be reliably detected, must produce a number of quantal absorptions that is large relative to any variations in the background absorptions. Consideration of the laws of probability governing quantal absorptions leads to the prediction that, if detection is limited only by quantal fluctuations, the average number of quanta absorbed at threshold will increase as the square root of test stimulus area and duration and of background luminance (Barlow, 1957; DeVries, 1943; Rose, 1948). The prediction does not hold with any generality (Barlow, 1958), indicating that other factors are also involved.

The second question concerns the role of neural summation. Areal summation has been widely supposed to involve spatial summation within receptive fields (Blackwell, 1963; Glezer, 1965; Graham *et al.,* 1939). The simplest interpretation takes areal summation as a direct manifestation of spatial summation within a single receptive field (Blackwell, 1963; Graham *et al.,* 1939). However, mammalian receptive fields generally have antagonistic surrounds, with the consequence that large stimuli are less effective in stimulating them than are stimuli of intermediate size (Wiesel, 1960). Psychophysical studies, on the other hand, show no corresponding reduction in sensitivity to large stimuli. Furthermore, when areal summation is investigated psychophysically by adding spots of light to test stimuli of different sizes, the pattern of spatial summation is found to vary with stimulus size (Bagrash, Kerr, & Thomas, 1971; Thomas, Padilla, & Rourke, 1969). That is, the increase in visibility produced by adding a fixed amount of light to the central region of the test stimulus is not fixed, but is smaller when the test stimulus is large than when it is small. These facts led Thomas (1970) to suggest that detection of stimuli of different sizes is mediated by receptive fields of different sizes and that areal summation cannot be interpreted as reflecting the characteristics of a single receptive field.

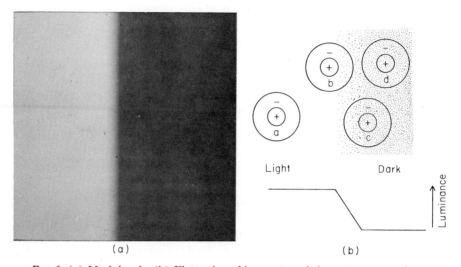

(a)   (b)

Fig. 6. (a) Mach bands. (b) Illustration of how antagonistic center–surround receptive fields might account for Mach bands. The antagonistic areas of fields *a* and
d are equally illuminated and a minimal response would be expected. In fields *b*
and *c*, the antagonistic areas are unequally illuminated and *b* would be expected
to give a greater positive response than *a*, and *c* would be expected to give a greater
negative response than *d*.

b. SHARPNESS OF TEST STIMULUS CONTOURS. Perception of the test
stimulus is influenced in several ways by the sharpness of its contours,
i.e., how well they approximate luminance steps. One consequence of
blurred or otherwise degraded contours is the appearance of Mach bands
(Mach, 1914), which are illustrated in Fig. 6a. Degrading the edges also
reduces the brightness of the stimulus (Enoch, 1958; Hood & Whiteside,
1968; Thomas & Kovar, 1965); the reduction is less in the bright Mach
bands than in other parts of the stimulus (Thomas, 1966). Finally, degrading the contours raises the detection threshold and makes the stimulus
appear somewhat larger (Thomas & Kerr, 1969).

Mach bands have received much attention. Ratliff (1965) has reviewed
the psychophysical and physiological findings and a number of theoretical
models. The bands are often attributed to the action of antagonistic center–
surround receptive fields. As is illustrated in Fig. 6b, such units might respond more vigorously to the edges of the luminance gradient than to other
parts of the display. One difficulty with this type of explanation is that
it requires the Mach bands to be more prominent at luminance steps than
at blurred edges or finite gradients, i.e., that the difference in brightness
(or darkness) between the bands and other parts of the stimulus be greatest

when the edge is a step. Empirically, however, finite gradients have been found to yield greater differences (Thomas, 1966).

2. EFFECTS OF CONDITIONING STIMULUS VARIABLES

a. BACKGROUND STIMULI. Superimposing the test stimulus on an illuminated background raises the luminance threshold. The magnitude of the rise increases with the luminance of the background, but also depends upon certain spatial relationships.

One spatial variable is the size of the background. In the case of a small test stimulus superimposed on the center of the background, the threshold for the test stimulus first rises and then falls as the area of the background is increased. The reduction in threshold for large backgrounds has been called sensitization (Westheimer, 1968). Westheimer (1967) found that for a 1-min test spot, viewed foveally, the greatest threshold elevation was produced by a background 5 min in diameter. The diameter yielding the highest threshold is larger if the stimuli are viewed peripherally (Westheimer, 1967) and is still larger, as much as 1 deg, at scotopic levels of illumination (Teller & Lindsey, 1970; Westheimer, 1965). The phenomenon is more marked at high background luminances than at low ones and is reduced if the background is exposed for only 10 msec (Westheimer, 1967). In the case of larger test stimuli, the threshold falls as the background becomes substantially larger than the test stimulus (Battersby & Wagman, 1964; Frumkes & Sturr, 1968; Ratoosh & Graham, 1951).

Another spatial variable is the location of the test stimulus with respect to the edges of the background. The increment threshold for a small test spot superimposed on a bright background is higher when the test spot is located just within the edge of the bright area than when the spot falls more toward the center of the background, even though the luminance of the background is the same at both locations (Fiorentini & Zoli, 1966; Kruger & Boname, 1955; Matthews, 1966). An analogous elevation of threshold is seen at the bright edge of a finite luminance gradient (Fiorentini, Jeanne, & Toraldo di Francia, 1955) and at the edges of a dark bar in the background (Novak & Sperling, 1963; Novak, 1969). These edge effects are most pronounced when the background containing the edge or gradient is exposed continuously. The effect is reduced when the edge is exposed for less than 500 msec and may be absent for exposures less than 10 msec (Matthews, 1966; Novak & Sperling, 1963).

Matthews (1971) and Thomas (1970) suggested that a common neural mechanism mediates both the sensitization and the edge phenomena just described. They suggested that detection of a small test stimulus is mediated by a pathway having a receptive field divided into antagonistic center and surround regions. The threshold for the test stimulus depends upon the activity that the background stimulus elicits in this pathway, increasing as the activity produced by the background increases. Thus, threshold is highest for those stimulus configurations in which the background most effectively stimulates the receptive field which mediates detection of the test stimulus. For a background disk concentric with the test stimulus, the most effective background is one of intermediate width, i.e., just large enough to illuminate the entire center region of the receptive field without illuminating the antagonistic surround. Large backgrounds most effectively stimulate receptive fields located adjacent to the background contours, because only a part of the antagonistic surround of each field is illuminated (see Fig. 6b). Thus, in the case of large backgrounds, threshold is highest when the test stimulus is superimposed near a border. Matthews (1971) examined spatial and temporal parameters of the two types of phenomena and found agreement which supports the suggestion of a common mechanism. He argued that the neural interactions which produce the phenomena require several hundred milliseconds to develop fully, hence the reduction or absence of the effects when background stimuli are flashed. However, such reductions would also occur if the effects depended upon eye movements. At present, there is not sufficient evidence to reject the latter interpretation, especially in the case of edge-effects.

b. INDUCING STIMULI. The appearance of the test stimulus is affected not only by its own physical properties and those of the background upon which it is superimposed, but also by other stimuli present in the visual field. The effect of a second, or inducing, stimulus depends upon the latter's luminance, size, and distance from the test stimulus.

Figure 7 shows the results of a study in which the luminance and distance of the inducing stimulus were varied (Leibowitz, Mote, & Thurlow, 1953). The test and inducing stimuli were seen by the right eye and the standard stimulus was seen by the left eye. Such binocular presentation is often used to minimize the effect of the inducing stimulus upon the standard. The luminance of the standard was constant and the subject adjusted the luminance of the test stimulus until the two stimuli were perceived as equally bright. Each curve in Fig. 7 shows the required test luminance as a function of the inducing luminance. The different curves are for different separations of the nearest edges of the test and inducing stimuli. The inducing stimulus exerts little effect until its luminance approximates that of the test stimulus. Above that point, as the inducing luminance increases, the test stimulus must be made more and more intense to match the brightness of the standard, indicating that the presence of the inducing stimulus dims the test stimulus. The rate of increase decreases with separation of the test and inducing stimuli up to a separation of 30 min, but is essentially constant for all greater separations.

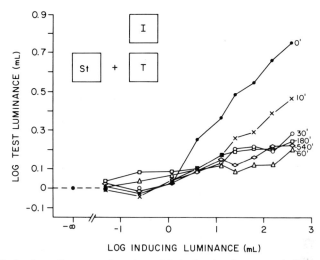

FIG. 7. Induction effect as a function of inducing luminance and distance between test (T) and inducing (I) fields. Distance for each curve is given in minutes of visual angle at right. Luminance of standard (St) was 1 mL. Each field was 30 min square. [Data from Leibowitz *et al.* (1953).]

Induction effects exhibit spatial summation. Up to a point, which depends on inducing luminance, the greater the area of the inducing stimulus, the more the test stimulus dims (Diamond, 1955). Similarly, increasing the number of inducing stimuli of a given size increases the induction effect. However, studies using multiple inducing stimuli have found summation to be nonlinear (Alpern & David, 1959; Thomas, 1963). That is, the total induction effect is not the linear sum of the individual effects produced by exposing the inducing stimuli one at a time.

Large induction effects are obtained when the inducing stimulus completely surrounds the test stimulus. Figure 8 shows results obtained by Heinemann (1955) using a 28-min test stimulus surrounded by an inducing annulus. In this experiment, the luminance of the test stimulus was constant and the subject adjusted the luminance of a comparison stimulus, seen by the other eye, to obtain the brightness match. As the inducing luminance increases, the test stimulus brightens slightly and then dims precipitously. As in the Leibowitz *et al.* (1953) study, the induced darkening begins as the inducing luminance approaches the test luminance. Once begun, the darkening increases rapidly and soon becomes unmeasurable, i.e., the test stimulus appears darker than the comparison stimulus can be made to appear, even if extinguished. In order to carry the measurements further, Heinemann surrounded the comparison field with its own inducing annulus.

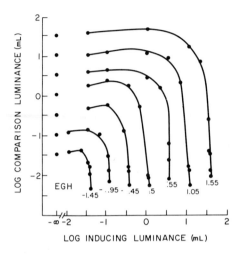

FIG. 8. Effect of inducing annulus. Subject adjusted comparison stimulus to match brightness of fixed test stimulus as luminance of annulus varied. Each curve is for a different test luminance, shown at foot of curve. [Data from Heinemann (1955).]

Heinemann's stimuli were at photopic and mesopic levels of illumination. Hollins (1971) obtained analogous results for purely scotopic vision.

Thomas (1968) investigated the variables of inducing luminance, area, and placement using low contrast stimuli superimposed on a photopic background. The test stimulus was a narrow line, 5 min wide by 9 deg high, which was viewed centrally and which was either more intense than its surround (bright test line) or less intense than its surround (dark test line). Inducing stimuli were introduced on both sides of the test line and their brightening or dimming effects measured by determining (a) the change in the luminance of the bright test line required to restore a brightness match with a standard bright line; or (b) the change in the luminance of the surround of the dark test line required to restore a match with a standard dark line. Figure 9 shows the effect of separating the test and inducing stimuli while inducing luminance is held constant. The ordinate shows the relative brightening (positive) or dimming (negative) effect produced by illuminating a unit area at the distance from the test stimulus, which is shown on the abscissa. More than one inducing stimulus was exposed at once and the two sets of points for each test line were obtained by using different combinations of inducing stimuli. The differences between corresponding points reflect the extent to which the effect of illuminating a given inducing area depends upon what other areas are also illuminated. Despite the scatter, there is general pattern that illumination in the test area or within a few minutes of it brightens the test stimulus; whereas more distant illumination darkens the test stimulus, the effect decreasing with distance from the test stimulus.

Patterns of spatial interaction analogous to that shown in Fig. 9 have been observed by Fiorentini and Mazzantini (1966) and, in scotopic

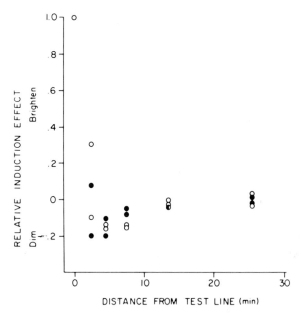

FIG. 9. Effect upon the brightness of test line of an inducing stimulus of unit area as a function of distance between the center of the test stimulus and center of the inducing stimulus: (○) bright test line; (●) dark test line. More than one inducing stimulus was exposed at once, and the two sets of points for each test line were obtained using different combinations of inducing stimuli. [Data from Thomas (1968).]

vision, by Fiorentini and Maffei (1968). Their measure of interaction was the change in the increment threshold for a small test spot. Fiorentini and Mazzantini found positive interactions (reduction of threshold) only when the contrast of the inducing stimulus was low.

c. MASKING AND ADAPTATION STIMULI. In masking experiments, the test stimulus is exposed briefly and its presence must be detected against the masking effects of a second briefly exposed stimulus. The effect of the masking stimulus is to raise the threshold for the test stimulus. The magnitude of the effect depends mainly upon the luminance of the masking stimulus and the temporal relationship between the two stimuli (see Chapter 6). However, the magnitude is also affected by the spatial relationships between the test and masking stimuli. If the test stimulus is a single line and the masking stimulus is another line (Parlee, 1969) or a grating (Sekuler, 1965), a large masking effect occurs only if the test and masking lines are parallel or nearly parallel. The same dependency is found if both test and masking stimuli are gratings (Campbell & Kulikowski, 1966). When the test and masking stimuli are disks of light, masking disks which approximate the size of the test disk produce greater effects than do larger masking stimuli (Battersby & Wagman, 1964; Frumkes & Sturr, 1968).

Analogous spatial dependencies occur when the conditioning stimulus is used to adapt the visual system prior to presentation of the test stimulus. That is, adaptation is greatest when the adapting and test stimuli have the same orientation (Fidell, 1970; Gilinsky, 1968; McCollough, 1965), have the same spatial frequency (Blakemore & Campbell, 1969), or are the same size (Bagrash, 1973; Kerr & Thomas, 1972).

B. General Considerations

Three mechanisms must be considered in interpreting the phenomena of spatial interaction: stray light, eye movements, and neural interaction.

1. STRAY LIGHT

The distribution of light in the retinal image differs from that in the distal display, for several reasons. The accuracy of image formation is limited by diffraction, aberrations in the eye's lens system, and scattering by the media of the eye. Furthermore, a small amount of light from the retinal image is reflected from and then scattered back over the retina. Thus, an inducing stimulus may alter the perception of the test stimulus because the presence of the inducing stimulus alters the retinal distribution of light within the test area. The optical mechanism is obviously important when the test stimulus is small and placed near inducing edges. If the inducing luminance is high, the mechanism is important even if the test and inducing stimuli are large and far apart. The loss in brightness or visibility produced by a remote inducing stimulus is equivalent in several ways to the loss produced by superimposing a faint veiling illumination on the test stimulus (Boynton, Bush, & Enoch, 1954; Fry & Alpern, 1953). Thus light scattered from the inducing stimulus appears to mediate such remote effects.

2. EYE MOVEMENTS

There is often the possibility that perception of the test stimulus is altered because eye movements image the stimulus on an area of the retina that has been previously illuminated, and altered in sensitivity, by other parts of the visual display. To assess this possibility, several interaction phenomena have been studied with stabilization of the retinal image, which eliminates the effects of eye movements. Mach bands are perceived in stabilized images (Riggs, Ratliff, & Keesey, 1961) and, thus, do not depend upon eye movements. The greater masking effects of intermediate backgrounds, as compared to large backgrounds (Westheimer, 1965, 1967), have also been observed under stabilization (Teller, Andrews, & Barlow, 1966). On the other hand, Teller (1968) investigated increment thresholds for a 2-min scotopic test spot when it was superimposed on black bars of various widths, and obtained different results with normal and stabilized viewing. In the normal case, the threshold first rose and then fell as bar width increased; in the stabilized case, the initial rise was absent. Thus, eye movements do play a role in some interaction phenomena.

3. NEURAL INTERACTION

Most theoretical speculation is directed toward neural mechanisms. The basic concept is the receptive field (Hartline, 1938; Sherrington, 1906): the portion of the retina, or visual field, in which illumination influences activity in the neural cell or pathway of interest. If the inducing stimulus falls within the receptive fields of pathways which mediate perception of the test stimulus, the neural signal and, hence, the perception is altered. Receptive fields in vertebrate visual systems are often divided into two or more parts that are antagonistic in the sense that illuminating one part tends to negate the effects of illuminating the other part (Barlow, 1953; Hubel & Wiesel, 1962; Kuffler, 1953). Within each part, however, there is spatial summation, i.e., the larger the area illuminated, the greater the effect for a given luminance. There is an obvious analogy between these neural interactions and the psychophysically defined negative and positive spatial interactions described earlier.

A receptive field arrangement which is commonly found in the retina and lateral geniculate body consists of a more or less oval or circular central area surrounded by an annular antagonistic area. Most theoretical speculation has dwelt on this type of receptive field (Békésy, 1960; Glezer, 1965; Matthews, 1971; Sperling, 1970; Thomas, 1970). The spatial frequency response of such a cell has the bandpass characteristic (higher sensitivity to middle frequencies than to either lower or higher ones) which is implied by the psychophysical results on contrast sensitivity described in the first half of this chapter (Enroth-Cugell & Robson, 1966). Thus, the antagonistic center–surround receptive field provides a common concept for the interpretation of data on both resolution and spatial interaction.

Specific application of the receptive field concept to psychophysical data requires additional assumptions about neural mechanisms. Where the psychophysical task is detection of a small test spot, it has been widely assumed that detection is mediated by the neural path whose center–surround receptive field is most nearly centered on the test spot. Using this assumption, Matthews (1971) and Thomas (1970) developed the explanation of edge effects and sensitization phenomena that was described in Section II.2a. In a different vein, Fiorentini and Maffei have shown parallels between the effect of a thin inducing annulus on the perception of a small test stimulus and the effect of such an annulus on activity in a cat ganglion cell with center–surround receptive field (Fiorentini & Maffei, 1968; Maffei, 1968).

Other types of test stimuli involve more extensive assumptions. Speculation has developed along two lines: a neural image approach and a detector approach. In the neural image approach, it is assumed that the spatial pattern of activity produced in the receptor mosaic by the retinal image is transmitted to some more central neural mosaic, where variations in neural activity produce a spatial analog of the retinal image. Because the neurons which transmit the image have center–surround receptive fields, the image is distorted. In terms of spatial frequency content, high- and low-frequency components are attenuated relative to intermediate frequency components. The central image is assumed to be processed according to specified detection rules (Kornfeld & Lawson, 1971; Sperling, 1970) or is simply assumed to be isomorphic with the perceived intensity distribution (Békésy, 1960; Cornsweet, 1970; Davidson & Whiteside, 1971; Ratliff, 1965). In either case, the interactions that are observed psychophysically are taken as a reflection of the distortion of the neural image produced by the action of the center–surround receptive fields. Appropriate analysis of the psychophysical data yields estimates of the characteristics of the receptive field, and such estimates have been obtained from data on (a) areal summation (Blackwell, 1963; Glezer, 1965), (b) Mach bands (Békésy, 1960; Lowry & DePalma, 1961; Thomas, 1965, 1966), (c) grating resolution (Bryngdahl, 1966; DePalma & Lowry, 1962; Patel, 1966), and (d) various patterns of grids and bars (Spillman, 1971). If the same neural mosaic and receptive fields mediate perception of all such stimuli, then these various estimates should agree. Empirically, however, the degree of agreement is equivocal and certain results are clearly inconsistent with the supposition of a single mosaic. For example, analysis of areal summation data yields a receptive field that has no antagonistic surround (Blackwell, 1963), whereas other data lead to the conclusion that there is such a surround; and Thomas, Rourke, and Wilder (1968) found that the receptive field characteristics that accounted for the visibility of a narrow test line could not account for the visibility of the larger inducing fields adjacent to the test line. Data on the resolution of gratings containing more than one spatial frequency are also inconsistent with the single mosaic hypothesis (Graham & Nachmias, 1971; Sachs, Nachmias, & Robson, 1971).

The detector approach emphasizes that the receptive field makes a neuron more sensitive to some stimuli than to others. Since the size and configuration of the receptive field varies from one neuron to another, particularly at the cortical level (Hubel & Wiesel, 1962, 1965, 1968), different neurons are sensitive to different stimuli. Thus, each neuron could function as a detector, signaling, by its activity, the presence of the stimulus or stimuli to which it is tuned. Thomas (1970) developed a model for the case of center–surround receptive fields of different sizes functioning as size detectors and applied the model to data on detection and apparent size. The concept of variously tuned spatial frequency filters (Blakemore & Campbell, 1969; Campbell & Robson, 1968; Graham & Nachmias, 1971; Sachs *et al.*, 1971) is closely related to the detector approach, although the frequency filters function to signal the presence of certain frequency components rather than the presence of certain stimulus objects.

The neural image and detector approaches lead to different interpretations of psychophysical data. Nevertheless, the two are not necessarily mutually exclusive. Rather, they can be thought of as representing neural processing at different levels of the visual system: the neural image approach representing more peripheral parts of the visual system, where there is greater similarity among receptive fields; and the detector approach representing more central levels, where there is greater diversity among receptive fields.

References

Alpern, M., & David, H. The additivity of contrast in the human eye. *Journal of General Physiology,* 1959, **43**, 109–126.

Bagrash, F. M. Size-selective adaptation: Psychophysical evidence for size-tuning and the effects of stimulus contour and adapting flux. *Vision Research,* 1973, **13**, 575–598.

Bagrash, F. M., Kerr, L. G., & Thomas, J. P. Patterns of spatial integration in the detection of compound visual stimuli. *Vision Research,* 1971, **11**, 635–645.

Baker, K. E. Some variables influencing vernier acuity. I. Illumination and exposure time. II. Wavelength of illumination. *Journal of the Optical Society of America,* 1949, **39**, 567–576.

Barlow, H. B. Summation and inhibition in the frog's retina. *Journal of Physiology,* 1953, **119**, 69–88.

Barlow, H. B. Increment thresholds at low intensities considered as signal/noise discriminations. *Journal of Physiology,* 1957, **136**, 469–488.

Barlow, H. B. Temporal and spatial summation in human vision at different background intensities. *Journal of Physiology,* 1958, **141**, 337–350.

Barlow, H. B., Fitzhugh, R., & Kuffler, S. W. Change of organization in the receptive fields of the cat's retina during dark adaptation. *Journal of Physiology,* 1957, **137**, 338–354.

Battersby, W. S., & Wagman, I. H. Light adaptation kinetics: The influence of spatial factors. *Science,* 1964, **143**, 1029–1031.

Beitel, R. J. Inhibition of threshold excitation in the human eye. *Journal of General Psychol.,* 1936, **14**, 31–61.

Békésy, G. Neural inhibitory units of the eye and skin. Quantitative description of contrast phenomena. *Journal of the Optical Society of America,* 1960, **50**, 1060–1070.

Berry, R. N. Quantitative relations among vernier, real depth, and stereoscopic depth acuities. *Journal of Experimental Psychology,* 1948, **38**, 708–721.

Blackwell, H. R. Contrast thresholds of the human eye. *Journal of the Optical Society of America,* 1946, **36,** 624–643.

Blackwell, H. R. Neural theories of simple visual discriminations. *Journal of the Optical Society of America,* 1963, **53,** 129–160.

Blakemore, C., & Campbell, F. W. On the existence of neurons in the human visual system selectively sensitive to the orientation and size of retinal images. *Journal of Physiology,* 1969, **203,** 237–260.

Boynton, R. M., Bush, W. R., & Enoch, J. M. Rapid changes in foveal sensitivity resulting from direct and indirect adapting stimuli. *Journal of the Optical Society of America,* 1954, **44,** 56–60.

Brown, J. L., Phares, L., & Fletcher, D. E. Spectral energy thresholds for the resolution of acuity targets. *Journal of the Optical Society of America,* 1960, **50,** 950–960.

Bryngdahl, O. Perceived contrast variation with eccentricity of spatial sine-wave stimuli. Size determination of receptive field centres. *Vision Research,* 1966, **6,** 553–565.

Campbell, F. W., Cooper, G. F., & Enroth-Cugell, C. The spatial selectivity of visual cells of the cat. *Journal of Physiology,* 1969, **203,** 223–235.

Campbell, F. W., & Green, D. G. Optical and retinal factors affecting visual resolution. *Journal of Physiology,* 1965, **181,** 576–593.

Campbell, F. W., & Gubisch, R. W. Optical quality of the human eye. *Journal of Physiology,* 1966, **186,** 558–578.

Campbell, F. W., Kulikowski, J. J., & Levinson, J. The effect of orientation on the visual resolution of gratings. *Journal of Physiology,* 1966, **187,** 427–436.

Campbell, F. W., & Robson, J. G. Application of fourier analysis to the visibility of gratings. *Journal of Physiology,* 1968, **197,** 551–566.

Cobb, P. W. The influence of pupillary diameter on visual acuity. *American Journal of Physiology,* 1915, **36,** 335–346.

Cornsweet, T. N. *Visual perception.* New York: Academic Press, 1970.

Craik, K. J. W. The effect of adaptation upon visual acuity. *British Journal of Psychology,* 1939, **29,** 252–266.

Daitch, J. M., & Green, D. G. Contrast sensitivity of the human peripheral retina. *Vision Research,* 1969, **9,** 947–952.

Davidson, M., & Whiteside, J. A. Human brightness perception near sharp contours. *Journal of the Optical Society of America,* 1971, **61,** 530–536.

DePalma, J. J., & Lowry, E. M. Sine-wave response of the visual system. II. Sine-wave and square-wave contrast sensitivity. *Journal of the Optical Society of America,* 1962, **52,** 328–335.

DeVries, H. The quantum character of light and its bearing upon the threshold of vision, the differential sensitivity and acuity of the eye. *Physica,* 1943, **10,** 553–564.

Diamond, A. L. Foveal simultaneous contrast as a function of inducing-field area. *Journal of Experimental Psychology,* 1955, **50,** 144–152.

Diamond, A. L. Brightness of a field as a function of its area. *Journal of the Optical Society of America,* 1962, **52,** 700–706.

Enoch, J. M. Summated response of the retina to light entering different parts of the pupil. *Journal of the Optical Society of America,* 1958, **48,** 392–405.

Enroth-Cugell, C., & Robson, J. G. The contrast sensitivity of retinal ganglion cells of the cat. *Journal of Physiology,* 1966, **187,** 517–552.

Fidell, L. S. Orientation specificity in chromatic adaptation of human "edge-detectors." *Perception & Psychophysics,* 1970, **8,** 235–237.

Fiorentini, A., Jeanne, M., & Toraldo di Francia, G. Measures photometriques visuelles sur un champ à gradient d'éclairement variable. *Optica Acta,* 1955, **1,** 192–193.

Fiorentini, A., & Maffei, L. Perceptual correlates of inhibitory and facilitatory spatial interactions in the visual system. *Vision Research,* 1968, **8,** 1195–1203.

Fiorentini, A., & Mazzantini, L. Neural inhibition in the human fovea: A study of interactions between two line stimuli. *Atti della Fondazione Giorgio Ronchi,* 1966, **21,** 738–747.

Fiorentini, A., & Zoli, M. T. Detection of a target superimposed to a step pattern of illumination. *Atti Fondazione Giorgio Ronchi,* 1966, **21,** 338–356.

Frumkes, T. E., & Sturr, J. F. Spatial and luminance factors determining visual excitability. *Journal of the Optical Society of America,* 1968, **58,** 1657–1662.

Fry, G. A., & Alpern, M. The effect of a peripheral glare source upon the apparent brightness of an object. *Journal of the Optical Society of America,* 1953, **43,** 189–195.

Gilinsky, A. S. Orientation-specific effects of patterns of adapting light on visual acuity. *Journal of the Optical Society of America,* 1968, **58,** 13–18.

Glezer, V. D. The receptive fields of the retina. *Vision Research,* 1965, **5,** 497–525.

Graham, C. H., Brown, R. H., & Mote, F. A. The relation of size of stimulus and intensity in the human eye. I. Intensity thresholds for white light. *Journal of Experimental Psychology,* 1939, **24,** 555–573.

Graham, N., & Nachmias, J. Detection of grating patterns containing two spatial frequencies: A comparison of single-channel and multiple-channels models. *Vision Research,* 1971, **11,** 251–259.

Hartline, H. K. The response of single optic nerve fibers of the vertebrate eye to illumination of the retina. *American Journal of Physiology,* 1938, **121,** 400–415.

Hecht, S. The relation between visual acuity and illumination. *Journal of General Physiology,* 1928, **11,** 255–281.

Hecht, S. Brightness, visual acuity and colour blindness. *Documenta Ophthalmologica,* 1949, **3,** 289–306.

Hecht, S., & Mintz, E. U. The visibility of single lines at various illuminations and the retinal basis of visual resolution. *Journal of General Physiology,* 1939, **22,** 593–612.

Heinemann, E. G. Simultaneous brightness induction as a function of inducing- and test-field luminances. *Journal of Experimental Psychology,* 1955, **50,** 89–96.

Higgins, G. C., & Stultz, K. Visual acuity as measured with various orientations of a parallel-line object. *Journal of the Optical Society of America,* 1948, **38,** 756–758.

Hollins, M. Brightness contrast at low luminances. *Vision Research,* 1971, **11,** 1459–1472.

Hood, D. C., & Whiteside, J. A. Brightness of ramp stimuli as a function of plateau and gradient widths. *Journal of the Optical Society of America,* 1968, **58,** 1310–1311.

Hubel, D. H., & Wiesel, T. N. Receptive fields, binocular interaction and functional architecture in the cat's striate cortex. *Journal of Physiology,* 1962, **160,** 106–154.

Hubel, D. H., & Wiesel, T. N. Receptive fields and functional architecture in two nonstriate visual areas (18 and 19) of the cat. *Journal of Neurophysiology,* 1965, **28,** 229–289.

Hubel, D. H., & Wiesel, T. N. Receptive fields and functional architecture of monkey striate cortex. *Journal of Physiology,* 1968, **195,** 215–243.

Jacobs, G. H., & Yolton, R. L. Center–surround balance in receptive fields of cells in the lateral geniculate nucleus. *Vision Research,* 1970, **10,** 1127–1144.

Kerr, L. G., & Thomas, J. P. Effect of selective adaptation on detection of simple and compound parafoveal stimuli. *Vision Research,* 1972, **12,** 1367–1379.

Kornfeld, G. H., & Lawson, W. R. Visual perception models. *Journal of the Optical Society of America,* 1971, **61,** 811–820.

Krauskopf, J. Light distribution in human retinal images. *Journal of the Optical Society of America,* 1962, **52,** 1046–1050.

Kruger, L., & Boname, J. R. A retinal excitation gradient in a uniform area of stimulation. *Journal of Experimental Psychology,* 1955, **49,** 220–224.

Kuffler, S. W. Discharge patterns and functional organization of mammalian retina. *Journal of Neurophysiology,* 1953, **16,** 37–68.

Leibowitz, H. The effect of pupil size on visual acuity for photometrically equated test fields at various levels of luminance. *Journal of the Optical Society of America,* 1952, **42,** 416–422.

Leibowitz, H., Mote, F. A., & Thurlow, W. R. Simultaneous contrast as a function of separation between test and inducing fields. *Journal of Experimental Psychology,* 1953, **46,** 453–456.

Lowry, E. M., & DePalma, J. J. Sine-wave response of the visual system. I. The Mach phenomenon. *Journal of the Optical Society of America,* 1961, **51,** 740–746.

Ludvigh, E. Extrafoveal visual acuity as measured with Snellen test-letters. *American Journal of Ophthalmology,* 1941, **24,** 303–310.

Lythgoe, R. J. The measurement of visual acuity. *Medical Research Council, Special Reports Series, No. 173 (Report of Committee upon the Physiology of Vision, No. X).* London: Her Majesty's Stationery Office, 1932.

Mach, E. *The analysis of sensations and the relation of the physical to the psychical.* Chicago and London: Open Court, 1914.

Maffei, L. Inhibitory and facilitatory spatial interactions in retinal receptive fields. *Vision Research,* 1968, **8,** 1187–1194.

Maffei, L., & Campbell, F. W. Neurophysiological localization of the vertical and horizontal visual coordinates in man. *Science,* 1970, **167,** 386–387.

Maffei, L., & Fiorentini, A. The visual cortex as a spatial frequency analyser. *Vision Research,* 1973, **13,** 1255–1267.

Mandelbaum, J., & Sloan, L. L. Peripheral visual acuity. *American Journal of Ophthalmology,* 1947, **30,** 581–588.

Matthews, M. L. Appearance of Mach bands for short durations and at sharply focused contours. *Journal of the Optical Society of America,* 1966, **56,** 1401–1402.

Matthews, M. L. Spatial and temporal factors in masking by edges and disks. *Perception & Psychophysics,* 1971, **9,** 15–22.

McCollough, C. Color adaptation of edge-detectors in the human visual system. *Science,* 1965, **149,** 1115–1116.

Miller, N. D. Variation of resolving power of the retina with distance from the foveal center. *Journal of the Optical Society of America,* 1961, **51,** 1462A.

Mitchell, D. E., Freeman, R. D., & Westheimer, G. Effect of orientation on the modulation sensitivity for interference fringes on the retina. *Journal of the Optical Society of America,* 1967, **57,** 246–249.

Novak, S. Comparison of increment and decrement thresholds near a light-dark boundary. *Journal of the Optical Society of America,* 1969, **59,** 1383–1384.

Novak, S., & Sperling, G. Visual thresholds near a continuously visible or a briefly presented light–dark boundary. *Optica Acta,* 1963, **10,** 187–191.

Ogilvie, J. C., & Taylor, M. M. Effect of orientation on the visibility of fine wires. *Journal of the Optical Society of America,* 1958, **48,** 628–629.

Parlee, M. B. Visual backward masking of a single line by a single line. *Vision Research,* 1969, **9,** 199–205.

Patel, A. S. Spatial resolution by the human visual system. The effect of mean retinal illuminance. *Journal of the Optical Society of America,* 1966, **56,** 689–694.

Piéron, H. De la sommation spatiale des impressions lumineuses au niveau de la fovea. *Annú Psychologique,* 1929, **30,** 87–105.

Pirenne, M. H. *Vision and the eye.* London: Science Paperbacks, 1967.

Pirenne, M. H., & Denton, E. J. Accuracy and sensitivity of the human eye. *Nature,* 1952, **170,** 1039–1042.

Pokorny, J. The effect of target area on grating acuity. *Vision Research,* 1968, **8,** 543–554.

Ratliff, F. *Mach bands: Quantitative studies on neural networks in the retina.* San Francisco: Holden-Day, 1965.

Ratoosh, P., & Graham, C. H. Areal effects in foveal brightness discrimination. *Journal of Experimental Psychology,* 1951, **42,** 367–375.

Riggs, L. A. Visual acuity. In C. H. Graham (Ed.), *Vision and visual perception.* New York: Wiley, 1965.

Riggs, L. A., Ratliff, F., & Keesey, U. T. Appearance of Mach bands with a motionless retinal image. *Journal of the Optical Society of America,* 1961, **51,** 702–703.

Rose, A. The sensitivity performance of the human eye on an absolute scale. *Journal of the Optical Society of America,* 1948, **38,** 196–208.

Sachs, M. B., Nachmias, J., & Robson, J. G. Spatial-frequency channels in human vision. *Journal of the Optical Society of America,* 1971, **61,** 1176–1186.

Schade, O. H. Optical and photoelectric analog of the eye. *Journal of the Optical Society of America,* 1956, **46,** 721–739.

Sekuler, R. W. Spatial and temporal determinants of visual backward masking. *Journal of Experimental Psychology,* 1965, **70,** 401–406.

Sherrington, C. *The integrative action of the nervous system.* New Haven, Connecticut: Yale Univ. Press, 1906.

Shlaer, S. The relation between visual acuity and illumination. *Journal of General Physiology,* 1937, **21,** 165–188.

Shlaer, S., Smith, E. C., & Chase, A. M. Visual acuity and illumination in different spectral regions. *Journal of General Physiology,* 1942, **25,** 553–569.

Sloan, L. L. Measurement of visual acuity. *Archives of Ophthalmology,* 1951, **45,** 704–725.

Sloan, L. L. The photopic acuity–luminance function with special reference to parafoveal vision. *Vision Research,* 1968, **8,** 901–911.

Sperling, G. Model of visual adaptation and contrast detection. *Perception & Psychophysics,* 1970, **8,** 143–157.

Spillmann, L. Foveal perceptive fields in the human visual system measured with simultaneous contrast in grids and bars. *Pflugers Archives,* 1971, **326,** 281–299.

Teller, D. Y. Increment thresholds on black bars. *Vision Research,* 1968, **8,** 713–718.

Teller, D. Y., Andrews, D. P., & Barlow, H. B. Local adaptation in stabilized vision, *Vision Research,* 1966, **6,** 701–705.

Teller, D. Y., & Lindsey, B. Sensitization by annular surrounds: Individual difference. *Vision Research,* 1970, **10,** 1045–1055.

Thomas, J. P. Relation of brightness contrast to inducing stimulus output. *Journal of the Optical Society of America,* 1963, **53,** 1033–1037.

Thomas, J. P. Threshold measurements of Mach bands. *Journal of the Optical Society of America,* 1965, **55,** 521–524.

Thomas, J. P. Brightness variations in stimuli with ramp-like contours. *Journal of the Optical Society of America,* 1966, **56,** 238–242.

Thomas, J. P. Linearity of spatial integrations involving inhibitory interactions. *Vision Research,* 1968, **8,** 49–60.

Thomas, J. P. Model of the function of receptive fields in human vision. *Psychological Review,* 1970, **77,** 121–134.

Thomas, J. P., & Kerr, L. G. Effect of ramp-like contours upon perceived size and detection threshold. *Perception & Psychophysics,* 1969, **5,** 381–384.

Thomas, J. P., & Kovar, C. W. The effect of contour sharpness on perceived brightness. *Vision Research,* 1965, **5,** 559–564.

Thomas, J. P., Padilla, G. J., & Rourke, D. L. Spatial interactions in identification and detection of compound visual stimuli. *Vision Research,* 1969, **9,** 283–292.

Thomas, J. P., Rourke, D. L., & Wilder, D. G. Inhibitory effect of less intense stimuli upon the increment threshold for a narrow test line. *Vision Research,* 1968, **8,** 537–542.

Watanabe, A., Mori, T., Nagata, S., & Hiwatashi, K. Spatial sine-wave responses of the human visual system. *Vision Research,* 1968, **8,** 1245–1263.

Westheimer, G. Optical and motor factors in the formation of the retinal image. *Journal of the Optical Society of America,* 1963, **53,** 86–93.

Westheimer, G. Pupil size and visual resolution. *Vision Research,* 1964, **4,** 39–45.

Westheimer, G. Spatial interaction in the human retina during scotopic vision. *Journal of Physiology,* 1965, **181,** 881–894.

Westheimer, G. Spatial interaction in human cone vision. *Journal of Physiology,* 1967, **190,** 139–154.

Westheimer, G. Bleached rhodopsin and retinal interaction. *Journal of Physiology,* 1968, **195,** 97–105.

Westheimer, G., & Campbell, F. W. Light distribution in the image formed by the living human eye. *Journal of the Optical Society of America,* 1962, **52,** 1040–1044.

Wiesel, T. N. Receptive fields of ganglion cells in the cat's retina. *Journal of Physiology,* 1960, **153,** 583–594.

Willmer, E. N. Subjective brightness and size of field in the central fovea. *Journal of Physiology,* 1954, **123,** 315–323.

Part IV

Pattern, Object, and Color

Chapter 8

PATTERN AND OBJECT PERCEPTION*

P. C. DODWELL

I. INTRODUCTION

Traditionally, the study of pattern perception has involved questions about figure and ground, the synthesis of "simple sensations" into "complex perceptions," perceptual learning and development, the nature of illusions and perceptual constancies, and the physiological substrata of all of these. To them we might add some topics that have more recently captured psychologists' interest, mainly under the heading of "information processing," such as the nature of short-term sensory memory, perceptual stability and clarity, and the nature of representation. These matters will be dealt with here chiefly in terms of human vision, although most of them also have manifestations in the other sense modalities and at other phylogenetic levels. Reviews and theoretical treatments of pattern and object recognition can be found in Dodwell (1970a, 1971), E. J. Gibson (1969), Uhr (1966), and Zusne (1970). The general relationship to cognitive psychol-

* Preparation of this chapter was supported in part by grants from the National Research Council of Canada (AOA44) and the Defence Research Board of Canada (DRB9425-12). This support is gratefully acknowledged, as is the able bibliographic assistance of Mrs. S. Smallman.

ogy is discussed, for example, by Lindsay and Norman (1971) and by Neisser (1967). Techniques for studying pattern perception have varied through the ages, starting perhaps with philosophical analyses of the nature of perception and knowledge (epistemology), and continuing through the experimental investigation of the physical nature of adequate stimulation, the physiological study of sensory systems, standard experimental psychological methods of inquiry down to the currently popular uses of computer simulation. The techniques vary, but the questions addressed remain remarkably persistent and in many cases somewhat intractable.

II. ORGANIZATION AND FORM

A. Figure and Ground

Consider the apparently simple question of discriminating a figure from its background: The phenomenon was brought to prominence by the Gestalt psychologists' insistence on it as a primary datum of perception (Koffka, 1935; Köhler, 1929) and has been the subject of a good deal of experimental investigation, particularly in regard to figural ambiguity (e.g., Rubin, 1921; Rock & Kremen, 1957), hidden or embedded figures (e.g., Gottschaldt, 1926; Witkin, Dyk, Faterson, Goodenough, & Karp, 1962) and the so-called Gestalt laws of organization (e.g., Kopferman, 1930; Hochberg & McAlister, 1953). There is no uniformly accepted interpretation of the nature of figural organization; although it is clear that set, motivation, and perceptual expectations play a role in many cases (see Section VII) there are also factors that are more in the nature of data-processing operations, as in the Julesz-type demonstrations of stereoptic form perception without monocular pattern cues. To show this contrast distinctly, Figs. 1 and 2 are presented. Figure 1 shows a typical ambiguous figure, although

Fig. 1. A typical ambiguous figure: Rat and professor compete for recognition. [Reproduced with permission from Bugelski, B. R., & Alampay, D. A. The role of frequency in developing perceptual sets. *Canadian Journal of Psychology,* 1961, **15**, 205–211.]

FIG. 2. A pair of random dot matrices. When fused binocularly as a stereogram a pattern emerges in depth to which no clue is obtained in the separate monocular images. [Reproduced with permission from Julesz, B. Binocular depth perception without familiarity cues. *Science,* 1964, **145,** 356–362. Copyright © 1964 by the American Association for the Advancement of Science.]

one not as familiar as Boring's famous "wife/mother-in-law" picture (Boring, 1930). With figures of this sort, it is hardly surprising that social and personal expectations should influence the way in which the picture is perceived. On the other hand, Fig. 2 (Julesz, 1964) shows a pair of random dot matrices which are a stereopair, now almost as familiar as the Boring picture, which, when fused, yield a striking effect: A square in the center of the fused array literally "pops out" in front of the reference plane in which the array is seen. Readers without stereovision or who cannot attain free stereoscopy must take the statement on trust: The phenomenon is very real. It is attained by arranging a phase shift between the central square area in one of the pair and the remainder of the two displays, which are otherwise identical. It is difficult to imagine that this form of stereoprocessing is due to anything but a built in disparity-detection system, which seems to be at the opposite pole, as a figure-organizing process, from whatever mediates the appearance and interpretation of pictures like Fig. 1.*

There are many arresting and subtle types of figural effects intermediate between these two extremes. One of the most interesting has been presented by Gregory (1972). Figure 3 shows marked illusory contours that occur at points quite far from the regions of sharp physical intensity difference. By removing parts of the figure, one can discover which features are needed to produce the effect, as for example, in Fig. 4. It appears that a sufficient—and perhaps necessary—condition to obtain the illusory contours

* Julesz has explored the possibilities of using random dot stereograms and similar materials for the analysis of pattern perception very thoroughly in *Foundations of Cyclopean Vision* (Julesz, 1971).

FIG. 3. An illusory shape induced by a configuration of pattern elements which, in themselves, do not explain the area of enhanced brightness. [Reproduced with permission from Gregory, R. L. Cognitive contours. *Nature,* 1972, **238,** 51–52.]

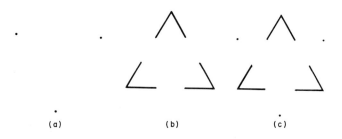

(a)   (b)   (c)

FIG. 4. Removal of certain features of the configuration of Fig. 3 (but not others) cause the disappearance of the illusory shape. [Reproduced with permission from Gregory, R. L. Cognitive contours. *Nature,* 1972, **238,** 51–52.]

is that the rest of the configuration suggest that another (probably rather simple) shape overlays it and thus blanks some parts of it. As Gregory points out, another possible explanation is that parts of the configuration (Fig. 3) weakly activate feature detectors for lines or edges at the physiological level, but it would be difficult then to explain why there is enhanced brightness over a large area within the hypothesized object. The former explanation seems more plausible, hence the term "cognitive contours" coined by him.

Another interesting example occurs when the density of points in a Julesz-type stereo display is much reduced (as in Fig. 5). In the display of Fig. 2 the in-depth contours of the inner square are not defined by continuous edges that share a common brightness gradient, but the density of the black squares tends to obscure this fact. As the density is reduced, it becomes obvious. Yet, when the density is very low the continuous in-depth central figure breaks down, and what is seen is just a set of isolated

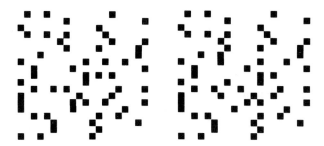

Fɪɢ. 5. A Julesz-type stereogram in which isolated points-in-depth can be observed, rather than the plane-in-depth of Fig. 2.

in-depth points. Here again is a true figural organizing process, which fails under some conditions. It might have a straightforward physiological basis, but perhaps depends on an interpretative leap beyond the immediately given sensory events.

B. Statistical Treatment

Attempts to deal with pattern organization from an information-theoretical point of view have been made by Attneave and his associates (Attneave, 1954, 1957; Attneave & Arnoult, 1956). Of particular interest was their attempt to show that figural "goodness" can be equated to a degree with the informational concept of redundancy (roughly, predictability). At one time—the late 1950s and early 1960s—it looked as if a methodology for constructing a "psychophysics of form," to use Attneave's phrase, was finally about to emerge. This line of work was developed by Garner (1962) in the search for an adequate definition of the concept of structure in psychology. So far as pattern recognition is concerned, one runs into the difficulty, which Garner recognized, of dealing with meaning as *structure,* and meaning as *signification.* In the latter case one is dealing with structure which is recognized as denoting an object in the real world. The amount of structure in the photographic negative of a face is the same as in the positive; yet recognizing the image as that of a face, and identifying whose face it is, is an entirely different matter from recognizing that both the negative and the positive have equal (physical) structure. In this sense, negative and positive are usually not at all equivalent. Thus information-theoretical concepts yield at best an ancillary set of operations for specifying and quantifying patterns. Unfortunately there is even confusion over the correct application of the concept of redundancy (Corcoran, 1971) and Garner (1970) also has recognized the limitation for applications of the theory inherent in the fact that human information *processing* (see Section VI) often requires a different definition of information than that which a straightforward application of information theory would specify.

C. Figural Completion and Synthesis

The informational analysis has also been challenged by Green and Courtis (1966) in an interesting way. Part of their argument hinges on technical inadequacies like those just referred to, but they also demonstrate that the useful features of a pattern which render it recognizable to the normal human observer are often distorted, exaggerated, seen by implication although not physically present, and generally are not quantifiable in the manner required for a statistical treatment of form perception. They illustrate this in a homely but effective way by referring to the work of cartoonists, and in particular to that of Haro Hodson, as illustrated in Fig. 6. These cartoons bear an obvious resemblance to the Gestalt completion figures (e.g., Street, 1931) that used to be popular, although, in the present case, the artist is intent on helping the perceiver rather than confusing him. In both cases, however, the observer has, in a clear sense, to "do the work" to complete the picture. The artistry consists in being able, in Green and Courtis's words, ". . . to convey a sense of spatial relationships in parts of the figure that are objectively empty, homogeneous and unstructured." How is this possible? We do not really know, but the processes evidently belong in that black box of "figure-organizing processes" we have drawn on in describing more technical investigations of pattern perception.

Green and Courtis draw attention to a characteristic of pattern perception that is currently at the center of most investigations of the topic. This is the view of pattern perception as essentially a *feature extraction* process. Of course, extracting features does not complete the job, because patterns are not just collections of features, however important those may be in the recognition process. Of great topical interest is the question of *feature synthesis,* and here some of the best progress has been made in the field of computer simulation; an entry to this literature is provided for the *Handbook* by Sutherland (1973), and an informal but quite thorough exploration of many of the possibilities of the approach expounded by Minsky and Papert (1972). Whether such simulations help us to understand the phenomena of figure–ground relationships any better than the early studies remains an open question. At least it is interesting to note that, in shifting emphasis away from patterns per se to the more central question of how perception of the world hinges on pattern analysis, but is not *only* pattern analysis, the modern approach brings us close once more to the questions which exercised the Gestalt psychologists.

FIG. 6. Contours that illustrate very vividly the presence of figure-organizing processes that have no physical counterpart in the arrays. [Reproduced with permission from Green, R. T., & Courtis, M. C. Information theory and figure perception: The metaphor that failed. *Acta Psychologica,* 1966, **25,** 12–36.]

III. PERCEPTUAL STABILITY AND CLARITY

A. The Problems

Two problems that are intimately related to the question of figural organization concern, (*a*) the manner in which the perception of a stable spatial frame of reference and the objects in it is possible, and (*b*) the reasons why clear and precise perceptions are possible, despite the very "noisy" nature of the proximal stimulus for vision. The first poses questions because organisms are mobile, so that self-produced movements induce changes in visual stimulation, and these changes are a priori not different from changes brought about by other forms of visual displacement, such as motion of objects in the environment; but the self-induced movements, unless distinguishable from the other type, should make stable orientation and perception of the environment impossible. The second question poses problems because examination of the physical properties of the pattern of stimulation at the retina, and of the nature of retinal transduction, suggest very strongly that clear and rapid detection of visual stimulation, and especially of changes of stimulation, should be impossible. Resolution of the first question—about perceptual stability—will give part of the solution to the second one—about acuity and clarity—but a complete solution requires additional postulates, and a different model of visual functioning.

B. Movement and Stability

The detection of movement is a primary function of virtually every sort of visual system, and it has obvious biological utility. There is good evidence for specialized motion detectors in vertebrates (e.g., Jacobson & Gaze, 1964; Barlow & Hill, 1963; Hubel & Wiesel, 1962) and even some evidence for relative velocity detectors, for instance in the frog's retina (Lettvin, Maturana, McCulloch, & Pitts, 1959). But, as we have seen, detection of motion, or even of relative velocities, is not sufficient to account for the way we perceive the environment as a stable frame of reference within which we orientate ourselves, in which we move and in which other objects are observed to be in motion: We must account for the ability to discriminate between the visual effects of self-produced movement and the visual effects of other forms of motion in the environment. An acceptable model for explaining perceptual stability was first suggested by Helmholtz as the motor outflow theory, and was elaborated on by von Holst and Mittelstaedt (1950) in their *principle of reafference.* These authors distinguish between reafference, which comprises all those changes in sensory stimulation resulting from self-produced movements of the organism (in our case, all visual stimulation arising from self-produced movements of the eye, head, torso, etc.) and changes not so induced, which is called exafference. The model states that commands to the motor system are preserved as an *efference copy,* and compared explicitly with consequent sensory stimulation. Where the efference copy and reafference match exactly, no movement of an external object is perceived: Or, we can say, the observed environment remains stable. Any discrepancy between efference copy and reafference is defined as exafference, and results (for the visual system) in perceived movement. Von Holst and Mittelstaedt demonstrate the viability of their principle in a number of ingenious ways, and indeed, as Gregory (1966) points out, its truth can be demonstrated by quite simple observations, for example, on the behavior of afterimages. There is as yet little direct physiological evidence for the efference copy or its cancellation (see, however, Bizzi, Kalil, & Tagliasco, 1971; Noda, Freeman, & Creutzfeldt, 1972). The major specific impact on psychological theorizing of von Holst's ideas has been in the adaptational model of Held (1961, 1967), although the general notion of systems analyses of visual functioning has been influential, as in the work of MacKay (1967).

C. Movement and Clarity

Elegant and successful though it is in explaining the gross stabilization of the visual world, the reafference principle is not the complete answer to our problems. It does not take into account the fact that "voluntary" movements are not the only ones which need to be neutralized in order to produce stabilization. The eyes are subject to saccades, tremor and drift which impose much unwanted movement on the retinal image. Saccades perhaps could be subsumed under the rubric of the reafference principle, but it seems highly unlikely that this can be true for drifts and tremor (physiological nystagmus) which are more in the nature of errors of alignment and stability in an organ maintained in position by sets of very powerful muscles acting antagonistically. Here the problem would seem to be not one of cancelling out a specific motor command, but rather of sorting out and correcting for random motions that serve no useful purpose but militate against clarity. It has been argued (Dodwell, 1971) that the development of the human eye and its extrinsic musculature arises from conflicting evolutionary pressures for a system that has both high acuity and capacity for detail vision, and also ability to track and fixate rapidly on moving objects. The former property would lead one to expect large receptor surfaces which integrate over time and can be maintained in steady orientation; the latter property leads to the expectation of small structures with high power-to-weight ratio. The second pressure seems to have won out, with the attendant characteristic but apparently nonadaptive noise-producing eye movements.

The importance of the involuntary eye movements in normal visual perception first became clear when methods were developed for stabilization* of the retinal image by Ditchburn and Ginsborg (1952) and Riggs, Ratliff,

---

* Stabilization of the retinal image refers to the absence of relative motion between the proximal retinal stimulus and the retina, not the larger-scale stabilization of the visual world discussed in the previous section.

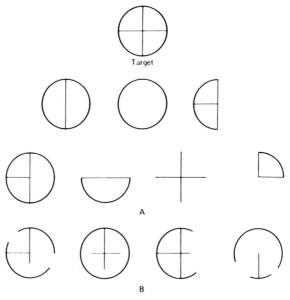

FIG. 7. Typical partial fading and regeneration of stopped images. Type A (organized) is much more prevalent than Type B (random). [Reproduced with permission from Evans, C. R. Some studies of pattern perception using a stabilized retinal image. *British Journal of Psychology*, 1965, **56**, 121–133.]

Cornsweet, and Cornsweet (1953). The first surprising and now well-known discovery was that properly stabilized (or stopped) retinal images fade quite rapidly and suffer little if any regeneration (Barlow, 1963; Yarbus, 1967). Under conditions of imperfect stabilization, regeneration occurs and generally does so in nonrandom ways. The typical finding here is that meaningful and well-structured wholes, or parts of a complex display, tend to fade and regenerate together. In most cases this appears to be affected by set and expectation (Pritchard, Heron, & Hebb, 1960) but in others to be a more automatic figure-organizing process (Evans, 1965) although still perhaps one that is subject to effects of perceptual learning. Figure 7 shows examples of the typical structured fadings and regenerations found by Evans in subjects who were naïve to the experimenter's expectations about what should be perceived. These effects are not limited to the viewing of artificially stabilized images, but can be observed in afterimages and even in steadily fixated targets (McKinnon, Forde, & Piggins, 1969).

The well-stabilized retinal image fades, so that some movement relative to the retina is a necessary condition of maintained clear vision; in single cell recording in the visual cortex sustained firing is usually best maintained when the retinal receptive field is stimulated with a moving display, and several authors have pointed out the likely connection between these two facts (Heckenmueller, 1965). Visual acuity is at least as good in the first few seconds of stabilized viewing as in normal vision, so that retinal image motion appears to be necessary only for the maintenance of clear vision, not its establishment, and as we have seen, the probable physiological basis for this fact is known. The power of the visual system to transcend the limitations imposed by the noise inherent in a nonstopped image is shown by the fineness of visual acuity, and particularly of stereoacuity. For instance a good observer's ability to maintain accurate binocular fixation is limited, and stereoacuity transcends it by a factor of about 100 (Krauskopf, Cornsweet, & Riggs, 1960). Such findings are striking in view of the fact that the retina is a time-integrator, and processes of storage are known to occur over periods of at least the order of hundreds of milliseconds. At the simplest level this is shown by Bloch's law, but also—and particularly for contoured displays—by the work on iconic memory and the voluminous literature on visual masking (Ganz, Chapter 6 of this volume and Thomas, Chapter 7 of this volume).

Thus there are four major points about visual clarity that need to be reconciled:

(*i*) The retinal image is "noisy" because of image motion.

(*ii*) Motion of the retinal image is a necessary condition of maintained clear vision.

(*iii*) The fineness of visual acuity implies that there is both smoothing and sharpening of retinal input over time.

(*iv*) One could expect blurring to occur in rapid sequences because of sensory storage.

The most straightforward way to make this reconciliation is to postulate that the visual system cross-correlates successive inputs over time and records some form of correlation function (Dodwell, 1971). Then the necessary and sufficient condition for distinguishing signal from noise and for maintaining visual clarity would be that the successive cross-correlations remain high and stable; image motion on the retina would actually contribute to formulation of the correlation functions. If short-term visual information storage is seen as the product of a correlational mechanism, then rapid processing is only possible as a function of the rate at which successive visual scenes are sampled. Various methods have been used for estimating the lower limit for quantization of perceptual time, and the figure of about 40 msec generally arrived at (Dodwell & Standing, 1970; Kristofferson, 1967) is quite consistent with the correlational model. The model can also accommodate the statistical smoothing process mentioned earlier to explain acuity in the presence of perturbations which are many times its angular magnitude.

D. Orientation and Repetition Clarity

Some other phenomena having to do with perceptual clarity are worthy of note: It has been known for a hundred years that visual detection is anisotropic. Perceptual performance is superior for stimuli aligned horizontally and/or vertically, as compared with other orientations. This is especially true for humans, but also for other organisms (Appelle, 1972), and has led to specific investigation of the probable causal antecedants. Blakemore and Cooper (1970) and Hirsch and Spinelli (1970) have shown that cats reared with selective exposure to lines in only one orientation are functionally blind to other orientations and show anomalies in the electrophysiology of the visual cortex, single cells being selectively tuned to fire only to lines in the previously exposed orientation, in contrast to the normal case (Hubel & Wiesel, 1962). In something of a *tour de force,* Pettigrew, Olson, and Barlow (1973) demonstrated tuning of single cells by appropriate stimuli over very short time periods in young kittens. It seems quite probable that such tuning also occurs in humans, and is the basis for differential sensitivity to various orientations (Freeman, Mitchell, & Millodot, 1972).

A somewhat different line of research is concerned with repetition clarity. Haber (1965) showed that repeated identical brief exposures of stimulus materials (seven-letter words) led to increasing ability to report what the words were, higher ratings for clarity and, in at least some subjects, reports that the brightness or duration of the displays must have been increasing over trials, because the perceived effects were so striking. A number of investigators have subsequently failed to obtain the effect, or have attributed it (when obtained) to a "multiple look" phenomenon whereby the information obtained on brief exposures is simply added to previous information to increase the observer's confidence in what is reported. This work has been reviewed in detail by Doherty and Keeley (1972). Using forced choice methodology, however, it can be shown that there is a real change in sensitivity with repetition for certain classes of stimuli, not just a criterion shift, and this is a form of sensory tuning which can be explained in terms of the correlational model already described (Dodwell, 1971). Haber's preferred explanation for repetition clarity was more cognitive, in terms of the multiple addressing of a central cell assembly (Hebb, 1949). The three sorts of explanations are not necessarily incompatible, and illustrate again the fact that perceptual phenomena are multiply determined and often not amenable to a single exhaustive explanation, either at the physiological, cognitive, or some other level.

IV. PERCEPTUAL CONSTANCIES

The classical work on perceptual constancies was reported by Thouless (1931a,b) and Brunswik (1944) and they were the subject of intensive investigation in the 1940s and 1950s. Perceptual constancies are said to occur whenever the variation in a perceived attribute, such as color, shape, or size, is less than the true physical variation of the proximal (retinal) stimulus leads one to expect. Thus size constancy occurs when an object's perceived linear dimensions (height and width) do not change in exact inverse proportion to any change in distance; brightness constancy occurs when proportionate changes in perceived brightness do not accompany changes in illumination, etc. There is an antithesis between one's general knowledge of the physical attributes of solid objects, such as size and shape, on the one hand, and the proximal effects on the receptors on the other. A popular conception of the resolution of the antithesis has been that what we judge to be the size, shape, color etc. of an object is a compromise between the two sorts of knowledge available; this is what Thouless called "phenomenal regression to the real object." Thus although we generally judge the size of an object to remain constant regardless of how far away it is, this judgment usually cannot be made entirely independently of retinal subtense. The compromise is perhaps not rational, but is nearly universal, at least among Westerners. The quantitative measure usually used is the ratio suggested by Brunswik (1929) for size, with similar interpretations for other constancies:

$$\text{Brunswik ratio} = \frac{P - R}{C - R},$$

where R is retinal size, C is constant (physical) size, and P is perceived or judged size. The ratio (or the Thouless ratio, in which logarithmic values are substituted in the expression for the ratio) has the property of being zero when there is no constancy, unity when constancy is perfect, i.e., when judgments are based on the proximal stimulus and the physical properties, respectively. As one might expect, the amount of constancy displayed varies with a number of situational and organismic factors. A useful review of this research is given by Forgus (1966). In general, the more information the observer has, such as cues to the real distance or orientation of an object, the higher will be the amount of constancy shown in his judgments; overconstancy has occasionally been reported. Under reduced conditions, perceptual judgments can be made to match the proximal stimulus values almost perfectly (e.g., Holway & Boring, 1941; Hastorf & Way, 1952).

The important question that the existence of the constancies raises for the psychology of perception is this: Do they throw any light on the nature and genesis of our perception of the world around us? Some psychologists would argue strongly that they are the very paradigm of what perception is all about. Physical stimulation is transduced in the receptors into electrochemical signals, which are processed in characteristic ways within the visual (or other sensory) system: But this information itself has to be assessed, or interpreted, within the framework of an existing set of attitudes, beliefs, and postulates about the nature of the physical world in which we live. The nature of the sensory input can be manipulated (e.g., richness of distance cues) and affect perceived size, but this can also be achieved by manipulation of context, (e.g., Beck & Gibson, 1955) by training and induced set (e.g., Thouless, 1932) and evidently by straight physiological processing, as in convergence micropsia and macropsia (e.g., Grant, 1942; see also Gogel, Wist, & Harker, 1963). Thus, perception of objects is held to be not a simple matter of discriminating relevant properties in the available stimulation, but rather a constructive process. The outstanding proponents of this view in recent times have been Piaget (1969) and the transactionalists (e.g., Ittleson, 1952). On the other hand, there are theorists (e.g., J. J. Gibson, 1966; E. J. Gibson, 1969) who dispute it. It should be possible to resolve the matter by appeal to existing evidence, which comes from two major sources: studies of perceptual deprivation and development, and cross-cultural work on perceptual differentiation. That evidence is also highly relevant to the topic of visual illusions, reviewed in the following section. In Section VI the evidence from developmental and cross-cultural studies will be considered.

V. PERCEPTUAL ILLUSIONS

A. Geometric Illusions

There are many different sorts of visual illusions, but probably the ones which have most intrigued psychologists are the so-called geometrical or spatial illusions, of which the Müller–Lyer (Fig. 8a) is the most celebrated. They are like the constancies in that systematic discrepancies are found between what is seen and what consideration of the retinal image leads one to expect. A general review is given by Over (1968).

Explicit attempts have been made to explain illusions as constancy phenomena: For instance, Gregory (1966) argues that the illusions arise because of "inappropriate constancy scaling." The arrowheads of the Müller–Lyer illusion, for example, give perspective cues to depth. These

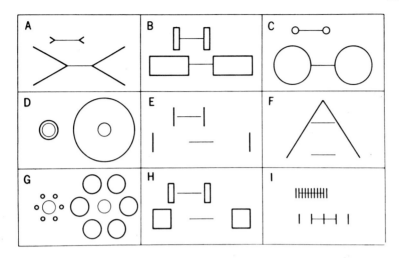

FIG. 8. Some of the many geometrical illusions that can be explained in terms of visual scaling. [Reproduced with permission from Day, R. H. Visual spatial illusions: A general explanation. *Science,* 1972, **175,** 1335–1340. Copyright © 1972 by the American Association for the Advancement of Science.]

cues are thought to trigger the depth-scaling system—in this case inappropriately, since the display is a plane figure. Clever as the idea is, it has been shown to be too narrow to encompass more than a few special cases (Fisher, 1968). A more general theory explaining illusions in terms of constancy phenomena has been put forward by Day (1972). Day's paper contains an excellent review of the relationship between illusion and constancy, and is recommended for the reader interested in pursuing this topic. Regarding illusions of size, he makes the point that there are many cues to distance, including accommodation, convergence, overlay, elevation, texture gradient, element size, and frequency, any or all of which can contribute to the maintenance of a degree of size constancy. Figure 8 shows some of the illusions of size that can be accounted for in terms of induction by various distance cues. A somewhat similar development by Merryman and Restle (1970) and by Restle (1971) has used adaptation-level theory (Helson, 1964) to predict the magnitudes of illusions like those in Fig. 8 in an exact way. The theory gives a quantitative expression for adaptation level, and the fit between predicted and obtained perceptual magnitudes of very simple illusory figures is, in general, rather good. A closely related contextual, but less quantitative, theory of the moon illusion was proposed by Rock and Kaufman (1962). Pressey's assimilation theory (Pressey, 1971) also belongs in this genre. Thus there is some agreement that at least one large class of illusions can be accounted for in terms of the scaling properties of the visual metric.

Day (1972) presents the display shown in Fig. 9 as an example of an

Fig. 9. An illusion of orientation which also illustrates the "acute angle" effect. [Reproduced with permission from Day, R. H. Visual spatial illusions: A general explanation. *Science,* 1972, **175,** 1335–1340. Copyright © 1972 by the American Association for the Advancement of Science.]

illusion of orientation. The display also illustrates an additional feature which has been thought to be important in the generation of another class of illusions; at a certain viewing distance (about 14 inches) the single vertical line appears to be broken into noncollinear segments at the points where it intersects with striations. The principle has been proposed that all acute angles are overestimated, and a possible neurological basis for such distortion in the cortical representation of an angle suggested (e.g., Chiang, 1968; Burns & Pritchard, 1971). This would explain the effect just described, and has been postulated as a major determinant of many geometrical illusions. The "acute angle" principle, like the inappropriate-constancy-scaling hypothesis, can be overgeneralized (as pointed out, e.g., by Pressey & Sweeney, 1972) yet undoubtedly cannot be dismissed as a possible factor in the genesis of illusions such as Zöllner's and Hering's (Coren, 1970; Wallace, 1969). Again one sees that a number of different factors affect illusions, making it difficult—and perhaps inappropriate—to attempt a single theoretical model to account for all of them. Distortion caused by certain special properties of the contour-coding apparatus of the visual system does, however, emerge as a second major factor currently accepted as underlying some of the geometrical illusions.

B. Figural Aftereffects

Distortions of another type are known as figural aftereffects. These are distortions that occur in the neighborhood of steadily fixated contours, and are typically measured in a successive observation paradigm: A contour is steadily fixated (the inspection figure), followed by observation of a test figure in which the distortion is observed. Interest in these effects was high for some years following the work of Köhler and Wallach (1944) in which they were first systematically explored, and some hundreds of papers were published. Many inconsistent and even contradictory findings were reported, but the experimental methodology used was frequently poor (Dodwell & Gendreau, 1969). Later studies have demonstrated the existence of figural aftereffects in a reliable way, and several authors have argued that they can be considered as special cases of effects that have usually been studied as simultaneous distortions, i.e., certain of the geometrical illusions (see, e.g., Over, 1968). Attempts to explain figural aftereffects have followed current neurophysiological findings and theory of the day, nearly all of them being based on the idea that adaptation or satiation in particular neural structures causes the aftereffects. It is not surprising, then, to find that the recent discoveries about contour-specific neural coding form the basis for the latest models (Dodwell & Gendreau, 1969; Coltheart, 1971; Over, 1971). Nor is it surprising, since the figural aftereffects have nearly always been thought to have a purely physiological basis, that interest in studying them developmentally or cross-culturally has been low.

VI. DEVELOPMENTAL AND CROSS-CULTURAL EVIDENCE

A. Selective Exposure

Questions about the effects of experience on perception have been posed and hotly debated for centuries. A most dramatic change in the nature and scope of possible evidence came about with the development of electrophysiological techniques for single unit recording in the mammalian brain (Hubel & Wiesel, 1962). It has been possible to demonstrate, (a) that contour coding of essentially the same type that is found in adult organisms exists in the neonatal kitten and, (b) that complete deprivation and selective rearing bias this coding in important ways. At least for selective rearing, the behavioral and physiological findings are in accord, as was mentioned earlier (e.g., Blakemore & Cooper, 1970). This evidence supports and amplifies a long line of reports on the effects of perceptual deprivation in animals, representative samples of which can be found in Dodwell (1970b). In general, it can be said that deprivation effects are most severe for complex discriminations, and that lower visual organisms tend to show less adaptability than higher.

Human studies of radical visual deprivation are much more limited, being restricted to clinical material (von Senden, 1932; Gregory & Wallace, 1963; White, Saunders, Scadden, Bach-y-Rita, & Collins, 1970) or only as of 1973, to the study of specific acuity deficits associated with uncorrected refractive errors (Mitchell, Freeman, Millodot, & Haegerstrom, 1973). Gregory and Wallace's evidence is important in confirming the notion, previously documented by von Senden, and used extensively by Hebb (1949) in theorizing about pattern perception, that attainment of object recognition and spatial orientation is a slow process for one who has been blind from birth, and probably never proceeds beyond a fairly rudimentary level. However, pattern perception is possible, and the most arresting of their findings is that transfer occurs between previously learned tactile discriminations and visual perception: In these extreme conditions at least, touch can educate vision. Additional evidence along these lines is provided by the work of White *et al.* (1970) on visual prosthetic devices. They investigated the possibility of educating the skin to act as a perceptual system that would substitute for vision. The optical image produced by a television camera was used to drive a 20 × 20 array of tactors (vibrators) in contact with the observer's back, the observer having at the time no direct visual input. Blindfolded and blind observers were able to learn simple form discriminations, but with high error rates unless they had control of the television camera. The observer who could control input by moving the camera himself to scan the presented visual display showed dramatic improvement in performance. Of considerable interest is the fact that with self-initiated movements of the sensor, external localization of the tactile image is readily achieved. As a practical aid for the blind, the device holds much promise, particularly in miniaturized form (for a review of sensory aids to the blind see Nye and Bliss, 1970); its significance for the psychology of pattern perception lies in its potential as a device for studying perceptual learning. The excitement and interest generated by the initial reports has perhaps not yet been adequately followed through with new findings, but the possibilities still exist. The skin for most people, even the blind, is an untutored sense, and the demonstration that it has a high capacity for pattern recognition must count as one of the few genuinely new discoveries of recent years in the field of pattern perception. The study of sensory substitution systems will not necessarily throw light on the normal course of perceptual development, but is more likely to do so than the investigation of recovery in a sensory system which has itself been severely deprived; the argument can always be made in such cases that the system in question has suffered irreversible damage in the course of depriving it. Interesting work on the behavioral effects of partial and selective deprivation on visual guidance has been reported, notably by Held and his associates (Held & Bossom, 1961; Held & Hein, 1963).

B. Infant Studies

Another question that has received much attention concerns the visual abilities of the human infant. Fantz (1961) found evidence of form discrimination in young infants by observing fixation preferences for different patterns, and since then, research has shown fairly consistently that the more infants are studied, the more their visual abilities appear to resemble those of adults (Bond, 1972). However, there are many methodological problems with research on infant vision, especially as to interpretation. The "visual cliff" experiments of Walk and Gibson (1961), for example, have been widely quoted as demonstrating an innate ability to perceive visual depth and to respond appropriately to it, and undoubtedly this is true for some species. Yet their human subjects were 6 months old and more, so the question of innateness scarcely arises. Bower's experiments on perceptual unity and constancy (Bower, 1965, 1966) have similarly led many psychologists to conclude that the constancies are "essentially" present in the newborn, although no such conclusion is justified, as the author himself points out, on the basis of that evidence (Bower, 1972).* In that later paper evidence is adduced to show that very young infants nevertheless can discriminate between solid objects and pictorial representations of them, making appropriate responses to the objects in terms of reaching and grasping. But this is also quite far from establishing object perception as a fact of the young infant's perceptual world. It demonstrates nicely that the rudiments are there—response to the distal properties of objects—but not more than that. Other findings of a more directly visual nature, in terms of eye movements, gives evidence of a still fairly primitive level of visual function in the newborn human infant (Kessen, Salapatek, & Haith, 1972). The careful observational reports of White (1971) also make it clear that sensory and motor functioning in the very young infant are quite primitive and undifferentiated.

C. Childhood Studies

A large volume of research has been devoted to the question of developmental changes in constancies (i.e., object-like perceptual properties as opposed to judgments based on proximal stimulus conditions) and in illusions, with very generally positive findings (Wohlwill, 1960; Piaget, 1969). E. J. Gibson (1969) has reviewed the literature on perceptual development from the point of view of the discrimination theory of perceptual learning (Gibson & Gibson, 1955; Gibson, 1966). She concludes that the constancies per se do not develop with experience; a view that is difficult to reconcile with the large number of contrary findings. It is no doubt true that more thorough and analytical studies in this area are badly needed. Some moves in this direction are represented by developmental studies of the ways infants look at patterns in terms of eye movements and fixations. Bond (1972) summarizes work on infants, and work on older children is reported by, for instance, O'Bryan and Boersma (1971) and Mackworth and Bruner (1970). Further interesting work on children, which supports a constructivist view of perceptual development, is reported by Elkind (1969). He shows that young children have difficulty in coping simultaneously with figures as wholes and with their constituent parts and links

---

* Some evidence (McKenzie & Day, 1972) using a different methodology lends no support to the notion that infants at 6–30 weeks of age manifest visual constancies.

this to the Piagetian concepts concerning logical multiplication and operational thinking (Piaget, 1957).

D. Cross-Cultural Studies

Interest in cross-cultural studies of illusions can be traced back at least to the work of Rivers (1901, 1905) who showed that Europeans are more susceptible to the Müller–Lyer illusion than certain South Sea Islanders, but less susceptible to the horizontal–vertical illusion. This he explained on ecological grounds, and an elaboration of his ideas has found fairly wide acceptance. The major work of Segall, Campbell, and Herskovits (1963, 1966) explored susceptibility to certain geometrical illusions in a number of cultures, and their findings generally support the notion that susceptibility is at least partly determined ecologically, i.e., by the type of environment in which the observer lives. Although the differences in illusion susceptibility between cultures tend to be small—of the order of a few percent—they are reliable and have been replicated a number of times. The principle hypothesis investigated has been that the degree of *carpenteredness* of an environment is the major factor determining susceptibility, and the evidence generally supports this: Unfortunately a number of confounding factors are usually present, such as differences in degree of education, test sophistication, and physiological factors, like age and retinal pigmentation, all or some of which may covary with degree of carpenteredness. Attempts have been made to tease some of them apart (e.g., Berry, 1968, 1971; Deregowski, 1968; Stewart, 1971) but as Jahoda (1971) says: "In general . . . the current position in this whole area is characterized by a good deal of uncertainty coupled with lively controversy." One logical puzzle here is that although susceptibility to various illusions, the Müller–Lyer included, tends to decrease with age and/or repeated exposure, the ecological genesis of the illusions is held to be a function of exposure and so also, presumably, of age as well. The constancies also tend to increase with age (Leibowitz, Graham, & Parrish, 1972) so that, for the class of illusions held to be mediated by constancies (Day, 1972), one would expect an increase with age plus a good correlation with constancy judgments. Little systematic work on shape and size constancy appears to have been done on non-Westernized subjects. The obvious next step seems to be to look for constancy–illusion correlations, especially in groups of observers reared in ecologically disparate environments.

So far as it goes, then, the evidence from developmental and cross-cultural research supports a position of moderate empiricism. There is evidence that young organisms respond appropriately to certain ecologically important features of their environments without specific training or experience, but no really convincing demonstration that object perception, shape and size constancy, or other features of an adult's visual world are present in the young infant. A certain amount of research has been done on the relationship of object perception to developmental change, and also to changes in susceptibility to illusions. This work reinforces the findings from cross-cultural research which show real, if mostly fairly small, differences between experientially disparate groups in the ways they perceive the visual world.

VII. INFORMATION PROCESSING

A. Scope of Field

A major development in psychology since about 1960 has been the emergence of the "information processing" movement. It is difficult to define what is to be regarded as the proper domain of information processing, or to circumscribe it by exclusion. To a large degree it is a point of view, rather than any fixed set of principles, findings, or research strategies. Heavily influenced by the concepts of systems engineering and computer science, the information processor tends to be interested in questions of representation, memory, and symbol manipulation—and pattern perception is certainly central to such matters. Representative sets of papers in the field have been put together by Haber (1969) and Coltheart (1972a). Computer simulation has also been a major influence (see Dodwell, 1970a, Chap. V for review) and the work on artificial intelligence, summarized by Sutherland (1973) is likely to remain prominent and a fertile source of ideas for psychologists.

B. Visual Input Processes

Much experimental effort has been spent on studying how symbols are read from very brief visual displays. The modern work on this topic was initiated by Sperling (1960) and has led to a number of important findings. The concept of an iconic memory, the accurate but ephemeral visual trace of a brief display, is now well established. Later work has concentrated on the manner in which the symbols, or information, in the icon are transferred to a more stable form of memory and made available for further use, and is reviewed by Coltheart (1972b). A number of models for the process have been proposed (e.g., Broadbent, 1967; Coltheart, 1972b; Sperling, 1967) all of which make use of the concept of different codes, or modes of representation at different processing stages for symbolic material, such as digits, letters, and words. It is not likely that all visual input must be processed in this way, although the theorists in the field might be taken to think so; the distinctly limited capacity for dealing with symbolic material is in striking contrast to the essentially limitless capacity for recording and recognizing pictorial material (Shepard, 1967; Standing, Comezio, & Haber, 1970; Standing, 1973).

Another related area of research has to do with visual scanning, typically studied by instructing subjects to search rapidly through sheets of printed materials to identify particular symbols. Much of the interest here has centered on the question of serial versus parallel processing: Can an observer search as efficiently for two or more symbol types simultaneously as for one? The answer seems to be that with practice he can, although the experiments are not as easy to interpret as one might think. Corcoran (1971) deals very thoroughly with the issue of serial versus parallel processing and how various experiments bear on the issue. Although the question has loomed large in the models and experiments of information processors, the issue has probably been overworked, since there is reason to think that, to quote Greeno (1972):

> . . . if the models are described in reasonably general ways, there is a serial processor that will mimic the behavior of any parallel processor, and there is a parallel processor that will mimic the behavior of almost any serial processor . . . . Townsend has shown that with a more general but still reasonable characterization, the two kinds of system are identical in their temporal characteristics [p. 99].

C. Reading

Research on information retrieval from brief displays and on scanning should, one would expect, be very relevant to understanding the process of reading. Many researchers in these areas have expressed such a hope, but so far the practical return has not been great. However, a good deal of work has been done specifically on reading, both by psychologists and educational researchers. The latter have been mainly concerned with finding efficient methods of teaching reading and the analysis of reading deficits such as specific developmental dyslexia; see, for example, Young and Lindsley (1970); Otto, Barrett, Smith, Dulin, & Johnson (1972). The more experimental approach has been reviewed by Gibson (1969), and her own work is some of the best in this area (Gibson, 1965). She and her associates have studied developmental trends in the recognition of letterlike forms (Gibson, Gibson, Pick, & Osser, 1962), the role of grapheme–phoneme correspondence in word recognition (Gibson, Pick, Osser, & Hammond, 1962) and other factors, such as meaningfulness and pronounceability (Gibson, Bishop, Schiff, & Smith, 1964). Kolers and Perkins (1969a,b) have studied the recognition of transformed text (rotated, inverted, etc.) and shown that an "orientation set" determines the interpretation of clues to letter recognition. The distinctive features, or clues, do not correspond directly to easily specifiable geometrical properties of letters. Also the speed at which good readers operate precludes the possibility that individual letters are recognized prior to word interpretation. It is as if the reader continually forms hypotheses about the to-be-read material which are at least minimally confirmed by the actual text (Kolers, 1972). However, whatever the constructive process that underlies letter and word recognition and ultimately reading may be, it still remains to be adequately characterized.

D. Lateral Asymmetry

A matter that has intrigued many information processors is the problem of how to explain the often-reported asymmetry for reporting materials from left and right visual fields (e.g., Mishkin & Forgays, 1952; Heron, 1957; White, 1969). For most types of material the right field superiority can be attributed to learned scanning (reading) habits, but not for all. Right field superiority may also be an effect of processing differences between the two cerebral hemispheres. A left hemisphere advantage in processing linguistic materials in normally right-handed individuals is well documented in hearing and vision (Bryden, 1970; Kimura, 1961, 1969). So far as visual pattern recognition per se is concerned, the major point of interest has been to give an account of how the two halves of the brain cortex, which receive separate visual inputs, can function together in a coherent manner. The history and current state of this field are considered by Corballis and Beale (1970) who argue, following Mach (1896), that the well-known left–right mirror image confusions found in humans (especially children) and animals are a function of the bilateral symmetry of the central nervous system, and may be overcome principally because of response asymmetries such as those that develop with learning to read. There is also evidence that organisms (in this case, children) can discriminate between left–right mirror images when they are presented simultaneously, but cannot perform successive discriminations which require them to remember which of the two displays is which. Thus visual memory is implicated in the problem, and this no doubt plays a major role in the difficulties which many children experience with certain letter reversals when learning to read (Frith, 1971).

E. Figural Synthesis

The relationship between pattern perception and visual short-term memory has been studied in an intriguing way by Hochberg (1968). By

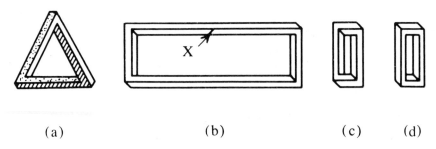

(a)   (b)   (c)   (d)

Fig. 10. Examples of "impossible"—and one possible—objects used to study figural synthesis. [Reproduced with permission from Hochberg, J. In the mind's eye. In R. N. Haber (Ed.), *Contemporary theory and research in visual perception.* New York: Holt, 1968.]

investigating the perception of ambiguous and "impossible" objects (Fig. 10), patterns briefly presented or seen part-by-part through a moving hole, he concludes that form perception comprises two separate components of processing, at least, which are very different from each other. First, the input of a single glance; second, the perceived structure or *schematic map,* which integrates information from successive glances, or within which such information is interpreted. Hochberg's notion is that the former, the local feature type of input, is relatively independent of learning, set, prior knowledge, etc., but that these influence the constructive process by which perceptual *Gestalten* are formed. A very similar notion, but based more on the electrophysiological and behavioral work on pattern processing in animals has been proposed by Dodwell (1970a). We thus come back to our original observations on figure-organizing processes: There are contour and perhaps other feature-detection operations in the visual system, but these are the primary data on which higher-order synthesis occurs. The experimental analysis of the higher-order processes is at least as important as the investigation of feature detectors, whether by physiological or psychophysical means. To understand the interactions of the two, and their relative importance in different types of pattern perception, remains a major goal of experimental and theoretical investigation.

VIII. ATTENTIONAL AND EMOTIONAL ASPECTS OF PATTERN PERCEPTION

Some years ago a so-called "new look" was introduced into research on perception, exemplified by studies demonstrating effects of set, motivation, and foreknowledge on the recognition of visual (and other) displays. The theme was not exactly new, having been studied experimentally by Bartlett (1932), Sherif (1935), and even, in certain respects, by Helmholtz and other nineteenth-century empiricists. Typical of the new look were reports by Bruner and Goodman (1947) on the influence which personal value has in size judgments; Postman, Bruner, and McGinnies (1948) on the relationship between personal values and recognition threshold for words, and the whole line of research on perceptual defense and subception initiated by McGinnies (1949) and Lazarus and McCleary (1951). The methodological objections to much of this early work are well known (Solomon & Howes, 1951; Eriksen, 1956, 1960) and hinge on questions about possible alternative explanations of the apparently perceptual effects. Thus, it has been argued, familiarity, guessing habits, partial cues to words presented tachistoscopically, response biases against saying "taboo" words and so on are possible determinants of perceptual reports, but do not necessarily entail changes in perception as such. Some of the difficulties encountered in making these distinctions are discussed by Natsoulas (1967), and Price (1966) has shown that the methodology of the theory of signal detectability (Swets, Tanner, & Birdsall, 1961) can be brought to bear on the separation of response factors in this type of research. To date, few experiments have used this methodology, but the findings are positive, and important in ruling out the possibility that response biases are responsible for the observed effects. A great deal of ingenuity has gone into the designing of experiments to show that, in some cases at least, genuine changes in sensory thresholds can be caused by manipulating the emotional content of visually presented materials (Natsoulas, 1965; Dixon, 1971). A related problem concerns the selective reporting of specified attributes in an otherwise neutral stimulus display. Improvement in performance can be produced by instructions to attend to different attributes or by sets induced by other means. It is not necessarily true that the improvement demonstrates superior processing of the items or attributes to which attention is directed. Other factors, such as order of report and selective fixation, are alternative possibilities that must be controlled for, and the question of whether the selective mechanism works in perception or in the short-term visual storage of perceived items remains troublesome (Haber, 1966). The great majority of studies of selective attention have been in the auditory mode (Moray, 1969), but some important results in vision have been reported, for example, by Eriksen and Colgate (1971) and by Estes (1972); see also Egeth (1967) and Swets & Kristofferson (1970).

Reservations about the interpretation of the exact site of action for motivational and similar factors in perceptual reports do not alter the important point that many perceptual judgments, and hence much actual behavior, are strongly influenced by social, emotional, and intellectual considerations. The study of social interaction takes this for granted, and several fields of research are concerned with the biasing of perceptual judgments explicitly, as in the work on person perception (see, for example, Anderson,

1968, 1973, and Cook, 1971). The questions of interest here are ones such as: How do initial (and subsequent) cues to a person's character get put together to form an overall judgment? How do prior reports of a person's attributes affect the perception of his speech? This may seem a long way from the matters discussed in earlier sections, but it serves to bring us back to a major theme of the chapter: Perception, or more specifically, pattern recognition, cannot be studied in isolation, or at a single level of discourse. Many influences bear on it, just as it has ramifications into most other areas of psychology.

IX. CONCLUSION

The study of pattern perception is one of the traditional areas of perception. It has had a respectable history, and has a lively present interest. Significant progress in the understanding of pattern recognition has been made in recent years, especially in knowledge of the perceptual attributes of young organisms, of the neurophysiological bases of contour and pattern vision, and the relationships between perception and short-term sensory storage. As was stated at the beginning of this chapter, the problems that are investigated in this field are large ones, and while the techniques and tactics of research vary, the problems in many cases defy definitive solution. And that, of course, is what ensures that the field will remain one of absorbing interest.

References

Anderson, N. H. Application of a linear-serial model to a personality-impression task using serial presentation. *Journal of Personality & Social Psychology,* 1968, **10**, 354–362.

Anderson, N. H. Algebraic models in perception. E. C. Carterette & M. P. Friedman (Eds.), *Handbook of perception,* Vol. 2. New York: Academic Press, 1973.

Appelle, S. Perception and discrimination as a function of stimulus orientation: The "oblique effect" in man and animals. *Psychological Bulletin,* 1972, **78**, 266–278.

Attneave, F. Some informational aspects of visual perception. *Psychological Review,* 1954, **61**, 183–193.

Attneave, F. Physical determinants of the judged complexity of shapes. *Journal of Experimental Psychology,* 1957, **53**, 221–227.

Attneave, F., & Arnoult, M. D. The quantitative study of shape and pattern perception. *Psychological Bulletin,* 1956, **53**, 452–471.

Barlow, H. B. Slippage of contact lenses and other artifacts in relation to fading and regeneration of supposedly stable retinal images. *Quarterly Journal of Experimental Psychology,* 1963, **15**, 36–51.

Barlow, H. B., & Hill, R. M. Selective sensitivity to direction of movement in ganglion cells of the rabbit retina. *Science,* 1963, **139**, 412–414.

Bartlett, F. C. *Remembering*. London and New York: Cambridge Univ. Press, 1932.

Beck, J., & Gibson, J. J. The relation of apparent shape to apparent slant in the perception of objects. *Journal of Experimental Psychology*, 1955, **50**, 125–133.

Berry, J. W. Ecology, perceptual development, and the Müller–Lyer illusion. *British Journal of Psychology*, 1968, **59**, 205–210.

Berry, J. W. Müller–Lyer susceptibility. Culture, ecology or race? *International Journal of Psychology*, 1971, **6**, 193–197.

Bizzi, E., Kalil, R. E., & Tagliasco, V. Eye–head co-ordination in monkeys: Evidence for centrally patterned organization. *Science*, 1971, **173**, 452–454.

Blakemore, C., & Cooper, G. F. Development of the brain depends on visual environment. *Nature*, 1970, **228**, 677–678.

Bond, E. K. Perception of form by the human infant. *Psychological Bulletin*, 1972, **77**, 225–245.

Boring, E. G. A new ambiguous picture. *American Journal of Psychology*, 1930, **42**, 444–445.

Bower, T. G. R. The determinants of perceptual unity in infancy. *Psychonomic Science*, 1965, **3**, 323–324.

Bower, T. G. R. Slant perception and shape constancy in infants. *Science*, 1966, **151**, 832–834.

Bower, T. G. R. Object perception in infants. *Perception*, 1972, **1**, 15–30.

Broadbent, D. E. The word frequency effect and response bias. *Psychological Review*, 1967, **74**, 1–15.

Bruner, J. S., & Goodman, C. C. Value and need as organizing factors in perception. *Journal of Abnormal & Social Psychology*, 1947, **42**, 33–44.

Brunswik, E. Zur Entwicklung der Albedowahrnehmung. *Zeitschrift für Psychologie*, 1929, **109**, 40–115.

Brunswik, E. Distal focusing of perception: Size constancy in a representative sample of situations. *Psychological Monographs*, 1944, Whole No. 254.

Bryden, M. P. Laterality effects in dichotic listening: Relations with handedness and reading ability in children. *Neuropsychologia*, 1970, **8**, 443–450.

Bugelski, B. R., & Alampay, D. A. The role of frequency in developing perceptual sets. *Canadian Journal of Psychology*, 1961, **15**, 205–211.

Burns, B. D., & Pritchard, R. Geometrical illusions and the response of neurons in the cat's visual cortex to angle patterns. *Journal of Physiology*, 1971, **213**, 599–616.

Chiang, C. A new theory to explain geometrical illusions produced by crossing lines. *Perception & Psychophysics*, 1968, **3**, 174–176.

Coltheart, M. Visual feature analyzers and after-effects of tilt and curvature. *Psychological Review*, 1971, **78**, 114–121.

Coltheart, M. *Readings in cognitive psychology*. Toronto: Holt of Canada, 1972. (a)

Coltheart, M. Visual information-processing. In P. C. Dodwell (Ed.), *New horizons in psychology II*. Baltimore: Penguin Books, 1972. Pp. 62–85. (b)

Cook, M. *Interpersonal perception*. Baltimore: Penguin Books, 1971.

Corballis, M. C., & Beale, I. L. Bilateral symmetry and behavior. *Psychological Review*, 1970, **77**, 451–464.

Corcoran, D. W. J. *Pattern recognition*. Baltimore: Penguin Books, 1971.

Coren, S. Lateral inhibition and the Wundt–Hering illusion. *Psychonomic Science*, 1970, **18**, 341–342.

Day, R. H. Visual spatial illusions: A general explanation. *Science*, 1972, **175**, 1335–1340.

Deregowski, J. B. Difficulties in pictorial depth perception in Africa. *British Journal of Psychology,* 1968, **59,** 195–204.

Ditchburn, R. W., & Ginsborg, B. L. Vision with a stabilized retinal image. *Nature,* 1952, **170,** 36–37.

Dixon, N. F. *Subliminal perception: The nature of a controversy.* New York: McGraw-Hill, 1971.

Dodwell, P. C. *Visual pattern recognition.* New York: Holt, 1970. (a)

Dodwell, P. C. *Perceptual learning and adaptation.* Baltimore: Penguin Books, 1970. (b)

Dodwell, P. C. On perceptual clarity. *Psychological Review,* 1971, **78,** 275–289.

Dodwell, P. C., & Gendreau, L. Figural after-effects, sensory coding, expectation and experience. *British Journal of Psychology,* 1969, **60,** 149–167.

Dodwell, P. C., & Standing, L. G. Studies of visual backward masking and a model for the Crawford effect. *Acta Psychologica,* 1970, **32,** 31–47.

Doherty, M. E., & Keeley, S. M. On the identification of repeatedly presented brief visual stimuli. *Psychological Bulletin,* 1972, **78,** 142–156.

Egeth, H. Selective attention. *Psychological Bulletin,* 1967, **67,** 41–57.

Elkind, D. Developmental studies of figurative perception. In L. P. Lipsitt & H. W. Reese (Eds.), *Advances in child development and behavior,* New York: Academic Press, 1969.

Eriksen, C. W. Subception: Fact or artifact? *Psychological Review,* 1956, **63,** 74–80.

Eriksen, C. W. Discrimination and learning without awareness: A methodological survey and evaluation. *Psychological Review,* 1960, **67,** 279–300.

Eriksen, C. W., & Colegate, R. L. Selective attention and serial processing in briefly presented visual displays. *Perception & Psychophysics,* 1971, **10,** 321–326.

Estes, W. K. Interactions of signal and background variables in visual processing. *Perception & Psychophysics,* 1972, **12,** 278–286.

Evans, C. R. Some studies of pattern perception using a stabilized retinal image. *British Journal of Psychology,* 1965, **56,** 121–133.

Fantz, R. L. The origin of form perception. *Scientific American,* 1961, **204**(5), 66–72.

Fisher, G. H. An experimental and theoretical appraisal of the inappropriate size-depth theories of illusions. *British Journal of Psychology,* 1968, **59,** 373–383.

Forgus, R. H. *Perception.* New York: McGraw-Hill, 1966.

Freeman, R. D., Mitchell, D. E., & Millodot, M. A neural effect of partial visual deprivation in humans. *Science,* 1972, **175,** 1382–1386.

Frith, U. Why do children reverse letters? *British Journal of Psychology,* 1971, **62,** 459–468.

Garner, W. R. *Uncertainty and structure as psychological concepts.* New York: Wiley, 1962.

Garner, W. R. The stimulus in information processing. *American Psychologist,* 1970, **25,** 350–358.

Gibson, E. J. Learning to read. *Science,* 1965, **148,** 1066–1072.

Gibson, E. J. *Principles of perceptual learning and development.* New York: Appleton, 1969.

Gibson, E. J., Bishop, C. H., Schiff, W., & Smith, J. Comparison of meaningfulness and pronounceability as grouping principles in the perception and retention of verbal material. *Journal of Experimental Psychology,* 1964, **67,** 173–182.

Gibson, E. J., Gibson, J. J., Pick, A. D., & Osser, H. A. A developmental study of the discrimination of letter-like forms. *Journal of Comparative & Physiological Psychology,* 1962, **55,** 897–906.

Gibson, E. J., Pick, A. D., Osser, H., & Hammond, M. The role of grapheme–phoneme correspondence in the perception of words. *American Journal of Psychology,* 1962, **75,** 554–570.

Gibson, J. J. *The senses considered as perceptual systems.* Boston: Houghton-Mifflin, 1966.

Gibson, J. J., & Gibson, E. J. Perceptual learning: Differentiation or enrichment? *Psychological Review,* 1955, **62,** 1–32.

Gogel, W. C, Wist, E. R., & Harker, G. S. A test of the invariance ratio of perceived size to perceived distance. *American Journal of Psychology,* 1963, **76,** 537–553.

Gottschaldt, K. Ueber den Einfluss der Erfahrung auf die Wahrnemung von Figuren I. Ueber den Einfluss gehäufter Einprägung von Figuren auf ihre Sicherheit in umfassen der Konfigurationen. *Psychologische Forschung,* 1926, **8,** 261–317.

Grant, V. W. Accommodation and convergence in visual space perception. *Journal of Experimental Psychology,* 1942, **31,** 89–104.

Green, R. T., & Courtis, M. C. Information theory and figure perception: The metaphor that failed. *Acta Psychologica,* 1966, **25,** 12–36.

Greeno, J. G. Mathematics in psychology. In P. C. Dodwell (Ed.), *New horizons in psychology II.* Baltimore: Penguin Books, 1972. Pp. 86–104.

Gregory, R. L. *Eye and brain.* London: Weidenfeld and Nicholson, 1966.

Gregory, R. L. Cognitive contours. *Nature,* 1972, **238,** 51–52.

Gregory, R. L., & Wallace, J. G. Recovery from early blindness. *Experimental Psychology Society Monograph,* 1963, No. 2.

Haber, R. N. Effect of prior knowledge of the stimulus on word-recognition processes. *Journal of Experimental Psychology,* 1965, **69,** 282–286.

Haber, R. N. Nature of the effect of set on perception. *Psychological Review,* 1966, **73,** 335–351.

Haber, R. N. *Information processing approaches to visual perception.* New York: Holt, 1969.

Hastorf, A. H., & Way, L. Apparent size with and without distant cues. *Journal of General Psychology,* 1952, **47,** 181–188.

Hebb, D. O. *The organization of behavior.* New York: Wiley, 1949.

Heckenmueller, E. G. Stabilization of the retinal image: A review of method, effects, and theory. *Psychological Bulletin,* 1965, **63,** 157–169.

Held, R. Exposure-history as a factor in maintaining stability of perception and co-ordination. *Journal of Nervous & Mental Diseases,* 1961, **132,** 26–32.

Held, R. Dissociation of visual functions by deprivation and rearrangement. *Psychologische Forschung,* 1967, **31,** 338–348.

Held, R., & Bossom, J. Neonatal deprivation and adult rearrangement: Complementary techniques for analyzing plastic sensori-motor co-ordinations. *Journal of Comparative & Physiological Psychology,* 1961, **54,** 33–37.

Held, R., & Hein, A. Movement-produced stimulation in the development of visually guided behavior. *Journal of Comparative & Physiological Psychology,* 1963, **56,** 607–673.

Helson, H. *Adaptation level theory.* New York: Harper, 1964.

Heron, W. Perception as a function of retinal locus and attention. *American Journal of Psychology,* 1957, **70,** 38–48.

Hirsch, H. V. B., & Spinelli, D. N. Visual experience modifies distribution of horizontally and vertically oriented receptive fields in cats. *Science,* 1970, **168,** 869–871.

Hochberg, J. In the mind's eye. In R. N. Haber (Ed.), *Contemporary theory and research in visual perception.* New York: Holt, 1968.

Hochberg, J., & McAlister, E. A quantitative approach to figural "goodness." *Journal of Experimental Psychology,* 1953, **46,** 361–364.

Holst, E. von, & Mittelstaedt, H. Das Reafferenzprinzip. *Die Naturwissenschaften,* 1950, **37,** 464–476. [Translated as: The Principle of reafference. In P. C. Dodwell (Ed.), *Perceptual processing.* New York: Appleton, 1971.]

Holway, A. H., & Boring, E. G. Determinants of apparent visual size with distance invariant. *American Journal of Psychology,* 1941, **54,** 21–37.

Hubel, D. H., & Wiesel, T. N. Receptive fields, binocular interaction and functional architecture in the cat's visual cortex. *Journal of Physiology,* 1962, **160,** 106–154.

Ittelson, H. The constancies in perceptual theory. In F. R. Kilpatrick (Ed.), *Human behavior from the transactional point of view.* Hanover, New Hampshire: Institute for Associated Research, 1952.

Jacobson, M., & Gaze, R. M. Types of visual response from single units in the optic tectum and optic nerve of the goldfish. *Quarterly Journal of Experimental Physiology,* 1964, **49,** 199–209.

Jahoda, G. Retinal pigmentation, illusion susceptibility and space perception. *International Journal of Psychology,* 1971, **6,** 199–208.

Julesz, B. Binocular depth perception without familiarity cues. *Science,* 1964, **145,** 356–362.

Julesz, B. *Foundations of cyclopean perception.* Chicago: Univ. of Chicago Press, 1971.

Kessen, W., Salapatek, P., & Haith, M. The visual response of the human newborn to linear contour. *Journal of Experimental Child Psychology,* 1972, **13,** 9–20.

Kimura, D. Cerebral dominance and the perception of verbal stimuli. *Canadian Journal of Psychology,* 1961, **15,** 166–171.

Kimura, D. Spatial localization in left and right visual fields. *Canadian Journal of Psychology,* 1969, **23,** 445–458.

Koffka, K. *Principles of Gestalt psychology.* New York: Harcourt, 1935.

Köhler, W. *Gestalt psychology.* New York: Liveright, 1929.

Köhler, W., & Wallach, H. Figural after-effects: An investigation of visual processes. *Proceedings of the American Philosophical Society,* 1944, **88,** 269–357.

Kolers, P. A., & Perkins, D. N. Orientation of letters and errors in their recognition. *Perception & Psychophysics,* 1969, **5,** 265–269. (a)

Kolers, P. A., & Perkins, D. N. Orientation of letters and their speed of recognition. *Perception & Psychophysics,* 1969, **5,** 275–280. (b)

Kolers, P. A. Experiments in reading. *Scientific American,* 1972, **227,** 84–91.

Kopferman, H. Psychologische Untersuchungen über die Wirkung zweidimensionaler Darstellung Körperliche Gebilde. *Psychologische Forschung,* 1930, **13,** 293–364.

Krauskopf, D., Cornsweet, T. N., & Riggs, L. A. Analysis of eye movements during monocular and binocular fixation. *Journal of the Optical Society of America,* 1960, **50,** 572–578.

Kristofferson, A. B. Attention and psychophysical time. *Acta Psychologica,* 1967, **27,** 93–100.

Lazarus, R. S., & McCleary, R. A. Autonomic discrimination without awareness: A study of subception. *Psychological Review,* 1951, **58,** 113–122.

Leibowitz, H. W., Graham, C. H., & Parrish, M. The effect of hypnotic age regression on size constancy. *American Journal of Psychology,* 1972, **85,** 271–276.

Lettvin, J. Y., Maturana, H. R., McCulloch, W. S., & Pitts, W. H. What the frog's eye tells the frog's brain. *Proceedings of the Institute of Radio Engineers,* 1959, **47,** 1940–1951.

Lindsay, P. H., & Norman, D. A. *Human information processing.* New York: Academic Press, 1971.

Mach, E. *The analysis of sensations.* New York: Dover, 1959. [Original edition: 1896.]

MacKay, D. M. Ways of looking at perception. In W. Wathen-Dunn (Ed.). *Models for the perception of speech and visual form.* Cambridge, Massachusetts: M.I.T. Press, 1967.

Mackworth, N. H., & Bruner, J. S. Measuring how adults and children search and recognize pictures. *Human Development,* 1970, **13,** 149–177.

Merryman, C. T., & Restle, F. Perceptual displacement of a test mark toward the larger of two objects. *Journal of Experimental Psychology,* 1970, **86,** 311–318.

Minsky, M., & Papert, S. Artificial intelligence progress report. *Artificial intelligence memo. No. 252.* Massachusetts Institute of Technology, 1972.

Mishkin, M., & Forgays, D. G. Word recognition as a function of retinal locus. *Journal of Experimental Psychology,* 1952, **43,** 43–48.

Mitchell, D. E., Freeman, R. D., Millodot, M., & Haegerstrom, G. Meridional amblyopia: Evidence for modification of the human visual system by early visual experience. *Vision Research,* 1973, **13,** 535–558.

Moray, N. *Attention: Selective processes in vision and hearing.* London: Hutchinson, 1969.

McGinnies, E. Emotionality and perceptual defense. *Psychological Review,* 1949, **56,** 244–251.

McKenzie, B. E., & Day, R. H. Object distance as a determinant of visual fixation in early infancy. *Science,* 1972, **178,** 1108–1109.

McKinnon, G. E., Forde, J., & Piggins, D. J. Stabilized images, steadily fixated figures, and proglonged after-images. *Canadian Journal of Psychology,* 1969, **23,** 184–195.

Natsoulas, T. Converging operations for perceptual defense. *Psychological Bulletin,* 1965, **64,** 393–401.

Natsoulas, T. What are perceptual reports about? *Psychological Bulletin,* 1967, **67,** 249–272.

Neisser, U. *Cognitive psychology.* New York: Appleton, 1967.

Noda, H., Freeman, R. B., & Creutzfeldt, O. D. Neuronal correlates of eye movements in the visual cortex of the cat. *Science,* 1972, **175,** 661–663.

Nye, P. W., & Bliss, J. C. Sensory aids for the blind: A challenging problem with lessons for the future. *Proceedings of the I.E.E.E.,* 1970, **58,** 1878–1898.

O'Bryan, K., & Boersma, F. J. Eye movements, perceptual activity and conservation development. *Journal of Experimental Child Psychology,* 1971, **12**(2), 157–169.

Otto, W., Barrett, C., Smith, R. J., Dulin, K. L., & Johnson, D. Summary and review of investigations relating to reading. *Journal of Educational Research,* 1972, **65,** 242–271.

Over, R. Explanations of geometrical illusions. *Psychological Bulletin,* 1968, **70,** 545–562.

Over, R. Comparison of normalization theory and neural enhancement explanation of negative after-effects. *Psychological Bulletin,* 1971, **75,** 225–243.

Pettigrew, J., Olson, C., & Barlow, H. B. Kitten visual cortex: Short term stimulus-induced changes in connectivity. *Science,* 1973, **180,** 1202–1203.

Piaget, J. *Logic and psychology.* New York: Basic Books, 1957.

Piaget, J. *The mechanisms of perception.* (Trans. by G. N. Seagrim.) London: Routledge and Kegan Paul, 1969.

Postman, L., Bruner, J. S., & McGinnies, E. Personal values as selective factors in perception. *Journal of Abnormal & Social Psychology,* 1948, **43,** 142–154.

Pressey, A. W. An extension of assimilation theory to illusions of size, area, and direction. *Perception & Psychophysics,* 1971, **9,** 172–176.

Pressey, A. W., & Sweeney, O. Acute angles and the Poggendorf illusion. *Quarterly Journal of Experimental Psychology,* 1972, **24,** 169–176.

Price, H. Signal-detection methods in personality and perception. *Psychological Bulletin,* 1966, **66,** 55–62.

Pritchard, R. M., Heron, W., & Hebb, D. O. Visual perception approached by the method of stabilized images. *Canadian Journal of Psychology,* 1960, **14,** 67–77.

Restle, F. *Mathematical models in psychology.* Baltimore: Penguin Books, 1971.

Riggs, L. A., Ratliff, F., Cornsweet, J. C., & Cornsweet, T. N. The disappearance of steadily fixated test objects. *Journal of the Optical Society of America,* 1953, **43,** 495–501.

Rivers, W. H. R. Vision. In A. C. Haddon (Ed.), *Reports of the Cambridge Anthropological Expedition to the Torres Straits.* Vol. II, Part 1. Cambridge: Cambridge Univ. Press, 1901.

Rivers, W. R. H. Observations on the senses of the Tobas. *British Journal of Psychology,* 1905, **1,** 321–396.

Rock, I., & Kaufman, L. The moon illusion. *Science,* 1962, **136,** 1023–1031.

Rock, I., & Kremen, I. A re-examination of Rubin's figural aftereffect. *Journal of Experimental Psychology,* 1957, **53,** 23–30.

Rubin, E. *Visuelle wahrgenommene Figuren.* Copenhagen: Gyldenalske, 1921.

Segall, M. H., Campbell, D. T., & Herskovits, M. J. Cultural differences in the perception of geometric illusions. *Science,* 1963, **139,** 769–771.

Segall, M. H., Campbell, D. T., & Herskovits, M. J. *The Influence of culture on visual perception.* Indianapolis: Bobbs-Merrill, 1966.

Senden, M. von. *Raum-und Gestalt-auffassung bei operierten Blindgeborenen vor und nach der Operation.* Leipzig: Barth, 1932. [Translated as: *Space and sight. The perception of space and shape in the congenitally blind before and after operation.* (Trans. by P. Heath.) Glencoe, Illinois: the Free Press, and London: Methuen, 1960.]

Shepard, R. Recognition memory for words, sentences, and pictures. *Journal of Verbal learning & Verbal behavior,* 1967, **6,** 156–163.

Sherif, M. A study of some social factors in perception. *Archives of Psychology,* 1935, **187,** 60.

Solomon, R. L., & Howes, D. Word frequency, personal values, and visual duration thresholds. *Psychological Review,* 1951, **58,** 256–270.

Sperling, G. The information available in brief visual presentations. *Psychological Monographs,* 1960, **74,** (Whole No. 498).

Sperling, G. Successive approximations to a model for short-term memory. *Acta Psychologica,* 1967, **27,** 285–292.

Standing, L. G. Learning 10,000 pictures. *Quarterly Journal of Experimental Psychology,* 1973, **25,** 207–222.

Standing, L. G., Conezio, J., & Haber, R. N. Perception and memory for pictures: Single-trial learning of 2500 visual stimuli. *Psychonomic Science,* 1970, **19,** 73–74.

Stewart, V. M. *A cross-cultural test of the "carpentered environment" hypothesis using three geometric illusions in Zambia.* Unpublished doctoral dissertation, University of Illinois, Urbana, Illinois, 1971.

Street, R. F. A Gestalt completion test: A study of a cross section of intellect. In *Teachers College Contributions to Education,* No. 481. New York: Teachers College, Columbia University, 1931.

Sutherland, N. S. Object recognition. In E. C. Carterette & M. P. Friedman (Eds.), *Handbook of perception,* Vol. 3. New York: Academic Press, 1973.

Swets, A. J., & Kristofferson, A. B. Attention. In P. Mussen & M. Rosenzweig (Eds.), *Annual review of psychology, 1970.* Palo Alto: Annual Reviews, 1970.

Swets, J. A., Tanner, W. P. Jr., & Bridsall, T. G. Decision processes in perception. *Psychological Review,* 1961, **68,** 301–340.

Thouless, R. H. Phenomenal regression to the real object I. *British Journal of Psychology,* 1931, **21,** 339–359. (a)

Thouless, R. H. Phenomenal regression to the real object II. *British Journal of Psychology,* 1931, **22,** 1–30. (b)

Thouless, R. H. Individual differences in phenomenal regression. *British Journal of Psychology,* 1932, **22,** 216–241.

Uhr, L. Pattern recognition. New York: Wiley, 1966.

Walk, R. D., & Gibson, E. J. A comparative and analytical study of visual depth perception. *Psychological Monographs,* 1961, **75,** No. 15 (Whole No. 519).

Wallace, G. K. The critical distance of interaction in the Zollner illusion. *Perception & Psychophysics,* 1969, **5,** 261–264.

White, B. L. *Human infants. Experience and psychological development.* Englewood Cliffs, New Jersey. Prentice-Hall, 1971.

White, B. W., Saunders, F. A., Scadden, L., Bach-y-Rita, P., & Collins, C. C. Seeing with the skin. *Perception and Psychophysics,* 1970, **7,** 23–27.

White, M. J. Laterality differences in perception: A review. *Psychological Bulletin,* 1969, **72,** 387–405.

Witkin, H. A., Dyk, R. B., Faterson, H. F., Goodenough, D. R., & Karp, S. A. *Psychological differentiation.* New York: Wiley, 1962.

Wohlwill, J. F. Developmental studies of perception. *Psychological Bulletin,* 1960, **57,** 249–288.

Yarbus, A. L. *Eye movements and vision.* New York: Plenum Press, 1967.

Young, F. A., & Lindsley, D. B. *Early experience and visual information processing in perceptual and reading disorders.* Washington: National Academy of Sciences, 1970.

Zusne, L. *Visual perception of form.* New York: Academic Press, 1970.

Chapter 9

COLOR, HUE, AND WAVELENGTH

ROBERT M. BOYNTON

I. INTRODUCTION

The flow chart of Fig. 1 is intended to represent 11 stages (A through K) of major questions concerned with the perception of colored objects. To provide a sample of some fundamentally wrong ideas about color perception, among many that have been seriously considered at one time or another, some rejected hypotheses are also included in Fig. 1. These statements are in thin-line boxes that are terminal, leading nowhere.

On the other hand, the selection of a correct hypothesis, at some stage of the chart, because it does not suffice to answer fully the initial question about how people perceive the colors of objects, merely leads in each instance to another question and then to more alternative hypotheses. The heavy arrows connecting the boxes of Fig. 1 define the path toward truth.

Although the stages are intended to form a logical sequence, the questions at each stage were not necessarily answered chronologically before a subsequent stage came under investigation. For example, the discovery of the retinal image (Stage D) occurred around 1600 (Polyak, 1957), yet the nature of light (Stage C) was quite unknown until the nineteenth century (Abrahamson & Japar, 1972). For the most part, however, these stages have been reached successively.

Although no answer can be regarded as final at any stage, the resolution of a choice from among major alternatives has allowed investigators to proceed more surely and swiftly toward each subsequent stage. For example, there is virtually unanimous agreement today (see the reviews by Abramov, 1972; Rushton, 1972; and Jameson, 1972) that the cone photoreceptors (Stage E) generate univariant responses (Stage F) that are broadly tuned to wavelength (Stage G), and it is also highly probable that these come in three types, whose differing spectral sensitivities are roughly known (Stage H). Yet the knowledge of facts about these stages does not preclude the need for still more detailed investigations of the photoreceptors of Stage E by a wide variety of techniques, including the established methods of electron microscopy, retinal densitometry, psychophysics, radioautography, electrophysiology, and microspectrophotometry. Nor would continued success with these methods eliminate the need for further studies using instruments and procedures yet to be imagined.

Some more examples may help.

(a) Although much has been learned about visual photochemistry, it remains to be discovered exactly how the absorption of photons by the cone photoreceptors manages to release responses from these structures (Stage F).

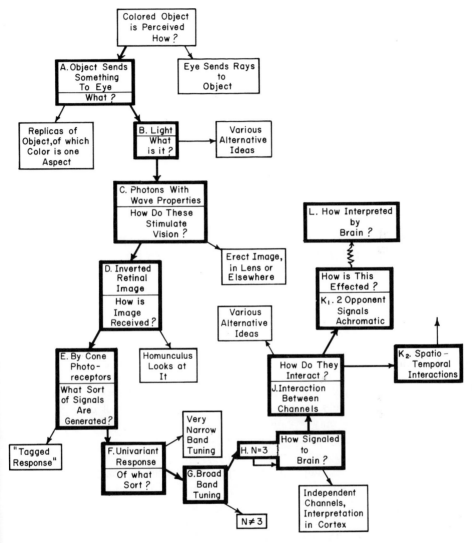

FIG. 1. Eleven stages of questions (A through K) about the perception of colored objects. Heavy arrows trace the pathways to verified hypotheses, which are in heavy boxes. Some alternative hypotheses that have been rejected are also indicated by light boxes.

(b) Because the precise shapes of the three fundamental spectral sensitivity curves (Stage H) are of theoretical importance, these are still under active investigation.

(c) Even at a very early stage, like D, detailed investigations of retinal images are still very much in order.

The "hot" topics at the present time are subsumed under Stages J and K, and L. As these questions are further pursued, it will almost certainly be found that the question posed at Stage K, how the brain interprets the chromatic signals that it receives, is much too general. Eventually, it may be predicted, there may be as many more stages as those already identified in Fig. 1 before the loop finally can be closed.

It should also be noted that many side issues are not represented on the flow chart—for example, color blindness. Interpretation of color blindness is not logically necessary as part of the description of normal human color vision. Yet, because it has turned out that color deficiencies frequently take the form of "reduced" normal color vision—for example, some people seem to possess only two of the normal three cone photopigments—the study of color-deficient individuals permits a look at simpler systems of color processing which helps to elucidate the nature of color vision in the normal observer. Thus, although the study of color deficiency is not represented in Fig. 1, knowledge gained from it is useful in helping to provide answers at Stages F through J.

II. BASIC CONCEPTS

A. Color

Color is the aspect of visual perception by which an observer may distinguish differences between two structure-free fields of view of the same size and shape, such as may be caused by differences in the spectral composition of the radiant energy concerned in the observation.

This definition of color, put forth by Wyszecki and Stiles (1967), can be elaborated by reference to a bipartite field. Assuming that the two components of the field are continuously present, or flashed simultaneously, a color difference is said to exist between them if they are seen as being different in any way. Such a difference ordinarily produces a contour that appears to divide the two halves of the field, although exceptions to this have been reported (Boynton & Greenspon, 1972).

B. Isomerism

Imagine a transilluminated circular field that is spatially homogeneous in color, except that a low-density neutral filter is placed in front of one half of it, as shown in Fig. 2. The physical change that this produces is shown in Fig. 3. The hue and saturation of the two half-fields will remain

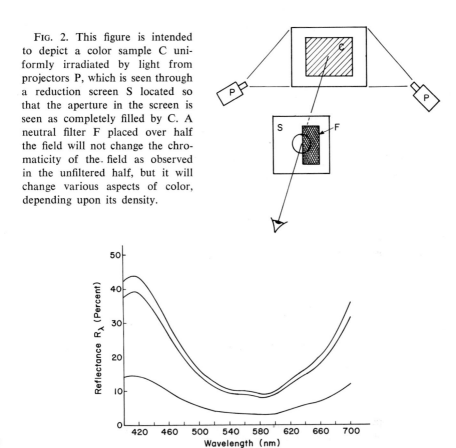

FIG. 2. This figure is intended to depict a color sample C uniformly irradiated by light from projectors P, which is seen through a reduction screen S located so that the aperture in the screen is seen as completely filled by C. A neutral filter F placed over half the field will not change the chromaticity of the field as observed in the unfiltered half, but it will change various aspects of color, depending upon its density.

FIG. 3. The uppermost curve shows the diffuse reflectance, as measured by Davidson and Hemmendinger, of Easton, Pennsylvania, of an actual Munsell paper chip having a nominal specification of 10PB/4/10. This is a rather light bluish purple of rather low saturation (see Wyszecki and Stiles, 1965, p. 476–478 for an explanation of the Munsell notation). The middle curve shows the result of reducing reflectance by about 12% at all wavelengths, which is equivalent to the use of a neutral filter of density .05 in the demonstration illustrated in Fig. 2. This would produce a small reduction in lightness, but little or no change in chromaticness. The bottom curve has a value at each wavelength of exactly ⅓ that of the uppermost one, equivalent to a filter density of .477 in Fig. 2. This sample would look much darker, and there would probably be a change in hue and saturation as well.

the same, the only perceptible difference being one of brightness. Now if the filter is removed, so that the absolute spectral energy distributions of the two half-fields are again made equal, a physically homogeneous field of light is again provided. The match of color between the two halves of such a field is termed *isomeric,* meaning that no physical difference exists between the half-fields. No discrimination between them is therefore possible, whether by eye or by physical instrument.

Depending upon the density of the inserted filter, there are actually three stages of differences that can be distinguished. If the density is very low, no difference will be perceived, despite the small physical difference that exists. This points up the fact that there is a *threshold* of color difference. For a filter of somewhat higher density, as already noted, only a brightness difference will be seen, and we may state this differently by saying that there is no difference in *chromaticness* between the half fields. For filters of higher density, hue and saturation (to be defined precisely later) may also change, although the relative spectral distribution still does not, which implies that some alteration of spectral distribution would be required to restore a chromatic match (for hue and saturation, but not brightness). The change in hue that often occurs with substantial changes in luminance is known as the *Bezold–Brücke hue shift.*

In order for a *chromatic* difference to exist, two conditions usually must be met:

(*a*) There must be a difference between the relative spectral distributions of the two half fields.

(*b*) This difference must produce a difference in the hue and/or saturation of the two fields.

An exception to the first rule may occur if the two parts of the retina upon which the half fields are imaged are asymmetrically adapted. A familiar example of this takes place in the perception of negative afterimages. If one fixates for a time upon a field that is, say, half red and half green, and then views a homogeneous white surface, the opposite hues are seen in each half of the afterimage, even though the same light reaches each eye. This chapter will not be concerned with the effects of chromatic adaptation. Emphasis will be upon the perception of the hue and saturation of real lights as mediated by the neutrally adapted, normal eye.

C. Metamerism

It is well known that there are many pairs of lights that appear the same, even though they are physically different. The rules for predicting such *metameric* matches are, to a first approximation, very simple.

In 1933, the *Commission Internationale de l'Eclairage* (CIE) established three "color-mixture" functions for a so-called "standard observer." From the CIE viewpoint, the standard observer consists, in effect, of three photocells, having the spectral sensitivities $\bar{x}_\lambda$, $\bar{y}_\lambda$, and $\bar{z}_\lambda$, each providing a measurable response that is linearly related to the irradiance of the light incident upon them.* These values vary, depending upon the amount and spectral distribution of the incident light. Readings of the outputs from three such photocells constitute quantities proportional to the "tristimulus values" X, Y, and Z, defined later in this section. The CIE has, in effect, defined the real observer out of the system. On the other hand, if the functions $\bar{x}_\lambda$, $\bar{y}_\lambda$, and $\bar{z}_\lambda$ did not bear a close resemblance to the color-matching behavior of real observers, the system would be useless. To the contrary, it has proved highly useful.

These three functions of wavelength are called *color-matching functions,* or more precisely *distribution coefficients for an equal energy spectrum.* These functions are related to a tripartitioning of signals that occurs in the three kinds of cones of the visual systems of real human beings, about which more will be said later. The result of metamerism is that, if lights have differing energy distributions $E_{1\lambda}$ and $E_{2\lambda}$ as a function of wavelength (λ) are integrated in turn with each of the three CIE functions, and if the same numerical values are obtained for each corresponding pair, then these will produce the same "responses" in all three "channels" for the ideal observer:

$$\int E_{1\lambda}\bar{x}\,d\lambda = \int E_{2\lambda}\bar{x}\,d\lambda; \tag{1a}$$

$$\int E_{1\lambda}\bar{y}\,d\lambda = \int E_{2\lambda}\bar{y}\,d\lambda; \tag{1b}$$

$$\int E_{1\lambda}\bar{z}\,d\lambda = \int E_{2\lambda}\bar{z}\,d\lambda. \tag{1c}$$

D. Chromaticity

If the three corresponding values for each side of the field all stand in the same ratios, even though they differ in absolute values, then the two halves of the field will have the same *chromaticity* at different luminances. This would happen if a neutral filter, no matter how dense, were placed in front of one half of a field. The two fields would not, of course, look alike, since one would appear darker than the other, and there might be a Bezold–Brücke hue shift as well. Nevertheless, if two fields have the same chromaticity, and if the radiance of one half of the field can be adjusted relative to the other without change in relative spectral distribution, then there must be some radiance of that field which will cause the fields to match for the standard observer.

The *chromaticity of a surface* depends upon the spectral distribution (E_λ) of the light irradiating it, the diffuse spectral reflectance of the surface (R_λ), and the CIE distribution functions $\bar{x}_\lambda$, $\bar{y}_\lambda$, and $\bar{z}_\lambda$. To calculate

---

* The subscript is usually omitted in this specification. It will be included here, but omitted later in the chapter.

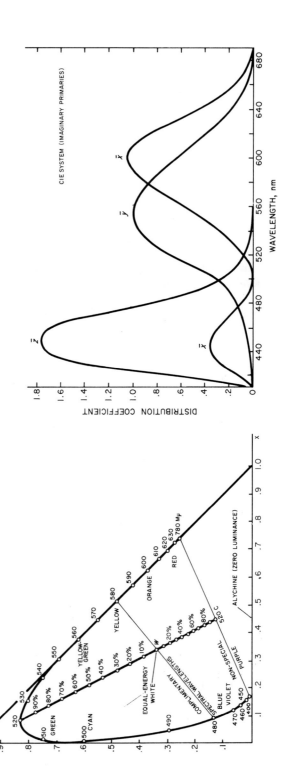

chromaticity, it is first necessary to determine three *tristimulus values X, Y,* and *Z* as follows:

$$X = \int E_\lambda R_\lambda \bar{x}_\lambda \, d\lambda; \tag{2a}$$

$$Y = \int E_\lambda R_\lambda \bar{y}_\lambda \, d\lambda; \tag{2b}$$

$$Z = \int E_\lambda R_\lambda \bar{z}_\lambda \, d\lambda. \tag{2c}$$

Then the three proportions, *x, y,* and *z,* which define the *chromaticity coefficients* must be determined:

$$x = X/(X + Y + Z); \tag{3a}$$
$$y = Y/(X + Y + Z); \tag{3b}$$
$$z = Z/(X + Y + Z); \tag{3c}$$

where $x + y + z = 1$.

Usually, *y* is plotted as a function of *x*, yielding the *chromaticity diagram* of Fig. 4, upon which the locus of spectral colors plots as a smooth, inverted U curve, and within which all other colors fall. Each point in the diagram represents all possible metamers of colors having that chromaticity.

Two surfaces of the same chromaticity, if also isomeric, will match at equal brightness for all observers under all conditions of illumination, whatever the state of adaptation of the eye. Two surfaces of equal luminance and chromaticity, if metameric, will not necessarily match exactly for any

---

FIG. 4. Color mixture functions of the CIE system are shown at the right. The CIE standard chromaticity diagram is shown at the left. The equal-energy white point, or achromatic point, is located at $x = y = .33$. The location of a given stimulus upon the chart can be specified either in terms of the chromaticity coordinates or by *dominant wavelength* and *excitation purity*. For example, the point labeled "30%" is located at approximately $x = .26$ and $y = .48$. It can also be specified as having a dominant wavelength of 520 mμ and an excitation purity of 30%. The dominant wavelength is determined by drawing a straight line from the white point through the point to be specified (sample point) until the line intersects the spectral locus; the spectral wavelength corresponding to the intersection point is the dominant wavelength. Excitation purity (OSA) is the "distance between achromatic and sample points, divided by the distance between achromatic point and the point on the spectrum locus representing the dominant wavelength of the sample." Examples of complementary chromaticities are also shown, e.g., 480 and 580 mμ on the spectral locus, or any two points along the line connecting them that fall on opposite sides of the white point. Note that the spectral color 520 mμ has no spectral complementary but intersects the line connecting nonspectral purples. This point is identified with the wavelength of the complementary chromaticity, followed by "C." Excitation purities for nonspectral chromaticities between the white point and 520 C are also shown; in this case 100% purity is defined by the intersection of the extension of the 520–white line with the nonspectral purple line. [From Boynton (1966).]

particular real observer, because real observers differ slightly from each other and from the ideal observer of the CIE system. Matches will break down seriously for color-defective individuals or if certain stipulated conditions of viewing are not met. These include a 2° field, centrally fixated and steadily viewed, in a luminance range from about 10 to 10,000 td. Also, any movement of the eyes—for example, one that would image the field on the peripheral retina—will usually destroy a match. Similarly, a gross change in field area, causing the centrally fixated field to be imaged upon the peripheral as well as central retina, may do likewise.

Even for the standard observer and stipulated viewing conditions, two fields that match metamerically under one illuminant will not, generally, do so under a different one, because the values X, Y, and Z of Eq. (1) usually will be differentially affected by changes in E_λ.

Whereas the three channels of the CIE system are, in effect, photocells, the three channels of the human eye are provided by the three different kinds of cone photoreceptors, whose initial signals are kept separate. The human eye is incredibly more complicated than a photocell, including the simple fact that, before reaching the cones, the light must pass through the eye media, which are selectively absorptive as a function of wavelength. If the spectral sensitivities of the cones are defined in terms of light reaching the cornea, rather than the retina, then an important relation exists between the cone sensitivity curves and the CIE distribution functions for an equal energy spectrum: For a real observer, whose matches are in accord with the predictions of the CIE system, it must be true that if S_λ, M_λ, and L_λ (representing the absorption spectra of the three kinds of cones, peaking in the short-, middle-, and longwave regions of the spectrum) were substituted in turn for $\bar{z}_\lambda$, $\bar{y}_\lambda$, and $\bar{x}_\lambda$ in Eqs. (1), identical predictions about color matches would be made.

E. Luminance

Two surfaces have equal *luminance* if $Y_1 = Y_2$. Such surfaces will appear approximately equal in brightness, but not necessarily exactly so. In general, the more saturated of two fields will appear brighter than the less saturated one. The photopic luminous efficiency function V_λ, which was standardized in 1931 by the CIE, is based primarily upon flicker photometry, a method that is able to tap the response of the achromatic channels of the human visual apparatus, while disregarding the chromatic ones (see Section VII).

That it proved possible to set y_λ proportional to V_λ is probably of theoretical as well as practical importance. Given the very different nature of the color mixture experiments from which the distribution coefficients were derived, when compared with the earlier flicker photometric experiments, the possibility of doing this was not preordained. That it can be done seems related to the physiology of the human visual system, which separates achromatic and chromatic signals to a high degree.

The practical importance of choosing a set of functions where $\bar{y}_\lambda = KV_\lambda$ is that calculations about luminance and chromaticity can be done with only three equations, rather than four.

An embarrassment to the CIE system, considered critical by some (e.g., see Graham, 1959) results from so-called additivity failure in human vision. This topic has been reexamined by Guth, Donley, and Marrocco (1969) and by Boynton and Kaiser (1968), where references to earlier papers can be found. The embarrassment can be most clearly described in terms of an example. In the CIE system, 580 nm and 480 nm are *complementary colors* (see Fig. 4). That is, when mixed in suitable proportions (about 80 and 20 td for the standard observer) they will match an equal-energy white light. According to the CIE system (recall the linear photocells) 80 td of yellow light at 580 nm and 20 td of blue-green light at 482.5 nm should (and do, by definition) when mixed produce 100 td of white light. The embarrassment comes about because the components of such a mixture field will in fact appear quite a bit brighter than white fields of equal luminance, whereas their mixture does not. The problem can be avoided by using criteria for comparing heterochromatic fields that do not produce additivity failure. The methods of flicker photometry and minimally distinct border are suitable for this purpose, but they do not predict the relative brightness of the fields of different chromaticity.

A way toward a solution has been pointed by Guth (1973). His work, and that of others, indicates that luminance should be regarded as a vector, rather than a scalar, quantity. Such *vector luminance* would then not predict additivity of stimuli of 580 and 480 nm. For example, if the luminance vectors were opposed, such a revised system would predict 80 — 20 or 60 td in the mixture.

F. Hue and Saturation

The term *hue* refers to that aspect of a field of light to which color names such as red, green, and purple, are assigned. (The word *color,* in the vernacular, almost always means *hue.*) A field that is strongly hued is said to be *chromatic*. In the absence of hue, a white, gray, or black is perceived. These sensations are said to be *achromatic* (without hue).

There exists a continuum of sensations running from an achromatic one, such as white, to a highly chromatic one, for example that sensation elicited by a longwave spectral light which appears vividly red. "Saturation has often been defined as 'the amount of hue in a color' and this adequately describes its independent status" according to Evans (1964). *Saturation* will be discussed in detail in Section VIII.

G. Correlations between Perceptual and Physical Variables

Two fields may be of different color because of hue, brightness, or saturation differences, existing singly or in combination. Hue is most highly correlated with spectral distribution, brightness with radiance or luminance, and saturation with the amount of monochromatic light in a mixture of monochromatic and white lights. But there are severe interactions in all cases. As already noted, luminance, can alter hue; it also can affect saturation. Therefore, neither spectral distribution (nor chromaticity, which it exactly predicts) can be the sole determiner of hue. Moreover, when a spectral light is mixed with white in various proportions, hue may change drastically. The most impressive example is the distinct redness that is produced in a pure blue by the addition of white light. And significant as these complications are between physical and perceptual variables, they fade into insignificance when compared to the alterations in hue, saturation, and lightness that can be produced by the influence of surround fields (Stage J_2 in Fig. 1). Land's (1959) elegant demonstrations have served as reminders of this. These complications will not be discussed further in this chapter.

III. SUBJECTIVE DESCRIPTION AND ORDERING OF COLORS

A. Color Diagram

If a large number of colored chips, for example, paint samples, are randomly tossed onto a table, with instructions to a human subject to "arrange these in some rational way," a possible outcome is a psychological color diagram of the sort illustrated in Fig. 5. The most saturated colors are placed toward the outside of the diagram, ordered according to hue. There are four hues that are considered to be "psychologically unique"; these are placed at the ends of vertical and horizontal diameters, with Y (for unique yellow) at the top. Y is intended to represent a yellow that is unique in the sense that it does not contain a trace of any other hue. Most yellows are tinged, more or less strongly, with a trace of green or red. The latter may be regarded as secondary components of two-valued hue sensations where yellow is dominant.

A patch of light, or area of visual space, usually has two hues associated with it, as, for example, a primary yellow and a secondary green. Some

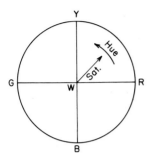

FIG. 5. Two-dimensional psychological color diagram, intended to represent, in an orderly way, colors of equal brightness. No reference to physical measurement is intended. The hues represented on the principal axes are psychologically unique.

combinations, specifically blue–yellow and red–green blends, are never seen. This fact, which is of fundamental importance, was seized upon by Hering (1964)* in the development of his opponent-colors theory, and any complete theory of color vision must indeed explain it (see Section VII).

B. Unique Hues

There are four psychologically unique hues: yellow, green, blue, and red. The relations among these four hues are shown in Table I, and are manifest also in Fig. 5, where contiguous hues represent perceivable blends, and opposite hues do not coexist. The arrangement shown in Fig. 5, though arbitrary in other respects, follows the rules of Table I and, for convenience, places the unique hues at the cardinal points of the compass, with red east, yellow north, green west, and blue south.

Because of the need to arrange hues in a circle, rather than in a straight line, it might be thought that sensations of hue should be regarded as being two-dimensional. Nevertheless, it is common and correct to speak of hue as a single dimension of a three-dimensional color sensation, with saturation and brightness as the other two. This is because, as is indicated by

TABLE I

PSYCHOLOGICALLY UNIQUE HUES: PERMISSIBLE AND PROHIBITED BLENDS

Psychologically unique hue	Permissible secondary hues	Prohibited secondary hues
Red	Yellow or Blue	Green
Yellow	Green or Red	Blue
Green	Blue or Yellow	Red
Blue	Red or Green	Yellow

* This is the date of publication of a translation by L. Hurvich and D. Jameson of material originally published by Hering much earlier, mostly between 1905 and 1911.

the psychological diagram described here [and others derived by more objective techniques (Section V)], hue and saturation *together* are representable in two dimensions, which can be separated by the simple device of using polar coordinates. If this is done, it then makes sense to assert that hue, as represented by the angle of a vector, is one of the dimensions of color sensation, while saturation, represented by the length of a vector, is another.

All colors falling on a particular radius of the circle of Fig. 5 are therefore to be regarded as being of the same hue. For example, unique yellow appears in its most saturated form at the top center of the diagram, and acquires progressively more white content toward the center, finally becoming white. Nowhere along the radius should it appear either reddish or greenish.

C. Balanced Hues

As one moves around the color circle, for example, counterclockwise from red toward yellow, a variety of yellowish reds are represented, with the yellow component gradually becoming stronger as the red is reduced. Moving clockwise from unique yellow toward red, a variety of reddish yellows are represented, with the initially weaker red component becoming progressively stronger. Somewhere, the two components must balance; this point is represented halfway between, at northeast on the compass. Similar balances may be imagined at three other points on the circle. These balances are also assumed to remain along the oblique radii that connect these four points to white at the center.

For anyone who has no cause to refer to the physical aspects of color, or who is not particularly concerned either about the physiological processes that intervene between stimulation of the eye by light and the resulting color perception, a psychological diagram like that of Fig. 5 is useful, and perhaps sufficient, as an ordered description of relevant facts about isolated patches of color. Diagrams like this, which are very commonly used by artists, interior decorators, and paint manufacturers, owe their origin to Newton, who had in mind the possibility that it might also prove useful as a device to describe the mixture of colors.

D. Color Names

The number of discriminably different colors is at least 100,000, in the sense that any two of them will look different if placed side by side and viewed under ideal circumstances. Yet our ability to identify single colors, on an absolute basis, is so limited that no more than seven different colors of signal lights may safely be used where life-and-death are at stake (Halsey, 1959a,b). When the ability to discriminate colors is tested by presenting them at different times, memory is required and it seems likely that verbal mediators are used to bridge even a few seconds of time. Color names are very widely used and there exist a bewildering variety of color terms, limited only by the imaginations of interior decorators, paint vendors, artists, and fashion designers to invent them.

On the other hand, color naming is by no means an entirely arbitrary process. A study by Berlin and Kay (1969) has recently been neatly summarized by Trandis, Malpass, and Davidson (1973) as follows:

> Humans give identical responses (as perceived by an observer) to discriminably different stimuli. This phenomenon is called categorization. Earlier views of the literature . . . established that categorization is universal, but what is categorized varies from culture to culture. Extensive cross-cultural work has been done with color categories, primarily because it is possible to establish relationships between the physical character of the stimuli and the responses of the subjects. Much of this research is reviewed by Berlin and Kay . . . who also provide evidence in favor of the conclusion that there are semantic universals in color terminology and basic color terms are acquired in every culture in the same order. Although different languages encode in their vocabularies different numbers of basic color categories, there are exactly 11 basic categories from which the color terms of every language always draw.
>
> The basic sequence is:

$$\left\{ \begin{array}{c} \text{white} \\ \text{black} \end{array} \right\} \rightarrow \{\text{red}\} \rightarrow \left\{ \begin{array}{c} \text{yellow} \\ \text{or} \\ \text{green} \end{array} \right\} \rightarrow \left\{ \begin{array}{c} \text{yellow} \\ \text{and} \\ \text{green} \end{array} \right\} \rightarrow \{\text{blue}\} \rightarrow \{\text{brown}\} \rightarrow \left\{ \begin{array}{c} \text{purple} \\ \text{pink} \\ \text{orange} \\ \text{gray} \end{array} \right\}$$

> The authors show that all languages have terms for white and black, and if they have a third term it is red; if they have four terms it is yellow or green; if they have five it is both yellow and green, etc. They suggest that this is also the order of color term development in children.

The work of Berlin and Kay and a great deal of other evidence has been reviewed by Bornstein (1973), who feels that black, white, red, yellow, green, and blue, chosen "from the vast vocabulary and array of color," can be used with confidence to form the "semantic base for cross-cultural comparison." [See also an instructive review of the Berlin–Kay book by Conklin (1973).]

E. Dark Colors

Brown, which comes next on the Berlin and Kay list, is a novel sensation produced by "induction," the darkening of a yellow or orange color by a brighter surround field. (The extreme of this process yields black, no matter what the initial hue of the test color.) Black is a color, but not properly a hue, sharing this achromatic property with white and gray. If the test area contains a saturated hue to begin with, grayness will be induced into it by a brighter surround, and a dark color is created. Of these, brown is certainly the most surprising, because it ceases almost entirely to resemble the original bright color. Other dark colors, such as maroons, navy blues, and dark greens seem much more to retain their original hues, becoming merely darkened versions of the original bright colors. The dark colors add substantially to the richness and variety of our chromatic experiences and undoubtedly improve our ability to identify, in an absolute sense, the apparent color of objects under ordinary viewing conditions. A chocolate bar and an orange have approximately the same chromaticity, and yet their colors are entirely different because their reflectances vary so greatly. For the chocolate, the sensation of brown arises *de novo* by induction from a brighter surround.

F. Other Hues

1. ORANGE AND PURPLE

The last four terms on the Berlin–Kay list are relatively dispensable, but they are of interest for various reasons. Two of them, namely, orange and purple, are frequently used to describe balanced, or nearly balanced hues. One dictionary, in dealing with the term "orange," begins with a discussion of fruit and finally provides, as a fourth definition, the information that orange is "any of the colors resembling those of oranges, varying in hue from reddish red–yellow to red–yellow, in saturation from high to very high, and in brilliance from medium to high." The primary definition of purple is: "a color of a hue between blue and red; one of the colors commonly called magenta, violet, lilac, mauve, etc. . . ." Equally common terms for balanced blue–greens and yellow–greens apparently do not exist in any language (the term *cyan,* which is widely used in technical color work, does not even appear in at least one unabridged dictionary). A possible explanation for this is the lack of anything perceptually novel in these blends. Orange, on the other hand, though it may be accurately described in terms of its red and yellow components (Sternheim & Boynton, 1966), contains (for some people at least) something that is rather different from just a blend of red and yellow. Perhaps the same can be said of purple.

2. GRAY

The term "gray" refers to a sensation produced by induction when a slightly brighter area surrounds a test color. Gray is somewhat special, perhaps, in the same sense as orange, appearing subjectively to be something other than a mixture of black and white. If a test area is chromatic to begin with, a brighter, white surround will introduce a "gray content" into the test area.

Evans (1964) distinguishes four dimensions of hue sensation for colored surfaces, which he has investigated extensively using test and surround fields of various chromaticities and luminances. In addition to hue, lightness, and saturation, his fourth scale begins, for achromatic colors, with black, passes through gray, becomes white (when it matches the surround) and then, at a slightly higher luminance, achieves an appearance of "fluorence" (similar to what fluorescent surfaces produce). Chromatic stimuli first appear fluorent when their luminances are less than a white surround, becoming more so, the more saturated the color (see Section VIII). Excepting fluorescent materials, the appearance of fluorence seems closely associated with conditions where the chromatic test area is brighter than it physically could be, were it produced by a reflecting pigment, since all chromatic pigments reduce luminance by selectively absorbing more light than does the white surround.

3. PINK

Among the saturated colors, strong unique reds are perhaps the most common. Many desaturated reds, however, in addition to being more whitish than their saturated counterparts, have a distinctly bluish cast; it is to such a desaturated, slightly bluish reds that the name "pink" is usually attached. Perhaps for pink, as for some of the other colors just described, there is something slightly more unique about it than can be fully described in terms of its red, white, and blue components.

In concluding this section, it should be emphasized again that Fig. 5 has. nothing whatever to do with the physics of color; it merely attempts to arrange subjectively perceived colors in an orderly way. There are hundreds of possible observations about color, requiring the manipulation of colored lights or the mixing of pigments, that this diagram does not attempt to represent. For example, it is found that when psychologically unique red and green *lights* are mixed, a yellow results that resembles neither component. When yellow and blue *pigments* are mixed, green results, although the mixture of yellow and blue lights yields white. When white light is added to blue light, a secondary red hue is introduced. And so on.

The concept of the psychologically unique hues has had a controversial history as reflected, for example, by arguments between Hering and Helmholtz in the nineteenth century, and there still exist strong feelings about the subject among experts. By and large, those with strong physical orientations tend to discount them as being irrelevant. Many feel that they are culturally induced and have no relevance for the physiology of vision. Yet the data summarized by Berlin and Kay and by Bornstein offer evidence that there is indeed something very fundamental about red, yellow, green, and blue.

IV. PHYSICAL BASIS OF THE ORDERING OF SPECTRAL COLORS

A. Thomas Young Updated

In a famous statement written in 1802, Thomas Young said:

> Now, as it is almost impossible to conceive each sensitive point of the retina to contain an infinite number of particles, each capable of vibrating in perfect unison with every possible undulation, it becomes necessary to suppose the number limited; for instance to the three principal colours, red, yellow, and blue . . . and that each of the particles is capable of being put in motion more or less forcibly by undulations differing less or more from perfect unison . . . each sensitive filament of the nerve may consist of three portions, one for each principal colour.

Although it would have been impossible, in view of the knowledge available to him at the time, to improve upon Young's prophetic statement, we may translate it into more modern terms as follows:

> The wavelength of light is continuous, and is related to its perceived color. It is almost impossible to conceive that each sensitive point of the retina contains an infinite number of photoreceptors, each capable of perfect resonance with, and exclusive response to, every possible wavelength. Thus it becomes necessary to suppose their number limited, for example, to three types of cone photoreceptors, with differing but overlapping sensitivities to light as a function of wavelength, so that each type of cone is activated more or less strongly by various wavelengths, depending upon the difference between each wavelength and the wavelength at which the cone is maximally sensitive.

In this and the two following sections, the implications of the foregoing statement will be examined in detail.

B. The Wavelength of Light Is Continuous

In 1792, the *Encyclopaedia Britannica* stated "It is obvious . . . that whatever side we take concerning the nature of light, many, indeed almost

TABLE II

Light differs from other forms of matter primarily in that photons have zero rest mass. The relation between momentum (p) and energy (E) takes on a special form for photons (top row). Wavelength (λ) depends on momentum and Planck's constant (h). When this universal relation is reexpressed as a dependence on energy, two forms result (second row). The equations are rewritten to permit the calculation of energy in the third row. The equations on the bottom row show that particle velocity (v) depends upon energy, except in the case of photons. (Adapted from Feinberg, 1968.)

	General Case	Photons ($m = 0$)
$p =$	$\dfrac{\sqrt{E^2 - m^2c^4}}{c}$	$\dfrac{E}{c}$
$\lambda = \dfrac{h}{p} =$	$\dfrac{hc}{\sqrt{E^2 - m^2c^4}}$	$\dfrac{hc}{E}$
$E =$	$\sqrt{\left(\dfrac{hc}{\lambda}\right)^2 + m^2c^4}$	$\dfrac{hc}{\lambda}$
$v = \dfrac{pc^2}{E} =$	$c\sqrt{1 - \dfrac{m^2c^4}{E^2}}$	c

all the circumstances concerning it, are incomprehensible, and beyond the reach of human understanding" (quotation from Henderson, 1970, p. 1).

One hundred and seventy-six years later, writing in a special edition of *Scientific American* concerned with light, Feinberg (1968) stated, "At present the photon theory gives us an accurate description of all we know about light. The notion that light is fundamentally just another kind of matter is likely to persist in any future theory. That idea is the distinctive contribution of twentieth-century physicists to the understanding of light, and it is one of which we can well be proud [p. 59]."

One of the triumphs of twentieth-century physics has indeed been the clarification of the relation between the wavelength of light and the energy of photons. A photon is now regarded as vibrating, and since it moves it also has wave properties, sharing this property with all physical particles. The quantitative relations between the wavelength of a particle and its energy are shown and defined in Table II.

In the general case, the velocity of a particle depends upon its rest mass. Particles of light (photons) differ from other particles by having zero rest mass. As shown in Table II, this greatly simplifies the equations compared to those which apply to particles more generally. The energy contained in a photon is inversely proportional to its wavelength. The constant of proportionality is the product of Planck's constant h, and the speed of light in free space, c. This velocity, about 3×10^8 m sec^{-1}, is the highest attainable by any particle.

The velocity of a photon decreases when it enters a homogeneous medium. The decrease in air is negligible, but it may be decreased by as much as one-third in a medium such as water or glass. The decrease in velocity depends upon the refractive index of the medium; the refractive index may be defined by Snell's law or, equally as well, by the velocity of a photon in the medium, divided into its velocity in free space.

Each photon vibrates, doing so at a frequency inversely proportional to its wavelength, according to the equation $v = c/\lambda$ where v is the frequency of vibration in reciprocal seconds (Hertz) and λ is the wavelength of the vibration.

A photon retains all of its energy as it enters a high-index medium from air or vacuum. Its frequency of vibration is also unchanged. But its velocity is reduced and its wavelength is shortened proportionally: in the eye, which has an index of refraction of about $\frac{4}{3}$, a photon of "blue–green" light at wavelength 500 nm outside the eye has an energy of about 4×10^{-12} erg and a frequency of vibration of about 6×10^{14} Hz. Upon entering the eye, neither the frequency nor the energy of the photon is altered, but its wavelength is shortened to about $\frac{3}{4} \times 500 = 375$ nm, and its velocity is reduced from about 3×10^8 m sec^{-1} to about 2.25×10^8 m sec^{-1}.

Table III shows the energy contained in one photon, as a function of wavelength, listed for 10-nm intervals throughout the visible spectrum. For visual purposes, energy per photon (or frequency of vibration, which is directly correlated with it) would be a better choice for specifying the spectral variable than is its wavelength. However, the use of wavelength for this purpose is so firmly established that we shall adhere to this convention in this chapter, keeping in mind that wherever wavelength is specified, this refers to light in a vacuum, and not within the eye. Table III provides the translation: For example, at a wavelength of 600 nm, each photon has an energy of 3.309 picoerg (10^{-12} erg) meaning that about a third of a million million photons would be required at this wavelength to produce just one erg of energy. When it is recalled that 10^7 erg sec^{-1} are required to produce 1 watt of power, and that about a half-dozen photons are sufficient, under ideal conditions, to elicit a visual sensation, two facts may be simultaneously appreciated: (a) Photons of light contain very little energy indeed. (b) The eye is an exquisitely sensitive device. In his book *Vision and the Eye*, M. H. Pirenne (1948) makes the latter point by noting that "the mechanical energy of a pea falling from a height of one inch would, if transformed into luminous energy, be sufficient to give a faint impression of light to every man that ever lived [p. 78]."

TABLE III

THE RELATION BETWEEN THE WAVELENGTH OF LIGHT IN FREE SPACE AND
SOME CORRELATED PHYSICAL AND PSYCHOPHYSICAL VALUES OF
IMPORTANCE FOR HUMAN VISION[a]

Wavelength λ (nm)	Energy per photon $E = h\nu$ in picoergs $(10^{-12}$ erg$)$	Millions of photons per second per square millimeter on the retina for 1 troland of retinal illumination	Number of photons per second per receptor for 1 troland of retinal illumination
390	5.092	150,000	1,000,000
400	4.964	24,660	165,000
410	4.843	9,247	62,000
420	4.728	2,791	18,600
430	4.618	986	6,580
440	4.513	510	3,400
450	4.413	798	2,100
460	4.317	204	1,360
470	4.225	137	918
480	4.137	92.1	613
490	4.052	62.8	419
500	3.972	41.2	275
510	3.893	27.0	180
520	3.819	19.5	130
530	3.746	16.4	109
540	3.678	15.1	101
550	3.611	14.7	98
555	3.578	14.8	99
560	3.546	15.0	100
570	3.483	16.0	106
580	3.424	17.8	118
590	3.366	20.8	139
600	3.309	25.4	169
610	3.255	32.3	216
620	3.202	43.3	289
630	3.152	63.4	423
640	3.102	94.4	650
650	3.055	162	1,080
660	3.008	288	1,920
670	2.963	558	3,720
680	2.920	1,064	7,100
690	2.878	2,242	15,000
700	2.837	4,623	31,000

[a] In calculating the number of incident photons/sec/receptor, a receptor population density of 150,000/mm² is assumed, which corresponds roughly to the central foveal region of the retina.

V. PSYCHOLOGICAL ORDERING OF SPECTRAL COLORS

A. The Wavelength of Light Is . . . Related to Its Perceived Color

The fact that perceived color is related to the wavelength of light is so widely accepted that it is surprising to learn that detailed attempts to specify this relation exactly have appeared only in recent years. Visual physicists have not been much interested in the problem, and others have approached it only indirectly. For example, Purdy (1931) published a classic and much-cited paper called "Spectral Hue as a Function of Intensity," in which he reported studies of the Bezold–Brücke effect. Purdy's experimental operation required that the subject vary the wavelength of a stimulus until it matched, for hue, another stimulus of a different intensity but fixed wavelength. Thus no attempt was actually made to measure hue, as promised by the title of his paper. Matches cannot, in themselves, provide information about the appearance of visual stimuli. Any inference concerning hue that one might draw from Purdy's data would require doing what he did not: directly assessing the relation between wavelength and hue at some intensity level. Three methods that have been used to make such assessments will now be considered and compared: color naming, hue cancellation, and the multidimensional scaling of perceived color differences.

B. Color Naming

Prior to 1965, most experiments involving the naming of spectral colors were concerned with the determination of the wavelengths of spectral stimuli corresponding to the psychologically unique hues. Many such studies have been summarized by Judd (1951), and those data are given here as Table IV. There are three studies prior to 1951 where direct color-naming techniques were used in an effort to establish the relation between hue and wavelength. Thomson (1954) and Dimmick and Hubbard (1939a,b) were concerned only with the appearance of hue in restricted spectral regions near those wavelengths corresponding to sensations of psychologically unique hues. The limitation of these studies is that they provide no information about the appearance of other parts of the spectrum. The first investigator to attempt the broader assessment was Beare (1963). Her observers were asked to provide either one or two responses to a large number of spectral stimuli, presented one at a time. The first response was required, being restricted to the hue names red, orange, green, yellow, and blue. Where a second, optional response was concerned, complete freedom was allowed. For example, her subjects could respond by saying

TABLE IV
STIMULI FOR COLOR PERCEPTION OF PSYCHOLOGICALLY UNIQUE HUES[a]

Experimenter	Date	Wavelength			
		Red	Yellow	Green	Blue
Bezold	1874	760–656	578	532	468
Donders	1884		582	535	485
Hess	1888		575	495	471
Rood	1890	700	581	527	473
Hering	1898		577	505	470
Voeste	1898		577	505	470
von Kries	1907		574	503	
Westphal	1909		574	506	479
Dreher	1911		575	509	477
Ridgway	1912	644	577	520	473
Goldytsch	1916				468
Bradley	1920	656	579	514	469
Goldmann	1922		568	504	468
Priest	1926	680	583	515	475
Brückner	1927		578	498	471
Schubert	1928		574	500	467
Purdy	1931		571	506	474
Ornstein, Eymers, Vermeulen	1934	630	578	528	487
Verbeek, Bazen	1935		580	530	
Schouten	1935		576	512	472
Dimmick, Hubbard	1939	495c	582	515	475
Theory					
Hering		498.2c	578.1	498.2	477.0
Ladd-Franklin		495.7c	574.3	510.6	468.9
von Kries, Schrödinger		495.7c	574.3	495.7	468.9
Müller		498.2c	578.1	498.2	477.0

[a] From Judd, 1951, after Dimmick and Hubbard (1939a,b).

"dark," "muddy," "pretty," or whatever else might come to mind, although they did, in fact, use color names much of the time for their secondary responses. Unfortunately, this procedure made Beare's secondary response data unsuitable for productive quantitative analysis.

With these limitations in mind, an experiment was reported in 1965 by Boynton and Gordon, in which an improved color naming technique was introduced. Working at two luminance levels (100 and 1000 td), they used 23 spectral stimuli of wavelengths from 440 to 660 nm, separated by

10-nm steps, presented in random order to the subjects. The surround was dark, and the stimuli, which were circular and 3° in diameter, were centrally fixated. Stimuli were presented as 300-msec flashes; during an experimental session, 230 flashes were presented—5 samples each of the 23 spectral stimuli at the 2 intensity levels.

Subjects were instructed as follows:

> You will be presented with single flashes of light of unpredictable color. You are to identify the hue of these flashes by the use of four, and only four color names: red, yellow, green, and blue. If you feel that you see only one of these hues, respond first with the [name of the] one that seems most intense [the primary component of the sensation] and second with the one that seems less intense. For example, the proper response to a greenish blue would be "blue, green," in that order.

There were, then, twelve possible responses that a subject could make: BR, B, BG, GB, G, GY, YG, Y, YR, RY, R, and RB (where BG, for example, means that the subject responded blue, then green, and Y, as another example, means that he reported seeing only yellow). Each response was assigned an arbitrary score value of three points. In those cases where only one name was given, the value 3 was assigned entirely to the appropriate response category. In those cases where two names were given, two points were assigned to the hue category of the first response, and one point was assigned to that of the second. Over 5 sessions, 25 stimuli were presented at each wavelength at each intensity, for each of three subjects. The computational procedure is illustrated by the example shown in Table V.

In Fig. 6, average data are plotted for three subjects. The form of this plot is different from that reported in the original paper, or in any of the various papers by others where the data have been replotted. Here, an opponent-colors representation has been used, and the computational procedure, whereby the data of the three subjects are averaged, is new. It is easiest to describe this in terms of an example, for which 510 nm will again be used. The adjusted totals for subject JG, as shown in Table V, are G = 68 and Y = 3. These have been added to those of the other two subjects and averaged as follows:

Subject	B	G	Y
JG	0	68	3
MB	0	52	16
TY	8	61	0
Mean	2.7	60.3	6.3
Adj. Mean	0	60.3	3.7
Normalized (90)	0	84.8	5.2

TABLE V

ILLUSTRATIVE DATA FROM COLOR-NAMING EXPERIMENT OF
BOYNTON AND GORDON (1965)

Subject JG. Wavelength 510 nm 1000 td
Responses recorded, 5 each in 5 sessions:

GB	GB	G	G	G
GY	G	G	G	G
GY	G	G	G	G
GY	G	G	G	G
GY	G	GY	G	G

Assignment of point values:

Category	Sole response	Primary response	Secondary response	Total	Adjusted
B	0	0	2	2	0
G	18	7	0	68	68
Y	0	0	5	5	3
				75	

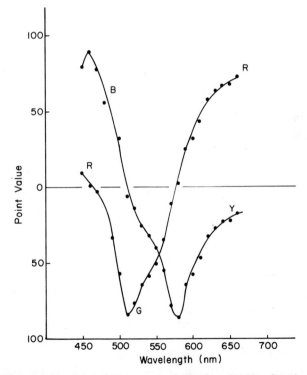

FIG. 6. Color naming data of Boynton and Gordon (1965), for the average of three subjects at 1000 td.

At this particular wavelength, green was always reported as the primary component of perceived hue, most frequently as the only one. All three subjects divided their secondary responses, from trial to trial, between blue and yellow. In order to estimate the most probable sensation to be associated with 510 nm, the smaller of the two secondary point values has been subtracted from each, to produce an adjusted total that eliminates the smaller value by reducing it to zero. In averaging the data, the problem arises again, since TY has an excess of 8 points in the B category, while the other subjects show B = 0. The problem has been solved by adjusting the mean data by the same procedure that has been used for the individual subjects. The adjusted total is then normalized so that the point values add to 90.

Plotted in this way, as in Fig. 6, only two hues are associated with each wavelength. The data are also represented in the polar plot of Fig. 7, where the spectral stimuli are ordered around the psychological hue circle that was described earlier. Here the distance between unique hues is taken as 90°, and the experimental wavelengths are plotted accordingly. This is perhaps the best possible way to present the relation between hue and wavelength.

C. Hue Discrimination

Figure 7 provides information about the rate at which hue varies with wavelength. The further apart two adjacent wavelengths are on the hue circle, the greater is the change in hue associated with that 10-nm wavelength difference. This rate of change appears to occur especially fast in two regions of the spectrum—from about 480 to 510 nm, and again at about 560–590 nm—and is especially slow around 530–540 nm, and at the spectral extremes.

This result is in obvious qualitative agreement with wavelength discrimination functions obtained by more traditional methods (e.g., Siegel, 1964). In such studies, λ_1 and λ_2, to be compared, are placed side by side. The object of the experiment is to compare λ_1 with $\lambda_2 + \Delta\lambda_2$, to find the value of λ_2 that is just discriminable.

The hue-discrimination ability that is implied by the color naming results can be estimated by plotting the angle of the hue vector of Fig. 7 as a function of wavelength, fitting a smooth curve to this, and then taking the first derivative of that function. This has been done, and the results are expressed in Fig. 8, together with other wavelength discrimination data to be described later.

Another means of comparison has been suggested by Smith (1971), who used the color-naming method of Boynton and Gordon with 10 sub-

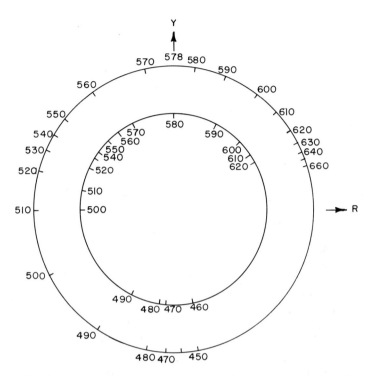

Fig. 7. The hue circle shown here is conceptually the same as that of Fig. 5, except that spectral stimuli have been indicated. Those on the outer circumference are derived from the color-naming data of Boynton and Gordon (1965), by a computational procedure described in the text. Those on the inner circumference are derived from the cancellation data of Jameson and Hurvich (1955).

jects. Point scores were normalized to 100 at each wavelength. The amount of hue change in the neighborhood of a given wavelength was gauged by summing the differences between the score for that wavelength and the two adjacent wavelengths ($\Delta\lambda = 10$ nm) across all four response categories. An "Index of Nameable Colour Difference" (INCD) was then computed by dividing this value into 100. Figure 8 also shows the results of this procedure as used by Smith, as well as a recomputation of the Boynton and Gordon data by this method.*

* Yet another method of deriving wavelength discrimination information from color naming data has been proposed by Graham (1973). The method permits a statistical test of the hypothesis that pairs of spectral stimuli cannot be discriminated as different, and for specifying the amount of difference in terms of bits of information available for discrimination.

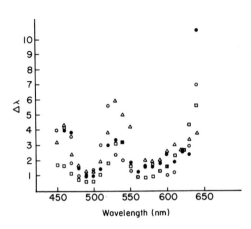

Fig. 8. Wavelength discrimination data derived form the evidence of two experiments by four methods. (●) Boynton and Gordon average data, 1000 td, using the INCD computational procedure of Smith. (□) Boynton and Gordon, average data, 1000 td, using the reciprocal rate of change of the chromatic vector. (○) Smith, using his INCD method for his 10 subjects. (△) Shepard's analysis of the Boynton–Gordon data.

In presenting his results, Smith quotes Graham (1965), who states that it is not possible to derive an accurate assessment of hue discrimination from color-naming data. The analysis presented here supports Smith in showing that Graham was incorrect in this belief. Also, these results strongly contradict Land and McCann (1971) who assert that "there is no predictable relationship between flux at various wavelengths and the color sensation associated with objects. . . ." One final point: although the functions resulting from side-by-side, traditional studies of wavelength discrimination are frequently called "hue discrimination" curves, they are not, since saturation also varies with wavelength, for spectral colors. The comparisons given here do, nevertheless, strongly suggest that change in hue, rather than change in saturation, is the critical factor in the discrimination of small wavelength-differences.

D. Chromatic Cancellation

Another method to gauge the appearance of the spectrum, one that avoids the direct use of color naming, is the cancellation method of Jameson and Hurvich (1955). They reasoned that it should be possible to cancel, in turn, the dominant and secondary hue components of spectral stimuli by the superposition of stimuli having dominant hues opposite to those being cancelled. For example, an orange at 600 nm contains both red and yellow components. Using a green cancellation stimulus, it is possible to cancel the red and leave a pure yellow, and the amount of green required to do this is used as a measure of the strength of the red component being cancelled. Using blue as a cancellation stimulus, it is possible to cancel yellow, leaving a pure red. This was done using four cancellation hues, two at a time in each of four regions of the spectrum, separated by those wavelengths corresponding to psychologically unique blue, green, and yellow.

To specify the units of the cancellation stimuli, a number of additional observations were made. First, opponent pairs of cancellation stimuli were superposed to produce cancellation of each other, and the relative energy required to do this was taken to represent equal intensities of the two stimuli. Then, after the cancellation experiment was done, the red–green and yellow–blue functions were related to one another as follows:

> The intersection loci of the two pairs [were] fixed empirically for a given luminance level by determining the wavelengths at which equal proportions of disparate hues are seen. Since equal ordinates are assumed to represent equal response levels, the intersection loci are isolated by determining experimentally those spectral loci where the observer reports the sensation as equal in redness and yellowness, equal in greenness and yellowness, etc. . . . Our procedure was to present successive spectral stimuli separated by 10 [nm] intervals all at the same luminance level, namely 10 mL. The observer simply specified the seen hue in terms of the four hue variables. Although this method does not lend itself to precise hue measurements, the transition points between, say, reddish-yellow and yellowish-red or between greenish-yellow and yellowish-green, are readily determinable. . . [p. 550].

Thus, a color-naming technique was used, despite the fact that it was not deemed suitable for precise measurements, as part of a procedure required to establish their "chromatic valence" curves, which are shown in Fig. 9. Before plotting, the 10-mL data "were then converted to an equal energy spectrum," presumably by multiplying the observed cancellation energy values by V_λ at each wavelength.

A more direct comparison between the Jameson–Hurvich and Boynton–Gordon data can be made by replotting the data for subject DJ, dividing 90 points at each wavelength according to the ratio implied by the difference between each pair of Jameson–Hurvich functions at each wavelength. For example, at 510 nm, Fig. 3 from their paper shows that the g function is .62 log unit above the y function. The antilogarithm of .62 (4.16) represents the ratio whereby the strength of the g component (evaluated with r) is greater than y. Ninety points divide in the proportions 73 for g and 17 for y. This determines the location of 510 nm in Fig. 7, where the Jameson–Hurvich results for subject J are represented. (It is not possible to do this analysis for subject H, because of missing data points near the unique-hue wavelengths. This is probably due to the relative insensitivity of the method, especially when the strength of the secondary component is low.)

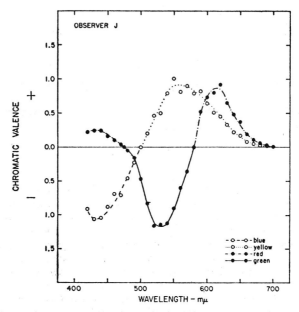

FIG. 9. Chromatic response functions obtained by Jameson and Hurvich (1955) for observer J, using a cancellation method described in the text.

E. Analysis of Proximities

Still another approach to the scaling of hue as a function of wavelength is to apply multidimensional scaling techniques to data of some kind, where the degree of difference between many pairs of stimuli has been evaluated. For example, Ekman (1954) used 14 colors, varying primarily in hue, that were projected two at a time upon transluscent windows. Subjects were instructed to rate the "qualitative similarity" of each pair of colors on a five-step scale. A procedure known as *analysis of proximities* was used to interpret the results.

Analysis of proximities is a multidimensional scaling technique described by Shepard, who applied it to Ekman's data (Shepard, 1962) and those of Boynton and Gordon (Shepard & Carroll, 1966), among others. The logic of the method is excellently described by Kruskal (1964) who pioneered with Shepard the development of the technique at Bell Laboratories.* Given N colors to be scaled, there will be $N(N-1)/2$ pairs, with a similarity (or difference) score associated with each pair. The objective of the method, in its metric form, would be to represent the N colors in

---

* A two-volume set on multidimensional scaling (Shepard *et al.*, 1972) has appeared, which summarizes this subject in all of its aspects.

an n-dimensional space, so that the relative distances between the various pairs of points in that space are related, as closely as possible, to the magnitudes of the difference ratings obtained experimentally. An important feature of the method is that it can also be used in a nonmetric form, in the sense that the experimental difference scores are first rank ordered, with their numerical values thereafter disregarded. The object then is to find an n-dimensional plot that will, as well as possible, recover the rank ordering of difference scores as represented by the rank ordering of diagram distances between the various pairs.

The advantage of the nonmetric analysis, where psychological data are concerned, is that typically (as in Ekman's study, for example) nothing is known about the mathematical properties of the psychological scale being used. To use the Shepard–Kruskal nonmetric analysis, the only necessary assumption is monotonicity, e.g., that a mean difference score of, say, 4.1 between two stimuli signifies a greater difference than, say, 3.5, within the limits implied by experimental error.

It can be shown that the method tends to recover the original metric, if known. For example, if the difference scores are taken as the distances between pairs of cities in the United States, and these are entered into the analysis, then these distances are rank ordered and the actual mileages are thereafter discarded. Yet, in the end, when a two-dimensional Euclidean representation of points is found (which will be the one that best recovers the original rank ordering of distances) it will come very close to recovering the actual (relative) distances as well. Moreover, in terms of this example, it can be shown that a one-dimensional analysis does very poorly and that a three-dimensional one shows insignificant improvement over two. Furthermore, a non-Euclidean space will do more poorly than a Euclidean one. Thus the original distances are correctly and consistently represented in a two-dimensional, Euclidean space, and this fact can be deduced through this type of analysis. Thus there is hope that, in the case of color scaling, the metric of the appropriate representational space can be deduced from the analysis despite the fact that (unlike the example of map distances) it is not known in the first place.

There are a number of technical difficulties with the method. Chief among these, related to the fact that it is basically a trial-and-error procedure, is that it is not possible to deduce with mathematical certainty that a particular solution is optimal. In practice, however, this difficulty can be overcome, and the method definitely works and is useful.

A nonmetric analysis of Ekman's data by Shepard (1962) yields the spatial configuration shown in Fig. 10, where the rank-ordering of the distances on the diagram correlates negatively with the rank ordering of the mean similarity data taken in Ekman's experiment. In another study, Ward

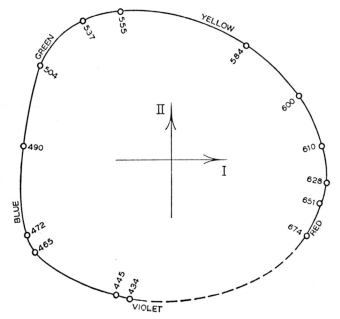

FIG. 10. Proximity analysis by Shepard (1962) of Ekman's (1954) data.

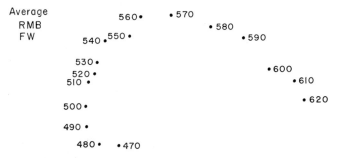

FIG. 11. Two-dimensional analysis of proximities applied to difference scores from data of Ward and Boynton (1974). Subjects were asked to rate the distinctness of minimally distinct borders formed between pairs of monochromatic stimuli.

and Boynton (1974) had subjects judge the distinctness of minimally distinct borders formed between all possible pairs of 16 monochromatic stimuli, and subjected these results to the same kind of analysis that Shepard had used for Ekman's data, with the results illustrated for one subject in Fig. 11. In still another calculation, Shepard applied his method to the Boynton and Gordon data, with the result shown in Fig. 12. The results stemming from the last of these analyses have also been represented in Fig. 8. Distances between adjacent pairs were measured from Fig. 6 of

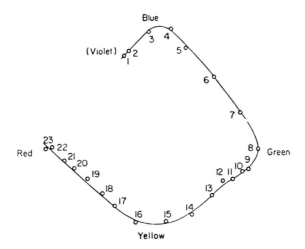

Fig. 12. Shepard and Carroll (1964) subjected the data of Boynton and Gordon (1965) to a "proximity analysis." Color-naming point values were used to derive an index of difference between all possible pairs of 23 wavelengths; these values were then subjected to a two-dimensional analysis with the result shown here. Stimulus 1 is at 440 nm, 2 is at 450 nm, etc. at 10-nm intervals to Stimulus 23 at 660 nm.

Shepard's paper, summed, and divided into 30 (a scaling constant). For example, 450 nm lies 2.0 mm from 550 on the shortwave side, and 7.5 mm from 460 on the longwave side. The plotted value of 3.15 is obtained as $30/(2.0 + 7.5)$.

It may be concluded that the results obtained by a variety of methods verify that spectral colors are well portrayed in a more-or-less circular arrangement of stimuli in a two-dimensional Euclidean space. Multidimensional scaling yields hue diagrams that are quite similar to those developed by other techniques.

VI. PRINCIPLE OF UNIVARIANCE AND THE CONE PHOTOPIGMENTS

A. It Is Almost Impossible to Conceive Each Sensitive Point of the Retina to Contain an Infinite Number of Receptors, Each Capable of Perfect Resonance and Exclusive Response to Every Possible Wavelength

In making the statement of which the title of this subsection is a paraphrase, Thomas Young had in mind that each "sensitive point" on the retina was tuned to respond, more or less, to the vibrations of incident light. Here he rejects the possibility of extremely narrowband tuning. In so doing, he evidently rejected beforehand a major alternative hypothesis (see Stage E of Fig. 1), namely, that each receptor might somehow be capable of producing a signal which, in addition to conveying information about the intensity of the light absorbed, could somehow signal information about its color. Instead he assumed, correctly as it turned out, that each "sensitive point" or receptor could respond only more or less vigorously and that nothing about the message thus generated could reveal anything about the wavelength of the light absorbed. The principle has since been called by Naka and Rushton (1966) the *Principle of Univariance*. The evidence in favor of it is by now so overwhelming that it is very generally accepted. This evidence is partly psychophysical: in particular, the results of trichromatic color mixture experiments, upon which the CIE system of colorimetry rests, are difficult to explain in any other way. But there is now much more direct, though less exact, evidence in the form of physical studies using the physical techniques of retinal densitometry and microspectrophotometry. Intracellular recordings from the cone receptors of fish and turtles and the data recorded extracellularly from primate cones are also consistent with the principle.

Assuming the principle of univariance to be true, the distinction that Young made is, as already noted, between a system containing receptors very sharply tuned, each one to a different wavelength, and another more probable system containing a smaller number of types of receptors, each having a broad-band type of sensitivity. Young found the first alternative "almost impossible to conceive," perhaps because it was clear to him that such a system would be tremendously inefficient. The photon-catching capacity of such a system will be severely limited, because a given receptor would in such a case yield no response at all to most visible wavelengths. High spatial acuity would, under such circumstances, be manifestly impossible except with broadband illumination.

B. Thus It Becomes Necessary to Suppose the Number Limited, for Example, to Three Types of Cones, Having Differing but Overlapping Sensitivities to Wavelength, So That Each Type of Cone Is Activated More or Less Strongly by Various Wavelengths, Depending upon How Different Each Wavelength Is in Comparison with the Wavelength of Peak Sensitivity

Perhaps Young made a lucky guess in suggesting the number three, since he offered this only as a "for instance." It remained for Helmholtz, later in the nineteenth century, to posit specifically three types of receptors, and

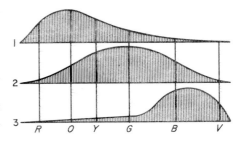

Fig. 13. These curves were pro-
posed by Helmholtz to represent the
three "sensations" of human color
vision, as a function of wavelength.
[These are reproduced from page 143
of the second volume of the 1924
Optical Society translation (J. P. C.
Southall, Editor) of Helmholtz's
Physiological Optics (Third German
Edition).]

to publish the hypothetical response curves shown in Fig. 13. By that time,
the nature of light was better understood, at least from the point of view
of wave theory, and the facts of visual trichromacy were better specified,
especially from the work of Maxwell who was the first to use monochromatic lights in color-mixing experiments.

To introduce the trichromatic scheme as it is understood today, it is
best to begin with a preliminary discussion of the simpler case of rod vision.
When the maximum luminance level of environmental objects is low—
below the threshold for cone vision—there is no hue discrimination, and
all color vision (excluding the effects of memory color) is black and white.
The reason for this is that scotopic vision is mediated by only one class
of receptor—the rod. Rods, in turn, contain only one class of visual photopigment, rhodopsin, a ubiquitous photosensitive substance which, though
not found in all seeing creatures, is found in most of them from insects
to man. The stimulation of rods by light at one wavelength leads in man
to the same sensation of scotopic white that is produced by stimulation
at any other wavelength, providing only that the relative intensities are
suitably adjusted.

When many photons are incident upon the eye, the resulting brightness
sensation depends upon the rate at which photons are being absorbed by
a collection of rods. Not only does a particular rod not know where, along
its length, the absorption of a given photon occurred, but the optic nerve
fiber to which a collection of rods is synaptically connected has no information concerning in which particular rods the photons were absorbed or
their angles of incidence. Moreover—and this is most important for the
present argument—the rod receptor also does not know what the wavelengths of the absorbed quanta were.

Whether or not a particular photon is absorbed is a matter of chance.
There is a peak frequency of resonance, at which absorption is most probable, which for rods is about 503 nm. Since the probability of absorption falls off for both shorter wavelengths (whose photons have more

energy) and longer ones (whose photons have less), this is clearly not just a matter of photon energy directly driving the receptors. Rather, the absorption of a photon changes the configuration of the molecule of visual photopigment that absorbs it, and in so doing somehow releases energy that is stored within the receptor, producing a much amplified receptor signal.

Once absorption has taken place, then, the effect produced by one photon is the same as that produced by another. The molecule of rhodopsin that absorbed the photon is considered to react in an all-or-none manner without receiving any information about what the energy of the photon was.

The psychophysical evidence in support of the view just presented lies mainly in the experimental work underlying the relation

$$E_{1\lambda}V_\lambda' = E_{2\lambda}V_\lambda'.$$

Here V' is the scotopic luminous efficiency function, and $E_{1\lambda}$ and $E_{2\lambda}$ are taken to be any two distributions of radiance for fields that match. For the standard observer, any two fields that satisfy this equation will match, all will have the same scotopic white color, and all potential information about the hue and saturation of objects is lost.

The trichromatic scheme implies the same assumptions for cone vision that have just been reviewed for rod vision, except that in this more complex case there are three classes of photopigment. One class has its maximum absorption at about 575 nm, meaning that photons having an energy of about 3.45 picoerg are most likely to be absorbed, with the probability falling off for photons of higher or lower energy. Another class of receptors has its maximum probability of absorption at about 540 nm, corresponding to 3.68 picoerg, and the third peak is at about 440 nm, corresponding to 4.51 picoerg. A given photon, for example, one having a wavelength to 550 nm (3.61 picoerg) may be absorbed by any one of the three kinds of photopigment, but it is more likely to be absorbed in the 540-nm pigment than in the others.

These pigments, though not yet directly extracted and measured in human cones, have absorption characteristics which by now are almost exactly specified by a variety of converging operations. Those shown in Fig. 14 cannot be far from correct. The pigments have been given a variety of names:

S_λ	P-440	Blue pigment (B)	cyanolabe	α
M_λ	P-540	Green pigment (G)	chlorolabe	β
L_λ	P-575	Red pigment (R)	erythrolabe	γ

These names are used interchangeably in the visual literature.

VII. APPEARANCE OF THE SPECTRUM: PHYSIOLOGICAL BASIS

A. Cone Sensitivities

Given that the appearance of the spectrum varies with wavelength as shown in Fig. 7, and that the three photopigments of human cone vision have the spectral sensitivities shown in Fig. 14, exactly how is it that the one is connected to the other?

Let us begin by seeing how far the simplest trichromatic scheme might take us. Given that there are three classes of cone receptors, (let us call them B, G, and R for short) assume that each contains only one of the three photopigments. Suppose further that B-cones, when uniquely activated, will send signals to the brain that are interpreted there as "blue," and that G-cones mediate "green" and R-cones "red" in analogous fashion.

The first problem would be that in many regions of the spectrum, one would expect to see all three hues simultaneously. For example, at 520 nm, where the G-cone sensitivity is highest, the highest percentage of incident photons would be absorbed in this class of receptors so that the dominant perceived hue would be green. So far, so good. But the R and B cones also have a finite sensitivity at that wavelength, this being approximately equal. Therefore R and B cones would absorb photons also, but in lesser amounts than the G-cones. The model predicts, then, that the observer should see blue as the primary hue, with a reddish-green as a secondary one. Actually, however, reddish-green is never seen, whether at 520 nm or under any other circumstance, and it is green alone that appears as the secondary component of hue at this wavelength.

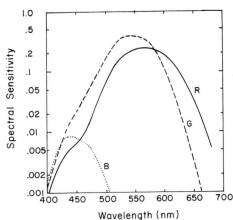

FIG. 14. Estimated spectral sensitivities of the three types of human cones. [After Vos and Walraven (1972); the R curve has been lowered by about .4 log unit, relative to the other two.]

Consider another type of problem that occurs at 600 nm. Here the B-cone has a sensitivity so low that its response may be disregarded. What should be seen is a greenish-red. What actually is seen is a yellowish-red, or orange. The problem becomes even more acute at the wavelength of about 580 nm, where the R- and G-cone sensitivity curves cross. Instead of seeing a balanced reddish-green, what is seen instead is yellow. On the simple trichromatic scheme, yellow thus emerges as a complete surprise and constitutes a considerable embarrassment; there is just no way to account for the sensation. In addition to these problems, the trichromatic scheme also does not account for the appearance of white. Yet an equal-energy spectrum, one which stimulates R-, G- and B-cones equally, is known to elicit a sensation of white, and not a balanced reddish-greenish-blue, as the trichromatic scheme would predict.

In the nineteenth century, the German physiologist Ewald Hering (1964) noted these and other such difficulties, and proposed an "opponent colors" theory of vision. There were two classes of receptor, he supposed, one of which could signal red *or* green and the other yellow *or* blue. The perceived hue would then depend upon blends of signals from these two classes of receptors. The scheme accounts at once for the impossibility of red–green and yellow–blue sensations, for the presence of yellow, and for the psychologically unique hues (yellow, for example, would arise when the YB system was stimulated in the yellow direction and the RG system was balanced). We recognize at once that this scheme does violence to the principle of univariance and this fact did not go unnoticed even by the scientists of Hering's day, or those of the early twentieth century, who swore by the doctrine of specific nerve energies and the all-or-none law of nerve impulse transmission.

The resolution of the problem has come with the adoption of various zone theories of vision. Those that were proposed during the first half of this century are well summarized by Judd (1951); there have been a number of others suggested since in various models of color vision.

B. A Color Model

The most ubiquitous of these is also the simplest and will be used here as an example. First, it must be realized that, although the $\bar{x}, \bar{y}, \bar{z}$ functions of the CIE system do not represent receptor sensitivity functions, they must be related to receptor sensitivity functions R_λ, G_λ, and B_λ. First, each receptor sensitivity function must be divided by the transmittance (τ) of the ocular media (mainly the lens) that selectively absorb photons on their way from the cornea to the photoreceptors. These modified functions will be called R' ($= \tau^{-1}R$), G' ($= \tau^{-1}G$) and B' ($= \tau^{-1}B$). It turns out that $\bar{x}$,

$\bar{y}$, and $\bar{z}$ must be linear transformations of R′, G′, and B′. This fact is related to a point noted earlier: If the equations that predict metameric matches are replaced by another sent of equations where R′ is substituted for $\bar{x}$, B′ for $\bar{y}$, and B′ for $\bar{z}$, exactly the same predictions will be made. There are infinitely many functions that can be derived for this purpose, but only one set will actually represent R′, G′, and B′. [See Graham (1959, p. 198), or Wyszecki & Stiles (1967, p. 235), for a more detailed treatment of this subject.]

Any set of equations, then, which is a linear transformation of $\bar{x}$, $\bar{y}$, and $\bar{z}$, will predict metameric matches. One such transformation, used by Judd to represent the Hering theory, is the following:

$$RG = \bar{x} - \bar{y}; \tag{4a}$$
$$YB = .4(\bar{y} - \bar{z}); \tag{4b}$$
$$W = \bar{y}. \tag{4c}$$

These functions are plotted in Fig. 15. As noted by Hurvich and Jameson, the RG and YB functions closely resemble the results of their color cancellation experiment, and it will be recalled that there is a reasonably good agreement between the results of color cancellation and direct color naming. This set of functions therefore provides a reasonable description of the change in hue with wavelength across the visible spectrum.

C. Electrophysiological Evidence

Considerable electrophysiological support for the opponent-colors conception has emerged over the past 15 or 20 years. The first, and most surprising evidence came from horizontal cells of the fish retina, which yield slow potentials that are negative or positive (depolarizing or hyperpolarizing) depending upon the wavelength of stimulation. Svaetichin (1956), who discovered these, immediately called attention to their possible significance for opponent-colors theory. Although this may have been premature, given that fish are not human and the exact role of the horizontal cells in chromatic processing was then and remains obscure, more recent evidence by DeValois is certainly germane.

DeValois's records were obtained from the lateral geniculate cells of old-world primates whose color vision has been shown by him (DeValois, 1965) to be identical to that of man. He finds that, in the absence of any light stimulation, such a unit typically fires at an intermediate spontaneous rate. This rate of firing is found to be modulatable, up or down, depending upon the wavelength of the light stimulating the eye. Although there is quite a spread of sensitivities, an argument can be made that they fall into

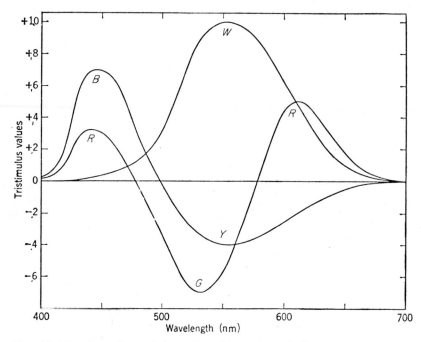

FIG. 15. Transformations of the color mixture data of the CIE system that are consistent with the Hering opponent-colors theory. [After Judd (1951).]

two classes, which at least resemble the functions of Fig. 6. Moreover, some units respond univariantly, and appear to be carrying an achromatic message. Readers are referred to DeValois (1966) for a detailed attempt by him to reconcile his results with those of human psychophysics, including the Boynton–Gordon color naming data.

VIII. SATURATION

It was pointed out in Section III that the psychological color diagram described there made no necessary reference to physics, and to this it may be added that it makes no reference either to the domain of physically or physiologically realizable experiences. The general idea is that colors arrayed around the perimeter of the hue circle are the most saturated imaginable—whatever exactly that might mean.

For aperture colors, assuming the eye to be in a neutral state of chromatic adaptation, the most saturated colors that are physically realizable are those produced by monochromatic spectral lights. This is because these lights come as close as possible to activating the three classes of receptor systems uniquely. It should be noted that all lights activate at least two of these, and that the activation of more than one always leads to desaturation.

Spectral colors are by no means equally saturated. A variety of saturation functions can be obtained by many different methods.

METHOD 1

Starting with a white field of light, monochromatic light is added to half of the field until a discriminable difference emerges. The function is calculated by $L_\lambda/L_\lambda + L_w$, where L_λ is the luminance of the chromatic component, monochromatic at wavelength λ, and L_w is the luminance of the white light.

METHOD 2

Starting with a white field of light, monochromatic light is added to half of it, while the luminance of the white component is reduced proportionately, until a discriminable difference emerges. Then monochromatic light is added to the other half of the field until (again with proportionate reduction of luminance of the white component) another discriminable difference is found, in the direction of a more saturated color. This procedure is continued until, finally, the more saturated field reaches the limit of a pure spectral color. The number of such steps (jnd's) is taken as a measure of saturation.

METHOD 3

A monochromatic light and a white light are exactly juxtaposed. One of these is varied until the border between them is rendered minimally distinct. The distinctness of the border thus formed is then evaluated by a matching technique.

METHOD 4

A monochromatic light is presented as a small field surrounded by white light. At low luminances, the field appears black. At higher luminances, a darker color is first seen, with a very strong gray content. At still higher luminances, the gray content diminishes and a pure hue emerges. At a slightly higher luminance, the hue takes on an appearance similar to that produced by fluorescent surfaces, the one called "fluorence" by Evans. Finally, it achieves the appearance of a self-contained source of light. The

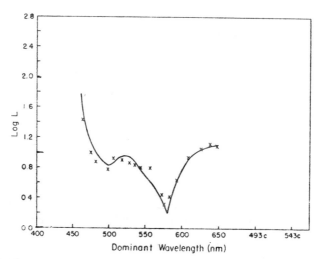

Fig. 16. The experimental points show the reciprocal of the log luminance required, at each wavelength tested, in order for the spectral sample to appear fluorent when seen as a one-degree spot presented in the center of a 1–10° annulus. The curve is that predicted by Hurvich and Jameson (1955).

reciprocal of the luminance required, as a function of wavelength, to achieve the appearance of fluorence, is plotted in Fig. 16.

METHOD 5

Complementary spectral colors are determined, which, when additively mixed, are metameric with a reference white. The relative luminances required to do this, for the CIE standard observer, can be calculated for each pair.

All of these results involve the fact that, as a function of wavelength, the coloring power, or what may be called *chrominance,* differs considerably, being highest at the spectral extremes, and minimum at 570 nm. This fact is easily interpreted by taking Eqs. (4) and deriving from them chrominance (C) and luminance (L) components:

$$C = [(\text{RG})^2 + (\text{YB})^2]^{1/2} = [(\bar{x} - \bar{y})^2 + .16(\bar{y} - \bar{z})^2]^{1/2}$$
$$L = \bar{y}.$$

These values are plotted in Fig. 17. If saturation is taken to be related to the ratio C/L, then a saturation function may also be derived; this is also presented in Fig. 17. Although differing in details, there are by now a very large number of color models, or theories, that make use of similar

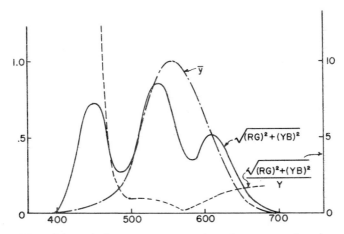

FIG. 17. The triple-peaked curve represents chrominance as a function of wavelength. Chrominance is here defined as the orthogonal vector sum of the two chromatic values $\bar{x} - \bar{y}$ and $.4\ (\bar{y} - \bar{z})$. When these values are divided by the achromatic value y, the result is the dashed curve whose values refer to the right-hand ordinate.

concepts. One of the earliest, and best known, is that of Jameson and Hurvich (1955).

Before leaving the subject of saturation, we should remind ourselves that only the saturation of aperture colors has been considered. When viewing monochromatic aperture colors, one is impressed with how relatively desaturated they appear and, moreover, with how quickly they desaturate further with prolonged viewing. Surface colors, though always physically less pure, often look more saturated than spectral colors viewed in the unrelated, or aperture mode. The explanations for this, undoubtedly complex, have to do with chromatic adaptation, lateral neural interaction, and the influence of achromatically mediated contours upon the appearance of the colors that they contain. These ideas, which are very important but cannot be dealt with further here, are under active investigation as a branch of Stage J_2 of Fig. 1.

IX. COLOR METRICS

This chapter will now conclude with a mercifully brief mention of a very complicated subject. It has been seen that spectral colors can be represented in two ways: (*a*) along a locus in the chromaticity diagram, where they plot in a continuous fashion, with no inversions; (*b*) around the circumference of a psychological color diagram, where the chromatic sensations represented there also vary in a smooth and continuous manner. Is there any simple relation between the two?

The answer is no. The matter has been exhaustively studied, both experimentally and theoretically. The question has also been generalized to colors inside the spectral locus of the chromaticity chart, and those which correspond, inside the circumference of the psychological color diagram, with saturation discrimination being the most intensively studied example. The answer is again no. Some of the most important experiments on this topic were done by MacAdam (1942), who then showed theoretically (MacAdam, 1944) that no chromaticity diagram can possibly exist, no matter what the choice of mixture primaries, that will represent sensory differences by equal distances in all regions and directions of the diagram. A great deal of work on this subject has been recently summarized in the report of a conference on *Color Metrices* (Vos, Friele, & Walraven, 1973). Attempts to find optimal nonlinear transformations of color mixture data that will account properly for sensory distances abound; this has been a happy hunting ground for the applied mathematician.

The basic reason for the difficulty is not too difficult to discern. The two diagrams stem, after all, from entirely different origins. The psychological color diagram is the result of paying attention to what colors look like, without any necessary reference whatever to their physical characteristics. If spectral colors are used, they may be represented in this kind of space by a variety of methods which have been discussed and compared here; the same is true in principle for all colors. The chromaticity diagram, on the other hand, results from experiments on color mixture where observers match stimuli but are never asked to judge anything at all about their appearance.

The tantalizing similarity between the two types of diagrams can be understood in the following terms. A chromaticity diagram based on cone photopigment curves would show, for each spectral color, the proportions of light absorbed in two of these. This proportion varies continuously with wavelength because the photopigment absorption curves are smooth, single-peaked, overlapping functions. If the discrimination of wavelength depended only on the rate of change of the absorption proportions of cone photopigments, then the two diagrams would agree. But this is clearly not so: (*a*) the visual system is nonlinear, (*b*) opponent colors signals are involved, and (*c*) in the end, achromatic and chromatic sensations, as a blend, form the final basis for sensory analysis. Because hue discrimination depends initially and *in part* upon the rate of absorption of pigment absorption proportions, there is *some* relation between the two diagrams. It has been part of the task of many explicit color theories to attempt a detailed explanation of what this relation is. Whereas all theories have succeeded to a degree (there are perhaps a dozen that can "explain" wavelength and saturation discrimination), they have also failed, because it is not yet possible to make a clear choice among them.

References

Abramov, I. Retinal mechanisms of colour vision. In M. G. F. Fuortes (Ed.), *Handbook of sensory physiology,* Vol. VII/2. Berlin: Springer-Verlag, 1972. Pp. 567–607.

Abrahamson, E. W., & S. M. Japar. Principles of interaction of light and matter. In H. J. A. Dartnall (Ed.), *Handbook of sensory physiology,* Vol. VII/1. Berlin: Springer-Verlag, 1972. Pp. 1–32.

Beare, A. C. Color-name as a function of wavelength. *American Journal of Psychology,* 1963, **76,** 248–256.

Berlin, B., & Kay, P. Basic color terms: their universality and evolution. Berkeley: Univ. of California Press, 1969.

Bornstein, M. H. Color vision and color naming: a psychophysiological hypothesis of cultural difference. *Psychological Bulletin,* 1973, **80,** 257–285.

Boynton, R. M. Vision. In J. Sidowski (Ed.), *Experimental methods and instrumentation in psychology.* New York: McGraw Hill, 1966. Pp. 273–330.

Boynton, R. M., & Gordon, J. Bezold-Brücke hue shift measured by color naming technique. *Journal of the Optical Society of America,* 1965, **55,** 78–86.

Boynton, R. M., & Greenspon, T. S. The distinctness of borders formed between equally saturated, psychologically unique fields. *Vision Research,* 1972, **12,** 495–507.

Boynton, R. M., & Kaiser, P. K. Vision: The additivity law made to work for heterochromatic photometry with bipartite fields. *Science,* 1968, **161,** 366–368.

Conklin, H. C. Color categorization. *American Anthropologist,* 1973, **75,** 931–942.

DeValois, R. L. Behavioral and electrophysiological studies of primate vision. In W. D. Neff (Ed.), *Contributions to sensory physiology,* Vol. 1. New York: Academic Press, 1965. Pp. 137–178.

DeValois, R. L. Analysis of response patterns of LGN cells. *Journal of the Optical Society of America,* 1966, **56,** 966–977.

Dimmick, F. L., & Hubbard, M. R. The spectral components of psychologically unique red. *American Journal of Psychology,* 1939, **52,** 348–353. (a)

Dimmick, F. L., & Hubbard, M. R. The spectral location of psychologically unique yellow, green, and blue. *American Journal of Psychology,* 1939, **52,** 242–254. (b)

Ekman, G. Dimensions of color vision. *Journal of Psychology,* 1954, **38,** 467–474.

Evans, R. M. Variables of perceived color. *Journal of the Optical Society of America,* 1964, **54,** 1467–1474.

Feinberg, G. Light. *Scientific American,* 1968, **219,** 50–59.

Graham, B. V., Turner, M. E., and Hurst, D. C. Derivation of wavelength discrimination from color naming. *Journal of the Optical Society of America,* 1973, **63,** 109-111.

Graham, C. H. Color theory. In S. Koch (Ed.), *Psychology: A study of a science,* Vol. 1: Sensory, perceptual, and physiological formulations. New York: McGraw-Hill, 1959. Pp. 145–287.

Graham, C. H. Discriminations that depend on wavelength. In C. H. Graham (Ed.), *Vision and visual perception.* New York: Wiley, 1965. Pp. 350–369.

Guth, S. L. Photometric and colormetric additivity at various intensities. In J. J. Vos, L. F. C. Friele, and P. L. Walraven (Eds.), *Color metrics.* Proceedings of the 1971 AIC Symposium on Color Metrics AIC/Holland, c/o Institute for Perception TNO, 1973. Ch. 2, pp. 26–35.

Guth, S. L., Donley, N. J., & Marrocco, R. T. On luminance additivity and related topics. *Vision Research,* 1969, **9,** 537–575.

Halsey, R. Identification of signal lights. I. Blue, green, white, and purple. *Journal of the Optical Society of America,* 1959, **49,** 45–55. (a)

Halsey, R. Identification of signal lights. II. Elimination of the purple category. *Journal of the Optical Society of America,* 1959, **49,** 167–169. (b)

Henderson, S. T. *Daylight and its spectrum.* New York: American Elsevier, 1970.

Hering, E. *Outlines of a theory of the light sense.* Translated by L. M. Hurvich and D. Jameson. Cambridge, Massachusetts: Harvard U. Press, 1964.

Jameson, D. Theoretical issues of color vision. In D. Jameson and L. M. Hurvich (Eds.), *Handbook of sensory physiology,* Vol. VII/4. Berlin: Springer-Verlag, 1972. Ch. 14, pp. 381–412.

Jameson, D., & Hurvich, L. M. Some quantitative aspects of an opponent-colors theory. I. Chromatic responses and spectral saturation. *Journal of the Optical Society of America,* 1955, **45,** 546–552.

Judd, D. B. Basic correlates of the visual stimulus. In S. S. Stevens (Ed.), *Handbook of experimental psychology.* New York: Wiley, 1951. Pp. 811–867.

Kruskal, J. B. Multidimensional scaling by optimizing goodness of fit to a nonmetric hypothesis. *Psychometrika,* 1964, **29,** 1–27.

Land, E. H. Experiments in color vision. *Scientific America,* May, 1959.

Land, E. H., & McCann, J. J. Lightness and retinex theory. *Journal of the Optical Society of America,* 1971, **61,** 1–11.

MacAdam, D. L. Visual sensitivities to color differences in daylight. *Journal of the Optical Society of America,* 1942, **32,** 247.

MacAdam, D. L. On the geometry of color space. *Journal of the Franklin Institute,* 1944, **238,** 195.

Pirenne, M. H. *Vision and the eye.* London: Chapman and Hall, 1948.

Polyak, S. L. *The vertebrate visual system.* (H. Klüver, Ed.). Chicago: Univ. of Chicago Press, 1957.

Purdy, D. M. Spectral hue as a function of intensity. *American Journal of Psychology,* 1931, **43,** 541–559.

Naka, K. I., & Rushton, W. A. H. S-potentials from colour units in the retina of fish (cyprinidae). *Journal of Physiology,* 1966, **185,** 536–555.

Rushton, W. A. H. Visual pigments in man. In H. J. A. Dartnall (Ed.), *Handbook of sensory physiology,* Vol. VII/1. Berlin: Springer-Verlag, 1972. Ch. 9, pp. 364–394.

Shepard, R. N. The analysis of proximities: multidimensional scaling with an unknown distance function. II. *Psychometrika,* 1962, **27,** 219–245.

Shepard, R. N., & Caroll, J. D. Parametric representation of nonlinear data structures. In P. R. Krishnaiah (Ed.), *International Symposium on Multivariate Analysis.* New York: Academic Press, 1966. Pp. 561–592.

Shepard, R. N., Kimball, A. K., & Nerlove, S. B. *Multidimensional scaling.* Vol. 1, Theory; Vol. 2, Applications. New York: Seminar Press, 1972.

Siegel, M. H. Discrimination of color: IV. Sensitivity as a function of spectral wavelength. *Journal of the Optical Society of America,* 1964, **54,** 821–832.

Smith, D. P. Derivation of wavelength discrimination data from colour-naming data. *Vision Research,* 1971, **11,** 739–742.

Sternheim, C. E., & Boynton, R. M. Uniqueness of perceived hues investigated with a continous judgmental technique. *Journal of Experimental Psychology,* 1966, **72,** 770–776.

Svaetichin, G. Spectral response curves of single cones. *Acta Physiologica Scandinavica,* 1956, **39**(Suppl. 134), 18–46.

Thomson, L. C. Sensations aroused by monochromatic stimuli and their prediction. *Optica Acta,* 1954, **1,** 93–101.

Trandis, H. C. Malpass, R. S., & Davidson, A. R. Psychology and culture. *Annual Review of Psychology,* 1973, **24,** 355–378.

Vos, J. J., Friele, L. F. C., & Walraven, P. L. (Eds.) *Color metrics.* Proceedings of the 1971 AIC Symposium on Color Metrics AIC/Holland, c/o Institute for Perception TNO, 1973.

Vos, J. J., & Walraven, P. L. An analytical description of the line element in the zone-fluctuation model of colour vision—I. Basic concepts. *Vision Research,* 1972, **12,** 1327–1344.

Ward, F., & Boynton, R. M. Scaling of large chromatic differences. *Vision Research,* 1974 (in press).

Wyszecki, G., & Stiles, W. S. *Color science.* New York: Wiley, 1967.

Young, T. On the theory of light and colours. *Philosophical Transactions,* 1802, 12–48.

Part V

Space and Motion Perception

Chapter 10

VISUAL SPACE PERCEPTION

WHITMAN RICHARDS

I. EGOCENTRIC COORDINATES

The three-dimensional environment around us provides a Euclidean framework for our own perception of spatial relations. The external Euclidean cues to these relations may be broadly categorized as static, if the observer is stationary, or dynamic, as when he locomotes or when objects move with respect to one another in the same neighborhood. Within these two broad categories, all the physical cues to spatial relations can be itemized as in the first column of Table I. Of course, having identified these available cues says very little about visual space perception, for we have not demonstrated that the human observer is, in fact, able to use these cues.

Although object relations in the environment can be described in terms of a Euclidean coordinate system, it is not clear that such a coordinate system offers the best framework for describing human space perception. Other obvious possibilities include cylindrical, polar, or spherical coordinate systems. Even though any one of these coordinate systems is just a transformation of the others, it is desirable that the coordinates we choose be close to those which the observer uses, for then we can see more directly how he is handling spatial information.

* This research was supported under NIH Grant EY-00742.

TABLE I
CUES TO SPATIAL LOCALIZATION

Physical cue	Notations	Neurophysiological basis	Physiological response
1. *Principal Axes*			
A. Primary (fore-aft body movement)	$\dfrac{d\theta}{dt} = \dfrac{d\phi}{dt} = 0$	No flow	Orienting, fixation
B. Secondary (gravity)	$\phi = \pm 90°$	Vestibular	Righting
C. Left–right	$\theta = \pm 90°$	Hemisphere	Turning
2. *Monocular*			
A. Static			
(*i*) Direction	θ, ϕ	Direction columns	Saccade
(*ii*) Size	$\Delta\theta, \Delta\phi$	Unknown	
(*iii*) Gradient	$d\theta/\theta$ $d\phi/\phi$	Orientation columns, Spatial frequency channels	
(*iv*) Intersections	"T"	Hypercomplex units	
B. Dynamic			
(*i*) Mean movement	$d\theta/dt, d\phi/dt$	Motion detector	Pursuit
(*ii*) Self-induced parallax	$d\theta/dt$	Unknown	
(*iii*) Shear rate	$\Delta(d\theta/dt)$	Unknown	
3. *Binocular*			
A. Static			
(*i*) Absolute distance	R	Unknown	Accommodation
(*ii*) Relative distance	ΔR	Disparity columns	Vergence
(*iii*) Gradients	dR/R	Unknown	
B. Dynamic			
(*i*) Flow	$dR/dt, dR/R \cdot dt$	Unknown	
(*ii*) Binocular shear	$\Delta(dR/dt)$	Unknown	Vergence tracking

The coordinate system we have chosen as the most informative is a spherical system centered on the observer (Fig. 1). This is an egocentric coordinate system. In such a system, two primary directions must be defined to represent the axes of the framework, as well as a unit of radial distance. The first obvious reference axis is "straight ahead." When the observer is moving, the straight ahead axis is defined unambiguously by the direction of his motion vector. When stationary, this reference axis is ambiguous, but is generally taken as the direction of forward movement. When the body is in motion the axis is particularly unique, because it corre-

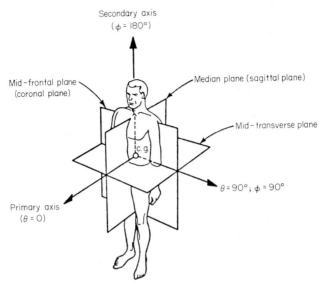

FIG. 1. Body-centered coordinate system. The primary axis points in the direction of forward motion. The secondary axis corresponds to the gravity axis. Angles θ and ϕ are taken, respectively, in the transverse and sagittal planes. [Adapted from Howard & Templeton (1966).]

sponds to the direction of the vanishing point of the flow patterns induced by the forward motion through an environment, as shown in Fig. 2. We define this direction as the primary direction. Orthogonal to this direction is a second axis naturally defined for the earthbound observer: the gravity axis. This axis may be determined in part by vestibular sensations but is primarily specified by the visual cues of the environment which are subject to gravity constraints, such as the verticality of trees and buildings as well as the horizon itself (Gibson, 1950).

Together, these two coordinates permit a specification of any visual direction in terms of the horizontal angle θ with respect to the primary visual direction $\theta = 0$ and the vertical elevation ϕ, with $\phi = 0$ in the horizontal plane and $\phi = 180$ in the vertical as determined by the gravity cue. Given a visual direction specified by θ and ϕ, a radial distance R must then be specified. We will arbitrarily chose as a unit for R the height of the observer's eyes above the ground. (This unit has the advantage of being correlated with interpupil distance, and, hence, tends to make the relation between radial distance and disparity invariant with the age of the observer.)

For a proper understanding of visual space perception, it is important to recognize that the two primary axes for the egocentric coordinate system

Fig. 2. Flow patterns induced by motion through an environment, in this case by a pilot during level flight (top) or during landing (bottom). The primary axis points toward the source of the flow. [From J. J. Gibson, *The Perception of the Visual World*, Boston: Houghton Mifflin, 1950. Reproduced by permission.]

are not necessarily absolute and fixed but instead are set to some degree by the observer himself based upon information available to him. For example, although the gravity sense provides an absolute reference for the vertical meridian, it is not necessary for the observer to have his own gravity detector. Because gravity acts upon everything in the environment, it is only necessary to know that trees are vertical and buildings have vertical edges and that the horizon is horizontal. With this knowledge, even if you tilt your head and had no vestibular sensations you could still deduce the secondary direction. In fact, these components of the visual scene may override the vestibular cues when an internal egocentric frame is constructed (Dichgans, Held, Young, & Brandt, 1972).

The primary direction is likewise indicated solely by relative information available to the observer through the visual input, regardless of head or body position. The primary direction is constrained only by the direction of locomotion of the whole body, regardless of where the observer fixates.

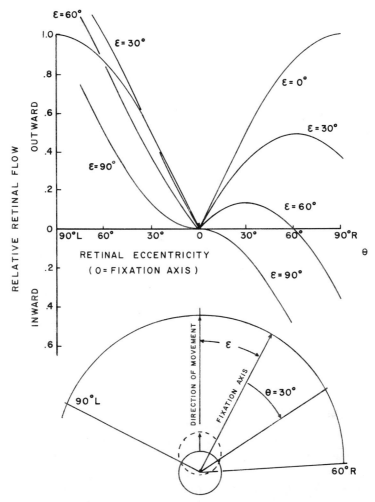

FIG. 3. Upper graph shows idealized horizontal retinal flow at any retinal angle from the fovea (θ) for several eccentricities of fixation (ϵ) relative to the direction of body (head) motion. When the fixation axis coincides with the direction of body movement, then the retinal flow pattern is symmetric on each side of the fovea ($\epsilon = 0°$). As the angle between the direction of body movement and fixation increases, the flow on each side of the fovea becomes more and more asymmetric ($\epsilon = 30, 60, 90°$).

For example, if the observer is fixating off to one side away from his direction of movement, the asymmetric flow patterns on the retina will indicate that fixation is not in the primary direction. As shown in Fig. 3, asymmetric flow patterns will result whenever the fixation point does not correspond to the vanishing point of flow set up by the body motion. Thus the primary visual direction can be determined by the relative visual information alone. The observer needs no visual information other than the visual flow pattern. In order to adjust his egocentric frame to proper orientation, the observer merely has to refixate so that the flow patterns are symmetrical on each half of the retina.

Although not yet studied in man, an excellent model for orienting may be drawn from studies of orienting by the fly (Reichardt, 1973; Poggio & Reichardt, 1973). Of particular interest is the orienting tendency produced by a moving stimulus located at various retinal eccentricities. To measure this tendency, these authors placed the fly in the middle of a cylinder the white inner wall of which had a single black stripe which could be positioned at any angular eccentricity in the fly's visual field. With the fly held rigid by a thin arm of a torque-compensator, the torque generated by the fly's attempt to orient to the oscillating bar may be measured for any eccentricity of the bar. Once such a stimulus strength versus eccentricity function had been determined, this function could in principle be applied to the flow rates of Fig. 3 to determine the orienting tendency for complex flow patterns. For the fly, this weighting function is given in Fig. 4. The abscissa of this figure shows the eccentricity of the stimulus presented to the fly, with the primary direction ($\theta = 0$) taken as the sagittal direction through the body. The abscissa is the torque that a moving bar will generate as the fly tries to orient toward the stimulus. The torque curve is S-shaped because, in one case, the fly attempts to turn counterclockwise, whereas when the stimulus is presented to the opposite side, there is a clockwise turning tendency. The curve in Fig. 4 is therefore a weighting function, which indicates how effective the stimulus is when it is off the primary axis. Because the curve is symmetrical about the primary direction, it is obvious that any asymmetric flow presented to the fly (as in Fig. 3) will cause it to orient toward a more stable position. The potential well in the lower part of the figure indicates the stable condition more clearly.

The same kind of weighting function can be applied to orienting (saccadic fixation) behavior in man. However, instead of using the two optic lobes as the fly, the presumed correlate will be the difference in stimulation between the two hemispheres. As we shall see later, a similar model may also be used to interpret vergence fixation along the primary axis.

The important conclusion to draw from Figs. 3 and 4 is that there is behavioral evidence demonstrating the ability of an animal to localize the straight ahead solely by relative visual information, without reference to any absolutes such as provided by vestibular sensations. Egocentric coordinates defined by such relative information are not necessarily very precise. But we must remember that the intent to orient to the primary direction need not be precision, but rather may be to provide a global orientation

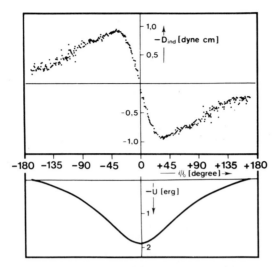

FIG. 4. The orienting torque of the fly induced by a stripe placed at various angular eccentricities, ψ_Ω off the primary direction. The lower figure is the potential well calculated from the torque measurements and shows the stable orientation is at $\psi = 0$. [From Poggio & Reichardt (1973).]

which will enable the organism to conduct a finer processing of information in a more limited region of visual space (Trevarthen, 1968; Schneider, 1967; Ingle, 1973). Such a refined processing of visual information in the neighborhood of the primary direction is not conducted in isolation, however, but rather must still be interpreted with reference to the entire visual scene. The global egocentric framework is thus not merely a basis for providing a semireflexive orienting mechanism. Instead, it may be vital to an interpretation of spatial relations in the neighborhood of fixation where acuity is high. Perhaps the strongest evidence supporting the dependence of detailed spatial analysis upon the global egocentric framework is provided by Hein and Diamond (1972); although antecedents appear earlier (Held, 1968). Hein has found that the development of sensory–motor coordination of guided reaching in kittens required the development first of an egocentric framework that relates the position of the body to its environment.

A. Translations of Coordinates

The Euclidean space around us is still. But if we operate in terms of an egocentric coordinate system, then whenever we twist, turn, or reorient, our egocentric coordinates have undergone some translation. Nevertheless, it is clear that when we move our egocentric reference frame we do not want to infer that the whole world has moved. Therefore, our specification for the coordinate system must be such that any transformation we are likely to make should leave the spatial relations within the coordinate system invariant. If the relations that our own brain is attempting to interpret remain invariant under translations of our coordinate system, then we will have a stable world.

Although many scientists have considered and studied this problem since Helmholtz, most current explanations for the stability of the world under active, self-produced movements still follow Helmholtz's original proposals. For example, it is possible that when a self-produced movement is initiated, there is an internal compensatory signal that in some way cancels or modifies the afferent change (Sperry, 1950; von Holst & Mittelstaedt, 1950; MacKay, 1956; Teuber, 1960). The extensive work on adaptation to prismatic distortions, whereby compensation proceeds much more rapidly with active, self-produced movements is strong evidence suggesting an internal readjustment tied to the egocentric coordinate system (Kohler, 1962; Held, 1965; Held & Freedman, 1963; Harris, 1965; Howard, 1973). However, one striking property of these adaptation effects is that following adaptation to a large shift in the frame (such as a 20° lateral displacement) there is only a small orienting error immediately after the subject is returned to the preadaptation condition. Because the error following adaptation is much smaller than the induced displacement of the frame, it is possible that the frame itself was invariant under translation and instead the observer adapted only to the local (prismatic) distortions in the flow or gradient patterns that now slightly redefine the axes of the coordinate system. Such an interpretation implies that the coordinate system itself is invariant under angular translation.*

Luneburg (1950) was the first to formalize precisely a coordinate system that would be invariant under changes in head and eye positions. This system was shortly followed by others cast along similar lines (Hardy, Rand, Rittler, Blank, & Boeder, 1953; Blank, 1957, 1958). One of the more recent formalisms of Luneburg's position is by Leibovic, Balslev, and Mathieson (1971), who derived a set of (eisekonic) coordinates† whose distance elements remain invariant under changes in fixation position (with head rigid). One such pair is represented by loci equidistant from the ob-

---

* The strong form of this hypothesis is that different body-centered frames are loosely coupled internally and tightly coupled only by external feedback through separate afferent pathways.

† An eisekonic transformation is one limited to translations or rotations. This is a special case of conformal transformations, which also include dilations and inversions. Dodwell (1970) proposes that the visual system makes use of conformal transformations, at least in adapting to optical distortions.

server (the equidistant horopter) and radii emanating from a cyclopean eye (an approximation to the Hillebrand hyperbolas). In essence, this is a polar coordinate system in the horizontal plane through the eyes, and, thus, a special case of our chosen egocentric coordinate system. Clearly, translations of fixation position along any arc will leave the remaining equidistant arcs invariant in that they will continue to excite the same neural populations. Similarly, changes in fixation along the radial loci (Hillebrand hyperbolas) will leave the remaining rays invariant. Leibovic notes that such a coordinate system fits nicely with Blakemore's (1970a) proposal that columns in the visual cortex of the cat appear distributed either as depth columns, whereby all cortical units in the column respond to a line at a particular orientation and locus of constant distance; or as direction columns, where all cortical units in the column respond to a line of a given orientation lying along a locus of constant visual direction.*

Perhaps the strongest evidence supporting the notion that distance and direction are encoded separately is the behavior of eye movements. Referring to Fig. 5, when fixation is altered from A to B, a saccade is first made to orient both eyes to the direction of B (i.e., to A'), and then a vergence

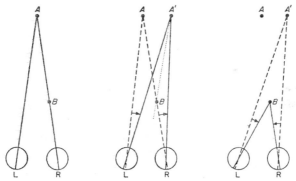

FIG. 5. Schematic diagrams illustrating sequence of movement in changing fixation from A to B. (1) Binocular fixation of A. (2) Conjugate lateral movement without change of convergence to A', so that bisector of angle of convergence passes through B. (3) Convergence movement from A to B. Steps (2) and (3) are to some extent superimposed; but in view of their time characteristics, they are easily distinguished. [From G. Westheimer & A. M. Mitchell, Eye movement responses to convergence and stimuli. *Archives of Ophthalmology. New York,* 1956, **55**, 848–856. Copyright 1956, American Medical Association.]

* Although such a division of the egocentric coordinate system appears necessary in principle, the distinction of depth versus direction columns may not be the appropriate correlate of behavior. Instead, we cannot yet exclude the very real possibility that these differences between cortical columns are merely a reflection of the variance in the encoding of position in three-space.

movement is initiated causing the eyes to slide down the new visual axis to the point B (Westheimer & Mitchell, 1956; Yarbus, 1967). The independence of these two sequential movements implies a separation of mechanisms, which has also been shown to have entirely different dynamics (Rashbass & Westheimer, 1961). Further support for the independence of visual direction and distance is provided by Foley (1972), on a more conceptual level. Curiously, when an observer is required to set up spatial configurations according to a preset Euclidean pattern, he will make size and distance judgments that may be in direct conflict with his separate judgments of visual angle. This suggests that angular judgments are encoded independently of size–distance judgments. Thus, there is strong support for a coordinate system based upon θ, ϕ, and R, with θ, ϕ, and R encoded by separate mechanisms or pathways.

However, it is still not clear why linear transformations of the egocentric system should leave object positions invariant, although von Schelling (1956) has shown that a metric invariant under such transformations can be found. One metric that is particularly appropriate is based upon ratios of distances. For example, consider the changes in object relations as the observer moves forward through his environment. As distant objects are approached, they become not only larger, but also move toward the periphery of the visual field. A possible mechanism for keeping object size invariant under such a translation would be one that compresses the apparent peripheral angles and expands the spatial representation of objects falling upon the central foveal region. The mapping of the retina onto the cortex is ideal in this respect, for the central fovea has a large representation at the expense of a smaller peripheral representation. Because the retino-cortical transformation is roughly a logarithmic function of retinal eccentricity (Fischer, 1973), ratios of spatial relations cast upon the fovea would remain invariant under forward translation by the observer. Thus, the cortical magnification factor could be an economy of neurons that yields high foveal acuity, while at the same time serving as a mechanism for leaving angular distances invariant under translations of egocentric coordinates (Cowan, 1974; Richards & Cowan, 1975).

More difficult to interpret is the stability of the visual environment under saccadic or vergence changes in fixation. The notion that such self-produced movements may generate "corollary discharges" that suppress or modify afferent input during this coordinate change has already been mentioned. Rather than invoking elaborate compensatory mechanisms, however, the brain may operate on a much simpler principle: namely, to assume that the world is stable unless afferent information proves otherwise (MacKay, 1970). Considering that the definition of the egocentric coordinate system is heavily dependent upon flow patterns and movement, so long as no apparent motion of the environment is observed, stability could be inferred. Suppression of visual input during saccades would facilitate such an inference (Latour, 1962; Zuber & Stark, 1966; Volkman, Schick, & Riggs, 1968; Richards, 1969). However, such suppression may not be necessary, for the retinal flow during the saccade, which may reach 100 deg/sec, greatly exceeds the optimal velocities for stimulating movement detectors, which respond in the neighborhood of 1–10 deg/sec. (Sekuler & Ganz, 1963; Barlow, Hill, & Levick, 1964; Sekuler, Chap. 11 of this volume). Movement suppression would therefore be more important during pursuit tracking (Richards & Steinbach, 1972) and vergence fixation, both of which are slower movements that yield flow patterns moving in the velocity range of the motion detectors.* Both of these latter types of movements, however, could invoke simple compensatory signals. For example, to compensate for the unidirectional lateral flow encountered during a pursuit movement, the brain only needs to suppress the hemispheric imbalance that would normally trigger a saccade (see Fig. 3). For vergence movements, the flow patterns to the hemispheres are symmetrical anyway, and the cancellation could occur directly at least in the frontal plane.

Such a model for visual stability of the environment also places a constraint upon the eye movement systems themselves. In order that no afferent information be available to the egocentric coordinate system during eye movements, it is critical that the eye positions themselves not be consciously sensed by this system (Merton, 1964; Hay, 1971). Thus, all major afferent signals for the primary visual directions that define the egocentric coordinates should come from the visual flow patterns alone and must not be perturbed by a proprioceptive sense of eye position. Instead, the sense or perception of eye position should be closely linked to the central eye movement command center (Skavenski, Haddad, & Steinman, 1972), whose primary coordinates would then be reset when necessary solely by retinal input (i.e., the flow pattern). By analogy, other egocentric coordinate systems defined for other sensory modalities should also not rely upon proprioceptive input for their definition of coordinates. Such multiple coordinate systems which are then only loosely coupled to one another should provide a stable framework for visual space under a variety of transformations of sensory input.

II. STEREOPSIS

With a global egocentric coordinate system that is stable and invariant under translation, this system may then be centered on particular regions in the visual field that may be subject to closer scrutiny. The objective

---

* The general rule will be that the closer the rate of eye movement approximates the optimal velocity of the motion detector, the greater the need for suppression or compensation. Blinks are a most useful suppressive device and occur frequently during vergence fixations which elicit object movement near optimal speeds.

will be to perform an analysis of objects in three-dimensional space in the neighborhood of the fixation point. The cues that can be used to analyze information in this smaller region will be the same as those put forth in Table I. However, rather than processing the more global θ, ϕ, and R values, it may be more efficient to examine the increments in these values: $\Delta\theta$, $\Delta\phi$, ΔR, and their various spatial–temporal derivatives. A first step in this direction is to consider how a three-dimensional space is constructed in the region of the fixation point. This is the problem of stereopsis.

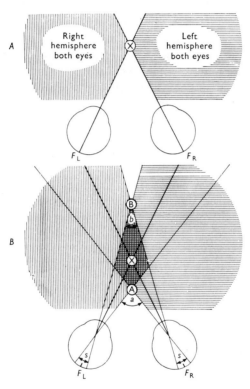

FIG. 6. (a) Assuming that partial decussation exactly divides the retinas through the foveas, F_L and F_R, the region of space shaded with vertical lines is entirely represented in the right hemisphere, since it projects upon nasal retina in the left eye and temporal in the right. The horizontally striped area is likewise represented in the left hemisphere. The areas of space nearer than the fixation point, X, and beyond it should project to separate hemispheres through the two eyes. (b) Now, if a central vertical strip of retina of angular width s is represented in *both* hemispheres, the striped regions of Fig. 6a are expanded to include the area around the fixation point, which projects to both hemispheres through both eyes. The precise location of the point X between A and B depends on the relative contribution of nasal and temporal retina to the region of double representation, which is determined by the exact position of each fovea within the strip s. The point X might, in fact, lie anywhere between A and B. [From Blakemore (1969).]

Crucial to an understanding of stereopsis is recognition of the significance of the overlap in the nasal and temporal portions of the retina of each eye. Consider the upper part of Fig. 6. The portion of the visual field indicated by horizontal cross-hatching goes to the left hemisphere, the vertical cross-hatching goes to the right hemisphere. Now, in the pie-shaped sector below the fixation point, stimuli will go to the left hemisphere via the left eye but to the right hemisphere via the right eye. The opposite is true for the sector above the fixation point. Thus, nearer and farther from the fixation point there is an hourglass shape which does not have representation in the same hemisphere and hence the binocular correlations needed for stereopsis become impossible. Yet if objects are to be analyzed in three-dimensional space about the fixation point, stereopsis is necessary. The brain solves this problem as indicated in the lower portion of the figure. Instead of having complete decussation through the fovea there is an overlap in the projections of the visual field that allows visual information to be correlated in the same hemisphere on one or the other side of fixation (Stone, 1966; Blakemore, 1969; Sanderson & Sherman, 1971). In each eye, this overlap will appear as an encroachment of nasal retina upon temporal retina and vice versa and is hence designated as the nasal–temporal overlap. This nasal–temporal overlap plays a major role in stereopsis.

With binocular information available to each hemisphere in the neighborhood of the fixation point as indicated in Fig. 6 stereoscopic information may be extracted from the three-dimensional space surrounding fixation. The manner in which this is done is still not clear. Proposals for the basis of stereopsis fall into two categories: (1) Those based upon a Keplerian model requiring disparity detectors and (2) those based upon global correlations and "disparity pools."

A. The Keplerian Model

The Keplerian model for stereopsis is merely an internal reflection of the external geometry of binocular parallax. As rays emanate from the nodal points of each eye, they cross and create a grid, as shown in Fig. 7. With the two focal axes F_L and F_R taken as reference, the distance of any object may be read off the grid in terms of its angular position in each eye. The difference in the angular position in each eye is retinal disparity, δ, which is zero at the intersection of the foveal projections as well as along the arc indicated by the heavy line. The object distance relative to the distance of the fixation point can thus be determined if retinal disparity can be sensed. The first demonstration that this is possible was by Wheatstone (1838), using his now famous stereoscope. More recently,

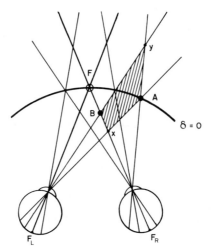

Fɪɢ. 7. Basic Keplerian model for stereopsis. The external geometry of binocular parallax is assumed to be reflected in the nervous system. Thus each intersection will activate a different binocular neuron or "disparity detector." The difficulty with the model is the presence of false intersections x and y arising from similar objects A and B located at different distances. Why are the "ghosts" not seen?

"disparity detectors" have been found in the visual cortex of the cat (Barlow, Blakemore, & Pettigrew, 1967; Pettigrew, Nikara, & Bishop, 1968; Joshua & Bishop, 1970) and monkey (Hubel & Wiesel, 1970) and have been inferred from psychophysical adaptation studies in man (Blakemore & Julesz, 1971; Blakemore & Hague, 1972; Felton, Richards, & Smith, 1972; Ronchi & Mariani, 1972; Long & Over, 1973).

The fact that detectors of retinal disparity have been found in visual cortex supports the basic Keplerian model, for these detectors would be responding to the points of intersection of the gridwork. Such a proposal was first clearly stated by Boring (1942), and subsequently modified by Charnwood (1951), Dodwell and Engel (1963, 1970), Julesz (1962, 1971), and Sperling (1970). Sperling's model may be reduced to two classes of neurons underlying stereopsis. The first class, designated as inflow neurons carry monocular signals along axons that cross at an angle similar to the Keplerian grid. A second type of neuron, a level detector, then indicates a correspondence in binocular activity at one level in the field created by the neural grid. These neurons are ingeniously designed with triangular dendritic arborizations to inhibit other level detectors. Accessory neurons in this class further tune up the disparity detection process. The output of the binocular level-detecting neurons is then combined with neurons analyzing shape and texture. Sperling, like others before him (Ogle, 1964; Mitchell, 1970) proposes two stereoscopic mechanisms, one global, handling large disparities without the need for feature-by-feature correlations and a second mechanism concerned with fine stereopsis (less than .25° disparity) that is more a part of the pattern recognition process.

The major difficulty with such Keplerian models is the elimination of "ghost" correlations. If two neighboring lines A and B are placed at different distances in visual space, a total of four intersections or disparity detectors are activated, as shown in Fig. 7. How does the brain choose the correct intersections? Although in the real world such confusions are unlikely because of slight textural, size, or shape differences between objects, the ghosts are also not seen in the laboratory where highly redundant patterns are used. The Julesz binary random-dot pattern is an example. To solve this problem, Julesz (1971) proposes cluster-by-cluster disparity matching rather than point-by-point matching. Sutro and Lerman (1973) on the other hand, merely truncate the nearest and farthest vertices of the quadrilateral, $AxBy$. These two methods represent examples of two classes of solutions to the problem of obtaining a single neural image from images that are disparate on each retina. In one case the problem is solved by (global) fusion, whereas, in the other, a process of suppression is invoked. Kaufman (1974) has provided an excellent review of the facts and theories related to fusion, suppression, and the problem of single binocular vision. This problem falls somewhere between that of object recognition and object localization (Dodwell, 1970), for the localization of objects in three-dimensional space will occur even when they are seen as diplopic (Mitchell, 1969; Jones & Kerr, 1972), and, in fact, the greatest depth generally occurs for disparities that do not yield single binocular images (Foley & Richards, 1972).

B. DISPARITY POOLS: GLOBAL CORRELATIONS

A completely different kind of model for stereopsis has been proposed that lies outside of the Keplerian framework (Richards, 1969, 1973). Rather than requiring disparity detection based upon correlations of local regions in space, the model states that only two global correlations are performed, one for a spectrum of convergent disparities and a second for divergent disparities. Earlier work that suggested such global, feature-free correlations appeared in studies by Kaufman (1964), and Kaufman and Pitblado (1965), and was also implied by a demonstration of the lability of disparity correlations by Fender and Julesz (1967). More recently, considerably more evidence has appeared showing that the disparity mechanism is capable of rather wide-field correlations, which need not be shape dependent (Westheimer & Tanzman, 1956; Mitchell, 1969; Jones & Kerr, 1972; Foley & Richards, 1972). Much earlier Linksz (1952) was also thinking in terms of a global separation of disparity correlation mechanisms. In order to make sense of the horopter, Linksz believed that the spectrum of disparities should be divided functionally into convergent and divergent regions. The horopter locus of zero disparity could then represent a functional equilibrium between two types of disparity analyzers (convergent and divergent). Although still thinking in Keplerian terms, Linksz (1952) elaborated earlier proposals of Bárány (1925) and Kleist (1926) that each type of disparity could be encoded separately in cortex, one above and the other below the stripe of Gennari (where the incoming geniculate fibers arrive).

The first demonstration of a separate encoding process for convergent and divergent disparities was by Richards (1970a), who found that some observers could process one type of disparity but not the other. Such individuals were designated as "stereoanomalous," and represented about 30% of the population.

Since this first demonstration that convergent and divergent disparities must be treated as separate functional entities, a large number of differences have been noted in the manner by which the visual system extracts these two kinds of disparity information (Richards & Regan, 1973). The visual system must therefore have at least two kinds of disparity filters: one for convergent and a second for divergent disparities.

The model proposed to account for these two types of disparity filters is quite simple. It is based upon the fact that stereopsis in the region of the fixation point requires an overlap in the nasal and temporal retinae or their projections. The consequence of this overlap is to cause a slight displacement in the correlations between retinal positions in each eye as they are projected onto the separate geniculate laminae. This is shown schematically in Fig. 8. As the temporal retina of the left eye is paired with the nasal retina of the right eye at the lateral geniculate body, the registration of the pairing will be off by the extent of the nasal–temporal overlap (estimated to be approximately .75° in man). For the first two pairs, the error will be a convergent disparity.* This model proposes that whenever the displacement in the registration of pairs of geniculate laminae does not occur, then a disparity filter will be missing.

Clearly, such a model is quite different from the Keplerian schemes, for only two types of correlations are performed, namely those between the adjacent laminae. There is not a series of difference-field operations, but only one for each class of disparity. The closer the stimulus disparity approaches that of the nasal–temporal shift, then the higher the correlation in activity. The two types of correlations of disparate stimuli thus serve to "pool" the disparity information. The simplicity of the model lies in

---

* For simplicity, Fig. 8 has been drawn with the displacement at the geniculate. Because the actual displacement is retinal, the correlations will be opposite to those shown.

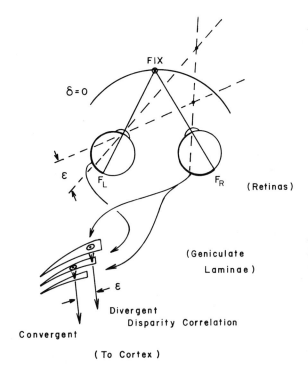

FiG. 8. Schematic showing effect of a nasal–temporal overlap upon binocular corre-lations. The retina of each eye projects to separate geniculate laminae, each of which are functionally displaced approximately by .75°, owing to the overlap of the nasal and temporal retinas. Because the displacement occurs twice, first between the upper two geniculate layers and again between the lower two, the total displacement will be $2 \times .75° = \epsilon$. Disparity correlations between each eye based on the upper genicu-late pairs will be biased toward divergent, whereas interocular correlations from the lower pair will be convergent. [See the footnote on page 366.]

the notion that the same anatomical constraint required for foveal stereop-sis (i.e., the nasal–temporal overlap) sets up the stereoscopic mechanism itself.

An estimate of the extent of two correlation processes corresponding to the convergent and divergent pooling of disparities is shown in the upper part of Fig. 9. The graph relates the depth sensation to disparity for two observers, one who lacks the divergent mechanism (ID) and a second who lacks the convergent correlation mechanism (RD). Only depth relative to the distance to the fixation point is plotted, ignoring the sign (front or back). For both observers, the flat region where depth remains constant is the region where disparities are not discriminated under a forced-choice method (Richards, 1971). Over the region of convergent disparities dis-

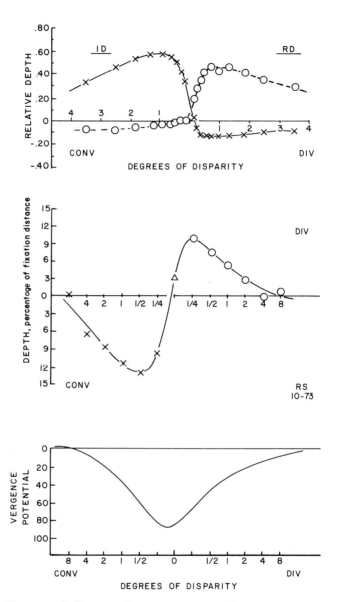

Fig. 9. Upper graph illustrates for two stereoanomalous observers the magnitude of the (unsigned) depth sensation associated with a given stimulus disparity. For both observers, the greatest depth is elicited by stimulus disparities near .75°, but for ID the stimulus must be convergent while RD requires a divergent stimulus. For the opposite disparities the depth sensation approximates that seen for monocular stimuli.

Middle graph shows the depth sensation for a third subject (RS) whose stereo-mechanism is a composite of the two separate components illustrated in the upper graph. The potential well associated with RS's depth-disparity sensation curve is given in the lower graph. The potential of this well is labeled "vergence potential" to stress the close relation between depth sensations and the vergence control mechanism.

criminated by ID, the depth sensation first rises and then falls as the stimulus disparity exceeds .75°. A similar, but symmetrical function is obtained from RD who discriminated only divergent disparities. The rise and fall in these depth sensation curves presumably represents the extent of the disparity correlation process, which is maximal at the value for the nasal-temporal shift.

For the complete stereoscopic mechanism, comprising both convergent and divergent mechanisms, the depth sensations may be approximated by subtracting the two types of correlation functions given in the upper part of Fig. 9. Such a difference comparison will yield a curve similar to that obtained for RS, shown in the middle portion of the figure. Of course, RS had been previously shown to possess both divergent and convergent disparity mechanisms.

The complete depth–disparity correlation function of RS now appears very similar to the weighting function used to direct fixation to the primary direction in the fly (see Fig. 4). Following the earlier analogy, we would now propose that this depth–disparity correlation function will be used to mediate vergence eye movements. Direct support for this construction has already been obtained by Jones (1972), who measured vergence movements in several types of stereo observers and found individuals whose pattern of vergence responses was formally similar to the depth functions shown in Fig. 9. It seems reasonable to assume, therefore, that both depth and vergence are mediated by a comparison of two global correlation processes that are set up by the same mechanism (Richards, 1970b, 1973; Jones, 1972).

III. FIXATION REFLEXES AND DISPARITY TUNING

When the two eyes converge onto a fixation point, two steps are involved: (1) the initial grasping or tracking of the target and (2) holding the target on the fovea. Three separate eye-movement systems are involved in this task: the saccadic, the pursuit, and the vergence systems (see Robinson, 1968 for a summary). Not surprisingly, each system utilizes separate sensory cues that are, respectively, positional displacement, velocity, and binocular disparity. Once stationary targets are acquired, both eyes do not necessarily orient the foveas directly at the target. Some observers fixate slightly behind the target (divergent phoria), whereas others fixate in front (convergent phoria). Such "fixation disparities" have been extensively studied by Ogle (1964) and his co-workers (Ogle, Martens, & Dyer, 1967). For any individual, these imbalances in fixation generally fall into one of four categories, which appear related to the stereoscopic abilities

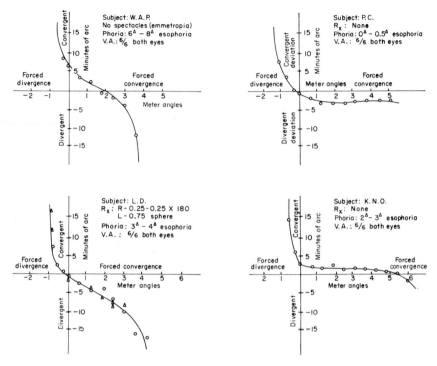

Fig. 10. Fixation disparity curves generated by forced vergence, indicated by meter angles. The ordinate shows the degree of misalignment of two nonius lines presented separately to each eye. [From Ogle (1964). Consult this reference for details.]

of the observer (Richards, in preparation). Examples taken from the two most common categories are shown in Fig. 10. Individuals lacking the divergent stereoscopic mechanism generally have a slightly divergent phoria and fixation disparity that remains constant over a wide range of forced convergence induced by prisms, as shown in the right-hand portion of the figure.

Normally, fixation disparity does not create a problem for space perception because depth judgments about object relations are made independent of the fixation point (i.e., the eye position is not sensed). However when excessive fixation disparity occurs on a larger scale, then squint or strabismus is observed, which may affect space perception. For example, when fixation imbalance reaches 5°, a value that approaches or exceeds the possible binocular correlations, then stereopsis on a fine scale becomes impossible. Perception of visual space must then be built up from the remaining cues, the spatial relations of objects in the Euclidean environment.

A further difficulty imposed upon the stereoscopic mechanism arises when objects are magnified in one eye but not the other. This situation

Fig. 11. The induced effect. The vertical magnification of an image in one eye acts like a horizontal disparity in the other, causing a rotation of the frontal plane (ordinate). Over the range from ±4%, the induced effect will exactly cancel the geometric effect caused by asymmetric fixation. [From Ogle (1964).]

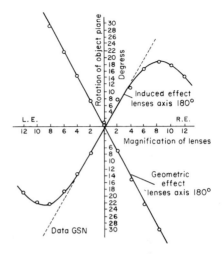

occurs naturally during asymmetric convergence at near distances, where the distance from the eye to the object is different for each eye.* Different image sizes may also occur when the eyeball length is greater in one eye, or when spectacle corrections are unequal, or when the refractive powers of the cornea are unequal. These conditions exist, to some degree, in all observers, and are called aneisekonia. The effect of these kinds of differences in the image sizes to the two eyes is to rotate the frontal plane about the vertical axis. For a known difference in magnification, such rotations may be predicted precisely from purely geometrical considerations (Ogle, 1964; Gillam, 1967; Smith & Wientzen, 1973; Kaye, 1973). Even for small magnification differences the effect is sizable. For example, at 50 cm a 10% magnification difference can lead to a rotation of 45° (Ogle, 1964; Blakemore, 1970c; Fiorentini & Maffei, 1971).

To prevent such rotations due to aneisekonia or asymmetric convergence, the visual system utilizes the vertical image disparity between the two eyes. The effect of a vertical disparity is to induce a tilt opposite to the geometric tilt, but about the same axis (Fig. 11). Thus, the vertical disparity in one eye is treated as a horizontal disparity in the other. This induced effect of vertical disparity has been studied extensively by Ogle (1964), who has shown that over its range it compensates precisely for the improper geometric tilt.† Thus, in order to prevent rotations of the

* For very near distances, excessive asymmetric convergence will also cause unequal blur in each eye. Problems of irradiation stereoscopy must also then be considered (Ogle, 1962; Cibis & Haber, 1951).

† Ocular dominance columns that run perpendicular to the vertical meridian could provide a substrate for vertical disparity detection. (See LeVay, Hubel, & Wiesel, 1975, for supporting anatomy.)

egocentric frame, vertical disparity is extracted and becomes an important participant in the analysis of visual space.

IV. THE HOROPTER

By definition, the horopter is the locus of points in space having equal visual direction in each eye. Ideally, the horopter locus would correspond to the circle defined by the nodal points of each eye and the fixation point (the Vieth–Müller circle). In practice, the horopter generally lies outside this locus.

The significance of the horopter in visual space perception has probably been exaggerated. Not only is its physiological significance obscure, but even its psychophysical definition has become ambiguous (Ogle, 1964, lists six different horopters!). Probably the horopter that is most closely related to visual physiology is the equidistant locus,* which yields the smallest standard errors and which probably corresponds to the locus of greatest visual acuity (Blakemore, 1970b). Such a horopter can be understood to represent a balance between the activities of convergent and divergent disparity analyzing mechanisms.† However, even this horopter, like all others, applies only to loci in the horizontal plane of the Vieth–Müller (V–M) circle. The geometric horopter does not exist outside this plane except for the special case when the two eyes are parallel.

Figure 12 illustrates the nature of the horopter locii in the horizontal plane. As fixation distance increases, the locus becomes more convex, deviating more and more from the geometric horopter (V–M circle). For the most part, this change in curvature is largely an artifact of the plotting method. If disparity rather than distance is plotted on the ordinate, the deviation of the horopter locus from the V–M circle remains constant over fixation distance for many observers (Shipley & Rawlings, 1970), at least for the nonius horopter based upon visual direction. When changes in curvature do occur, they may be due solely to shifts in the nodal points of the eyes rather than to any neural mechanism (Bourdy, 1972; Blank & Enoch, 1973). The equidistant horopter, on the other hand, is known to undergo modifications from neural factors, particularly during asymmetric convergence (Ogle, 1964; Lazarus, 1970). The nature of these modifica-

---

* The fact that the fovea lies 5° off the optical axis produces a close approximation to an equidistant horopter for a fixation distance of 50 cm.

† However, note that stereoacuity near the horopter may be upset by peripheral factors (Luria, 1969) suggesting that even "fine" stereo mechanisms may be subject to more global constraints.

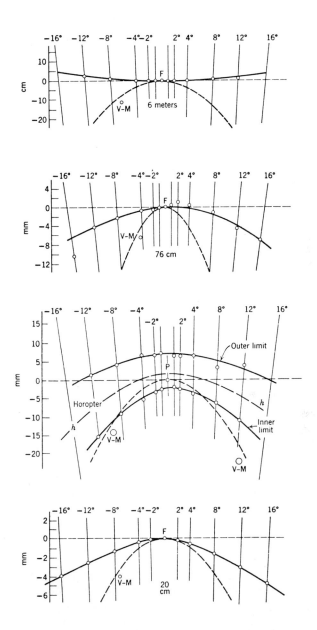

FIG. 12. Data for the apparent frontoparallel plane for different observation distances. In each case, F is the point of fixation. The data for 40 cm are based on the criterion of single vision. The vertical dimensions have been magnified. [From Ogle (1964).]

tions is in the direction of keeping the equidistant frontal plane normal to the axis of fixation.

V. DYNAMIC STEREOPSIS

A complete analysis of objects in visual space must also include the dynamic situation where objects move relative to one another. Clearly, the stereoscopic mechanisms detecting the flow of patterns toward and away from the observer are particularly important for many everyday problems, including understanding an answer to the simple question of *How do we catch a ball?* Yet information about the dynamics of the disparity detecting mechanisms has only just begun to become available (Lee, 1970; Richards, 1971; Tyler, 1971; Harker, 1973). The study most directly related to this problem is that by Regan and Beverley (1973; see also Beverley & Regan, 1973). These authors have shown that the detection of motion in three-dimensional space may be subdivided into three regions: a central region lying between the fixation axes where forward-moving objects would eventually strike the head, and the two regions to the left or right of the fixation axes. Within the central region, two subpopulations of in–out motion detectors were also suggested, each with different directional tuning curves. Together, these two populations would help to yield a high sensitivity to object direction in the central region of vision. These mechanisms could easily be set up by the nasal–temporal overlap, with the introduction of a time delay analogous to that proposed by Barlow *et al.* (1964) for motion detectors. Clearly, a considerable amount of further study about the dynamics of the stereoscopic process is needed. Perhaps of particular interest might be the relation between this dynamic binocular process and the dynamic monocular cue of motion parallax (Wallach, Moore, & Davidson, 1963; Epstein, 1969). Does one serve as a substrate for the other?

VI. MOTION PARALLAX

Although parallax induced by head movement is an effective cue to depth even with one eye (Ferris, 1972), the fact that this cue is monocular does not require that it precede stereopsis when extracted by the visual system. In fact, the motion parallax cue probably follows stereopsis in the sequence of information processing by the visual system. One test of the hypothesis that motion parallax cues are processed after stereopsis is to present to each eye dynamic noise patterns that individually contain no flow gradients, but when seen binocularly do generate a gradient. The fact

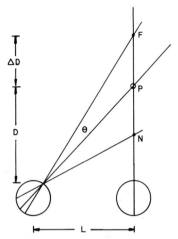

FIG. 13. Motion parallax cue to distance. Observer fixates P while moving laterally through a distance L. The relative displacements ΔD of F and N cause both points to sweep through angle θ.

that a moving gradient may be seen demonstrates that at least a portion of the movement parallax cue is extracted after stereopsis (Julesz, 1971). Enright (1970) also has demonstrated the strong dependency of the parallax cue upon stereopsis by a completely different method. If a neutral density filter is placed before one eye, the visual signal is delayed slightly (Lit, 1949), but the rate of change of flow patterns will remain unaltered. When the observer is stationary but the object moves in the frontal plane, this interocular delay elicits a disparity sensation and the object will appear to move off the frontal plane (Pulfrich effect; Lit, 1949; Levick *et al.*, 1972). On the other hand, if it is not the object but the observer who moves with one eye attenuated (as when riding a motor vehicle), then the objects moving by will still move in one plane but their relative depths will be altered. This change in the depth sensation in turn alters the perception of the rate of motion, suggesting that the motion information depends upon and hence follows the processing of the stereoscopic cue.

The actual manner in which the visual system extracts the parallax information induced by head movement is not clear (Gogel & Tietz, 1972; Eriksson, 1973). The geometric basis for this cue is straightforward, however. Referring to Fig. 13, if the observer moves laterally through a distance L while fixating a point P, then for small movements the angular change of points F and N lying at distance $\pm\Delta D$ from P will be

$$\theta = L \cdot \frac{\Delta D}{D^2}.$$

If ΔD is positive for objects farther than P and negative for closer objects, then a positive angle corresponds to movement in the same direction as the head movement whereas a negative angle will correspond to angular changes opposite to the change in head position. This equation is formally identical to the equation relating binocular parallax to retinal disparity, except that in the latter case, L remains fixed at the interpupil distance. Considering this formal equivalence, it is of interest to determine whether movement is the cue extracted during self-produced parallax, or whether only positional change is noted.

If motion is the relevant cue, then the rate of angular change across the retina will be

$$\omega = \frac{d\theta}{dt} = \frac{L\,\Delta D}{D^2\,\Delta t}.$$

The motion parallax cue becomes most useful at large distances. Consider, at a distance of 10 m, the relative velocity induced in an object lying at 11 m by a head translation of 5 cm in 1 sec. The relative velocity, ω will be about 2'/sec. This rate is well below the 1–2°/sec optimal rate for stimulating bar and edge detectors in the cortex (Hubel & Wiesel, 1962; Pettigrew, Nikara, & Bishop, 1968; Jung, 1973), and also below the optimal rate of 2 to 6° for motion detection in man (Sekuler & Ganz, 1963; Richards, 1971a). Yet Graham, Baker, Hecht, and Lloyd (1948) have shown that parallax changes occurring at rates as low as .5'/sec may be detected even if the average speed of movement of the display is near 6°/sec. Detection at these low rates suggests that if the parallax cue utilizes the movement information, then it must do so by comparing relative motions of objects as they flow past one another. The cue would thus be the "shear rate" between objects in motion. If motion detectors responded optimally near 4°/sec, then the detection of shear might be optimal for objects moving near these speeds. If this motion system is assumed to have an accuracy of one part in 50 (a reasonable Weber fraction for a sensitive sensory system), then the detection of shear would approach the measured values.

When shear does not occur, the parallax cue would become ambiguous, for there are no differential velocities to signal relative motion. Other cues to depth will then prevail, or in their absence, the object may be assumed to retain its shape but rotate in an orthogonal dimension in space. Ames's trapezoid window (Ames, 1951) is an example of an illusion of the first kind, where a trapezoidal object rotating through 36° about the vertical axis may be seen to oscillate back and forth through about 150°, centering about the perpendicular to the frontal plane. The stimulus conditions providing this type of ambiguity in rotation in depth have been specified by Graham (1965), Guastella (1966), and Jansson and Börjesson (1969).

Examples of the second kind of illusion induced by ambiguous motion cues have been studied extensively by Johansson (1964, 1974) and his coworkers (Johansson & Jansson, 1968; Börjesson & v. Hofsten, 1972; Eriksson, 1973). The typical display is a two-dimensional pattern which undergoes linear distortion along the x or y axes or both. These distortions confined to the frontal plane nevertheless induce an illusion of rotation of an object in depth, in the direction predicted by assuming shape invariance. The fact that motion in the absence of shear will induce depth may be taken as support for the notion that the shear rate between two objects is the relevant cue for motion parallax.

VII. PERSPECTIVE AND GRADIENTS: CONTEXTUAL CUES

Two railroad tracks separated by a fixed distance subtend smaller and smaller angles as the tracks disappear into the horizon. Similarly, the angular size of a long corridor will shrink as it recedes away from the observer. These are examples of the linear perspective cue to distance (Fry, 1952). When combined with linear and texture gradients, these cues together provide a powerful stimulus to depth, as shown in Fig. 14.

Despite the obvious importance of perspective cues to interpreting visual space, little experimental work has been done. J. J. Gibson (1950) has contributed the most to this field through his studies of "ecological optics." This is an optics of projective geometry and perspective in which the point sources are the vanishing points of the railroad tracks and the rays are the linear perspective cues to distance. Such projections, as well as gradients of texture, carry information about the orientation, slope, and distances of objects on surfaces. The scale is set by the texture density or

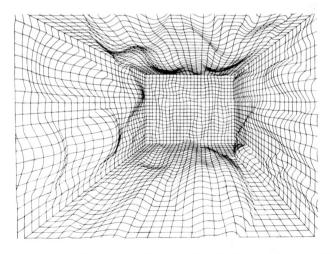

FIG. 14. Drawing of a "wire" room. This drawing depicts a wire room with fluctuation in the walls drawn to enhance the feeling of depth. [Courtesty of the Carpenter Center for the Visual Arts, Harvard University.]

the angular dimensions of the projection lines. These cues provide an important background or context for the estimation of object sizes, and remain relatively invariant under translation of the egocentric coordinate system.

Although the physiological basis for the perspective and gradient cues to visual space are little understood, they clearly represent a special static case of the dynamic flow patterns set up by the moving observer. However, the dynamic flow patterns appear to be more peripheral and more appropriate for guiding an orienting response or to defining a primary visual direction. In contrast to this more global function, the perspective cues are more local and are most important in the foveal region where objects are to be localized in three-dimensional space (Gogel, 1971, 1972). Thus, it would not be surprising to learn that the contextual cues provided by linear perspective and gradients were extracted quite separately from the dynamic flow patterns. Perhaps our understanding of the physiological basis for an ecological optics will progress more rapidly once we have understood how textures are analyzed, for certainly a texture analysis must underly the perception of texture gradients. Until then, the physiological interrelations among texture, distance, and relative retinal sizes will remain obscure.

VIII. INTERPOSITION AND SHADOW

Interposition is the cue offered when one object overlaps the other, as in Fig. 15. Because the overlapping object cuts off a view of part of the second object, the overlapping object appears nearer. Although it may not be immediately obvious, shadows and highlighting aid in the use of the interposition cue, for they help to define edges or surfaces that may be occluded (Waltz, 1972). In isolation, shading and highlights may provide

A.

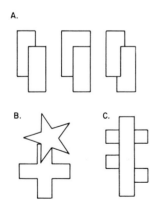

B.

C.

FIG. 15. Examples of interposition as a cue for the perception of relative distance. In part A, the first two outlines give obvious cues, whereas the third is ambiguous. In B, the star and cross intersect at junction points that have no continuous first derivatives and hence should be seen ambiguously in depth according to a modification of Helmholtz's model. The star is obviously in front of the cross, however. In C, the interposition cue may be slightly stronger when the intersected parts of the partly hidden bar may be completed by extrapolation across the occluding object. [Adapted from Ratoosh (1949) and Chapanis & McCleary (1953).]

FIG. 16. Turn this upside down and you will see the optical illusion of two craters from what really is a photograph of two cones in the desolate Ka'u Desert lava fields on Island of Hawaii. The illusion was photographed on a helicopter trip over the area. [From Wide World Photos, November, 1972.]

ambiguous information about depth, such as when the direction of the light source is misinterpreted (see Fig. 16).

One of the first attempts to define the conditions for the interposition cue was by Helmholtz (republished in 1962). A more recent formalization of Helmholtz's definition states that the sole determinant of the cue is whether the first spatial derivative of the object's contour is continuous at the points of intersection (Ratoosh, 1949). If two contours meet at a point of intersection and if both contours have continuous derivatives, then no interposition cue will be provided. However, Chapanis and Mc-Cleary (1953) have devised a number of patterns (Fig. 15) which raise difficulties for Ratoosh's simple formulation. Clearly, the interposition cue can be utilized even if the derivatives of both contours are discontinuous.

Still more recently, a simpler model has been developed at M.I.T.'s Artificial Intelligence Laboratory (Minsky & Papert, 1969). This approach attempts to identify objects in three-dimensional space by examining the nature of the intersections appearing in the scene. The attempt is to use the local properties of the intersections to constrain decisions about the global properties of the display (Guzmán, 1968). To accomplish this, the scene is first analyzed in terms of five types of vertices:

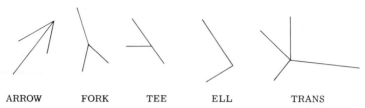

ARROW   FORK   TEE   ELL   TRANS

Each type of vertex is considered to provide some evidence about how the regions they abut may be grouped together, and then decisions are made as to whether "links" should be formed between regions. For example, the most usual physical cause of a TEE is an edge of one object that has disappeared behind an edge of another object. Hence the TEE junction should be taken as evidence against linking the regions lying on each side of the intersected line. Alternatively, the presence of a FORK, which is usually due to the intersection of three planes of one object, would be taken as evidence for linking the adjacent regions. Extensions of this scheme have been made by Winston (1970), Huffman (1970), Clowes (1971), and Waltz (1972). Quite naturally, the most informative of these studies is the most recent. Waltz's primary contribution was the discovery that objects in three-dimensional space may be identified quite accurately with only a few rules about their intersections, provided that shadow was taken into account to define the nature of an edge or junction more precisely. This reduction became possible only by an exhaustive computer search, which revealed that the possible real-life features greatly constrained the independence of the labeled junctions.

Perhaps the most striking finding of the object-recognition process devised by Waltz (1972) is the similarity between the important elements of his artificial analysis and those actually used by the visual system. The most useful junctions were found to be the ELL and the TEE, both of which are typical features detected by the hypercomplex units of Hubel and Wiesel (1965). Clearly, at this level of object identification, the localization must now be encoded simultaneously with an analysis of object properties. The problem of visual space perception has thus merged with the problem of pattern recognition.

Acknowledgments

R. Held, M. E. Jernigan, M. G. Kaye, and S. Purks all provided excellent feedback and comments on the development and exposition of the ideas presented in this chapter. Irene Bonner was most helpful in compiling the figures and manuscript in time to meet deadlines.

References

Ames, A. J. Visual perception and the rotating trapezoidal window. *Psychological Monographs*, 1951, **65**(7), 1–32.

Bárány, R. Ist die Zwerteilung der inneren Körnerschichte der anatomische Ausdruck gesonderter Repräsentation der monoculören Gesichtsfelder? *Journal fur Psychologie und Neurologie*, 1925, **31**, 289.

Barlow, H. B., Blakemore, C., & Pettigrew, J. D. The neural mechanism of binocular depth discrimination. *Journal of Physiology (London)*, 1967, **193**, 327–342.

Barlow, H. B., Hill, R. M., & Levick, W. R. Retinal ganglion cells responding selectively to direction and speed of image motion in the rabbit. *Journal of Physiology (London)*, 1964, **173**, 377–407.

Beverley, K. I. & Regan, D. Evidence for the existence of neural mechanisms selectively sensitive to direction of movement in space. *Journal of Physiology (London)*, 1973, **235**, 17–29.

Blakemore, C. Binocular depth discrimination and the nasotemporal division. *Journal of Physiology (London)*, 1969, **205**, 471–497.

Blakemore, C. The representation of three dimensional visual space in the cat's striate cortex. *Journal of Physiology (London)*, 1970, **209**, 155–178. (a)

Blakemore, C. The range and scope of binocular depth discrimination in man. *Journal of Physiology (London)*, 1970, **211**, 599–622. (b)

Blakemore, C. A new kind of stereoscopic vision. *Vision Research*, 1970, **10**, 1181–1199. (c)

Blakemore, C., & Hague, B. Evidence for disparity detecting neurons in the human visual system. *Journal of Physiology (London)*, 1972, **225**, 437–455.

Blakemore, C., & Julesz, B. Stereoscopic depth aftereffect produced without monocular cues. *Science*, 1971, **171**, 286–288.

Blank, A. A. The geometry of vision. *British Journal of Physiological Optics*, 1957, **14**, 154–169, 222–235.

Blank, A. A. Analysis of experiments in binocular space perception. *Journal of the Optical Society of America*, 1958, **48**, 911–925.

Blank, K., & Enoch, J. M. Monocular spatial distortions induced by marked accommodation. *Science*, 1973, **182**, 393–395.

Boring, E. G. *Sensation and perception in the history of experimental Psychology*. New York: Appleton, 1942.

Börjesson, E., & v. Hofsten, C. Spatial determinants of depth perception in two-dot motion patterns. *Perception & Psychophysics*, 1972, **11**, 263–268.

Bourdy, C. Directionnalité Optique des récepteurs et points correspondants. *Vision Research*, 1970, **12**, 1831–1839.

Chapanis, A., & McCleary, R. A. Interposition as a cue for the perception of relative distance. *Journal of General Psychology*, 1953, **48**, 113–132.

Charnwood, J. R. B. *Essay on binocular vision*, 6th ed. London: Hatton Press, 1951.

Cibis, P. A., & Haber, H. Anisopia and perception of visual space. *Journal of the Optical Society of America*, 1951, **41**, 676–683.

Clowes, M. B. On seeing things. *Artificial Intelligence*, 1971, **2**, 76–119.

Cowan, J. The visual field: Psychophysics and neurophysiology. Neurosciences Research Program Work Session, Dec. 9–11, 1973. (To appear in the *Neurosciences Research Program Bulletin.*)

Dichgans, J., Held, R., Young, L. R., & Brandt, T. Moving visual scenes influence the apparent direction of gravity. *Science*, 1972, **178**, 1217–1219.

Dodwell, P. C. *Visual pattern recognition*. New York: Holt, 1970.

Dodwell, P. C., & Engel, G. R. A theory of binocular fusion. *Nature*, 1963, **198**, 39–40, 73–74.

Enright, J. T. Distortions of apparent velocity: A new optical illusion. *Science*, 1970, **168**, 464–467.

Epstein, W. Modification of disparity-depth relationship as a result of conflicting cues. *American Journal of Psychology*, 1969, **81**, 189–197.

Eriksson, E. S. Distance perception and the ambiguity of visual stimulation. *Perception & Psychophysics*, 1973, **13**, 379–381.

Felton, T. B., Richards, W., & Smith, R. A. Jr. Disparity processing of spatial frequencies in man. *Journal of Physiology (London)*, 1972, **225**, 349–362.

Fender, D., & Julesz, B. Extension of Panum's fusional area in binocularly stabilized vision. *Journal of the Optical Society of America*, 1967, **57**, 819–830.

Ferris, S. H. Motion parallax and absolute distance. *Journal of Experimental Psychology*, 1972, **95**, 258–263.

Fiorentini, A., & Maffei, L. Binocular depth perception without geometrical cues. *Vision Research*, 1971, **11**, 1299–1305.

Fischer, B. Overlap in receptive field centers and representation of the visual field in the cat's optic tract. *Vision Research*, 1973, **13**, 2113–2120.

Foley, J. M. The size-distance relation and intrinsic geometry of visual space: Implications for processing. *Vision Research*, 1972, **12**, 323–332.

Foley, J., & Richards, W. Effects of voluntary eye movement and convergence on the binocular appreciation of depth. *Perception & Psychophysics*, 1972, **11**, 423–427.

Fry, G. A. The relationship between geometrical perspective and stereo cues. *American Journal of Optometry & Archives of the American Academy of Optometry*, 1952, **29**, 353–368.

Gibson, J. J. *The perception of the visual world*. Boston: Houghton Mifflin, 1950.

Gillam, B. Changes in the direction of induced aniseikonic slant as a function of distance. *Vision Research*, 1967, **7**, 777–783.

Gogel, W. C. Adjacency principle and three-dimensional visual illusions. *Psychological Monographs*, 1971, **45**, 16–32.

Gogel, W. C. Scalar perceptions with binocular cues of distance. *American Journal of Psychology*, 1972, **85**, 477–497.

Gogel, W. C., & Tietz, J. D. Absolute motion parallax and the specific distance tendency. *Perception & Psychophysics*, 1972, **13**, 284–292.

Graham, C. H. *Vision and visual perception*. New York: Wiley, 1965.

Graham, C. H., Baker, K. E., Hecht, M., & Lloyd, V. V. Factors influencing thresholds for monocular movement parallax. *Journal of Experimental Psychology*, 1948, **38**, 205–223.

Guastella, M. J. New theory on apparent movement. *Journal of the Optical Society of America*, 1966, **56**, 960–966.

Guzmán, A. Computer recognition of three-dimensional objects in a visual scene. (Tech. Report AI-TR-228) M.I.T. Artificial Intelligence Lab., 1968.

Hardy, L. H., Rand, G., Rittler, M. C., Blank, A. A., & Boeder, P. *The Geometry of Binocular Space Perception*. (Report to U.S. Office of Naval Research Project NR 143–638, Contract N6onr27119) New York: Columbia University, 1953.

Harker, G. S. The Mach–Dvorak phenomenon and binocular fusion of moving stimuli. *Vision Research*, 1973, **13**, 1041–1058.

Harris, C. S. Perceptual adaptation to inverted, reversed, and displaced vision. *Psychological Review*, 1965, **72**, 419–444.

Hay, J. C. Does head-movement feedback calibrate the perceived direction of optical motions? *Perception & Psychophysics*, 1971, **10**, 286–288.

Hein, A. & Diamond, R. M. Locomotory space as a prerequisite for acquiring visually guided reaching in kittens. *Journal of Comparative & Physiological Psychology*, 1972, **81**, 394–398.

Held, R. Plasticity in sensory-motor systems. *Scientific American*, 1965, **213(5)**, 84–94.

Held, R. Dissociation of visual functions by deprivation and rearrangement. *Psychologische Forschung*, 1968, **31**, 338–348.

Helmholtz, H. L. F. von *Treatise on physiological optics*. J. P. C. Southall (Trans.). New York: Dover, 1962.

Hering, E. *Spatial sense and movements of the eye*. A Raddle (Trans.). Baltimore: American Academy of Optometry, 1942.

Holst, E. von, & Mittelstaedt, H. Das Reafferenzprinzip. *Die Naturwissenschaften*, 1950, **37**, 464–476.

Howard, I. P. Orientation and motion in space. In E. C. Carterette & M. P. Friedman (Eds.), *Handbook of perception*, Vol. III. New York: Academic Press, 1973.

Howard, I. P. & Templeton, W. B. *Human spatial orientation*. London: Wiley, 1966.

Hubel, D., & Wiesel, T. N. Receptive fields, binocular interaction and functional architecture in the cat's visual cortex. *Journal of Physiology, London*, 1962, **160**, 106–154.

Hubel, D. H., & Wiesel, T. N. Receptive fields and functional architecture in two non-striate visual areas (18 and 19) of the cat. *Journal of Neurophysiology*, 1965, **28**, 229–289.

Hubel, D. H., & Wiesel, T. N. Stereoscopic vision in Macaque monkey. *Nature*, 1970, **225**, 41–42.

Huffman, D. A. Impossible objects as nonsense sentences. *Machine Intelligence*, 1970, **6**.

Ingle, D. Evolutionary perspectives on the function of the optic tectum. *Brain, Behavior & Evolution*, 1973, **8**, 211–237.

Jansson, G., & Borjesson, E. Perceived direction of rotary motion. *Perception & Psychophysics*, 1969, **6**, 19–26.

Johansson, G. Perception of motion and changing form. *Scandinavian Journal of Psychology*, 1964, **5**, 181–208.

Johansson, G. Visual motion perception. *Studia Psychologica*. In press, 1975.

Johansson, G., & Jansson, G. Perceived rotary motion from changes in a straight line. *Perception Psychophysics*, 1968, **4**, 165–170.

Jones, R. Psychophysical and oculomotor responses of normal and stereoanomalous observers to disparate retinal stimulation. Doctoral dissertation, Ohio State University, 1972. Dissertation Abstracts N. 72-20970.

Jones, R., & Kerr, K. E. Vergence eye movements to pairs of disparity stimuli with shape selection cues. *Vision Research*, 1972, **12**, 1425–1430.

Joshua, D. E., & Bishop, P. O. Binocular single vision and depth discrimination. *Experimental Brain Research*, 1970, **10**, 389–416.

Julesz, B. Towards the automation of binocular depth perception (AUTOMAP-1). In C. M. Popplewell (Ed.), *Proc. IFIPS Congress, Munich, 1962*. Amsterdam: North-Holland, 1963.

Julesz, B. *Foundations of cyclopean perception*. Chicago: Univ. of Chicago Press, 1971.

Jung, R. Visual perception and neurophysiology. In R. Jung (Ed.), *Handbook of sensory physiology*, Vol. III. Berlin: Springer-Verlag, 1973.

Kaufman, L. On the nature of binocular disparity. *American Journal of Psychology*, 1964, **77**, 393–402.

Kaufman, L. *Sight & mind: An introduction to visual perception*. Cambridge: Oxford Univ. Press, 1974.

Kaufman, L., & Pitblado, C. B. Further observations on the nature of effective binocular disparities. *American Journal of Psychology*, 1965, **78**, 386–389.

Kaye, M. Rivalry between two stereoscopic cues. *Journal of the Optical Society of America*, 1973, **63**, 1297A.

Kleist, K. Die einzelangigen Gesichtsfleder und ihre Vertretung in in den beiden Lagen der verdoppelten inneren Kornerschicht der Sehrinde. *Klinische Wochenschrift*, 1926, **5**, 3–9.

Kohler, I. Experiments with goggles. *Scientific American*, 1962, **206(5)**, 62–72.

Latour, P. L. Visual threshold during eye movements. *Vision Research*, 1962, **2**, 261–262.

Lazarus, M. A quantitative theory of the horopter. Unpublished doctoral dissertation, M.I.T., 1970.

Lee, D. N. Spatio-temporal integration in binocular-kinetic space perception. *Vision Research*, 1970, **10**, 65–78.

Leibovic, K. N. Balslev, E., & Mathieson, T. A. Binocular vision and pattern recognition. *Kybernetik*, 1971, **8**, 14–23.

LeVay, S., Hubel, D. H., & Wiesel, T. N. The pattern of ocular dominance columns in Macaque visual cortex revealed by a reduced silver stain. *Journal of Comparative Neurology*, 1975, **159**, 559–576.

Levick, W. R., Cleland, B. G., & Coombs, J. S. On the apparent orbit of the Pulfrich pendulum. *Vision Research*, 1972, **12**, 1381–1388.

Linksz, A. *Physiology of the Eye*, Vol. II (2nd ed.). New York: Grune & Stratton, 1952.

Lit, A. The magnitude of the Pulfrich stereophenomenon as a function of binocular-differences of intensity at various levels of illumination. *American Journal of Psychology*, 1949, **62**, 159–181.

Long, N., & Over, R. Stereoscopic depth aftereffects with random-dot patterns. *Vision Research*, 1973, **13**, 1283–1287.

Luneburg, R. K. The metric of binocular visual space. *Journal of the Optical Society of America*, 1950, **40**, 627–642.

Luria, S. M. Stereoscopic and resolution acuity with various fields of view. *Science*, 1969, **164**, 452–453.

MacKay, D. M. Towards an information-flow model of human behavior. *British Journal of Psychology*, 1956, **47**, 30–43.

MacKay, D. M. Perception and brain function. In F. O. Schmitt (Ed.), *The neurosciences: Second study program*. New York: Rockefeller Univ. Press, 1970.

Merton, P. A. Absence of conscious position sense in the human eyes. In M. B. Bender, (Ed.), *The oculomotor system*. New York: Harper and Row, 1964.

Minsky, M., & Papert, S. *Perceptrons: An introduction to computational Geometry*. Cambridge, Massachusetts: M.I.T. Press, 1969.

Mitchell, D. E. Qualitative depth localization with diplopic images of dissimilar shape. *Vision Research*, 1969, **9**, 991–993.

Mitchell, D. E. Properties of stimuli eliciting vergence eye movements and stereopsis. *Vision Research*, 1970, **10**, 145–162.

Ogle, K. N. The optical space sense. In H. Davson (Ed.), *The eye,* Vol. 4. London: Academic Press, 1962.

Ogle, K. N. *Researches in binocular vision.* New York: Hafner, 1964.

Ogle, K. N., Martens, I. G., & Dyer, J. A. *Oculomotor imbalance in binocular vision and fixation disparity.* Philadelphia: Lea & Febiger, 1967.

Pettigrew, J. D., Nikara, T., & Bishop, P. O. Responses to moving slits by single units in cat striate cortex. *Experimental Brain Research,* 1968, **6**, 373–390.

Poggio, T., & Reichardt, W. A theory of pattern induced flight orientation of the fly *Musca domestica. Kybernetik,* 1973, **12**, 185–203.

Rashbass, C., & Westheimer, G. Disjunctive eye movements. *Journal of Physiology (London),* 1961, **159**, 339–360.

Ratoosh, P. On interposition as a cue for the perception of distance. *Proceedings of the National Academy of Sciences,* 1949, **35**, 257–259.

Reichardt, W. Musterinduzierte flugorientierung. *Die Naturwissenschaften,* 1973, **60**, 122–138.

Regan, D., & Beverley, K. I. Disparity detectors in human depth perception: evidence for directional selectivity. *Science,* 1973, **181**, 877–879.

Richards, W. Saccadic Suppression. *Journal of the Optical Society of America,* 1969, **59**, 617–623.

Richards, W. Stereopsis and stereoblindness. *Experimental Brain Research,* 1970, **10**, 380–388. (a)

Richards, W. Size–distance transformations. Paper presented at the Fourth Congress of the Deutsche Gesellschaft fur Kybernetik, Berlin, April, 1970. (b) [In O.-J Grusser & R. Klinke (Eds.), *Pattern Recognition in biological and technical systems.* Berlin: Springer-Verlag, 1971.]

Richards, W. Motion detection in man and other animals. *Brain, Behavior and Evolution,* 1971, **4**, 162–181. (a)

Richards, W. Anomalous stereoscopic depth perception. *Journal of the Optical Society of America,* 1971, **61**, 410–414. (b)

Richards, W. Response functions for sine- and square-wave modulations of disparity. *Journal of the Optical Society of America,* 1972, **62**, 907–911.

Richards, W. Factors affecting depth perception. (Tech. Report, AFOSR-TR-73-0439) Arlington, Virginia: Air Force Office of Scientific Research, 1973.

Richards, W. The visual field: Psychophysics and neurophysiology. Neurosciences Research Program Work Session, Dec. 9–11, 1973. (To appear in the *Neurosciences Research Program Bulletin*).

Richards, W., & Steinbach, M. J. Impaired motion detection preceding smooth eye movements. *Vision Research,* 1972, **12**, 353–356.

Richards, W., & Regan, D. Stereo field map with implications for disparity processing. *Investigative Ophthalmology,* 1973, **12**, 904–909.

Richards, W., & Cowan, J. Size scaling by the visual system. (In preparation, 1975.)

Robinson, D. Eye movement control in primates. *Science,* 1968, **161**, 1219–1224.

Ronchi, L., & Mariani, A. On a long-term temporal aspect of stereoscopic depth sensation. *Vision Research,* 1972, **12**, 1661–1668.

Sanderson, K. J., & Sherman, S. M. Nasotemporal overlap in the visual field projected to the lateral geniculate nucleus in the cat. *Journal of Neurophysiology,* 1971, **34**, 453–466.

Schelling, H. von. Concept of distance in affine geometry and its applications in theories of vision. *Journal of the Optical Society of America,* 1956, **46**, 309–315.

Schneider, G. E. Contrasting visuomotor functions of tectum and cortex in the Golden Hamster. *Psychologische Forschung,* 1967, **31,** 52–62.

Sekuler, R. W., & Ganz, L. After effect of seen motion with a stabilized retinal image. *Science,* 1963, **139,** 419–420.

Shipley, T., & Rawlings, S. C. The nonius horopter. *Vision Research,* 1970, **10,** 1225–1299.

Skavenski, A., Haddad, G., & Steinman, R. M. The extraretinal signal for the visual perception of direction. *Perception & Psychophysics,* 1972, **11,** 287–290.

Smith, F. D., & Wientzen, R. V. Prediction of visual effects from the warpage of spectacle lenses. *American Journal of Optometry & Archives of the American Academy of Optometry,* 1973, **50,** 616–631.

Sperling, G. Binocular vision: A physical and a neural theory. *American Journal of Psychology,* 1970, **83,** 461–534.

Sperry, R. W. Neural basis of the spontaneous optokinetic response produced by inverted vision. *Journal of Comparative & Physiological Psychology,* 1950, **43,** 482–489.

Stone, J. The nasotemporal division of the cat's retina. *Journal of Comparative Neurology,* 1966, **126,** 585–599.

Sutro, L. L., & Lerman, J. B. Robot vision. (Report R-635) Cambridge, Massachusetts: Draper Laboratory, M.I.T., 1973.

Teuber, H.-L. Perception. In J. Field (Ed.), *Handbook of physiology,* Vol. III, *Neurophysiology.* Baltimore: Williams & Wilkins, 1960.

Trevarthen, C. B. Two mechanisms of vision in primates. *Psychologische Forschung,* 1968, **31,** 299–337.

Tyler, C. W. Stereoscopic depth movement: Two eyes less sensitive than one. *Science,* 1971, **174,** 958–961.

Volkman, F. C., Schick, A. M. L., & Riggs, L. A. Time course of visual inhibition during voluntary saccades. *Journal of the Optical Society of America,* 1968, **58,** 562–569.

Wallach, H., Moore, M. E., & Davidson, L. Modification of stereoscopic depth perception. *American Journal of Psychology,* 1963, **76,** 191–204.

Waltz, D. L. Generating semantic descriptions from drawings of scenes with shadows. (Tech. Report AI-TR-271) Cambridge, Massachusetts: Artificial Intelligence Laboratory, M.I.T., 1972.

Westheimer, G., & Mitchell, A. M. Eye movement responses to convergence and stimuli. *Archives of Ophthalmology, New York,* 1956, **55,** 848–856.

Westheimer, G., & Tanzman, I. J. Qualitative depth localization with diplopic images. *Journal of the Optical Society of America,* 1956, **46,** 116–117.

Wheatstone, C. Contributions to the physiology of vision. *Philosophical Transactions of the Royal Society, London,* 1838, **142,** 371–394.

Winston, P. H. Learning structural descriptions from examples. (Tech. Report MAC-TR-76) Cambridge, Massachusetts: Artificial Intelligence Laboratory, M.I.T., 1970.

Yarbus, A. L. *Eye movements and vision.* New York: Plenum, 1967.

Zuber, B. L., & Stark, L. Saccadic suppression: Elevation of visual threshold associated with saccadic eye movements. *Experimental Neurology,* 1966, **16,** 65–79.

Chapter 11

VISUAL MOTION PERCEPTION

ROBERT SEKULER

I. INTRODUCTION

During evolution, motion perception was probably shaped by selective pressures that were stronger and more direct than those shaping other aspects of vision. As you may know from your own experience, a rapid response to a moving object is often more important than the recognition of precisely *what* has moved. As a result of such selective pressures, our visual systems contain neural mechanisms specialized for the analysis of motion.

* I thank Allan Pantle for his careful reading of an early version of this chapter. My thanks also go to those people who generously allowed me to discuss their unpublished observations. Preparation of this chapter and some of the work it describes has been supported by Grants EY-00321, NB-06354 and NS-EY-10094 from the National Institutes of Health and by grants from the Research Committee of Northwestern University.

The physiology of motion perception reflects the importance of motion to the survival of individual organisms and whole species. For example, when brain injuries in human adults cause temporary loss of all visual functions, movement perception is often recovered first (Riddoch, 1917). Moreover, motion perception is also given special treatment in the physiology of the visually immature animal. In the cerebral cortex of newborn mammals, many visual functions need environmental stimulation to develop, but sensitivity to direction of visual motion is present from the outset; little priming is needed (Blakemore, 1974; Barlow & Pettigrew, 1971). In fact, the importance of visual motion has long been recognized. Centuries ago, one student of psychophysics, William Shakespeare, summed up its importance in a statement that contains more truth than many other generalizations: "Things in motion sooner catch the eye than what stirs not."

Motion perception has had a long and distinguished history of scientific study, the highlights of which have been well summarized elsewhere (Teuber, 1960; Graham, 1965). Unlike most earlier treatments of the same topic, this chapter is organized to emphasize and boost a recent change in direction that work on motion perception has taken. Thus, this chapter will ignore much of the classical work on motion as well as the arbitrary categories used to organize that work. Instead, it will concentrate on the mechanisms of human vision that are specialized for response to motion, emphasizing insights from psychophysics.

In order to gain some perspective on what follows, we should note that recent work on visual motion defies a major tradition in perception: that of Gestalt psychology. The Gestaltists doubted the value of analyzing perceptual experience into component parts. They demonstrated repeatedly that the whole of perceptual experience was more than the sum of its parts, at least its obvious parts. Despite the Gestalt demonstrations, there is a renewed effort to decompose perceptual experience into some *nonobvious* parts by considering the filter properties of various neural mechanisms (Gouras, 1973). It is assumed that once the characteristics of various feature filters are understood, most perceptual phenomena can be described by linear combinations of filter outputs. This approach has had much success in color vision; its incipient success in spatial vision augers well for success in the perception of motion (Sekuler, 1974).

This new approach to motion perception is part of a developing structuralism in the life sciences and sensory psychology:

> Both materialism and idealism take it for granted that all information gathered by our senses actually reaches our mind; materialism envisions that thanks to this information reality is mirrored in the mind, whereas idealism envisions that thanks to this information reality is constructed by

mind. Structuralism, on the other hand, has provided the insight that knowledge about the world enters the mind not as raw data but in highly abstracted form, namely as structures. In the preconscious process of converting the primary data of our experience step by step into structures, information is necessarily lost, because the creation of structures, or the recognition of patterns, is nothing else than the selective destruction of information. Thus since the mind does not gain access to the full set of data about the world, it can neither mirror nor construct reality. Instead for the mind reality is a set of structural transforms of primary data taken from the world. This transformation process is hierarchical, in that "stronger" structures are formed from "weaker" structures through selective destruction of information. Any set of primary data becomes meaningful only after a series of such operations has so transformed it that it has become congruent with a stronger structure pre-existing in the mind. Neurophysiological studies carried out in recent years on the process of visual perception in higher mammals have not only shown directly that the brain actually operates according to the tenets of a structuralism but also offers an easily understood illustration of those tenets [Stent (1972, pp. 92–93)].

The physiological state of the organism filters and distorts the response to any sensory input. Moreover, each input affects the organism's state, and thereby its response to succeeding inputs. Perceptual experience then, results from an interplay among genetics, physiology, and sensory environment. Although we know very little about the genetics of motion perception (but see Richards & Dichgans, 1974), we know quite a bit about (1) the physiology of motion perception and (2) how motion perception is altered by various sensory inputs. As the structuralist framework implies that we ought to, we shall give much attention to these classes of facts in this chapter.

II. A GENERAL ORIENTATION TO MOTION PERCEPTION

"Motion" means a directional component in either the stimulus or its percept. This directional component makes motion different from other forms of spatio-temporal modulation. The proximal stimulus for the vast majority of motion experiences is some corresponding movement of the retinal image. This correspondence has led some students of perception to "explain" motion perception in terms of various physical correlates in the stimulus (e.g., Gibson, 1966). I find this approach unsatisfactory, because it diverts attention from observations that *cannot* be reduced to some aspect of the stimulus, and such observations are crucial for understanding the mechanisms by which we come to perceive the world—its motion in particular.

To illustrate this argument, consider a few of the many observations that *cannot* be explained by the characteristics of the stimulus.

(*1*) Prolonged observation produces strong and systematic change in the apparent speed of a target which moves at a fixed rate (Gibson, 1937; Carlson, 1962; Goldstein, 1957; Beck & Stevens, 1972; Clymer, 1972).

(*2*) Many different kinds of stationary targets appear to move (Duncker, 1929; MacKay, 1961; Wertheimer, 1912; Robinson, 1972, Chap. 9).

(*3*) Successive presentation of two stimulus points, close enough in space to appear fused, gives a strong impression of motion (Biederman-Thorson, Thorson, & Lange, 1971). In addition, motion between the points sometimes seems to cover distances of more than ten times the real separation between points.

For now, these examples are enough. The point is made: We cannot reduce motion perception to obvious aspects of the stimulus. We must consider the contribution of our sensory apparatus.

Others have assumed that motion perception is built from a series of stopped frames (Dimmick & Karl, 1930; Kinchla & Allan, 1969). According to this viewpoint, motion is a kind of "inference." First the observer recognizes that on two successive inputs, the same object is seen; he then notes its changed position relative to visual field boundaries or other objects. The inference of motion comes from a comparison of seen position and remembered position. This scheme may be appropriate for extremely slow rates of motion (as the "movement" of a clock's hour hand), but it is not appropriate for most responses to moving stimuli. For example, Cynader, Berman, and Hein (1973) reared newborn kittens in stroboscopic illumination. The strobe flashes were brief enough to rule out the possibility of retinal image motion. Cynader and his colleagues found a dramatic reduction in the proportion of cortical direction-sensitive cells in their kittens. The stopped-images produced by the strobe illumination apparently do not do a good job of stimulating motion (direction) sensitive mechanisms—at least at the low flicker rates used by Cynader *et al.* Croft's (1971) comments on the difficulties of catching a beanbag under low-frequency stroboscopic illumination reinforce this point.

If motion perception is more than inference, it is also more than a response to spatio-temporal modulation. In fact, spatio-temporal modulation can sometimes be detected separately from direction of motion (Julesz & Hesse, 1970; Keesey, 1972; Richards, 1971; Van Nes, Koenderink, Nas, & Bouman, 1967; Watanabe *et al.*, 1968; Kulikowski, 1971). For example, Richards (1971) showed that a moving stimulus has several different effects on the human visual system. He measured the minimum contrast

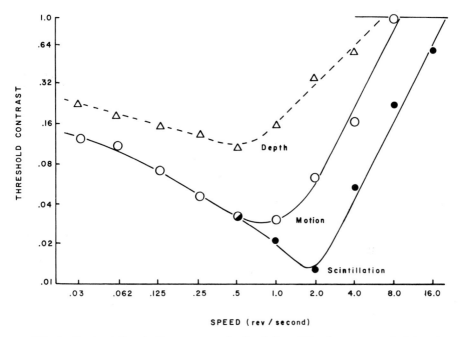

FIG. 1. Contrast threshold versus speed of rotation. Stimulus was a spiral target. Thresholds are given for three different and distinct sensory impressions: scintillation, directional movement (in the frontal plane), and movement in depth (approach or recession). [From Richards (1971).]

at which a rotating spiral just evoked various sensations of scintillation (local flicker), motion, or depth. Measurements were repeated with various speeds of spiral rotation. Several features of the data shown in Fig. 1 are noteworthy. First, at slow speed, motion is perceptible *before* scintillation. Subjects could not see scintillation without some impression of directional movement. Second, at these same low rates of rotation, when the contrast of the spiral is about twice that required for the sensation of motion, another sensation is evoked: The spiral seems to be moving in depth. Third, at higher rates of rotation, less contrast is needed to see the scintillation than to see motion. The contrast needed to see motion in depth is again highest of all. Look at the data in a slightly different way. Consider the rate of rotation at which the contrast required for any of the three sensations is at its own minimum. The minimum for depth experience is at the slowest rate of rotation, that for motion at a somewhat higher rate, and the minimum for seeing flicker or scintillation is highest. When the spiral rotates, it obviously affects several different, functionally separable stimulus-analyzing mechanisms. (In Section V, we will show that Richards's findings need slight adjustment to take certain account of spatial factors.)

In summary, this chapter will emphasize anomalous aspects of motion perception. The anomalies, like those of color vision, focus attention on the properties of the stimulus-analyzing mechanisms; they are the phenomena of motion perception that cannot be reduced to the properties of the optic array. The idiosyncrasies of visual motion force us to consider the nature of the perceptual machinery itself.

III. DIRECTION-SPECIFIC MECHANISMS

Many cells in the mammalian visual brain provide information about a target's direction of movement. These direction-selective cells discharge strongly when a properly oriented stimulus drifts in one direction through the visual field. The same cell fires less strongly, or not at all, when the same stimulus moves through the field in the opposite direction (Hubel & Wiesel, 1962; Wurtz, 1969). Similar cells, capable of responding differentially to various directions of motion, could be the basis for our own perception of moving targets.

Although we cannot be certain that our brains have exactly the same sort of direction-selective cells as the monkey brain does, there is circumstantial evidence that they do. First, some of our other visual abilities are virtually identical to those of certain monkeys, particularly the *macaque* monkeys (DeValois, Morgan, & Snodderly, 1974). So far as motion perception itself is concerned, we really know almost nothing about the perceptual experience of monkeys. In fact, all we do know is that they experience at least one aftereffect of seen motion in much the same way we do (Scott & Powell, 1963). For the time being, then, we must content ourselves with psychophysical evidence on human direction-sensitive mechanisms, leaving aside speculation on the parallels between such mechanisms and single cells in other animals.

How exactly do we make psychophysical observations that tell us something about direction-sensitive mechanisms? A basic strategy for analyzing the response of visual mechanisms is *selective adaptation*. By comparing sensitivity across some stimulus dimension before and after adaptation we can estimate the response characteristics of mechanisms sensitive to the adapting target. The assumptions and data formats of this procedure have been most fully developed by Stiles, in his studies of color-vision mechanisms (cf. Enoch, 1972).

Consider how selective adaptation has been applied to motion. Sekuler and Ganz (1963) used the technique of retinal image stabilization to lock stimuli onto one retinal area. They first presented adapting gratings of vertical bars moving either leftward or rightward through the field. Then lumi-

Fig. 2. (a–c) Percentage of direction specific threshold elevation as a function of stimulus velocity. Each panel shows data for one subject with each point the mean of 170 to 300 measurements. (d–f) Duration of motion aftereffect as a function of stimulus velocity for the same observers as in the lefthand panels. (g) Comparable data from Kinoshita did not involve points for velocities intermediate to 8°/sec and 28°/sec. [From Sekuler and Ganz (1963).]

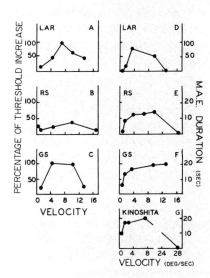

nance thresholds were measured for similar gratings. When test and adapting gratings moved in the *same* direction, thresholds were about twice as high as when they moved in the *opposite* direction. Obviously, the adapting grating had a strong direction-specific effect on the threshold.

Threshold elevations were measured with a variety of stimulus velocities—ranging from the point where motion was just perceptible to the point where the grating seemed quite blurred (from 0.17 to 15°/sec). In all cases, test and adapting speeds were equal. The amount of direction-specific threshold elevation increased with stimulus velocity, reaching a maximum in the region of 3–6°/sec, and dropping off with further increases in speed. The results are shown in panels a–c of Fig. 2.

Sekuler and Ganz (1963) tried to establish a parallel between the threshold measure, direction-specific adaptation (DSA), and the motion aftereffect (MAE)—or waterfall illusion—produced when you view a train of contours moving across the visual field. If, after a while, you look at a stationary target, the stationary target seems to be in motion in a direction opposite that which was seen originally.

Both the threshold elevation found by Sekuler and Ganz (1963) and MAE could be interpreted in terms of the poststimulation depression in the response of motion-sensitive cells like those described by Barlow and Hill (1963). So also could a related phenomenon: The apparent velocity of a steadily moving target decreases with prolonged observation (Goldstein, 1957). This decrease could manifest the development of the same adaptation that produces DSA or MAE.

To test whether they had really found a threshold correlate of motion aftereffect, Sekuler and Ganz (1963) measured the duration of MAE produced by various speeds of adapting motion.Their adapting stimulus was a stabilized retinal image; the test stimulus was not stabilized. The duration of MAE was a quadratic function of adapting speed, like the function for threshold elevation. Similar data for MAE had been reported earlier by Kinoshita (1909). These results are shown in panels d–g of Fig. 2. These similarities have been taken as evidence that DSA and MAE reflect the same physiological states. We will consider this assumption later, in Sections IV and XI. To anticipate, the parallels drawn between DSA and MAE need some adjustment. While the operations that produce the two effects are similar, the discrepancies between them reflect what may be a general difference between the neural bases of threshold and suprathreshold phenomena.

Sekuler and Wolf (unpublished) examined the time course of the *development* of direction-specific adaptation. Their experiments used gratings of low spatial frequency, .33 to .5 cycles per degree at moderate photopic levels. Subjects were exposed for 0, 5, 10, 20, 40, 80, 160, or 320 sec to an adapting pattern of horizontal bars moving either upward or downward. Thresholds were measured for test targets that moved downward. For both observers, DSA increased with exposure duration, and then reached a plateau well within the range of durations used. These results are shown in Fig. 3. A pair of line segments was fit to the data, assuming there is some duration beyond which threshold is constant.

The inflection point in these data is at about 100 sec of adaptation. Additional observations were made using extended adapting periods, 35–45 min. The resulting DSA was nearly identical to that found with only 100 sec. Moreover, recovery to control levels occurred within 45 sec or so after

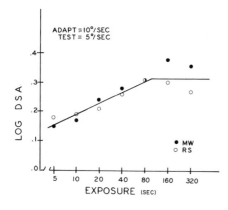

Fig. 3. Direction-specific threshold elevation as a function of exposure duration. Note that the ordinate shows logarithmic values. Data for two observers.

exposures ranging from 5 to 320 sec. There was some evidence that recovery from protracted exposures requires extra time.

Direction-sensitive mechanisms may also have a role in the detection of certain *non*moving targets (cf. Kulikowski & Tolhurst, 1973). A good example of this comes from work with counterphase gratings. In a counterphase grating, the luminance of the bars varies with time: Dark bars become bright while bright bars become dark. Neighboring bars are modulated in opposite phase. For a sinusoidal spatial grating modulated sinusoidally in time, luminance at point x and time τ is proportional to

$$1 + m(\cos \alpha x)(\cos \omega \tau),$$

where $\alpha/2\pi$ is the spatial frequency in cycles per degree of visual angle, $\omega/2\pi$ is the temporal frequency in hertz, and m is the depth of modulation.

This sort of grating can be produced in various ways; one is to combine two gratings of the same spatial frequency which drift at the same rate but in opposite directions. The combination is a counterphase grating; it may not seem to drift systematically in any direction—provided good fixation is maintained (Kulikowski, 1971).

Levinson and Sekuler (1973) report several observations supporting the idea that the counterphase gratings are detected by direction-sensitive mechanisms. We will consider only one of their observations here. Subjects viewed a normal sinusoidal grating that moved *rightward*. After adaptation to this grating, a subsequently seen counterphase grating appeared as a single sinusoidal grating drifting *leftward*. The rightward component of the counterphase grating was not visible because channels sensitive to rightward motion had been adapted. As adaptation dissipated, the counterphase test grating ceased its leftward drift and resumed its normal, stationary, pulsating appearance. Other, quantitative observations more strongly support the idea that counterphase gratings are detected by independent direction-specific channels.

These psychophysical observations are complemented nicely by preliminary electrophysiological evidence for direction selectivity in human vision. Clarke (1974) measured the averaged scalp potential evoked by a pattern which moved first in one direction then in the opposite. Adaptation produced a change in the brain's response to motion in the same direction as the adapting motion; the response to motion in the opposite direction was unaffected.

IV. A CODE FOR PERCEIVED MOTION

Although psychophysical results tell us that we have direction-sensitive mechanisms in our visual systems, we are not certain how the information such mechanisms produce is handled subsequently. Various ideas have been proposed, but arguments about a code for perceived motion boil down to this: Does the visual system combine at all the information it receives from mechanisms tuned to different directions of motion?

Sutherland (1961) suggested that we see something moving down because of an imbalance in the *ratio* of activities in two sets of direction-specific mechanisms: one set sensitive to downward motion, the other to upward motion. The MAE, according to this hypothesis, results from post-stimulatory imbalance (see also Cornsweet, 1970). Sutherland's ratio hypothesis was consistent with the early observation by Wohlgemuth (1911) that repeated alternation between inspection targets moving up ward and downward gives zero net MAE. Sutherland's ratio hypothesis is important because it is one of the few detailed psychophysical linking hypotheses in perception (cf. Brindley, 1970). It postulates a specific sensory code for perceived motion.

To test various ideas about how information from direction analyzers might be combined, we can use a procedure called *subthreshold summation* (cf. Kulikowski & King-Smith, 1973). Like selective adaptation, subthreshold summation can be used to study not only motion perception, but other sensory responses as well. Imagine that we have measured the threshold for some stimulus—say, how much contrast is needed to make a certain stimulus just detectable. By definition, that amount of contrast is one threshold unit. Now we can present that same stimulus but at a reduced, subthreshold contrast and determine how much contrast must be added to that subthreshold amount to restore the stimulus to threshold. If our original threshold contrast is one threshold unit and we reduce its contrast by half, we will obviously need another half-threshold unit to get back up to threshold. If we reduced the threshold stimulus by a factor of 4, we would require an additional .75 threshold units of contrast to restore the stimulus to threshold; and so on. Call the subthreshold stimulus the background, and the amount we add to it the test stimulus. At each of several different subthreshold background contrasts we can measure how much more contrast must be supplied, in the form of the test target, in order for the observer to see something. We can make this manipulation more than an exercise in arithmetic by using test and background targets that differ in some way—spatial frequency, direction, etc. Essentially, subthreshold summation allows us to measure the interaction, if any, between mechanisms that detect the test target and mechanisms that detect the background.

If there is zero background contrast, then, logically, the background can neither help nor hinder the detection of the test; so we would have to present the test target at a contrast equal to its own threshold. If the background is presented with high enough contrast so that, by itself, it is at threshold, no additional contrast has to be added in the form of a test

FIG. 4. Logic of subthreshold summation experiments. Test target intensity needed for detection when presented against backgrounds of increasing, but subthreshold intensity. Both test and background intensities are scaled relative to their own threshold intensities when each is presented alone. Path of data points for complete summation between background and test targets is shown by oblique line, test intensity = background intensity; path of points for independence between background and test targets is shown by horizontal line, test intensity = constant = 1.0 threshold unit. Three other regions indicate possible data paths for facilitation (bottom), partial summation (middle) and inhibition (top) between test and background targets.

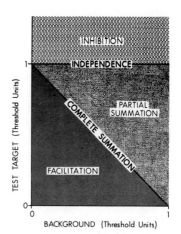

target. Figure 4 shows the possible outcomes of subthreshold summation experiments. If things work as simple arithmetic implies, the data should fall on the line marked "complete summation" in Fig. 4. Along that line the amount of background *plus* the amount of test stimulus sum to unity.

But there are other interesting ways that the data could come out. Again, take the original threshold stimulus, reduce it by a factor of two and present it to one eye. Now present a test stimulus to another eye and find out how much contrast must be added to the second eye to restore the combination of test plus background to visibility. To make things really interesting, let us use one eye in one head and the other eye in another head—and both heads on different bodies. Now we are not surprised that having the half-threshold amount present in the first eye does not help us see the added test stimulus in the other eye. In fact, we need a full threshold amount of contrast in the second eye before the stimulus is seen. This means that there is no summation between the background and the test. When the subthreshold background present neither helps nor hurts the ability to detect a test target, we say there is independence of detection of the two stimuli. Data points that correspond to this case fall along the horizontal line marked independence. As we shall see, background and test do not have to be put in different eyes to be detected independently of one another.

Take another possibility, one implied by Sutherland's (1961) ratio hypothesis discussed earlier. Suppose the background and test stimuli are targets which move in opposite directions. Suppose, in addition, that the visual system takes a *ratio* between the responses produced by (*1*) targets that move in one direction and (*2*) targets that move in the opposite direction. Assume further that this ratio determines the perception. On these assumptions, it should be easier to detect the test target when no background is present than when a background is present. Data should fall along a line that decreases in height as the amount of background increases. There are many such lines possible; which one the data obeys depends upon how much weight the system gives to the denominator in the ratio. But each of these lines corresponds to what is termed *inhibition*. Finally, there is the possibility of facilitation: Having some background present does more good toward helping detection of the test target than having an equivalent amount of test target present would have.

Levinson and Sekuler (1973) used subthreshold summation to see whether oppositely moving contours were detected by independent mechanisms. They measured the contrast threshold for a grating drifting rightward. The test grating was superimposed on a subthreshold background grating, which drifted leftward. Test and background gratings had the same spatial frequency and drift rate. By repeating these measurements at different background contrasts the sensitivity of a motion analyzer to the direction of movement *opposite* that which it prefers could be estimated. No summation was found between background and test gratings—even with background contrasts as high as .85 of threshold contrast. Lack of interaction between oppositely moving gratings—at threshold—shows the independence of detectors for the two directions of motion. This result is quite different from what would be expected if detection were based on a ratio of responses in mechanisms tuned to opposite directions of motion. Another test of Sutherland's (1961) ratio theory of motion detection was made by Sekuler *et al.* (1971). Using a selective adaptation procedure with compound adapting stimuli, they too rejected the idea that detection of motion depended upon a ratio of activity.

Although the MAE seems to be a function of the relative or pooled response of visual mechanisms sensitive to opposite directions of motion, the detection threshold for motion in a particular direction depends only upon the sensitivity of one mechanism "tuned" to that direction. The parallels to color vision and other sensory domains are obvious. Sensitivity, as a general rule, is determined at threshold by whichever single channel is most responsive to the particular test target employed. Suprathreshold appearance is not controlled by a single channel, but is the product of the pooled response of several channels, all responding in different degrees to the test target (cf. Tolhurst, Sharpe, & Hart, 1973).

V. VELOCITY AND SPATIO-TEMPORAL MODULATION

Mechanisms for motion are sensitive not only to direction of motion but also to its speed. Our ability to perceive moving stimuli over a wide range of speeds could be explained by either of two models.

(*1*) All mechanisms sensitive to one direction respond over the entire speed range and all have essentially the same monotonic function relating response rate to velocity.

(*2*) Mechanisms sensitive to one direction differ in their responses to velocity, with subsets differentially tuned to stimulus speed.

On the first hypothesis, speed is coded by the integrated response within one direction analyzer; on the second hypothesis, speed is coded by *which* of several, differentially tuned speed subsets is maximally responsive. The following experiment permits a clear choice between these two hypotheses.

Pantle and Sekuler (1968b) adapted subjects to gratings moving at various velocities from .5°/sec to 45°/sec. Thresholds were measured for targets which moved at 2, 5, or 9°/sec. For each combination of test and adapting speed, Pantle and Sekuler measured the difference between threshold for targets that moved in the same direction as the adapting grating and test targets that moved in the opposite direction. This measure, it will be remembered, defines direction-specific adaptation (DSA). There was a clear separation of three velocity–response profiles, with one distributed about each test speed.

This outcome suggests that there are several channels responsive to somewhat different (but overlapping) ranges of velocity (Hypothesis 2). Consider the following arguments: Assume that a motion mechanism is desensitized in proportion to that mechanism's response to an adapting stimulus. If there were just one general mechanism for motion detection (Hypothesis 1), the adaptation functions measured with any *test* velocity would, of course, be dependent upon the sensitivity of the same, single detector. The functions would each have the same shape and maximum point on the *x* axis. This was clearly not the outcome. These observations have been replicated and extended by Tolhurst *et al.* (1973).

Pantle and Sekuler (1968b) found most DSA when the adapting velocity was slightly greater than the test velocity. This peak shift can be explained as follows: If we change velocity but hold spatial frequency constant, as Pantle and Sekuler did, the rate of temporal stimulation varies along with velocity. Temporal rate (in hertz) can be thought of as the number of contours that pass a given retinal point per unit time. If temporal rate of stimulation were an important factor, DSA ought to vary with spatial frequency. Pantle and Sekuler (Sekuler, 1967), examined this possibility. The test target was a grating of low spatial frequency (.3 cycles/degree), which always moved at 5°/sec. For each adapting stimulus, threshold was measured with (*1*) the test moving in the same direction as the adaptation stimulus and (*2*) the test moving in the opposite direction. One set of conditions measured the effect of temporal rate, independent of adaptation

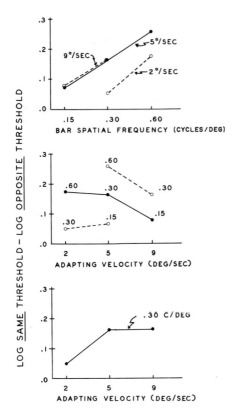

Fig. 5. Top panel. Log threshold elevation as a function of inspection pattern spatial frequency. The parameter is the speed of inspection motion. Central panel. Log threshold elevation as a function of inspection stimulus velocity. Above each data point is shown the spatial frequency of the inspection pattern in cycles per degree. Each curve represents the path of data points generated with constant product of spatial frequency and velocity. This constant product means that a constant number of contours per degrees per second pass a given retinal point, making for a constant temporal rate of stimulation. Lowest panel. Log threshold elevation as a function of inspection velocity. Spatial frequency of the inspection target was .3 cycles/degree. In all panels the test velocity was 5°/sec and test pattern spatial frequency was .3 cycles per degree. All data shown are for one observer. [From Sekuler (1967).]

speed. Adaptation was produced by gratings of various spatial frequencies all moving at 5°/sec. The results are shown with the curve labeled 5°/sec in the top panel of Fig. 5. The horizontal axis is the spatial frequency of the adaptation stimulus; the vertical axis is the amount of DSA. With constant adaptation *velocity,* DSA increases as adaptation spatial frequency increases. Note that in these conditions, temporal frequency of the adaptation stimulus covaries with its spatial frequency.

Other conditions show the effect of adaptation velocity without complicating variation in temporal frequency. In these conditions adaptation velocity was 2°20′, 4°40′, or 9°20′/sec. As speed increased, the spatial frequency of the adapting target was reduced, keeping temporal rate of stimulation constant. Data from these conditions are shown in the middle panel of Fig. 5. The data indicate that stimulus velocity itself has some control over DSA. Vertical differences among points plotted against any single velocity value reflect the effects of temporal frequency.

In a final set of conditions, adaptation velocity was varied over the same range as before, but with spatial frequency held constant. This confounded velocity and temporal frequency. The DSA produced under these conditions is shown in the lowest panel of Fig. 5. The function is approximately what one obtains if one adds the appropriate functions from each of the upper panels. In other words, the combined effect of velocity and temporal frequency approximates the sum of the independent effects of both variables. It seems that the adapting effects of a moving grating may be decomposed into an effect due to its velocity and an effect due to its temporal frequency.

The motion aftereffect also shows reciprocity between velocity and spatial frequency. Pantle (1974) measured the duration and initial apparent velocity of MAE with sinusoidal gratings of 3 and 6 cycles/degree. The same grating served as both adapting and test target. Pantle varied the drift rate of each grating over several decades. As Fig. 6 shows, MAE velocity with both gratings was a quadratic function of drift rate, peaking at 5 Hz. The MAE was reduced at higher or lower drift rates. Note that if the x axis in Fig. 6 were scaled for velocity rather than drift rate, the two curves would not have the same mean value. The same sort of result occurred with the MAE duration as dependent variable.

Crook (1937) measured the luminance threshold for seeing the direction of movement of a square wave grating. With various grating spatial frequencies and velocities, his results show best sensitivity for stimuli in which the product of grating spatial frequency and velocity is approximately constant, 2–4 Hz. This constant is the number of contours per second that stimulate a given retinal point.

The reciprocity between the spatial frequency of a grating (cycles per

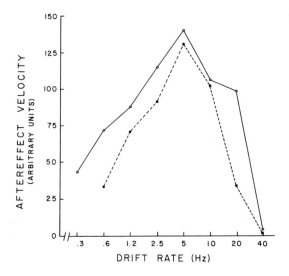

Fig. 6. Initial apparent velocity of motion aftereffect as a function of temporal drift rate of adaptation gratings. Solid curve: 3 cycle/degree grating; dashed curve: 6 cycle/degree grating. Data are from 8 observers. [From Pantle (1974).]

degree) and its rate of translation (degrees per second) is consistent with a relationship noted by Enroth-Cugell and Robson (1966) in their study of cat retinal ganglion cells. For any cell, the most effective stimulus was defined by a constant product of grating spatial frequency and rate of translation. Ganz and Lange (1973) reported a similar result.

Reciprocity between spatial frequency and velocity implies a relationship between (1) the velocity to which a mechanism is most responsive and (2) its preferred spatial frequency. Mechanisms that are maximally sensitive to slowly moving targets should respond preferentially to stimuli of high spatial frequency; mechanisms sensitive to fast rates of movement should respond preferentially to stimuli of low spatial frequency. This idea was tested in selective adaptation experiments by Pantle (1970) and by Breitmeyer (1973). Pantle measured detection thresholds for square-wave gratings that moved across the visual field at various speeds—0 to 22°/sec. The spatial frequency of the moving gratings was kept at .38 cycles/degree. Adaptation targets were stationary square-wave gratings of varying spatial frequency—from 0 cycles/degree (a uniform field) to 23 cycles/degree.

The outcome was clear. The visibility of high-velocity test targets was most degraded by adaptation to stationary gratings of low spatial frequency; visibility of slowly moving test gratings was maximally degraded by adaptation to a stationary grating of high spatial frequency. Mechanisms that detect rapidly moving targets are most sensitive to low spatial frequencies; mechanisms that detect slowly moving targets are most sensitive to higher spatial frequencies.

Breitmeyer (1973) did the converse of Pantle's experiment: Adaptation to high-velocity targets most raised the threshold for low spatial frequency stationary test gratings; adaptation to low-velocity targets most raised the threshold for high spatial frequency stationary test gratings. Moreover, adaptation to a 4 cycle/degree grating maximally raised the threshold for a grating moving at about 2.5°/sec; adaptation to a grating of 1.5 cycles/degree yielded peak threshold elevations at a velocity of 7°/cycle. There is an approximate reciprocity in these data between adapting spatial frequency and the test velocity that it affects most strongly. Obviously, additional observations are required to establish this reciprocity more securely.

VI. MOTION VARIES WITH RETINAL LOCATION

Is the periphery of the visual field specialized for response to motion? As with many important questions about perimetry, this one is hard to answer. We already know that different parts of the human retina vary in their response to temporal or spatial stimulation. As we shall see later in this section, perimetric results parallel anatomical and physiological variation in related species. But first let us consider how motion responses do vary with retinal region.

Using a technique introduced by Westheimer (1967), Richards (1971) tried to estimate the size of motion analyzers in various retinal regions. With a small stationary test target and adaptation targets of various diameters, Richards determined the minimum adapting contrast for which a motion aftereffect (MAE) could be seen. In general, adapting targets of about 3–4° diameter required less contrast to produce MAE than other size target. Richards inferred that motion detectors in the center of vision subtend about 3.5°. This value rises rapidly as measurements are extended to the periphery, being nearly a logarithmic function of eccentricity over the range 0° (fovea) to 16°. Before generalizing from Richards's data we should wait for comparable estimates at other adaptation levels and target spatial frequencies (cf. McColgin, 1960). In addition, work by Leibowitz and his colleagues (to be discussed later in this section) shows that we must exercise caution in adopting Richards's estimates of peripheral receptive field size. Those estimates may very well need correction for substantial refractive errors.

A paper by Brown (1972) substantiates the idea that the peripheral retina is specialized for motion perception. Foveal acuity for a moving target declined linearly with angular velocity; parafoveal acuity showed a more interesting relationship to angular velocity. Parafoveal acuity for a slowly moving target was, in fact, somewhat better than for a stationary target. As velocity increased further, acuity was degraded. The independence of visual resolution measured by dynamic and static tests in normal subjects of varying ages should be noted in this context (Reading, 1972).

Tyler and Torres (1972), too, showed that retinal regions differ in their response to motion. Their subjects saw a bright vertical line oscillating back and forth sinusoidally. At each of several frequencies of oscillation they found the smallest lateral excursion (depth of modulation) for which movement could still be seen. The frequency-response of the detector can be determined by plotting threshold modulation against temporal frequency. Similar curves for spatially uniform, flickering fields are standard in the analysis of the temporal response characteristics of the visual system.

Tyler and Torres repeated their observations at four retinal positions: foveal, 5, 10, and 20° peripheral. Although peak sensitivity was somewhat greater in the fovea, the envelope of sensitivity was more narrowly tuned in the periphery than in the fovea. There is one trouble with Tyler and Torre's technique: It probably does not really reflect the response of *motion* detectors. Their procedure favors the response of mechanisms capable of mediating very fine spatial discriminations; Kulikowski and Tolhurst (1973) have shown that motion detectors are not likely to be in this population (see p. 405).

We should examine some data that do not support peripheral specialization for response to motion. Lichtenstein (1963) used a stimulus that falls midway between real and apparent motion. When the frequency of a square wave imposed on the y axis of an oscilloscope is slightly less than a whole multiple of the sawtooth sweep frequency, a train of square waves is seen drifting left to right across the face of the oscilloscope. By manipulating sweep speed and the relationship between sweep frequency and the external square-wave superimposed on that sweep, Lichtenstein produced various stimulus velocities. He measured how much the subject had to avert his gaze from the display in order for the appearance of movement to disappear. As eccentricity of viewing increased, stimulus velocity seemed to drop; finally, the apparent drift stopped. As stimulus velocity increased from .08 to 1.25°/sec the disappearance of apparent motion required increasingly greater eccentricity of viewing. Although the data are quite scattered, the effect does seem real.

A straightforward interpretation of Lichtenstein's finding is that the fovea is more sensitive to very slow motion than is the periphery. Averting the gaze shifts the target more peripherally, toward an area of reduced motion sensitivity. We should be careful in extrapolating from Lichtenstein's data to other, higher velocities. In fact, it may be the case that with *higher* velocities the relationship between foveal and peripheral motion sensitivity is reversed (see Bhatia, 1975). R. Armstrong (personal communication) tested this idea with an oscilloscope display similar to Lichtenstein's but with target velocity raised to 50°/sec. When the display was viewed directly (foveally), no motion was seen. However, when the observers shifted their gaze to a point some 10° above the display, motion became visible again. A similar difference between retinal regions could be demonstrated with real, continuous motion as well. By feeding the same frequency sinusoid into both x- and y-inputs of an oscilloscope and adjusting the phase, Armstrong produced a spot that moved rapidly along a circular path on the CRT face. The path radius was adjusted to 3° visual angle and the spot velocity raised to 100°/sec. When they fixated the center of the circular path, subjects could not perceive the direction of the dot's motion; when they fixated a point 10° eccentric, the direction was easily discerned. Moreover, apparent speed of the moving dot dropped very noticeably as eccentricity increased (cf. Teuber, 1960, p. 1644; Sharpe, 1974).

Having established the differences between peripheral and foveal responses to motion we can consider possible physiological bases for these differences. The X and Y channels of both retinogeniculate and geniculostriate pathways (Enroth-Cugell & Robson, 1966; Hoffman, 1973) differ in their receptive field size, linearity, and conduction velocity. Also, the neurons of the two channels respond best over very different stimulus speed ranges (Hoffman, 1973). The Y cells are faster conducting and have a more pronounced transient response to spatio-temporal modulation.

There is another difference between the channels that we should consider: The X channel carries information primarily from the center of vision, whereas the Y channel is responsible for much of the analysis of peripheral stimulation. This proposal is based, first, on the *relative* distribution of X- and Y-type retinal ganglion cells across the retina and, second, on the segregation of the two channels, which is maintained from retina to visual cortex (Stone, 1972; Stone & Dreher, 1973). Since Y cells predominate in the periphery of the cat retina we wonder whether the specialization of the human periphery for motion results from similar Y-cell concentration. (cf. Day, 1973).

An important characteristic of Y cells (transient type) is that compared to X cells (sustained type) they are more sensitive to stimuli of low spatial frequency. In addition, Y cells are relatively *less* sensitive to stimuli of high spatial frequency. Tolhurst (1973) provided convincing data that motion-sensitive mechanisms in humans, like Y cells, give a far greater response to stimuli of *low* spatial frequency than do mechanisms sensitive to stationary stimuli. In fact, it is likely that a briefly presented stationary stimulus of low spatial frequency is detected, under some conditions, by mechanisms that ordinarily respond to moving targets. Breitmeyer, Love, and Wepman (1974) explored some of the interesting perceptual consequences of this possibility.

Although the existing psychophysical data are persuasive, it may turn out that the simple dichotomy between transient and sustained mechanisms is too gross. For example, might there not be separate mechanisms for detecting the temporal modulation of the entire field and for detecting local flicker (cf. Foster, 1971; Schouten, 1967)?

Before we can compare motion responses at various retinal locations we must take account of possible variation in dioptric factors (Leibowitz, Johnson, & Isabelle, 1972). Leibowitz and his colleagues determined the spherical and stigmatic refractive errors for each subject. *Peripheral* refractive errors, in particular, were substantial. When motion thresholds were measured with the appropriate optical correction, individual differences virtually disappeared. Refractive correction also reduced—but did not eliminate—the difference between peripheral and foveal thresholds for motion.

Leibowitz *et al.* noted that the "relative degradation with off-axis viewing is less for motion than for resolution. In the periphery, all visual functions are degraded, but motion suffers the least [p. 1208]." The lesson is that psychophysical estimates of receptive field size in various retinal locations may need to be adjusted for optical factors (cf. Hilz & Cavonius, 1974; Richards, 1971).

The preceding discussion can be summarized easily. Foveal and peripheral motion responses differ in the spatial and temporal properties of those moving targets to which they respond best. The periphery shows a distinct preference for targets of low spatial frequency and high rates of temporal modulation or velocity. A complication in this picture is the fact that any single retinal region contains several relatively independent sets of motion detectors, tuned to different spatio-temporal ranges. A complete parametric elaboration of these basic facts would be a monumental and difficult undertaking.

VI. MOVEMENT, ORIENTATION, AND SPATIAL FREQUENCY

Moving stimuli have properties not directly connected with their movement. For example, moving gratings have a characteristic orientation or spatial frequency. The preceding section suggested a connection between the spatial and temporal selectivities of motion analyzers; this section examines their orientation and other configural properties. To anticipate somewhat, there is considerable agreement that the visual system separates information about the motion of a stimulus from information about its pattern properties. There is no consensus, however, on the details of that separation.

Graham and Hunter (1931) were among the first to compare sensitivity to direction of motion and to orientation. Their study lacks some of the technical and methodological sophistication that one would insist upon in a contemporary paper, but it contains enough important information to make discussion of it worthwhile. Graham and Hunter measured the luminance thresholds for two kinds of discriminations with varying spatial frequency. A vertically oriented square-wave grating could move either left or right. The subject had to identify the *direction* in which it moved. The same grating could be presented vertically or horizontally without movement. The subject had to identify the *orientation*. Testing was done at photopic levels. Unfortunately, gratings were moved manually by the experimenters ("sharply, but not rapidly"), making it difficult to know the actual velocity. Fortunately, for the sake of comparison between the two conditions, stimulus exposures though unspecified, are said to be equal. Figure 7 shows the mean results from five observers.

The upper curve shows the relationship between spatial frequency and

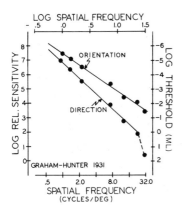

FIG. 7. Log relative sensitivity to the orientation (top curve) and direction of motion (bottom curve) of a grating as a function of its spatial frequency. Data are replotted from Graham and Hunter (1931). Computations from their published tables of data indicated that Graham and Hunter had misplotted one of their data points. Their error has been rectified in this figure.

sensitivity to orientation. Sensitivity is the reciprocal of threshold luminance for discrimination of orientation. On log–log coordinates the data are approximately linear. The lower set of data are for discrimination of direction. Again, for all the spatial frequencies used except the highest, the data are linear on the axes shown. The major findings of Graham and Hunter, then, are as follows:

(1) At low spatial frequencies, sensitivity for orientation and direction is nearly the same.

(2) Increasing test target spatial frequency differentially affects the two kinds of discriminations.

This second finding provides a good way to separate the response to the orientation of a grating from the response to its direction of motion.

It has been proposed that orientation-sensitive mechanisms provide a major input to mechanisms that analyze directional information (Hubel & Wiesel, 1962). Although this idea, derived from studies of single cells in cat visual cortex, has needed revision, we might consider the relevant psychophysical data. Many different tasks concerned with the perception of orientation show strong meridional anisotropies (Taylor, 1963; Appelle, 1972). For example, detection of a grating is best when it is vertical or horizontal and poorest at orientations between. Similar anisotropies may exist in motion perception. Richards (1971) compared sensitivity to motion along various meridians: Sensitivity was highest along or near the horizontal meridian with nearly equal sensitivity along with vertical meridian. Other meridians show reduced sensitivity. Although far from conclusive, this similarity is consistent with the idea that orientation analyzers provide major inputs to the motion-analyzing system.

Frisby's (1972b) work on apparent movement sheds more light on the relationship between orientation and direction analysis. Although his data are noisy, there are clear effects of orientation. Apparent motion is most easily seen when the two alternating targets have the same orientation. Apparent movement deteriorates with differing orientations. Note that Frisby's experiments cannot define the *order* in which orientation and directional information are extracted from the stimulus; they merely suggest a relationship between the two dimensions. More recently, Frisby and Clatworthy (1974) have argued that information about direction of movement is extracted in parallel with information about stimulus orientation.

Related observations on orientation and the MAE have been reported by Over, Broerse, Crassini, and Lovegrove (1973). With a stationary vertical test grating, MAE strength decreased as the orientation of the inspection grating departed from the vertical. Over *et al.* note the similarity of their results to those reported for DSA (Sekuler, Rubin, & Cushman, 1968). Unfortunately in both studies, orientation and direction of motion covaried, making clear interpretations difficult.

Stimulus-analyzing mechanisms for orientation and direction have been separated in other ways. Pantle and Sekuler (1969) measured thresholds for five different kinds of test targets following exposure to an adaptation grating which moved continuously downward through the field. The mean luminance of the adaptation grating was held constant while its contrast was varied from 0 to .83. The test targets were: (*1*) a homogeneous field; (*2*) a stationary grating of vertical bars; (*3*) a stationary grating of horizontal bars; (*4*) a grating of horizontal bars moving in the *same* direction as the adapting grating; and (*5*) a grating of horizontal bars moving in the direction *opposite* to that of the adaptation grating. As the contrast of the adaptation grating increased, differential effects on the threshold for the two stationary gratings would reflect the contrast response of visual mechanisms sensitive to contour orientation. As the contrast of the adaptation grating varied, differences between the thresholds for the two moving gratings would reflect the direction-specific effect of the adaptation grating. This difference reflects the contrast response of directionally sensitive mechanisms.

The orientation component of the visual response increased throughout the range of contrast studied, whereas the directional component increased only over the very low portion of the contrast range (up to about .16). The data are shown in Fig. 8. The different contrast responses of orientation- and direction-sensitive elements suggests their functional separation.

Keck, Palella, and Pantle (in press) argued that the response of direction-sensitive elements saturates at a very low contrast level. Measurements of MAE duration and velocity were made with a variety of combinations of inspection and test target contrasts (all targets were sinusoidal gratings). For a constant level of test contrast, MAE increased as inspection target contrast increased over the range from threshold to .03; it was nearly con-

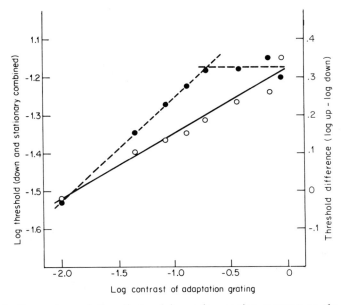

FIG. 8. Comparison of the effects of inspection grating contrast on the response of orientation sensitive (open circles) and direction-sensitive (filled circles) elements. See text for explanation. [From Pantle and Sekuler (1969).]

stant thereafter. Whereas the saturation level is slightly lower than that estimated by Pantle and Sekuler (1969), the basic point is sustained: Direction-sensitive mechanisms have an extremely restricted contrast response range, saturating at contrast levels perhaps no more than 4–5 times threshold.

How do these data relate to the known properties of motion sensitive neurons? Maffei and Fiorentini (1973) measured the contrast response of simple and complex neurons in the cat's visual cortex. The simple cells may be the targets of the sustained mechanisms of lower visual centers (the X channel described in Section VI); the complex cells may be targets of transient mechanisms of lower centers (the Y channel). The response of simple cells increased linearly with log input contrast and did so over a very large range of contrast. The response of many (but not all) complex cells saturated at contrast levels not far above their own contrast thresholds. These two facts resemble the psychophysical data just described: The contrast response of human direction-sensitive elements is restricted and saturates at low levels; the response of human orientation-sensitive elements spans a much wider range of contrasts.

Though there may be striking parallels between simple and complex cells, on one hand, and psychophysically defined orientation and motion mechanisms, on the other, we must be careful not to put too much theoretical burden on these parallels. For one thing, it is not at all clear that the properties of complex cells are completely determined by the Y channel, nor that the properties of simple cells are completely determined by the X channel. It may well be that the two channels each dominate one particular cell type, but the details of velocity tuning in simple and complex cells of the cat's visual cortex, make it unlikely that either cell type is the exclusive product of either X or Y channel (Movshon, personal communication). In addition, any psychophysical response we observe is probably not the result of activity in either simple or complex cells alone; it is probably the product of rather complicated interactions among and between cell types (cf. Singer & Bedworth, 1973; Breitmeyer, Love & Wepman, 1974).

Returning to psychophysics, direction-sensitive elements differ in the spatial properties of the stimuli to which they respond best. Sekuler and Armstrong (1971) measured thresholds for moving vertical bars displayed on a computer controlled CRT. Exposure to a moving, spatially random field of small bright points produced no direction-specific adaptation. When the computer rearranged the components of the random field into vertical lines, considerable DSA resulted. Moreover, a moving random adapting field produced DSA when the test target was a similar random field but not when the test field was a pattern of vertical bars.

Pantle (1973) extended these preliminary observations, showing that DSA depends specifically on the spatial frequency content of adapting and test patterns. After adaptation to a moving sinusoidal grating, Pantle found direction-specific losses of sensitivity with a test grating of the same spatial frequency, but not with a grating whose spatial frequency was an octave away. The directional effect is evidence that, as with nonmoving targets, there are spatial frequency channels each tuned to a somewhat different region of the spatial frequency spectrum (Pantle & Sekuler, 1968a). As a result of these observations we may assume that human movement-perception is not dependent upon one general speed-sensitive mechanism but, rather, is built upon mechanisms segregated by (1) the directionality of their response, (2) their velocity response, and (3) the configural properties of their optimal stimuli.

Other, nonthreshold phenomena show that direction-selective mechanisms vary in their preferred configurations. One such phenomenon is a texture-contingent MAE (Walker, 1972; Mayhew, 1973). Walker used two disks of quite different textures as inspection and test targets. One disk of a fine texture had very many randomly placed small dots scattered over its surface. The other disk was a coarsely textured photographic enlargement of the fine disk. When both disks were of the same diameter, the dots in the coarse disk were fewer in number (i.e., number of dots per unit area) and were larger than those in the fine disk. The subject alternately viewed the coarse disk rotating counterclockwise and the fine disk rotating clockwise. After many cycles of alternation a stationary *coarse* disk seemed to move clockwise; a stationary *fine* disk seemed to move counterclockwise. In a related study Bonnet and Pouthaus (1972) found that when inspection and test fields have similar patterns, the MAE lasts longer. We have to separate the effects of (*1*) adaptation field pattern, (*2*) test field pattern, and (*3*) the similarity of these two patterns. Each component could independently influence MAE.

A final point on this matter. For the sake of methodological clarity it would be useful in future studies of motion phenomena to define the stimulus dimensions in a more theoretically useful fashion. For example, if a field with random texture is used, it would be useful to know its spatial frequency characteristics. Surely, if the response to a moving target is partly determined by the product of its velocity and spatial frequency, it would be easier to compare one study with another if a full description of the stimuli is given. That description should include the spatial frequency spectrum of the pattern.

VIII. OCULOMOTOR INFLUENCES ON MOTION PERCEPTION

Motion of the retinal image can come from various sources: movement of the distal stimulus object, movement of the eyes, or combinations of the two. Usually, we can discriminate retinal image motion caused by *eye* movements from that which is caused by *target* motion. This means our visual system receives information about oculomotor activity. The information could arise either from feedback from extraocular muscles (Skavenski, 1972) or from the corollary discharge of centers that control extraocular movements (Teuber, 1960). Regardless of source, the existence of some oculomotor input to the visual pathway is critical for the apparent stability of the perceptual world (Jung, 1961).

An initial attempt to identify the relative loci of motion adaptation and input from the extraocular system was made by Anstis and Gregory (1965). When observers followed the motion of an inspection target with their eyes the magnitude of MAE dropped to zero. In other words, when the net retinal motion went to zero, so did MAE. More recently there was another attempt to show that the analysis of retinal image motion is carried at a neural site *prior* to the receipt of influences from the oculomotor system. Tolhurst and Hart (1972) found a constant amount of elevation of the threshold of a moving grating regardless of whether the adapting motion had been produced by movements of the distal grating with conditions of good fixation or by eye movements across a stationary grating. Retinal image motion—not the target motion—controlled the amount of direction specific threshold elevation. The signals from the oculomotor system would have been different in the two adapting conditions just described. As a result, it is likely that oculomotor signals enter the visual pathways central to the point at which adaptation occurs. (Johnstone and Mark, 1973, have raised some possible objections to the logic of Tolhurst and Hart's experiments.)

Tolhurst and Hart speculate that DSA occurs at or after the striate cortex. Two sets of facts support their argument: First, single neurons in the monkey and cat striate cortex do not discriminate between retinal image motion contingent upon distal stimulus motion and that which is contingent upon eye movements (Wurtz, 1969; Noda, Freeman, & Creutzfeldt, 1972). Second, evoked potentials from cat cortex give similar results (Jeannerod & Sakai, 1971).

The gaze-contingent MAE's reported by Mayhew (1973) seem to contradict the work of Anstis and Gregory (1965) and Tolhurst and Hart (1972). Recall that the earlier reports showed the amount of MAE and DSA could be predicted from the net retinal motion. But Mayhew generated MAE under conditions where the net retinal motion (over time) was zero! When Mayhew's observers gazed leftward they saw a pattern moving in one direction; when they gazed rightward they saw a pattern moving in the opposite direction. Since both patterns fell on the same area of the retina the net retinal image motion produced by one stimulus was cancelled by the other stimulus. Repeated presentation of the two oppositely moving targets was contingent upon direction of gaze. After this inspection period the subjects experienced opposite MAEs, also contingent upon direction of gaze. Looking leftward at a stationary target, subjects saw one direction of MAE, looking rightward they saw the opposite. A similar finding for the tilt aftereffect was reported some years ago (Hein & Sekuler, 1959).

More to the point are the obvious facts that Mayhew's data force on us: First, the visual system codes and segregates information about retinal image motion according to the direction of gaze with which it is associated; second, and just as surprising, the system can retrieve the stored information selectively, depending upon direction of gaze.

A final methodological point. Many studies of visual motion could be improved if the psychophysical observations were supplemented by measurements of the eye movements elicited by the moving stimuli. Data on *tracking* eye movements could be used for computation of the actual retinal-image motion vectors. Where patterns do elicit substantial tracking movements there are likely to be significant differences between the nominal stimulus the observer is shown and the real stimulus, on his retina. Specifying stimuli in terms of the retinal image motion, thereby discounting eye movement, is analogous to specifying the retinal illuminance (in trolands) of stimuli, thereby discounting the effect of pupil area.

IX. SUPRATHRESHOLD DIRECTION-SPECIFIC EFFECTS

Many of the threshold effects we have discussed can be reproduced at suprathreshold levels of stimulation. Some of these suprathreshold effects have, in fact, already been described, and their resemblance to their threshold counterparts noted. This section will consider a different kind of suprathreshold direction-specific effect: one that demonstrates an important property of sensitive mechanisms, not easily demonstrated at threshold levels.

A. Interaction between Real and Apparent Movement

Among the issues that have generated much theoretical heat without the help of much experimental light, is the relationship between real and apparent motion (cf. the exchange between Frisby, 1972a and Kolers, 1972). Obviously, the two phenomena cannot be the product of *precisely* the same visual mechanisms (cf. Kolers, 1963). However, the two types of motion may share some processes. Consider the following facts: Induced motion is the apparent motion of a stationary target that is surrounded by a moving field. This compelling illusion of movement can be produced by either real, continuous motion or stroboscopic apparent motion in the surround (Duncker, 1929). In addition, we already know about kinds of motion that logically are part way between real motion (continuous) and apparent motion or phi (Lichtenstein, 1963; Banks & Kane, 1972). One good way to operationalize the extent to which the two kinds of motion share common mechanisms is to see how much an exposure to one type of motion adapts the response to the other. We need such data on cross-adaptation between stroboscopic and real motion.

This chapter has described several forms of adaptation measured with continuous motion. Analogous results can be produced with apparent motion (Beck & Stevens, 1972). With closely spaced briefly flashed circular targets, only ten massed presentations (with timing adjusted to make them seem to move in one direction, say, leftward) were sufficient to produce a large decrease in the apparent speed of targets that moved in the same direction. Similar, rapid adaptation of *induced* motion (see p. 415) was described by Duncker (1929).

B. Hue-Contingent Motion Phenomena

Moving objects differ in hue. There have been several demonstrations that direction-sensitive mechanisms use this information about the hue of a target hue. The first of these demonstrations was Hepler's (1968). Her observers alternately viewed green stripes that moved up and red stripes that moved down (the chromatic stripes were separated by black stripes). After prolonged exposure, subjects were tested with black and white stripes. The stripes that moved up appeared "pink"; those that moved down appeared "green." Color appearance was contingent upon the direction in which contours moved. Even more surprising is the persistence of this phenomenon: some subjects continue to experience the hue aftereffect for more than 20 hr.

A more systematic study of the same effect has been published by Stromeyer and Mansfield (1970). Among other things, they report the effect does not transfer interocularly and is restricted, like MAE, to the area of the retina upon which the adapting stimulus fell (cf. Sekuler & Pantle, 1967; Masland, 1969). With the report of normal MAEs that last more than 24 hr after prolonged inspection periods (Masland, 1969), the persistence of the two types of effects does not differentiate them, except *quantitatively*. Another point of similarity is that, according to Stromeyer and Mansfield, their direction-contingent colors can be induced when the subject sweeps his eyes in one direction or the other across a field of stationary stripes. This resembles the fact that retinal image motion, whatever its source, is sufficient to produce the motion aftereffect (Anstis & Gregory, 1965).

Mayhew and Anstis (1972) reported experiments that are the logical inverse of the Stromeyer and Mansfield experiments. Instead of producing colored afterimages contingent upon direction of test motion, Mayhew and Anstis analyzed the segregation of chromatic and directional information by producing motion aftereffects contingent upon the hue of the test targets. A disk with radial stripes alternated between clockwise and counterclockwise directions of motion. When the disk moved clockwise, it was illuminated with red light; when it rotated counterclockwise, it was illuminated with green light. When the disk was stopped, illuminating it with green light caused it to appear to rotate clockwise, and illuminating it with red light caused its apparent rotation to be counterclockwise. These very persistent effects could be made contingent upon the *width* of the stripes and level of stimulus illumination. Similar observations were reported by Favreau, Emerson, and Corballis (1972).

Although these hue-contingent aftereffects are fascinating they do pose a problem: Is theory building helped by a proliferation of contingent motion effects? If these effects are to prove more than intriguing scientific curiosities (like certain geometrical illusions) investigators must design experiments so that meaningful conclusions about the mechanisms of motion perception will be possible. The study of motion perception has matured sufficiently to require more than an expanding catalog of various contingent curiosities.

C. Relative Motion and Storage of MAE

Most responses to objects moving through the visual field are actually responses to the motion of an object *relative* to its surround or to other objects (Gibson, 1966). We should not be surprised, therefore, that there are single cells in the mammalian visual system that are sensitive not to motion in general but to relative motion in particular (Bridgeman, 1972; Burns, Gassanov, & Webb, 1972; Phelps, 1974; Mandl, 1974). Because of involuntary and voluntary eye movements, there is always motion in the retinal image. This causes motion detectors to be stimulated constantly—even when there is no motion in the outside world. If we are to detect motion of objects, without many "false alarms" being set off by involuntary eye movements, it must be arranged that the relative motion of a *portion* of the retinal image is a potent stimulus in its own right (above and beyond some uniform movement of the entire retinal image).

Burns, Gassanov, and Webb (1972) studied cells in Area 17 of the cat cortex. Most of the cells responded more strongly to relative motion (i.e., a moving contour presented at the same time as a stationary one) than to absolute motion (i.e., just the moving contour present). Although more work on analyzers of relative motion is needed, we might consider some of the perceptual phenomena which might be related to these analyzers. First, the velocity of a target moving through a uniform, contourless field seems less than when the same target moves through a field of stationary dots or lines (Teuber, 1960; Mandl, 1974). Second, a frame surrounds a stationary dot; when the frame is moved leftward the dot appears to move rightward—with the frame appearing stationary (Duncker, 1929).

Induced movement can also be produced by more complex arrays. Tynan and Sekuler (in press, a) displayed an annulus of spatially random dots on a CRT screen surrounding a smaller, central section of similar dots. When the annular dots drifted across the screen the stationary central dots appeared to move in the opposite direction. In addition, when the center dots moved either in the same direction as the surround or in the opposite direction, surround speed affected the perceived speed of the center in a systematic but complex fashion. The changes in perceived speed were accompanied by illusory depth effects: Often the central dots seemed to occupy a different depth plane than that of the surround. Like Gogel and Koslow (1972) who used simpler targets, Tynan and Sekuler found that induced movement decreased as the apparent difference in depth between center and surround grew. Tynan and Sekuler explained their induced motion effects in terms of lateral inhibition between motion analyzers sensitive to opposite directions of motion. Imagine that the elements which respond to the movement of the surround *inhibit* neighboring elements (in the center of the field) sensitive to that same direction of motion. Induced motion might then result from the imbalance (in the field center) of spontaneous activities in (*1*) elements sensitive to the surround direction and (*2*) elements sensitive to the opposite direction. This explanation of induced motion is quite speculative, but we already have good demonstrations of one key ingredient in this story: inhibition, over some distance, between mechanisms tuned to the same direction (Holmgren, 1974; Loomis & Nakayama, 1973).

Day and Strelow (1971) reported an effect which may also depend upon interactions between neighboring motion analyzers. They found that MAE is reduced or abolished completely when there are not stationary contours *surrounding* the inspection and/or test areas. This large and dramatic effect shows the prepotence of relative motion; it also resembles two other effects. The first is that a moving pattern that fills the whole visual field produces a very small MAE (Wohlgemuth, 1911). The second effect, MAE storage, was reported some years ago by Spigel (1962a). The following protocol defines storage. The subject is exposed to a moving inspection stimulus which normally produces 10 sec of MAE. Instead of testing the MAE duration immediately after the end of the inspection period, the subject is kept in darkness for 10 sec. The period of interpolated darkness was so long that all of the MAE should have dissipated before testing began. Surprisingly, nearly all (about 70–80% of the usual MAE) was still intact after the interpolated dark period. A dark period two or even three times as long as the to-be-expected MAE duration leaves some residual MAE when the long postponed testing begins (Spigel, 1962b).

An interpolated stimulus can inhibit the decay of MAE if the interpolated stimulus contains contours. Interpolation of contourless patterns, whether bright or dark, does not keep MAE from decaying. From extensive observations on this MAE storage effect, Honig (1967) concluded that there are really two different exponential processes involved in the decay of the MAE. The decay measured under normal conditions of testing (without interpolation) has a shorter time constant than decay during interpolated stimulation. Finally, Honig found the amount of storage is inversely related to the *similarity* of the interpolated pattern to the test field. These studies remind us that in studying motion perception by any of the selective adaptation procedures we must pay attention not only to the configural properties of the adaptation and test targets but also to the similarity of one to the other.

The full explanation of the motion aftereffect, which has been known for more than 150 years, needs more complication than recent theories dared (Sekuler & Pantle, 1967; and see final section of this chapter). The observation of aftereffects of extraordinary duration (Masland, 1969; Kalfin & Locke, 1972) presents another challenge to theory building. Aftereffects of long duration lie on the interface of sensory psychology and memory. They should be pursued vigorously using paradigms from both domains.

D. Inhibition between Direction-Specific Mechanisms

In color vision, many phenomena require the existence of antagonistic interactions between mechanisms tuned to different wavelengths. As we have already seen, certain motion phenomena require the existence of inhibitory interactions between opponent mechanisms tuned to opposite directions of motion. Let us now consider additional evidence for direction-specific inhibition.

Erke and Graser (1972) and K. T. Brown (1962) have studied reversals in the perceived direction of an ambiguous stimulus. The stimulus is simple: a shadow containing both leftward and rightward motion vectors. As the subject watches it, he experiences spontaneous reversals of apparent direction. The rate of apparent reversal grows with inspection time and finally asymptotes. Erke and Graser (1972) derived good insights into the mechanisms of human motion-perception from variations on this simple phenomenon.

What sort of model can be used for reversals in apparent direction or, for that matter, for other more well-known, reversible perceptions? Attneave (1971) used an astable multivibrator (oscillator) to model reversible figures. Although it was not intended to be a detailed explanation of perceptual reversal or to deal with motion effects, Attneave's model is a good heuristic. Simple additions to Attneave's model could account for most of the data on the rate of reversal in apparent direction of an ambiguous stimulus. The details of the model are not important; what is important is that suppression or inhibition between direction-specific mechanisms is a necessary part of that model.

Consider a somewhat clearer demonstration of direction-specific inhibition. Levinson and Sekuler (1973) measured the threshold for a rightward-moving grating after adaptation to two kinds of stimuli: (1) a standard,

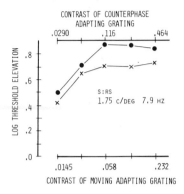

Fig. 9. Log relative threshold for rightward moving grating. The lower x-axis shows the contrast of a rightward adapting grating (●); the upper x-axis shows the contrast of a counterphase adapting grating (×). [From Sekuler & Levinson (1974).]

rightward-moving grating; and (2) a combination of that same rightward grating *plus* a similar grating, which moved leftward. Possible inhibition between mechanisms for opposite directions should make the combination of leftward grating plus rightward grating less effective as an adapting stimulus than either of its components alone.

Test and adapting gratings had spatial frequencies of 1.75 cycles/degree and all stimuli drifted at a rate of 7.9 Hz. The peak-to-peak contrast of the combination adapting grating is twice that of either of its components—when the two components are added in equal amplitudes. If one wanted to compare adaptation gratings that contained equal amounts of rightward-moving gratings, one should adjust the combination (or counterphase) grating to twice the contrast of the rightward adapting grating alone. Levinson and Sekuler (1973) compared the threshold raising abilities of the two kinds of adapting gratings, testing each at five different contrast levels. Some of their data are shown in Fig. 9. The upper curve shows thresholds measured after adaptation to a rightward grating; the lower curve shows similar data measured after adaptation to a combination, counterphase stimulus (see Section II for other work with counterphase gratings). The two x-axes, one for each type of adapting stimulus, are adjusted so that points at any x value are taken with the same contrast of rightward grating present in both types of adapting stimuli. Over the adapting contrasts studied, the counterphase grating consistently produced less threshold elevation than was produced by its rightward component alone. Adding a leftward component to the adapting stimulus, keeping the rightward component constant, actually reduces the effectiveness of the rightward component. This is strong evidence for direction-specific inhibition.

The existence of direction-specific inhibition is consistent with observations on the response of direction-sensitive cells in the visual cortex of cats. Benevento *et al.* (1972) found that some cells were inhibited by target motion in a direction opposite its preferred direction. In addition to the demonstration of direction-specific inhibition, Benevento and his associates offer a plausible model of the neural connections which could support the inhibition.

Direction-specific inhibition will receive greater attention in the coming years. It is a force that must be taken into account when we try to model various motion phenomena.

X. BINOCULAR ASPECTS OF MOTION PERCEPTION

There are undoubtedly several different neural loci in the human visual system that are specialized for the analysis of visual motion. Good support for this idea comes from studies of the relationship between monocular and binocular motion perception. Although we cannot specify all the loci for motion analysis, this section will show that there are multiple sites for motion analysis, each with its own idiosyncrasies and defining characteristics.

In one attempt to identify the neural locus of motion responses, Papert (1964) found monocular motion is not necessary to generate the motion aftereffect (MAE). Papert made random-dot stereogram movies which, to either eye alone, looked like random visual noise. This random monocular noise contained motion in all directions and did not produce MAE. But when the noise was presented to both eyes, with the aid of a stereoscope, the frame-by-frame correlation between the inputs to the two eyes caused the subject to see squares that stood out in depth and moved continuously downward. This stereo image produced a strong MAE. Note that Papert's stimulus had no systematic directional vectors prior to the point of binocular combination. The stimulus could affect only motion analyzers *central* to the point of binocular combination (Area 17 of the visual cortex). This kind of stimulus, which Julesz (1971) terms "cyclopean," demonstrates that monocular motion vectors are not necessary to MAE. This does not imply the monocular vectors are not *sufficient* for MAE.

Enlarging on Papert's observations, Anstis and Moulden (1970) showed that *both* cyclopean and monocular motion components separately can produce MAE. Their first experiment was really a replication of one reported by Wohlgemuth (1911) in his classic monograph on MAE. Anstis and Moulden presented clockwise rotation to one eye, while the other eye saw counterclockwise motion. Stimulation fell on corresponding retinal regions of the two eyes. The monocular aftereffect was counterclockwise for one eye and clockwise for the other eye. This MAE, Anstis and Moulden argue, has to be peripheral (i.e., monocular) since the *cyclopean* stimulus would have no net rotation vector. In their last experiment, stimulation was so arranged that each eye independently saw clockwise rotation, but both eyes together saw counterclockwise rotation. When the stationary test field was viewed monocularly, the MAE was in the direction determined by the cyclopean (central) inspection motion, i.e., clockwise. All these studies add up to the conclusion: There are *both* central and peripheral determinants of the MAE. We must be careful not to generalize, however, beyond the specific case of MAE.

Among the good, older measurements of binocular motion perception are those of Ammons and Weitz (1951), Howard (1961), and Smith and Gulick (1957). Ammons and Weitz found that the perception of apparent movement (phi) was significantly improved when both stimuli for apparent movement projected to the same rather than to opposite hemispheres. Over and above the difference between ipsilateral and contralateral hemispheric projection, apparent movement was more easily seen with monocular rather than binocular stimulation. The inferiority of binocular relative to monocular motion perception is apparently a general rule. The basis for this observation remains uncertain.

Howard (1961) examined the time taken for the first reversal in the apparent direction of an ambiguous moving stimulus. Subjects viewed a slowly rotating wire cube and reported when the apparent direction of rotation reversed. The findings relevant to the present discussion are as follows:

(*1*) The effect transfers interocularly; i.e., a short viewing period with one eye reduced the time to reversal when viewing was switched to the other eye.

(*2*) The effect seem to be relatively well localized to a particular position in space, i.e., a brief period of viewing at one retinal locus did not affect time to reversal at other, nonhomologous locations.

(*3*) Binocular time to reversal was longer than monocular time to reversal.

This last finding reinforces the possibility of *inhibitory* interaction between each eye's motion inputs. Erke and Graser (1972) and Brown (1962) found near perfect interocular transfer of a similar effect.

Several other recent observations show how binocular and monocular motion responses differ. This difference is crucial because (*1*) nearly all cells in the striate cortex of the cat receive excitatory input from both eyes (Pettigrew, 1972); (*2*) binocular viewing is the common extralaboratory way of looking at the world; and (*3*) there are certain indications that binocular experience may not always be predictable from the separate monocular responses to a moving stimulus.

In their study of cyclopean apparent movement, Julesz and Payne (1968) made some observations that suggest greater sensitivity with monocular than with binocular viewing. Julesz (1971) has since amplified this point and described other discrepancies between monocular and binocular motion. Among the discrepancies is a phenomenon Julesz terms "binocular standstill [p. 251]."

The variety of cyclopean and monocular motion phenomena Julesz (1971) describes in his book shows that (*1*) all analysis of visual movement is *not* carried out at a single stage, and (*2*) under some conditions extraction of disparity information precedes extraction of movement information.

Wohlgemuth (1911) examined the binocular summation of the MAE generated by independent and oppositely moving, monocular inspection targets. He found that, whereas eye-specific MAEs could be generated under conditions of monocular testing, they seemed to cancel one another under binocular test viewing.

Ware and Mitchell (1974) report differences between interocular transfer of MAE for normal and stereoblind observers. Their stereoblind observers had strabismus which would have produced discordant visual input from the two eyes. If the human visual system was modified by its early input, Ware and Mitchell argue that binocularity could be lost in such cases. The fact that their stereoblind subjects showed no interocular transfer of MAE, whereas their normal subjects showed considerable transfer, strengthened the idea that stereoblind subjects possess very few or no binocular neurons.

XI. THE VARIETY OF MOTION

The preceding discussion makes one conclusion inescapable: Similar percepts can arise under different conditions of stimulation. Perceived motion could arise in various ways, involving different sensory mechanisms. This fact may help reconcile otherwise incompatible findings.

Consider the variety of effects produced by exposure to a moving target. A scheme that has been useful elsewhere (Sekuler & Pantle, 1967; Blakemore, Muncey, & Ridley, 1973) gives a convenient framework. Imagine that viewing a moving stimulus desensitizes channels which normally respond to that stimulus. Their reduced sensitivity leads us to expect these effects:

(*1*) Response to the moving target should decrease over time (e.g., Goldstein, 1957).

(*2*) Adaptation should make it harder to detect any target processed by the same channels (e.g., Sekuler & Ganz, 1963).

(*3*) Detection of targets processed over *other* channels should be unaffected (e.g., Pantle & Sekuler, 1969).

(4) The imbalance between "opponent" channels—those which have been adapted and those which have not—should produce a negative aftereffect with a suprathreshold test target (e.g., MAE).

(5) The appearance of targets similar to the adaptation stimulus should be distorted (e.g., Scott, Jordan, & Powell, 1963; Levinson & Sekuler, 1975).

This list does not include all the "contingent" effects a stimulus probably exerts; it does not even consider that *both* adaptation and test targets are likely to be multidimensional. Clearly, the list is far from exhaustive.

One general point has been made several times previously but bears repetition: There is a difference between threshold and suprathreshold aspects of motion. This distinction is crucial for a theory of motion perception. It is trivial to say that the visual system operates differently at threshold and suprathreshold levels. If nothing else, the existence of a threshold implies a strong nonlinearity. Because of this nonlinearity, in a multiple-channel system the *threshold* visual response is determined exclusively by the single most sensitive channel (mechanism). The identity of that most sensitive channel will vary with the parameters of adaptation and test.

Threshold measures of adaptation produced by a moving target reflect this rule: The threshold for contours moving in one direction is controlled exclusively by the sensitivity of a channel sensitive to that direction of motion. Contrary to the ratio hypothesis (Sutherland, 1961), it does not appear as if the sensitivity of other channels enters into the threshold determination (Sekuler, Lehr, Stone, & Wolf, 1971; Sekuler & Levinson, 1974).

Different rules govern *suprathreshold* responses. As a general principle, we may assume that motion perception at suprathreshold levels is the result of activity in all the channels which respond above their individual threshold levels. Insisting upon a theoretical distinction between threshold and suprathreshold phenomena permits the reconciliation of apparently discrepant findings. For example, Scott, Jordan and Powell (1963) reported that the perceived velocity of a test stimulus was the algebraic sum of its actual physical velocity and the velocity of a superimposed MAE. Note that this experiment departs from the standard conditions for measuring MAE. In almost all other studies the test target is stationary. We might expect that after adaptation to leftward-moving inspection targets, the residual adaptation might *sum* with rightward-moving test targets. Summation between the adaptation process and the test target might facilitate detection of test targets moving rightward. But this kind of facilitation at threshold has not been found (Pantle & Sekuler, 1969).

Lack of interaction between the adaptation process and the test target is interpreted by assuming that (1) threshold for a test target is determined by the sensitivity of a single channel, whereas (2) suprathreshold appearances, including aftereffects, result from pooled activity from many or all responding channels.

In addition, suprathreshold appearance represents a summation across a considerable spatial region. Extensive spatial averaging is usually not the case at threshold. An observation on the MAE illustrates this point. Sekuler and Pantle (1967) varied the overlap between (1) the area of the retina stimulated by the adapting pattern and (2) the area of the retina stimulated by the stationary test pattern. The aftereffect's apparent velocity increased as the overlap between inspection and test areas increased. We can explain this by supposing the apparent velocity in the test area was governed by the ratio of activity, within the *entire* test area, of motion analyzers (1) sensitive to the inspection direction and (2) sensitive to the opposite direction. As overlap between inspection and test areas increased, the test area contained more motion analyzers that had been stimulated by the inspection target and fewer that had not.

There is another set of motion data that demonstrates the difference between threshold and suprathreshold spatial integration. Tynan and Sekuler (in press, a, and see Section IX,C) used a computer driven display to study various kinds of simultaneous motion contrast. In one experiment, an annulus of moving, spatially random dots induced apparent movement in a center cluster of stationary dots. The center cluster was 1° square and the outside of the annulus was 8° square. This same stimulus produced another strange phenomenon: When no dots at all were presented in the central 1° square, movement in the surround caused subjects to see phantom moving dots in the center (Tynan & Sekuler, in press, b). Both the induced movement and the phantom dots show that movement in one area of the field (the surround) can affect the motion response in another (the center). In contrast to these suprathreshold effects, which spread across the visual field, are some results with detection thresholds. With the same display configuration as before, Tynan and Sekuler (in press, a) used a forced-choice procedure to measure the detection thresholds for center dots that moved either in the same direction as the surround dots or in the opposite direction. Surprisingly, they found no evidence of direction-specific adaptation: thresholds were identical for the two conditions. Control measures, with spatially overlapping adapting and test regions showed that the moving dots could produce considerable direction adaptation. Here then we see no spatial spread of the threshold-raising effects of visual motion. Using exactly the same stimulus to measure threshold and suprathreshold effects, Tynan and Sekuler (in press, a) found areal spread of the suprathreshold and no spread of the threshold effects.

We already know that the visual system integrates across large areas in other suprathreshold responses (cf. Section IX). The same sort of spatial integration is seen in color vision where the wavelength of one patch can affect the hue of very distant areas. In fact, this inducing effect works over distances far greater than the spatial resolving ability of the system.

Another, more speculative analogy to color vision may be in order. In the same way that hue is controlled by the weighted responses in all the color channels, the direction and velocity of suprathreshold moving targets may be similarly controlled—by the combination of responses from separate detectors (see Wohlgemuth, 1911; Expt. 26). This weighted outcome would include excitatory as well as inhibitory responses produced by the stimulus (cf. Section IX,D).

While we learn a lot about motion perception from measurements at threshold levels, we should not ignore measurements of various aftereffects and suprathreshold effects. The goal of visual psychophysics is the explanation of why the world appears as it does. Therefore, theory building must incorporate data from the entire gamut of visual phenomena—suprathreshold as well as threshold measures.

The past decade has seen the development of a coherent picture of the mechanisms which mediate motion perception. The mechanisms we hypothesize are complex; but perceived motion is complex. At the very least we now know something about the spatio-temporal stimulation to which motion analyzers are tuned, their nonuniform distribution across the retina, and the variety of effects produced by exposure to a moving target.

As this chapter indicates, motion perception is a complicated business. It is fortunate that, in science as well as in nature itself, "Things in motion sooner catch the eye than what stirs not." If moving things were *not* so potent in capturing the eye and the brain, many of us might have turned to more easily solved, but less interesting problems.

References

Ammons, C. H., & Weitz, J. Central and peripheral factors in the phi phenomenon. *Journal of Experimental Psychology,* 1951, **42,** 327–332.

Anstis, S. M., & Gregory, R. L. The aftereffect of seen motion: The role of retinal stimulation and of eye movements. *Quarterly Journal of Experimental Psychology,* 1965, **17,** 173–174.

Anstis, S. M., & Moulden, B. P. Aftereffect of seen movement: Evidence for peripheral and central components. *Quarterly Journal of Experimental Psychology,* 1970, **22,** 222–229.

Appelle, S. Perception and discrimination as a function of stimulus orientation. *Psychological Bulletin,* 1972, **78,** 266–278.

Attneave, F. Multistability in perception. *Scientific American,* 1971, **225** (No. 6), 62–71.

Banks, W. P., & Kane, D. A. Discontinuity of seen motion reduces the motion aftereffect. *Perception & Psychophysics,* 1972, **12,** 69–72.

Barlow, H. B., & Hill, R. M. Evidence for a physiological explanation of the waterfall illusion and figural aftereffects. *Nature,* 1963, **200,** 1434–1435.

Barlow, H. B., & Pettigrew, J. O. Lack of specificity of neurones in the visual cortex of young kittens. *Journal of Physiology,* 1971, **218,** 98–100.

Beck, J., & Stevens, A. An aftereffect to discrete stimuli producing apparent movement and succession. *Perception & Psychophysics,* 1972, **12,** 482–486.

Benevento, L. A., Creutzfeldt, O. D., & Kuhnt, U. Significance of intra-cortical inhibition in visual-cortex. *Nature,* 1972, **238,** 124–126.

Bhatia, B. Minimum separable as a function of speed of a moving object. *Vision Research,* 1975, **15,** 23–33.

Biederman-Thorson, M., Thorson, J., & Lange, G. D. Apparent movement due to closely spaced sequentially flashed dots in the human peripheral field of vision. *Vision Research,* 1971, **11,** 889–903.

Blakemore, C. Developmental factors in the formation of feature extracting neurons. In F. O. Schmitt & F. G. Worden (Eds.), *The neurosciences: Third study program.* Cambridge, Massachusetts: M.I.T. Press, 1974.

Blakemore, C., & Campbell, F. W. On the existence of neurons in the human visual system selectively sensitive to the orientation and size of retinal images. *Journal of Physiology,* 1969, **203,** 237–260.

Blakemore, C., Carpenter, R. H. S., & Georgeson, M. A. Lateral inhibition between orientation detectors in the human visual system. *Nature,* 1970, **228,** 37–41.

Blakemore, C., Muncey, J. P. J., & Ridley, R. M. Stimulus specificity in the human visual system. *Vision Research,* 1973, **13,** 1915–1931.

Bonnet, C., & Pouthas, V. Interactions between spatial and kinetic dimensions in movement aftereffect. *Perception & Psychophysics,* 1972, **12,** 193–200.

Breitmeyer, B. G. A relationship between the detection of size, rate, orientation and direction in the human visual system. *Vision Research,* 1973, **13,** 41–58.

Breitmeyer, B., Love, R., & Wepman, B. Contour Supression during stroboscopic motion and metacontrast. *Vision Research,* 1974, **14,** 1451–1456.

Bridgeman, B. Visual receptive fields sensitive to absolute and relative motion during tracking. *Science,* 1972, **178,** 1106–1108.

Brindley, G. S. *Physiology of the retina and visual pathway.* Baltimore, Maryland: Williams & Wilkins, 1970.

Brown, B. Resolution thresholds for moving targets at the fovea and in the peripheral retina. *Vision Research,* 1972, **12,** 293–304.

Brown, K. T. Complete interocular transfer of an adaptation process responsible for perceptual fluctuations with an ambiguous visual figure. *Vision Research,* 1962, **2,** 469–475.

Burns, B. D., Gassanov, U., & Webb, A. C. Responses of neurones in the cat's visual cerebral cortex to relative movement of patterns. *Journal of Physiology,* 1972, **226,** 133–151.

Carlson, V. R. Adaptation in the perception of visual velocity. *Journal of Experimental Psychology,* 1962, **64,** 192–197.

Clarke, P. G. H. Are visual evoked potentials to motion-reversal produced by direction-sensitive brain mechanisms? *Vision Research,* 14, 1281–1284.

Clatworthy, J. L., & Frisby, J. P. Real and apparent visual movement: Evidence for a unitary mechanism. *Perception,* 1973, **2,** 161–164.

Clymer, A. The effect of seen motion on the apparent speed of subsequently viewed test velocities: A new approach to movement after-effects. Paper presented at meetings of Association for Research in Vision and Ophthalmology, 1972, Sarasota, Florida.

Cornsweet, T. N. *Visual perception*. New York: Academic Press, 1970.

Craik, K. J. W. The effect of adaptation upon visual acuity. *British Journal of Psychology*, 1939, **29**, 252–266.

Croft, T. A. Failure of visual estimation of motion under strobe. *Nature*, 1971, **231**, 397.

Crook, M. N. Visual discrimination of movement. *Journal of Psychology*, 1937, **3**, 541–558.

Cynader, M., Berman, N., & Hein, A. Cats reared in stroboscopic illumination: Effects on receptive fields in visual cortex. *Proceedings of the National Academy of Science*, 1973, **70**, 1353–1354.

Day, R. H. Apparent contraction and disappearance of moving objects in the peripheral visual field. *Vision Research*, 1973, **13**, 959–975.

Day, R. H., & Strelow, E. R. Visual aftereffect of movement: Partial or complete reduction in the absence of a patterned surround. *Nature*, 1971, **230**, 55–56.

DeValois, R. L., Morgan, H. C., & Snodderly, D. M. Psychophysical of monkey vision—III. Spatial luminance contrast sensitivity tests of macaque and human observers. *Vision Research*, 1974, **14**, 75–82.

Dimmick, R. L., & Karl, J. C. The effect of exposure time upon the Reiz Limen of visible motion. *Journal of Experimental Psychology*, 1930, **13**, 365–369.

Duncker, K. Ueber induzierte bewegung. *Psychologische Forschungen*, 1929, **12**, 180–259.

Enoch, J. M. The two-color threshold technique of Stiles and derived component color mechanisms. In D. Jameson & L. M. Hurvich (Eds.), *Visual psychophysics*. Berlin: Springer, 1972.

Enroth-Cugell, C., & Robson, J. G. The contrast sensitivity of retinal cells of the cat. *Journal of Physiology*, 1966, **187**, 517–552.

Erke, H., & Graser, H. Reversibility of perceived motion: Selective adaptation of the human visual system to speed, size and orientation. *Vision Research*, 1972, **12**, 69–87.

Favreau, O. P., Emerson, V. F., & Corballis, M. C. Motion perception: A color-contingent aftereffect. *Science*, 1972, **176**, 78–79.

Foster, D. H. A model of the human visual system in its response to certain classes of moving stimuli. *Kybernetik*, 1971, **8**, 69–84.

Frisby, J. P. Real and apparent movement—same or different mechanisms? *Vision Research*, 1972, **12**, 1051–1055. (a)

Frisby, J. P. The effect of stimulus orientations on the phi phenomenon. *Vision Research*, 1972, **12**, 1145–1166. (b)

Frisby, J. P., & Clatworthy, J. L. Evidence for separate movement and form channels in the human visual system. *Perception*, 1974, **3**, 87–96.

Ganz, L., & Lange, A. Changes in motion sensitivity of cat visual cortex neurones during the course of dark adaptation. Paper presented at meetings of Association of Research in Vision and Ophthalmology, 1973, Sarasota, Florida.

Gibson, J. J. *The senses considered as perceptual systems*. Boston: Houghton Mifflin, 1966.

Gibson, J. J. Adaptation with negative aftereffect. *Psychological Review*, 1937, **44**, 222–244.

Gogel, W. C., & Koslow, M. The adjacency principle and induced movement. *Perception & Psychophysics*, 1972, **11**, 309–314.

Goldstein, A. G. Judgments of visual velocity as a function of length of observation time. *Journal of Experimental Psychology*, 1957, **54**, 457–461.

Gouras, P. Visual neurophysiology: Feature detecting channels. *Investigative Ophthalmology,* 1973, **12,** 2–3.

Graham, C. H. Perception. In C. H. Graham *et al.* (Eds.), *Vision and visual perception.* New York: Wiley, 1965.

Graham, C. H., & Hunter, W. S. Thresholds of illumination for the visual discrimination of direction of movement and for the discrimination of discreteness. *Journal of General Psychology,* 1931, **5,** 178–190.

Harris, P. L., Cassel, T. Z., & Bamborough, P. Tracking by young infants. *British Journal of Psychology,* 1974, **65,** 345–349.

Hein, A. V., & Sekuler, R. A technique for producing displacement aftereffects contingent upon eye and head position. *American Psychologist,* 1959, **16,** 437.

Hepler, N. Color: A motion-contingent after-effect. *Science,* 1968, **162,** 376–377.

Hilz, R., & Cavonius, C. R. Functional organization of the peripheral retina: Sensitivity to periodic stimuli. *Vision Research,* 1974, **14,** 1333–1337.

Hoffman, K.-P. Conduction velocity in pathways from retina to superior colliculus in the cat: A correlation with receptive-field properties. *Journal of Neurophysiology,* 1973, **36,** 409–424.

Holland, H. C. Differential disinhibition and reminiscence in the spiral after-effect. *Nature,* 1963, **198,** 1074–1075.

Holmgren, S. On searching for Mach band type phenomena in the visual perception of spatial velocity distributions. Report 151, Dept. of Psychology, Univ. Uppsala, Sweden.

Honig, W. K. Studies of the 'storage' of the after-effect of seen movement. Paper presented at meetings of the Psychonomic Society, 1967, Chicago, Illinois.

Howard, I. P. An investigation of a satiation process in reversible perspective of revolving skeletal shapes. *Quarterly Journal of Experimental Psychology,* 1961, **13,** 19–33.

Hubel, D. H., & Wiesel, T. N. Receptive fields, binocular interaction and functional architecture in the cat's visual cortex. *Journal of Physiology,* 1962, **160,** 106–154.

Jeannerod, M., & Sakai, K., Potentials related to visual field motions as compared to eye movement potentials in the cat's visual system. *Vision Research,* 1971, **11,** 161–165.

Johnstone, J. R., & Mark, R. F. Corollary discharge. *Vision Research,* 1973, **13,** 1621, 1622.

Julesz, B. *The foundations of cyclopean perception.* Chicago, Illinois: Univ. of Chicago Press, 1971.

Julesz, B., & Hesse, R. I. Inability to perceive the direction of rotation movement of line segments. *Nature,* 1970, **225,** 243–244.

Julesz, B., & Payne, R. A. Differences between monocular and binocular stroboscopic movement perception. *Vision Research,* 1968, **8,** 433–444.

Jung, R. Neuronal integration in the visual cortex and its significance for visual information. In W. A. Rosenblith (Ed.), *Sensory communication.* Cambridge, Massachusetts: M.I.T. Press, 1961.

Kalfin, K., & Locke, S. Evaluation of long term visual motion afterimage following monocular stimulation. *Vision Research,* 1972, **12,** 359–361.

Keck, M. J., Palella, T. D., & Pantle, A. Motion aftereffect as a function of the contrast of sinusoidal gratings. *Vision Research* (in press).

Keesey, U. T. Flicker and pattern detection: A comparison of thresholds. *Journal of Optical Society of America,* 1972, **62,** 446–448.

Kinchla, R. A., & Allan, L. G. A theory of visual movement perception. *Psychological Review,* 1969, **76,** 537–558.

Kinoshita, T. Ueber die dauer des negativen bewegungsnachbildes. *Zeitschrift für Sinnesphysiologie,* 1909, **43,** 434–442.

Kolers, P. A problem for theory. *Vision Research,* 1972, **12,** 1057–1058.

Kolers, P. Some differences between real and apparent visual movement. *Vision Research,* 1963, **3,** 191–206.

Kulikowski, J. J. Effect of eye movements on the contrast sensitivity of spatio-temporal patterns. *Vision Research,* 1971, **11,** 261–274.

Kulikowski, J. J., & King-Smith, P. E. Spatial arrangement of line, edge and grating detectors revealed by subthreshold summation. *Vision Research,* 1973, **13,** 1455–1478.

Kulikowski, J. J., & Tolhurst, D. J. Psychophysical evidence for sustained and transient neurones in the human visual system. *Journal of Physiology,* 1973, **232,** 149–162.

Leibowitz, H. W., Johnson, C. A., & Isabelle, E. Peripheral motion detection and refractive error. *Science,* 1972, **177,** 1207–1208.

Levinson, E., & Sekuler, R. Spatio-temporal contrast sensitivities for moving and flickering stimuli. Paper presented at meetings of the Optical Society of America, 1973, Rochester, New York.

Levinson, E., & Sekuler, R. Adaptation shifts perceived direction of motion. Paper presented at meetings of the Association for Research in Vision and Ophthalmology, 1975, Sarasota, Florida.

Lichtenstein, M. Spatio-temporal factors in cessation of smooth apparent motion. *Journal of Optical Society of America,* 1963, **53,** 302–306.

Loomis, J. M., & Nakayama, K. A velocity analogue of brightness contrast. *Perception,* 1973, **2,** 425–428.

MacKay, D. M. Interactive processes in visual perception. In W. A. Rosenblith (Ed.), *Sensory communication.* New York: Wiley, 1961. Pp. 339–355.

Maffei, L., & Fiorentini, A. The visual cortex as a spatial frequency analyzer. *Vision Research,* 1973, **13,** 1255–1267.

Mandl, G. The influence of visual pattern combinations on responses of movement sensitive cells in the cat's superior colliculus. *Brain Research,* 1974, **75,** 215–240.

Masland, R. H. Visual motion perception: Experimental modification. *Science,* 1969, **165,** 819–821.

Mayhew, J. E. W., & Anstis, S. M. Movement after-effects contingent on color, intensity, and pattern. *Perception & Psychophysics,* 1972, **12,** 77–85.

McColgin, F. H. Movement threshold in peripheral vision. *Journal of the Optical Society of America,* 1960, **50,** 774–779.

Noda, H., Freeman, R. B., & Creutzfeldt, O. D. Neuronal correlates of eye movements in the cat visual cortex. *Science,* 1972, **175,** 661–664.

Over, R., Broerse, J., Crassini, B., & Lovegrove, W. Spatial determinants of the after-effect of seen motion. *Vision Research,* 1973, **13,** 1681–1690.

Pantle, A. Adaptation to pattern spatial frequency: Effects on visual movement sensitivity in humans. *Journal of Optical Society of America,* 1970, **60,** 1120–1124.

Pantle, A. Motion aftereffect magnitude as a measure of the spatiotemporal response properties of direction-sensitive analyzers. *Vision Research,* 1974, **14,** 1229–1236.

Pantle, A., & Sekuler, R. Size detecting mechanisms in human vision. *Science,* 1968, **162,** 1146–1148. (a)

Pantle, A., & Sekuler, R. Velocity sensitive mechanisms in human vision. *Vision Research,* 1968, **8,** 445–450. (b)

Pantle, A., & Sekuler, R. Contrast response of human visual mechanisms sensitive to orientation and direction of motion. *Vision Research,* 1969, **9,** 397–406.

Papert, S. Stereoscopic synthesis as a technique for localizing visual mechanisms. *M.I.T. Quarterly Progress Report*, 1973, **239**, 243.

Pettigrew, J. D. The neurophysiology of binocular vision. *Scientific American*, 1972, **227** (No. 2), 84–96.

Phelps, R. W. Effects of interactions of two moving lines on single unit responses in the cat's visual cortex. *Vision Research*, 1974, **14**, 1371–1376.

Reading, V. M. Visual resolution as measured by dynamic and static tests. *Pflügers Archives*, 1972, **333**, 17–26.

Richards, W. Motion perception in man and other animals. *Brain, Behavior & Evolution*, 1971, **4**, 162–181.

Richards, W., & Dichgans, J. Effect of directional-flow patterns motion thresholds. *Journal of Optical Society of America*, 1974, **64**, 1148–1149.

Riddoch, G. Dissociation of visual perceptions due to occipital injuries with special reference to appreciation of movement. *Brain*, 1917, **40**, 15–57.

Robinson, J. O. *The psychology of visual illusions*. London: Hutchinson, 1972. Pp. 206–252.

Schouten, J. F. Subjective stroboscopy and a model of visual movement detectors. In W. Wathen-Dunn (Ed.), *Models for the perception of speech and visual Form*. Cambridge, Massachusetts: M.I.T. Press, 1967. Pp. 44–55.

Scott, T. R., Jordan, A. E., & Powell, D. A. Does the visual aftereffect of motion add algebraically to objective motion of the test stimulus? *Journal of Experimental Psychology*, 1963, **66**, 500–505.

Scott, T. R., & Powell, D. A. Measurement of a visual motion aftereffect in the Rhesus monkey. *Science*, 1963, **140**, 57–59.

Sekuler, R. Movement analyzers in human vision. Paper presented in Symposium on Sensory Mechanisms in Visual Perception. Meetings of American Psychological Association, 1967, Philadelphia, Pennsylvania.

Sekuler, R. Spatial vision. *Annual Review of Psychology*, 1974, **25**, 195–232.

Sekuler, R., & Armstrong, R. Luminance control of a small computer CRT display: A very cheap technique. *Behavior Research Methods & Instrumentation*, 1971, **3**, 48–49.

Sekuler, R., & Ganz, L. A new aftereffect of seen movement with a stabilized retinal image. *Science*, 1963, **139**, 419–420.

Sekuler, R., Lehr, D., Stone, W., & Wolf, M. Human visual motion sensitivity: Evidence against a ratio theory. *Perception & Psychophysics*, 1971, **9**, 483–484.

Sekuler, R., & Levinson, E. Mechanisms of motion perception. *Psychologia* (Kyoto), 1974, **17**, 38–49.

Sekuler, R., & Pantle, A. A model for after-effects of seen motion. *Vision Research*, 1967, **7**, 427–439.

Sekuler, R., Rubin, R., & Cushman, W. Selectivity of human visual mechanisms for direction of movement and contour orientation. *Journal of Optical Society of America*, 1968, **58**, 1146–1148.

Sharpe, C. R. The contrast sensitivity of the peripheral visual field to drifting sinusoidal gratings. *Vision Research*, 1974, **14**, 905–906.

Singer, W., & Bedworth, N. Inhibitory interaction between X and Y units in the cat lateral geniculate nucleus. *Brain Research*, 1973, **49**, 291–307.

Skavenski, A. A. Inflow as a source of extraretinal eye position information. *Vision Research*, 1972, **12**, 221–229.

Smith, W. M., & Gulick, W. L. Dynamic contour perception. *Journal of Experimental Psychology*, 1957, **53**, 145–151.

Spigel, I. M. Relation of movement aftereffect duration to interpolated darkness intervals. *Life Sciences,* 1962, **1,** 239–242. (a)

Spigel, I. M. Contour absence as a critical factor in the inhibition of the decay
of a movement aftereffect. *Journal of Psychology,* 1962, **54,** 221–228. (b)

Stent, G. S. Prematurity and uniqueness in scientific discovery. *Scientific American,*
1972, **227** (No. 6), 84–93.

Stone, J. Morphology and physiology of the geniculocortical synapse in the cat:
The question of parallel input to the striate cortex. *Investigative Ophthalmology,*
1972, **11,** 338–344.

Stone, J., & Dreher, B. Projection of X- and Y-cells of the cat's lateral geniculate
nucleus to areas 17 and 18 of visual cortex. *Journal of Neurophysiology,* 1973,
36, 551–567.

Stromeyer, C. F., III, & Mansfield, R. J. W. Colored after-effects produced with
moving edges. *Perception & Psychophysics,* 1970, **7,** 108–114.

Sutherland, N. S. Figural after-effects and apparent size. *Quarterly Journal Experimental Psychology,* 1961, **13,** 222–228.

Taylor, M. M. Visual discrimination and orientation. *Journal of Optical Society of
America,* 1963, **53,** 763–765.

Teuber, H. L. Perception. In H. W. Magoun (Ed.), *Handbook of physiology: Neurophysiology, 3.* Washington, D. C.: American Physiological Society, 1960. Pp.
1595–1668.

Tolhurst, D. J. Separate channels for the analysis of the shape and the movement
of a moving visual stimulus. *Journal of Physiology,* 1973, **231,** 385–402.

Tolhurst, D. J., & Hart, G. Psychophysical investigation of effects of controlled eye-
movement on movement detectors of human visual system. *Vision Research,*
1972, **12,** 1441–1446.

Tolhurst, D. J., Sharpe, C. R., & Hart, G. The analysis of the drift rate of moving
sinusoidal gratings. *Vision Research,* 1973, **13,** 2545–2556.

Tyler, C. W., & Torres, J. Frequency response characteristics for sinusoidal movement
in the fovea and periphery. *Perception & Psychophysics,* 1972, **12,** 232–236.

Tynan, P., & Sekuler, R. Simultaneous motion contrast: Velocity, sensitivity and
depth response. *Vision Research,* in press. (a)

Tynan, P., & Sekuler, R. Moving visual phantoms: A new contour completion effect.
Science, in press. (b)

Van Nes, F. L., Koenderink, J. J., Nas, H., & Bouman, M. A. Spatio-temporal modulation transfer in the human eye. *Journal of the Optical Society of America,*
1967, **57,** 1082–1088.

Walker, J. T. A texture-contingent visual motion aftereffect. *Psychonomic Science,*
1972, **28,** 333–335.

Ware, C., & Mitchell, D. E. On interocular transfer of various after effects in normal
and stereoblind observers. *Vision Research,* 1974, **14,** 731–734.

Watanabe, A., Mori, T., Nagata, S., & Hiwatashi, K. Spatial sine-wave response of
the human visual system. *Vision Research,* 1968, **8,** 1245–1263.

Wertheimer, M. Experimentelle studien ueber das sehen von bewegung. *Zeitschrift
fur Psychologie,* 1912, **61,** 161–265.

Westheimer, G. Spatial interaction in human cone vision. *Journal of Physiology,*
1967, **190,** 139–154.

Wohlgemuth, A. On the after-effect of seen movement. *British Journal of Psychology.*
Monograph Suppl., Nov. 1, 1911.

Wurtz, R. H. Comparison of eye movements and stimulus movements on striate
cortex neurones of the monkey. *Journal of Neurophysiology,* 1969, **32,** 987–994.

Part VI

Painting and Photography

Chapter 12

VISION AND ART

*M. H. PIRENNE**

*Member of the Royal Belgian Academy of Sciences.

I. INTRODUCTION

This chapter does not attempt to cover the whole of the immense subject of the relationship of the visual sciences to the art of painting, which would be an impossible task.

Its main purpose is to reexamine in simple terms the significance of linear perspective in painting, and thus to demonstrate the fundamental importance of the pattern on the picture surface in our everyday perception of ordinary paintings and photographs. The present discussion of perspective may appear as an oversimplification to some readers, and raise further questions in their minds. But I have tried to answer many of these questions in advance, in a book entitled *Optics, Painting and Photography* (1970). In this book, however, my main thesis may to some extent have become lost precisely because I attempted to discuss fully all the important points. Although some reviewers gave excellent summaries of the main thesis, they have been relatively few, as far as I know, so it seemed advisable to restate it here: I have done so, partly on the basis of new experiments.

This chapter ends with a section on irradiation, which shows the links of the "pointillist" method of the painter Seurat and his followers to earlier techniques including those of the artists who made mosaics and illuminated manuscripts. All this again refers to the surface pattern of the picture.

Other problems, not dealt with here, relating for instance to the depiction of night-scenes, are briefly examined in my book, *Vision and the Eye* (1967), and its French translation, with additions by R. Crouzy (Pirenne, 1972).

I wish to dedicate the present chapter to the memory of my late professor Léon Rosenfeld, disciple and collaborator of the physicist Niels Bohr, who told me when I was still a student to read the original accounts of the discoveries made by great scientists, even of many centuries ago, because they often were much more accurately and vividly written than later accounts given in textbooks. I have found this advice most valuable—while being, of course, immensely grateful to Léon Rosenfeld for teaching me the theory of quantum physics, which he always kept in close link with the crucial experimental findings.

II. NATURAL PERSPECTIVE

A. Pyramid of Sight

Even though we can hear around corners, we cannot see around corners. Through a medium of even density we see in straight lines. The earliest treatise on vision still extant, Euclid's *Optics* (ca. 300 B.C.) rests on this essential fact.

It is true that Euclid adopted the strange theory—now of historical interest only—that the eye *emitted* visual rays, reaching out like long straight tentacles to the objects seen; but in some of his theorems he also deals with the shadows thrown by the light rays coming from the sun. In fact it is the rectilinearity of the rays—not their direction from the eye or to the eye—which alone matters in the main part of his *Optics,* namely "natural perspective."

B. Visual Angles

Natural perspective deals with many fundamental properties of direct vision, solely on the geometrical basis of visual angles. These are the angles subtended at the eye by any pair of points belonging to the visual scene. Thus in the case of the triangular object in Fig. 1, there are three main visual angles, namely, those subtended at the eye by the three sides of this triangular object. Needless to say, if the eye changes its position, or if the triangle is moved, all these visual angles may become altered.

A certain point inside the eye is the apex of all these angles, which form what may be conveniently called the pyramid of sight, as illustrated in Fig. 1 for the cases of a flat triangle, a cube, a man, and a horse. The exact position of the apex of the visual pyramid is not discussed by Euclid, who calls it simply "the eye." It will be seen later that in ordinary vision, this apex is at the center of rotation of the eye, close to the center of the eyeball.

1. EUCLID'S VISUAL MAGNITUDES ARE VISUAL ANGLES

Euclid's *Optics* is written as a systematic mathematical synthesis—even though, like his famous *Elements of Geometry,* it obviously rests in part on old-established knowledge and observations. Now according to the "axioms" listed at the beginning of his book, what Euclid means by "visual magnitude" is the size of the corresponding visual angle: His axioms do *define* these magnitudes as visual angles.

It is on this rigorous mathematical basis that Euclid, for instance, demonstrates that, "Objects of equal size unequally distant appear unequal—the ones lying nearer the eye always appearing larger"; and that, "Parallel lines, when seen from a distance, appear not to be equally distant from one another" (Burton's translation, 1945; Ver Eecke, 1938).

What these two theorems mean is, for example, that if a spectator stands in front of a long straight horizontal wall, the angle subtended at his eye by the height of the wall is greatest for the part of the wall nearest to

FIG. 1. Instances of pyramids of sight. [From Malton (1800), *Perspective.*]

his eye, and that the size of this visual angle decreases progressively both toward the right and toward the left.

This is an objective fact, which applies as well to inanimate objects as to the human eye: Thus, in the case of a pinhole *camera obscura* the angles corresponding to Euclid's visual angles have their apex at the center of the pinhole. Strictly speaking, therefore, there is nothing "psychological" about visual angles. The problem of the *subjective* appearance (and of the depiction) of straight parallel lines, however, is still the subject of many controversies.*

It is on the same objective basis that Euclid studied not only the problem of parallel lines, but, say, that of motion parallax, and that he even touched on the problem of binocular vision.

C. Modern Optics

1. LINES OF SIGHT

It was only some 1900 years after Euclid that the formation of the retinal image on the very strongly curved inner surface of the human eyeball—the retina extending over more than one hemisphere inside the eye—became first understood, by the astronomer Kepler (1604).

Since Kepler, our knowledge of the physical properties of light, and of the structure and functioning of the eye, has increased enormously. Yet modern optics still uses a notion—indeed a geometrical abstraction—which corresponds to the visual rays of Euclid, namely the *lines of sight* which join external object-points to the center of rotation of the eye. Thus, the geometrical concept of the visual angles, which constitute the pyramid of sight, remains valid now as it was in Euclid's day. The same is of course true of natural perspective, which rests on this geometrical concept: all men have always seen the outside world in *natural perspective*.

2. ROTATION OF THE EYE

Euclid already alluded to the movements of the eye. The apex of the pyramid of sight, in ordinary vision, is the center of the rotary motions of the eyeball in its orbit. When we look around us, we shift our gaze onto the various parts of the scene: We rotate our eye so as to bring the image of whatever attracts our attention onto the most accurate region of the retina, the *fovea centralis*.

Whereas we may think that we let our eye "roam" over, say, a landscape, our eye in fact jumps in jerky, *saccadic,* motions from one part of the

---

* Experiments made on the eye of a dead albino rabbit, in which the bright retinal images of small electric bulbs can be observed from outside the eyeball through its translucent white wall, give results in full agreement with the theorems of the *Optics* of Euclid—who knew nothing of the dioptrics of the human eye (Pirenne, 1970).

landscape to another. Even when we try to fix our gaze exactly onto one point, our eye still undergoes small continual movements. These motions of the eye are essential to normal vision: If artificial means are used to keep the image steady on the retina, after the lapse of a few seconds, vision fades and becomes very blurred and imperfect.*

III. LINEAR PERSPECTIVE

A. Sections of the Pyramid of Sight

A picture delineated in exact, "scientific," linear perspective on a surface is the central projection of the scene or object to be depicted, on this surface, the center of projection or center of perspective being the apex of the pyramid of sight. The intersection by the picture surface of each and every line of sight that joins an object-point to the eye defines a corresponding image-point on the picture surface, that is, on the surface of projection.

In other words, the picture in linear perspective of a given scene, on a given surface, for a given position of the center of rotation of the eye, is the intersection of the relevant pyramid of sight by the surface concerned. Thus, linear perspective defines, point by point, the size, shape, and disposition of the components of the scene on the picture surface, with their foreshortening, and with the overlapping of some near objects upon more distant objects. Figure 2 shows how the same pyramid of sight, relating to the same real object, here the cube A B C D, can thus be intersected by different transparent surfaces. The result is the formation, on each surface, of a different picture in linear perspective, since—*all other things remaining the same*—the surfaces are in different positions.

All this simply means that, shutting one eye and keeping my head steady, I can, in principle at least, draw on my study window a picture, in exact linear perspective, of the view outside my window, by tracing (say, with a grease pencil) the outline of all the objects I see on the glass pane of the window.

Note that, keeping my head steady, I could do this on different "windows," placed in different positions, or on windows whose shape is curved instead of plane. Yet, all these outlines in perspective would be seen to cover each other and to cover exactly the real objects, by virtue of their very construction, as illustrated in Fig. 2.

This is so even though the eye is continually rotating around a fixed center of rotation, because the images projected successively on the retina, as the eye is rotating, always remain superimposed on one another for each position of the eye. Contrary to widespread misconceptions, the physical and physiological basis of linear perspective does not in the least entail

---

* For a critical discussion of this phenomenon, see e.g., Barlow (1963).

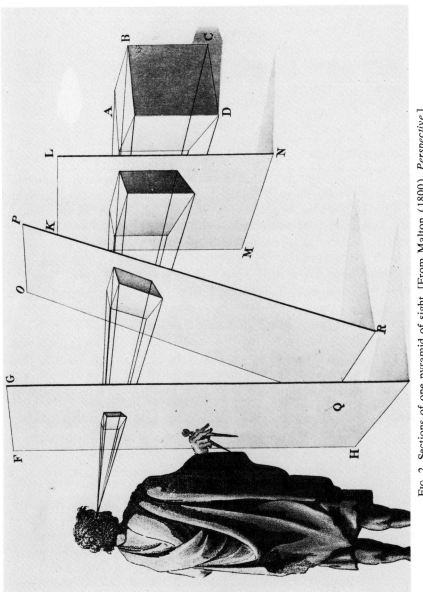

Fig. 2. Sections of one pyramid of sight. [From Malton (1800), *Perspective.*]

the immobility of the eye—which in any case would lead to the utter failure of vision. The foveal retinal images of a real object, and those of the perspective image of the object, always remain in exact coincidence even though the eye is rotating—always provided that everything else, including the center of rotation of the eye, remains unchanged. And this is ultimately due to the rectilinear propagation of light in the air outside the eye.*

IV. TROMPE L'OEIL

A. Experiment

Pinhole photographs give pictures in exact linear perspective, the center of the pinhole being the center of perspective. Figure 3 shows such a photograph, taken with the plate tilted at an angle of 20° from the vertical, of a Greek temple at Paestum in southern Italy. (This photograph, of course, reproduces approximately the distribution of light and shade, as well as the outlines of the various parts of the building.) Like all architectural photographs taken with a plate which is not vertical, this figure, as seen printed in this book, looks peculiar: The columns, for instance, appear to be falling backward.

Now an enlargement of this photograph was set up at the correct angle, and in the right position, relative to a small aperture (1 mm in diameter), which was at the center of perspective of the enlarged photograph (Fig. 4). While keeping one eye shut, the observer looks at the photograph with the other eye through the small aperture (Fig. 5). Such a small "artificial pupil," as is well-known, gives a very great depth of field, showing as clearly to most observers objects near or far without the need of lenses or spectacles. This small aperture, however, limits the field of view, so that the whole picture, and especially its frame, cannot be seen as a whole because the photograph is a wide-angle one (covering about 90° from top to bottom).

The essential result of this experiment—which surprises many observers—was that the observer sees the temple standing upright, as a solid object, and looking truly three-dimensional. What the observer sees is very similar to what he would have seen if he had looked with both eyes at a pair of stereoscopic photographs of the same building, say, with the help

---

* It will be noted that since the same pyramid of sight—that is to say the same "natural perspective"—of a given scene can be intersected by any number of different surfaces, each giving a different "linear perspective" of the same scene. The *natural perspective* of Euclid, dealing with angles only, is a much more basic concept than that of linear perspective.

FIG. 3. Pinhole photograph of a Greek temple. [From Pirenne (1970), *Optics, Painting, and Photography*. London and New York: Cambridge Univ. Press.]

FIGS. 4 and 5. Trompe l'oeil experiment made with enlargement of Fig. 3. [Photo by A. S. Evett.]

of a Brewster-type refracting stereoscope. The arrangement of Fig. 5 is a "trompe l'oeil," in the sense that it gives an excellent visual illusion of three-dimensionality, and that the surface of the photograph has become "invisible," *qua* surface. Thus, a "stereoscopic" illusion is produced, using only one eye. The photograph viewed through the device of Fig. 4 looks extremely different from the way Fig. 3 appears when we look at it with both eyes in the usual manner.

The explanation of the experiment of Fig. 5 is that the observer receives from the enlarged photograph a (very complicated) flux of light, the *geometrical* properties of which were very closely similar to those of the light flux he would have received if he had looked at the real temple, from the right position, through the same artificial pupil. As only one eye is used, there are no binocular stereoscopic clues to show the flatness of the photograph; neither is there any possibility of parallactic clues due to any displacement of the eye; and uniocular clues for depth are also missing since accommodation was made inoperative by the use of the small artificial pupil. The only clues that remain operative are precisely those typically used by photographers and representational painters, namely linear perspective—which includes foreshortening and overlapping—and light and shade.

This particular experiment was included in a practical class of about a hundred students in the Laboratory of Physiology of the University of Oxford. No student reported that it did not work.*

It must be added that, according to all this, the same "stereoscopic" illusion as in the experiment of Fig. 5 should be obtained using other sections, suitably positioned, of the visual pyramid corresponding to the temple—always on the principle illustrated by Fig. 2. This was indeed found to be the case using suitable pairs of pinhole photographs depicting sets of cubes and spheres: Both sections of the same pyramid of sight then looked truly three-dimensional, and most observers were unable to tell which section, that is, which photograph, was being used (Pirenne, 1970).

B. "Deceiving the Eye"

As a rule, "trompe l'oeil" arrangements of the type just described, despite the literal meaning of their name, fail to "deceive the eye" entirely, but they can deceive entirely with regard to depth and relief, that is, with regard to the third dimension. It is precisely by comparing them with ordinary photographs viewed binocularly in the usual manner that one fully realizes that the latter do *not* look fully three-dimensional.

In his *Physiological Optics,* while discussing the difference between monocular and binocular vision, Helmholtz describes the following ideal experiment. Suppose, he explains, that I find myself in a room well-known to me and brightly lit. Now if, while looking at the room without moving the head, I close one eye, I may believe that I see the room just as clearly and precisely as when I was using both eyes. Yet, thus using one eye only, I would still receive exactly the same visual perception of the room if all the points of the room had been moved along their respective lines of sight, their distances from the eye being changed at will (Helmholtz, 1896, pp. 609–610; 1962).

Accordingly, imagine that all the points of the room have been moved along their lines of sight until they have reached a given surface. This surface would then contain a perfect picture of the room in perspective, which would be an exact section of the pyramid of sight. And I would be unable to distinguish this "picture" from the room itself and all the real objects contained in it.

This would be so because in monocular vision, as Helmholtz of course knew, the degree of accommodation of the eye, by itself, gives almost no

* This is not the case for experiments on binocular stereoscopic vision: Some human subjects lack stereopsis even though both their eyes appear normal when tested separately. The number of people lacking stereopsis is probably greater than is usually believed (Julesz, 1971).

clue to the distance of objects. Consequently, in the experiment of Fig. 5 the use of the small artificial pupil is not essential—except to limit the field of view, since Helmholtz's ideal picture would have no frame.

Helmholtz's experiment is an ideal one because it implies that his "picture"—his section of his pyramid of sight—would be made with the utmost degree of perfection with regard to the physical intensity, and to the spectral composition, of the light that each part of the "picture" would send to his eye. This, in most cases, cannot be achieved. For instance, even if Fig. 3 were a color photograph, the effect of dazzling sunshine would still not be fully reproduced, because the range of luminances in a photographic print on paper, or in a painting, is much more restricted than the actual range in the sunlit scene, especially with regard to the sky.

These limitations constitute a different problem, which Helmholtz himself studied in his lectures on optics and painting (Helmholtz, 1871–1873, 1878, 1903).

1. PERSPECTIVE PEEPSHOWS

Thus devices giving a true three-dimensional illusion can be made simply by using a hole (say, 1 inch wide) that keeps the eye in the right position. This is the principle of the peepshows painted in perspective on the inside surface of a box; the spectator looks with one eye only through a hole in the wall of the box. Here the pyramid of sight is sectioned by a continuous surface consisting of several planes at right angles to one another. A cabinet containing two peepshows of this kind by S. Van Hoogstraeten (1627–1678) is on show in the National Gallery in London. One of these peepshows represents a Dutch interior consisting of a hall with a black and white tiled pavement, opening on two furnished rooms with a view of a street and a canal. All this appears in three dimensions when viewed through the peephole. This peepshow looks very much like a real interior, extending far beyond the dimensions of the cabinet. The painting is carried over in a continuous fashion from one wall of the box to another. In the hall the tiles, two chairs and a dog are painted partly on the wall, and partly on the floor of the box. It is hardly possible to tell on which surface of the cabinet the various parts are painted. But when something of the actual wall of the cabinet can be distinguished, the painted view is seen "through" the wall.

A painting by A. Wiertz (1806–1865), *L'Inhumation Précipitée* ("Buried Alive") used to be arranged in the Wiertz Museum in Brussels so that it could be seen through a peephole in the wall of a room in the museum. This macabre picture, showing a man trying to break out of his coffin in a vault, then made a much more startling impression than when simply hanging on a wall, partly because it acquired a three-dimensional appearance.

Similar arrangements have been used in psychological experiments on visual perception (see, e.g., Piéron, 1952).

2. BRUNELLESCHI'S EXPERIMENT

The earliest recorded peepshows giving a trompe l'oeil based on exact perspective were made at the beginning of the fifteenth century by Brunelleschi (1377–1446), the architect of the dome of the Cathedral in Florence. Brunelleschi, for instance, constructed, on the basis of the section of the visual pyramid, a flat painting of the Florence Baptistry, and arranged it to be viewed through an aperture placed at the apex of the pyramid of sight. The painting (now lost) was executed with the precision of a miniature and the sky was represented by burnished silver that was to reflect the real sky with its moving clouds. Manetti, Brunelleschi's biographer, wrote, "When one looked at it thus . . . the perspective of the piazza and the fixing of the point of vision made the scene absolutely real." (See the article, "Perspective" by Carter in Osborne (Ed.), 1970, p. 860; and Gioseffi, 1966.)

The evidence concerning Brunelleschi's experiments is second-hand and incomplete. Yet there seems to be no doubt that his is the first well-established instance of someone who definitely understood the principle of the section of the visual pyramid, and proved its validity by experiments; his experiments astonished contemporary painters because they made his painting look truly three-dimensional.

Leonardo da Vinci (1452–1519) may have alluded to Brunelleschi's experiments when, after having explained that a painting cannot produce the same effect as a real scene in relief when it is seen with both eyes, he added ". . . and why does a picture seen with one eye give the same effect of relief as the real relief, having the same qualities of light and shade [as the real relief]?"*

Even if Leonardo does not allude here to Brunelleschi's experiments, it is a fact that paintings, drawn in more or less accurately in perspective, do acquire a marked three-dimensional appearance, quite different from their usual appearance, merely as a result of the spectator shutting one of his eyes. Today, this effect can also be observed, for instance, in the case of large photographs published in magazines, especially photographs of landscapes.

Yet there does not seem to be any indication that Leonardo da Vinci set out to arrange—as a work of art—any trompe l'oeil of the type Brunel-

---

* Richter and Richter (1939; 1970, vol. 1, p. 122, No. 29). The above translation in quotes is mine; I think that the translators did not really understand Leonardo's sentence: "e perche la pittura veduta con ū ochio parrà di relievo, come il proprio relievo, auēte le medesime qualità di lumi e d'ōbre?"

leschi had made. Even though in his writings Leonardo insists so much on the study and on the "imitation" of nature as the basis of art, it does not appear that he made any special endeavor to imitate fully the three-dimensionality of a scene in this manner.

It seems probable that Leonardo and his contemporaries sensed, rightly, that to do so would have meant abandoning the art of painting, as they understood it, for something of an entirely different kind. Yet later, especially in the seventeenth century, trompe l'oeil was rather extensively practiced: But it is quite a different genre from ordinary painting, having affinities with colored sculpture and with theatre settings.

V. DEFORMATION OF THREE-DIMENSIONAL ILLUSIONS VIEWED FROM THE WRONG POSITION

A. Binocular Stereoscopy

Referring to Fig. 2, the principle of binocular stereoscopy rests on the fact that, for the same scene, there are two *different* pyramids of sight, corresponding to the two eyes of the spectator. The pupils of his eyes are, of course, in different positions—about 65 mm apart. Accordingly, the sections of a given surface of these two pyramids will give two different perspective pictures on the surface. This becomes clear if we look at a scene through a window and shut one eye at a time: We see that we could draw two different outlines of the scene on the transparent surface, one for each eye, in different positions on the surface, and that these two outlines would be *different*.*

Wheatstone's stereoscope uses two mirrors to present two such pictures *separately* to the eyes of the spectator, each picture being presented to the eye to which it corresponds. This gives rise to the well-known three-dimensional illusion of binocular stereoscopy.

1. Anaglyphs

Although in most stereoscopes, such as Wheatstone's and Brewster's, the positions of the two eyes are fixed as the spectator looks into the instrument, this is not the case for the stereoscopic devices called *anaglyphs*. In anaglyphs, the two different pictures corresponding to the two eyes are drawn or printed on top of one another, on the same card. They corre-

---

* Leonardo da Vinci already understood the principle of this (Richter & Richter, 1970, No. 29) but it is only in 1833 that the first stereoscope was invented by Wheatstone (see Helmholtz, 1896; Pirenne, 1970, p. 96n).

spond, therefore, to the two pictures, one for each eye, which the spectator of Fig. 2 could try to draw, on top of one another, on the same window. But in anaglyphs one picture is drawn in red and the other in green, so that by using suitable red and green glasses, each eye only sees the picture relevant to it. Through a red transparent sheet only the green picture is seen, and vice versa. Viewed with the naked eyes, the two pictures of course appear as a jumble.

Similar arrangements rely on the polarization of light to achieve the same result. A striking arrangement of this kind is that of the "Polaroid House Fly Test for Binocular Vision,"* which consists of two different, greatly enlarged, photographs of an ordinary housefly, printed on top of each other but reflecting light polarized in different planes. Using a suitable pair of polarizing glasses, the subject of the experiment sees a huge fly in three dimensions—provided he possesses stereoscopic vision. This is precisely a test of stereopsis, especially devised for children.

If the "Polaroid Fly" picture is tilted, or if it is brought nearer or farther from the eye, the shape of the fly changes in a definite manner with every move. Thus, increasing the viewing distance increases the apparent depth of the fly.

Similar deformations occur in the case of other anaglyphic pictures. This is entirely in keeping with theoretical expectations. For, as the two sections of the pyramids of sight are moved together in exactly the same fashion, they automatically produce two new, altered, visual pyramids, which correspond to the "deformed" object or scene which is then perceived.

B. Single Perspective Pictures Seen from the Wrong Position

According to the theory of linear perspective, similar deformations should occur when we look with one eye, from the wrong position, at a scene drawn in perspective. La Gournerie's treatise on perspective (1859), which is perhaps the best book ever written on the subject, discusses this matter exhaustively (his conclusions are summarized in Pirenne, 1970). Yet in this case, it usually takes some practice to see the deformations predicted by the theory, and they are much less striking than with anaglyphs.

One of the reasons for this is that a stereoscopic double view of solid objects is unambiguous. But our view of a single perspective picture is, in theory, quite ambiguous, because the same pyramid of sight might correspond to any number of different scenes or objects. Consequently, what we see depends a great deal on what we expect to see. Now, this expecta-

* Manufactured by the Titmus Optical Company, Petersburg, Virginia.

tion is not always very precise in the case of a picture, even though we know what it represents. Moreover, we can, and do, make intuitive compensations for these deformations, on the basis of the foreshortening of the frame of the picture.

None of these factors comes into effect in the case of binocular stereoscopic views, where there are two different visual pyramids which together define exactly the three-dimensional objects depicted.

1. Pozzo's Ceilings

There are a few trompe l'oeil paintings, however, where this ambiguity cannot really arise. This is the case for the painting on the vast hemicylindrical ceiling of the nave of the Church of St. Ignazio in Rome. On this ceiling Pozzo (also called A. Putei, 1642–1709) painted a vast array of architecture which *continues* the real architecture of the church, and appears like an extension of it which almost doubles the real size of the building—thus there is no obvious frame to the picture.

Here it is impossible to see where the real architecture stops and where the painted architecture begins. This is so even when the spectator uses both eyes, because Pozzo's painted ceiling is about 30 m high, and, thus, too far to give significant binocular clues about the real shape of the painted surface. From the correct position, that is from the center of perspective which is indicated by a marble disk on the floor, the painted ceiling is therefore seen, fully in three dimensions, as forming part of the church. When the spectator moves away from the correct position, however, the painted architecture gets out of line with the real architecture; straight architectural elements also become curved, because the painted surface is curved. Yet everything still looks fully three-dimensional. This immense trompe l'oeil painting is discussed in detail elsewhere (Pirenne, 1970).

The three photographs reproduced here (Figs. 6, 7, and 8) are three views of another painting by Pozzo in the same church, made on a spherical surface situated behind the main altar. The first photograph is taken from the right position, the center of projection of the painting, and looks like an ordinary architectural scene (Fig. 6). The two other photographs (Figs. 7 and 8) are taken from points away from the correct position: They show that the columns get out of line with the real architecture and that they now look curved. Seen in the church, the painted architecture looks *fully three-dimensional* while undergoing these deformations.

There also is, in the same church, a vast flat horizontal painting representing a complicated cupola, which from the right position, looks quite real and seems to be part of the church (Pirenne, 1970). This cupola, seen in three dimensions, also becomes deformed, getting out of line with the real church, when the spectator moves away from the right position.

Fig. 6. Photograph of a painting made on a spherical surface by Pozzo, taken from the center of perspective. [Photo by S. Calza-Bini.]

FIG. 7. Photographs of the painting of Fig. 6, taken from a position away from the center of perspective. (Photos by S. Calza-Bini.)

Fig. 8. Photograph of the painting of Fig. 6, taken from a position away from the center of perspective. [Photo by S. Calza-Bini.]

A similar cupola painted by Pozzo in the Jesuit Church in Vienna, produces a similar, compelling, illusion, according to a personal communication from Mr. J. M. Duesberg, of Brussels, who has seen it *in situ.**

It must be noted that in his book on perspective for painters and architects (Putei, 1693–1700; Pozzo, 1707), Pozzo stresses the fact that he drew these vast paintings in exact linear perspective, in all particulars; that is, he drew in each case a painting which was an *exact* section of the visual pyramid corresponding to the *whole* scene he wished to represent, by the relevant picture surface, from the relevant position.

Pozzo's successors did not closely imitate his works: For instance, they depicted instead figures seated in clouds, seen through architectural frameworks irregular in shape. One, if not the main, reason for this may be precisely that Pozzo's paintings were executed in a manner which shows most strikingly the deformations just discussed. These deformations, according to his own book, must have been considered a drawback already in his lifetime: Thus Pozzo seems, in effect, to have defeated his own purpose, while at the same time producing on a colossal scale illusions of great interest for students of optics.

VI. ORDINARY PICTURES SEEN WITH BOTH EYES

A. The Pattern of the Picture Surface

The two pinhole photographs reproduced in Figs. 9 and 10 give two different perspectives of the same building, the Arch of Janus in Rome, taken from exactly the same position. Contrary to what might be thought, the camera was *not* carried from one position to another to take them: The camera was simply rotated around a vertical axis passing through its small pinhole (i.e., the centre of projection) which was left in exactly the same position.

What we have here, therefore, are two different plane vertical sections of the same pyramid of sight, relating to exactly the same scene viewed monocularly from exactly the same position. The two photographs correspond to the picture which the spectator could have drawn on the two vertical transparent surfaces AB and A_1B_1, AB (corresponding to Fig. 9) being parallel to the façade of the Arch, whereas A_1B_1 (corresponding to Fig. 10) was at an angle of 25° to it, the spectator using only one eye kept at the same position O, as shown in the diagram of Fig. 11.

The spectator's view of the real building when his eye is at O would of course remain entirely unchanged when seen through either of the trans-

---

* An important monograph on Pozzo's paintings and architecture has been written by Kerber (1971).

FIGURE 9

FIGURE 10

FIGS. 9 and 10. Pinhole photographs of an Arch taken from the same position 0 in Fig. 11. [From Pirenne (1970), *Optics, Painting and Photography*. London and New York: Cambridge Univ. Press.]

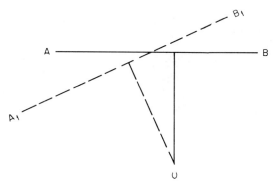

FIG. 11. Diagram explaining Figs. 9 and 10.

parent surfaces. Accordingly, what can be seen in Fig. 9 can be seen in Fig. 10; and what cannot be seen in one cannot be seen in the other. Thus the right inside wall of the Arch going through the building is just seen, in extreme foreshortening, in one photograph as in the other; again, the distant round temple seen through the arch appears in the same position in both pictures.

The obvious differences seen here between Fig. 9 and Fig. 10 are due to the fact that we see them as flat patterns printed on the page of the book. Viewed monocularly with an arrangement similar to that of Fig. 5, they should both give the *same,* fully three-dimensional, view of the Arch.

2. EXPERIMENT WITH A PAINTING

It was possible to make a similar experiment with a reproduction of an early Renaissance painting Fig. 13, the *Flagellation* by Piero della Francesca (1410/20–1492), thanks to the fact that Mr. B. A. R. Carter has been able to reconstruct the plan and elevation of the scene represented, together with the position of the center of perspective, i.e., the apex of the pyramid of sight ("eye"), and the position of the picture plane ("intersection") of this painting (Fig. 12).

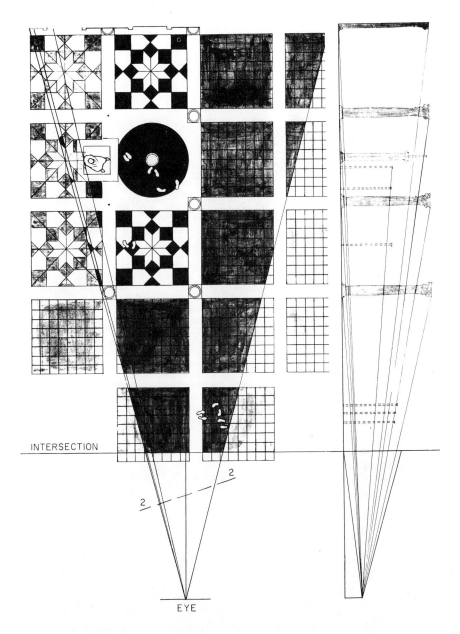

INTERSECTION

2

2

EYE

FIG. 12. Plan and elevation of the scene represented in Piero della Francesca's *Flagellation*.

This is a reconstruction made by Mr. B. A. R. Carter. The center of perspective is the point marked "eye," and the plane of projection, i.e., the picture plane, is called "intersection." The visual pyramid is shown in plan and elevation. In the plan, the part of the scene which is included in the painting is shown in a darker shade.

The broken line marked 22 shows the angular position of the new intersection of the visual pyramid obtained in Figs. 14 and 18. [From Wittkower and Carter (1953), *J. Warburg and Courtauld Institutes*, **16**, 292–302.]

FIG. 13. Frontal pinhole photograph of Piero della Francesca's *Flagellation*. [Photo by A. S. Evett.]

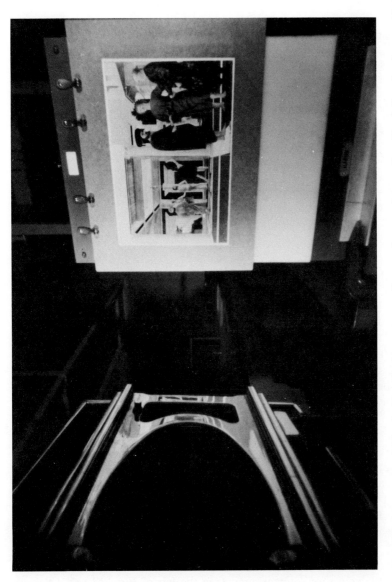

Fig. 14. Pinhole photograph of Piero's *Flagellation* corresponding to the new intersection 22 of the visual pyramid, indicated in Fig. 12. [Photo by A. S. Evett.]

Figs. 15 and 16. Arrangement, similar to that of Figs. 4 and 5, to view Figs. 13 and 14. [Photo by A. S. Evett.]

Two pinhole photographs were made of a reduced reproduction of this painting, one on a plate parallel to the plane of this reproduction (Fig. 13) and the other with a vertical plate at an angle of 20° to the first (Fig. 14). It must be stressed that the pinhole was in each case at the position marked "eye" in Fig. 12, that is, at the center of perspective of the painting.

The arrangement therefore was essentially similar to that of Fig. 11, relating to the photographs of the Arch of Janus, the center of projection always being kept at the apex of the pyramid of sight corresponding to the scene depicted. But instead of photographing an actual scene, here of course Fig. 13 gives an ordinary reproduction of Piero's painting, while Fig. 14 gives in effect a photograph which is another section, by another plane, of Piero's original pyramid of sight. The angular position of this other plane, or intersection, is given by the broken line 2- - -2 in Fig. 12.

Then an experiment (Figs. 15 and 16) was made on the principle of that of Fig. 5. To a spectator looking through the same small artificial pupil at Fig. 14 placed at the right angle and position (i.e., at the apex of the visual pyramid of the painting) the Piero reproduction looked essentially the same as when the spectator looked at Fig. 13 placed in the position relevant to it. Furthermore, in both cases the Piero reproduction now looked genuinely three-dimensional. (On the left of Figs. 13 and 14 there is a close view of the metallic flap of the camera, which, of course, turned with the camera when the latter was turned by 20°.)

All this is what is to be expected of two different sections of the same pyramid of sight, except that here the pyramid of sight is that corresponding to a scene depicted by an artist, whereas in Figs. 9 and 10 the pyramid of sight related to a real building.

B. Importance of the Flat Painted Pattern

These two photographs of Piero's *Flagellation* (Figs. 13 and 14) were enlarged and printed as Fig. 17 and Fig. 18, but here the photos were cut so as to be both of the same rectangular shape. Thus Fig. 17 is an ordinary reproduction of the main part of the original painting, whereas Fig. 18 is a different, but equally correct perspective view of most of the same scene.

The result is that in Fig. 18 the composition of the picture is altered: For instance, the horizontal lines of the architecture which are parallel to the horizontal sides of the frame in Fig. 17 are now converging toward a point to the left of the picture—instead of being depicted as horizontal lines. This is the result neither of a change in the three-dimensional composition of the scene depicted by the artist, nor of a change in the position of the artist's eye—but *only* of a change in the angle of the vertical picture plane relative to the scene.

The picture of Fig. 18 is no longer in the style of Piero della Francesca or of the Quatro Cento. In my opinion at any rate, its harmony has been destroyed—because the composition of the *flat pattern* of the picture has been altered.

The frame of the picture—which here merely consists of its outline—is very important in defining this flat pattern in Fig. 18: The rectangular frame helps to make us see this flat pattern printed on the page of the book.

In Fig. 14, on the other hand, the outline of the painting is not a rectangle on the sheet of paper: It is a foreshortened photograph of a rectangular picture and, especially with the help of its surroundings, it is recognized as such. So that any art historian would recognize Fig. 14 at once as Piero's famous "Flagellation," or rather a reproduction of it, whereas he would probably be puzzled by Fig. 18.

VII. WHAT IS A PAINTING?

Piero della Francesca's *Flagellation* is a typical example of a Renaissance painting executed in central perspective—Piero himself wrote a treatise on perspective based on the principle of the section of the visual pyramid.

FIGURE 17

FIGURE 18

FIGS. 17 and 18. Enlargements of Figs. 13 and 14, cut to the same shape and size. [Photo by A. S. Evett.]

This would seem to imply that the spectator also should view this painting with one eye only, placed at the right position, namely where the artist placed the apex of his visual pyramid—as in the case of Brunelleschi's experiments. But probably this is not the way in which Piero intended his painting to be seen, and it is certainly not the way in which spectators normally look at it.

In practice such paintings are almost always viewed with both eyes, neither of which is at the center of perspective, and the spectators tend to move about in front of the painting. Accordingly, on account of binocular stereopsis and of motion parallax, the spectator cannot help being aware of the shape and position of the picture plane, of the flatness of the painting surface, and also of some at least of the features of the geometrical composition of the flat painted pattern, qua surface pattern. Even if he concentrated his attention on the scene represented, the spectator must remain aware of all this, but he is then only "subsidiarily aware" of it, in the sense in which Polanyi uses this term (Polanyi, 1958, 1969, 1970).

That is to say, as the spectator is attending to the three-dimensional scene represented, being "focally aware" of this scene and of its meaning, he is at the same time aware, in a much less positive way, of many clues relating to the flat pattern of pigments which constitutes the painting as executed by the artist.

Subsidiary awareness lies between unawareness and full awareness. It is aptly described as a set of clues. The importance of clues is, of course too well-known to experimental psychologists to have to be emphasized here.

Thus in the trompe l'oeil experiment of Fig. 5 special precautions were always taken to try to remove all clues relating to the flat pattern on the surface of the picture, especially its position, which is easily revealed when its frame can be seen. The experimenter in arranging these experiments took great care to attend *focally* to the existence of any such clues, precisely in an attempt to be able, if possible, to remove them entirely.

Although it is not possible to attend focally at the same time to the scene represented, and to the pattern of pigments on the surface of the painting, it is possible to be focally aware of the three-dimensional scene represented while being at the same time *subsidiarily* aware of the flat-painted pattern. In fact, it is then impossible not to be subsidiarily aware of the painted pattern, since it is impossible to be quite unaware that one is looking at a painting which is placed, say, on the wall of a building one has just walked into to look at the painting.

Accordingly a psychological integration must occur between these two elements: the focal awareness of the scene in depth, and the subsidiary awareness of the flat painted pattern. And this is an integration of *incompatible* things: depth and flatness. It is not the mere integration of the parts of a single whole, as studied in Gestalt psychology. This special kind of psychological integration is of the greatest importance from an artistic point of view—as well as in other respects.

A. The "Music" of the Painting

"There is a kind of emotion which is quite particular to painting," wrote the painter Delacroix (1798–1863), "and which results from such and such arrangements of colour, lights, etc. That is what one may call 'the music of the painting.' Even before knowing what the painting represents, being at too great distance to see what it represents, often you are taken by its magical accord" (Roger Marx, 1963). Since this aesthetic effect takes place before the scene represented can even be identified, it can only be produced by the harmonious characteristics of the flat pattern of the surface of the painting.

Even though it is a poor reproduction, Fig. 17 retains much of the "music" of Piero's original painting, whereas in Fig. 18 this music has at any rate been changed—even though the scene represented is the same as in Fig. 17.

This is the essential point of my theory, the gist of which happens to coincide with ideas developed independently by Polanyi, who has discussed them further with regard to painting, and with regard to other representational arts. Thus, in poetry, there is an integration of the focal awareness of the meaning of the poetry with the subsidiary awareness of the music of the verse: This explains why a great poem may be almost impossible to translate since its "music" is most easily lost in the process of its translation into another language (Polanyi, 1970).

At this point I may perhaps add that I was driven to the preceding conclusions (against earlier misconceptions I had entertained over many years) when I saw Pozzo's ceilings for the first time (Pirenne, 1963, 1970). Further study of Pozzo's trompe l'oeil paintings and of his book relating to them, and the setting up of experiments, such as those described in this chapter, only confirmed my two main conclusions. First, linear perspective does work in a straightforward manner *only* when the surface of the picture is "invisible," qua surface; and it then gives a fully three-dimensional illusion of the kind which must have astonished Brunellischi's contemporaries in Florence. Second, our everyday perception of ordinary pictures is a very complex process, which does not give a fully three-dimensional illusion. So far as I know, the complexity of this psychological process has not hitherto been clearly and definitely recognized—and it deserves further study.

Trompe l'oeil illusions often are regarded as rather puzzling oddities, whereas ordinary paintings and photographs tend to be taken for granted, largely, no doubt, because we are so familiar with them. Yet I am now convinced that it is the perception of these ordinary pictures—not the perception of trompe l'oeil illusions—which presents the student of optics with a really puzzling problem.*

---

* There are many indications that the existence of this problem was sensed by Leonardo da Vinci, who was both artist and scientist; and that it is this which led him to his extensive studies in optics and perspective—of which unfortunately no complete and systematic first-hand account has reached us.

VIII. STABILITY OF ORDINARY PAINTINGS

In ordinary paintings viewed binocularly in the usual manner the scene represented hardly becomes deformed when the spectator is at the wrong position: In this case, as I have tried to demonstrate, the spectator is at least subsidiarily aware of the flat pattern of the painting. In the case of devices giving a fully three-dimensional illusion, on the other hand, the spectator is not aware of this flat pattern; and then strong deformations appear when the spectator is at the wrong position. This appears to me to lead inescapably to the conclusion that the stability of our perception of ordinary paintings is due to our subsidiary awareness of their flat pattern, since this is the only essential difference between the two cases.

This is also of considerable practical importance. It also occurs in the case of ordinary photographs: Otherwise, say, two different officials could not examine the photograph in a traveler's passport at the same time.

An intuitive compensation takes place when we look at ordinary pictures in the usual manner, and this compensation must be based on our subsidiary awareness of the picture surface, and also, of course, on our preconceived ideas concerning the scene or objects represented by the picture.

A. A Chinese Instance

An instance of this stability of ordinary pictures is given by the brush drawing on the foreshortened screen contained in the Chinese painting of Fig. 19. Part of this screen is reproduced in Fig. 20, but with the top and bottom of the screen cut off horizontally.

Thus Fig. 20 gives an accurate reproduction of the screen, corresponding to what one would get by cutting out the relevant part of the actual silk canvas of the painting and pasting it onto a page 465 of the present book. The result is a Chinese landscape of traditional design—which could be blown up to be used, unchanged, as an imitation of a traditional Chinese screen.

B. Marginal Distortions

The existence of this intuitive compensation was pointed out to me as early as 1955 by Einstein—who added that if the visual angle subtended by a picture were too large, this compensation would fail (A. Einstein, 1955, personal communication published in Pirenne, 1970). Einstein's letter was so politely and tactfully written that I completely failed to understand that it meant that the views on perspective I held at the time were,

Fig. 19. Reproduction of a Chinese painting on silk, nineteenth century. (private collection.) [Photo by A. Austin.]

in effect, *wrong*. It took me about 7 years to come to realize this, on the basis of my own observations and experiments. This is why I felt it would be worthwhile to give here a systematic summary of the facts that have driven me to the present thesis.

The problem of the total angular extent by a painting is an old one, already discussed at the time of the Italian Renaissance. It is, in fact, the same problem as that of the so-called "marginal distortions" of wide-angle photographs. These marginal "distortions" are *not* distortions of perspective: They are simply strange shapes, given by exact perspective, of objects placed at too great an angle from the line falling perpendicularly from the "eye," the center of perspective, onto the picture plane.

1. Depiction of a Sphere

The problem of these so-called distortions is discussed in detail elsewhere (Pirenne, 1970). Here, the case of the depiction of a sphere will be briefly examined. Figure 21 is a wide-angle pinhole photograph showing a spherical architectural ornament, which appears elliptical on the surface of the photograph. This is so because the central projection of a sphere is a circle only if the plane of projection is normal to the straight line

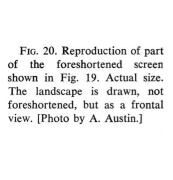

FIG. 20. Reproduction of part of the foreshortened screen shown in Fig. 19. Actual size. The landscape is drawn, not foreshortened, but as a frontal view. [Photo by A. Austin.]

joining the center of the sphere to the center of projection—which is not the case in Fig. 21.

In experiments similar to that of Fig. 5, which give a full three-dimensional illusion, such elliptical perspective images of spheres appear truly spherical, always looking circular in outline. This is so because, even though the eye is moving around its center of rotation, the image formed in the retina by this flat elliptical image always remains, for each and every position of the eye, the same as the retinal image which would be given by a real, solid, sphere of the right size at the right position (Pirenne, 1970).

Even contemporary textbooks on perspective still show misunderstanding in this respect. The miscalled "distortions" in wide-angle pictures are

FIG. 21. Wide-angle pinhole photograph of a stone sphere. [From Pirenne (1970), *Optics, Painting, and Photography*. London and New York: Cambridge Univ. Press.]

not due to the fact that seeing "out of the corner" of the eye differs from central vision. In an accurate trompe l'oeil arrangement like that of Fig. 5, the eye rotates and *looks at each part of the scene in turn,* turning its gaze so as to form a succession of images on the fovea, the *central* part of the retina, which mediates the most accurate vision. Central vision is used to look straight at each and every part of the picture, including its marginal parts.

The reason why such shapes as that of the sphere in Fig. 19 have been called "distortions" must be that ordinarily we are aware of the flat pattern of the picture.

Leonardo da Vinci already knew that the true central perspective of the outline of a sphere is, in most cases, an ellipse; but apparently he never depicted a sphere in any of his paintings. Raphael (1483–1520) on the other hand, represented at the right hand of his "School of Athens" two spheres as circles, whereas their exact perspectives should be elliptical. At this point I must refer the reader to my book (Pirenne, 1970) for a fuller discussion of these problems, and I can only repeat that I see no way of solving them without a full realization of the importance of our subsidiary awareness of the flat surface pattern of the painting.

This awareness of the flat surface of ordinary pictures, while giving stability to the pictures—and being essential to produce the "music" of a painting considered as a work of art—does, in the case of the miscalled "marginal distortions" of wide-angle plane pictures, work against verisimilitude. This is so especially in the case of objects having curved surface of known shape, including human figures. This is extensively discussed by La Gournerie (1859) who shows that Renaissance painters, in fact, did not draw human figures in exact perspective from the main center of perspective of their paintings. This is the case even for Piero della Francesca's "Flagellation." It was *not* the case, however, for the trompe l'oeil made later by Pozzo, who states explicitly in his book that he drew in each painting an exact section of his pyramid of sight, in all particulars, including curved ornaments and figures.*

IX. THE PAINTER'S TASK

A few representational painters, such as the brothers Van Eyck, Leonardo da Vinci, Vermeer, and Seurat, did strive to copy what they saw:

* Professor Sir Ernst Gombrich, in his book, *Art and Illusion* (1951), and in his other publications, appears to reject—explicitly or implicitly—the thesis I have tried to restate in this chapter. Professor Gombrich recently gave a review lecture on these problems to the Royal Society of London; as this lecture has not yet been published, however, it is not possible to discuss it here.

Leonardo, at any rate, stated that this was his primary aim. But first-hand information as to how such painters regarded their task is hard to come by. That is why I feel that I may here mention my father, Maurice Pirenne (1872–1968), who, toward the end of his long life, told an art historian, or rather an archaeologist, who came to see him, that he was very astonished that this visitor could be interested in the paintings and drawings of someone "qui essayait tout bêtement de copier ce qu'il voyait"—that is, roughly, "who simply tried to copy what he saw." Indeed, he considered himself a surviving specimen of a species of a "fossil" genus.

Figures 22, 23, 24, and 25 are reduced reproductions in black and white of paintings that were readily available to me and that cover a span of about half a century. They do not indicate any systematic trend in the choice of his motifs; after 1954, Maurice Pirenne continued to make pictures of the most varied kinds, ceasing to paint only a few days before his sudden death.*

I discussed the painter's problem with my father in innumerable conversations. Here is a brief and forthright summary of his views:

> The artist is a man who is fond of looking.
> By dint of looking, he sees.
> He then strives to reproduce what he sees.
> The mass of the public does not look:
> consequently they do not see.

* The crystalline lens of the eye is yellow: That is, it absorbs preferentially short-wave radiations such as "blue" light. Moreover this yellow color is said to increase with age, even though it may differ in degree in the two eyes of the same person (M. H. Pirenne, 1970). At the end of his life, my father suffered from cataract, but continued to paint. His paintings of course then became blurred. But a comparison among a number of original pictures covering a span of about 50 years, *viewed side by side,* revealed little effect of such a yellowing, with one exception: When he was 90 or so, he used dashes of deep blue in the very dark parts of his pictures. This blue, of course, must have looked black to him if his crystalline lenses were a rather deep yellow.

This may help to settle the controversy concerning the effect with increase of age of the increased yellow color of the eye lenses, since the present case refers to a painter who is definitely known to have "tried simply to copy what he saw."

Since the beginning of the present century—if not earlier—many of the painters in the public eye deliberately did the opposite. Thus it has often been reported that Pablo Picasso stated, "I paint what I *think,* not what I see." In effect, it may be argued that such paintings reverted to the method of depiction used in *pre*-Greek art, for instance, in Egyptian, Assyrian, and Sumerian art. It is an open secret that this "modern" art emerged as a reaction against the invention of photography. But it is impossible here to establish that sweeping statement: The present chapter deals with the psychology and physiology of vision in relation to the craft of picture-making. It is not a treatise on aesthetics.

But some people go and look at paintings. They
do so because they see what the artist has
represented: the pictures speak to them.
And then, naively, they believe that what they
see in the paintings has been *invented* by the
painter.

Again, Maurice Pirenne said that he believed that the famous "secret of the Mona Lisa smile" was simply that Leonardo attempted to "represent an ordinary woman just as he saw her"—avoiding the mere imitation of paintings already done—according to the precept that Leonardo explicitly stated in his writings (Richter & Richter 1939).

Leonardo saw much more than most people—especially us, with our "dull modern eye." This may account for the difficulties encountered by some art theorists who still try to explain the "secret of the Mona Lisa" in increasingly complex and varied fashion. For if such writers on art are theorists only, and not practitioners of the craft of painting, they must mainly look at paintings already done: If so, they must see very little of aesthetic interest in the world around them.

Here art meets science. The artist's seeing differs from the scientist's seeing—even though the same man may be both artist and scientist. But their ways of seeing the world have something in common: They are *personal* ways of seeing the world. They constitute *personal knowledge.*

All human knowledge is personal knowledge: How could it be otherwise? And one's personal knowledge is, perforce, always limited. This fact has been stressed by Michael Polanyi, who expounded many of its more important consequences (Polanyi, 1958, 1969, 1970).

Of course, no painter, especially today, can avoid being influenced almost from his birth by the innumerable pictures—photographs included—which he sees around him. However, photography does not give a complete, exact, imitation of reality. As Mr. A. Austin, a scientific photographer in Oxford, put it: "They say that the camera cannot lie: The problem is to make it tell the truth!" The idea that a "mere imitation of reality" is possible to achieve in a picture is a myth. For it implies that a man could see, and represent (photographically or otherwise) the "infinite" number of aspects of the things which can be seen in even the simplest scene, *if* he really looks for them. Everyone knows that a man, a woman, a doctor, a detective, and a farmer see different things in the world around them: For example, a farmer may tend to disregard the weeds at the edges of his fields, whereas a botanist may concentrate his interest on those very weeds.

Roughly speaking, the first problem of those interested in painting is therefore *not* to explain how a painter will simplify and arrange in an "ar-

FIG. 22. Maurice Pirenne, ca. 1896: "Young Woman." Charcoal drawing.

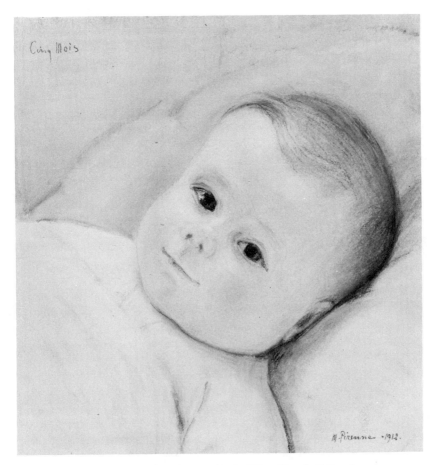

Cinq Mois

M. Pirenne. 1912.

Fig. 23. Maurice Pirenne, 1912: "Five Months." Pastel.

tistic" manner a scene he could represent exactly as it is: This is an impossible task.

On the contrary, the problem is to find out how a truly original artist succeeds in seeing and in representing—out of a world which is boundless in its variety—things which no one before him has represented. The original artist is first and foremost a discoverer. His discoveries—artistic discoveries—which provide the raw material that is used, quite legitimately, by those who make decorative pictures, or illustrations such as posters.

At almost all periods of history, there have been at the same time original representational artists, decorative artists, illustrators—as well as nonrepresentational, or miscalled "abstract" artists. One has only to think of Vermeer and of the so-called "Delft" ceramic tiles—which appear in some

FIG. 24. Maurice Pirenne, 1934: "Landscape." Pastel. [Photo by A. Austin.]

of Vermeer's own paintings. Again there are Oriental carpets of geometrical design, which are called in the trade "Holbein Carpets," precisely because Holbein has represented them in his meticulously made paintings. (Such carpets àre also depicted in several of Vermeer's paintings.)

To this sketchy outline it may be added that, in Michael Polanyi's words, "We know more than we can tell." Again, in Hazlitt's words, "Genius [that is, the ability to discover truely original things in art], is unconscious of its own powers."

Thus Leonardo knew that a representational painting, seen with one eye kept in a fixed position, does take a truly stereoscopic appearance, appearing as a "hole in the wall"—whereas ordinary paintings seen with both eyes do not. Leonardo da Vinci presumably sensed that this was not the kind of art he was aiming at. So far as I know, he never built an ar-

Fig. 25. Maurice Pirenne, 1954: "The Stone." Drawing with some color. [Photo by A. Austin.]

rangement to produce such a truely three-dimensional effect, at any rate for an important painting.

But in later times peepshow boxes were built to do so; afterward they were rather despised; and now they are beginning again to attract increasing interest.

It may be added here that complicated effects of contour and contrast, only recently studied by scientists (O'Brien, 1958; Ratliff, 1971, 1968), have been known and used by artists for at least a thousand years. A striking example is that of a Corean vase of the Yi dynasty, which represents the moon, which looks brighter than the surrounding sky; yet the physical luminance of the moon disk is actually *lower* than that of the sky some distance away from its limbus. (Similar effects were used in porcelain ware of the Chinese Sung dynasty.) Photographs can be found in Ratliff (1971).

Again Chinese Yin bones of about the twelfth century B.C. (more than 3000 years ago), give drawings of the crescent of the moon which suggest that the artist might have represented the appearance of the crescent—seen with the dilated pupil—when, in fact, several crescents are usually seen, a fact noted by Helmholtz in his *Physiological Optics* and explained by the complicated structure of the crystalline lens of the eye. (Drawings reproduced in Karlgren, 1940.)

This tends to show that artists jumped in *medias res,* using psychological or physiological effects long before they were studied, or at any rate, published by scientists—who try, in the words of Pasteur, "never to advance anything which cannot be proved in a simple and decisive manner [Valery-Radot, 1911, Vol. 2, p. 112]."

X. EFFECTS OF IRRADIATION

A. Visual Acuity

Visual acuity defines the limits of our ability to distinguish fine details of forms and shapes, and also to detect, say, single spots or lines. This complex subject cannot be discussed here: A simple account of some of its problems will be found, for instance, in Pirenne (1967, 1972), and a much more extensive one in LeGrand (1952). In daylight, under the best conditions, and for certain types of test objects, human visual acuity seems to come near to the limits set by the wave properties of physical light. On account of these properties of light itself, the retinal image of a "point source" of light (i.e., a source of very small angular extent) must always be a small, finite patch, the intensity of which fades out toward its edges: This is the phenomenon of diffraction, which limits the resolving power of all optical instruments. Inaccurate focusing of the eye, and any defects in the optical system of the eye, can only extend further the size of the patch that is the retinal image of a point source.

Consequently, the retinal images of two contiguous colored dots must always be patches that overlap. Thus there occurs retinal mixing of the two overlapping colored luminous images, even if the actual dots are sharply defined. This is what the physiologist Brücke discussed under the name of *irradiation* in his book on the scientific aspects of pictorial art (Brücke, 1877, 1878).

B. Illuminations in Manuscripts

Because of the limit of our vision acuity, it might appear pointless to paint details finer than those which can be distinguished by the normal eye at reading distance. Yet this has often been done. If one examines medieval manuscripts with a strong magnifying lens, one is often surprised by the amount of detail they contain. This is so for the famous *Lindisfarne Gospels* (698–721 A.D.), and for the *Book of Kells* (760–820 A.D.). It is also a frequent feature of later manuscripts (see Rickert, 1954; D'Ancona & Aeschliman, 1969).

A curious instance was discovered by Miss D. Callard in the Bodleian Library in Oxford. In a manuscript of the middle of the fourteenth century, a small disk, about 15 millimeters in diameter, contains the whole of the *Magnificat* and part of the *Ave Maria*, in writing so small that modern copyists and students of manuscripts wonder how it was written: perhaps with a fine metal nib, rather than with a "brush" consisting of a single hair. Figure 26 reproduces, actual size, part of Folio 199r of Manuscript Canon. Liturg. 192, in which the small disk is seen, held with both hands by a grotesque figure, in the bottom left part of the folio. Even the very existence of the inscription (in medieval script) may be difficult to detect in Fig. 26. But enlarged color slides of this disk have been published and can now be obtained from the Bodleian Library, Oxford (Ref. No. 170 E/15), making it possible to project on a screen an enlarged image of the inscription. The reader is referred to these slides, because ordinary black and white photographic enlargements of the disk have proved to be unsatisfactory.

Figure 27 reproduces, actual size, Folio 150r of Manuscript Douce 223 of the Bodleian Library (Flanders, ca. 1480). Figure 28 gives an enlargement of part of the border of this folio. The roses contained in this border are specimens of *Rosa gallica officinalis,* a famous medieval red rose, which is still in cultivation today. The white butterfly is almost certainly a specimen of *Aporia crataegi,* a butterfly widespread in continental Europe (Higgins & Riley, 1970).*

These illustrations are extraordinarily accurate with regard to details, and to color—as I could verify, particularly in the case of the *Rosa gallica,* which used to grow in my garden. There are many illuminations of the same kind, in which the details might appear to be unnecessarily fine, since

* Figures 26, 27, and 28 are reproduced by kind permission of the Bodleian Library, Oxford. I am greatly indebted to Dr. W. O. Hassall and to Miss D. Callard for all their help and for invaluable information on the subject of illuminated manuscripts.

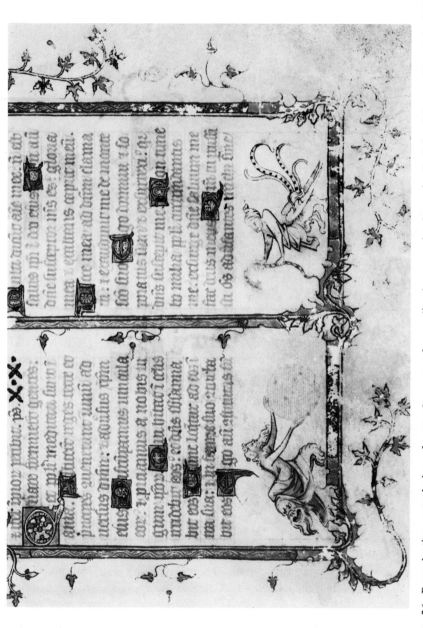

Fig. 26. Reproduction, actual size, of part of a page of a medieval manuscript from the Bodleian Library. The circle held by a figure at bottom left of the page contains a long inscription; see text. [Reproduced by courtesy of the Bodleian Library, Oxford.]

FIG. 27. Reproduction, actual size, of a page of a medieval manuscript from the Bodleian Library; see text. [Reproduced by courtesy of the Bodleian Library, Oxford.]

they can only be seen with a strong magnifier. The same applies to some extent to Flemish paintings of the fifteenth century: A magnifying glass is sometimes made available to examine these paintings in the galleries where they are exhibited.

This "unnecessary" fineness of detail does not by itself detract from realism, verisimilitude, or truth to nature. Owing to irradiation, such finely painted details will partly fuse and overlap in the retinal image formed in our eye, and yet, *if* accurately depicted, they will give precisely the same retinal image as the details of the real object. Thus details too fine to be clearly seen will give a blurred or fuzzy retinal image, but this blurred image will be about the *same* in the case of the painting and of the real object. The difficulty of this genre of painting is, of course, that the artist while giving care to the details may be led to neglect general shapes and proportions, which are all-important—but this did not occur in the cases discussed here, however.

FIG. 28. Enlargement of part of the border of Fig. 21. A millimeter scale is added to the enlargement. [Photo by A. S. Evett.]

Positive lenses and spectacles probably came into use in about 1300 (Meiss, 1967). Thus Figs. 26 and 27 may have been painted with the help of such devices. This, however, is unlikely for, say, the *Lindisfarne Gospels* which date from the eighth century. It seems possible that myopic and strongly myopic artists did specialize in this kind of illumination, and continued to do so even after the introduction of magnifying lenses. This would be in keeping with what ophthalmologists say of myopic persons (Mann & Pirie, 1946). (The objection arises that myopes do not see clearly at a distance, but they may have simply copied—or reduced—paintings of distant scenes made by other artists.)

C. Seurat: Pointillism

In the fine miniatures just discussed, retinal mixing of colors takes place unavoidably. In the paintings Seurat (1859–1891) executed in his typical pointillist technique, on the other hand, the effect of retinal mixing occurs only within a suitable range of distances. At close range the colored dots or spots of pigment on the canvas are clearly seen separately. At too long a distance, the mixing is too complete and efficient, so that the paintings look as if they were painted in even tones, sometimes tending to gray. At a suitable distance, however, the effect aimed at by Seurat does fully take place: The surface of the painting acquires a peculiar shimmering appearance. This, in his sunny landscapes, suggests admirably the shimmering effect of full sunshine. Indeed I know of no other colored pictures—paintings or photographs—representing this so realistically. At the same time, Seurat was a master in the composition of his paintings and in suggesting the solidity of things. (Seurat's paintings are most difficult to reproduce adequately; the best reproductions are perhaps those edited by Sir Anthony Blunt, 1965.)

In his comprehensive study on Seurat and the science of painting, Homer (1964) has discussed Seurat's pointillist technique and the books on optics and color Seurat is definitely known to have read. Homer, however, does not give much attention to Brücke's *Principes Scientifiques des Beaux-Arts,* published in French in 1878, in the same volume of the "Bibliothèque Scientifique Internationale" as Helmholtz's lectures on *L'Optique et la Peinture.* This book was published in Paris *before* Seurat developed fully his technique; and Brücke, in effect, describes clearly in advance the basis of the technique Seurat was going to use. It seems very hard to believe that Seurat did not read Brücke. Yet there appears to be no written evidence that he did so: This may explain why Homer rather neglected this French book. It is worthwhile here to give some relevant quotations from Brücke, who was famous as a physiologist in his day, and whose studies on irradiation may, in any case, have provided the basis of the writings which Seurat is definitely known to have read.*

Brücke, in his chapter on irradiation, wrote

> Consider for instance the same tree at different distances. At a short distance we see the leaves, monochrome in themselves, as having a rich variety of colours: highlights; thick dark green shadows, sometimes brownish, sometimes almost black; and the saturated green of medium tones.

* A copy of this 1878 book by Brücke and Helmholtz was in the City Library of Verviers, a provincial town in Belgium, when I was a school boy. This is one of the reasons why I believe that it cannot have escaped the attention of Seurat when it was first published in Paris.

My father Maurice Pirenne (1872–1968) made me read this book. I accompanied him when he went to paint in the country and questioned him about what Brücke said. My father knew Léon Fredericq: I remember that once he told Fredericq that this book by Brücke and Helmholtz was the *only* book which dealt adequately with the problems encountered by artists who tried to represent what they see. Fredericq simply answered that this book was based on sensory physiology, and that its two authors, were famous physiologists, Helmholtz being the more famous of the two. (With reference to Léon Fredericq, who was one of the founders of modern physiology, see Figs. 32a and b.)

As my father earned his living as Curator of the Museum of Art and Archeology of Verviers, and as this museum contained many valuable antiquities and paintings of all kinds—regional, European, and exotic—he took a keen interest in everything pertaining to representational and to decorative art. He was a voracious reader, describing himself a "painter infected with literature."

Maurice Pirenne painted steadily for more than 80 years, until he died, suddenly, at the age of 96. He was of a thoroughly independent turn of mind, and since his marriage in 1905 hardly ever exhibited outside his home town. His immense talent was indeed fully recognized by a few friends and a few relations, including some with whom he was at variance. (His elder brother, the medieval historian Henri Pirenne, born in 1862, died in 1935.) The final outcome of my father's fierce independence, combined with the fact that he sold his pictures at ridiculously low prices, was that he remained almost unknown and unacknowledged, to his death. [During his lifetime he published at his own expense two sets of reproductions of his works (M. Pirenne, 1954 and 1958). A posthumous book has now appeared (Vandeloise, 1970).]

When I called on Selig Hecht in 1939 with a view to working in his laboratory, most of what I knew about vision still came from this book by Brücke and Helmholtz. The present chapter is in part inspired by the same book, and by what my father taught me. Maurice Pirenne considered Seurat's *La Grande Jatte,* now in Chicago, as one of *the* three great paintings of the nineteenth century.

He insisted on the fact that he was almost entirely self-taught: No teacher, he said, had taught him anything of real practical value with regard to painting—except, however, for Roll, in whose studio he worked in Paris around 1900. Roll told him: "You must put so many colors on your canvas, make it so rich in colors, that finally it looks [from a distance] gray." That, said my father, was a painter's advice—which of course went back to Seurat's time which then was not far away.

But at a certain distance, all this is fused in a smooth medium green, little saturated, out of which come out only the great masses of shadows which serve to model the tree as a whole. . . .

Another result of irradiation, which is of no less importance for the artist, is that which the colors produce in the painting itself. When they are close to one another in an area such that, from the right standpoint, one cannot distinguish them separately, their retinal images also overlap one another to some extent. The colors then combine themselves in a manner which is essentially different from that of colors mixed by the artist on his palette. Ultramarine and chrome yellow together produce gray, not green as pigments mixed on the palette; the mixture of cinnabar red with green gives yellow. In brief the mixture occurs according to the same laws as it would on a rotating color disk; I have given an account of these laws in my book on the physiology of colours. Here I want only to point out that, by this mode of mixture, one can obtain effects which cannot be obtained by any other method. *The uncertainty, the lack of distinctness, of the different colors gives to the painted surface a certain* life *which it would not have if covered with an even tint . . . and produce a special illusion on the nature of the painted surface.* [Brücke, 1877, 1878. English translation and italics mine.]

Brücke goes on to state that the idea of knowingly arranging to mix colors in this manner on the retina was by no means a new one. He mentions as instances certain paintings by Murillo, antique mosaics and paintings, as well as the embroideries and tapestries of the Gobelins.

A brilliant color, covering a small area on a dark ground, must expand itself in the retina according to the laws of irradiation; at the same time its brightness must decrease because the same quantity of colored light is now spread over an area greater than that corresponding to the geometrical retinal image. Thereon rests the effect of the dashes of cinnabar red which P. P. Rubens has introduced in his shadows to paint reflections more strongly. At the right distance, one no longer sees the red of the cinnabar, but a red–brown shimmer which, to use the language of artists, produces a particularly warm tone [Brücke, 1877; English translation mine].

In his books on the physiology of color, published in the same year in German and French, Brücke (1866a,b) discusses textiles in the same context, saying,

I remember a beautiful Lyons cloth of the sixteenth century in the Museum here [no doubt in Vienna.] It is a blue silk damask. In the web, the yellow threads cross the blue threads, and the two colors are so well weighted against each other that they precisely neutralize each other to gray, and in strong light to white. This arrangement leads to a shimmering appearance; at a suitable distance and in suitable lighting the cloth appears with a pleasing silvery color, such as could not be produced by the direct use of real white. [Brücke, 1887; English translation mine.]

FIG. 29. Reproduction, actual size, of part of an aquatint, nineteenth century, representing the Pont-Neuf in Paris. [Photo by A. Austin.]

FIG. 30. Enlargement of part of the aquatint, Fig. 23. [Photo by A. Austin.]

D. Engravings

Figure 29 reproduces, actual size, part of an aquatint which was made at the beginning of the nineteenth century. Figure 30 shows an enlargement of a smaller part of the same aquatint: This gives a good idea of what the original aquatint looks like when examined with a good magnifier. Now it happens that the *enlarged* aquatint looks very much like the well-known drawings made with Conté crayon on rough paper by Seurat. I have verified

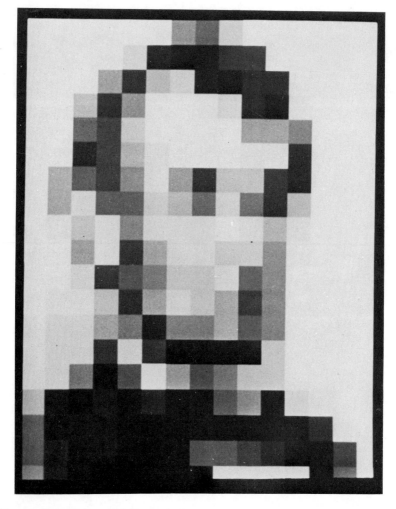

FIG. 31. "Mosaic" artificially made by computer, on the basis of a photographic picture of Abraham Lincoln; see text. [Courtesy of Leon D. Harmon, Bell Laboratories. Copyright Bell Telephone Laboratories, Inc. Reproduced in Julesz (1971).]

FIG. 32. A small lead pencil sketch of the Belgian physiologist Léon Fredericq (1851–1935; discoverer of hemocyanin—see Florkin, 1943). Actual size of the original. This was made in 1930 during a walk near Botrange in Belgium, by the present writer (M.H.P.) who then, at 18, had very good eyesight (visual acuity probably almost equal to 2). [Photo by A. Austin.]

this by examining the original Seurat drawings which are kept in the British Museum; but this can also be seen by examining the reproductions of Seurat's drawings published by Kahn (1971), especially plate 77.

In both cases, there are hardly any continuous lines: There is a transition from pure white to pure black, through areas containing black spots on a white background and then white spots on a black background, the spots varying in shape and size. Again in both cases, irradiation plays an important role, by giving "life" to the surface. Whether or not Seurat was led to this technique of drawing after studying such aquatints is open to question. In any case, the similarity is mainly one of technique: The outstanding quality of many of Seurat's drawings resides in his skill in constructing the broad masses of his drawings. Seurat's pictures give a very strong impression of stability, which is lacking in many Impressionist paintings.

The phenomenon of irradiation played a great role in many kinds of engravings, centuries before Seurat's time. Copper engravings, for instance, represent an apparently even tone with a complex array of lines and dots—the result of a vast amount of work. Again, many tones are not even, but are made to fade off to lighter ones, with great skill. The sky of landscapes is represented by many lines: this technique gives to the sky a "life" and "brilliance," which it would not have if represented by an even tone. The book on prints by Ivins (1943) gives magnified reproductions of engravings that illustrate the present argument.

FIG. 33. Enlargement of part of the sketch of Fig. 32. The enlargement factor
is about 6×, the head in the original being about 18 mm high from the top of
the beret to the end of the beard. Thus the present enlargement should be looked
at, say, from a distance of about 1.50 meter to look like the original at reading
distance. [Photo by A. Austin.]

E. Mosaics

The artificial "mosaic" of Fig. 31 was made by using a computer, from a photograph of Abraham Lincoln. At close range it is hardly possible to say what it represents, but at a certain distance the likeness comes forward. Julesz (1971) puts forward an interesting theory of why this happens; however, the main point here is that it does happen. Thus makers of real mosaics may have had to work at close range to make pictures to be seen from a much greater distance.

The art of mosaic was much more widely practiced in antiquity than today, judging on the basis of all those which have been found at Pompeii and Herculaneum, two of the cities which were buried, and thus preserved, by the eruption of Vesuvius in A.D. 79. There are various types of mosaics, and it must have been an extremely difficult art to practice. A clear and scholarly description of these mosaics—and of Greco–Roman paintings—can be found in the illustrated book on the Cities of Vesuvius by M. Grant (1971).

F. Addendum

It is often difficult to obtain first hand information about what an "artist," or, rather, someone who makes pictures actually did, or rather about what he wished to do. Accordingly I am reproducing here, rather diffidently, a small drawing I made myself when I was a youth, together with an enlargement of it. Details are given in the caption of Fig. 32.

This may help to illustrate some of the points discussed above, notably about "fine" drawings. My aim, of course, was simply to obtain as good a likeness as I could. (This portrait was probably an amateur's lucky shot, and I was surprised myself when I looked at it with a lens after more than 40 years.)

References

Barlow, H. B. Slippage of contact lenses and other artefacts in relation to fading and regeneration of supposedly stable retinal images. *Quarterly Journal of Experimental Psychology*, 1963, **15**, 36–51.

Blunt, A. *Seurat: Fifty plates in full colour.* London: Phaidon, 1965.

Brücke, E. *Les couleurs au points de vue physique, physiologique, artistique et industriel.* Traduit de l'Allemand sous les yeux de l'Auteur par J. Schutzenberg. Paris: G. Bailliere, 1866b. [Translation from German of Brücke (1866a), i.e., first edition of Brücke *Physiologie des Farben.*]

Brücke, E. *Bruchstücke aus der Theorie der bildenden Künste.* Leipzig: Brockhaus, 1877. [French translation, *see* Brücke (1878).]

Brücke, E. *Principes scientifiques des beaux-arts: essais et fragments de théorie.* Paris: Bibliothèque Scientifique Internationale, Librairie Germer Baillière, 1878. [Trans. of Brücke, 1877. Published in one volume with H. Helmholtz, *L'Optique et la Peinture* (trans. of Helmholtz, 1871–1873). A fourth edition was published in 1891 by Alcan.]

Brücke, E. *Die Physiologie der Farben fur die Zwecke der Kunstgewerbe, auf Auregung der Direction des Kaiserlich Oesterreichischen Museum fur Kunst und Industrie* (2nd increased and improved ed.). Leipzig: S. Hirzel, 1887. [According to the Preface, the first edition was published in 1866.]

Burton, H. E. The optics of Euclid. *Journal of the Optical Society of America,* 1945, **35**, 357–372.

Carter, B. A. R. The perspective of Piero della Francesca's *Flagellation. Journal of the Warburg and Courtauld Institute,* 1953, **16**, 292–302. This is Pt II of the paper by Wittkower and Carter (1953).]

Carter, B. A. R. Perspective. In H. Osborne (Ed.), *The Oxford companion to art.* Oxford: Clarendon, 1970.

D'Ancona, P., & Aeschliman, E. *The art of illumination: An anthology of manuscripts from the sixth to the sixteenth century.* London and New York: Phaidon, 1969.

Florkin, M. *Léon Fredericq et les débuts de la physiologie en Belgique.* Brussels: Office de Publicité 1943. [Anciens Etablissements J. Lebèque.]

Gioseffi, D. Perspective. In *Encyclopedia of world art,* Vol. XI. New York: McGraw-Hill, 1966. [English language edition of *Enciclopedia universale dell'arte.* Venice and Rome: Istituto per la Collaborazione Culturale.]

Gombrich, E. H. *Art and illusion: A study of the psychology of pictorial representation.* New York: Pantheon, 1951.

Grant, M. *Cities of Vesuvius: Pompeii and Herculaneum.* London: Weidenfeld and Nicolson, 1971.

Helmholtz, H. von *Handbuch der Physiologischen Optik,* 1st ed. Hamburg and Leipzig: Leopold Voss, 1866 [2nd German edition, see Helmholtz (1896). 3rd German edition. see Helmholtz (1909–1911).]

Helmholtz, H. von *Optisches über Malerei,* 1871–1873. Republished in Helmholtz (1884). [For French translation, *see* Brücke (1878).]

Helmholtz, H. von *Vorträge and Reden.* 2 vols. Brunswick: Vieweg, 1884.

Helmholtz, H. von *Handbuch der Physiologischen Optik.* 2nd edn. Hamburg and Leipzig: Leopold Voss, 1896. [This edition, revised by Helmholtz, contains new material based mostly on the work of his collaborator A. König. It also contains a bibliography, complete to the year 1894, prepared by König.]

Helmholtz, H. von On the relation of Optics to Painting. In *Popular lectures on scientific subjects,* 2nd series, London: Longmans, Green, 1903. Pp. 73–138. [Translation of Helmholtz 1871–1873.]

Helmholtz, H. von *Handbuch der Physiologischen Optik.* 3rd, posthumous, ed., 3 vols. Hamburg and Leipzig: Leopold Voss, 1909–1911. [This consists of the text of the first edition (1866) with supplements by A. Gullstrand, T. von Kries and W. Nagel.]

Helmholtz, H. von *Treatise on physiological optics.* (Trans. and ed. by J. P. C. Southall), 3 vols. bound as 2. New York: Dover, 1962. [This edition, first published by the Optical Society of America in 1924–1925, is a translation of Helmholtz (1909–1911).]

Higgins, L. G., & Riley, N. D. *A field guide to the butterflies of Britain and Europe*. London: Collins, 1970.

Homer, W. I. *Seurat and the science of painting*. Cambridge, Massachusetts: M.I.T. Press, 1964.

Ivins, W., Jr. *How prints look: Photographs with a commentary*. Boston: Beacon Hill Press, 1943.

Julesz, B. *Foundations of cyclopean perception*. Chicago: Univ. of Chicago Press, 1971.

Kahn, G. *The drawings of George Seurat*. New York: Dover, 1976.

Karlgren, B. *Grammata Serica*, p. 204, 306a–f. Reprinted from *The Museum of Far Eastern Antiquities Bulletin*, No. 17, Stockholm, 1940.

Kepler, J. *Ad Vitellionem paralipomena, quibus astronomiae pars optica traditur*. Francofurti, 1604.

Kerber, B. *Andrea Pozzo*. Berlin and New York: Walter de Gruyter, 1971. (In German.)

La Gournerie, J. de *Traité de perspective linéaire contenant les tracés pour les tableaux plans et courbes, les bas-reliefs et les décorations théatrales, avec une théorie des effets de perspective*. 1. vol. and 1 atlas of plates. Paris: Dalmont et Dunod; Mallet-Bachelier, 1859.

Le Grand, Y. *Optique physiologique*, Vol. 1. *La dioptrique de l'oeil et sa correction*. (2nd ed.). Paris: Editions de la Revue d'Optique, 1952.

Malton, J. *The young painter's maulstick; Being a practical treatise on perspective*. London: Griffiths, 1800.

Mann, I., & Pirie, A. *The science of seeing*. New York: Penguin, 1946.

Meiss, M. *French painting in the time of Jean de Berry*, London and New York: Phaidon, 1967.

O'Brien, V. Contour, perception, illusion and reality. *Journal of the Optical Society of America*, 1958, **48**, 112–119.

Osborne, H., Ed. *The Oxford companion to art*, Oxford: Clarendon Press, 1970.

Piéron, H. *The sensations: Their functions, processes and mechanisms* (Trans. by M. H. Pirenne and B. C. Abbott). London: Frederick Muller, 1952.

Pirenne, M. *99 Reproductions d'oeuvres de Peintre*. Texte d'André Blavier. Verviers: Ed. "Temps Mélés," 23 Place Général Jacques, 1954.

Pirenne, M. *Dessins*. Verviers: Ed. "Temps Mélés," 23 Place Général Jacques, 1958.

Pirenne, M. H. Les lois de l'optique et la liberté de l'artiste. *Journal de Psychologie Normale et Pathologie*, 1963, **60**, 151–166.

Pirenne, M. H. *Vision and the eye*, 2nd ed. London: Chapman and Hall, 1967.

Pirenne, M. H. *Optics, painting, and photography*. London and New York: Cambridge Univ. Press, 1970.

Polanyi, M. *Personal knowledge: Towards a post-critical philosophy*. London: Routledge and Kegan Paul, 1958.

Polanyi, M. *Knowing and being*. London: Routledge and Kegan Paul, 1969.

Polanyi, M. What is a painting? *British Journal of Aesthetics*, 1970, **10**, 225–236. [Also published in *The American Scholar, 39*, 655–669.]

Pozzo, A. (A. Putei) *Rules and examples of perspective proper for painters and architects. In English and Latin. Done into English by Mr. John James*. London, 1707. [English edition of Putei, 1693.]

Putei, A. (A. Pozzo). *Perspectiva Pictorum et Architectorum Pars Prima— Secunda*. (Latin and Italian.) Rome, 1693–1700. [For the English edition see Pozzo, 1707.]

Ratliff, F. *Mach bands: Quantitative studies on neural networks in the retina.* San Francisco: Holden-Day, 1965.

Ratliff, F. Contour and contrast. *Proceedings of the American Philosophical Society,* 1971, **115**, 150–163.

Richter, J. P., & Richter, I. A. (Eds.) *The literary works of Leonardo da Vinci compiled and edited from the original MSS. by J. P. Richter,* 2nd ed. enlarged and revised by J. P. and I. A. Richter, 2 vols. London: Oxford Univ. Press, 1939. (Italian and English.) [Reprinted 1970, New York: Phaidon.]

Rickert, M. *Painting in Britain: The middle ages.* London: Penguin, 1954.

Roger Marx, C. Centenaire de Delacroix. Le plus grand des critiques d'art. *Revue de Paris,* April, 1963, 101–111.

Valery-Radot, R. *The life of Pasteur* [Trans. by Mrs. R. L. Devonshire], 2 vols. London, Constable, 1911.

Vandeloise, G. *Maurice Pirenne.* Verviers: Ed. 'Temps Mèlés', 23 Place Général Jacques, 1970.

Ver Eecke, P. *Euclide: l'optique et la catoptrique.* Paris, Bruges: Desclée de Brouwer, 1938.

Wittkower, R., & Carter, B. A. R. The perspective of Piero della Francesca's *Flagellation,* I and II. *Journal of the Warburg and Courtauld Institute,* 1953, **16**, 292–302.

AUTHOR INDEX

Numbers in italics refer to the pages on which the complete references are listed.

SUBJECT INDEX

A

Abney's law, 45
Achromatic light (Newton), 19
Accommodation
  critical distances for focus, 241
  early findings on, 7, 8
  uniocular clues, 442
Action potential, discovered at onset of illumination, 12
Acuity, *see also* Clarity, Spatial resolution
  alignment of two lines, 17
  bases of, 16
  contrast sensitivity limiting, 243
  detail in manuscript illuminations, 475–479
  dioptrical defects of the eye, 16
  irradiation affecting detail, 477
  early measurement of, 15
  illumination intensity in relation to, 237–238
  maximum at fovea, 38
  monocular, 17
  optimal pupil size for grating, 239–240
  quality of retinal image, 16
  scotopic performance poor, 16
  stereoscopic, 17
  stray light affecting, 16
  test patterns described, 233–235
Adaptation, *see also* Dark adaptation, Direction-specific adaptation, Selective adaptation
  chromatic adaptation, 150
  color-contingent motion aftereffects, 62
  in cone input studies, 129–130
  critical duration related to level of, 171, 178
  to prismatic distortions, 358
  simultaneous, 39–40

summation effect, 40
temporal, 39
Adaptation-level theory, 281
Aftereffects, *see also* Figural aftereffects, Motion aftereffects
  in color vision, 151–156
  contrast effects, 151
  luminance of positive over time, 183
  negative and positive, 151
  stability of image, 275
  successive induction, 151
  tilt, 412
Afterimage, *see* Aftereffects
Age effects, *see also* Developmental studies, Infants, Kittens
  on constancies, 286
  crystalline lens in youth, 27
  diffraction of light for young people, 16
  height of observer's eyes, 353
  position of crystalline lens for young people, 16
  for scotopic observers, 47
  spectral transmission factor of lens varying, 48
  in susceptibility to illusions, 286
  yellowing of crystalline lens of artist, 468
Alhazen (Ibn Al Haitham) *see* Optics, physiological
Ambiguous figures, *see also* Illusions
  direction reversals, 417
  cartoons as, 272
  cognitive contours, 269–270
  rat and professor, 268
  stereograms, 268, 269, 270, 271
  trapezoid window (Ames), 376
  wife/mother-in-law (Boring), 269
Ametropia, 16
Anaglyphs, 446–447
Anesthesia, effects of, 98, 101

HANDBOOK OF PERCEPTION

EDITORS: *Edward C. Carterette and Morton P. Friedman*

Department of Psychology
University of California
Los Angeles, California 90024

Volume I: Historical and Philosophical Roots of Perception. 1974
Volume II: Psychophysical Judgment and Measurement. 1974
Volume III: Biology of Perceptual Systems. 1973
Volume V: Seeing. 1975

IN PREPARATION

Volume IV. Hearing

A	5
B	6
C	7
D	8
E	9
F	0
G	1
H	2
I	3
J	4